LITIGATION LIBRARY

DISCLOSURE

Second Supplement
Third Edition

LITIGATION LIBRARY

DISCLOSURE

SECOND SUPPLEMENT
THIRD EDITION

by

Paul Matthews, B.C.L. (Oxon), LL.D. (Lond.)
Solicitor Advocate (Higher Courts: Civil), Withers
HM Coroner for the City of London
Visiting Professor, King's College, London
Deputy Master, High Court, Chancery Division
A Recorder (Civil)

and

Hodge M. Malek, B.C.L., M.A. (Oxon)
One of Her Majesty's Counsel,
A Bencher of Gray's Inn
A Recorder of the Crown Court

SWEET & MAXWELL

THOMSON REUTERS

HOW TO USE THIS SUPPLEMENT

This is the Second Supplement to *Disclosure* (being the third edition of *Discovery*), and has been compiled according to the structure of the main volume.

At the beginning of each chapter of this Supplement is a mini table of contents from the main volume. Where a heading in this table of contents has been marked by an asterisk, this indicates that there is relevant information in the Supplement to which the reader should refer.

Within each chapter, updating information is referenced to the relevant paragraph in the main volume.

The Table of Cases refers to all the cases cited in the main volume and this Supplement. References to paragraph numbers in the Supplement are in bold.

CONTENTS

	page
How to use this Supplement	v
Table of Cases	xi
Table of Statutes	cxli
Table of Statutory Instruments	cxliii
Table of Civil Procedure Rules	cxliv

para.

Chapter 1
Introduction

D)	Comparative Discovery	1.15
F)	Reform and the Civil Procedure Rules 1998	1.28

Chapter 2
Time of Discloure

A)	Before Proceedings Commenced	2.02
B)	At the Time that Proceedings are Commenced	2.10
C)	After Proceedings have been Commenced	2.31
D)	Discloure after Judgment has been Given	2.46
F)	Foreign Disclosure for English Proceedings	2.57

Chapter 3
Norwich Pharmacal and other Pre-Action Disclosure

A)	Norwich Pharmacal Order	3.02
B)	Pre-Action Disclosure: CPR Rule 31.16	3.26
C)	Corporate Insolvency	3.40
D)	Application to Inspect Court File	3.45

Chapter 4
Persons Who Must Give Disclosure

A)	General Position of Substantive Parties to Proceedings	4.01
B)	Special Cases	4.18
D)	Non-Parties	4.47

Chapter 5
What Must be Disclosed

A) What is a Document 5.02
B) Scope of the Obligation 5.08
C) Particular Instances 5.19
D) Special Cases 5.33
E) "Possession, Custody or Power" "Control" 5.39

Chapter 6
Means of Disclosure

A) Lists of Documents 6.01
C) Verification on Affidavit 6.37
E) Conclusiveness of List or Affidavit 6.41
F) Application for Specific Disclosure 6.45
H) Publicity 6.58

Chapter 7
Electronic Disclosure

A) What are Electronic Documents? 7.02
B) Duty of Search 7.06
C) Form of Disclosure 7.13

Chapter 8
Objections to Disclosure

B) Objections as of Right 8.06
F) Other Objections 8.18

Chapter 9
Inspection of Documents

C) Documents Mentioned in Statements of Case etc. 9.04
G) Translations 9.22
H) Electronically Held Documents and Equipment 9.23
N) Sealing Up 9.37

Chapter 10
Production by Non-Parties

B)	Witness Summons	10.02
C)	Banker's Books Evidence Act 1879	10.37
D)	Evidence (Proceedings in other Jurisdictions) Act 1975	10.54

Chapter 11
Objections to Inspection

A)	The General Rule	11.01
C)	Legal Professional Privilege	11.05
D)	Legal Advice Privilege	11.09
E)	Litigation Privilege	11.30
F)	Exceptions to Legal Professional Privilege	11.63
G)	Public Interest Immunity	11.81
H)	Privilege Against Incrimination	11.104
I)	"Without Prejudice" Privilege	11.121
M)	Other Statutory Objections to Inspection	11.143
O)	Disproportionality	11.156
P)	Conditional or Restricted Inspection	11.157

Chapter 12
Loss of Privilege

B)	Who Can Waive?	12.02
C)	What is a Waiver?	12.03
E)	Inclusion in List of Documents	12.16
F)	Reference in Affidavit or Witness Statement	12.19
K)	Waiver on Taxation of Costs	12.30
L)	Extent of Waiver	12.31
M)	Privilege against Self-incrimination	12.37
N)	"Without Prejudice" Privilege	12.39

Chapter 13
Failure to Comply with Disclosure Obligation

C)	Striking Out	13.07
F)	Contempt	13.27
G)	Other Consequences	13.30

Chapter 14
Solicitor's Obligations

B) Solicitor's Duties 14.02

Chapter 15
Collateral Use of Documents

B) CPR Rule 31.22 15.03
C) Rationale 15.05
E) On Whom Binding 15.09
F) Documents or Information 15.11
I) Duration of Obligation 15.25
J) Release from or Modification of Obligation 15.33
L) Arbitration 15.47
N) Criminal Proceedings 15.56

Chapter 16
Information Requests

A) Background 16.01
D) Applications for Order Under Part 18 16.20
G) Particular Instances 16.38
H) Necessity and Proportionality 16.51
J) Special Cases 16.54

Chapter 17
Other Disclsoure of Facts

B) Letters of Request 17.10
C) Witness Statements 17.20

Chapter 18
Experts' Reports

A) General 18.01
B) Direction of the Court 18.04
C) Single Joint Experts 18.09
D) Ruling on Admissibility 18.11

E) Duties of Expert 18.12
F) Privilege 18.16
G) Questions for Expert 18.17
H) Requests for Information 18.18
I) Meeting of Experts 18.19
J) Expert's Request for Directions 18.20
K) Procedure at Trial 18.21
L) Assessors 18.23

Chapter 19
Real Evidence

A) Inspection of Property 19.02

Chapter 20
Disclosure in other Courts and Tribunals

C) Arbitrations 20.04
M) Employment Tribunals (Formerly Industrial Tribunals) 20.27
N) European Court of Justice and the European Court of First Instance 20.32
O) Financial Services and Markets Tribunal 20.38
W) Mediation 20.55

Chapter 21
The Impact of the Human Rights Act 1998

C) The Right to Respect for Private Life 21.08
D) The Right to Freedom of Expression 21.14

Appendix 1 A.54A
Appendix 2 B.02

TABLE OF CASES IN MAINWORK AND SUPPLEMENT

[*References to the Supplement are printed in* **bold**]

789 Ten Pty Ltd v Westpac (2005) 215 A.L.R. 131, Sup. Ct. (NSW) 11.26

A, Re. *See* R. (on the application of Malik) v Manchester Crown Court

A v A (Ancillary Relief) B v B (Ancillary Relief) [2000] 1 F.L.R. 701 [2000] 1 F.C.R. 577 [2000] Fam. Law 470, Fam Div 2.03, 3.45, 15.05, 15.11, 15.34, 15.37, 15.43, 20.69

A v B (2001–02) 4 I.T.E.L.R. 877, HC (Cook I) 8.09

A v B Bank (Bank of England Intervening) [1993] Q.B. 311 [1992] 3 W.L.R. 705 [1992] 1 All E.R. 778 (1991) 135 S.J. 11, Q.B.D. (Comm.) .. 8.13, 8.15

A v B Plc sub nom. A v B (A Firm) B and C v A [2002] EWCA Civ 337 [2003] Q.B. 195 [2002] 3 W.L.R. 542 [2002] 2 All E.R. 545 [2002] E.M.L.R. 21 [2002] 1 F.L.R. 1021 [2002] 2 F.C.R. 158 [2002] H.R.L.R. 25 [2002] U.K.H.R.R. 457 12 B.H.R.C. 466 [2002] Fam. Law 415 (2002) 99(17) L.S.G. 36 (2002) 152 N.L.J. 434 (2002) 146 S.J.L.B. 77, CA (Civ Div) 21.08, 21.14

A v Boulton (2004) 204 A.L.R. 598, Fed. Ct. Aus. 11.114

A v C (No.1) sub nom. A & B v C, D, E, F, G and H (No.1) [1981] Q.B. 956 [1981] 2 W.L.R. 629 [1980] 2 All E.R. 347 [1980] 2 Lloyd's Rep. 200, Q.B.D. (Comm.) 2.13, 3.11, 4.63, 4.64, 16.68

A v France (A/277–B) (1994) 17 E.H.R.R. 462, ECHR 21.10

A v Hayden (No.2) (1984) 56 A.L.R. 82 .... 12.42

A v X (Disclosure: Non-Party Medical Records) [2004] EWHC 447, Q.B.D. ... 4.55, 4.58

AB v John Wyeth & Brother Ltd (No.1) sub nom. A v John Wyeth & Brother Ltd B v John Wyeth & Brother Ltd [1992] 1 W.L.R. 168 [1992] 1 All E.R. 443 [1992] P.I.Q.R. P437 [1992] 3 Med. L.R. 190, CA (Civ Div) ... 12.24

ABB AG v Hochtief Airport GmbH [2006] EWHC 388 [2006] 1 All E.R. (Comm.) 529 [2006] 2 Lloyd's Rep. 1, Q.B.D. (Comm.) 20.04, 20.08

ACCC v Allphones (No.3) [2009] FCA 1075; 259 A.L.R. 541 .... 11.123

ACCC v Pratt (2009) 250 A.L.R. 661, Fed Ct (Aus) 10.11

ACCC v Visy (No.2) [2007] FCA 444, Fed. Ct of Australia 11.38, 11.44

AE Farr Ltd, Re [1992] B.C.C. 150 [1992] B.C.L.C. 333, Ch.D (Companies Ct) 11.113

AF Noonan (Architectural Practice) Ltd v Bournemouth & Boscombe Athletic Community Football Club Ltd; sub nom. Bournemouth & Boscombe Athletic Community Football Club Ltd, Re [2007] EWCA Civ 848; [2007] 1 W.L.R. 2614; [2007] C.P. Rep. 44; (2007) 151 S.J.L.B. 923 .... 2.03, 6.58

AG (NT) v Maurice (1986) 161 C.L.R. 475, H Ct (Aus) 12.15, 12.34

AG für Autogene Aluminium Schweissung v London Aluminium Co Ltd [1919] 2 Ch. 67 (1919) 36 R.P.C. 199, CA 5.34, 16.72

AJ Bekhor & Co Ltd v Bilton [1981] Q.B. 923 [1981] 2 W.L.R. 601 [1981] 2 All E.R. 565 [1981] 1 Lloyd's Rep. 491 [1981] Com. L.R. 50 125 S.J. 203, CA (Civ Div) 2.13, 2.15, 2.51, 6.30, 8.12, 11.106, 16.68
AKZO Chemie BV v Commission of the European Communities (C–62/86) [1991] E.C.R. I–3359 [1993] 5 C.M.L.R. 215 [1994] F.S.R. 25, ECJ 20.35
AM&S Europe Ltd v Commission of the European Communities. *See* Australian Mining & Smelting Europe Ltd v Commission of the European Communities
AM&S Ltd v EC Commission. *See* Australian Mining & Smelting Europe Ltd v Commission of the European Communities (155/79)
AMP Society v Architectural Widows Ltd [1986] 2 N.Z.L.R. 190, H Ct (NZ) 4.60
AOOT Kalmneft v Denton Wilde Sapte [2002] 1 Lloyd's Rep. 417, Q.B.D. (Merc) 3.11, 11.69, 11.71
AP v Switzerland (1998) 26 E.H.R.R. 541, ECHR 21.05
ARC Ltd v Scholfield [1990] 2 E.G.L R. 52 .... 5.28
ASIC v Lindberg [2009] VSCA 234; 261 A.L.R. 207 .... 11.76
ASIC v P Dawson Nominees Pty Ltd [2008] FCAFC 123; (2008) 247 A.L.R. 646, Fed. Ct of Australia 11.103
AT&T Istel Ltd v Tully [1993] A.C. 45 [1992] 3 W.L.R. 344 [1992] 3 All E.R. 523 (1992) 142 N.L.J. 1088 [1992] 136 S.J.L.B. 227, HL reversing [1992] Q.B. 315 [1992] 2 W.L.R. 112 [1992] 2 All E.R. 28 (1992) 89(2) L.S.G. 32 (1992) 142 N.L.J. 88, CA (Civ Div) 2.25, 2.26, 4.23, 11.104, 11.116
AWA Ltd v Daniels (1992) 7 A.C.S.R. 463 .... 20.56
AWB Ltd v Cole [2006] F.C.A. 571, Fed. Ct of Australia 11.31
AWB Ltd v Cole (No.5) [2006] F.C.A. 1234; 234 A.L.R. 651, Fed. Ct of Australia 11.09, 11.10, 11.32, 11.69, 11.70, 12.06, 12.07, 12.09, 12.36
AXA China Region Insurance Co Ltd v Pacific Century Insurance Co Ltd (No.2) [2005] 3 HKC 359 .... 12.19
AXA Equity & Law Life Assurance Society Plc v National Westminster Bank Plc [1998] C.L.C. 1177, CA (Civ Div) affirming [1998] P.N.L.R. 433, Ch.D 3.06, 3.11, 3.14
A (A Minor), Re, *The Times*, August 21, 1998, CA 4.04
A (Children) (Contact: Expert Evidence), Re sub nom. A (Children) (Family Proceedings: Expert Witnesses), Re [2001] 1 F.L.R. 723 (2001) 98(16) L.S.G. 32 (2001) 151 N.L.J. 224, Fam Div 18.02
A (Disclosure of Medical Records to GMC), Re [1998] 2 F.L.R. 641 [1999] 1 F.C.R. 30 (1999) 47 B.M.L.R. 84 [1998] Fam. Law, Fam Div 3.45
A (Disclosure to Third Party), Re [2002] N.I. Fam. 5 .... 4.04
A Co v B Co [2002] H.K.C.F.I. 261 .... 3.03, 3.15
A Company, Re [1985] B.C.L.C. 333 .... 2.13, 16.68
A Health Authority v X (No.1) sub nom. A Health Authority v X (Discovery: Medical Conduct) (No.1) [2001] EWCA Civ 2014 [2002] 2 All E.R. 780 [2002] 1 F.L.R. 1045 [2002] 2 F.C.R. 357 [2002] Lloyd's Rep. Med. 139 [2002] Fam. Law 342, CA (Civ Div) affirming [2001] 2 F.L.R. 673 [2001] 2 F.C.R. 634 [2001] U.K.H.R.R. 1213 [2001] Lloyd's Rep. Med. 349 (2001) 61 B.M.L.R. 22 [2001] Fam. Law 653 , Fam Div ... 21.12
Aamer v Secretary of State for Foreign and Commonwealth Affairs [2009] EWHC 3316 (Admin); [2010] A.C.D. 25 .... 3.07, 3.10, 3.11
Abacha v Secretary of State for the Home Department. *See* R. (on the application of Abacha) v Secretary of State for the Home Department (No.2)

Abalian & Tossounian v Innous [1936] 2 All E.R. 834 (1936) 55 Ll. L. Rep. 219, CA 13.06
Abas v Netherlands (1997) 88B D.R. 120, Eur Comm. HR 21.05
Abbey National Mortgages Plc v Key Surveyors Nationwide Ltd [1996] 1 W.L.R. 1534 [1996] 3 All E.R. 184 80 B.L.R. 52 53 Con. L.R. 93 [1996] P.N.L.R. 120 [1996] 2 E.G.L.R. 99 [1996] 33 E.G. 88 [1996] E.G.C.S. 23 [1996] N.P.C. 14 (1996) 72 P. & C.R. D1, CA (Civ Div) 18.09
Abbey National Plc v Clive Travers & Co [1999] Lloyd's Rep. P.N. 753 [1999] P.N.L.R. 819, CA (Civ Div) ... 11.67, 11.68, 11.69, 11.06, 11.08, 12.02
Abdulaziz v United Kingdom (A/94) Cabales v United Kingdom (9473/81) Balkandali v United Kingdom (9474/81) (1985) 7 E.H.R.R. 471, ECHR 21.08
Abelene Ltd v Cranbrook Finance Inc, unreported, July 24, 2000, CA (Civ Div) 13.32
Ablitt v Mills & Reeve, *The Times*, October 25, 1995, Ch.D 6.29, 11.76, 12.18
Abraham v Thompson [1997] 4 All E.R. 362 [1997] C.L.C. 1377 (1997) 94(37) L.S.G. 41 (1997) 141 S.J.L.B. 217, CA (Civ Div) 2.40
Abu Dhabi National Tanker Co v Product Star Shipping The Product Star (No.1) [1992] 2 All E.R. 20 [1991] 2 Lloyd's Rep. 508, QBD (Comm.) 4.21, 4.25
Accident Exchange Ltd v Autofocus Ltd [2009] EWHC 3304 (QB) 17.30
Accident Insurance Mutual Holdings Ltd v Fadden (1993) 31 N.S.W.L.R. 412 .... 11.106, 11.111, 11.110, 11.112, 12.38
Ackbar v CF Green & Co Ltd [1975] Q.B. 582 [1975] 2 W.L.R. 773 [1975] 2 All E.R. 65 [1975] 1 Lloyd's Rep. 673 119 S.J. 219, Q.B.D. 3.28
Ackroyd v Mersey Care NHS Trust (No.2). *See* Mersey Care NHS Trust v Ackroyd (No.2)
Adams v Adams (Att.-Gen. intervening) [1971] P. 188 [1970] 3 W.L.R. 934 [1970] 3 All E.R. 572 114 S.J. 605, PDAD 11.89
Adams v Batley Cole v Francis (1887) L.R. 18 Q.B.D. 625, CA 8.06, 16.86
Adams v Sunday Pictorial Newspapers (1920) Ltd [1951] 1 K.B. 354 [1951] 1 All E.R. 865 66 T.L.R. (Pt. 2) 771 94 S.J. 741, CA 16.63
Adams Steamship Co. Ltd v London Assurance Corp [1914] 3 K.B. 1256, CA 11.39
Adham v BCCI. *See* El Jawhary v Bank of Credit and Commerce International SA (No.2)
Admiral Management Services Ltd v Para Protect Europe Ltd [2002] EWHC 233 [2002] 1 W.L.R. 2722 [2003] 2 All E.R. 1017 [2002] C.P. Rep. 37 [2003] 1 Costs L.R. 1 [2002] F.S.R. 59 (2002) 99(16) L.S.G. 37 (2002) 152 N.L.J. 518 (2002) 146 S.J.L.B. 93, Ch.D 11.129, 11.130, 18.12
Advanced Specialist Treatment Engineering Ltd v Cleveland Structural Engineering (Hong Kong) Ltd sub nom. Cleveland Structural Engineering (Hong Kong) Ltd v Advanced Specialist Treatment Engineering Ltd [2000] 1 W.L.R. 558 [2000] 2 All E.R. (Comm.) 189, Q.B.D. (Comm.) 3.45
Aegis Blaze, The [1986] 1 Lloyd's Rep. 203 (1986) 130 S.J. 15, CA (Civ Div) 11.06
Ahmed v University of Oxford sub nom. Ahmed v Governing Body of the University of Oxford [2002] EWCA Civ 1907 [2003] 1 W.L.R. 995 [2003] 1 All E.R. 915 [2003] I.C.R. 733 (2003) 100(10) L.S.G. 27, CA (Civ Div) 18.23
Aid, The (1881) L.R. 6 P.D. 84, PDAD 18.24
Ainsworth Lumber Co. v Canada (Attorney-General) (2003) 326 D.L.R. (4th) 93, CA (British Columbia) 10.31

Ainsworth v Hanrahan (1991) 25 N.S.W.L.R. 155, CA (NSW) 16.117
Ainsworth v Wilding (No.2) [1900] 2 Ch. 315, Ch.D 11.09, 11.28, 11.31
Air Canada v Secretary of State for Trade (No.2) [1983] 2 A.C. 394 [1983] 2 W.L.R. 494 [1983] 1 All E.R. 910, HL affirming [1983] 2 W.L.R. 494 [1983] 1 All E.R. 161 (1983) 127 S.J. 205, CA (Civ Div) 8.22, 11.92, 11.93, 11.94, 11.98, 11.83, 11.02, 12.42
Aird v Prime Meridian Ltd [2006] EWHC 2338 (TCC), 108 ConLR 1, [2006] BLR 494, [2006] All ER (D) 88 (Sep), TCC .. 11.129, 11.133, 18.19, 20.56
Airey v Ireland (1977) 8 D.R. 42 .... 21.17
Airey v Ireland (A/32) (1979–80) 2 E.H.R.R. 305, ECHR 21.18
Airservices v Transfield (1999) 164 A.L.R. 330 .... 3.03
Aiscough, Ex p. (1730) 2 P. Wms 591 .... 19.20
Akai Holdings Ltd (in liquidation) v Ernst & Young [2009] HKFCA 14 ...... 3.42, 11.08, 11.45
Akers v Lomas sub nom. Trading Partners Ltd, Re [2002] 1 B.C.L.C. 655 [2002] B.P.I.R. 606, Ch.D 3.44
Akhtar v Muhammad [2002] EWHC 673, Ch.D 17.23
Akiba on Behalf of the Torrest Strait Regional Sea Claim Group v State of Queensland [2010] FCA 321 .... 10.35
Akins v Abigroup Ltd (1998) 43 N.S.W.L.R. 539, CA (NSW) 12.10
Akinsete v South Pacific Investments Ltd, 1992 J.L.R.1 .... 1.17
Aktiebolaget Hassle v Pacific Pharmaceuticals Ltd [1991] 3 N.Z.L.R. 186 ... 8.25, 11.36, 11.160
Aktiengesellschaft für Autogene Aluminium v London Aluminium Co. *See* AG für Autogene Aluminium Schweissung v London Aluminium Co. Ltd
Akzo Nobel Chemicals Ltd v Commission of the European Communities (T–125/03, T–253/03) [2007] 4 C.M.L.R. 23, CFI 11.19, 20.37
Al-Fayed v Al-Tajir [1988] Q.B. 712 [1987] 3 W.L.R. 102 [1987] 2 All E.R. 396 [1987] 1 F.T.L.R. 441 (1987) 84 L.S.G. 1055 (1987) 131 S.J. 744, CA (Civ Div) 11.140
Al-Fayed v Central Intelligence Agency, 229 F.3d 272 (D.C. Cir. 2002) 2.62
Al-Fayed v Commissioner of Police of the Metropolis (No.1) [2002] EWCA Civ 780 (2002) 99(30) L.S.G. 39 (2002) 146 S.J.L.B. 153, CA (Civ Div) ... 6.28, 12.17, 12.18
Al-Fayed v United Kingdom (A/294–B) (1994) 18 E.H.R.R. 393, ECHR 21.
Alberta Treasury Branches v Leahy, 2000 A.B.Q.B. 575, QB (Alberta) 3.03, 3.11, 3.15, 3.25, 15.22
Al Haq v Shah. *See* Ul-Haq v Shah
Al Rawi v Security Service [2010] EWCA Civ 482; [2010] 3 W.L.R. 1069; [2010] C.P. Rep. 37; [2010] U.K.H.R.R. 728; (2010) 107(20) L.S.G. 19; [2010] N.P.C. 51 .... 2.03, 2.33, 11.82A, 11.88, 21.15
Al Rushaid Petroleum v TSJ Engineering, April 20, 2010, HC (BVI) 3.08, 3.15, 3.25
Al-Sabah v Grupo Torras SA, unreported, October 10, 2000, PC 6.57
Alcoota v CLC [2001] N.T.S.C. 30, Sup. Ct. (NT) 11.98, 11.94, 11.02, 11.09
Alcoy & Gandia Railway & Harbour Co. v Greenhill [1896] 1 Ch. 19 (1896) 74 L.T. 345, CA 4.12, 4.15, 16.29
Alderton and Barry's Application, Re (1941) 59 R.P.C. 56 .... 5.04
Alexandra Palace Co (No.1), Re (1880–81) L.R. 16 Ch. D. 58, Ch.D 4.37, 16.66

Alfred Crompton Amusement Machines Ltd v Customs and Excise Commissioners (No.2) [1974] A.C. 405 [1973] 3 W.L.R. 268 [1972] 1 W.L.R. 833 [1973] 2 All E.R. 1169 117 S.J. 602, HL affirming [1972] 2 Q.B. 102 [1972] 2 W.L.R. 835 [1972] 2 All E.R. 353 116 S.J. 198, CA (Civ Div) 5.39, 5.44, 8.01, 11.19, 11.38, 11.44, 11.99, 11.35, 11.144
Alfred Crompton Amusement Machines Ltd v Customs and Excise Commissioners (No.1) [1971] 2 All E.R. 843 (1971) 115 S.J. 307, Q.B.D. .. 6.15, 11.89
Alhamrani v Alhamrani, 2009 J.L.R. 301, CA (Jer) 13.07
Ali Shipping Corp v Shipyard Trogir [1999] 1 W.L.R. 314 [1998] 2 All E.R. 136 [1998] 1 Lloyd's Rep. 643 [1998] C.L.C., CA (Civ Div) 2.03, 8.17, 11.147, 15.48, 15.49, 15.52, 15.54
Alizadeh v Nikbin, *The Times*, March 19, 1992, CA (Civ Div) ... 11.122, 11.129
Allan v U.K., *The Times*, November 12, 2002, E.Ct.H.R 21.07
Allan v United Kingdom (App. No.48539/99) (2003) 36 E.H.R.R. 12 13 B.H.R.C. 652, ECHR 11.107, 11.118
Allhusen v Labouchere (1877–78) L.R. 3 Q.B.D. 654, CA ... 16.38, 16.52, 16.53, 16.85
Alliance Flooring Co v Winsorflor (Discovery) [1961] R.P.C. 375 .... 16.72
Allington Investments Corp v First Pacific Bancshares Holdings Ltd [1995] 2 H.K.C. 139, CA (HK) 5.12
Alliott v Smith [1895] 2 Ch. 111, Ch.D 16.95, 16.97
Allitt v Sullivan [1988] V.L.R. 621 .... 11.08
Alphapharm Pty Ltd v Merck & Co Inc [2006] F.C.A. 1227, Fed. Ct. Aus. ... 5.35
Alpine Zurich Insurance v Bain Clarkson, *The Times*, January 23, 1989 ... 18.21
Alterskye v Scott [1948] 1 All E.R. 469 92 S.J. 220, Ch.D .. 15.01, 15.02, 15.18, 15.21, 15.24, 15.45
Altertext Inc v Advanced Data Communications Ltd [1985] 1 W.L.R. 457 [1985] 1 All E.R. 395 [1985] E.C.C. 375 [1986] F.S.R. 21 (1985) 82 L.S.G. 1715 (1985) 129 S.J. 247, Ch.D 2.17, 2.22, 19.04
Amann v Switzerland (2000) 30 E.H.R.R. 843, ECHR 21.12
Ambiorix Ltd v Minister for the Environment [1992] 1 I.R. 277, Sup. Ct. (Irl) 11.82, 11.93, 11.94, 11.98, 15.01
American Cyanamid Co v Ethicon Ltd (No.2) [1977] F.S.R. 593 [1978] R.P.C. 667, CA (Civ Div) 5.35, 19.19
American Endeavour Fund Ltd v Trueger, unreported, January 23, 1998, R Ct (Jersey) 9.18, 9.20
American Home Products Corp v Novartis Pharmaceuticals UK Ltd [2001] F.S.R. 784, CA (Civ Div) 4.55, 4.56
Amery v Long (1808) 9 East 472 .... 10.08
Ampolex Ltd v Perpetual Trustee Co (Canberra) Ltd (1995) 37 N.S.W.L.R. 405, Sup. Ct. (NSW) 11.62, 11.64, 12.02, 12.06
Ampthill Peerage, The [1977] A.C. 547 [1976] 2 W.L.R. 777 [1976] 2 All E.R. 411 120 S.J. 367, HL 20.11
Amwell View School (Chairman & Governors of) v Dogherty, unreported, September 15, 2006, EAT 11.99, 19.25, 21.11
Anderson v Bank of British Columbia (1875–76) L.R. 2 Ch. D. 644, CA ... 4.63, 11.39, 11.40, 11.05, 11.06, 1.14, 11.15, 11.16, 11.23, 11.31, 11.53, 11.153, 12.02, 16.95
Anderson v Halifax Plc [2000] N.I. 1, Ch.D (NI) 3.03
Anderson v John Zivanovic Holdings Ltd (2000) 195 D.L.R. (4th) 713, Sup. Ct. (Div Ct) (Ont) 11.62

Anglo Group Plc v Winther Browne & Co Ltd sub nom. Winther Brown & Co Ltd v Anglo Group Plc [2000] 1 W.L.R. 820 72 Con. L.R. 118 [1999–2000] Info. T.L.R. 61 [2000] I.T.C.L.R. 559 [2000] Masons C.L.R. 13 (2000) 144 S.J.L.B. 197, Q.B.D. (TCC) 18.14
Anglo Irish Bank Corp Plc v West LB AG [2009] EWHC 207 (Comm) 3.31, 3.34
Ankerl v Switzerland (App. No. 17748/91) (2001) 32 E.H.R.R. 1, ECHR 21.06
Annandale (Earldom of) and Hartfell sub nom. Annandale and Hartfell Peerage Claim [1986] A.C. 319 [1986] 2 W.L.R. 43 [1985] 3 All E.R. 577 1986 S.L.T. (Lyon Ct.) 18, HL 20.11
Anon [1876] W.N. 39 .... 6.07
Antares II and Victory, The [1996] 2 Lloyd's Rep. 482, Q.B.D. (Admlty) 18.26
Anti-Dumping Documents, Re sub nom. Greece v Council of Ministers (C–129/86 R) [1989] E.C.R. 3963 [1986] E.C.R. 2071 [1988] 3 C.M.L.R. 728, ECJ 20.36
Anton Piller KG v Manufacturing Processes Ltd [1976] Ch. 55 [1976] 2 W.L.R. 162 [1976] 1 All E.R. 779 [1976] F.S.R. 129 [1976] R.P.C. 719 (1975) 120 S.J. 63, CA (Civ Div) 2.20, 2.21
Applause Store Productions Ltd v Raphael [2008] EWHC 1781 (QB) 3.11
Apple Corps Ltd v Apple Computer Inc (Use of Documents in EC Commission Proceedings) [1992] 1 C.M.L.R. 969 [1992] F.S.R. 389, Ch.D 15.07, 15.31, 15.37, 15.39, 15.41
Applicant v Inspector of Taxes [1999] S.T.C. (S.C.D.) 128 .... 20.79, 20.82
Application by Bayer AG, Re [1999] I.L. Pr. 786, Ct. of Appeals (3rd Cir.) (US) 2.63
Application of Cojuangco, Re (1986) 4 N.S.W.L.R. 513 .... 1.10
Application of Nicholas Basil Cannar, Re Sharon Y. Eubanks [2003] N.S.W.S.C. 802, Sup. Ct. (NSW) 10.55, 10.59
Application of Technostrogexport, Re, 853 F. Supp. 695 (S.D.N.Y., 1994) 2.62
Application Pursuant to r.7.28 of the Insolvency Rules 1986, Re [1994] B.C.C. 369 [1994] 1 B.C.L.C. 104, Ch.D 3.46
Arab Monetary Fund v Hashim, unreported, January 21, 1993 .... 6.22
Arab Monetary Fund v Hashim, unreported, March 2, 1993, affirmed, September 30, 1993, CA (Civ Div) 11.30, 11.78, 12.27, 12.35
Arab Monetary Fund v Hashim (No.4) [1992] 1 W.L.R. 1176 [1992] 4 All E.R. 860, CA (Civ Div) affirming [1992] 1 W.L.R. 553 [1992] 1 All E.R. 645, Ch.D 1.14, 4.47
Arab Monetary Fund v Hashim (No.5) [1992] 2 All E.R. 911, Ch.D 3.06, 3.10, 3.11, 3.14, 3.15, 5.44, 8.23
Arab Monetary Fund v Hashim (No.8) (1994) 6 Admin. L.R. 348, CA (Civ Div) affirming [1989] 1 W.L.R. 565 [1989] 3 All E.R. 466 (1989) 133 S.J. 749, Ch.D 11.105, 11.150, 11.159
Arbitration between Fenner and Lord, Re [1897] 1 Q.B. 667, CA 9.07
Arbuthnott v Fagan (Discovery) Arbuthnott v Feltrim Underwriting Agencies Ltd (In Liquidation) (Discovery) [1996] L.R.L.R. 143, CA (Civ Div) 8.09, **11.143**
Arbuthnott v Fagan. *See* Henderson v Merrett Syndicates Ltd (No.1)
Arbuthnott v Feltrim Underwriting Agencies Ltd (In Liquidation) (Discovery). *See* Arbuthnott v Fagan (Discovery)
Arhill Pty Ltd v General Terminal Company Pty Ltd (1991) 23 N.S.W.L.R. 545 .... 10.09, 10.10, 10.13, 10.31
Armchair Passenger Transport Ltd v Helical Bar Plc [2003] EWHC 367, Q.B.D. 18.12
Armco In. v Donohue, unreported, October 25, 1999, R Ct (Jersey) 2.14
Armour v Walker (1884) L.R. 25 Ch. D. 673, CA 2.61, 17.12

Armstrong v First York Ltd [2005] EWCA Civ 277 [2005] 1 W.L.R. 2751 [2005] C.P. Rep. 25 [2005] R.T.R. 19, CA (Civ Div) 18.22
Arnold & Butler v Bottomley [1908] 2 K.B. 151, CA 5.33, 16.65
Arnott, Re (1888) 60 L.T.N.S. 109 .... 11.13
Arnott v Hayes (1887) L.R. 36 Ch. D. 731, CA 10.44, 10.45
Arrow Nominees Inc v Blackledge [2000] C.P. Rep. 59 [2001] B.C.C. 591 [2000] 2 B.C.L.C. 167 [2000] All E.R. (D), CA (Civ Div) 13.07, 13.17
Arrow Pharmaceuticals Ltd v Merck & Co Inc (2004) 210 A.L.R. 593, Fed. Ct. Aus. 11.19, 11.45, 12.07, 12.08
Arrow Trading & Investments Est 1920 v Edwardian Group Ltd (No.2) [2004] EWHC 1319 [2004] B.C.C. 955 [2005] 1 B.C.L.C. 696, Ch.D (Companies Ct) 6.06, 6.07, 11.73
Arrows Ltd (No.2), Re [1994] 1 B.C.L.C. 355 .... 3.41
Arrows Ltd (No.4), Re [1992] B.C.C. 446 [1992] B.C.L.C. 1176 (1992) 136 S.J.L.B. 164, Ch.D 11.113
Arrows Ltd (No.5), Re sub nom. Hamilton v Naviede Adviser (188), Re Trachtenberg, Ex p. Bishopsgate Investment Management Ltd, Re Headington Investments Ltd, Re [1995] 2 A.C. 75 [1994] 3 W.L.R. 656 [1994] 3 All E.R. 814 [1994] B.C.C. 641 [1994] 2 B.C.L.C. 738 [1995] 1 Cr. App. R. 95 (1994) 144 N.L.J. 1203, HL affirming [1993] Ch. 452 [1993] 3 W.L.R. 513 [1993] 3 All E.R. 861 [1993] B.C.C. 473 [1993] B.C.L.C. 1222 (1993) 143 N.L.J. 688, CA (Civ Div) 2.26, 3.42, 3.44, 11.102, 11.113, 11.114
Arsenal Football Club Plc v Elite Sports Distribution Ltd (No.1) [2002] EWHC 3057 [2003] F.S.R. 26 (2003) 26(3) I.P.D. 26017 (2003) 100(7) L.S.G. 36, Ch.D 3.34
Artisan Scaffolding Co v The Antique Hypermarket Ltd, unreported, February 10, 1993, CA 13.11, 13.13
Asbestos Insurance Coverage Cases, Re. *See* Sedgwick Group Plc v Johns-Manville Fibreboard Corp
Asda Stores Ltd v Thompson [2004] I.R.L.R. 598, EAT 20.30
Asda Stores Ltd v Thompson. *See* Thompson v Asda Stores Ltd
Ash v Buxted Poultry Ltd, *The Times*, May 17, 1990 .... 5.41
Ash v Buxted Poultry Ltd, *The Times*, November 29, 1989, Q.B.D. 19.07
Ashburton (Lord) v Pape [1913] 2 Ch. 469, CA 6.26, 11.76
Ashdown v Telegraph Group Ltd [2001] EWCA Civ 1142 [2002] Ch. 149 [2001] 3 W.L.R. 1368 [2001] 4 All E.R. 666 [2002] E.C.C. 19 [2002] E.C.D.R. 32 [2001] E.M.L.R. 44 [2001] H.R.L.R. 57 [2001] U.K.H.R.R. 1242 [2002] R.P.C. 5 (2001) 24(9) I.P.D. 24058 (2001) 98(33) L.S.G. 29 (2001) 145 S.J.L.B. 201, CA (Civ Div) 21.14
Ashley v Chief Constable of Sussex (Disclosure of documents) [2008] EWHC 3152 (QB) **5.12**
Ashtiani v Kashi [1987] Q.B. 888 [1986] 3 W.L.R. 647 [1986] 2 All E.R. 970 (1986) 83 L.S.G. 3248 (1986) 136 N.L.J. 753 (1985) 130 S.J. 730, CA (Civ Div) 2.15, 16.68
Ashworth Hospital Authority v MGN Ltd sub nom. Ashworth Security Hospital v MGN Ltd [2002] UKHL 29 [2002] 1 W.L.R. 2033 [2002] 4 All E.R. 193 [2002] C.P.L.R. 712 [2002] E.M.L.R. 36 [2002] H.R.L.R. 41 [2002] U.K.H.R.R. 1263 12 B.H.R.C. 443 [2003] F.S.R. 17 (2002) 67 B.M.L.R. 175 (2002) 99(30) L.S.G. 37 (2002) 146 S.J.L.B. 168, HL affirming [2001] 1 W.L.R. 515 [2001] 1 All E.R. 991 [2001] E.M.L.R. 11 [2001] F.S.R. 33 (2001) 61 B.M.L.R. 48 (2001) 98(6) L.S.G. 46 (2001) 145 S.J.L.B. 20, CA (Civ Div) .. 3.05, 3.06, 3.07, 3.18, 3.20, 3.21, 3.25, 21.15

Ashworth Special Hospital, Re, unreported, December 1991 .... 20.68
Ashworth v Roberts (1890) L.R. 45 Ch. D. 623, Ch.D 16.72
Asian Properties Limited, Re (1993–95) M.L.R. 404 .... 1.17
Asiatic Petroleum Co Ltd v Anglo-Persian Oil Co Ltd [1916] 1 K.B. 822, CA 11.96
ASIC v Rich [2003] N.S.W.S.C. 25710.11, 10.14
ASIC v Rich [2005] N.S.W.C.A. 152 (2005) 218 A.L.R. 764 .... 18.14
Aspinall v Sterling Mansell [1981] 3 All E.R. 866, Q.B.D. 19.22
Assi v Dina Foods Ltd [2005] EWHC 1099, Q.B.D. 17.22
Assimina Maritime Ltd v Pakistan National Shipping Corp The Tasman Spirit [2004] EWHC 3005 [2005] 1 All E.R. (Comm.) 460 [2005] 1 Lloyd's Rep. 525 [2005] 2 C.L.C. 448, Q.B.D. (Comm.) ... 10.06, 10.24, 20.05
Assistant Deputy Coroner for Inner West London v Channel 4 Television Corp [2007] EWHC 2513 (QB); [2008] 1 W.L.R. 945; (2008) 100 B.M.L.R. 44 .... 10.10, 10.15, 10.24
Associated Electric & Gas Insurance Services Ltd v European Reinsurance Co of Zurich [2003] UKPC 11 [2003] 1 W.L.R. 1041 [2003] 1 All E.R. (Comm.) 253 [2003] 2 C.L.C. 340 (2003) 100(11) L.S.G. 31 (2003) 147 S.J.L.B. 148, PC (Ber) 15.48, 15.53
Associated Newspapers Ltd Ex p. sub nom. Practice Note (CA: Ex p. Application) [1959] 1 W.L.R. 993 [1959] 3 All E.R. 878 103 S.J. 797, CA 3.45
Associated Newspapers Ltd v United Kingdom, unreported, November 30, 1994, ECHR 21.15
Astra Holdings Plc, Re sub nom. Secretary of State for Trade and Industry v Anderson [1999] B.C.C. 121 [1998] 2 B.C.L.C. 44, Ch.D 5.14, 5.30
Astra National Production v Neo-Art Productions [1928] W.N.218 .... 6.51
Asylum for Idiots v Handyside (1906) 22 T.L.R. 573, CA 10.40
Atari Inc v Philips Electronics and Associated Industries Ltd [1988] F.S.R. 416, Ch.D 11.162
Atherton, Re [1912] 2 K.B. 251, KBD 11.104, 11.113
Athlete's Foot Australia Pty Ltd v Divergent Technologies Pty Ltd (1997) 78 F.C.R. 283, Fed. Ct. Aus. 3.27, 9.28, 19.02
Athletic Union of Constantinople (AEK) v National Basketball Association (Application to Strike Out) sub nom. National Basketball Association v Athletic Union of Constantinople (AEK) (Application to Strike Out) Athletic Union of Constantinople (AEK) v National Basketball Association (No.2) [2002] EWCA Civ 830 [2002] 1 W.L.R. 2863 [2002] 3 All E.R. 897 [2002] 2 All E.R. (Comm.) 385 (2002) 99(29) L.S.G. 33 (2002) 146 S.J.L.B. 153, CA (Civ Div) 6.57
Atikin v Ettershank (1885) 7 A.L.T. 21 .... 9.04
Atkinson v Fosbroke (1866) L.R. 1 Q.B. 628, QB 16.26, 16.60
Atkinson v Stewart and Partners Ltd [1954] N.I.L.R 146, CA 16.49
Atkinson v T&P Fabrications [2001] TAS.S.C. 38, Sup. Ct. (Tas) 12.08, 12.22
Atlan v United Kingdom (App. No.36533/97) (2002) 34 E.H.R.R. 33 [2001] Crim. L.R. 819, ECHR 11.82
Atlanta Gas Light Co v Aetna Casualty & Surety, unreported, February 7, 1993 .... 10.57
Att.-Gen. v Barker (1900) 83 L.T. 245 .... 4.33
Att.-Gen. v Castleford (1872) 21 W.R. 117 .... 4.33
Att.-Gen. v Clapham (1853) 10 Hare Appx. lxviii 4.33
Att.-Gen. v Clough [1963] 1 Q.B. 773 [1963] 2 W.L.R. 343 [1963] 1 All E.R. 420 107 S.J. 96, Q.B.D. 10.15
Att.-Gen. v Emerson (1882–83) L.R. 10 Q.B.D. 191, CA 6.41, 11.51

Att.-Gen. v Gaskill (Interrogatories) (1881–82) L.R. 20 Ch. D. 519, CA 1.12, 16.34, 16.35
Att.-Gen. v Guardian Newspapers Ltd (No.2) Att.-Gen. v Observer Ltd (No.2) Att.-Gen. v Times Newspapers Ltd (No.2) [1990] 1 A.C. 109 [1988] 3 W.L.R. 776 [1988] 3 All E.R. 545 [1989] 2 F.S.R. 181 (1988) 85(42) L.S.G. 45 (1988) 138 N.L.J. Rep. 296 (1988) 132 S.J. 1496, HL 15.08
Att.-Gen. v Jonathan Cape Ltd Att.-Gen. v Times Newspapers Ltd [1976] Q.B. 752 [1975] 3 W.L.R. 606 [1975] 3 All E.R. 484 119 S.J. 696, Q.B.D. 11.98
Att.-Gen. v Landau, unreported, July 10, 1991, Div Ct 4.41
Att.-Gen. v Leveller Magazine Ltd Att.-Gen. v National Union of Journalists Att.-Gen. v Peace News Ltd [1979] A.C. 440 [1979] 2 W.L.R. 247 [1979] 1 All E.R. 745 (1979) 68 Cr. App. R. 342 [1979] Crim. L.R. 247 123 S.J. 129, HL 2.03
Att.-Gen. v Limbrick, *The Times*, March 28, 1996, Q.B.D. 3.45
Att.-Gen. v Lundin (1982) 75 Cr. App. R. 90 [1982] Crim. L.R. 296, DC 11.153
Att.-Gen. v Maurice (1986) 161 C.L.R. 475 .... 11.05
Att.-Gen. v Mulholland Att.-Gen. v Foster [1963] 2 Q.B. 477 [1963] 2 W.L.R. 658 [1963] 1 All E.R. 767 107 S.J. 154, CA 10.15, 11.153
Att.-Gen. v Newcastle-upon-Tyne Corp [1897] 2 Q.B. 384, CA 4.39
Att.-Gen. v Newspaper Publishing Plc sub nom. R. v Blackledge (William Stuart) [1997] 1 W.L.R. 926 [1997] 3 All E.R. 159 [1997] E.M.L.R. 429 (1997) 147 N.L.J. 757, CA (Crim Div) 15.45
Att.-Gen. v North Metropolitan Tramways Co [1892] 3 Ch. 70, Ch.D 8.20, 8.22
Att.-Gen. v Punch Ltd sub nom. Steen v Att.-Gen. [2002] UKHL 50 [2003] 1 A.C. 1046 [2003] 2 W.L.R. 49 [2003] 1 All E.R. 289 [2003] E.M.L.R. 7 [2003] H.R.L.R. 14, HL 15.45, 21.14
Att.-Gen. v Scotcher [2005] UKHL 36 [2005] 1 W.L.R. 1867 [2005] 3 All E.R. 1 [2005] 2 Cr. App. R. 35 [2005] U.K.H.R.R. 637 [2005] Crim. L.R. 791 (2005) 155 N.L.J., HL 21.15
Att.-Gen. v Wang NZ [1990] 3 N.Z.L.R. 148, CA (NZ) 16.45
Att.-Gen. v Whitwood Local Board (1871) 40 L.J. Ch. 592 .... 9.11
Att.-Gen. v Wilson (1829) 9 Sim. 52610.08, 10.10
Att.-Gen.'s Reference (No.7 of 2000), Re [2001] EWCA Crim 888 [2001] 1 W.L.R. 1879 [2001] 2 Cr. App. R. 19 [2001] H.R.L.R. 41 [2001] B.P.I.R. 953 [2001] Crim. L.R. 736 (2001) 98(22) L.S.G. 35 (2001) 145 S.J.L.B. 109, CA (Crim Div) 11.107, 11.118
Att.-Gen.v. Birss [1991] 1 N.Z.L.R. 669 .... 11.99
Att.-Gen. of British Columbia v Davies (2009) 308 D.L.R. (4th) 577, CA (BC) 11.07
Att.-Gen. for New South Wales v Chidgey [2008] NSWSCCA 65 .... 10.11
Att.-Gen. for the Northern Territory v Kearney (1985) 158 C.L.R. 500, H Ct (Aus) 11.19, 11.70
Att.-Gen. for the Northern Territory v Maurice (1986) 161 C.L.R. 475 ..... 11.08, 12.06
Att.-Gen. of Gibraltar v May [1999] 1 W.L.R., CA (Civ Div) 11.105, 15.11, 15.42, 15.43
Att.-Gen. of Gibraltar v May [1999] 1 W.L.R. 998, CA (Civ Div) 2.29
Atos Consulting Ltd v Avis Plc [2007] EWHC 323 (TCC); [2008] Bus. L.R. D20 .... 6.14, 6.18, 9.33, 9.39, 11.14, 11.46, 11.88, 12.36
Au Shui-yuen v Ford [1991] 1 H.K.L.R. 525 .... 11.01
Austin v DPP, *The Times*, November 26, 1992, DC 11.103

Austintel Ltd, Re Applications Pursuant to r.7.28 of the Insolvency Rules 1986, Re Creditnet Ltd, Re Debtor Management Ltd, Re [1997] 1 W.L.R. 616 [1997] B.C.C. 362 [1997] 1 B.C.L.C. 233 [2000] B.P.I.R. 223 (1996) 93(43) L.S.G. 26 (1996) 140 S.J.L.B. 254, CA (Civ Div) 3.46
Australia and New Zealand Banking Group Ltd v National Westminster Bank Plc (2002) 99(12) L.S.G. 35 (2002) 146 S.J.L.B. 51, Ch.D 3.23
Australian Blue Metal v Hughes [1960] N.S.W.R. 673 .... 16.34
Australian Broadcasting Corporation v Seven Network Ltd [2005] F.C.A. 1851 .... 3.34
Australian Competition & Consumer Commission v Advanced Medical Institute Pty Ltd [2005] F.C.A. 366 .... 6.49
Australian Competition and Consumer Commission v Amcor Printing Papers Group Ltd (1999) 163 A.L.R. 465 .... 17.21
Australian Competition and Consumer Commission v Australian Safeway Stores Pty Ltd (1998) 81 F.C.R. 526, Fed. Ct. Aus. 11.31, 11.38, 11.44, 11.46
Australian Competition and Consumer Commission v Cadbury Schweppes Pty Ltd [2009] FCAFC 32 .... 12.10
Australian Competition and Consumer Commission v Shell Co of Australia Ltd (1999) 161 A.L.R. 686, Fed. Ct. Aus. 10.06, 10.10, 10.12, 10.13
Australian Hospital Care (Pindara) Pty Ltd v Duggan [1999] V.S.C. 131, Sup. Ct. (Vic) 11.18
Australian Mining & Smelting Europe Ltd v Commission of the European Communities sub nom. AM&S Europe Ltd v Commisson of the European Communities (155/79) [1983] Q.B. 878 [1983] 3 W.L.R. 17 [1983] 1 All E.R. 705 [1982] E.C.R. 1575 [1982] 2 C.M.L.R. 264 [1982] F.S.R. 474 (1983) 127 S.J. 410, ECJ 11.19, 20.37
Australian National Airlines Commission v Commonwealth of Australia [1975] 49 A.J.L.R. 3385.06, 11.94
Australian Rugby Union Ltd v Hospitality Group Pty Ltd (1999) 165 A.L.R. 25311.14, 12.08
Australian Rugby Union Ltd v Hospitality Group Pty Ltd (2000) 173 A.L.R. 70210.14, 10.15
Australian Securities & Investments Commission (No.3) [2006] F.C.A. 772, Fed. Ct. Aus. 11.70
Australian Securities and Investments Commission v Michalik (2003) 211 A.L.R. 285, Sup. Ct. (NSW) 11.107, 11.111
Australian Securities Commission v Ampolex Ltd (1995) 38 N.S.W.L.R. 504 .... 8.16
Australian Securities Commission v Zorro [1992] A.C.L. Rep.195 F.C.3 ... 12.42
Auten v Rayner (No.2) Auten v Baker Todman & Co [1960] 1 Q.B. 669 [1960] 2 W.L.R. 562 [1960] 1 All E.R. 692 104 S.J. 252, Q.B.D. 10.31, 11.25
Author of a Blog v Times Newspapers Ltd [2009] EWHC 1358 (QB); [2009] E.M.L.R. 22; (2009) 106(26) L.S.G. 18; (2009) 159 N.L.J. 924; (2009) 153(24) S.J.L.B. 33 .... 11.13, 21.11, 21.15
Autronic AG v Switzerland (A/178) (1990) 12 E.H.R.R. 485 [1991] F.S.R. 55, ECHR 21.14
Avanes v Marshall [2007] NSWSC 191: (2007) 69 N.S.W.L.R. 595 .... 4.22
Aveling Barford Ltd, Re [1989] 1 W.L.R. 360 [1988] 3 All E.R. 1019 (1988) 4 B.C.C. 548 [1989] B.C.L.C. 122 [1989] P.C.C. 240 (1988) 138 N.L.J. Rep. 275 (1989) 133 S.J. 512, Ch.D 3.44
Averill v Sunday Pictorial Newspapers Ltd, *The Times*, April 22, 1959 ..... 5.06

Avory Ltd v Ashworth Son & Co Ltd (1915) 32 R.P.C. 463 aff. 32 R.P.C. 560, CA 5.08, 5.25, 5.34
Axen v Germany (A/72) (1984) 6 E.H.R.R. 195, ECHR 21.15
Ayres v Levy (1868) 19 L.T. 8 .... 9.37
Azzi v Volvo [2006] N.S.W.S.C. 283 .... 10.06, 10.13

BBGP Managing General Partner v Babcock & Brown Global Partners [2010] EWHC 2176 (Ch) 11.09, 11.14, 11.67, 11.71, 11.74
B (A) v D (C) (2008) 291 D.L.R. (4th) 359, Alberta CA 3.15
BC v A; D, Re. *See* **Reading BC v D (Angela)**
BC Children's Hospital v Air Products Canada (2003) 224 D.L.R. (4th) 47, CA (BC) 11.124, 11.128
BCCI SA (No.12), Re. *See* Bank of Credit and Commerce International SA (In Liquidation) (No.12)
BCCI SA v Al-Kaylani, unreported, December 13, 1999 .... 16.53
BCCI SA v Al-Kaylani, unreported, July 7, 1999 .... 16.53
BCCI v Rahim, unreported, November 11, 2005, Ch.D 17.03, 17.12
BMG Canada Inc v John Doe (2005) 252 D.L.R. (4th) 342, FCA (Canada) 3.03, 3.06
BNP Paribas v Deloitte & Touche LLP [2003] EWHC 2874 [2004] 1 Lloyd's Rep. 233 [2004] 1 C.L.C. 530 [2004] B.L.R. 90 (2003) 153 N.L.J. 1841, Q.B.D. (Comm.) 2.56, 10.24, 20.05
BNP Paribas v Mezzotero [2004] I.R.L.R. 508 (2004) 148 S.J.L.B. 666, EAT 11.127
BNP Paribas v TH Global Ltd [2009] EWHC 37 (Ch) 3.24
BNZ Investments Ltd v Commissioner of Inland Revenue [2008] 2 N.Z.L.R. 709, Sup Ct of New Zealand 11.98
BOC Ltd v Instrument Technology Ltd sub nom. BOC Ltd v Barlow Barlow v BOC Ltd [2001] EWCA Civ 854 [2002] Q.B. 537 [2001] 3 W.L.R. 1687, CA (Civ Div) 10.54
BPA Industries Ltd v Black (1987) 11 N.S.W.L.R. 609, Sup. Ct. (NSW) 11.116
BPB Industries Plc v Commission of the European Communities (C–310/93 P) sub nom. BPB Industries Plc v Commission of the European Communities (T–65/89) British Gypsum Ltd v Commission of the European Communities (C–310/93 P) [1995] E.C.R. I–865 [1997] 4 C.M.L.R. 238, ECJ 20.35
BSW Ltd v Balltec Ltd [2006] EWHC 822 (Pat); [2007] F.S.R. 1; (2006) 29(6) I.P.D. 29050 .... 3.31
BX v Secretary of State for the Home Department [2010] EWCA Civ 481; [2010] 1 W.L.R. 2463; [2010] U.K.H.R.R. 766 .... 5.38A
B v Auckland District Law Society sub nom. Russell McVeagh McKenzie Bartleet & Co v Auckland District Law Society [2003] UKPC 38 [2003] 2 A.C. 736 [2003] 3 W.L.R. 859 [2004] 4 All E.R. 269 (2003) 100(26) L.S.G. 38 (2003) 147 S.J.L.B. 627, PC (NZ) 11.06, 11.76, 11.77, 12.06, 12.08
B v B (Matrimonial Proceedings: Discovery) [1978] Fam. 181 [1978] 3 W.L.R. 624 [1979] 1 All E.R. 801 122 S.J. 643, Fam Div .. 4.03, 5.39, 5.43, 5.45, 5.46, 5.49
B v N (1994) 35 N.S.W.L.R. 140, Sup. Ct. (NSW) 11.99, 12.43
B v Dentists Disciplinary Tribunal [1994] 1 N.Z.L.R. 95 .... 2.61
B v Scottish National Blood Transfusion Service, 1993 S.L.T. 36 1990 S.C.L.R. 263, OH 11.103

B v United Kingdom (App. No.36337/97) P v United Kingdom (App. No.35974/97) [2001] 2 F.L.R. 261 [2001] 2 F.C.R. 221 (2002) 34 E.H.R.R. 19 11 B.H.R.C. 667 [2001] Fam. Law 506, ECHR 21.15
B v United Kingdom. (1984) 38 D.R. 213 .... 21.05
BR v Germany, unreported, October 23, 1997 .... 21.13
BSB Holdings Ltd (Joinder), Re [1992] B.C.C. 915 [1993] B.C.L.C. 246, Ch.D 10.23
BSW Ltd v Balltec Ltd [2006] EWHC 822 (2006) 29(6) I.P.D. 29050, Ch.D (Patents Ct) 3.34
B (A Child) (Sexual Abuse: Expert's Report), Re sub nom. B (A Child) (Sexual Abuse: Independent Expert), Re [2000] 1 F.L.R. 871 [2000] 2 F.C.R. 8 [2000] Fam. Law 479 (2000) 164 J.P.N. 624, CA (Civ Div) 18.09
B (A Child) (Split Hearings: Jurisdiction), Re [2000] 1 W.L.R. 790 [2000] 1 F.L.R. 334 [2000] 1 F.C.R. 297 [2000] Fam. Law 320 (2000) 164 J.P.N. 441 (1999) 96(48) L.S.G. 39 (2000) 144 S.J.L.B. 23, CA (Civ Div) ... 18.22
B (A Minor) (Contempt of Court: Affidavit Evidence), Re [1996] 1 W.L.R. 627 [1996] 1 F.L.R. 239 [1996] 1 F.C.R. 158 [1996] Fam. Law 147 (1995) 92(44) L.S.G. 30 (1996) 140 S.J.L.B. 12, Fam Div 11.109
B (A Minor) (Disclosure of Evidence), Re sub nom. B (A Minor) (Confidential Evidence: Disclosure), Re [1993] Fam. 142 [1993] 2 W.L.R. 20 [1993] 1 All E.R. 931 [1993] 1 F.L.R. 191 [1992] 2 F.C.R. 617 [1993] Fam. Law 26, CA (Civ Div) 4.04
B (L) (M) v B (R) (Note) [1968] 1 W.L.R. 1182 [1968] 3 All E.R. 170 112 S.J. 504, CA (Civ Div) 19.20
B (LM) v B (IJ) (2005) 251 D.L.R. (4th), CA (Alberta) 11.153
B Johnson & Co (Builders) Ltd v Minister of Health [1947] 2 All E.R. 395 111 J.P. 508 45 L.G.R. 617 [1947] W.N. 251 [1948] L.J.R. 155 177 L.T. 455, CA 20.66
B&S Displays v Inland Revenue Commissioners sub nom. B&S Displays v Special Commissioners of Income Tax [1978] S.T.C. 331 [1978] T.R. 61, Ch.D 20.82
B, R and C (Children), Re [2002] EWCA Civ 1825 [2003] Fam. Law 305, CA (Civ Div) 4.04
Babanaft International Co SA v Bassatne (No.2), unreported, May 23, 1989, CA 10.12, 10.26
Babanaft International Co SA v Bassatne [1990] Ch. 13 [1989] 2 W.L.R. 232 [1989] 1 All E.R. 433 [1988] 2 Lloyd's Rep. 435 [1989] E.C.C. 151 (1988) 138 N.L.J. Rep. 203 (1989) 133 S.J. 46, CA (Civ Div) 2.18, 4.66, 4.67
Babcock v Attorney-General of Canada (2002) 214 D.L.R. (4th) 193, SCC ... 11.98, 12.42
Bailey v Beagle Management Pty Ltd (2001) 182 A.L.R. 264, Fed. Ct. Aus. ... 11.44, 11.124
Bailey v Beagle Management Pty Ltd [2001] F.C.A. 60, Fed. Ct. Aus. 2.39, 5.30, 6.51
Bailey v IBC Vehicles Ltd [1998] 3 All E.R. 570 [1998] 2 Costs L.R. 46 (1998) 142 S.J.L.B. 126, CA (Civ Div) 2.39
Bailie v Bloomfield Bakery [1926] N.I. 53 .... 4.19
Baker v Campbell (1983) 153 C.L.R. 52, H Ct (Aus) 11.05, 11.08, 11.12
Baker v Campbell (1983) 49 A.L.R. 38511.56, 11.57
Baker v Newton (1875) Bitt. Prac. Cas. 80 .... 16.38
Balabel v Air India [1988] Ch. 317 [1988] 2 W.L.R. 1036 [1988] 2 All E.R. 246 [1988] E.G.C.S. 38 (1988) 138 N.L.J. Rep. 85 (1988) 132 S.J. 699, CA (Civ Div) 11.05, 11.08, 11.09, 11.10, 11.11

Balcombe Group Plc v London Development Agency [2008] EWHC 1392 (TCC) 18.23
Baldock v Addison [1995] 1 W.L.R. 158 [1995] 3 All E.R. 437 [1994] F.S.R. 665 (1995) 92(3) L.S.G. 38, Ch.D 2.33, 5.12, 5.21, 8.20, 8.29, 8.30
Balfour v Foreign and Commonwealth Office [1994] 1 W.L.R. 681 [1994] 2 All E.R. 588 [1994] I.C.R. 277, CA (Civ Div) affirming [1993] I.C.R. 663, EAT 11.94, 11.96
Balkanbank v Taher (No.1) [1994] 4 All E.R. 239, Q.B.D. ... 12.10, 12.23, 12.36
Balmoral Group Ltd v Borealis (UK) Ltd [2006] EWHC 2531, Q.B.D. (Comm.) 18.15
Baltic Shipping Co v Translink Shipping Ltd [1995] 1 Lloyd's Rep. 673, Q.B.D. (Comm.) 2.18
Banco Nacional de Comercio Exterior SNC v Empresa de Telecomunicationes de Cuba SA [2007] EWCA Civ 662; [2008] Bus. L.R. 1265; [2007] 1 W.L.R. 1936; [2007] 2 All E.R. (Comm) 1093; [2007] 2 Lloyd's Rep. 484; [2007] C.P. Rep. 39; [2007] 2 C.L.C. 34; [2007] I.L.Pr. 51; (2007) 104(29) L.S.G. 22; (2007) 151 S.J.L.B. 923 .... 2.19
Bank Geselleschaft Berlin International SA v Zihnali sub nom. Bankgesellschaft Berlin International SA v Zihnali, unreported, July 16, 2001, Q.B.D. (Comm.) 2.28, 11.105, 11.150
Bank Mellat v Helleniki Techniki SA [1984] Q.B. 291 [1983] 3 W.L.R. 783 [1983] 3 All E.R. 428 [1983] Com. L.R. 273 (1983) 133 N.L.J. 597 (1983) 127 S.J. 618, CA (Civ Div) 8.08
Bank Mellat v HM Treasury [2010] EWCA Civ 483; [2010] 3 W.L.R. 1090; [2010] U.K.H.R.R. 760; [2010] Lloyd's Rep. F.C. 499 .... 5.38A
Bank Mellat v Kazmi [1989] Q.B. 541 [1989] 2 W.L.R. 613 [1989] 1 All E.R. 925 (1989) 133 S.J. 185, CA (Civ Div) 4.65
Bank of Baroda v Panessar [1987] Ch. 335 [1987] 2 W.L.R. 208 [1986] 3 All E.R. 751 [1987] P.C.C. 165 (1987) 84 L.S.G. 339 (1986) 136 N.L.J. 963 (1987) 131 S.J. 21, Ch.D 8.08
Bank of China v NBM LLC [2001] EWCA Civ 1933 [2002] 1 W.L.R. 844 [2002] 1 All E.R. 717 [2002] 1 All E.R. (Comm.) 472 [2002] 1 Lloyd's Rep. 506 [2002] C.P. Rep. 19 [2002] C.L.C. 477 (2002) 99(9) L.S.G. 29 (2002) 146 S.J.L.B. 22, CA (Civ Div) 2.18
Bank of China v Xu Chao Fan [2003] B.C.S.C. 1672, Sup. Ct. (BC) 15.42
Bank of Columbia v CBC(1995) 126 D.L.R. (4th) 644, CA (BC) 5.08
Bank of Credit and Commerce International (Overseas) Ltd (In Liquidation) v Price Waterhouse (No.3) Bank of Credit and Commerce International (Overseas) Ltd (In Liquidation) v Ernst & Whinney [1998] Ch. 84 [1997] 3 W.L.R. 849 [1997] 4 All E.R. 781 [1997] 6 Bank. L.R. 216 [1998] B.C.C., Ch.D 8.09, 10.31, 11.143, 16.90
Bank of Credit and Commerce International SA (In Liquidation) (No.12), Re sub nom. Morris v Bank of America National Trust and Savings Association [1997] B.C.C. 561 [1997] 1 B.C.L.C. 526, Ch.D 3.40, 3.41
Bank of Crete SA v Koskotas (No.2) [1992] 1 W.L.R. 919 [1993] 1 All E.R. 748, Ch.D 15.21, 15.42
Bank of Crete SA v Koskotas [1991] 2 Lloyd's Rep. 587 [1992] I.L.Pr. 356, CA (Civ Div) 2.14, 5.30, 8.26, 11.154
Bank of England v Riley [1992] Ch. 475 [1992] 2 W.L.R. 840 [1992] 1 All E.R. 769, CA (Civ Div) 11.114
Bank of New South Wales v Withers (1981) 35 A.L.R. 21 .... 10.35
Bank of Nova Scotia v Hellenic Mutual War Risks Association (Bermuda) Ltd The Good Luck (Disclosure) [1992] 2 Lloyd's Rep. 540 (Note), Q.B.D. (Comm.) 6.18, 9.38, 11.14, 11.27, 11.60, 11.62, 12.35

Bank of Russian Trade Ltd v British Screen Productions Ltd [1930] 2 K.B. 90, CA 16.94, 16.99, 16.102
Bankers Trust Co v Shapira [1980] 1 W.L.R. 1274 [1980] 3 All E.R. 353 124 S.J. 480, CA (Civ Div) ... 2.13, 3.03, 3.05, 3.11, 3.15, 3.23, 4.64, 10.44, 11.69, 15.22
Bankers Trust International v PT Dharmala Sakti Sejahtera, unreported, October 19, 1995, Q.B.D. (Comm.) 2.58
Banks v Cox, unreported, July 17, 2000, CA (Civ Div) 2.53
Banque Bruxelles Lambert SA v Eagle Star Insurance Co Ltd, unreported, February 26, 1993 .... 10.13
Banque Bruxelles Lambert SA v Simmons & Simmons, unreported, November 24, 1995 .... 12.04
Banque Keyser Ullman SA v Skandia (UK) Insurance Co Ltd, unreported, July 2, ... 19858.26, 11.141, 11.154
Banque Keyser Ullmann SA v Skandia (UK) Insurance Co (No.1) [1986] 1 Lloyd's Rep. 336, CA (Civ Div) 11.67, 1.68
Banque Keyser Ullmann SA v Skandia (UK) Insurance Co Ltd, unreported, July 11, 1986, CA (Civ Div) 12.28
Barbados Redifusion v asha Mirchandani (No.2) [2006] CCJ1 (AJ); (2006) 69 W.I.R. 52 .... 13.10
Barclays Bank Plc v Ellis [2001] C.P. Rep. 50, CA (Civ Div) 21.01
Barclays Bank Plc v Eustice [1995] 1 W.L.R. 1238 [1995] 4 All E.R. 511 [1995] B.C.C. 978 [1995] 2 B.C.L.C. 630 (1995) 145 N.L.J. 1503 (1995) 70 P. & C.R. D29, CA (Civ Div) 11.69, 11.67, 11.70
Barclays Bank Plc v Taylor Trustee Savings Bank of Wales and Border Counties v Taylor [1989] 1 W.L.R. 1066 [1989] 3 All E.R. 563 [1989] Fin. L.R. 304 (1990) 87(4) L.S.G. 66 (1989) 133 S.J. 1372, CA (Civ Div) 10.15, 10.28
Barham v Lord Huntingfield [1913] 2 K.B. 193, CA 16.42, 16.60
Barings plc, Re. *See* Secretary of State for Trade and Industry v Baker (No.2)
Barings Plc (In Liquidation) v Coopers & Lybrand (No.1) sub nom. Barings Futures (Singapore) PTE Ltd (In Liquidation) v Mattar (No.1) [2000] 1 W.L.R. 2353 [2000] 3 All E.R. 910 [2000] Lloyd's Rep. Bank. 225 (2000) 150 N.L.J. 681, CA (Civ Div) 8.09, 11.143, 12.42
Barings Plc (In Liquidation) v Coopers & Lybrand (No.2) Barings Futures (Singapore) Pte Ltd (In Liquidation) v Mattar (No.2) [2001] Lloyd's Rep. Bank. 85 [2001] Lloyd's Rep. P.N. 379 [2001] P.N.L.R. 22 (2001) 98(13) L.S.G. 40, Ch.D 18.11
Barker v Wilson [1980] 1 W.L.R. 884 [1980] 2 All E.R. 81 (1980) 70 Cr. App. R. 283 [1980] Crim. L.R. 373 124 S.J. 326, DC 5.02, 5.05, 10.40
Barlow Clowes Gilt Managers Ltd, Re [1992] Ch. 208 [1992] 2 W.L.R. 36 [1991] 4 All E.R. 385 [1991] B.C.C. 608 [1991] B.C.L.C. 750 (1991) 141 N.L.J. 999 [1991] N.P.C. 73, Ch.D 3.42, 11.102, 15.01
Barned's Banking Co Ex p. Contract Corp, Re (1866–67) L.R. 2 Ch. App. 350, CA in Chancery 4.37, 16.29, 16.66
Barnes v FCT [2007] FCAFC 88; 242 A.L.R. 601 .... 11.31, 11.32
Barnes (t/a Pool Motors) v Seabrook [2010] EWHC 1849 (Admin) 13.27
Barnetson v Framlington Group Ltd; sub nom. Framlington Group Ltd v Barnetson [2007] EWCA Civ 502; [2007] 1 W.L.R. 2443; [2007] 3 All E.R. 1054; [2007] C.P. Rep. 42; [2007] I.C.R. 1439; [2007] I.R.L.R. 598; (2007) 23 Const. L.J. 665 .... 11.127
Baron v Lovell [1999] C.P.L.R. 630 [2000] P.I.Q.R. P20, CA (Civ Div) 18.08, 18.15

Barratt v Kearns [1905] 1 K.B. 504, CA 11.138, 16.62
Barrett v Ministry of Defence (1990), *The Times*, January 24, 1990 *Independent*, January 23, 1990 *Guardian*, April 13, 1990 *Daily Telegraph*, February 5, 1990, Q.B.D. 3.36, 11.93, 11.101
Barristers (Wasted Costs Order: Criminal Proceedings) (No.5 of 1997), Re, *The Times*, September 7, 1999, CA (Crim Div) 10.12, 10.35, 14.16
Bartram & Son v EA Clark & Son Pty Ltd [1905] V.R. 442 .... 11.39
Bates v Burchell [1884] W.N. 108 .... 16.29
Bates v Microstar Ltd [2003] EWHC 661 (2003) 100(22) L.S.G. 30, Ch.D ... 15.39
Baugh v Delta Water Fittings, Ltd [1971] 1 W.L.R. 1295 [1971] 3 All E.R. 258 115 S.J. 485, Q.B.D. 19.22
Baxter v RMC Group plc [2003] 1 N.Z.L.R. 304 .... 12.08
Bay Milk Products Ltd v Earthquake and War Damage Commission [1990] 1 N.Z.L.R. 139, CA (NZ) 5.22, 5.24
Bayer AG v Harris Pharmaceuticals Ltd [1991] F.S.R. 170, Ch.D 9.22
Bayer AG v Winter (No.2) [1986] 1 W.L.R. 540 [1986] 2 All E.R. 43 (1985) 130 S.J. 373, Ch.D 2.13, 2.15
Bayer AG v Winter (No.3) [1986] E.C.C. 465 [1986] F.S.R. 357, Ch.D 2.14
Beachley Property Ltd v Edgar [1997] P.N.L.R. 197 (1997) 13 Const. L.J. 67, CA (Civ Div) 17.21
Beal v Pilling (1878) 38 L.T. 846 .... 16.26
Beaumont v Ministry of Defence [2009] EWHC 1258 (QB) 18.08
Beazer Homes Ltd v Stroude. *See* Stroude v Beazer Homes Ltd
Beck v Canadian Imperial Bank of Commerce [2009] EWCA Civ 619; [2009] I.R.L.R. 740; (2009) 153(26) S.J.L.B. 28 .... 6.53
Beck v Ministry of Defence [2003] EWCA Civ 1043 [2005] 1 W.L.R. 2206 [2003] C.P. Rep. 62 [2004] P.I.Q.R. P1 (2003) 100(31) L.S.G. 31, CA (Civ Div) 18.07, 19.22
Beeforth v Beeforth, *The Times*, September 17, 1998, CA (Civ Div) 13.10, 13.24
Beer v Ward (1821) Jac. 77 .... 10.15
Beeston Shipping Ltd v Babanaft International SA The Eastern Venture [1985] 1 All E.R. 923 (1983) 80 L.S.G. 2683 (1983) 127 S.J. 682, CA (Civ Div) 2.49
Begum (Runa) v Tower Hamlets LBC sub nom. Tower Hamlets LBC v Begum (Runa) [2003] UKHL 5 [2003] 2 A.C. 430 [2003] 2 W.L.R. 388 [2003] 1 All E.R. 731 [2003] H.R.L.R. 16 [2003] U.K.H.R.R. 419 14 B.H.R.C. 400 [2003] H.L.R. 32 [2003] B.L.G.R. 205 2003 Hous. L.R. 20 [2003] A.C.D. 41 (2003) 100(13) L.S.G. 28 (2003) 147 S.J.L.B. 232 [2003] N.P.C. 21, HL 21.05
Belegging-en Exploitatiemaatschapij Lavender BV v Witten Industrial Diamonds Ltd [1979] F.S.R. 59, CA (Civ Div) 5.34
Belgian Linguistic Case (A/6) (1979–80) 1 E.H.R.R. 252, ECHR 21.08, 21.18
Bell Group Ltd v Westpac [2004] WASC 162, (2004) 208 A.L.R. 491, Sup. Ct. (W Aus) 2.61, 17.12
Bellet, Ex p. (1786) 1 Cox. 297 .... 19.20
Belletti v Morici [2009] EWHC 2316 (Comm); [2010] 1 All E.R. (Comm) 412; [2009] 2 C.L.C. 525; [2009] I.L.Pr. 57; (2009) 153(37) S.J.L.B. 37; [2010] Bus. L.R. D49 .... 2.19
Bellis v U.S., 417 U.S. 85 (1974) 11.107
Belt v Basildon & Thurrock NHS Trust [2004] EWHC 783, Q.B.D. 11.127
Benchmark v Standards Australia [2004] F.C.A. 1489, (2005) 212 A.L.R. 464 .... 3.34
Bendenoun v France (A/284) (1994) 18 E.H.R.R. 54, ECHR 21.05

Benecke v National Australia Bank Ltd (1993) 35 N.S.W.L.R. 110, CA (NSW) 11.64, 12.06
Beneficial Finance Corp Co Ltd v Conway [1970] V.R. 321 .... 5.06
Beneficial Finance Corp Ltd v Price Waterhouse (1996) 68 S.A.S.R. 19, Sup. Ct. (Full Ct) (s Aus) 5.23, 20.55
Benfield Holdings Ltd v Richardson (Elliott) [2007] EWHC 171 (QB) 2.58, 2.63
Bengalla Mining Co Pty Ltd v Barclay Mowlem Construction [2001] N.S.W.S.C. 93, Sup. Ct. (NSW) 101.06, 10.29, 20.05
Benham v United Kingdom (App. No.19380/92) (1996) 22 E.H.R.R. 293, ECHR 21.05, 21.17
Bennett v Chief Executive Officer, Australian Customs Service (2004) 210 A.L.R. 220, Fed. Ct. Aus. 12.26
Bennett v Commissioner of Police of the Metropolis (1994) [1995] 1 W.L.R. 488 [1995] 2 All E.R. 1, Ch.D 11.89, 12.42
Bennett v Compass Group UK & Ireland Ltd [2002] EWCA Civ 642 [2002] C.P. Rep. 58 [2002] C.P.L.R. 452 [2002] I.C.R. 1177, CA (Civ Div) 9.34
Bennett v Greenland Houchen & Co [1998] P.N.L.R. 458, CA (Civ Div) 3.28
Benno Jaffe and Darmstädter Lanolin Fabrik v Richardson & Co (1893) 62 L.J. Ch. 710 .... 2.33, 16.72
Berezovsky v Abramovich [2010] EWHC 2010 (Comm) 5.10
Berg v IML London Ltd [2002] 1 W.L.R. 3271 [2002] 4 All E.R. 87, Q.B.D. 11.122
Berkeley Administration Inc v McClelland (Specific Discovery) [1990] F.S.R. 381, CA (Civ Div) 5.30, 6.44, 6.53, 6.56, 8.19, 8.20, 8.29
Berkeley Administration Ltd v McClelland, unreported, May 1, 1991, CA ... 8.20
Berkeley v Standard Discount Co (1879–80) L.R. 13 Ch. D. 97, CA 16.104, 16.102
Berlei Hestia (NZ) Ltd v Fernyhough [1980] 2 N.Z.L.R. 150 .... 5.52
Bermuda International Securities Ltd v KPMG [2001] EWCA Civ 269 [2001] C.P. Rep. 73 [2001] C.P.L.R. 252 [2001] Lloyd's Rep. P.N. 392 (2001) 98(15) L.S.G. 33 (2001) 145 S.J.L.B. 70, CA (Civ Div) 3.30, 3.39
Bernard, The [1905] W.N. 73, CA 16.54
Bernarus v Haughton [2005] IEHC 240, High Ct of Ireland 10.40
Berry Trade Ltd v Moussavi (No.3) [2003] EWCA Civ 715 (2003) 100(29) L.S.G. 36 (2003) 147 S.J.L.B. 625, CA (Civ Div) 11.129
Berry v Tottenham Hotspur Football & Athletic Co Ltd Stewart v Tottenham Hotspur Football & Athletic Co Ltd [1935] Ch. 718, Ch.D 8.08
Betfair Pty Ltd v Racing New South Wales (No.7) [2009] FCA 1140 .... 11.98, 11.129
Bevan v Hastings Jones [1978] 1 W.L.R. 294 [1978] 1 All E.R. 479 122 S.J. 146, Ch.D 11.58
Bevan v Webb (Inspection of Books) sub nom. Bevan v Webb [1901] 2 Ch. 59, CA 5.53
Bewicke v Graham (1880–81) L.R. 7 Q.B.D. 400, CA 6.41, 11.51
Bhimji v Chatwani (No.1) [1991] 1 W.L.R. 989 [1991] 1 All E.R. 705, Ch.D 2.20
Bhimji v Chatwani (No.2) sub nom. Chatwani v Bhimji [1992] 1 W.L.R. 1158 [1992] 4 All E.R. 912 [1992] B.C.L.C. 387, Ch.D ... 2.14, 2.15, 10.52, 11.109, 15.11, 15.33
Biala Pty Ltd v Mallina Holdings Ltd [1990] W.A.R., 174 .... 11.144
Bibby & Baron Ltd v Duerden (1910) 27 R.P.C. 283 .... 5.35
Bibby Bulk Carriers v Cansulex [1989] Q.B. 155 [1989] 2 W.L.R. 182 [1988] 2 All E.R. 820 [1988] 1 Lloyd's Rep. 565 [1988] 1 F.T.L.R. 113 (1988) 132 S.J. 1640, Q.B.D. (Comm.) 15.27, 15.37, 15.31, 15.41

Bidder v Bridges (No.2) (1885) L.R. 29 Ch. D. 29, CA 16.83
Biguzzi v Rank Leisure Plc [1999] 1 W.L.R. 1926 [1999] 4 All E.R. 934 [2000] C.P. Rep. 6 [1999] C.P.L.R. 675 [2000] 1 Costs L.R., CA (Civ Div) 13.07
Biola, The (1876) 34 L.T. (N.S.) 185 .... 16.54
Birch v Islands' Insurance Company Ltd (1993) 16 G.L.J. 47 .... 1.17
Birch v Mather (1883) L.R. 22 Ch. D. 629, Ch.D 16.72
Birchal v Birch Crisp & Co [1913] 2 Ch. 375, CA 4.11, 16.27
Bird v Hadkinson [2000] C.P. Rep. 21 [1999] B.P.I.R. 653, Ch.D 2.13, 13.29, 16.95, 16.113
Bird v Malzy (1856) 1 C.B. (N.S.) 308 .... 8.21
Birds Eye Walls Ltd v Harrison [1985] I.C.R. 278 [1985] I.R.L.R. 47 (1985) 82 L.S.G. 1006, EAT 20.31, 20.88
Birmingham & Midland Motor Omnibus Co Ltd v London & North Western Railway Co [1913] 3 K.B. 850, CA 6.44, 11.39, 11.46
Birmingham Banking Co, Re, Ex p. Brinsley (1866) 36 L.J. Ch. 1504.36, 15.02
Birmingham City Council v O. *See* R. v Birmingham City Council Ex p. O
Birmingham Midshires Mortgage Services Ltd v Ansell [1998] P.N.L.R. 237, Ch.D 11.69
Birrell v ANA Commission (1994) 55 A.L.R. 211 .... 12.03, 12.37
Bishopsgate Investment Management Ltd (In Provisional Liquidation) v Maxwell Cooper (Provisional Liquidator of Bishopsgate Investment Management Ltd) v Maxwell Mirror Group Newspapers Plc v Maxwell [1993] Ch. 1 [1992] 2 W.L.R. 991 [1992] 2 All E.R. 856 [1992] B.C.C. 222 (1992) 136 S.J.L.B. 69, CA (Civ Div) 3.44, 11.113, 11.120, 12.38
Bishopsgate Management Ltd, Re. *See* Arrows Ltd (No.5), Re
Black v Sumitomo Corp [2001] EWCA Civ 1819 [2002] 1 W.L.R. 1562 [2003] 3 All E.R. 643 [2002] 1 Lloyd's Rep. 693 [2002] C.P.L.R. 148, CA (Civ Div) 3.30, 3.31, 3.33, 3.34
Black & Decker Inc v Flymo Ltd [1991] 1 W.L.R. 753 [1991] 3 All E.R. 158 [1991] F.S.R. 93, Ch.D 1.02, 11.08, 11.136, 12.10
Blackpool Corp v Locker [1948] 1 K.B. 349 [1948] 1 All E.R. 85 (1948) 112 J.P. 130 46 L.G.R. 58 [1948] L.J.R. 847, CA 11.19
Blair v Haycock Cadle Co (1917) 34 T.L.R. 39, HL 16.35
Blakebrough v British Motor Corp (1969) 113 S.J. 366, CA (Civ Div) 5.25
Blanco v Scottish Ministers. *See* Somerville v Scottish Ministers
Blank v Canada (Minister of Justice) 2006 SCC 31, SCC 11.33
Blunt v Park Lane Hotel Ltd [1942] 2 K.B. 253, CA 11.104, 11.105, 11.110
Board v Thomas Hedley & Co [1951] 2 All E.R. 431 [1951] 2 T.L.R. 779 [1951] W.N. 422 95 S.J. 546, CA 5.25
Boeing Co v PPG Industries [1988] 3 All E.R. 839 (1988) 138 N.L.J. Rep. 259, CA (Civ Div) 10.29, 10.54, 10.61
Bolckow Vaughn & Co v Fisher sub nom. Bolckow v Fisher Bolckow Vaughan & Co v Fisher (1882–83) L.R. 10 Q.B.D. 161, CA 1.12, 4.20, 16.97, 16.103, 16.95, 16.97, 16.98
Bolckow, Vaughan & Co v Young (1880) 42 L.T. 690 .... 16.44
Bolkiah v KPMG sub nom. HRH Prince Jefri Bolkiah v KPMG [1999] 2 A.C. 222 [1999] 2 W.L.R. 215 [1999] 1 All E.R. 517 [1999] 1 B.C.L.C. 1 [1999] C.L.C. 175 [1999] P.N.L.R. 220 (1999) 149 N.L.J. 16 (1999) 143 S.J.L.B. 35, 1999, HL 15.46
Bolton Borough v W, unreported, April 3, 1987, Fam D (Manchester) 5.06
Bonisch v Austria (A/92) sub nom. Bonisch v Austria (App. No.8658/79) (1987) 9 E.H.R.R. 191, ECHR 21.06

Bonnardet v Taylor (1861) 1 J. & H. 383 .... 9.11, 9.31
Bonzel (T) v Intervention Ltd (No.2) [1991] R.P.C. 231, Ch.D (Patents Ct) ... 12.33
Bookbinder v Tebbit (No.2) [1992] 1 W.L.R. 217, Q.B.D. ... 10.13, 10.31, 11.99, 11.143
Booth v Warrington HA [1992] P.I.Q.R. P137, Q.B.D. 12.23
Borgers v Belgium, unreported, October 30, 1999, ECHR 21.06, 21.16
Borough Council (A) v A (Chief Constable of Thames Valley Police intervening). ***See*** **Reading BC v D (Angela)**
Botany Bay Instrumentation & Control Pty Ltd v Stewart [1984] 3 N.S.W.L.R. 98 .... 10.29
Botta v Italy (App. No.21439/93) (1998) 26 E.H.R.R. 241 4 B.H.R.C. 81 (1999) 2 C.C.L. Rep. 53 [1998] H.R.C.D. 302, ECHR 21.18
Bournemouth & Boscombe Athletic Community Football Club Ltd, Re. ***See*** **Noonan (Architectural Practice) Ltd v Bournemouth & Boscombe Athletic Community Football Club Ltd**
Bourns Inc v Raychem Corp (No.3) [1999] 3 All E.R. 154 [1999] C.L.C. 1029 [1999] 2 Costs L.R. 72 [1999] F.S.R. 641 (1999) 22(7) I.P.D. 22063, CA (Civ Div) 12.07, 12.10, 12.20, 12.22, 12.23, 12.29, 12.30, 12.32, 15.07, 15.11, 15.42, 15.55
Bova v Avati [2009] NSWSC 921 .... 5.48
Bovill v Cowan (1869–70) L.R. 5 Ch. App. 495, CA in Chancery 6.14
Bown v Gould & Swayne [1996] P.N.L.R. 130 [1996] N.P.C. 5, CA (Civ Div) 18.11
Boyle v United Kingdom (1985) 41 D.R. 90, Eur Comm. HR 21.10
Boyse (No.2), Re sub nom. Crofton v Crofton (1881–82) L.R. 20 Ch. D. 760, Ch.D 2.61, 17.12
Bozkurt v Thames Magistrates Court. *See* R. (on the application of Bozkurt) v Thames Magistrates Court sub nom. Bozkurt v Thames Magistrates Court
Bradbrook Ex p. Hawkins, Re (1889) L.R. 23 Q.B.D. 226, CA 17.04
Bradbury v Cooper (1883–84) L.R. 12 Q.B.D. 94, Q.B.D. 16.60
Bradford & Bingley Plc v Rashid [2006] UKHL 37 [2006] 1 W.L.R. 2066 (2006) 103(30) L.S.G. 30 (2006) 156 N.L.J. 1172 (2006) 150 S.J.L.B. 983, HL 11.122, 11.125, 11.128, 11.129
Bradley v Eagle Star Insurance Co Ltd [1989] A.C. 957 [1989] 2 W.L.R. 568, HL affirming [1988] 2 Lloyd's Rep. 233 [1988] Fin. L.R. 238, CA (Civ Div) 3.31
Bradshaw v Widdington (1902) 86 L.T. 726 .... 10.06
Braegrove Pty Ltd v Benedeich [1993] 2 Qd.R. 239, Sup. Ct. (Queensland) 6.15
Bramblevale, Re [1970] Ch. 128 [1969] 3 W.L.R. 699 [1969] 3 All E.R. 1062 113 S.J. 775, CA (Civ Div) 11.109
Brannigan v Davison [1997] A.C. 238 [1996] 3 W.L.R. 859 2 B.H.R.C. 395 (1996) 140 S.J.L.B. 231, PC (NZ) 11.104
Braswell v U.S., 487 U.S. 99 (1988) 11.107
Breakspear v Ackland [2008] EWHC 220 (Ch); [2008] 2 All E.R. (Comm) 62; [2008] W.T.L.R. 777; (2007–08) 10 I.T.E.L.R. 852; (2008) 105(9) L.S.G. 29 .... 4.23, 5.52
Brebner v Perry [1961] S.A.S.R. 177 .... 11.111
Breen v Williams (1996) 70 A.L.J.R. 772, HC (Aus) 5.52
Breeze v Ahmad [2005] EWCA Civ 223 [2005] C.P. Rep. 29, CA (Civ Div) 18.14
Breeze v John Stacey and Sons Ltd, *The Times*, July 8, 1999, CA 6.27, 11.76, 12.17, 12.18

Brennan v Sunderland City Council [2009] I.C.R. 479, EAT 12.19
Breslin v McKenna [2007] NICA 14; [2007] N.I. 201 ..... 11.105, 11.113, 15.34, 15.56
Bre-X Minerals Ltd, Re (2002) 206 D.L.R. (4th) 280, CA (Alberta) 12.02
Briamore Manufacturing Ltd (In Liquidation), Re [1986] 1 W.L.R. 1429 [1986] 3 All E.R. 132 (1987) 84 L.S.G. 36 (1986) 136 N.L.J. 608 (1986) 130 S.J. 924, Ch.D 6.25, 6.26, 12.17
Brickman's Settlement, Brickman v Goddard Trustees (Jersey) Ltd (Note), Re. *See* Practice Note (Ch.D: Evidence by Deposition: Conduct of Examination)
Bridal Fashions Pty Ltd v Comptroller-General of Customs (1997) 17 W.A.R. 499, Sup. Ct. (Full Ct) (W Aus) 11.107
Bridgmont v Associated Newspapers (No.2) [1951] 2 K.B. 578 [1951] 2 All E.R. 285 [1951] 2 T.L.R. 682 95 S.J. 529, CA 16.64
Briggs v Morgan (1820) 2 Hag. Con. 324 .... 19.20
Briggs & Forrester Electrical Ltd v Southfield School for Girls Governors [2005] EWHC 1734 [2005] B.L.R. 468, Q.B.D. (TCC) 3.34
Bristol Corp v Cox sub nom. Mayor of Bristol v Cox (1884) L.R. 26 Ch. D. 678, Ch.D 9.04, 9.08, 11.18, 11.38, 11.72
Bristol Corp v Cox sub nom. Mayor of Bristol v Cox (1884) L.R. 26 Ch. D. 678, Ch.D 6.11, 6.13
British & Commonwealth Holdings Plc (In Administration) v Barclays de Zoete Wedd Ltd (No.1) sub nom. Atlantic Computers Plc (In Administration), Re [1998] B.C.C. 200, Ch.D 3.41
British & Commonwealth Holdings Plc (In Administration) v Barclays de Zoete Wedd Ltd (No.2) British & Commonwealth Holdings Plc (In Administration) v Atlantic Computers Plc British & Commonwealth Holdings Plc (In Administration) v Spicer & Oppenheim British & Commonwealth Holdings Plc (In Administration) v NM Rothschild & Sons Ltd [1999] 1 B.C.L.C. 86 (1998) 95(45) L.S.G. 41 (1999) 143 S.J.L.B. 14, Ch.D 11.01, 11.02
British & Commonwealth Holdings Plc (Joint Administrators) v Spicer & Oppenheim sub nom. British & Commonwealth Holdings Plc (Nos.1 and 2), Re [1993] A.C. 426 [1992] 3 W.L.R. 853 [1992] 4 All E.R. 876 [1992] B.C.C. 977 [1993] B.C.L.C. 168 (1992) 142 N.L.J. 1611, HL 3.43
British & Commonwealth Holdings v Quadrex Holdings Inc, unreported, July 4, ... 19909.38, 11.14, 12.35
British Aerospace Plc v Green [1995] I.C.R. 1006 [1995] I.R.L.R. 433, CA (Civ Div) 5.26, 5.30, 20.29
British American Tobacco (Investments) Ltd v United States of America [2004] EWCA Civ 1064, CA (Civ Div) 12.03, 12.07, 12.09
British American Tobacco Australia Services v McCabe [2002] V.S.C.A. 197, Sup. Ct. (Victoria) 13.18, 13.38, 14.04
British and Commonwealth Holdings plc (Nos 1 & 2), Re. *See* British & Commonwealth Holdings Plc (Joint Administrators) v Spicer & Oppenheim
British Association of Glass Bottle Manufacturers Ltd v Nettlefold [1912] A.C. 709, HL 6.41
British Coal Corp v Dennis Rye (No.2) [1988] 1 W.L.R. 1113 [1988] 3 All E.R. 816, CA (Civ Div) 11.66, 11.76, 12.08, 12.32
British Columbia (Securities Commission) v BDS (2003) 226 D.L.R. (4th) 393, CA (BC) 12.06
British Data Management Plc v Boxer Commercial Removals Plc [1996] 3 All E.R. 707 [1996] E.M.L.R. 349, CA (Civ Div) 5.33

British Leyland Motor Corp Ltd v TI Silencers Ltd [1980] 1 C.M.L.R. 598 [1979] F.S.R. 591, Ch.D 8.12, 11.109
British Leyland Motor Corp Ltd v Wyatt Interpart Co Ltd (No.1) sub nom. British Leyland Motor Corp Ltd, British Leyland UK Ltd, Pressed Steel Fisher Ltd and British Leyland (Austin-Morris) v Wyatt Interpart Co Ltd [1979] 1 C.M.L.R. 395 [1979] F.S.R. 39, Ch.D 5.30
British Sky Broadcasting Plc v Virgin Media Communications Ltd (formerly NTL Communications Ltd) [2008] EWCA Civ 612; (2008) 105(29) L.S.G. 33 .... 14.15, 15.05, 15.06
British Steel Corp v Granada Television Ltd [1981] A.C. 1096 [1980] 3 W.L.R. 774 [1981] 1 All E.R. 417 124 S.J. 812, HL 3.05, 3.07, 3.16, 3.17, 11.102, 11.112
British Thomson Houston Co Ltd v Duram Ltd [1915] 1 Ch. 823, CA 2.33
British Thomson-Houston Co Ltd v Durham Ltd (1920) 37 R.P.C. 121 .... 19.11
British Thomson-Houston Co Ltd v Tungstalite Ltd (1938) 55 R.P.C. 280 .... 19.19
British Xylonite Co v Fibrenyle [1959] R.P.C. 252, CA 11.159, 19.10, 19.11
Broadcasting Corp of New Zealand & Horton Ltd [1991] 1 N.Z.L.R. ... 33511.09, 11.31, 11.45
Broadmoor Hospital v Hyde, *The Times*, March 18, 1994 *Independent*, March 4, 1994, Q.B.D. 3.21
Broere v Mourant & Co (Trustees) Ltd [2004] J.C.A. 009, CA (Jersey) 1.17, 4.24
Brook Martin & Co, Re [1993] B.C.L.C. 328 [1992] E.G.C.S. 138, Ch.D ... 3.44, 11.74
Brookes v Prescott sub nom. Brooks v Prescott [1948] 2 K.B. 133 [1948] 1 All E.R. 907 64 T.L.R. 302 (1948) 112 J.P. 312 46 L.G.R. 301 92 S.J. 349, CA 6.41, 11.51
Brookfield v McPherson's Ltd [2003] F.C.A. 1237, Fed. Ct. Aus. 13.38
Brookfield v Yevad Products Pty Ltd [2004] F.C.A.F.C. 117 .... 13.36
Brookfield Multiplex Ltd v International Litigation Funding Partners Pte Ltd (No.2) [2009] FCA 449 .... 11.05, 11.07, 11.10, 15.12, 15.45
Brooks v Medical Defence Association of Western Australia (1999) 94 F.C.R. 164, Fed. Ct. Aus. 11.34
Broome v Broome [1955] P. 190 [1955] 2 W.L.R. 401 [1955] 1 All E.R. 201 99 S.J. 114, PDAD 11.134
Brown, Re (1792) 4 Bro. C.C. 91 .... 19.20
Brown, Re (1864) 33 L.J.Q.B. 193 .... 10.09, 11.105
Brown v Bennett (Wasted Costs) (No.1) [2002] 1 W.L.R. 713 [2002] 2 All E.R. 273 [2002] Lloyd's Rep. P.N. 155 [2002] P.N.L.R. 17 (2002) 99(2) L.S.G. 27 (2001) 151 N.L.J. 1733 (2001) 145 S.J.L.B. 267, Ch.D 12.05
Brown v Bennett (Wasted Costs) (No.2) [2002] Lloyd's Rep. P.N. 242 (2002) 99(8) L.S.G. 35, Ch.D 11.13
Brown v Bennett (Witness Summons), *The Times*, November 2, 2000, Ch.D 10.31, 18.16
Brown v Commissioner of Taxation [2002] F.C.A. 318, Fed. Ct. Aus. 11.123
Brown v Executors of the Estate of HM Queen Elizabeth the Queen Mother [2008] EWCA Civ 56; [2008] W.T.L.R. 425 .... 3.45A
Brown v Foster (1857) 1 H. & N. 736 .... 11.12, 11.13
Brown v Guardian Royal Exchange Assurance Plc [1994] 2 Lloyd's Rep. 325 (1994) 91(9) L.S.G. 40 (1994) 138 S.J.L.B. 35 [1994] N.P.C. 8, CA (Civ Div) 11.62, 12.03
Brown v Matthews sub nom. B v M (Disclosure of Welfare Reports) [1990] Ch. 662 [1990] 2 W.L.R. 879 [1990] 2 All E.R. 155 [1990] 2 F.L.R. 46 [1990] F.C.R. 581 (1990) 154 J.P.N. 547 (1990) 87(14) L.S.G. 44, CA (Civ Div) 11.99

Brown v Patel. *See* Brown v Rice and Patel
Brown v Procurator Fiscal. *See* Brown v Stott sub nom. Stott (Procurator Fiscal) v Brown
Brown v Rice and Patel [2007] EWHC 625 (Ch); [2007] B.P.I.R. 305; [2008] F.S.R. 3; (2008) 24 Const. L.J. 238; [2007] C.I.L.L. 2467 ... 11.130, 11.133, 20.506
Brown v Sewell (1880–81) L.R. 16 Ch. D. 517, CA 9.11
Brown v Stott sub nom. Stott (Procurator Fiscal) v Brown [2003] 1 A.C. 681 [2001] 2 W.L.R. 817 [2001] 2 All E.R. 97 2001 S.C. (P.C.) 43 2001 S.L.T. 59 2001 S.C.C.R. 62 [2001] R.T.R. 11 [2001] H.R.L.R. 9 [2001] U.K.H.R.R. 333 11 B.H.R.C. 179 (2001) 3 L.G.L.R. 24 (2001) 145 S.J.L.B. 100 2000 G.W.D. 40–1513, PC (Sc) reversing 2000 J.C. 328 2000 S.L.T. 379 2000 S.C.C.R. 314 [2000] R.T.R. 394 [2000] U.K.H.R.R. 239 2000 G.W.D. 6–237, HCJ ... 11.105, 11.113, 11.115, 11.118, 11.119, 21.05, 21.07
Brown & Co v Watkins & Co (1885–86) L.R. 16 Q.B.D. 125, QBD 4.09, 4.11, 16.27
Brue Ltd v Solly, *The Times*, February 9, 1988, Ch.D 5.53, 9.21, 15.45
Brunel University v Vaseghi; sub nom. Brunel University v Webster [2007] EWCA Civ 482; [2007] I.R.L.R. 592; (2007) 151 S.J.L.B. 709 ... 11.129, 12.39
Brunel University v Webster. *See* Brunel University v Vaseghi
Buchanan Turf Supplies Pty Ltd v Premier Turf Supplies Pty Ltd [2003] FCA 230, Fed. Ct. Aus. 13.34
Buchanan v Taylor [1896] W.N. 73 .... 16.65
Buchanan-Michaelson v Rubinstein [1965] 1 W.L.R. 390 [1965] 1 All E.R. 599 109 S.J. 111, CA reversing [1965] Ch. 258 [1964] 3 W.L.R. 1235 [1964] 3 All E.R. 850 108 S.J. 1013, Ch.D 4.24, 4.26, 6.08, 8.28
Buckingham v Daily News [1956] 2 Q.B. 534 [1956] 3 W.L.R. 375 [1956] 2 All E.R. 904 100 S.J. 528, CA 19.13
Buckinghamshire CC v Moran [1990] Ch. 623 [1989] 3 W.L.R. 152 [1989] 2 All E.R. 225 88 L.G.R. 145 (1989) 58 P. & C.R. 236 [1989] E.G.C.S. 21 (1989) 139 N.L.J. 257 (1989) 133 S.J. 849, CA (Civ Div) 11.127
Buckley v Law Society (No.2) [1984] 1 W.L.R. 1101 [1984] 3 All E.R. 313 (1984) 81 L.S.G. 3017 (1984) 128 S.J. 505, Ch.D 11.103
Buckley v United Kingdom (App. No.20348/92) (1997) 23 E.H.R.R. 101 [1997] 2 P.L.R. 10 [1996] J.P.L. 1018, ECHR 21.09
Budden v Wilkinson [1893] 2 Q.B. 432, CA 6.11, 6.13, 6.14, 6.41
Bula Ltd v Tara Mines Ltd [1994] I.L.R.M. 111, Sup. Ct. (Irl) 5.43, 5.46
Bula Ltd v Tara Mines Ltd (No.5) [1994] 1 I.R. 487, Sup. Ct. (Irl) 1.16, 5.41
Bulk Materials (Coal Handling) Services Pty Ltd v Coal and Allied Operations Pty Ltd (1988) 13 N.S.W.L.R., 68 .... 11.60
Bull v Clarke (1864) 15 C.B. (N.S.) 851 .... 9.37
Bullivant v Att.-Gen. of Victoria sub nom. R. v Bullivant [1901] A.C. 196, HL 11.06, 11.67, 11.69
Bullock & Co v Corry & Co (1877–78) L.R. 3 Q.B.D. 356, Q.B.D. 11.38
Bulman and Dixon v Young, Ehlers and Co (1884) 49 L.T. 736, CA .. 6.14, 6.41
Bulut v Austria (App. No.17358/90) (1997) 24 E.H.R.R. 84, ECHR ... 21.06, 21.13
Bunbury v Bunbury (1839) 2 Beav. 173 .... 11.21
Burchard v MacFarlane [1891] 2 Q.B. 241 .... 10.06, 10.12
Burchard v Macfarlane, exp. Tindall [1891] 2 Q.B. 241, CA 10.55
Burg Design Pty Ltd v Wolki (1999) 162 A.L.R. 639, Fed. Ct. Aus. 12.39
Burkle Holdings Ltd v Laing (No.2) [2005] EWHC 2022, Q.B.D. (TCC) 11.76, 12.07, 12.19

Burmah Oil Co Ltd v Bank of England [1980] A.C. 1090 [1979] 3 W.L.R. 722 [1979] 3 All E.R. 700 123 S.J. 786, HL 11.02, 11.83, 11.94, 11.98
Burnell v British Transport Commission [1956] 1 Q.B. 187 [1956] 2 W.L.R. 61 [1955] 3 All E.R. 822 [1955] 2 Lloyd's Rep. 549 100 S.J. 33, CA 12.19, 12.28, 12.34
Burns v National Bank of New Zealand [2003] N.Z.C.A. 232 [2004] 3 N.Z.L.R. 289, CA (NZ) 13.38
Burns v Shuttlehurst Ltd sub nom. Burns v General Accident Fire and Life Assurance Corp Plc [1999] 1 W.L.R. 1449 [1999] 2 All E.R. 27 [1999] P.I.Q.R. P229 (1999) 96(6) L.S.G. 35, CA (Civ Div) 3.28, 3.31
Burrells Wharf Freeholds Ltd v Galliard Homes Ltd [2000] C.P. Rep. 4 (2000) 2 T.C.L.R. 54 65 Con. L.R. 1 [1999] 2 E.G.L.R. 81 [1999] 33 E.G. 82 [1999] N.P.C. 79, Q.B.D. (TCC) 3.26, 4.50
Bursill v Tanner (1885–86) L.R. 16 Q.B.D. 1, CA 11.13, 11.34
Burstall v Beyfus (1884) L.R. 26 Ch. D. 35, CA 4.45
Burton v Dodd (1890) S.J. 39 .... 11.09
Bustros v Bustros (1882) 30 W.R. 374, CA 9.13
Bustros v White (1875–76) L.R. 1 Q.B.D. 423, CA 5.14
Bute (Marquess of) v James (1886) L.R. 33 Ch. D. 157, Ch.D 17.06
Butler v Board of Trade [1971] Ch. 680 [1970] 3 W.L.R. 822 [1970] 3 All E.R. 593 114 S.J. 604, Ch.D 11.66, 11.67
Butler v GKN Foundations Ltd, unreported, May 22, 1992 .... 16.41
Butler v Police Ombudsman for Northern Ireland [2003] N.I.Q.B. 64 .... 10.11, 11.100
Butterfield, Re (1890) 7 Morr. 293 .... 11.113
Buttes Gas & Oil Co v Hammer (No.3) Occidental Petroleum Corp v Buttes Gas & Oil Co (No.2) [1982] A.C. 888 [1981] 3 W.L.R. 787 [1981] 3 All E.R. 616 [1981] Com. L.R. 257 125 S.J. 776, HL reversing [1981] Q.B. 223 [1980] 3 W.L.R. 668 [1980] 3 All E.R. 475 124 S.J. 630, CA (Civ Div) 4.44, 11.33, 11.56, 11.59, 11.69, 11.60, 11.89, 11.97, 11.140, 12.14, 12.15, 12.25
Byers v Burleson, 100 F.R.D. 436 (1983) 12.06
Byrne v Shannon Foynes Port Co [2007] IEHC 315; [2008] P.N.L.R. 5 .... 12.18

C's Application for Judicial Review, Re [2009] UKHL 15; [2009] 1 A.C. 908; [2009] 2 W.L.R. 782; [2009] 4 All E.R. 335; [2009] N.I. 258; [2009] 2 Cr. App. R. 1; [2009] E.M.L.R. 19; [2009] H.R.L.R. 20; [2009] U.K.H.R.R. 853; [2009] Crim. L.R. 525; (2009) 153(11) S.J.L.B. 28 .... 11.77
C v C (Privilege) [2006] EWHC 336 (Fam); [2008] 1 F.L.R. 115; [2007] W.T.L.R. 753; [2008] Fam. Law 121 .... 11.09, 11.12, 11.67
C v C (Privilege: Criminal Communications) sub nom. C v C (Evidence: Privilege) GC v JC C v C (Custody: Affidavit) [2001] EWCA Civ 469 [2002] Fam. 42 [2001] 3 W.L.R. 446 [2001] 2 F.L.R. 184 [2001] 1 F.C.R. 756 [2001] Fam. Law 496, CA (Civ Div) 11.10, 11.67
C v S (Money Laundering: Discovery of Documents) (Practice Note) sub nom. Practice Note (CA: Money Laundering: Discovery of Documents) [1999] 1 W.L.R. 1551 [1999] 2 All E.R. 343 [1999] Lloyd's Rep. Bank. 26 (1998) 148 N.L.J. 1723, CA (Civ Div) 8.13, 11.146
C Plc v P; sub nom. W v P [2007] EWCA Civ 493; [2008] Ch. 1; [2007] 3 W.L.R. 437; [2007] 3 All E.R. 1034; [2007] C.P. Rep. 35 .... 2.23, 11.105, 11.106, 11.108, 11.118, 12.37, 15.11, 15.34, 15.43

CAS (Nominees) Ltd v Nottingham Forest FC Plc (Application for Disclosure) sub nom. Nottingham Forest Plc, Re [2001] 1 All E.R. 954 [2002] B.C.C. 145 (2000) 97(40) L.S.G. 42 (2000) 150 N.L.J. 1264, Ch.D 11.73
CBS United Kingdom Ltd v Lambert [1983] Ch. 37 [1982] 3 W.L.R. 746 [1982] 3 All E.R. 237 [1983] F.S.R. 127 (1983) 80 L.S.G. 36 126 S.J. 691, CA (Civ Div) 2.13, 16.68
CGU v Malaysia Corp [2001] FCA 1223, (2001) 187 A.L.R. 279, Fed. Ct. Aus. 3.34
CH Beazer (Commercial & Industrial) Ltd v Smith (RM) (1984) 1 Const. L.J. 196 .... 6.25
CHC Software Care Ltd v Hopkins & Wood [1993] F.S.R. 241, Ch.D 3.06, 3.14, 11.151, 16.42, 16.60
CHC Software Care Ltd v Hopkins & Wood, unreported, February 18, 1994 .... 11.06, 12.02, 12.15
CI v NS [2004] EWHC 659 [2004] W.T.L.R. 1113, Fam Div 4.26, 5.52
CIA Barca de Panama SA v George Wimpey & Co Ltd (No.1) [1980] 1 Lloyd's Rep. 598, CA (Civ Div) 11.61, 11.62, 11.74
CIBC Mellon Trust Co v Stolzenberg (Sanctions: Non-compliance) [2004] EWCA Civ 827 (2004) 148 S.J.L.B. 824, CA (Civ Div) affirming [2003] EWHC 13, Ch.D 2.13, **13.10**
CIBC Mellon Trust Co v Stolzenberg [2001] E.W.C.A. Civ. 1222, CA (Civ Div) 11.128
CIBC Mellon Trust Co v Stolzenberg, unreported, November 15, 2000, Ch.D affd. [2001] E.W.C.A. Civ. 1222, CA 11.13
CJ O'Shea Construction Ltd v Bassi [1998] I.C.R. 1130, EAT 20.31
CTC Resources NL v Australian Stock Exchange [2001] W.A.S.C. 40 .... 16.40
C (A Child) (HIV Testing), Re sub nom. C (A Minor) (HIV Test), Re [1999] 2 F.L.R. 1004 [2000] Fam. Law 16, CA (Civ Div) [2000] Fam. 48 [2000] 2 W.L.R. 270 [1999] 3 F.C.R. 289 (1999) 50 B.M.L.R. 283, Fam Div 19.20
C (A Minor) (Care Proceedings: Disclosure), Re sub nom. EC (A Minor) (Care Proceedings: Disclosure), Re EC (Disclosure of Material), Re [1997] Fam. 76 [1997] 2 W.L.R. 322 [1996] 2 F.L.R. 725 [1996] 3 F.C.R. 521 [1997] Fam. Law 160, CA (Civ Div) 4.04
C (A Minor) (Evidence: Confidential Information), Re [1991] 2 F.L.R. 478 [1991] F.C.R. 553 [1991] Fam. Law 524 (1991) 155 L.G. Rev. 744, CA (Civ Div) 11.153
C (Children Act 1989: Expert Evidence), Re sub nom. C (Child Cases: Evidence and Disclosure Practice), Re [1995] 1 F.L.R. 204 [1995] 2 F.C.R. 97 [1995] Fam. Law 176 (1995) 159 L.G. Rev. 849, Fam Div 11.99
C (Disclosure) , Re [1996] 1 F.L.R. 797 [1996] 3 F.C.R. 765 (1996) 160 J.P.N. 732, Fam Div 4.04
C (Restraint Orders: Identification), Re [1995] C.O.D. 263, Q.B.D. 2.26
C Corp v P, 1994–95 C.I.L.R. 189 .... 3.03
C Inc Plc v L [2001] 2 All E.R. (Comm.) 446 [2001] 2 Lloyd's Rep. 459 [2001] C.L.C. 1054 (2001) 151 N.L.J. 535, Q.B.D. (Comm.) 2.51
C Ltd v United Kingdom (1989) 61 D.R. 285 .... 21.15
C Plc v P [2006] EWHC 1226 [2006] 4 All E.R. 311 (2006) 156 N.L.J. 988, Ch.D 2.23, 11.105, 11.106, 11.107, 11.118, 12.37, 15.11, 15.34, 15.43
C Van der Lely NV v Watveare Overseas Ltd [1982] F.S.R. 122, Ch.D (Patents Ct) 19.19
Cadbury Schweppes Pty Ltd v Darrell Lea Chocolate Shops Pty Ltd [2007] FCAFC 70, Fed. Ct of Australia 18.22

Cadogan Petroleum Plc v Tolley [2009] EWHC 3291 (Ch) ... 8.24, 11.82A, 11.128, 11.151
Cairnstores Ltd v Aktiebolaget Hassle Generics (UK) Ltd v Aktiebolaget Hassle [2002] EWCA Civ 1504 [2003] F.S.R. 23 (2002) 25(12) I.P.D. 25081, CA (Civ Div) ... 18.12
Calcraft v Guest [1898] 1 Q.B. 759, CA ... 11.06, 11.76, 12.02
Calderbank v Calderbank [1976] Fam. 93 [1975] 3 W.L.R. 586 [1975] 3 All E.R. 333 (1975) 5 Fam. Law 190 119 S.J. 490, CA (Civ Div) ... 11.132
Calenti v North Middlesex NHS Trust, unreported, March 2, 2001 ... 18.05
Calley v Richards (1854) 19 Beav. 401 ... 11.07
Caltex Refining Co Pty Ltd (1990) 51 I.R. 113 ... 5.30
Calvet v Tomkies [1963] 1 W.L.R. 1397 [1963] 3 All E.R. 610 107 S.J. 791, CA ... 5.21
Cambers v Times Newspaper Ltd [1999] 1 I.L.R.M. 504 ... 4.60
Camden London Borough Council v Dempster, unreported, January 16, 1998, EAT ... 11.94
Camelot Group Plc v Centaur Communications Ltd [1999] Q.B. 124 [1998] 2 W.L.R. 379 [1998] 1 All E.R. 251 [1998] I.R.L.R. 80 [1998] E.M.L.R. 1 (1997) 94(43) L.S.G. 30 (1997) 147 N.L.J. 1618 (1998) 142 S.J.L.B. 19, CA (Civ Div) ... 3.21, 21.15
Campaign Against Arms Trade v BAE Systems Plc [2007] EWHC 330 (QB) 3.11, 3.14
Campaign Master v Forty Two [2010] FCA 76, (2010) 269 ALR 76 ... 10.28
Campaign Master v Forty Two [2010] FCA 398, (2010) 269 ALR 7 ... 10.11
Campbell v French (1792) 1 Anst. 58 ... 9.37
Campbell v Mirror Group Newspapers Ltd sub nom. Campbell v MGN Ltd [2004] UKHL 22 [2004] 2 A.C. 457 [2004] 2 W.L.R. 1232 [2004] 2 All E.R. 995 [2004] E.M.L.R. 15 [2004] H.R.L.R. 24 [2004] U.K.H.R.R. 648 16 B.H.R.C. 500 (2004) 101(21) L.S.G. 36 (2004) 154 N.L.J. 733 (2004) 148 S.J.L.B. 572, HL reversing [2002] EWCA Civ 1373 [2003] Q.B. 633 [2003] 2 W.L.R. 80 [2003] 1 All E.R. 224 [2003] E.M.L.R. 2 [2003] H.R.L.R. 2 (2002) 99(42) L.S.G. 38 (2002) 146 S.J.L.B. 234, CA (Civ Div) ... 21.11, 21.15
Campbell v Tameside MBC [1982] Q.B. 1065 [1982] 3 W.L.R. 74 [1982] 2 All E.R. 791 80 L.G.R. 700 126 S.J. 361, CA (Civ Div) 3.36, 8.24, 11.99
Campbell v United Kingdom (A/233A) (1993) 15 E.H.R.R. 137, ECHR 21.08, 21.10, 21.13
Campbell v United Kingdom (A/80) Fell v United Kingdom (A/80) (1985) 7 E.H.R.R. 165, ECHR ... 21.05
Canada Post Corp v Euclide Cormier Plumbing and Heating Inc (2008) 296 D.L.R. (4th) 738, CA (NB) ... 12.18
Canada (Privacy Commissioner) v Blood Tribe Department of Health (2008) 294 D.L.R. (4th) 385, SCC ... 11.08
Canada Trust Co v Stolzenberg (1997) 1 O.F.L.R. 606, Ch.D ... 11.150
Canada Trust Co v Stolzenberg (No.1) [1997] 1 W.L.R. 1582 [1997] 4 All E.R. 983 [1997] C.L.C. 1083 [1998] I.L.Pr. 30, CA (Civ Div) ... 2.39
Canada Trust Company v Stolzenberg, The (1997) 1 O.F.L.R. 606, Ch.D 11.154
Canadian Association of Regulated Importers v Canada (1992) 87 D.L.R. (4th) ... 7301.19, 11.81
Canadian Derivatives Clearing Corp v EFA Software Services Ltd, 2001 A.B.Q.B. 425, QB (Alberta) ... 3.03
Canadian Imperial Bank of Commerce v Beck. *See* Beck v Canadian Imperial Bank of Commerce

Candacal Pty Ltd v Industry Research & Development Board [2005] F.C.A. 649, Fed. Ct. Aus. 11.05, 12.06
Cank v Broadyard Associates Ltd, unreported, July 11, 2000, CA (Civ Div) 13.07, 13.12
Cannar, re Application of, re Eubanks [2003] N.S.W.S.C. 802, Sup. Ct. (NSW) 12.03, 12.06
Cannock v Jauncy (1853) 1 Dr. 497 .... 5.09
Cannon v United Kingdom, unreported, January 17, 1997, ECHR 21.06
Cantabrica Coach Holdings Ltd v Vehicle Inspectorate. *See* Vehicle Inspectorate v Cantabrica Coach Holdings Ltd
Canter v Stone, Odell & Frankson, unreported, April 19, 1991, CA 13.07
Capar v Commissioner of Police (1994) 34 N.S.W.L.R. 715 ..... 11.39, 11.48, 11.68
Cardwell v Tomlinson (1885) 52 L.T. 746 .... 13.15
Care Canada v Canadian Broadcasting Corp (1999) 175 D.L.R. (4th) 743, Div Ct (Ont) 4.60
Carew v White (1842) 5 Beav. 172 .... 9.38
Caribbean General Insurance Ltd v Frizzell Insurance Brokers [1994] 2 Lloyd's Rep. 32 (1994) 91(3) L.S.G. 47, CA (Civ Div) 13.12, 13.24
Carl Zeiss Stiftung v Rayner & Keeler Ltd Rayner & Keeler Ltd v Courts & Co [1967] 1 A.C. 853 [1966] 3 W.L.R. 125 [1966] 2 All E.R. 536 [1967] R.P.C. 497 110 S.J. 425, HL 1.01
Carlco Ltd v Chief Constable of Dyfed Powys [2002] EWCA Civ 1754, CA (Civ Div) 6.06, 13.09
Carlson v Townsend [2001] EWCA Civ 511 [2001] 1 W.L.R. 2415 [2001] 3 All E.R. 663 [2001] C.P. Rep. 86 [2001] C.P.L.R. 405 [2001] P.I.Q.R. P24 (2001) 62 B.M.L.R. 50, CA (Civ Div) 18.07
Carlton Cranes Ltd v Consolidated Hotels Ltd [1988] 2 N.Z.L.R. 555 ..... 11.45
Carnduff v Rock [2001] EWCA Civ 680 [2001] 1 W.L.R. 1786 (2001) 98(25) L.S.G. 47 (2001) 145 S.J.L.B. 141, CA (Civ Div) 11.103, 12.42
Carrington v Helix Lighting [1990] I.C.R. 125 [1990] I.R.L.R. 6 (1990) 87(1) L.S.G. 30, EAT 5.41, 20.28
Carter v Gardner [2003] F.C.A. 653, Fed. Ct. Aus. 3.42
Carter v Leeds Daily News [1876] W.N. 11 .... 16.62
Carter v Northmore, Hale, Dary & Leake (1995) 183 C.L.R. 121, H Ct (Aus) 11.65
Carter v The Managing Partner, Northmore Hale Davy & Leake (1995) 183 C.L.R. 121 .... 11.08
Carver v Pinto Leite (1871–72) L.R. 7 Ch. App. 90, CA in Chancery 8.25
Casado Coca v Spain (A/285) (1994) 18 E.H.R.R. 1, ECHR 21.14
Casey v Cartwright [2006] EWCA Civ 1280, CA 18.09
Casley-Smith v District Council of Stirling (1989) 51 S.A.S.R. 447 .... 4.60
Cass v Fitzgerald [1884] W.N. 18 .... 9.07
Cassidy v Engwirda Constructions Co [1976] Q.W.N. 16 .... 5.06
Cassidy v Hawcroft, [2000] All E.R. (D) 1082, CA 15.13
Castle New Homes, Re [1979] 1 W.L.R. 1075 [1979] 2 All E.R. 775 123 S.J. 569, Ch.D 3.40, 3.43
Cathcart Ex p. Campbell, Re (1869–70) L.R. 5 Ch. App. 703, CA in Chancery 11.1
Catt v Church of Scientology Religious Education College In. (2001) 5 C.L.17 .... 5.50
Cattley v Pollard [2006] EWHC 3130 (Ch); [2007] Ch. 353; [2007] 3 W.L.R. 317; [2007] 2 All E.R. 1086; [2007] P.N.L.R. 19; [2007] W.T.L.R. 245; (2007–08) 10 I.T.E.L.R. 1 .... 20.56

Caudle v LD Law Ltd [2008] EWHC 374 (QB); [2008] 1 W.L.R. 1540; [2008] W.T.L.R. 587, QBD 2.08
Causton v Mann Egerton (Johnsons) Ltd [1974] 1 W.L.R. 162 [1974] 1 All E.R. 453 [1974] 1 Lloyd's Rep. 197 117 S.J. 877, CA (Civ Div) ... 11.37, 12.02, 12.10
Caven-Atack v Church of Scientology Religious Education College Inc, unreported, October 31, 1994, CA 13.08, 13.24
Cayley v Sandycroft Brick (1885) 33 W.R 557 .... 16.75
C-C Bottlers Ltd v Lion Nathan Ltd [1993] 2 N.Z.L.R. 445 .... 11.14, 11.32, 12.08, 12.34
Cedenco Foods Ltd v State Insurance Ltd [1996] 3 N.Z.L.R. 205, H Ct (NZ) 11.129, 11.130
Celanese Canada Inc v Murray Demolition Corp [2006] 2 S.C.R. 189, Sup. Ct of Canada 2.22
Central Exchange Ltd v Anaconda Nickel Ltd [2001] W.A.S.C. 128, Sup. Ct. (WA) 3.34
Cepheus Shipping Corp v Guardian Royal Exchange Assurance Plc The Capricorn [1995] 1 Lloyd's Rep. 622, Q.B.D. 13.14, 13.35
Ceval Alimentos SA v Agrimpex Trading Co Ltd (No.1) [1995] 2 Lloyd's Rep. 380, Q.B.D. (Comm.) 13.34
Chaddock v British South Africa Co [1896] 2 Q.B. 153, CA 16.104
Chadwick v Bowman (1885–86) L.R. 16 Q.B.D. 561, Q.B.D. 11.33, 11.34
Chambers v Times Newspapers Ltd [1999] 1 I.L.R.M. 504, H Ct (Eire) ... 4.60
Chan Mei Yiu v Secretary for Justice [2007] HKCFI 664 ... 4.06, 8.24, 10.54, 11.85
Chan U Seek v Alvis Vehicles Ltd sub nom. Guardian Newspapers Ltd (Court Record: Disclosure), Re [2004] EWHC 3092 [2005] 1 W.L.R. 2965 [2005] 3 All E.R. 155 [2005] E.M.L.R. 19, Ch.D 3.45
Chandler v Church (1987) 137 N.L.J. 451, Ch.D 11.67, 11.69, 11.71
Chandler v Water Corporation [2004] W.A.S.C. 95, Sup. Ct. (W Aus) 5.12, 11.130
Chandris Lines Ltd v Wilson & Horton Ltd [1981] 2 N.Z.L.R. 600 .... 12.08
Chanel Ltd v 3 Pears Wholesale Cash & Carry Co [1979] F.S.R. 393, Ch.D 2.20
Chant v Brown (1849) 7 Hare 84 .... 11.06
Chant v Brown (1852) 9 Hare 790 .... 11.09
Chantrey Martin & Co v Martin [1953] 2 Q.B. 286 [1953] 3 W.L.R. 459 [1953] 2 All E.R. 691 46 R. & I.T. 516 38 A.L.R.2d 663 97 S.J. 539, CA 5.43, 11.06, 11.21, 11.144, 11.145
Chapman v Luminis Pty Ltd (No.3) (2000) 179 A.L.R. 702, Fed. Ct. Aus. 10.35
Chappell v United Kingdom (A/152) sub nom. Chappell v United Kingdom (10461/83) (1990) 12 E.H.R.R. 1 [1989] 1 F.S.R. 617, ECHR .. 2.22, 21.09, 21.12
Chapple v Williams [1999] C.P.L.R. 731, CA (Civ Div) 1.32
Charles of the Ritz Group Ltd v Jory [1986] F.S.R. 14, Ch.D 11.116, 11.150
Charman v Charman [2005] EWCA Civ 1606 [2006] 1 W.L.R. 1053 [2006] W.T.L.R. 1 [2006] Fam. Law 516 (2006) 103(5) L.S.G. 28, CA (Civ Div) 2.61, 4.03, **10.10**, 10.54
Chase v News Group Newspapers Ltd sub nom. Chase v Newsgroup Newspapers Ltd [2002] EWCA Civ 1772 [2003] E.M.L.R. 11 (2002) 146 S.J.L.B. 279, CA (Civ Div) affirming [2002] EWHC 1101, Q.B.D. 15.37
Chater & Chater Productions Ltd v Rose [1994] E.M.L.R. 217 [1994] F.S.R. 491, Ch.D 2.32, 6.51
Cheddar Valley Engineering Ltd v Chaddlewood Homes Ltd [1992] 1 W.L.R. 820 [1992] 4 All E.R. 942 (1992) 89(27) L.S.G. 35, Ch.D 11.127

Cheeseman v Bowaters United Kingdom Paper Mills [1971] 1 W.L.R. 1773 [1971] 3 All E.R. 513 115 S.J. 931, CA (Civ Div) 16.49
Cherrywood Restaurants Ltd v Gamma Investments Ltd [2004] EWHC 3227 [2004] All E.R. (D) 260, Ch.D 9.10
Chertkow v Retail Credit [1932] 1 W.W.R. 905 .... 16.60
Cheshire CC v C [1995] 2 F.L.R. 862 [1996] 2 F.C.R. 365 [1996] Fam. Law 72, Fam Div 10.09
Chesterfield v North Derbyshire Royal Hospital NHS Trust. *See* ES v Chesterfield and North Derbyshire Royal Hospital NHS Trust
Cheung Kai Wing v Mak Sheum Shum [1993] H.K. Digest, G134, CA (HK) 5.26
Chief Constable of Greater Manchester v McNally sub nom. McNally v Chief Constable of Greater Manchester [2002] EWCA Civ 14 [2002] 2 Cr. App. R. 37 [2002] Crim. L.R. 832, CA (Civ Div) 11.103
Chilcott and Clarkson Co Ltd, Re (1985) 13 D.L.R. (4th) 481, CA (Ont) 12.02
Child Maintenance Enforcement Commission v Forrest [2010] EWHC 1264 (Admin); (2010) 174 J.P. 449; [2010] 2 F.C.R. 631; [2010] A.C.D. 74; [2010] Fam. Law 911; (2010) 107(21) L.S.G. 16 .... 11.114
Childs v Vernon & Butcher [2007] EWCA Civ 305 .... 18.09
Chimera v Nguyen (1993) 104 D.L.R. (4th) 244, CA (Man) 5.06
China National Petroleum Corp v Fenwick Elliott (A Firm) [2002] EWHC 60 [2002] T.C.L.R. 19, Ch.D 3.05, 11.48
China Traders Insurance Co Ltd v Royal Exchange Assurance Corp [1898] 2 Q.B. 187, CA 4.21
Chipchase v Rosemond [1965] 1 W.L.R. 153 [1965] 1 All E.R. 145 108 S.J. 940, Ch.D 13.18
Chiron Corp v Evans Medical Ltd (No.2) [1997] F.S.R. 268, Ch.D (Patents Ct) 15.11
Chiron Corp v Organon Tekenika Ltd (1994) I.P.D. 18032 .... 11.158, 11.161, 11.163
Chmara v Nguyen (1993) 104 D.L.R. (4th) 244, CA (Manitoba) 11.31
Chocoladefabriken Lindt & Sprunghi AG v Nestlé Co Ltd [1978] R.P.C. 287, CA 11.124
Chorherr v Austria (A/266–B) (1994) 17 E.H.R.R. 358, ECHR 21.14
Chowood Ltd v Lyall (No.1) [1929] 2 Ch. 406, Ch.D 6.41
Choy v Nissei Sangyo America Ltd [1992] H.K.L.R. 177, CA (HK) 1.18, 3.11
Chrzanowska v Glaxo Laboratories Ltd, *The Times*, March 16, 1990 .... 4.10
Church of Scientology of California v Department of Health and Social Security [1979] 1 W.L.R. 723 [1979] 3 All E.R. 97 123 S.J. 304, CA (Civ Div) 4.52, 9.30, 11.159, 11.163, 15.19, 15.21, 15.24
Church v Perry (1877) 36 L.T. 57316.79, 16.93
Churton v Frewen (1865) 2 Dr. & Sm. 390 .... 9.38
Cimenteries CBR SA v Commission of the European Communities (T10/92) (No.2) [1992] E.C.R. II–2667 [1993] 4 C.M.L.R. 259, CFI 20.35
Cinepoly Records Co Ltd v Hong Kong Broadband Network Ltd [2006] H.K.C.F.I. 84 .... 3.03, 3.05
City of Baroda, The (1926) 134 L.T. 576 .... 6.15
Clapson v British Airways Plc [2001] I.R.L.R. 184, EAT 20.27
Clare v Health Insurance Commission [2003] F.C.A. 1279 .... 4.06
Clark v Perks, unreported, September 1, 2000, CA 6.57
Clarke v Bennett (1884) 32 W.R. 550 .... 16.39
Clarke (Executor of the Will of Francis Bacon) v Marlborough Fine Art (London) Ltd [2002] EWHC 11 [2003] C.P. Rep. 30, Ch.D 18.11

Clauss v Pir [1988] Ch. 267 [1987] 3 W.L.R. 493 [1987] 2 All E.R. 752 (1987) 84 L.S.G. 2767 (1987) 131 S.J. 1087, Ch.D 6.38
Clayson v Rolls Royce Ltd [1951] 1 K.B. 746 [1950] 2 All E.R. 884 66 T.L.R. (Pt. 2) 827 94 S.J. 741, CA 4.13, 16.27
Clements, Dunne & Bell Pty Ltd v Commissioner of Australian Federal Police (2001) 188 A.L.R. 515, Fed. Ct. Aus. 11.05, 11.67, 11.68, 11.70
Cleveland Bridge UK Ltd v Multiplex Constructions (UK) Ltd [2005] EWHC 2101, Q.B.D. (TCC) 3.45
Cleveland CC v F [1995] 1 W.L.R. 785 [1995] 2 All E.R. 236 [1995] 1 F.L.R. 797 [1995] 3 F.C.R. 174 93 L.G.R. 449 [1995] Fam. Law 473 (1995) 159 J.P.N. 459, Fam Div 11.107, 15.21, 15.42, 15.43
Clibbery v Allan [2002] EWCA Civ 45, [2002] Fam 261, CA 6.58, 15.11
Clinch v Inland Revenue Commissioners [1974] Q.B. 76 [1973] 2 W.L.R. 862 [1973] 1 All E.R. 977 [1973] S.T.C. 155 49 T.C. 52 [1973] T.R. 157 117 S.J. 342, Q.B.D. 20.77
Clingham v Kensington and Chelsea RLBC sub nom. R. (on the application of Clingham) v Marylebone Magistrates Court [2001] EWHC Admin 1 (2001) 165 J.P. 322 (2001) 165 J.P.N. 306, Q.B.D. (Admin) 21.07
Clough v Tameside and Glossop HA [1998] 1 W.L.R. 1478 [1998] 2 All E.R. 971 [1998] 3 F.C.R. 133 [1998] P.I.Q.R. P219 [1998] Lloyd's Rep. Med. 69 (1998) 42 B.M.L.R. 166, Q.B.D. 12.23, 18.18
Cloverbay Ltd (Joint Administrators) v Bank of Credit and Commerce International SA [1991] Ch. 90 [1990] 3 W.L.R. 574 [1991] 1 All E.R. 894 [1991] B.C.L.C. 135, CA (Civ Div) 3.43
Coal Cliff Collieries v CE Heath Insurance (1988) 5 N.S.W.L.R 703 .... 16.45
Cobra Golf Inc v Rata (No.2) [1998] Ch. 109 [1997] 2 W.L.R. 629 [1997] 2 All E.R. 150 [1997] F.S.R. 317 (1997) 20(2) I.P.D. 20013, Ch.D 2.25, 11.109, 11.116, 15.22, 15.24, 15.39
Coca Cola Co v British Telecommunications Plc [1999] I.T.C.L.R. 365 [1999] F.S.R. 518, Ch.D 3.02, 3.05, 3.14, 3.23, 3.24
Coca-Cola Co v Gilbey Schweppes Ltd v Gilbey [1995] 4 All E.R. 711 (1995) 145 N.L.J. 1688, Ch.D 11.116
Coch v Allcock & Co (1888) L.R. 21 Q.B.D. 178, CA 2.61, 17.12
Cocks v Royskill Steel Erection Ltd, unreported, November 20, 1991, CA ... 16.39
Coco v AN Clark (Engineers) Ltd [1968] F.S.R. 415 [1969] R.P.C. 41, Ch.D 15.08
Coflexip SA v Stolt Comex Seaway MS Ltd (Interrogatories) sub nom. Coflexip SA v Stolt Comex Seaways MS Ltd (No.2) [1999] F.S.R. 911, Ch.D (Patents Ct) 16.51
Colbeck v Ferguson, unreported, January 1, 2002, Q.B.D. 15.28
Cole v Elders Finance & Investment Co Ltd [1993] 2 V.R. 356, Sup. Ct. (Vic) 11.32
Cole v Kivells, *The Times*, May 2, 1997, CA (Civ Div) 17.25
Coleman v Dunlop Ltd, unreported, October 20, 1999, CA (Civ Div) 13.13
Colley v Hart (1890) L.R. 44 Ch. D. 179 (1890) 7 R.P.C. 101, Ch.D 11.159
Collins v Jones [1955] 1 Q.B. 564 [1955] 2 W.L.R. 813 [1955] 2 All E.R. 145 99 S.J. 258, CA 16.57
Collins v London General Omnibus Co (1893) 68 L.T. 831 .... 11.38
Colne Valley Water Co v Watford and St Albans Gas Co [1948] 1 K.B. 500 [1948] 1 All E.R. 104 64 T.L.R. 44 112 J.P. 113 46 L.G.R. 120 [1948] L.J.R. 385 92 S.J. 40, CA 8.06, 8.07, 16.86
Coloured Asphalt Co Ltd v British Asphalt & Bitumen Ltd (1936) 53 R.P.C. 89 .... 11.159

Columbia Pictures Industries v Robinson [1987] Ch. 38 [1986] 3 W.L.R. 542 [1986] 3 All E.R. 338 [1986] F.S.R. 367 (1986) 83 L.S.G. 3424 (1986) 130 S.J. 766, Ch.D 2.22
Comalco New Zealand Ltd v Broadcasting Standards Authority [1995] 3 N.Z.L.R. 469 .... 11.99
Comaplex Resources International Ltd v Schaffhauser Kantonalbank (1992) 84 D.L.R. (4th) 343 .... 11.154
Comaplex Resources International Ltd v Schaffhauser Kantonalbank [1990] I.L.Pr. 319, Sup. Ct. (Can) 11.154
Comeau, Re (1986) 77 N.S.R. (2d) 47, Sup. Ct. (Nova Scotia) 3.03
Comet Products (UK) Ltd v Hawkex Plastics Ltd [1971] 2 Q.B. 67 [1971] 2 W.L.R. 361 [1971] 1 All E.R. 1141 [1971] F.S.R. 7 [1972] R.P.C. 691 114 S.J. 975, CA (Civ Div) 11.109
Comfort Hotels v Wembley Stadium [1988] 1 W.L.R. 872 [1988] 3 All E.R. 53 (1988) 132 S.J. 967, Ch.D 12.10
Comfort v Department of Constitutional Affairs (2005) 102(35) L.S.G. 42, EAT 5.32, 11.28, 11.31
Commerce & Industry Insurance Co (Canada) v Lloyd's Underwriters sub nom. Viking Insurance Co v Rossdale [2002] 1 W.L.R. 1323 [2002] 2 All E.R. (Comm.) 204 [2002] 1 Lloyd's Rep. 219 [2002] C.L.C. 26, Q.B.D. (Comm.) 2.56, 10.54, 20.07
Commercial Bank of Australia Ltd v Amadio (1983) 151 C.L.R. 447 .... 12.06
Commercial Union Assurance Co Plc v Mander [1996] 2 Lloyd's Rep. 640 [1997] C.L.C. 32, Q.B.D. (Comm.) 11.60, 11.61, 11.62, 11.151
Commission for the New Towns v Edwards Commission for the New Towns v Freeman Design & Packaging Machinery Ltd, unreported, July 10, 2000, Q.B.D. 13.07
Commissioner of Police v Bermuda Broadcasting Co Ltd [2008] UKPC 5, PC (Ber) 21.15
Commissioner of Police of the Metropolis v Locker [1993] 3 All E.R. 584 [1993] I.C.R. 440 [1991] I.R.L.R. 319, EAT 11.101
Commissioner of Taxation v Pratt Holdings Ltd (2004) 207 A.L.R. 217, Fed. Ct. (Full Ct) Aus. 11.26
Commissioner of Taxation v Pratt Holdings Pty Ltd (2005) 225 A.L.R. 266, Fed. Ct. Aus. 11.09, 11.14
Commissioner of Taxation v Pratt Holdings Pty Ltd [2003] F.C.A. 6, Fed. Ct. Aus. 12.08
Commissioner of Taxation v Rio Tinto Ltd (2006) 229 A.L.R. 304, Fed. Ct. (Full Ct) Aus. 12.06
Commissioner, Australian Federal Police v Propend Finance Pty Ltd (1997) 71 A.L.J.R. 327 .... 11.12, 11.32, 11.34, 11.36
Commissioner, Australian Federal Police v Propend Finance Pty Ltd (1997) 188 C.L.R. 501, H.Ct.Aus 11.33, 11.69
Commissioners of the Sewers of the City of London v Glasse (1873) L.R. 15 Eq. 302 .... 16.83
Commonwealth Bank of Australia v Quade (1991) 178 C.L.R. 134 .... 13.36
Commonwealth of Australia v Northern Land Council (1993) 67 A.L.J.R. 405, HC (Aus) 5.08, 11.98
Commonwealth of Australia v Vance (2005) 158 A.C.T.R. 47, CA (Aus Cap Terr) 11.18, 11.19
Commonwealth of Australia, Re (1991) 103 A.L.R. 267, Fed. Ct. (Full Ct) Aus. 4.39
Commonwealth v CFMEU (2000) 98 F.C.R. 31 .... 11.98

Commonwealth v Northern Land Council (1992–93) 176 C.L.R. 604 .... 11.02, 11.94
Compagnie Financière du Pacifique v Peruvian Guano Co (1882) 28 S.J. 410 .... 16.104
Compagnie Financière du Pacifique v Peruvian Guano Co (1882–83) L.R. 11 Q.B.D. 55, CA 5.08, 5.09, 5.10, 5.14, 5.33, 6.41, 6.56
Compagnie Noga D'Importation et D'Exportation SA v Australia & New Zealand Banking Group Ltd, unreported, December 10, 1999, CA 11.122
Compania Naviera Vascongada v Hall (No.2) (1906) 40 I.L.T. 246 .... 4.21
Companies W, X, Y, Z v Austria (1976) 7 D.R. 148, Eur Comm. HR 21.16
Company (No.005374 of 1993), Re [1993] B.C.C. 734, Ch.D (Companies Ct) 3.42
Complete Technology Pty Ltd v Toshiba (Australia) Pty Ltd (1994) 124 A.L.R. 493, Fed. Ct. Aus. 11.136
Computerland Corporaton v Yew Seng Computers Pte Ltd [1985] H.K.C.A. 201 .... 3.03
Computershare Ltd v Perpetual Registrars Ltd [2000] V.S.C. 139 .... 2.32, 3.03, 3.05, 3.14
Condliffe v Hislop [1996] 1 W.L.R. 753 [1996] 1 All E.R. 431 [1996] E.M.L.R. 25, CA (Civ Div) 2.40, 4.33
Conerney v Jacklin sub nom. Cornarney v Jacklin [1985] Crim. L.R. 234 (1985) 82 L.S.G. 1092 (1985) 129 S.J. 285, CA (Civ Div) 11.100
Coni v Robertson [1969] 1 W.L.R. 1007 [1969] 2 All E.R. 609 113 S.J. 549, Ch.D 4.02
Conlon v Conlons sub nom. Conlon v Conlans [1952] 2 All E.R. 462 [1952] 2 T.L.R. 343 [1952] W.N. 403 96 S.J. 547, CA 11.10, 11.64
Connolly v Dale [1996] Q.B. 120 [1995] 3 W.L.R. 786 [1996] 1 All E.R. 224 [1996] 1 Cr. App. R. 200, DC 12.24, 18.16
Connolly v Taylor, unreported, May 11, 2001 .... 15.38
Connor (Debtors), Re, Ex p. Carter Holt Harvey Ltd [1996] 1 N.Z.L.R. 244 .... 11.129
Conoco (UK) Ltd v Commercial Law Practice, 1997 S.L.T. 372, OH 1.16, 11.13
Conopco v Ernst & Young, unreported, September 1, 1993, CA 10.57
Consolidated NBS Inc v Price Waterhouse (1992) 94 D.L.R. (4th) 176, Ont Ct 15.41, 15.56
Consolidated NBS Inc v Price Waterhouse (1994) 111 D.L.R. (4th) 656 ... 15.56
Consul Corfitzon, The [1917] A.C. 550, PC (UK) 5.08, 8.26, 11.154, 20.65
Continental Bank N.A. v Aeakos Compania Naviera SA, unreported, January 20, 1993, CA 9.09
Continental Reinsurance Corp (UK) Ltd v Pine Top Insurance Ltd [1986] 1 Lloyd's Rep. 8, CA (Civ Div) 10.11, 11.83, 11.94, 11.98, 11.103, 16.84
Contract Corp (Winding Up: Production of Documents), Re sub nom. Gooch's Case (1871–72) L.R. 7 Ch. App. 207, CA in Chancery 4.37, 16.29, 16.66
Controlled Consultants Proprietary Ltd v Commissioner for Corporate Affairs (1984) 156 C.L.R. 385, H Ct (Aus) 11.105, 11.115
Conway v Petronius Clothing Co Ltd [1978] 1 W.L.R. 72 [1978] 1 All E.R. 185 122 S.J. 15, Ch.D 5.52
Conway v Rimmer [1968] A.C. 910 [1968] 2 W.L.R. 998 [1968] 1 All E.R. 874 112 S.J. 191, HL 11.82, 11.83, 11.89, 11.96, 11.98, 11.101
Cook Industries Inc v Galliher [1979] Ch. 439 [1978] 3 W.L.R. 637 [1978] 3 All E.R. 945 122 S.J. 367, Ch.D 2.17, 2.22, 19.04
Cook v Carroll [1945] I.R. 515 .... 11.153

Cooke v Australia National Railways Commission [1985] 39 S.A.S.R. 146 .... 5.41
Cooke v Smith (No.2) [1891] 1 Ch. 509, CA 6.11, 6.13
Cooper Flynn v RTE [2001] 1 I.L.R.M. 208,H Ct (Irl) ... 5.33, 8.23, 11.153, 11.159
Coopers Payen Ltd v Southampton Container Terminal Ltd [2003] EWCA Civ 1223 [2004] 1 Lloyd's Rep. 331, CA (Civ Div) 18.22
Cordis Corp v Pfizer Inc, I.P.D. 18109 .... 4.46, 5.35
Cornelius v De Taranto [2001] EWCA Civ 1511 [2002] E.M.L.R. 6 (2002) 68 B.M.L.R. 62, CA (Civ Div) 18.17
Cornwall Coast Country Club v Cardgrange [1987] 1 E.G.L.R. 146 (1987) 282 E.G. 1664, Ch.D 5.28
Corporacion Nacional del Cobre de Chile v Metallgesellschaft AG Ltd sub nom. Corporacion Nacional del Cobre de Chile v Metallgesellschaft Ltd AG [1999] C.P.L.R. 309, Ch.D 16.26, 16.85
Corporation of the Trustees of the Roman Catholic Archdiocese of Brisbane v Discovery Bay Developments Pty Ltd [1995] 2 Qd.R. 121 .... 16.103
Corporation of Trustees of Roman Catholic Archdiocese of Brisbane v Discovery Bay Developments Pty Ltd [1995] 2 Qd.R. 121 .... 16.45
Corsellis, Re, Lawton v Elwes (1883) 52 L.J. Ch.339 .... 4.28
Cosgrove v Pattison [2001] 2 C.P.L.R. 177 .... 18.10
Costa Rica v Erlanger (1875) L.R. 2 Eq. 659 .... 4.43
Costa Rica v Strousberg (No.2) (1880–81) L.R. 16 Ch. D. 8, CA 2.47
Costello v Customs & Excise Commissioners, unreported, June 9, 2000, V&DTr 20.89
Coston v Blackburn (1872–73) L.R. 8 Q.B. 54, QB 13.27
Council of Civil Service Unions v Minister for the Civil Service [1985] A.C. 374 [1984] 1 W.L.R. 1174 [1984] 3 All E.R. 935 [1985] I.C.R. 14 [1985] I.R.L.R. 28 (1985) 82 L.S.G. 437 (1984) 128 S.J. 837, HL 11.96
Coventry Newspapers, Ex p. [1993] Q.B. 278 [1992] 3 W.L.R. 916 [1993] 1 All E.R. 86, CA (Civ Div) 11.100, 15.41, 15.56
Cowan v Carlill (1885) 33 W.R. 583 .... 2.48
Cowgate Ltd, Re [2004] EWHC 1773, Ch.D 5.16
Cowland v District Judges of West London County Court, unreported, July 20, 1999, CA 17.21
Cowley (Earl) v Countess Cowley [1901] A.C. 450 .... 20.10
Cox v Bankside Members Agency Ltd (1994) 145 N.L.J. 313, CA (Civ Div) 5.23, 9.37
Cox v Jones [2004] EWHC 1006, Ch.D 17.28
Cox v Royskill Steel Erection Ltd, unreported, November 20, 1991, CA 16.50
Cramp v Hastings BC Phillips v Camden LBC [2005] EWCA Civ 1005 [2005] 4 All E.R. 1014 [2005] H.L.R. 48 [2005] N.P.C. 109, CA (Civ Div) 6.57
Crane v Cooper (1838) 4 Myl. & Cr. 263 .... 9.13
Credit Suisse Fides Trust SA v Cuoghi [1998] Q.B. 818 [1998] 1 W.L.R. 474 [1997] 3 W.L.R. 871 [1997] 3 All E.R. 724 [1997] C.L.C. 1187 [1998] I.L.Pr. 41, CA (Civ Div) 11.150
Creditnet Ltd, Ex p. *See* Austintel Ltd, Re
Crescent Farm (Sidcup) Sports v Sterling Offices [1972] Ch. 553 [1972] 2 W.L.R. 91 [1971] 3 All E.R. 1192 116 S.J. 59, Ch.D 11.06, 11.70
Crest Homes Plc v Marks [1987] A.C. 829 [1987] 3 W.L.R. 293 [1987] 2 All E.R. 1074 [1988] R.P.C. 21 (1987) 84 L.S.G. 2362 (1987) 137 N.L.J. 662 (1987) 131 S.J. 1003, HL 11.116, 15.01, 15.05, 15.14, 15.19, 15.35, 15.37, 15.39
Crisford v Hazard [2000] 2 N.Z.L.R. 729, CA (NZ) 11.13

Croft House Care Ltd v Durham CC [2010] EWHC 909 (TCC) 11.159
Crompton (Lynn Alexander) v Lancashire CC, *The Times*, November 24, 1994, Q.B.D. 19.23
Cropper v Smith. *See* Smith v Cropper (t/a HS Cropper & Co)
Crow v Columbine (1843) 2 L.T. (O.S.) 454 .... 9.37
Crown Prosecution Service v Holman, Fenwick & Willan, unreported, December 13, 1993, DC 11.33
Crowther v Appleby (1873–74) L.R. 9 C.P. 23, CCP 10.08
Crowther v Elgood (1887) L.R. 34 Ch. D. 691, CA (Civ Div) 6.57
Crozier v Wishart Books Ltd [1936] 1 K.B. 471, CA 16.99
Cumberland Queen, The (1921) 126 L.T. 679, CA 19.09
Cumbria Waste Management Ltd v Baines Wilson (A Firm) [2008] EWHC 786 (QB); [2008] B.L.R. 330, QBD (Merc) (Birmingham) .. 11.125, 11.133, 20.56
Cumming v Matheson (1970) 92 W.N.(N.S.W.) 339 .... 16.34
Cunningham v Essex CC, *The Times*, March 31, 1997, Q.B.D. 15.11, 15.56, 15.57
Cunningham v North Manchester HA [1997] 8 Med. L.R. 135 , CA (Civ Div) 13.36
Curd v Curd (1842) 1 Hare. 274 .... 9.37
Curlex Manufacturing Pty Ltd v Carlingford Australia General Insurance Ltd [1987] 2 Qd. R. 335 .... 9.37, 12.35
Currie v Chief Constable of Surrey [1982] 1 W.L.R. 215 [1982] 1 All E.R. 89 125 S.J. 121, Q.B.D. 10.24
Curtis v Beaney [1911] P. 181, PDAD 11.18
Customs & Excise v Turnstem Ltd, May 19, 2004, unpreported Ch.D 2.39
Customs and Excise Commissioners v AE Hamlin & Co [1984] 1 W.L.R. 509 [1983] 3 All E.R. 654 [1983] S.T.C. 780 (1983) 80 L.S.G. 2140 (1984) 128 S.J. 246, Ch.D 15.21
Customs and Excise Commissioners v Harz sub nom. R. v Harz (Samuel Mendel) R. v Power (Jack) Customs and Excise Commissioners v Power [1967] 1 A.C. 760 [1967] 2 W.L.R. 297 [1967] 1 All E.R. 177 (1967) 51 Cr. App. R. 123 (1967) 131 J.P. 146 111 S.J. 15, HL 11.114
Cutts v Head [1984] Ch. 290 [1984] 2 W.L.R. 349 [1984] 1 All E.R. 597 (1984) 81 L.S.G. 509 (1984) 128 S.J. 117, CA (Civ Div) 11.122

D v Australian Red Cross Society (1993) 30 N.S.W.L.R. 376, CA (NSW) 11.103
D v D (County Court Jurisdiction: Injunctions) [1993] 2 F.L.R. 802; [1994] Fam. Law 8; (1993) 137 S.J.L.B. 199, CA (Civ Div) 4.04
D v East Berkshire Community NHS. Trust. *See* JD v East Berkshire Community Health NHS Trust
D v National Society for the Prevention of Cruelty to Children (NSPCC) [1978] A.C. 171; [1977] 2 W.L.R. 201; [1977] 1 All E.R. 589; 76 L.G.R. 5; 121 S.J. 119, HL 8.23, 11.37, 11.103, 11.134
DB Deniz Nakliyati TAS v Yugopetrol [1992] 1 W.L.R. 437; [1992] 1 All E.R. 205, CA (Civ Div) 10.46, 10.53
DC v United Kingdom (App. No.39031/97), September 14, 1999, ECHR 21.05
DCT v Law Institute of Victoria [2010] VSCA 127; (2010) 267 ALR 127 ...... 11.84, 11.98
DN v Greenwich LBC [2004] EWCA Civ 1659; [2005] 1 F.C.R. 112; [2005] B.L.G.R. 597; [2005] E.L.R. 133; (2005) 149 S.J.L.B. 25, CA (Civ Div) 18.14
DORMEUIL Trade Mark [1983] R.P.C. 131, Ch.D 11.42

DSE Holdings Ltd v Intertan (2003) 135 F.C.R. 151, 203 A.L.R. 348, Fed. Ct. Aus. 11.09, 11.14
DSL Group Ltd v Unisys International Services Ltd (1994) 67 B.L.R. 117 .... 11.125, 12.04
D (A Child) v Walker; sub nom. Walker v D (A Child) [2000] 1 W.L.R. 1382; [2000] C.P.L.R. 462; [2001] H.R.L.R. 1; [2000] U.K.H.R.R. 648; [2000] P.I.Q.R. P193; (2000) 97(22) L.S.G. 44, CA (Civ Div) .. 18.10, 21.01
D (Infants), Re [1970] 1 W.L.R. 599; [1970] 1 All E.R. 1088; 68 L.G.R. 183; 114 S.J. 188, CA (Civ Div) 4.04, 11.37, 11.99
D (Minors) (Adoption Reports: Confidentiality), Re [1996] A.C. 593; [1995] 3 W.L.R. 483; [1995] 4 All E.R. 385; [1995] 2 F.L.R. 687; [1996] 1 F.C.R. 205; [1996] Fam. Law 8; (1995) 145 N.L.J. 1612, HL 4.04
D (Minors) (Conciliation: Disclosure of Information), Re; sub nom. D (Minors) (Conciliation: Privilege), Re [1993] Fam. 231; [1993] 2 W.L.R. 721; [1993] 2 All E.R. 693; [1993] 1 F.L.R. 932; [1993] 1 F.C.R. 877; [1993] Fam. Law 410; (1993) 143 N.L.J. 438, CA (Civ Div) 11.135, 20.56
D (Minors) (Wardship: Disclosure), Re [1994] 1 F.L.R. 346; [1992] F.C.R. 297; [1994] Fam. Law 247; (1992) 156 L.G. Rev. 522, CA (Civ Div) 15.43
Dadourian Group International Inc v Simms [2006] EWCA 1745; [2006] All E.R. (D) 305 (Dec) 11.107, 12.37, 15.21, 15.24, 15.37
Dadourian Group International Inc v Simms [2006] EWCA Civ 399; [2006] 3 All E.R. 48; [2006] 1 All E.R. (Comm.) 709, CA (Civ Div) 2.18
Dadourian Group International v Simms [2007] EWHC 2634 (Ch) 11.76, 15.45
Dadourian Group International Inc v Simms [2008] EWHC 1784 (Ch) 11.09, 11.18, 11.25, 11.59, 11.71, 12.19
Dadourian Group International Inc v Simms (Damages) [2009] EWCA Civ 169; [2009] 1 Lloyd's Rep. 601 .... 13.07, 13.17, 13.37
Daily Express (1908) Ltd v Mountain (1916) 32 T.L.R. 592 .... 11.09
Daintrey Ex p. Holt, Re [1893] 2 Q.B. 116, QBD 11.129
Dalgleish v Lowther [1899] 2 Q.B. 590, CA ... 11.64, 16.42, 16.60, 16.79, 16.91
Dallas v Dallas (1960) 24 D.L.R. 2d 746 .... 5.49
Dalleagles Pty Ltd v Ausralian Securities Commission (1991) 4 W.A.R. 325 .... 11.10
Dalrymple v Leslie (1881–82) L.R. 8 Q.B.D. 5, QBD 16.41, 16.94
Daltel Europe Ltd (In Liquidation) v Makki (Committal for Contempt) [2006] EWCA Civ 94, CA (Civ Div); affirming [2005] EWHC 749, Ch.D 2.15, 2.20, 13.27, 13.29
Daltel Europe Ltd (In Liquidation) v Makki (No.1) [2004] EWHC 726; [2005] 1 B.C.L.C. 594, Ch.D 3.43
Danieletto v Khera (1995) 35 N.S.W.L.R. 684 .... 10.35
Daniels v TAB Ltd [2009] FMCA 148 .... 15.03
Daniels v Walker. *See* D (A Child) v Walker
Daniels Corp International Pty Ltd v Australian Compensation and Consumer Commission (2002) 213 .... 8.10
Daniels Corp International Pty Ltd v Australian Competition and Consumer Commission (2002) 194 A.L.R. 561, H Ct (Aus) 11.77
Daniels Corp International Pty Ltd v Australian Competition and Consumer Commission (2002) 213 C.L.R. 543, H Ct (Aus) 11.08
Danvillier v Myers [1883] W.N. 58, CA 13.07, 13.08
Darby v Sweden (A/187) (1991) 13 E.H.R.R. 774, ECHR 21.18

Darker v Chief Constable of the West Midlands [2001] 1 A.C. 435; [2000] 3 W.L.R. 747; [2000] 4 All E.R. 193; [2000] Po. L.R. 305; (2000) 97(32) L.S.G. 38; (2000) 150 N.L.J. 1421; (2000) 144 S.J.L.B. 243, HL **17.30**
Dartberg Pty Ltd v Wealthcare Financial Planning Pty Ltd [2007] FCA 1216 .... 3.34
Darthez Brothers v Lee (1836) 2 Y. & C. 5 .... 3.14
Data Access Corp v Powerflex Services [1994] A.I.P.C. 91 .... 12.06
David Agmashenebeli, The [2001] C.L.C. 942; [2000] All E.R. (D.) 2324 ..... 11.70, 11.71
David Kahn Inc v Conway Stewart & Co Ltd (No.1) [1972] F.S.R. 169; [1972] R.P.C. 572, Ch.D 6.49, 8.20, 8.28
Davidson v Financial Services Authority [2004] UKFSM FSM011 .... 20.39
Davies (Joy Rosalie) v Eli Lilly & Co (No.1) [1987] 1 W.L.R. 428; [1987] 1 All E.R. 801; [1987] E.C.C. 340; (1987) 84 L.S.G. 826; (1987) 131 S.J. 360, CA (Civ Div) 9.31, 11.08, 11.161, 11.163
Davies v American Home Assurance Co (2002) 217 D.L.R. (4th) 157, Div Ct (Ont) 11.45
Davies (Joy Rosalie) v Eli Lilly & Co (No.1) [1987] 1 W.L.R. 428; [1987] 1 All E.R. 801; [1987] E.C.C. 340; (1987) 84 L.S.G. 826; (1987) 131 S.J. 360, CA (Civ Div) 1.02, 1.25
Davis v Dale (1830) 173 E.R. 142 .... **10.27**
Davis v Stena Line Ltd [2005] EWHC 420; [2005] 2 Lloyd's Rep. 13, QBD 18.12
Davis v Turning Properties [2005] N.S.W.S.C. 742; (2006) 222 A.L.R. 676 .... 3.08
Davison v Farmer (1851) 6 Exch. Rep. 242 .... 10.09, 11.105
Dawkins v Lord Rokeby (1874–75) L.R. 7 H.L. 744, HL; affirming (1872–73) L.R. 8 Q.B. 255; [1874–80] All E.R. Rep. 994, Ex Chamber 11.101, 11.138
Dayman v Canyon Holdings Ltd, unreported, January 11, 2006, Ch.D 6.47
De Mata v Menfred Properties (Pty) Ltd 1969 (3) S.A.L.R. 332 .... 5.06
De Molestina v Ponton (Application for Specific Discovery); sub nom. Molestina v Ponto [2002] EWHC 366, QBD 6.53
Deacons v White & Case [2003] H.K.C.F.I. 227 .... 5.12, 6.51
Debtor (No.7 of 1910), Re [1910] 2 K.B. 59, CA 16.26, 16.86
Decor Corp Pty Ltd v Australian Housewares Pty Ltd, unreported, November 25, 1998, Fed. Ct. Aus. 11.159, 11.161, 11.163
Def American Inc v Phonogram Ltd, *The Times*, August 16, 1994, Ch.D 12.28
Defendant, Re, *Independent, April 2, 1987, QBD* *2.25*
Delta Metal Co Ltd v Maxim Nordenfeldt Guns and Ammunition Co Ltd (1891) 8 R.P.C. 169 .... 5.35
Den Norske Bank ASA v Antonatos [1999] Q.B. 271; [1998] 3 W.L.R. 711; [1998] 3 All E.R. 74; [1998] Lloyd's Rep. Bank. 253, CA (Civ Div) 2.14, 2.24, 2.25, 11.111, 11.112
Dendron GmbH v University of California (Parallel Proceedings: Use of Evidence) [2004] EWHC 589; [2005] 1 W.L.R. 200; [2004] I.L.Pr. 35; [2004] F.S.R. 42; (2004) 27(6) I.P.D. 27063, Ch.D (Patents Ct) ... 10.36, 10.54, 11.160, 15.11, 15.38, 17.13, 17.14

Department of Economic Policy and Development of the City of Moscow v Bankers Trust Co; sub nom. Moscow City Council v Bankers Trust Co; Department of Economics, Policy and Development of the City of Moscow v Bankers Trust Co. [2004] EWCA Civ 314; [2005] Q.B. 207; [2004] 3 W.L.R. 533; [2004] 4 All E.R. 746; [2004] 2 All E.R. (Comm.) 193; [2004] 2 Lloyd's Rep. 179; [2004] 1 C.L.C. 1099; [2004] B.L.R. 229; (2004) 148 S.J.L.B. 389, CA (Civ Div) 2.03
Derby & Co Ltd v Weldon, unreported, July 24, 1990 .... 10.10, 10.13, 10.26
Derby & Co Ltd v Weldon, unreported, November 2, 1988 .... 16.107
Derby & Co Ltd v Weldon, unreported, November 4, 1988 .... 15.31
Derby & Co Ltd v Weldon, unreported, October 19, 1988 .... 2.06, 20.69
Derby & Co Ltd v Weldon (No.1) [1990] Ch. 48; [1989] 2 W.L.R. 276; [1989] 1 All E.R. 469; [1989] 1 Lloyd's Rep. 122; [1989] E.C.C. 283; (1988) 138 N.L.J. Rep. 236; (1989) 133 S.J. 83, CA (Civ Div) 2.18, 2.29
Derby & Co Ltd v Weldon (No.2), *The Times*, October 20, 1988; *Independent*, November 2, 1988; *Independent*, October 31, 1988 (C.S.), Ch.D 15.07, 15.11, 15.12, 15.29, 15.30, 15.31, 15.42
Derby & Co Ltd v Weldon (Nos.3 and No.4) [1990] Ch. 65; [1989] 2 W.L.R. 412; [1989] 1 All E.R. 1002; [1989] E.C.C. 322; (1989) 139 N.L.J. 11; (1989) 133 S.J. 83, CA (Civ Div) 2.18, 4.67
Derby & Co Ltd v Weldon (No.7) [1990] 1 W.L.R. 1156; [1990] 3 All E.R. 161, Ch.D 6.14, 6.15, 11.67, 11.69, 11.171
Derby & Co Ltd v Weldon (No.8) [1991] 1 W.L.R. 73; [1990] 3 All E.R. 762; (1991) 88(2) L.S.G. 33; (1991) 135 S.J. 84, CA (Civ Div) 6.26, 11.76, 12.18
Derby & Co Ltd v Weldon (No.9), *The Times*, November 9, 1990, CA (Civ Div); affirming [1991] 1 W.L.R. 652; [1991] 2 All E.R. 901, Ch.D ... 5.41, 9.25, 12.10, 18.16
Derby & Co Ltd v Weldon (No.10) [1991] 1 W.L.R. 660; [1991] 2 All E.R. 908, Ch.D 12.19, 12.27, 12.34, 12.36
Derco Industries Ltd v A.R. Grimwood Ltd (1984) 47 C.P.C. 82 .... 11.124
Derham v Anev (1978) 20 A.C.T.R. 23 .... 16.97
Desborough v Rawlins (1838) 3 My. & Cr.515 .... 6.14
Desilla v Fells & Co (1879) 40 L.T. 423 .... 10.56, 10.62
Det Danske Hedelskabet v KDM International Plc [1994] 2 Lloyd's Rep. 534, Q.B.D. (Comm.) 16.26, 16.52
Deutsch-Südamerikanische Bank v Codelco, 1996 C.I.L.R. 1 .... 3.03
Dew Pitchmastic Plc v Birse Construction Ltd, 78 Con. L.R. 162, Q.B.D. (TCC) 18.05
Deweer v Belgium (A/35); sub nom. De Weer v Belgium [1980] E.C.C. 169; (1979–80) 2 E.H.R.R. 439, ECHR 21.13
Dian AO v Davis Frankel & Mead (A Firm) [2004] EWHC 2662; [2005] 1 W.L.R. 2951; [2005] 1 All E.R. 1074; [2005] 1 All E.R. (Comm.) 482; [2005] C.P. Rep. 18, Q.B.D. (Comm.) 3.45
Dickenson v Rushmer [2001] EWHC 9018; [2001] All E.R. (D) 369 (Dec) 11.09, 11.10
Dickinson, Re [1992] 2 N.Z.L.R., 43, CA (NZ) 5.29, 10.11, 10.15
Dickinson (t/a John Dickinson Equipment Finance) v Rushmer (t/a FJ Associates) (Costs) [2002] 1 Costs L.R. 128; (2002) 152 N.L.J. 58, Ch.D 12.30
Dickson v Enoch (1871) L.R. 13 Eq. 394 .... 16.62
Digby v Essex CC [1994] P.I.Q.R. P53, CA (Civ Div) 19.23
Digicel (St Lucia) Ltd v Cable & Wireless Plc [2008] EWHC 2522 (Ch); [2009] 2 All E.R. 1094 .... 6.33, 7.01, 7.11, 12.19

Director of Assets Recovery Agency v Szepietowski, *The Times*, October 25, 2006 .... 15.12
Director of Consumer Affairs and Fair Trading v Sugar Distributors [1991] 1 I.R. 225, Sup Ct (Eire) 11.103
Director of Investigation & Research and Shell Canada Lt, Re (1975) 55 D.L.R. (3d) 713 .... 11.19
Disney v Longbourne (1875–76) L.R. 2 Ch. D. 704, Ch.D 2.32, 16.26
Distillers Co (Biochemicals) Ltd v Times Newspapers Ltd; Distillers Co (Biochemicals) Ltdv Phillips [1975] Q.B. 613; [1974] 3 W.L.R. 728; [1975] 1 All E.R. 41; 118 S.J. 864, QBD 15.01, 15.05, 15.09, 15.21, 15.45
Dixons Stores Group Ltd v Thames Television Plc [1993] 1 All E.R. 349, QBD 11.128
Dobson v Hastings [1992] Ch. 394; [1992] 2 W.L.R. 414; [1992] 2 All E.R. 94; (1992) 89(8) L.S.G. 27; (1991) 141 N.L.J. 1625, Ch.D 3.45
Dobson v Richardson (1867–68) L.R. 3 Q.B. 778, QB 16.39
Dolling-Baker v Merrett [1990] 1 W.L.R. 1205; [1991] 2 All E.R. 890; (1990) 134 S.J. 806, CA (Civ Div) 2.003, 5.08, 8.01, 8.17, 8.28, 11.01, 11.147, 11.151, 15.47, 15.52
Dombo Beheer BV v Netherlands (A/274–A) (1994) 18 E.H.R.R. 213, ECHR 21.06
Domsalla v Barr (t/a AB Construction) [1969] 1 W.L.R. 630; [1969] 3 All E.R. 487; 113 S.J. 265, CA (Civ Div) 16.39
Donaldson v Harris (1973) 4 S.A.S.R. 299, Sup Ct (S Aust) 5.08, 5.12, 5.14
Donaldson Judicial Review, Re [2010] NIQB 47 .... 12.19, 12.22
Doncaster BC, Ex p. *See* R. v Secretary of State for the Environment Ex p. Doncaster BC
Donnelly v Weybridge Construction Ltd [2006] EWHC 348; [2006] B.L.R. 158, Q.B.D. (TCC) 11.38, 12.02
Donovan v DCT (1992) 105 A.L.R. 661 .... 11.114
Donovan v Deputy Commissioner of Taxation (1992) 105 A.L.R. 661, Fed. Ct. Aus. 11.109
Doorson v Netherlands (1996) 22 E.H.R.R. 330, ECHR 21.07
Dora v Simper [2000] 2 B.C.L.C. 561, CA (Civ Div); affirming [1999] B.C.C. 836, Ch.D 11.125
Doran Constructions, Re [2002] N.S.W.S.C. 215, (2002) 194 A.L.R. 101, Sup. Ct. of N.S.W 11.74, 12.06, 18.14
Dorajay Pty Ltd v Aristocrat Leisure Ltd [2006] FCA 335; (2007) 230 A.L.R. 549 .... 10.08
Dore v Leicestershire CC [2010] EWHC 34 (Ch) 12.34, 12.36
Dory v Richard Wolf GmbH [1990] F.S.R. 266, Ch.D (Patents Ct) 15.11, 15.39
Dos Santos v Sun Life Assurance Co of Canada (2005) 249 D.L.R. (4th) 416, CA (BC) 11.130
Double K Oil Products 1996 Ltd v Neste Oil Oy [2009] EWHC 3380 (Comm); [2010] 1 Lloyd's Rep. 141; (2010) 160 N.L.J. 68 .... 12.07
Douglas v Hello! Ltd (No.1) [2001] Q.B. 967; [2001] 2 W.L.R. 992; [2001] 2 All E.R. 289; [2001] E.M.L.R. 9; [2001] 1 F.L.R. 982; [2002] 1 F.C.R. 289; [2001] H.R.L.R. 26; [2001] U.K.H.R.R. 223; 9 B.H.R.C. 543; [2001] F.S.R. 40 , CA (Civ Div) 21.08
Douglas v Hello! Ltd (No.3) [2003] EWHC 55; [2003] 1 All E.R. 1087 (Note); [2003] E.M.L.R. 29; (2003) 100(11) L.S.G. 34; (2003) 153 N.L.J. 175, Ch.D 13.18, 14.04
Douglas v Hello! Ltd (No.5) [2003] EWCA Civ 332; [2003] C.P. Rep. 42; [2003] E.M.L.R. 30; (2003) 147 S.J.L.B. 297, CA (Civ Div) 17.26

Douglas v Hello! Ltd (No.6); sub nom. Douglas v Hello! Ltd (Trial Action: Breach of Confidence) (No.3) [2005] EWCA Civ 595; [2006] Q.B. 125; [2005] 3 W.L.R. 881; [2005] 4 All E.R. 128; [2005] E.M.L.R. 28; [2005] 2 F.C.R. 487; [2005] H.R.L.R. 27; (2005) 28(8) I.P.D. 28057; (2005) 155 N.L.J. 828, CA (Civ Div) 21.14
Douglas v Lloyds Bank Ltd (1929) 34 Com. Cas. 263 .... 10.38
Douglas v Morning Post (1923) 39 T.L.R. 404, CA 16.94
Douglas v Pindling [1996] A.C. 890; [1996] 3 W.L.R. 242; (1996) 93(20) L.S.G. 30; (1996) 140 S.J.L.B. 128, PC (Bah) 8.23, 10.42, 10.47, 11.151
Douglas-Hamilton, Petitioner, 1996 S.L.T. (Lyon Ct) 8, Lyon Ct 20.11
Douglas-Hill v Parke-Davis Pty Ltd (1990) 54 S.A.S.R. 346 .... 5.46
Douihech v Findlay [1990] 1 W.L.R. 269; [1990] 3 All E.R. 118, DC 4.45, 19.07
Dow Chemical Co and Distrene Ltd v Monsanto Chemicals Ltd [1969] F.S.R. 504, Ch.D 19.10
Dowles Manor Properties Ltd v Bank of Namibia [1999] C.P.L.R. 259, CA (Civ Div) 13.10, 13.15, 13.24, 13.38
Downie v Coe, *The Times*, November 28, 1997, CA (Civ Div) 11.106
Downing v Falmouth United Sewerage Board (1888) L.R. 37 Ch. D. 234, CA 8.19, 8.29
Doyle v Commissioner of An Garda Siochana [1999] 1 I.R. 147 .... 3.03
DPP v Morrow (1993) 14 B.M.L.R. 54, D.C 11.99
DPP v Wilson [2001] EWHC Admin 198; (2001) 165 J.P. 715; [2002] R.T.R. 6; (2001) 165 J.P.N. 845; (2001) 98(18) L.S.G. 45, DC 11.119, 21.05
DPR Futures Ltd, Re [1989] 1 W.L.R. 778; (1989) 5 B.C.C. 603; [1989] B.C.L.C. 634; (1989) 133 S.J. 977, Ch.D 2.13, 4.36
Draper v Manchester, Sheffield & Lincolnshire Railway Co (1861) 3 De G.F. & J. 23 .... 9.31
Drennan v Brooke Marine; Robinson v Brooke Marine; Walker v Brooke Marine; Smith v Brooke Marine, *The Times*, June 21, 1983, QBD 5.24, 5.25
Dreyfus v Peruvian Guano Co (Discovery) (1889) L.R. 41 Ch. D. 151, Ch.D ... 2.54, 3.07, 3.23, 10.54
Drums & Packaging Ltd v Freeman, unreported, August 6, 1999 .... 12.05
Du Barré v Livette (1791) Peake 108 .... 11.14
Dubai Aluminium Co Ltd v Al-Alawi [1999] 1 W.L.R. 1964; [1999] 1 All E.R. 703; [1999] 1 All E.R. (Comm.) 1; [1999] 1 Lloyd's Rep. 478, Q.B.D. (Comm.) 11.69, 11.70, 11.71
Dubai Bank v Galadari, unreported, February 26, 1992 .... 16.107
Dubai Bank Ltd v Galadari [1990] Ch. 98; [1989] 3 W.L.R. 1044; [1989] 3 All E.R. 769; (1989) 86(37) L.S.G. 44; (1989) 139 N.L.J. 1301; (1989) 133 S.J. 1261, CA (Civ Div) 11.33, 11.34
Dubai Bank Ltd v Galadari (Mareva Injunction) [1990] 1 Lloyd's Rep. 120; [1990] B.C.L.C. 90, CA (Civ Div) 11.31, 11.45
Dubai Bank Ltd v Galadari (No.2). *See* Dubai Bank Ltd v Galadari (No.3)
Dubai Bank Ltd v Galadari (No.3) [1990] 1 W.L.R. 731; [1990] 2 All E.R. 738; (1990) 134 S.J. 986, CA (Civ Div); reversing in part, *The Times*, December 11, 1989, Ch.D 1.17, 8.29, 9.07, 9.08, 9.09
Dubai Bank Ltd v Galadari (No.6), *The Times*, October 14, 1992; *Independent*, November 24, 1992, CA (Civ Div); reversing, *The Times*, April 22, 1991; *Independent*, May 6, 1991 (C.S.), Ch.D 5.41, 11.67, 11.69, 11.71, 12.07
Dubai Bank Ltd v Galadari (No.7) [1992] 1 W.L.R. 106; [1992] 1 All E.R. 658; (1992) 89(7) L.S.G. 31, Ch.D 5.04, 6.09, 6.15, 11.33
Dudgeon v United Kingdom (A/45) (1982) 4 E.H.R.R. 149, ECHR 21.08, 21.12

Dummer v Chippenham Corp (1807) 14 Ves. Jun. 245 .... 11.16, 11.17, 4.63
Dun & Bradstreet Ltd v Typesetting Facilities Ltd [1992] F.S.R. 320, Ch.D 2.32, 2.41, 3.27, 19.03
Duncan v Cammell Laird & Co Ltd (Discovery); Craven v Cammell Laird & Co Ltd; The Thetis (Discovery) [1942] A.C. 624; [1942] 1 All E.R. 587; (1942) 73 Ll. L. Rep. 109; (1942) 86 S.J. 287, HL ... 4.39, 11.81, 11.82, 11.89, 11.96, 12.42
Duncan v Governor of Portlaiose Prison [1997] 1 I.R. 558, H Ct (Eire) 6.44, 11.94
Duncan (Deceased), Re; sub nom. Garfield v Fay [1968] P. 306; [1968] 2 W.L.R. 1479; [1968] 2 All E.R. 395; 112 S.J. 254, PDAD 11.21, 11.35
Dunlop Slazenger International Ltd v Joe Bloggs Sports Ltd [2003] EWCA Civ 901, CA (Civ Div) 12.19
Dunn v British Coal Corp [1993] I.C.R. 591; [1993] I.R.L.R. 396; [1993] P.I.Q.R. P275; (1993) 137 S.J.L.B. 81, CA (Civ Div) 4.33, 4.61, 5.21, 10.11, 11.153, 11.159, 15.11
Dunning v United Liverpool Hospital's Board of Governors [1973] 1 W.L.R. 586; [1973] 2 All E.R. 454; 117 S.J. 167, CA (Civ Div) 3.31, 3.35
Durrant International Corporation v HM Att.-Gen. [2006] J.C.A. 039, CA (Jersey) 10.54
Dwyer v Collins (1852) 7 Exch. 639 .... 11.12
Dyke v Stephens (1885) L.R. 30 Ch. D. 189, Ch.D 4.28
Dyson Appliances Ltd v Hoover Ltd (No.3); sub nom. Dyson Ltd v Hoover Ltd (No.3) [2002] EWHC 500; [2002] R.P.C. 42; (2002) 25(5) I.P.D. 25032, Ch.D (Patents Ct) 5.37
Dyson v Foster, unreported, February 7, 1908 .... 10.20

E v A (2003) 5 I.T.E.L.R. 760, CA (Cook Islands) 11.67, 11.69
EAA Securities Ltd v Chan Lin Mui [2008] HKDC 205 .... 5.09, 5.12, 5.24
EB v BA [2006] EWCA Civ 132; [2006] I.R.L.R. 471; (2006) 150 S.J.L.B. 266, CA (Civ Div) 20.31
EDC v United Kingdom [1998] B.C.C. 370, Eur Comm HR 21.05
EDO Corp v Ultra Electronics Ltd [2009] EWHC 682 (Ch); [2009] Bus. L.R. 1306; [2009] 2 Lloyd's Rep. 349 .... 3.31, 20.04
EDS v South Pacific Aluminium [1981] 1 N.Z.L.R. 146, CA (NZ) 16.42
EG Music v SF (Film) Distributors Ltd [1978] F.S.R. 121, Ch.D 5.31
EG, Re [1914] 1 Ch. 927, CA 11.74
EH v Information Commissioner [2001] 2 I.R. 463, H Ct (Irl) 15.25, 15.27, 15.35
EL v Switzerland [1997] H.R.C.D. 3/10, 668 ECHR 21.05
EMI Records Ltd v Spillane [1986] 1 W.L.R. 967; [1986] 2 All E.R. 1016; [1986] S.T.C. 374; (1986) 83 L.S.G. 2659; (1986) 136 N.L.J. 633; (1986) 130 S.J. 555, Ch.D 15.07, 15.11, 15.21, 15.35, 15.42
ES v Chesterfield and North Derbyshire Royal Hospital NHS Trust; sub nom. S v A Health Authority [2003] EWCA Civ 1284; [2004] C.P. Rep. 9; [2004] Lloyd's Rep. Med. 90; (2003) 100(38) L.S.G. 34, CA (Civ Div) 18.08
ETI Euro Telecom International NV v Bolivia [2008] EWCA Civ 880; (2008) 105(32) L.S.G. 20 .... 2.19, 3.08, 19.04
E (Mental Health Patient), Re [1985] 1 W.L.R. 245; [1985] 1 All E.R. 609; (1985) 82 L.S.G. 523; (1985) 129 S.J. 67, CA (Civ Div) 4.31, 20.22
Eade v Jacobs (1877) 3 Ex. D.335 .... 16.34
Eadie v Addison (1882) 52 L.J. Ch. 80 .... 11.06, 11.28

Eagle Star Insurance Co Ltd v Arab Bank plc, unreported, February 25, 1991 .... 9.09, 15.13
Earles v Barclays Bank Plc [2009] EWHC 2500 (QB); [2010] Bus. L.R. 566; [2009] 6 Costs L.R. 906; (2009) 106(43) L.S.G. 24 .... 7.08, 13.18, 13.34
Easey v Webber (1870) 18 W.R. 1064 .... 16.91
East India Company v Kynaston (1821) 3 Bligh 153 .... 19.06
Eaton v Lewis (1853) 20 L.T. (O.S.) 243 .... 9.37
Ebert v Birch; Ebert v Venvil [2000] Ch. 484; [1999] 3 W.L.R. 670; [2000] B.P.I.R. 14; (1999) 96(19) L.S.G. 28; (1999) 149 N.L.J. 608; (1999) 143 S.J.L.B. 130; [1999] N.P.C. 46, CA (Civ Div) 21.05
Eccles & Co v Louisville & Nashville Railroad Co [1912] 1 K.B. 135, CA 10.08, 10.56
Edelston v Russell (1888) 57 L.T. 927 .... 6.51, 8.19
Eden v Weardale Iron & Coal Co (No.1) (1887) L.R. 34 Ch. D. 223, CA 4.16
Eden v Weardale Iron & Coal Co (No.2) (1887) L.R. 35 Ch. D. 287, CA 16.29
Edge Technology v Wang [2001] F.C.A. 247, Fed. Ct. Aus. 15.41
Edison & Swan Electric Light Co v Holland (1888) 5 R.P.C. 213 .... 5.34
Edmeades v Thames Board Mills Ltd [1969] 2 Q.B. 67; [1969] 2 W.L.R. 668; [1969] 2 All E.R. 127; [1969] 1 Lloyd's Rep. 221; 113 S.J. 88, CA (Civ Div) 4.33, 19.21
Edmiston v British Transport Commission; sub nom. Practice Note (CA: Discovery) [1956] 1 Q.B. 191; [1956] 2 W.L.R. 21; [1955] 3 All E.R. 823; 100 S.J. 12, CA 5.26, 6.42
Edmondson v Birch & Co Ltd [1905] 2 K.B. 523, CA 16.63
Edwards v Bruce & Hyslop (Brucast) Ltd [2009] EWHC 2970 (QB) 18.09
Edwards v United Kingdom (A/247B) (1993) 15 E.H.R.R. 417, ECHR 21.06
Edwards v United Kingdom (App. No.39647/98); Lewis v United Kingdom (App. No.40461/98)15 B.H.R.C. 189; [2003] Crim. L.R. 891; (2005) 40 E.H.R.R. 24, ECHR 11.82
Egan v Chadwick (1999) 46 N.S.W.L.R. 563, CA (NSW) 11.98
Egan v Chadwick, unreported, June 10, 1999, CA (NSW) 11.79
Egan v Willis (1998) 158 A.L.R. 527, H Ct (Aus) 11.79
Egerton v Jones [1939] 3 All E.R. 889, CA 6.57
Egglishaw v ACC (No.2) [2009] FCA 12; (209) 253 A.L.R. 354, Fed Ct (Aus) 9.37
Ehrmann v Ehrmann (No.2) [1896] 2 Ch. 826, Ch.D 6.17
Ehrmann v Ehrmann [1896] 2 Ch. 611, CA 2.61, 17.12
El Jawhary v Bank of Credit and Commerce International SA (No.1); Pharaon v Bank of Credit and Commerce International SA; Adham v Bank of Credit and Commerce International SA (No.1) [1993] B.C.L.C. 396, Ch.D 8.15, 8.17
El Jawhary v Bank of Credit and Commerce International SA (No.2); Adham v Bank of Credit and Commerce International SA (No.2) [1995] 2 B.C.L.C. 581, Ch.D 8.15
Elanay Contracts Ltd v The Vestry, unreported, August 30, 2000, ... 21.05
Elder v Carter; sub nom. Slide and Spur Gold Mining Co Ex p., Re (1890) L.R. 25 Q.B.D. 194, CA 4.47, 10.23
Electricity Supply Nominees Ltd v London Clubs Ltd [1988] 2 E.G.L.R. 152; [1988] 34 E.G. 71 .... 5.29
Electrolux Northern Ltd v Black & Decker, unreported, April 25, 1996 ... 19.19
Eleftheria (Owners) v Hakki Deval (Owners) [2006] EWHC 2809 (Admlty); [2006] All E.R. (D) 96 (Nov) 18.26

Eli Lilly & Co Ltd v Neopharma Ltd; sub nom. Eli Lilly & Co Ltd v Neolab Ltd [2008] EWHC 415 (Ch); [2008] F.S.R. 25; (2008) 31(4) I.P.D. 31027, Ch D (Patents Ct) 3.23
Elliott (Janet Denise) v MEM Ltd,unreported, March 11, 1993, CA (Civ Div) 4.61, 11.159
Ellis v Home Office [1953] 2 Q.B. 135; [1953] 3 W.L.R. 105; [1953] 2 All E.R. 149; 97 S.J. 436, CA 11.82, 11.101
Elmer v Creasy (1873–74) L.R. 9 Ch. App. 69, CA in Chancery 8.20
Elvee Ltd v Taylor [2001] EWCA Civ 1943; [2002] F.S.R. 48; (2002) 25(3) I.P.D. 25017; (2002) 99(7) L.S.G. 34, CA (Civ Div) 2.20, 2.21
Emanuel v Emanuel [1982] 1 W.L.R. 669; [1982] 2 All E.R. 342; (1982) 12 Fam. Law 62, Fam Div 2.21
Emmanuel v Soltykoff (1892) 8 T.L.R. 33 .... 12.61, 17.12
Emmott v Michael Wilson & Partners Ltd. *See* Michael Wilson & Partners Ltd v Emmott

Emmott v Star Newspaper Co (1892) 62 L.J.Q.B. 77 .... 10.42
Emmott & Co v Walters [1891] WN 79 .... 16.100
Endeavour Wines v Martin and Martin [1948] W.N. 338; 92 S.J. 574 .... 16.116
Energy Financing Team Ltd v Director of the Serious Fraud Office. *See* R. (on the application of Energy Financing Team Ltd) v Bow Street Magistrates' Court
Engel v Netherlands (A/22) (1979–80) 1 E.H.R.R. 647, ECHR 21.05, 21.17
England v Purves. *See* JN Taylor Finance Pty Ltd, Re
England v Smith; sub nom. Southern Equities Corp Ltd (In Liquidation), Re [2001] Ch. 419; [2000] 2 W.L.R. 1141; [2000] B.C.C. 123; [2000] 2 B.C.L.C. 21; [2000] I.L.Pr. 730; [2000] B.P.I.R. 28; (1999) 96(47) L.S.G. 29; (2000) 144 S.J.L.B. 8, CA (Civ Div) 3.44
English & American Insurance Co Ltd v Herbert Smith & Co [1988] F.S.R. 232; (1987) 137 N.L.J. 148, Ch.D 6.26, 11.76, 12.18
Enoch and Zaretsky Bock & Co's Arbitration, Re [1910] 1 K.B. 327, CA 10.19
Environment Agency v Lewin Fryer & Partners [2006] EWHC 1597 (TCC) 4.59
Environment Protection Agency v Caltex Refining Co Pty Ltd (1993) 178 C.L.R. 477, H Ct (Aus) 11.107, 11.112
Epikhiriseon Metalleftikon Viomikhanikon Kai Naftiliakon AE v Council of Ministers (C–121/86 R) [1986] E.C.R. 2063; [1987] 1 C.M.L.R. 57, ECJ 20.33
Equatorial Guinea v Royal Bank of Scotland International [2006] UKPC 7, PC (Gue 3.03, 3.08
Equiticorp Industries Group Ltd v Hawkins [1990] 2 N.Z.L.R. 175 .... 12.08, 12.19
Equiticorp Industries Group Ltd v Hawkins [1994] 2 N.Z.L.R. 738, H Ct (NZ) 4.20, 5.43, 5.46, 8.20, 11.149
Eronat v Tabbah [2002] EWCA Civ 950, CA (Civ Div) 15.42
Esal Commodities Ltd, Re (No.2) [1990] B.C.C. 708, Ch.D (Companies Ct) ... 3.42, 15.01
Essex v Inland Revenue Commissioners [1980] S.T.C. 378; 53 T.C. 720, CA (Civ Div) 20.77
Esso Australia Resources Ltd v Dawson (1999) 162 A.L.R. 79, Fed. Ct. (Full Ct) Aus. 11.77
Esso Australia Resources Ltd v Federal Commissioner of Taxation (1998) 159 A.L.R. 664, Fed. Ct. (Full Ct) Aus. 11.44
Esso Australia Resources Ltd v Plowman (1995) 183 C.L.R. 10, H Ct (Aus) 8.16, 15.48

Esso Australia Resources Ltd v The Commissioner of Taxation (1999) 201 C.L.R. 49, 168 A.L.R. 123, H Ct (Aus) 11.08, 11.44
Esterhuysen v Lonrho, *The Times*, May 29, 1989; *Independent*, June 12, 1989, CA (Civ Div) 15.12
Ethemi (Blerim) v Shiels (Robert) [2008] EWHC 291 (QB) 13.07, 13.10
Eurobell (Holdings) Plc v Barker [1998] I.C.R. 299, EAT 20.27
Euromepa SA v R. Esmerian Inc [1999] I.L. Pr. 694, U.S. Ct. of Appeals (2nd Cir.) 2.62
Euromepa SA, Re, 51 F.3d. 1095 (2nd. Cir., 1995) 2.62, 2.63
European Pacific Banking Corp v Television New Zealand Ltd [1994] 3 N.Z.L.R. 43, CA 11.102, 11.153
Evans v Bartlam; sub nom. Bartlam v Evans [1937] A.C. 473; [1937] 2 All E.R. 646, HL 6.57
Evans v Chief Constable of Surrey [1988] Q.B. 588; [1988] 3 W.L.R. 127; [1989] 2 All E.R. 594; (1988) 85(28) L.S.G. 45; (1988) 132 S.J. 898, QBD 11.89, 11.101
Evans v Granada Television Ltd, unreported, April 2, 1993 .... 10.11, 11.100
Evans v Granada Television Ltd, unreported, February 19, 1993, CA 5.33
Evans (Michael) v Inspector of the Serious Fraud Office. *See* R. (on the application of Evans) v Director of the Serious Fraud Office
Evans Deakin Pty Ltd v Sebel Furniture Ltd [2003] FCA 171, Fed. Ct. Aus. 18.14
Exagym Pty Ltd v Professional Gymnasium Equipment Pty Ltd (No.2) [1994] 2 Qd. R. 129 .... 2.15
Expandable Ltd v Rubin [2008] EWCA Civ 59; [2008] 1 W.L.R. 1099; [2008] C.P. Rep. 22; [2008] B.P.I.R. 314; [2008] N.P.C. 16 ... 9.05, 9.10, 12.19
Expanded Metal Manufacturing Pte Ltd v Expanded Metal Co Ltd [1995] 1 S.L.R. 673, CA (Singapore) 2.22, 11.111
Eyre v Rodgers (1891) 40 W.R. 137 .... 16.75

FDR Ltd v Holloway [1995] I.R.L.R. 400, EAT 5.26, 5.30, 20.29
F and L Valks Ltd v BNZ Offices Provident Association [1996] N.Z.L.R. 735 .... 4.60
F Hoffmann-La Roche AG v Chiron Corp (2000) 171 A.L.R. 295, Fed. Ct. Aus. 5.35
F(K) v White (2001) 198 D.L.R. 541, CA (Ontario) 11.153
Factortame Ltd v Secretary of State for the Environment, Transport and the Regions (Costs) (No.1); sub nom. R. v Secretary of State for Transport Ex p. Factortame Ltd (Costs: Part 36 Payments) [2002] EWCA Civ 22; [2002] 1 W.L.R. 2438; [2002] 2 All E.R. 838; [2002] C.P.L.R. 385; (2002) 152 N.L.J. 171, CA (Civ Div) 13.37
Factortame Ltd v Secretary of State for the Environment, Transport and the Regions (Costs) (No.2); sub nom. R. (on the application of Factortame Ltd) v Secretary of State for Transport, Local Government and the Regions (Costs: Champertous Agreement) [2002] EWCA Civ 932; [2003] Q.B. 381; [2002] 3 W.L.R. 1104; [2002] 4 All E.R. 97; [2003] B.L.R. 1; [2002] 3 Costs L.R. 467; (2002) 99(35) L.S.G. 34; (2002) 152 N.L.J. 1313; (2002) 146 S.J.L.B. 178, CA (Civ Div) 18.12
Fairfield-Mabey Ltd v Shell UK Metallurgical Testing Services (Scotland) Ltd [1989] 1 All E.R. 576; 45 B.L.R. 113; 27 Con. L.R. 1, QBD 12.10
Falmouth v Moss (1822) 11 Price 455 .... 10.08
Family Housing Association (Manchester) v Michael Hyde & Partners [1993] 1 W.L.R. 354; [1993] 2 All E.R. 567; [1993] 2 E.G.L.R. 239; [1992] E.G.C.S. 150, CA (Civ Div) 11.129, 11.130

Fanmail.com Ltd v Cooper [2010] EWHC 2647 (Ch) 4.56, 4.57
Farden v Richter (1889) L.R. 23 Q.B.D. 124, QBD 13.09, 13.25
Farm Assist Ltd (In Liquidation) v Secretary of State for the Environment, Food and Rural Affairs [2009] EWHC 1102 (TCC); [2009] B.L.R. 399; 125 Con. L.R. 154 .... 10.32, 11.64, 12.04, 12.08, 20.56
Farrow Mortgage Services Pty Ltd v Webb (1995) 13 A.C.L.C. 1329, affd. July 5, 1996, CA (NSW) 11.59, 12.02, 12.08
Fecht v Deloitte & Touche [2000] I.L.Pr. 398, CJ (Gen Div) (Ont) 10.55
Federal Commissioner of Taxation v Coombes (No.2) (1998) 160 A.L.R. 456, Fed. Ct. Aus., reversed by the Full Court, (1999) 92 F.C.R. 240 ...... 11.13, 12.02
Federal Savings v Molinaro, 1988–89 C.I.L.R.6 .... 3.03
Feldbrugge v Netherlands (A/99); sub nom. A v Netherlands (8562/79) (1986) 8 E.H.R.R. 425, ECHR 21.06
Felthouse v Bailey (1866) 14 W. R.827 .... 17.08
Fenner and Lord, Re. *See* Arbitration between Fenner and Lord, Re
Fenton Textile Association Ltd v Lodge [1928] 1 K.B. 1, CA 4.24, 4.34, 11.145
Fenton v Hughes (1802) 7 Vest. 287 .... 4.19
Fenwick v Johnston (1876) Bitt. Prac. Cas. 120 .... 16.26
Festing v Canada (Att.-Gen.) (2002) 206 D.L.R. (4th) 98, CA (BC) 11.08
Feuerheerd v London General Omnibus Co Ltd [1918] 2 K.B. 565, CA 11.31
Few v Guppy (1836) 13 Beav. 457 .... 4.23, 11.145
Fiddes v Channel 4 Television Corp [2010] EWCA Civ 516 .... 6.53, 7.11
Field v Bennett (1885) 2 T.L.R. 122 .... 16.107
Field v Leeds City Council [2001] C.P.L.R. 129; [1999] C.P.L.R. 833; (2000) 32 H.L.R. 618; [2000] 1 E.G.L.R. 54; [2000] 17 E.G. 165, CA (Civ Div) 18.09, 18.12
Financial Services Authority v Amro. *See* R. (on the application of Amro International SA) v Financial Services Authority
Financial Services Compensation Scheme Ltd v Abbey National Treasury Services Plc [2007] EWHC 2868 (Ch) 11.02, 11.09
Financial Times Ltd v United Kingdom (821/03) [2010] E.M.L.R. 21; (2010) 50 E.H.R.R. 46; 28 B.H.R.C. 616 .... 3.18, 3.21, 21.15
Findel plc v White Arrow Express Ltd, unreported, December 19, 2002, Q.B.D. (Merc) 3.33
Finers v Miro [1991] 1 W.L.R. 35; [1991] 1 All E.R. 182; (1990) 140 N.L.J. 1387; (1990) 134 S.J. 1039, CA (Civ Div) 11.68, 11.71
First American Corp v Price Waterhouse LLP [1999] I.L.Pr. 745, US Ct 10.57
First American Corp v Sheikh Zayed Al-Nahyan; sub nom. First American Corp v Al-Nahyan; Clifford v First American Corp [1999] 1 W.L.R. 1154; [1998] 4 All E.R. 439; [1998] Lloyd's Rep. Bank. 213; [1998] C.L.C. 1225; [1999] I.L.Pr. 179, CA (Civ Div) 10.56, 10.59
First Gulf Bank v Wachovia Bank National Association (formerly First Union National Bank) [2005] EWHC 2827, Q.B.D. (Comm.) 3.34
First Malaysia Finance Bbhd v Mohd Fathi Haji Ahmad [1993] 2 A.M.R. 1293 .... 3.03
First National Tricity Finance Ltd v OT Computers Ltd (In Administration) [2004] EWCA Civ 653, [2004] 3 W.L.R. 886, CA 5.23
Fischer v City Hotels Pty (1970) 92 W.N.(N.S.W.) 322 .... 16.34
Fisher v Hughes (1887) 25 W.R. 528 .... 13.09
Fisher v Owen (1878) L.R. 8 Ch. D. 645, CA 16.52, 16.53, 16.85
Fitzherbert v Faisandier (1995) 8 P.R.N.Z. 592 .... 3.03

Flamar Interocean v Denmac; The Flamar Pride and The Flamar Progress [1990] 1 Lloyd's Rep. 434; Lloyd's List, January 5, 1990, Q.B.D. (Comm.) 5.23, 16.44
Flannery v Halifax Estate Agencies Ltd (t/a Colleys Professional Services) [2000] 1 W.L.R. 377; [2000] 1 All E.R. 373; [2000] C.P. Rep. 18; [1999] B.L.R. 107; (1999) 11 Admin. L.R. 465; (1999) 15 Const. L.J. 313; (1999) 96(13) L.S.G. 32; (1999) 149 N.L.J. 284; [1999] N.P.C. 22, CA (Civ Div) 18.22
Flood v Times Newspapers Ltd [2009] EWHC 411 (QB); [2009] E.M.L.R. 18 .... 4.58
Flett v North Tyneside HA [1989] C.L.Y. 2968 .... 11.99
Flynn v Scougall [2004] EWCA Civ 873; [2004] 1 W.L.R. 3069; [2004] 3 All E.R. 609; [2004] C.P. Rep. 37; [2005] 1 Costs L.R. 38; (2004) 148 S.J.L.B. 880, CA (Civ Div) 1.32
Foakes v Webb (1885) L.R. 28 Ch. D. 287, Ch.D 16.80, 16.94, 16.95
Fonseca v Blumenthal, 620 F.2d. 322 (2nd Cir., 1980) 2.62
Fookes v Samuel [1913] 3 K.B. 706 .... 10.08
Football League Ltd v Football Association Ltd, unreported, September 20, 1991, CA 9.02
Forbes v Smith [1998] 1 All E.R. 973; [1998] 1 F.L.R. 835; [1998] 2 F.C.R. 342; [1998] F.S.R. 295; [1998] Fam. Law 256, Ch.D 2.03, 6.58
Ford v GKR Construction Ltd [2000] 1 W.L.R. 1397; [2000] 1 All E.R. 802; [1999] C.P.L.R. 788, CA (Civ Div) 19.25
Ford v GKR Construction Ltd, unreported, October 22, 1999, CA 13.37
Ford v Tennant (1863) 32 Beav. 162 .... 11.28
Format Communications MFG Ltd v ITT (United Kingdom) Ltd [1983] F.S.R. 473, CA (Civ Div) 5.07, 5.09, 6.51, 8.01, 11.162, 11.163
Formica Ltd v Export Credits Guarantee Department [1995] 1 Lloyd's Rep. 692; [1994] C.L.C. 1078, Q.B.D. (Comm.) ... 5.43, 11.60, 11.61, 11.62, 11.74
Forrester v British Railways Board, *The Times*, April 8, 1996, CA (Civ Div) 5.24
Forster v Friedland, unreported, November 10, 1992, CA (Civ Div) 11.125, 11.127, 11.129, 12.39
Forum (Holdings) Ltd v Brook Street Computers Ltd, unreported, May 5, 1998, CA 5.24
Foster v Perryman (1891) 8 T.L.R. 115 .... 16.64
Foucher v France (1998) 25 E.H.R.R. 234, ECHR 21.06
Fox v H Wood (Harrow) [1963] 2 Q.B. 601; [1962] 3 W.L.R. 1513; [1962] 3 All E.R. 1100; (1962) 106 S.J. 570, CA 16.49
Foxley v United Kingdom (2001) 31 E.H.R.R. 25; 8 B.H.R.C. 571, ECHR 11.77, 21.10, 21.12, 21.13
Framlington Group Ltd v Barnetson. *See* Barnetson v Framlington Group Ltd
Framus Ltd v CRH plc [2004] 2 I.R. 20, Sup Ct (Irl) 5.30
Francome v Mirror Group Newspapers Ltd [1984] 1 W.L.R. 892; [1984] 2 All E.R. 408; (1984) 81 L.S.G. 2225; (1984) 128 S.J. 484, CA (Civ Div) 3.19
Frankenstein v Gavin's Cycle Cleaning and Insurance Co [1897] 2 Q.B. 62, CA 6.41
Franklin v Daily Mirror Newspapers (1933) 149 L.T. 443 .... 16.64
Franks v Towse [2001] EWCA Civ 9; [2002] R.V.R. 15, CA (Civ Div) 18.12
Frankson v Home Office [2003] EWCA Civ 655, [2003] 1 W.L.R. 1952, CA ... 4.55, 4.58

Frankson v Secretary of State for the Home Department; sub nom. Rowe v Fryers; Johns v Secretary of State for the Home Department [2003] EWCA Civ 655; [2003] 1 W.L.R. 1952; [2003] C.P. Rep. 52, CA (Civ Div) 11.100
Frary v Frary [1993] 2 F.L.R. 696; [1994] 1 F.C.R. 595; [1993] Fam. Law 628, CA (Civ Div) 4.03, 10.13
Fraser v Thames Television Ltd [1984] Q.B. 44; [1983] 2 W.L.R. 917; [1983] 2 All E.R. 101; (1983) 133 N.L.J. 281; (1983) 127 S.J. 379, QBD 15.08
Freeman v Health Insurance Commission (1997) 78 F.C.R. 91, Fed. Ct. Aus. 11.70
Frenette v Metropolitan Life Insurance [1992] 1 S.C.R. 647, SCC 11.153
Fressoz and Roire v France [1999] E.H.R.L.R. 339 .... 21.15
Friction Division Products Inc, Re v EI Du Pont de Nemours & Co (No.2) (1986) 32 D.L.R. (4th) 105 .... 10.54
Fritz, Re [1995] 2 Qd.R.580, CA (Queensland) 11.64
Frogmore Estates Ltd v Berish Berger, cited [1993] B.C.L.C. 254 .... 3.14
Frost v Brooke (1875) 32 L.T. 312 .... 16.39
Frucor Beverages Ltd v Rio Beverages Ltd [2001] 2 N.Z.L.R. 604 .... 11.22
Fruehauf Finance v Zurich Australian Insurance Ltd (1990) 20 N.S.W.L.R. 359 .... 6.44
Fuel Express Ltd v.L.M. Ericsson Pty Ltd (1987) 75 A.L.R. 284 .... 10.35
Fuji Photo Film Co v Carr's Paper [1989] R.P.C. 713, Ch.D (Patents Ct) 5.34, 5.35
Fuld (Deceased) (No.2 A), In the Estate of; sub nom. Hartley v Fuld (Privilege: Witness of the Court) [1965] P. 405; [1965] 3 W.L.R. 162; [1965] 2 All E.R. 657; 109 S.J. 394, PDAD 11.32
Fullam v Newcastle Chronicle & Journal Ltd [1977] 1 W.L.R. 651; 121 S.J. 376, CA (Civ Div) 16.57
Fulham Leisure Holdings Ltd v Nicholson Graham & Jones (Application for Disclosure) [2006] EWHC 158; [2006] 2 All E.R. 599; [2006] P.N.L.R. 23, Ch.D 12.34, 12.36
Fuller v Strum [2001] EWCA Civ 1879; [2002] 1 W.L.R. 1097; [2002] 2 All E.R. 87; [2002] 1 F.C.R. 608; [2002] W.T.L.R. 199; (2001–02) 4 I.T.E.L.R. 454; (2002) 99(7) L.S.G. 35; (2002) 146 S.J.L.B. 21, CA (Civ Div) 18.22
Funke v France (A/256–A) [1993] 1 C.M.L.R. 897; (1993) 16 E.H.R.R. 297, ECHR 21.07, 21.09, 21.12
Fyffes Plc v DCC Plc [2005] I.E.S.C. 3, Sup Ct (Irl) 12.08

G v France (1988) 57 D.R. 100, 106 .... 21.07
G v G (Financial Provision: Discovery), Re; sub nom. G v G (Matrimonial Proceedings), Re [1992] 1 F.L.R. 40; [1991] F.C.R. 808; [1992] Fam. Law 66, Fam Div 4.03
G v Wikimedia Foundation Inc [2009] EWHC 3148 (QB); [2010] E.M.L.R. 14 .... 3.11, 3.45
GE Capital Commercial Finance Ltd v Sutton, unreported, July 4, 2003 ... 11.28
GE Capital Commercial Finance Ltd v Sutton; sub nom. Sutton v GE Capital Commercial Finance Ltd; Anglo Petroleum Ltd v GE Capital Commercial Finance Ltd [2004] EWCA Civ 315; [2004] 2 B.C.L.C. 662; (2004) 101(14) L.S.G. 25, CA (Civ Div) 11.76, 11.77, 12.07
GE Capital Corporate Finance Group v Bankers Trust Co [1995] 1 W.L.R. 172; [1995] 2 All E.R. 993; (1994) 91(37) L.S.G. 50; (1994) 138 S.J.L.B. 178, CA (Civ Div) 5.31, 6.41, 9.37, 9.38, 12.35

GEA Group AG v Ventra Group Co (2010) 312 D.L.R. (4th) 160, CA (Ont) **3.10**
GEC Marconi Systems Pty Ltd v BHP Information Technology Pty Ltd [2000] F.C.A. 593 .... 12.08
GMTC Tools and Equipment Ltd v Yuasa Warwick Machinery Ltd (1994) 73 B.L.R. 102; 44 Con. L.R. 68; (1995) 11 Const. L.J. 370, CA (Civ Div) 13.13
GS v Minister for Justice [2004] 2 I.R. 417 .... 4.06
G (A Child) (Litigants In Person), Re; sub nom. G (A Child) (Disclosure: Prohibition), Re [2003] EWCA Civ 1055; [2003] 2 F.L.R. 963; [2003] Fam. Law 808, CA (Civ Div) 4.04
G (A Minor) (Social Worker: Disclosure), Re; sub nom. G (A Minor) (Care Proceedings: Disclosure), Re; G (A Minor) (Child Protection: Investigations), Re [1996] 1 W.L.R. 1407; [1996] 2 All E.R. 65; [1996] 1 F.L.R. 276; [1996] 3 F.C.R. 77; (1996) 31 B.M.L.R. 175; [1996] Fam. Law 143; (1996) 146 N.L.J. 85, CA (Civ Div) 11.107
G (Minors) (Care Proceedings: Wasted Costs), Re [2002] Fam.104 .... 18.21
Gadget Shop Ltd v Bug.Com Ltd [2001] C.P. Rep. 13; [2001] F.S.R. 26; (2001) 24(1) I.P.D. 24004; (2000) 97(27) L.S.G. 38, Ch.D 2.20
Gait v Osbaldeston (1826) 1 Russ 158 .... 3.02
Gale v Denman Picture Houses Ltd [1930] 1 K.B. 588, CA 2.32
Galileo Group Ltd, Re; sub nom. Company (No.003025 of 1997), Re; Elles v Hambros Bank Ltd [1999] Ch. 100; [1998] 2 W.L.R. 364; [1998] 1 All E.R. 545; [1998] B.C.C. 228; [1998] 1 B.C.L.C. 318; (1997) 94(46) L.S.G. 30; (1998) 142 S.J.L.B. 21, Ch.D 3.41, 8.09, 9.38, 11.143
Gall v Chief Constable of the West Midlands [2006] EWHC 2638 (QB) ... **18.02**
Gallaher International Ltd v Tlais Enterprises Ltd [2007] EWHC 527 (Comm) 18.08
Gallaher International Ltd v Tlais Enterprises Ltd; Gallaher International Ltd v Ptolemeos Tlais [2007] EWHC 464 (Comm) **18.12**
Galliford Try Construction Ltd v Mott MacDonald Ltd [2008] EWHC 603 (TCC); [2008] T.C.L.R. 6 .... **12.39**
Gambro Pty Ltd v Fresenius Medical Care Australia Pty Ltd [2001] FCA 235, Fed. Ct. Aus. 5.35
Gamlen Chemical Co (UK) Ltd v Rochem Ltd (No.1) [1980] 1 W.L.R. 614; [1980] 1 All E.R. 1049; [1983] R.P.C. 1; 123 S.J. 838, CA (Civ Div) 11.69
Gannon v Gannon (1971) 125 C.L.R. 629 .... 16.116
Garcin v Amerindo Investment Advisors Ltd [1991] 1 W.L.R. 1140; [1991] 4 All E.R. 655; [1992] I.L.Pr. 496; (1991) 135 S.J.L.B. 53, Ch.D 5.06
Garden Cottage Foods Ltd v Milk Marketing Board [1984] A.C. 130; [1983] 3 W.L.R. 143; [1983] 2 All E.R. 770; [1983] Com. L.R. 198; [1983] 3 C.M.L.R. 43; [1984] F.S.R. 23; (1983) 127 S.J. 460, HL 6.57
Gardner v Irvin (1878) 4 Ex.D.49, CA 6.07, 6.14, 6.15, 6.41
Garnaut v Bennett (No.1) (1909) 29 N.Z.L.R. 378 .... 16.60
Garner v Garner (1920) 36 T.L.R. 196 .... 11.153
Garrard v Edge (1889) 37 W.R. 501 .... 19.07
Garratt v Saxby [2004] EWCA Civ 341; [2004] 1 W.L.R. 2152; [2004] C.P. Rep. 32; (2004) 101(11) L.S.G. 35; (2004) 148 S.J.L.B. 237, CA (Civ Div) 1.32
Garratt's Ltd v Thanga Thangathurai [2002] N.S.W.S.C. 39, Sup Ct (NSW) 12.06

Gartner v Carter [2004] F.C.A. 258, Fed. Ct. Aus. 11.70, 11.71
Garvin v Domus Publishing Ltd [1989] Ch. 335; [1988] 3 W.L.R. 314; [1989] 2 All E.R. 344; (1988) 85(33) L.S.G. 44; (1988) 132 S.J. 1091, Ch.D 11.109, 11.112, 15.39
Gaskin v Liverpool City Council [1980] 1 W.L.R. 1549; 124 S.J. 498, CA (Civ Div) 11.99
Gaskin v United Kingdom (A/160); sub nom. Gaskin v United Kingdom (App. No.10454/83) [1990] 1 F.L.R. 167; (1990) 12 E.H.R.R. 36, ECHR 21.08, 21.11
Gates v Pirate's Lure Beverage Room (2004) 237 D.L.R. (4th), Nova Scotia CA 13.13
Guardian Newspapers Ltd, Re [1999] 1 W.L.R. 2130; [1999] 1 All E.R. 65; [1999] 1 Cr. App. R. 284; (1998) 95(39) L.S.G. 34; (1998) 148 N.L.J. 1514; (1998) 142 S.J.L.B. 255, CA (Crim Div) 2.05
Geary v Buxton (1860) 29 L.J. Ex. 280 .... 13.27
Geffen v Goodman Estate (1991) 81 D.L.R. (4th) 211 .... 11.12
Gemini Personnel Ltd v Morgan Banks Ltd [2001] 1 N.Z.L.R. 14 and 672, CA (NZ) 11.69, 11.70, 11.74
General Accident Assurance Co v Chrusz (2000) 180 D.L.R. (4th) 241, CA (Ont) 11.46
General Accident Fire & Life Assurance Corp Ltd v Tanter; The Zephyr [1985] 2 Lloyd's Rep. 529, CA (Civ Div); reversing in part [1984] 1 W.L.R. 100; [1984] 1 All E.R. 35; [1984] 1 Lloyd's Rep. 58; (1984) 134 N.L.J. 35; (1983) 127 S.J. 733, Q.B.D. (Comm.) 12.04, 12.34, 12.36
General Manager, WorkCover Authority of New South Wales v Law Society of New South Wales [2006] N.S.W.C.A. 84, CA (NSW) 11.05, 11.09
General Mediterranean Holdings SA v Patel [2000] 1 W.L.R. 272; [1999] 3 All E.R. 673; [1999] C.P.L.R. 425; [1999] 2 Costs L.R. 10; [2000] H.R.L.R. 54; [2000] U.K.H.R.R. 273; [1999] Lloyd's Rep. P.N. 919; [1999] P.N.L.R. 852; (1999) 149 N.L.J. 1145; [1999] N.P.C. 98, Q.B.D. (Comm.) 11.08, 11.136, 12.41, 15.28, 18.16, 21.06
General Nutrition Ltd v Pattni [1984] F.S.R. 403; (1984) 81 L.S.G. 2223, Ch.D 15.21, 15.21
Genese, Re (1885) 34 W.R. 79 .... 11.111
Genira Trade & Finance Inc v CS First Boston and Standard Bank (London) Ltd. *See* Refco Capital Markets Ltd v Credit Suisse First Boston Ltd
George Ballantine & Son Ltd v FER Dixon & Son Ltd [1974] 1 W.L.R. 1125; [1974] 2 All E.R. 503; [1974] F.S.R. 415; [1975] R.P.C. 111; 118 S.J. 566, Ch.D 5.31
George Doland Ltd v Blackburn Robson Coates & Co [1972] 1 W.L.R. 1338; [1972] 3 All E.R. 959; 116 S.J. 713, QBD 12.28, 12.36
Georgiadis v Greece (App. No.21522/93) (1997) 24 E.H.R.R. 606, ECHR 21.07
Georgius v Oxford University Press [1949] 1 K.B. 729; [1949] 1 All E.R. 342; 65 T.L.R. 101; [1949] L.J.R. 454; 93 S.J. 87, CA 16.63
Geraghty v Minister for Local Government [1975] I.R. 300, Sup Ct 11.19
Gerald R Smith & Partners v Wylie, unreported, July 28, 1994, CA 5.23
Gerard v Penswick (1818) 1 Wils. Ch. Ca. 222; 1 Swan. 534 .... 9.13

Ghaidan v Godin-Mendoza; sub nom. Ghaidan v Mendoza; Godin-Mendoza v Ghaidan; Mendoza v Ghaidan [2004] UKHL 30; [2004] 2 A.C. 557; [2004] 3 W.L.R. 113; [2004] 3 All E.R. 411; [2004] 2 F.L.R. 600; [2004] 2 F.C.R. 481; [2004] H.R.L.R. 31; [2004] U.K.H.R.R. 827; 16 B.H.R.C. 671; [2004] H.L.R. 46; [2005] 1 P. & C.R. 18; [2005] L. & T.R. 3; [2004] 2 E.G.L.R. 132; [2004] Fam. Law 641; [2004] 27 E.G.C.S. 128; (2004) 101(27) L.S.G. 30; (2004) 154 N.L.J. 1013; (2004) 148 S.J.L.B. 792; [2004] N.P.C. 100; [2004] 2 P. & C.R. DG17, HL 21.18
Giambrone v JMC Holidays Ltd (formerly t/a Sunworld Holidays Ltd) [2002] EWHC 495; [2002] C.P.L.R. 440; [2002] 2 Costs L.R. 294, QBD 12.30
Gianola, Re, 3 F.3d. 54 (2nd Cir., 1993) 2.63
Gibson v Evans (1889) L.R. 23 Q.B.D. 384, QBD 16.63
Gibson v Sykes (1884) 28 S.J. 533 .... 13.09
Gidrxslme Shipping Co Ltd v Tantomar Transportes Maritimos Lda; The Naftilos [1995] 1 W.L.R. 299; [1994] 4 All E.R. 507; [1994] 2 Lloyd's Rep. 392; [1994] C.L.C. 544; (1994) 91(27) L.S.G. 37; (1994) 138 S.J.L.B. 127, Q.B.D. (Comm.) 2.46, 2.51
Gilchrist v Wallace [1972] V.R. 481 .... 16.94
Gillespie (t/a Gillespie Transport) v Anglo Irish Beef Processors Ltd [1994] N.I. 65, Q.B.D. (NI) 4.16
Gillingham v Gillingham [2001] EWCA Civ 906; [2001] C.P. Rep. 89; [2001] C.P.L.R. 355, CA (Civ Div) 2.53, 13.36
Gillow v United Kingdom (A/109); sub nom. Gillow v United Kingdom (App. No.9063/80) (1989) 11 E.H.R.R. 335, ECHR 21.09
Gio Personal Investment Services Ltd v Liverpool and London Steamship Protection & Indemnity Association Ltd [1999] 1 W.L.R. 984; (1999) 96(6) L.S.G. 35, CA (Civ Div) 2.03, 17.28
Giovanna, The. *See* Gulf Interstate Oil Co v ANT Trade & Transport Ltd of Malta; The Giovanna
Girdlestone v North British Mercantile Insurance (1870) LR 11 Eq. 197 .... 16.47
Glaverbel SA's Patent, I.P.D 18043 .... 5.35
Glaverbel SA v British Coal Corp (No.1) [1992] F.S.R. 642, Ch.D (Patents Ct) 8.19
Glaverbel SA v British Coal Corp (No.2) [1993] R.P.C. 90, Ch.D (Patents Ct) 5.35
Glaverbel SA v British Coal Corp (No.4) [1995] F.S.R. 254; [1995] R.P.C. 255, CA (Civ Div) 5.22
Glaxo Wellcome plc v Minister of National Revenue (1998) 172 D.L.R. (4th) 433, FCA 3.03
Gleeson v J Wippell & Co Ltd [1977] 1 W.L.R. 510; [1977] 3 All E.R. 54; [1977] F.S.R. 301; 121 S.J. 157, Ch.D 5.22
Glencore v Selwyn Mines [2005] F.C.A. 801, (2006) 223 A.L.R. 238 .... 3.34
Glidepath BV v Thompson [2005] EWHC 818; [2005] 2 All E.R. (Comm.) 833; [2005] 2 Lloyd's Rep. 549; [2005] 1 C.L.C. 1090, Q.B.D. (Comm.) 3.45
Global Funds Management (NSW) Ltd v Rooney (1994) 36 N.S.W.L.R. 122, Sup Ct (NSW) 11.07
Global Info Ltd, Re; sub nom. Secretary of State for Trade and Industry v Wiper [1999] C.P.L.R. 76; [1999] 1 B.C.L.C. 74, Ch.D 10.10, 10.12, 10.13, 10.32
Global Mariner (Owner) v Atlantic Crusader (Owners). *See* Owners of the Global Mariner v Owners of the Atlantic Crusader

Gloucester v R. (1981) 129 D.L.R. (3d) 275, CA (BC) 11.98
Glyn v Sorres (1836) 1 T. & C. 644 .... 4.25
Glyn v Western Feature Film Co [1916] 1 Ch. 36 .... 5.05
Gnitrow Ltd v Cape Plc [2000] 1 W.L.R. 2327; [2000] 3 All E.R. 763; [2001] C.P. Rep. 21; (2000) 150 N.L.J. 1109, CA (Civ Div) 11.125, 11.130
Goddard v Nationwide Building Society [1987] Q.B. 670; [1986] 3 W.L.R. 734; [1986] 3 All E.R. 264; (1986) 83 L.S.G. 3592; (1986) 137 N.L.J. 775; (1986) 130 S.J. 803, CA (Civ Div) 6.26, 10.15, 11.06, 11.28, 11.76
Godman v Times Publishing Co Ltd [1926] 2 K.B. 273, CA 5.33
Goldberg v Ng (1995) 185 C.L.R. 83 .... 11.08, 12.06
Goldberg v Ng (1994) 33 N.S.W.L.R. 639, CA (NSW) 11.99
Golden Eagle Refinery Company v The Associated International Insurance Company [1998] EWCA Civ 428 .... 10.56
Golder v United Kingdom (A/18) (1979–80) 1 E.H.R.R. 524, ECHR 21.05
Goldlion Properties Ltd v Regent National Enterprises Ltd [2005] HKCA 331, [2005] H.K.C.F.I. 166 .... 1.18, 12.06, 12.19
Goldman v Hesper [1988] 1 W.L.R. 1238; [1988] 3 All E.R. 97; [1997] Costs L.R. (Core Vol.) 99; [1989] 1 F.L.R. 195; [1989] Fam. Law 152; (1988) 138 N.L.J. Rep. 272, CA (Civ Div) 12.03, 12.07, 12.30, 12.32
Goldstone v Williams Deacon & Co [1899] 1 Ch. 47, Ch.D 11.06, 11.28, 12.20, 12.28
Gomba Holdings (UK) Ltd v Minories Finance Ltd (formerly Johnson Matthey Bankers) (No.1) [1988] 1 W.L.R. 1231; [1989] 1 All E.R. 261; (1989) 5 B.C.C. 27; [1989] B.C.L.C. 115; [1989] P.C.C. 107; (1988) 85(36) L.S.G. 41; (1988) 132 S.J. 1323, CA (Civ Div) 4.34, 5.43, 11.145
Good Luck, The. *See* Bank of Nova Scotia v Hellenic Mutual War Risks Association (Bermuda) Ltd; The Good Luck
Goodale v Ministry of Justice [2010] EWHC B40 (QB) 7.12
Goodis v Ontario 2006 SCC 31, Sup. Ct of Canada 11.65
Goodman v Holroyd (1864) 15 C.B.(N.S.) 839 .... 16.35
Goodman v Ross (1995) 125 D.L.R. (4th) 613, CA (Ontario) 15.05, 15.45, 16.117
Goodridge v Chief Constable of Hampshire [1999] 1 W.L.R. 1558; [1999] 1 All E.R. 896, QBD 11.01, 11.02, 11.44, 11.94, 11.84, 11.101
Goodwin v Chief Constable of Lancashire, *The Times*, November 3, 1992, CA 11.101
Goodwin v United Kingdom (App. No.17488/90) (1996) 22 E.H.R.R. 123; 1 B.H.R.C. 81, ECHR 3.21, 11.153, 21.15
Goold v Evans & Co [1951] 2 T.L.R. 1189, CA 19.13
Gore v Harris (1851) 21 L.J.Ch. 10 .... 11.28
Gotha City v Sotheby's (No.1) [1998] 1 W.L.R. 114; (1997) 94(30) L.S.G. 28; (1997) 141 S.J.L.B. 152, CA (Civ Div 6.49, 6.50, 11.27, 12.07, 12.08
Gould v National Provincial Bank [1960] Ch. 337; [1960] 2 W.L.R. 417; [1960] 1 All E.R. 544; 104 S.J. 188, Ch.D 4.09, 4.19, 4.45, 5.09
Gourard v Edison Co (1988) 57 L.J. Ch. 498 .... 11.72
Gourley v Plimsoll (1872–73) L.R. 8 C.P. 362, CCP 16.65
Government Trading Corp v Tate & Lyle. *See* Tate & Lyle International v Government Trading Corp
Gower v Tolko Manibota Inc (2001) 196 D.L.R. (4th) 716, CA (Manitoba) 11.21, 12.15
Gower Chemicals Group Litigation v Gower Chemicals Ltd [2008] EWHC 735 (QB) 12.30
Grace v U.K. (1988) 62 D.R. 22, Eur Comm. HR 21.10
Graham v Bogle [1924] 1 I.R. 68 .... 11.34

Graham v Sutton Carden & Co [1897] 1 Ch. 761, CA 6.17, 9.37
Grand Metropolitan Nominee Co (No.2) v Evans [1992] 1 W.L.R. 1191; [1993] 1 All E.R. 642; (1992) 136 S.J.L.B. 166, CA (Civ Div) 13.07
Grant v Downs, 135 C.L.R. 674; (1977) 51 A.L.J.R. 198, HC (Aus) ... 11.05, 11.08, 11.12, 11.38, 11.44
Grant v Southwestern and County Properties Ltd [1975] Ch. 185; [1974] 3 W.L.R. 221; [1974] 2 All E.R. 465; 118 S.J. 548, Ch.D 5.05, 5.06, 9.28, 11.31
Grapha Holding AG v Quebecor Printing (UK) Plc [1996] F.S.R. 711; (1996) 19(8) I.P.D. 19070, Ch.D 15.01, 15.11, 19.06
Grappelli v Derek Block (Holdings) Ltd [1981] 1 W.L.R. 822; [1981] 2 All E.R. 272; 125 S.J. 169, CA (Civ Div) 16.57
Gray v Associated Book Publishers (Aust) Pty Ltd [2002] F.C.A. 1045 ...... 9.37
Gray v Bateman (1872) 21 W.R. 137 .... 16.91
Gray v Haig & Son (1855) 20 Beav. 219 .... 13.34
Gray v Malton Bacon Factory Ltd [1995] P.I.Q.R. P175, CA (Civ Div) 5.26, 13.36
Great Atlantic Insurance Co v Home Insurance Co; sub nom. Great Atlantic Insurance Co v American Foreign Insurance Association; Great Atlantic Insurance Co v CE Heath & Co (International); Great Atlantic Insurance Co v Frank Elger & Co [1981] 1 W.L.R. 529; [1981] 2 All E.R. 485; [1981] 2 Lloyd's Rep. 138; 125 S.J. 203, CA (Civ Div) ... 11.21, 11.30, 12.02, 12.19, 12.28, 12.34
Great Western Colliery Co v Tucker (1873–74) L.R. 9 Ch. App. 376, CA in Chancery 8.20, 8.25
Greater Beijing Region Expressway Ltd, Re [2000] H.K.C.F.I. 171 ...... 3.03, 3.07
Green Opal, The. *See* Tsavliris Russ (Worldwide Salvage & Towage) Ltd v RL Baron Shipping Co. SA; The Green Opal
Green v Green (1913) 13 S.R.(N.S.W.) 126 .... 16.34
Greencore Group Plc v Murphy [1995] 3 I.R. 520 .... 15.01
Greenfield v Reay (1874–75) L.R. 10 Q.B. 217, QBD 16.61, 16.85
Greenough v Gaskell (1833) 1 Myl. & K. 98 .... 11.05, 11.07, 11.23
Gresley v Mousley (1856) 2 K. & J. 288 .... 5.09
Griebart v Morris [1920] 1 K.B. 659, CA 16.50
Griffin (Paul), Re, *The Times*, November 6, 1996, CA (Civ Div) 2.03
Griffin v Pantzer (2004) 207 A.L.R. 169, Fed. Ct. Aus. 11.113
Griffin v Sogalease Australia Ltd (2003) 57 N.S.W.L.R. 257, CA (NSW) 11.106, 11.111, 11.112
Griffiths McBurney & Parnters v Ernst & Young YBM Inc (2000) ABCA 284, Alberta CA 11.60, 12.02
Grobbelaar v Sun Newspapers Ltd, *The Times*, August 12, 1999, CA (Civ Div) 18.04
Grofam Pty Ltd v Australia and New Zealand Banking Group Ltd (1993) 117 A.L.R. 669, Fed. Ct. (Full Ct) Aus. 11.07, 11.19
Grosvenor Hotel, London (No.1), Re [1964] Ch. 464; [1964] 2 W.L.R. 184; [1964] 1 All E.R. 92; 107 S.J. 1002, CA 6.44, 11.90
Grosvenor Hotel, London (No.2), Re [1965] Ch. 1210; [1964] 3 W.L.R. 992; [1964] 3 All E.R. 354; 108 S.J. 674, CA 11.98, 15.28
Groves v Groves (1853) 2 W.R. 86 .... 9.11
Grubb v Bristol United Press [1963] 1 Q.B. 309; [1962] 3 W.L.R. 25; [1962] 2 All E.R. 380; 106 S.J. 262, CA 16.57
Grundy v Naqvi [2001] EWCA Civ 139, CA (Civ Div) 13.19, 13.21, 17.21
Grupo Mexicano de Desarrollo SA v Alliance Bond Fund Inc, 527 U.S. 308, 119 S. Ct. 1961 (1999) 1.21

Grupo Torras SA v Al-Sabah (No.3); Jaffar v Grupo Torras SA [1997] C.L.C. 1553; [1998] Masons C.L.R. Rep. 90; (1997) 94(30) L.S.G. 28; (1997) 141 S.J.L.B. 169, QBD 9.20
Grupo Torras SA v Al-Sabah [1998] Masons C.L.R. 90 .... 9.22, 9.27
Grupo Torras SA v Al-Sabah, unreported, February 16, 1994, CA 2.18
Grupo Torras SA v Al-Sabah, unreported, June 5, 1997 .... 4.09, 4.11, 4.15, 5.43, 5.46, 11.33
Grupo Torras SA v Royal Bank of Scotland [1994] J.L.R. 42 .... 3.03
Grupo Torras v Butterfield Bank, 2000 C.I.L.R. 442 .... 3.03
Guardian Newspapers Ltd (Court Records: Disclosure), Re, *The Times*, December 8, 2004, Ch.D 3.45
Guardian Royal Assurance of New Zealand Ltd v Stuart [1985] 1 N.Z.L.R. 596, CA (NZ) 11.15, 11.31, 11.44, 11.45
Gündem Özgür v Turkey. *See* Özgür Gündem v Turkey (App. No.23144/93)
Guerra v Italy (1998) 26 E.H.R.R. 357; 4 B.H.R.C. 63; [1998] H.R.C.D. 277, ECHR 21.14
Guidelines are set out at [1982] 1 All E.R. 734 .... 11.76
Guinness Peat Properties Ltd v Fitzroy Robinson Partnership [1987] 1 W.L.R. 1027; [1987] 2 All E.R. 716; 38 B.L.R. 57; (1987) 84 L.S.G. 1882; (1987) 137 N.L.J. 452; (1987) 131 S.J. 807, CA (Civ Div) 6.11, 6.25, 6.26, 11.31, 11.38, 11.45, 11.46, 11.59, 11.60, 12.17, 12.18
Gulf Interstate Oil Co v ANT Trade & Transport Ltd of Malta; The Giovanna [1999] 1 All E.R. (Comm.) 97; [1999] 1 Lloyd's Rep. 867; [1999] C.L.C. 554, Q.B.D. (Comm.) 11.130
Gunn-Russo v Nugent Care Society; sub nom. R. (on the application of Gunn-Russo) v Nugent Care Society [2001] EWHC Admin 566; [2002] 1 F.L.R. 1; [2001] U.K.H.R.R. 1320; [2001] A.C.D. 86; [2002] Fam. Law 92; (2001) 151 N.L.J. 1250, Q.B.D. (Admin) 11.99
Gurney Consulting Engineers v Gleeds Health & Safety Ltd (No.1) [2006] EWHC 43, Q.B.D. (TCC) 18.21
Gus Consulting GmbH v Leboeuf Lamb Greene & Macrae; sub nom. CAIB InvestmentBank AG v Leboeuf [2006] EWCA Civ 683; [2006] P.N.L.R. 32; (2006) 103(25) L.S.G. 31, CA (Civ Div) 15.46
Guyer v Walton (Inspector of Taxes) [2001] S.T.C. (S.C.D.) 75; [2001] S.T.I. 732, Sp Comm. 20.79
Gwelhayl Ltd v Midas Construction Ltd [2008] EWHC 2316 (TCC); 123 Con. L.R. 91; [2008] C.I.L.L. 2637 .... 3.31, 3.34, 19.07

H v Lambeth, Southwark and Lewisham HA [2001] EWCA Civ 1455; [2001] C.P. Rep. 117; [2002] P.I.Q.R. P14; [2002] Lloyd's Rep. Med. 8, CA (Civ Div) 18.19, 21.05, 21.06
H (A Healthcare Worker) v Associated Newspapers Ltd; H (A Healthcare Worker) v N (A Health Authority) [2002] EWCA Civ 195; [2002] E.M.L.R. 23; [2002] Lloyd's Rep. Med. 210; (2002) 65 B.M.L.R. 132, CA (Civ Div) 6.58, 21.14
H (A Minor) (Blood Tests: Parental Rights), Re [1997] Fam. 89; [1996] 3 W.L.R. 506; [1996] 4 All E.R. 28; [1996] 2 F.L.R. 65; [1996] 3 F.C.R. 201; (1996) 160 J.P.N. 576; (1996) 146 N.L.J. 406, CA (Civ Div) 19.20
H (A Minor) (Originating Application in Adoption Proceedings), Re; sub nom. H (Criminal Proceedings: Disclosure of Adoption Records), Re [1995] 1 F.L.R. 964; [1995] 2 F.C.R. 711; [1995] Fam. Law 470, Fam Div 11.99

H&R Johnson Tiles Ltd v Candy Tiles Ltd [1985] F.S.R. 253, Ch.D 19.19
Haddon's Patent, Re (1885) 54 L.J. Ch. 126 .... 16.72
Hadmor Productions v Hamilton [1983] 1 A.C. 191; [1982] 2 W.L.R. 322; [1982] 1 All E.R. 1042; [1982] I.C.R. 114; [1982] I.R.L.R. 102; 126 S.J. 134, HL 6.57
Hafner v Secretary of State for the Home Department. *See* R. (on the application of Hafner) v Secretary of State for the Home Department
Haig v Aitken [2001] Ch. 110; [2000] 3 W.L.R. 1117; [2000] 3 All E.R. 80; [2000] B.P.I.R. 462, Ch.D 21.02, 21.10
Haigh v Haigh (1886) L.R. 31 Ch. D. 478, Ch.D 13.09
Haiti v Duvalier (Mareva Injunction) (No.2) [1990] 1 Q.B. 202; [1989] 2 W.L.R. 261; [1989] 1 All E.R. 456; [1989] 1 Lloyd's Rep. 111; [1989] E.C.C. 449; (1988) 138 N.L.J. Rep. 234; (1988) 132 S.J. 1495, CA (Civ Div) 2.18, 3.08, 4.66
Hajigeorgiou v Vasiliou. *See* Vasiliou v Hajigeorgiou
Hakansson v Sweden (A/171); sub nom. Sturesson v Sweden (A/171); Hakansson v Sweden (11855/85) (1991) 13 E.H.R.R. 1, ECHR 21.13
Halcon International Inc v Shell Transport and Trading Co (Discovery: No.2) [1979] R.P.C. 459, Ch.D (Patents Ct) 5.35
Halcon International Inc v Shell Transport and Trading Co (Discovery: Confidential Documents) [1979] R.P.C. 97; 122 S.J. 645, CA (Civ Div) 15.01, 15.05, 15.38, 15.39, 15.45
Hale v Henkel, 201 U.S. 43 (1906) 11.107
Halford v Brookes (No.2); sub nom. Halford v Brookes and Brookes; *Independent*, September 12, 1991; *Guardian*, August 7, 1991, CA (Civ Div) 10.06
Halford v Sharples; sub nom. Sharples v Halford [1992] 1 W.L.R. 736; [1992] 3 All E.R. 624; [1992] I.C.R. 583, CA (Civ Div); affirming [1992] I.C.R. 146, EAT 11.81, 11.100, 11.101, 12.42, 20.29, 20.30
Halford v United Kingdom (App. No.20605/92) [1997] I.R.L.R. 471; (1997) 24 E.H.R.R. 523; 3 B.H.R.C. 31; [1998] Crim. L.R. 753; (1997) 94(27) L.S.G. 24, ECHR 21.10
Hall v Avon AHA [1980] 1 W.L.R. 481; [1980] 1 All E.R. 516; 124 S.J. 293, CA (Civ Div) 19.22
Hall v LNWR Co (1879) 35 L.T. 848 .... 8.20
Hall v Pertemps Group Ltd., *The Times*, December 23, 2005, Ch.D 11.129, 11.133, 12.40, 20.56
Hall v Sevalco Ltd; Crompton v Sevalco Ltd [1996] P.I.Q.R. P344, CA (Civ Div), CA 16.26, 16.51
Hall v Truman Hanbury & Co (1885) L.R. 29 Ch. D. 307, CA 6.41, 6.43, 16.40
Hall v Wandsworth Health Authority, *The Times*, February 16, 1985 .... 3.39
Halliburton Energy Services Inc v Smith International (North Sea) Ltd [2006] EWCA Civ 1599 .... 18.23, 18.26
Halsey v Milton Keynes General NHS Trust; Steel v Joy [2004] EWCA Civ 576; [2004] 1 W.L.R. 3002; [2004] 4 All E.R. 920; [2004] C.P. Rep. 34; [2004] 3 Costs L.R. 393; (2005) 81 B.M.L.R. 108; (2004) 101(22) L.S.G. 31; (2004) 154 N.L.J. 769; (2004) 148 S.J.L.B. 629, CA (Civ Div) 11.133, 20.55, 20.56
Hamdan v MIMIA (2004) 211 A.L.R. 642, Fed. Ct. Aus. 11.13
Hamer v France (1996) 23 E.H.R.R. 313, ECHR 21.05
Hamilton v Al Fayed (No.2) [2001] E.M.L.R. 394, CA 2.53
Hamilton v Nott (1873) L.R.16 Eq. 112 .... 11.15
Hammer v Sunman, unreported, October 2, 1998, Fed. Ct. Aus. 12.06, 12.26

Hammersley Iron Pty Ltd v.Lovell (1998) 19 W.A.R. 316, Sup Ct (Full Ct) (W Aus) 15.25
Hammerstone Pty Ltd v Lewis [1994] 2 Qd. R.267, Sup Ct (Queensland) 11.148
Hammond v Mitchell [1991] 1 W.L.R. 1127; [1992] 2 All E.R. 109, Fam Div 4.03
Han v Cho (2008) 297 D.L.R. (4th) 572, Sup Ct (BC) 9.22, 11.33
Han (t/a Murdishaw Supper Bar) v Customs and Excise Commissioners; Martins v Customs and Excise Commissioners; Morris v Customs and Excise Commissioners; Yau v Customs and Excise Commissioners [2001] EWCA Civ 1048; [2001] 1 W.L.R. 2253; [2001] 4 All E.R. 687; [2001] S.T.C. 1188; [2001] H.R.L.R. 54; [2001] U.K.H.R.R. 1341; [2001] B.V.C. 415; 3 I.T.L. Rep. 873; [2001] S.T.I. 1015; (2001) 98(32) L.S.G. 37; (2001) 151 N.L.J. 1033; (2001) 145 S.J.L.B. 174, CA (Civ Div) 21.05
Handmade Films (Productions) Ltd v Express Newspapers Plc [1986] F.S.R. 463, Ch.D 3.18, 3.23
Hands v Morrison Construction Services Ltd [2006] EWHC 2018, Ch.D 3.34
Handyside v United Kingdom (A/24) (1979–80) 1 E.H.R.R. 737, ECHR 21.12
Hanley v Stage and Catwalk Ltd [2001] EWCA Civ 1739, CA (Civ Div) 18.05
Hannibal, The (1867) L.R. 2 Ad. & E. 53 .... 18.24
Hannigan v D.P.P. [2002] I.E.S.C. 92, Sup Ct (Irl) 12.19
Hannigan v Hannigan [2000] 2 F.C.R. 650; [2006] W.T.L.R. 597, CA (Civ Div) 1.30
Hansfield Developments v Irish Asphalt [2009] IEHC 90 .... 11.44, 11.60
Harbour Inn Seafoods Ltd v Switzerland General Insurance Co Ltd [1990] 2 N.Z.L.R. 381 .... 12.07, 12.08
Harcourt v FEF Griffin [2007] EWHC 1500 (QB); [2008] Lloyd's Rep. I.R. 386; [2007] P.I.Q.R. Q9 .... 5.23, 16.44
Hardie Rubber Co v General Tire & Rubber Co (1972) 46 A.J.L.R. 326; (1973) 47 A.J.L.R. 462 .... 2.61
Harding v Royal Canadian Legion (1999) 166 D.L.R. (4th) 570, Sup Ct (Newfoundland) 11.46
Harding v Williams (1880) L.R. 14 Ch. D. 197, Ch.D 10.38
Harich v Stamp (1979) 27 O.R. (2d.) 395, CA (Ont) 12.06
Harman v United Kingdom (1984) 38 D.R. 53 .... 21.05
Harmony Precious Metals Services SAS v BCPMS (Europe) Ltd [2002] EWHC 1687, Q.B.D. (TCC) 11.130
Harmony Shipping Co SA v Davis; Harmony Shipping Co. SA v Saudi Europe Line Ltd; Harmony Shipping Co SA v Orri (t/a Saudi Europe Line Ltd) [1979] 1 W.L.R. 1380; [1979] 3 All E.R. 177; [1980] 1 Lloyd's Rep. 44, CA (Civ Div) 11.48, 12.24, 18.16
Harrington v North London Polytechnic [1984] 1 W.L.R. 1293; [1984] 3 All E.R. 666; (1984) 81 L.S.G. 3341; (1984) 128 S.J. 800, CA (Civ Div) ... 3.12, 4.63
Harris v Newcastle upon Tyne HA [1989] 1 W.L.R. 96; [1989] 2 All E.R. 273; (1989) 133 S.J. 47, CA (Civ Div) 3.31
Harris v Society of Lloyd's [2008] EWHC 1433 (Comm) 2.39
Harris v Warre (1878–79) L.R. 4 C.P.D. 125, CPD 16.57
Harrison v Bloom Camillin, unreported, March 30, 1999, May 4, 1999 ... 17.32
Harrison v Bloom Camillin, unreported, May 12, 1999 .... 10.15, 10.18, 10.29, 10.35
Harrison v Bloom Camillin, unreported, May 19, 1999 .... 5.23
Harrods Ltd v Times Newspapers Ltd [2006] EWCA Civ 294, CA (Civ Div) ... 5.12, 6.53

Harvey v Lovekin (otherwise Harvey) (1885) L.R. 10 P.D. 122, CA 16.85
Hassneh Insurance Co of Israel v Stuart J Mew [1993] 2 Lloyd's Rep. 243, Q.B.D. (Comm.) 8.17, 10.15, 11.147, 15.51, 15.53
Hastings Corp v Ivall (No.1); sub nom. Corp of Hastings v Ivall (No.1) (1872–73) L.R. 8 Ch. App. 1017, CA in Chancery 6.41
Hatfield v TCN Channel Nine Pty Ltd [2010] NSWCA 69 .... 3.34
Hawick Jersey International Ltd v Caplan, *The Times*, March 11, 1988, QBD 11.71, 11.124, 11.129
Hawley v Fearn-Stewart (2004) 233 D.L.R. (4th) 160, Sup Ct (Ont) 11.103
Hawley v Reade [1876] W.N. 64, ... 16.26
Hayes v Brown [1920] 1 K.B. 250, KBD 5.04
Hayes v Dowding [1996] P.N.L.R. 578, Ch.D ... 11.13, 11.28, 11.64, 12.04, 12.18, 12.36
Hayes v Transco Plc [2003] EWCA Civ 1261; (2003) 147 S.J.L.B. 1089, CA (Civ Div) 17.29
Hays Specialist Recruitment (Holdings) Ltd v Ions [2008] EWHC 745 (Ch) 3.33, 3.34
Headington Investments Ltd, Re. *See* Arrows Ltd (No.5), Re
Health & Life Care Ltd v Price Waterhouse (1997) 69 S.A.S.R. 362, Sup Ct (Full Ct) (S Aus) 11.31
Hearn v Rhay, 68 F.R.D. 574 (1975) 12.06
Hearne v Street [2008] HCA 36 .... 15.03, 15.09
Heath v Crealock (1873) L.R. 15 Eq. 257 .... 11.13
Heaton v Goldney [1910] 1 Q.B. 754, CA 16.39, 16.64
Hedrich v Standard Bank London Ltd [2008] EWCA Civ 905 .... 13.37, 14.02
Hehir v Commissioner of Police of the Metropolis [1982] 1 W.L.R. 715; [1982] 2 All E.R. 335; 126 S.J. 330, CA (Civ Div) 11.100, 12.42
Helitune Ltd v Stewart Hughes Ltd (No.2) [1994] F.S.R. 422, Ch.D 5.37, 11.159
Hellard v Money, unreported, April 28, 2008, Ch D 7.03
Helle v Finland (1998) 26 E.H.R.R. 159; [1998] H.R.C.D. 186, ECHR 21.06, 21.07
Hellenic Mutual War Risks Association (Bermuda) Ltd v Harrison; The Sagheera [1997] 1 Lloyd's Rep. 160, Q.B.D. (Comm.) 2.33, 8.29, 9.38, 11.30, 11.60, 11.74, 12.02
Hemmersley Iron Pty Ltd v Lovell (1998) 19 W.A.R. 316, Sup Ct (Full Ct) (W Aus) 15.07
Henderson v Merrett Syndicates Ltd (No.1); sub nom. McLarnon Deeney v Gooda Walker Ltd; Gooda Walker Ltd v Deeny; Arbuthnott v Fagan; Hallam-Eames v Merrett Syndicates Ltd; Hughes v Merrett Syndicates Ltd; Feltrim Underwriting Agencies Ltd v Arbuthnott; Deeny v Gooda Walker Ltd (Duty of Care) [1995] 2 A.C. 145; [1994] 3 W.L.R. 761; [1994] 3 All E.R. 506; [1994] 2 Lloyd's Rep. 468; [1994] C.L.C. 918; (1994) 144 N.L.J. 1204, HL 11.01, 11.99, 11.143
Henderson v Overall, unreported, December 13, 2001, QBD 6.55
Henderson v Scottish Ministers. *See* Somerville v Scottish Ministers
Henley v Henley (Bligh cited) [1955] P. 202; [1955] 2 W.L.R. 851; [1955] 1 All E.R. 590 (Note); 119 J.P. 215; 99 S.J. 260, PDAD 11.134
Henly Cosmosair [1995] C.L.Y. 449 .... 5.46
Hennessy v Wright (No 2) (1890) L.R. 24 Q.B.D. 445, CA 16.42, 16.63
Hennessy v Wright [1897] 2 Q.B. 188, CA 16.35
Henriksen v Tallon Ltd (No.1) [1963] R.P.C. 308 .... 16.72

Hercules Chemicals NV v Commission of the European Communities (C–51/92 P); sub nom. Polypropylene Cartel, Re (T–7/89); Hercules Chemicals NV v Commission of the European Communities (T–7/89) [1999] E.C.R. I–4235; [1999] 5 C.M.L.R. 976, ECJ; affirming [1991] E.C.R. II–1711; [1992] 4 C.M.L.R. 84; [1999] E.C.R. I–4235, AGO 20.35
Herczegfalvy v Austria (A/242–B) (1993) 15 E.H.R.R. 437, ECHR 21.10
Hermon v Yorkshire Television Ltd [1992] N.I. 27, Q.B.D. (NI) 5.21
Hershfield v Clarke (1856) 11 Exch. 712 .... 16.41
Hertfordshire Investments Ltd v Bubb [2000] 1 W.L.R. 2318; [2001] C.P. Rep. 38; [2000] C.P.L.R. 588, CA (Civ Div) 2.53
Hewitson v United Kingdom (App. No.50015/99) (2003) 37 E.H.R.R. 31, ECHR 21.10
Heyward v Plymouth Hospital NHS Trust [2005] EWCA Civ 939; [2006] C.P. Rep. 3, CA (Civ Div) 18.08
Hickey v Marks, unreported, July 6, 2000, CA (Civ Div) 1.32
Hickling v Baker. ***See*** **Mason v Richard Freeman & Co**
Higginson v Hall (1878–79) L.R. 10 Ch. D. 235, Ch.D 4.28
Highberry Ltd v Colt Telecom Group Plc (No.1); sub nom. Colt Telecom Group Plc (No.1), Re [2002] EWHC 2503; [2003] 1 B.C.L.C. 290; [2003] B.P.I.R. 311; (2003) 100(5) L.S.G. 32, Ch.D (Companies Ct) 4.05, 4.35
Highgrade Traders Ltd, Re [1984] B.C.L.C. 151, CA (Civ Div) 3.44, 11.15, 11.31, 11.38, 11.44, 11.45, 11.46
Hildebrand v Germany, unreported, April 16, 1998, Eur Comm. HR 21.09
Hildebrand v Hildebrand [1992] 1 F.L.R. 244; [1992] Fam. Law 235 ...... 4.03, **6.26**
Hill v Arcola School Division No. 72 (2000) 179 D.L.R. (4th) 539, CA (Sask) 11.46
Hill v Hart-Davies; sub nom. Hill v Hart-Davis (1884) L.R. 26 Ch. D. 470, CA 6.10, 6.19
Hill v R. [1945] K.B. 329, KBD 5.04
Hillman's Airways Ltd v Societe Anonyme d'Editions Aeronautiques Internationales [1934] 2 K.B. 356, KBD 16.63
Hinchliffe (Deceased), Re [1895] 1 Ch. 117, CA 9.07
Hindlip v Mudford (1890) 6 T.L.R. 367 .... 16.65
Hipwood v Gloucester HA [1995] I.C.R. 999; [1995] P.I.Q.R. P447; [1995] 6 Med. L.R. 187; (1995) 139 S.J.L.B. 67, CA (Civ Div) 3.35, 4.52, 5.21, 11.159
Hiro Balani v Spain (A/303–B) (1995) 19 E.H.R.R. 566, ECHR 21.07
Hiscox Underwriting Ltd v Dickson Manchester & Co Ltd [2004] EWHC 479; [2004] 1 All E.R. (Comm.) 753; [2004] 2 Lloyd's Rep. 438, Q.B.D. (Comm.) 4.20, 20.06
HIV Haemophiliac Litigation, Re [1996] P.I.Q.R. P220; (1998) 41 B.M.L.R. 171; [1996] P.N.L.R. 290; (1990) 140 N.L.J. 1349, CA (Civ Div) 11.94
Hoad v Nationwide News Pty Ltd (1998) 19 W.A.R. 468, Sup Ct (W Aus) 12.17, 12.34
Hobbs & Co v Hudson. *See* TW Hobbs & Co Ltd v Hudson
Hobbs v Hobbs and Cousens [1960] P. 112; [1959] 3 W.L.R. 942; [1959] 3 All E.R. 827; 103 S.J. 1005, PDAD 11.48
Hodgkinson & Corby Ltd v Wards Mobility Services Ltd (No.2) [1998] F.S.R. 530, CA (Civ Div); reversing [1997] F.S.R. 178, Ch.D 11.129
Hodgkinson v Simms (1988) 55 D.L.R. (4th) 577 .... 11.34

Hodgson v Imperial Tobacco Ltd (No.1) [1998] 1 W.L.R. 1056; [1998] 2 All E.R. 673; [1998] 1 Costs L.R. 14; [1999] P.I.Q.R. Q1; (1998) 41 B.M.L.R. 1; (1998) 95(15) L.S.G. 31; (1998) 148 N.L.J. 241; (1998) 142 S.J.L.B. 93, CA (Civ Div) 2.03, 6.58
Hodgson v United Kingdom (1987) 51 D.R. 136 .... 21.15
Hodkin v Caven Atack, unreported, March 9, 1995 .... 5.33
Hodsoll v Taylor (1873–74) L.R. 9 Q.B. 79, QB 8.21
Hoechst Celanese Corp v BP Chemicals Ltd (No.1); Hoechst Celanese Corp v Purolite International Ltd [1999] F.S.R. 319; (1998) 21(10) I.P.D. 21105, CA (Civ Div); affirming [1997] F.S.R. 547; (1997) 20(5) I.P.D. 20045, Ch.D (Patents Ct) 5.35
Hoffman-La Roche & Co A.G. v Secretary of State for Trade and Industry, *The Times*, April 18, 1975 .... 11.99
Hogg v Aggarwal, *The Times*, August 1, 1995; *Independent*, August 28, 1995 (C.S.), QBD 13.12, 13.24
Holden v Liquidator of Scottish Heritable Security Co Ltd (1887) 14 R. 663 .... 4.36
Holland v Marshall (2009) 301 D.L.R. (4th) 371, CA (NB) 13.38
Hollins v Russell; Tichband v Hurdman; Dunn v Ward; Pratt v Bull; Worth v McKenna; Sharratt v London Central Bus Co Ltd (No.3) [2003] EWCA Civ 718; [2003] 1 W.L.R. 2487; [2003] 4 All E.R. 590; [2003] 3 Costs L.R. 423; (2003) 100(28) L.S.G. 30; (2003) 153 N.L.J. 920; (2003) 147 S.J.L.B. 662, CA (Civ Div) 11.31, 12.30
Holloway, Re; sub nom. Young v Holloway (1887) L.R. 12 P.D. 167, CA 11.39, 11.48, 11.55, 11.57, 11.58
Holmes v Amerex Rent-a-Car 710A 2d 846, 854 (1998) CA (Columbia) 13.38
Holmes v SGB Services Plc [2001] EWCA Civ 354, CA (Civ Div) ... 18.05, 18.10
Home Office v Harman; sub nom. Harman v Home Office [1983] 1 A.C. 280; [1982] 2 W.L.R. 338; [1982] 1 All E.R. 532; 126 S.J. 136, HL ... 11.98, 14.15, 15.01, 15.05, 15.07, 15.09, 15.18, 15.27, 15.31, 15.44, 15.45
Honda Giken Kogyou Kabushiki Kaisha v KJM Superbikes Ltd [2007] EWCA Civ 313; [2007] C.P. Rep. 28; (2007) 151 S.J.L.B. 431 ... 2.58, 10.59
Honeyrose Products v Joslin [1981] I.C.R. 317; [1981] I.R.L.R. 80, EAT 20.29
Honeywell Ltd v Appliance Components Ltd, unreported, February 22, 1996, Ch.D (Patents Ct) 19.19
Hong Kong Bank of Australia Ltd v Murphy [1993] 2 V.R. 419, Sup Ct (Vic) 12.06, 12.15
Hong Kong Special Administrative Region v Lee Ming Tee [2001] 4 H.K.C.F.A.R. 133, Ct. Final App (HK) 11.113, 11.115
Hongkong Bank of Australia Ltd v Murphy [1993] 2 V.R. 419, Sup Ct (Vic) 11.30
Hookham v Wiggins Teape Fine Papers Ltd [1995] P.I.Q.R. P392, CA (Civ Div) 19.21
Hooton v Dalby [1907] 2 K.B. 18, CA 16.34, 16.42
Hope v Liddell (1855) 7 De G.M. & G. 331 .... 11.149
Hope v McLoughlin [1976] 1 N.Z.L.R. 715 .... 16.45
Hopkinson v Lord Burghley (1866–67) L.R. 2 Ch. App. 447, CA in Chancery 15.02
Horgan v Murray [1999] 1 I.R.L.M. 257, H Ct (Irl) 5.46
Horne v Hough (1873–74) L.R. 9 C.P. 135, CCP 16.39
Horrocks v Ford Motor Co Ltd, *The Times*, February 15, 1990, CA (Civ Div) 4.10
Horton v Donnington (1886) T.L.R. 73 .... 16.75

Hospira Inc v Amgen Inc [2010] EWHC 176 (Pat) 5.34
House of Spring Gardens Ltd v Waite (No.1) [1985] F.S.R. 173; [1985] J.P.L. 173; (1985) 82 L.S.G. 443; (1985) 129 S.J. 64, CA (Civ Div); reversing [1984] F.S.R. 277, Ch.D 2.13, 6.44
Howard v Beall (1889) L.R. 23 Q.B.D. 1, QBD 10.45, 10.48
Howe v David Brown Tractors (Retail) Ltd [1991] 4 All E.R. 30, CA (Civ Div) 3.28
Howglen Ltd (Application for Disclosure), Re [2001] 1 All E.R. 376; [2001] B.C.C. 245; [2001] 2 B.C.L.C. 695, Ch.D 4.55, 4.56, 4.58, 4.59, 10.05, 10.35, 10.40
Hubbard v Lambeth, Southwark and Lewisham HA. *See* H v Lambeth, Southwark and Lewisham HA
Huddleston v Control Risks Information Services Ltd [1987] 1 W.L.R. 701; [1987] 2 All E.R. 1035; (1987) 84 L.S.G. 1494; (1987) 131 S.J. 776, QBD 3.27, 4.50, 19.03, 19.07
Hudson Bay Mining and Smelting Co v Cummings (2007) 272 D.L.R. (4th) 419, Manitoba CA 11.37
Hughes v Biddulph (1827) 4 Russ. 190 .... 11.48
Hughes v Carratu International Plc [2006] EWHC 1791, QBD 3.05
Hunnings v Williamson (1882–83) L.R. 11 Q.B.D. 533, CA (1882–83) L.R. 10 Q.B.D. 459, QBD 8.06, 11.106
Hunt v Judge Russell (1995) 63 S.A.S.R. 402 .... 10.10, 10.29
Hunt v Peasegood (Set Aside), *The Times*, October 20, 2000, CA (Civ Div) 6.57
Hunter v Blackburn, 128 U.S. 464, 9 S.Ct. 125 (1888) 12.06
Hunter v Dublin, Wicklow and Wexford Railway Co (1891) 28 Ir. R. 489 .... 9.05, 9.07
Hunter v Mann [1974] Q.B. 767; [1974] 2 W.L.R. 742; [1974] 2 All E.R. 414; (1974) 59 Cr. App. R. 37; [1974] R.T.R. 338; [1974] Crim. L.R. 260; 118 S.J. 171, DC 11.153
Husband's of Marchwood v Drummond Walker Developments [1975] 1 W.L.R. 603; [1975] 2 All E.R. 30; 119 S.J. 286, CA (Civ Div) 13.05, 13.18
Hussein v William Hill Group [2004] EWHC 208, QBD 18.15
Hutchinson v Glover (1875–76) L.R. 1 Q.B.D. 138, QBD 5.08
Hutchison 3G UK Ltd v O2 (UK) Ltd [2008] EWHC 50 (Comm) 3.33, 3.34
Hutt v Haileybury College (1888) 4 T.L.R. 277, CA 11.15
Huvig v France (A/176–B); sub nom. Huvig v France (11105/84) (1990) 12 E.H.R.R. 528, ECHR 21.10, 21.12
Hydro-Dynamic Products Ltd v AH Products Ltd, unreported, August 21, 1986 .... 9.05
Hydrosan, Re [1991] B.C.C. 19; [1991] B.C.L.C. 418, Ch.D (Companies Ct) 11.73
Hytec Information Systems Ltd v Coventry City Council [1997] 1 W.L.R. 1666; (1997) 13 Const. L.J. 344, CA (Civ Div) 13.10, 13.15, 13.24
Hytrac Conveyors Ltd v Conveyors International Ltd [1983] 1 W.L.R. 44; [1982] 3 All E.R. 415; [1983] F.S.R. 63; 126 S.J. 728, CA (Civ Div) 2.22, 2.32

IFAW v European Commission (C–64/05 P) [2008] 3 W.L.R. 756, ECJ 20.37
INA Corp v Iran (1985) 8 Iran-U.S. Claims Tribunals Reports 373, 382 .... 13.34, 20.47
ITC Film Distributors Ltd v Video Exchange Ltd (No.1) [1983] E.C.C. 43, CA (Civ Div); affirming [1982] Ch. 431; [1982] 3 W.L.R. 125; [1982] 2 All E.R. 241; [1982] Crim. L.R. 237; 125 S.J. 863, Ch.D 11.76

I Waxman & Sons Ltd v Texaco Canada Ltd [1968] 2 O.R. 452, CA (Ont) ... 11.124
IBEW Local 213 v Hochstein (2010) 11 D.L.R. (4th) 389 .... 15.25
IBEW Local 213 v Pacific Newspaper Group Inc (2005) 249 D.L.R. (4th) 647, CA (BC) 5.33
IBL v Planet [1990] J.L.R. 294 .... 3.03
IBM Corp v Phoenix International (Computers) Ltd. *See* International Business Machines Corp v Phoenix International (Computers) Ltd (Discovery)
IBM United Kingdom Ltd v Prima Data International Ltd [1994] 1 W.L.R. 719; [1994] 4 All E.R. 748, Ch.D 2.27
IC Mutual Ltd v Raven [2005] EWHC 2680, Ch.D 13.27
Idoport Pty Ltd v National Australia Bank Ltd [2001] N.S.W.S.C. 22, Sup Ct (NSW) 11.70
Idoport Pty Ltd v National Australia Bank Ltd [2004] N.S.W.C.S. 695 .... 3.03, 3.07
Ikarian Reefer, The. *See* National Justice Compania Naviera SA v Prudential Assurance Co Ltd; The Ikarian Reefer
Implied Waiver of Privilege, [2000] N.Z.L.R. 355 .... 12.04
Imutran Ltd v Uncaged Campaigns Ltd [2001] 2 All E.R. 385; [2001] C.P. Rep. 28; [2001] E.C.D.R. 16; [2001] E.M.L.R. 21; [2001] H.R.L.R. 31; [2002] F.S.R. 2; (2001) 24(5) I.P.D. 24031; (2001) 98(14) L.S.G. 40, Ch.D 21.14
Independent Insurance Co Ltd (In Provisional Liquidation) (No.1), Re [2002] EWHC 1577; [2004] B.C.C. 919; [2002] 2 B.C.L.C. 709; [2003] B.P.I.R. 562, Ch.D (Companies Ct) 18.23
Independent Research Services v Catterall [1993] I.C.R. 1, EAT 11.130
Individual Homes Ltd v Macbream Investments Ltd; sub nom. Individual Homes v Macbreams Investments (2002) 99(46) L.S.G. 32, Ch.D 10.05, 10.35
Infabrics Ltd v Jaytex Ltd (No.2) [1987] F.S.R. 529, CA (Civ Div); affirming [1985] F.S.R. 75, Ch.D 13.34, 14.04
Infields Ltd v P Rosen & Son [1938] 3 All E.R. 591, CA 12.13, 12.20
Ingot v MacQuarie [2006] NSWSC 530; (2007) 233 A.L.R. 369 .... 11.37
Ingram v Little (1882–83) L.R. 11 Q.B.D. 251, QBD 4.28
Inland Revenue Commissioners v Blueslate Ltd [2003] EWHC 2022, Ch.D 3.34
Innovative Health Group Inc Calgary Health Region (2008) 294 D.L.R. (4th) 83, CA (Alta) 9.29
Innovisions Ltd v Chan Sing-Chuck [1992] 2 H.K.L.R. 306, H Ct (HK) 5.49, 11.01
Inquests into the deaths of Toman, McKerr, Re, unreported, July 11, 1994, H Ct (NI) 10.11, 11.96
Inquiry under the Company Securities (Insider Dealing) Act 1985 (No.1), Re [1988] A.C. 660; [1988] 2 W.L.R. 33; [1988] 1 All E.R. 203; (1988) 4 B.C.C. 35; [1988] B.C.L.C. 153; [1988] P.C.C. 133; (1988) 85(4) L.S.G. 33; (1987) 137 N.L.J. 1181; (1988) 132 S.J. 21, HL 3.20
Instance v Denny Bros Printing Ltd (Interim Injunction) [2000] F.S.R. 869; (2000) 23(11) I.P.D. 23090; (2000) 97(5) L.S.G. 35; (2000) 144 S.J.L.B. 56, Ch.D (Patents Ct) 11.122, 12.39
Insurance Co v Lloyd's Syndicate [1995] 1 Lloyd's Rep. 272 ..... 8.17, 11.147, 15.52
Intalite International NV v Cellular Ceilings (No.1) [1987] R.P.C. 532, Ch.D (Patents Ct) 5.34
Intel Corp v General Instrument Corp (No.1) [1989] 1 F.S.R. 640, Ch.D (Patents Ct) 2.32, 5.34

Intel Corp v Advanced Micro Devices, Inc,542 U.S. 241, 124 S.Ct. 2466 (2004), Sup Ct (US) 2.63
Intelsec Systems Ltd v Grech Cini [2000] 1 W.L.R. 1190; [1999] 4 All E.R. 11; [1999] Masons C.L.R. 296, Ch.D 2.12
Interbrew SA v Financial Times Ltd [2002] EWCA Civ 274; [2002] 2 Lloyd's Rep. 229; [2002] E.M.L.R. 24; (2002) 99(16) L.S.G. 37, CA (Civ Div); affirming [2002] 1 Lloyd's Rep. 542; (2002) 99(9) L.S.G. 28, Ch.D 3.05, 3.18, 3.21, **21.15**
Interchase Corp Ltd v Grosvenor Hill (Queensland) Pty Ltd (No.1) [1999] 1 Qd. R. 141, CA (Queensland) 11.48
Interchase Corp Ltd v Grosvenor Hill (Queensland) Pty Ltd (No.2) [1999] 1 Qd. R. 163, CA (Queensland) 6.15
InterDigital Technology Corp v Nokia Corp [2008] EWHC 969 (Pat), Ch D (Patents Ct) 11.157
International Business Machines Corp v Phoenix International (Computers) Ltd (Discovery) [1995] 1 All E.R. 413; [1995] F.S.R. 184, Ch.D 6.27, 11.09, 11.21, 11.76, 12.18
International Credit and Investment Co (Overseas) Ltd v Adham (Disclosure); sub nom. ICIC (Overseas) Ltd v Adham (1997) 94(9) L.S.G. 31; (1997) 141 S.J.L.B. 56, Ch.D 11.13
International Fund for Agricultural Development v Jazayeri, March 8, 2001, Q.B.D. (Comm.) 2.14
International Minerals & Chemical Corpoation (Canada) v Commonwealth Insurance Co (1991) 47 C.C.C.I. 196 .... 11.09
International Operations Ltd v Silver Falcon Enterprises Ltd (1994) 17 G.L.J. 61, CA (Guernsey) 1.17
International Power Industries Inc, Re [1985] B.C.L.C. 128 .... 10.55, 11.06, 11.08, 12.02
Interpool v Galani [1988] Q.B. 738; [1987] 3 W.L.R. 1042; [1987] 2 All E.R. 981; [1987] 2 F.T.L.R. 315; (1987) 137 N.L.J. 613; (1987) 131 S.J. 1392, CA (Civ Div) 2.48
Interporc Im- und Export GmbH v Commission of the European Communities (C–41/00P); sub nom. Interporc Im- und Export GmbH v Commission of the European Communities (T–92/98) [2003] E.C.R. I–2125; [2005] 2 C.M.L.R. 17, ECJ; affirming [1999] E.C.R. II–3521; [2000] 1 C.M.L.R. 181; [2000] C.E.C. 337; [2003] E.C.R. I–2125, AGO 20.35
Irish Press plc v Ingersoll Irish Publications Ltd [1994] 1 I.R. 208, Sup Ct 4.60
Ironmonger & Co v Dyne (1928) 44 T.L.R. 579 .... 10.44, 10.53
Irvin v Donaghy [1996] P.I.Q.R. 207, H Ct (NI) 3.35, 4.60, 6.17
Irwell v Eden (1887) L.R. 18 Q.B.D. 588, CA 2.48
Isle of Cyprus, The (1890) 15 P.D. 134 .... 16.26, 16.54
Islington LBC, Ex p. *See* R. v Secretary of State for the Environment Ex p. Islington LBC
Ismail v Richards Butler [1996] Q.B. 711; [1996] 3 W.L.R. 129; [1996] 2 All E.R. 506; (1996) 146 N.L.J. 442; (1996) 140 S.J.L.B. 66, QBD 11.148
Istel Ltd v Tully. *See* AT&T Istel Ltd v Tully
Istil Group Inc v Zahoor [2003] EWHC 165; [2003] 2 All E.R. 252; [2003] C.P. Rep. 39, Ch.D 6.29
Istil Group Inc v Zahoor; Metalsukraine Corp Ltd v Reventox Consulting Ltd [2004] EWHC 452, Ch.D 11.31, 11.71, 11.76
Italy v High Authority (2/54) [1954–56] E.C.R. 37, ECJ 20.33, 20.37

J, Ex p. *See* R. v Secretary of State for Education and Science Ex p. J

JC (Care Proceedings: Procedure), Re [1995] 2 F.L.R. 77; [1995] Fam. Law 543, Fam Div 4.04
J-Corp Pty Ltd v Australian Builders' Labourers Federated Union of Workers (1992) 110 A.L.R. 520, Fed. Ct. Aus. 5.06, 11.12, 11.31
JD v East Berkshire Community Health NHS Trust; sub nom. MAK v Dewsbury Healthcare NHS Trust; D v East Berkshire Community NHS Trust; K v Dewsbury Healthcare NHS Trust; RK v Oldham NHS Trust [2005] UKHL 23; [2005] 2 A.C. 373, HL; affirming [2003] EWCA Civ 1151; [2004] Q.B. 558; [2004] 2 W.L.R. 58; [2003] 4 All E.R. 796; [2003] 2 F.L.R. 1166; [2003] 3 F.C.R. 1; [2003] H.R.L.R. 35; [2003] U.K.H.R.R. 1200; (2004) 7 C.C.L. Rep. 63; [2003] Lloyd's Rep. Med. 552; (2004) 76 B.M.L.R. 61; [2003] Fam. Law 816; (2003) 100(36) L.S.G. 37, CA (Civ Div) 21.02
JJ Gallagher Ltd v Secretary of State for Local Government Transport and the Regions [2002] EWHC 1195 (Admin) 4.06
JMA Accounting Pty Ltd v Commissioner of Taxation (2004) 211 A.L.R. 380, Fed. Ct. Aus. 11.08, 20.80
JN Taylor Finance Pty Ltd, Re; sub nom. England v Purves [1999] B.C.C. 197; [1999] 2 B.C.L.C. 256; [1998] B.P.I.R. 347, Ch.D 3.44
JP Morgan Chase Bank v Springwell Navigation Corp [2006] EWHC 2755, Q.B.D. (Comm.) 18.08, 18.11
JSC BTA Bank v Ablyazov [2009] EWCA Civ 1124; [2010] 1 W.L.R. 976; [2010] C.P. Rep. 8; [2010] 1 Cr. App. R. 9; [2010] Lloyd's Rep. F.C. 105 .... 11.113
JSC BTA Bank v Ablyazov [2009] EWCA Civ 1125; [2010] 1 All E.R. (Comm) 1029 .... 2.15
JSC BTA Bank v Ablyazov [2010] EWHC 2352 (Comm) 2.15
J (A Child) (Care Proceedings: Disclosure), Re; sub nom. A MBC v JJ [2003] EWHC 976; [2003] 2 F.L.R. 522; [2003] Fam. Law 634; (2003) 100(31) L.S.G. 31, Fam Div 11.99
J (A Child) v Smith (Deceased) [2001] EWCA Civ 1264; [2001] C.P.L.R. 489, CA (Civ Div) 18.05
J (A Minor) (Child Abuse: Expert Evidence), Re [1991] F.C.R. 193, Fam Div 18.02
J Barber & Sons v Lloyd's Underwriters; J Barber & Sons v Toplis Harding Inc [1987] Q.B. 103; [1986] 3 W.L.R. 515; [1986] 2 All E.R. 845; [1987] E.C.C. 154; (1986) 83 L.S.G. 3253; (1986) 136 N.L.J. 658; (1986) 130 S.J. 730, QBD 10.62
J Boag & Son Brewing Ltd v Cascade Brewery Co Pty Ltd (1997) 7 Tas.R.119 .... 10.23
J Corp Pty Ltd v Australian Builders Labourers Federation Union of Workers (1992) 110 A.L.R. 510, Fed. Ct. Aus. 11.28
J(P) v Canada (Att.-Gen.) (2002) 198 D.L.R. (4th) 733, Sup Ct (BC) 11.103
Jackson v Marley Davenport Ltd [2004] EWCA Civ 1225; [2004] 1 W.L.R. 2926; [2005] C.P. Rep. 8; [2005] B.L.R. 13; [2005] P.I.Q.R. P10; [2005] 1 E.G.L.R. 103; (2004) 101(38) L.S.G. 29; (2004) 148 S.J.L.B. 1121, CA (Civ Div) 9.06, 18.16, 11.48
Jacobs v GW Ry Co [1884] W.N. 33 .... 16.40
Jacobson v Dafna Nominees Pty Ltd [1999] V.S.C. 529, Sup Ct (Victoria) 4.22
Jacubowski v Germany (1994) 19 E.H.R.R. 64 .... 21.14
Jade Engineering (Coventry) Ltd v Antiference Window Systems Ltd [1996] F.S.R. 461; (1996) 19(9) I.P.D. 19085, Ch.D 3.06, 3.08, 3.14, 3.16
Jaffray v Society of Lloyd's; sub nom. Society of Lloyd's v Jaffray [2002] EWCA Civ 1101; (2002) 146 S.J.L.B. 214, CA (Civ Div) 17.27

Jameel v Wall Street Journal Europe Sprl [2006] UKHL 44, HL 11.137
James McHale Automobiles Ltd, Re [1997] B.C.C. 202; [1997] 1 B.C.L.C. 273, Ch.D 3.40
James Nelson & Sons Ltd v Nelson Line (Liverpool) Ltd (No.1) [1906] 2 K.B. 217, CA 4.21, 13.07
James v Baily Gibson & Co [2002] EWCA Civ 1690; [2003] C.P. Rep. 24; (2002) 99(46) L.S.G. 33, CA (Civ Div) 19.22
James v Carr (1890) 7 T.L.R. 4 .... 16.62
Jameson v Smith. *See* J (A Child) v Smith (Deceased)
Janson v Solarte (1836) 2 Y. & Co 127 .... 8.25
Jawett, Re [1929] 1 Ch. 108, Ch.D 11.113
Jay (Baron) v Wilder Coe (A Firm) [2003] EWHC 1786, QBD ... 3.31, 3.34, 5.30
Jeffrey S Levitt Ltd, Re [1992] Ch. 457; [1992] 2 W.L.R. 975; [1992] 2 All E.R. 509; [1992] B.C.C. 137; [1992] B.C.L.C. 250, Ch.D 3.44, 11.113
Jenkins v Grocott, unreported, July 30, 1999 .... 17.21
Jenkyns v Busby (1866) L.R. 2 Eq. 547 .... 11.15, 11.59
Jennings v Jennings [2009] SC (Bda) 62 Civ 2.61, 10.57
Jespers v Belgium (1981) 27 D.R. 61 .... 21.06
Jessop (Alexander Smethhurst) v Rae, 1990 J.C. 292; 1991 S.L.T. 267; 1990 S.C.C.R. 228, HCJ 10.39
Jilani v Wilhelm [2005] FCAFC 269, (2006) 227 A.L.R. 93, Fed. Ct. Aus. 4.07
Jobson v Johnson,unreported, December 12, 1986, CA 12.15
Jockey Club v Buffham [2002] EWHC 1866; [2003] Q.B. 462; [2003] 2 W.L.R. 178; [2003] C.P. Rep. 22; [2003] E.M.L.R. 5; (2002) 99(40) L.S.G. 32, QBD 21.14
Johansen v Norway (1985) 44 D.R. 155 .... 21.17
John Cochrane & Sons v Shipton, *The Times*, October 5, 1966 .... 11.111
John Guest (Southern)'s Patent [1987] R.P.C. 259, Ch.D (Patents Ct) 5.35
John Tanner Holdings v Mortgage Management [2001] F.C.A. 194, Fed. Ct. Aus. 12.06
John v Express Newspapers [2000] 1 W.L.R. 1931; [2000] 3 All E.R. 257; [2000] E.M.L.R. 606; (2000) 97(21) L.S.G. 38; (2000) 150 N.L.J. 615; (2000) 144 S.J.L.B. 217, CA (Civ Div) 3.21
John Walker & Sons Ltd v Henry Ost & Co Ltd [1970] 1 W.L.R. 917; [1970] 2 All E.R. 106; [1970] F.S.R. 63; [1970] R.P.C. 489; 114 S.J. 417, Ch.D 13.25
Johnson Matthey Bankers Ltd v Arthur Young Ltd, *Independent*, May 6, 1988 .... 11.98
Johnson v Blackpool General Commissioners [1997] S.T.C. 1202; 70 T.C. 1; [1997] B.T.C. 501; (1997) 94(34) L.S.G. 28, CA (Civ Div) 20.74
Johnson v Church of Scientology [2004] 2 I.L.R.M. 110, Sup Ct (Irl) 5.43, 5.46
Johnson v Medical Defence Union Ltd [2005] F.S.R. 657, Ch.D 8.24, 11.152
Johnson v Valks (Permission to Appeal) [2000] 1 W.L.R. 1502; [2000] 1 All E.R. 450; [2000] C.P. Rep. 36; (1999) 96(46) L.S.G. 40; (2000) 144 S.J.L.B. 10, CA (Civ Div) 13.06, 13.09
Johnston and Johnston Restaurants, Re (1980) 93 A.P.R. 341, CA (Prince Edward Island) 3.03
Johnston v Ireland (A/112); sub nom. Johnston v Ireland (9697/82) (1987) 9 E.H.R.R. 203, ECHR 21.08, 21.18
Johnston v Jackson (1860) 6 V.L.R. 1 .... 12.40
Johnstone v National Coal Board, 1968 S.C. 128; 1968 S.L.T. 233, IH (1 Div) 11.143
Joint & Several Liquidtors of Kong Wah Holdings v Grande Holdings Ltd (2006) 9 HKCFAR 766 .... 3.41

Joint & Several Liquidtors of Kong Wah Holdings v HSBC [2007] HKCFI 1056 .... **6.15**
Jokai Tea Holdings, Re [1992] 1 W.L.R. 1196; [1993] 1 All E.R. 630, CA (Civ Div) 13.07, 13.10, 13.24
Jonal Properties Pty Ltd v Ms McLeod Holdings Ltd [1994] S.A.S.C. 4380, Sup Ct (S Aus) 10.29
Jones v Andrews (1888) 58 L.T. 601, CA 6.17, 9.37
Jones v GD Searle & Co [1979] 1 W.L.R. 101; [1978] 3 All E.R. 654; 122 S.J. 435, CA (Civ Div) 11.78
Jones v Great Central Railway Co [1910] A.C. 4, HL ... 11.05, 11.40, 11.44, 11.49, 11.55
Jones v Jones (1889) L.R. 22 Q.B.D. 425, QBD 8.06, 11.09
Jones v Kaney [2010] EWHC 61 (QB); [2010] 2 All E.R. 649; [2010] P.N.L.R. 18 .... **17.30, 18.15**
Jones v Money Expert Ltd UKEAT/0231/08/DM, EAT 13.32, 20.31
Jones v Monte Video Gas Co (1879–80) L.R. 5 Q.B.D. 556, CA 1.10, 1.12, 6.41, 6.43, 16.40
Jones v National Coal Board [1957] 2 Q.B. 55; [1957] 2 W.L.R. 760; [1957] 2 All E.R. 155; 101 S.J. 319, CA 10.19
Jones v Richards (1884–85) L.R. 15 Q.B.D. 439, QBD 16.41, 16.61
Jones v Smith [1999] 1 S.C.R. 455, Sup Ct (Can) 11.48, 11.80
Jones v Warwick University; sub nom. Jones v University of Warwick [2003] EWCA Civ 151; [2003] 1 W.L.R. 954; [2003] 3 All E.R. 760; [2003] C.P. Rep. 36; [2003] P.I.Q.R. P23; (2003) 72 B.M.L.R. 119; (2003) 100(11) L.S.G. 32; (2003) 153 N.L.J. 231; (2003) 147 S.J.L.B. 179, CA (Civ Div) 19.25, 21.11
Jordan v Sanders [1934] S.A.S.R. 424 .... 16.41
Jourdain v Palmer (1866) L.R. 1 Exch. 102 .... 16.39
Juman v Doucette 2008 SCC 8 .... **15.42**
Jyske Bank Ltd v Spjeldnaes 1993 J.L.R. 99, R Ct (Jersey) 15.43

K (Infants), Re. *See* Official Solicitor v K
K (Minors) (Disclosure of Privileged Material), Re; sub nom. Kent CC v K [1994] 1 W.L.R. 912; [1994] 3 All E.R. 230; [1994] 1 F.L.R. 377; [1994] 2 F.C.R. 805; [1994] Fam. Law 247, Fam Div 15.43
Kabadains v Panagiotou (1970) 47 F.L.R. 221 .... 16.116
Kadlunga v Electricity Trust of South Australia (1986) 39 S.A.S.R. 410, Sup Ct (S Aus) 6.15
Kain v Farrer (1887) 37 L.T. 469 .... 6.15
Kamasinski v Austria (A/168); sub nom. Kamasinski v Austria (9783/82) (1991) 13 E.H.R.R. 36, ECHR 21.06
Kansal v United Kingdom (App. No.21413/02) (2004) 39 E.H.R.R. 31; [2004] B.P.I.R. 740, ECHR 11.113, 21.07
Kanthak v Germany (1988) 58 D.R. 94 .... 21.09
Kapadia v Lambeth LBC [2000] EWCA Civ 81; [2000] I.R.L.R. 699; (2001) 57 B.M.L.R. 170, CA (Civ Div) 18.21, 19.21
Kapur v JW Francis & Co (No.1), *The Times*, March 4, 1998, CA (Civ Div) ... 2.33, 5.12, 5.21, 8.29
Kaufmann v Credit Lyonnais Bank [1995] C.L.C. 300 ... 11.94, 11.89, 11.93, 11.99

Kay v Lambeth LBC; sub nom. Lambeth LBC v Kay; Leeds City Council v Price; Gorman v Lambeth LBC; Constantine v Lambeth LBC; Barnett v Lambeth LBC; Cole v Lambeth LBC; Price v Leeds City Council; Dymny v Lambeth LBC [2006] UKHL 10; [2006] 2 W.L.R. 570; [2006] 4 All E.R. 128; [2006] 2 F.C.R. 20; [2006] H.R.L.R. 17; 20 B.H.R.C. 33; [2006] H.L.R. 22; [2006] B.L.G.R. 323; [2006] 11 E.G.C.S. 194; (2006) 150 S.J.L.B. 365; [2006] N.P.C. 29, HL 11.105, 21.02
Kaya v Haringey LBC [2001] EWCA Civ 677; [2002] H.L.R. 1; (2001) 98(25) L.S.G. 46, CA (Civ Div) 11.105, 21.02
Kearsley v Philips (No.1); sub nom. Kearsley v Phillips (1882–83) L.R. 10 Q.B.D. 465, CA; affirming (1882–83) L.R. 10 Q.B.D. 36, QBD 1.12, 5.44, 11.144
Keith v CPM Field Marketing Ltd [2001] C.P. Rep. 35, CA (Civ Div) 13.06, 13.07, 13.12, 13.17, 13.21, 13.24
Kelly v Colhoun [1899] 2 I.R. 199 .... 11.112
Kelly v Commissioner of Police of the Metropolis, *The Times*, August 20, 1997, CA (Civ Div) 11.84, 11.100, 11.101
Kelly v Denman, unreported, February 21, 1996, CA (Civ Div) 11.07, 11.09
Kelly v Wyman (1869) 17 W.R. 399 .... 16.71
Kemble v Hope (1894) 10 T.L.R. 371, CA 16.53
Kempton v Special Commissioners of Income Tax [1992] S.T.C. 823; 66 T.C. 249; [1992] S.T.I. 891; (1992) 89(43) L.S.G. 31, Ch.D 20.77
Kennedy v Dodson [1895] 1 Ch. 334, CA 5.31, 16.34, 16.38
Kennedy v Lyell (No.5) [1882] W.N. 137, CA 13.07, 16.109
Kennedy v Wallace (2004) 213 A.L.R. 108, Full Fed. Ct. Aus. 11.14, 11.21
Kenny v Loewen (1999) 64 B.C.L.R. (3d) 346, Sup Ct (BC) 3.03
Kensington International Ltd v Congo [2006] EWHC 1848, Q.B.D. (Comm.) 2.13, 3.11, 17–29
Kensington International Ltd v Congo [2007] EWCA Civ 1128; [2008] 1 W.L.R. 1144; [2008] 1 All E.R. (Comm) 934; [2008] 1 Lloyd's Rep. 161; [2008] C.P. Rep. 6; [2007] 2 C.L.C. 791; (2007) 104(45) L.S.G. 31 .... 2.25, 3.17, 11.113
Kent CC v B (A Child); sub nom. B (A Child) (Disclosure), Re [2004] EWHC 411; [2004] 2 F.L.R. 142; [2004] 3 F.C.R. 1; [2004] Lloyd's Rep. Med. 303; [2004] Fam. Law 493; (2004) 154 N.L.J. 498, Fam Div ... 4.04, 21.12, 21.15
Kent CC v B (A Child); sub nom. B (A Child) (Disclosure), Re [2004] EWHC 411; [2004] 2 F.L.R. 142; [2004] 3 F.C.R. 1; [2004] Lloyd's Rep. Med. 303; [2004] Fam. Law 493; (2004) 154 N.L.J. 498, Fam Div 21.12
Kent v Kehoe (2000) 1 D.L.R. (4th) 50, CA (Nova Scotia) 5.33
Kerojavi v Finland [1996] E.H.R.L.R. 66 .... 21.06
Kershaw v Whelan [1996] 1 W.L.R. 358; [1996] 2 All E.R. 404, QBD 12.04
Kesse v Secretary of State for the Home Department [2001] EWCA Civ 177; [2001] Imm. A.R. 366, CA (Civ Div) 10.19
Kettlewell v Barstow (No.2) (1871–72) L.R. 7 Ch. App. 686, CA in Chancery 6.17
Khan v Armaguard Ltd [1994] 1 W.L.R. 1204; [1994] 3 All E.R. 545; [1994] P.I.Q.R. P286, CA (Civ Div) 8.18, 11.01, 11.08, 11.31, 19.23
Khan v Khan [1982] 1 W.L.R. 513, CA (Civ Div) 11.115
Khan v United Kingdom (2000) 30 E.H.R.R. 1016, ECHR 21.12
Khanna v Lovell White Durrant [1995] 1 W.L.R. 121; [1994] 4 All E.R. 267; (1994) 91(45) L.S.G. 38, Ch.D 10.23
Kilderkin Investments v Player, 1980–83 C.I.L.R. 403 .... 3.03

Kimber v Brookman Solicitors [2004] 2 F.L.R. 221; [2004] Fam. Law 649, Fam Div 11.67
Kimberley Mineral Holdings Ltd v McEwan [1980] 1 N.S.W.L.R. 210, CA (NSW) 15.01
Kimberly Clark Worldwide Inc v Procter & Gamble Ltd (No.1) [2000] F.S.R. 235; [2000] R.P.C. 422; (1999) 96(47) L.S.G. 32; (2000) 144 S.J.L.B. 9, CA (Civ Div) 12.05
King of the Two Sicilies v Willcox (1851) 1 Sim. (N.S.) 301 .... 11.104
King v AG Australia Holdings Ltd (2002) 191 A.L.R. 697, Fed. Ct. Aus. 12.19
King v Commercial Bank [1920] V.L.R. 218 .... 16.45
King v Commercial Bank of Australia [1920] V.L.R. 218 .... 16.41
King v Davenport (1878–79) L.R. 4 Q.B.D. 402, QBD 13.23
King v Telegraph Group Ltd [2004] EWCA Civ 613; [2005] 1 W.L.R. 2282; [2004] C.P. Rep. 35; [2004] 3 Costs L.R. 449; [2004] E.M.L.R. 23; (2004) 101(25) L.S.G. 27; (2004) 154 N.L.J. 823; (2004) 148 S.J.L.B. 664, CA (Civ Div) 16.51
Kingsley v Inland Revenue Commissioners [1987] 2 E.G.L.R. 217; (1987) 283 E.G. 1518; [1987] R.V.R. 251, Lands Tr 20.50
Kingston's (Duchess of) Case (1776) 20 St.Tr. 355 .... 11.153
Kirella Pty Ltd v Hooper (1999) 161 A.L.R. 447 .... 3.03
Kirin-Amgen Inc v Boehringer Mannheim GmbH, unreported, March 3, 1995 .... 11.159
Kirkman v Euro Exide Corp (CMP Batteries Ltd) [2007] EWCA Civ 66; [2007] C.P. Rep. 19; (2007) 104(6) L.S.G. 31; (2007) 151 S.J.L.B. 164 .... 18.02
Kissam v Link [1896] 1 Q.B. 574, CA 10.49
Kistler v Tettmar [1905] 1 K.B. 39, CA 2.49
Kitcat v Sharp (1882) 48 L.T. 64 .... 11.129
Kitchenham v AXA Insurance (2009) 306 D.L.R. (4th) 68, CA (Ont) 15.05, 15.18
Kizon v Palmer (No.2) (1998) 82 F.C.R.310, Fed. Ct. Aus. 4.07
Klabin v Technocom Ltd, September 20, 2002, CA (Guernsey) 1.17, 9.09
Klass v Germany (A/28) (1979–80) 2 E.H.R.R. 214, ECHR 21.08, 21.10
Kneale v Barclays Bank Plc (t/a Barclaycard) [2010] EWHC 1900 (Comm) 3.31, 3.34, 3.39
Knight v Department of Social Security [2002] I.R.L.R. 249, EAT 20.30
Knight v Truss-Michaelis, unreported, April 14, 1993, District Ct (Queensland) 20.56
Knightstone Housing Association v Crawford, unreported, October 27, 1999, EAT 11.130
Koca v Customs and Excise Commissioners [1996] S.T.C. 58, QBD 20.88
Koch Shipping Inc v Richards Butler [2002] EWCA Civ 1280; [2002] 2 All E.R. (Comm.) 957; [2003] C.P. Rep. 10; [2002] Lloyd's Rep. P.N. 604; [2003] P.N.L.R. 11; (2002) 99(37) L.S.G. 39; (2002) 146 S.J.L.B. 197, CA (Civ Div) 15.46
Koger Inc v O'Donnell [2009] IEHC 385 .... 8.25, 11.159
Koh Tech Hee v Leow Swee Lim [1992] 1 S.L.R. 905, H Ct (Singapore) ... 13.32, 14.03, 14.07
Komarek v Ramco Energy plc, unreported, November 21, 2002, QBD 11.09
Konigsberg (A Bankrupt), Re [1989] 1 W.L.R. 1257; [1989] 3 All E.R. 289; [1990] Fam. Law 94; (1989) 86(40) L.S.G. 44; (1989) 139 N.L.J. 1302; (1989) 133 S.J. 1337, Ch.D 11.06, 11.09, 11.74, 11.77, 12.02, 12.36

KOO Golden East Mongolia v Bank of Nova Scotia [2007] EWCA Civ 1443; [2008] Q.B. 717; [2008] 2 W.L.R. 1160; [2008] Bus. L.R. 744; [2008] 2 All E.R. (Comm) 314 .... 4.44, 11.141
Kooltrade Ltd v XTS Ltd [2001] F.S.R. 158, Ch.D 11.129
Koowarta v Bjelke-Petersen (1989) 92 F.L.R. 104, Sup Ct (Qld) 11.98
Kopp v Switzerland (1999) 27 E.H.R.R. 91; 4 B.H.R.C. 277; [1998] H.R.C.D. 356, ECHR 21.10
Korean Airlines v ACCC (No.3) [2008] FCA 701; (2008) 247 A.L.R. 781, Fed. Ct of Australia 11.123
Kostovski v Netherlands (A/166) (1990) 12 E.H.R.R. 434, ECHR 21.07
Kranidiotes v Paschali [2001] EWCA Civ 357; [2001] C.P. Rep. 81; [2003] B.C.C. 353, CA (Civ Div) 18.09
Krcmar v Czech Republic (App. No.35376/97) (2001) 31 E.H.R.R. 41, ECHR 21.06
Kronprinzessin Victoria, The [1919] A.C. 261, PC (UK) 20.65
Kroon v Netherlands (A/297–C) [1995] 2 F.C.R. 28; (1995) 19 E.H.R.R. 263, ECHR 21.08
Kruslin v France (A176–B); sub nom. Kruslin v France (App. No.11801/85) (1990) 12 E.H.R.R. 547, ECHR 21.10
Kuah Kok Kim v Ernst & Young [1996] 2 S.L.R. 364, HC (Singapore) ... 1.19, 3.31, 4.60
Kumar v United Air Travel (Services) Ltd, unreported, January 14, 1993, CA 6.13, 13.11, 13.24
Kuopila v Finland (App. No.27752/95) (2001) 33 E.H.R.R. 25, ECHR 21.06
Kupe Group Ltd v Seamar Holdings Ltd [1993] 3 N.Z.L.R. 209 ..... 11.02, 11.28
Kurtz v Spence (1887) 58 L.T. 438 .... 11.129
Kuwait Airways Corp v Iraqi Airways Co (Disclosure: Fraud Exception) [2005] EWCA Civ 286; [2005] 1 W.L.R. 2734; [2005] C.P. Rep. 32; (2005) 102(21) L.S.G. 33; (2005) 155 N.L.J. 468, CA (Civ Div) ... 11.67, 11.69
Kuwait Airways Corp v Iraq Airways Co [2010] EWCA Civ 741 ...... 2.48, 2.51, 17.14
Kyshe v Holt [1888] W.N. 128 .... 11.53, 11.55

L v L and H [2007] EWHC 140 (QB); [2007] 2 F.L.R. 171; [2007] Fam. Law 692 .... 2.22
L v United Kingdom (App. No.34222/96) (1999) 21.12
LTE Scientific Ltd v Thomas [2005] EWHC 7, Q.B.D. 2.20, 13.27, 13.29
L (A Child) (Care: Assessment: Fair Trial), Re; sub nom. C (A Child) (Care Proceedings: Disclosure of Local Authority's Decision Making Process), Re [2002] EWHC 1379; [2002] 2 F.L.R. 730; [2002] 2 F.C.R. 673; [2002] Fam. Law 802, Fam Div 4.04
L (A Child) v United Kingdom (Disclosure of Expert Evidence) [2000] 2 F.L.R. 322; [2000] 2 F.C.R. 145; [2000] Fam. Law 708, ECHR 21.07
L (A Minor) (Police Investigation: Privilege), Re; sub nom. L (Minors) (Disclosure of Medical Reports), Re; L (Minors) (Police Investigation: Privilege), Re [1997] A.C. 16; [1996] 2 W.L.R. 395; [1996] 2 All E.R. 78; [1996] 1 F.L.R. 731; [1996] 2 F.C.R. 145; (1996) 32 B.M.L.R. 160; [1996] Fam. Law 400; (1996) 160 L.G. Rev. 417; (1996) 93(15) L.S.G. 30; (1996) 146 N.L.J. 441; (1996) 140 S.J.L.B. 116, HL; affirming [1995] 1 F.L.R. 999; [1996] 1 F.C.R. 419; [1995] Fam. Law 474; (1995) 159 J.P.N. 624, CA (Civ Div) 11.05, 11.08, 11.36, 11.37, 11.48, 11.78, 11.107, 11.117, 12.08, 12.10, 12.37, 15.21, 15.42, 21.06

L Brown & Sons Ltd v Crosby Homes (North West) Ltd [2008] EWHC 817 (TCC); [2008] B.L.R. 366 .... 13.36, 20.09
La Societe les Affreteurs Reunis v Shipping Controller; sub nom. Arbitration between La Societe les Affreteurs Reunis and Shipping Controller, Re [1921] 3 K.B. 1; (1921) 6 Ll. L. Rep. 408, KBD 4.39
Lac d'Amiante du Québec Ltée v 2858–0702 Québec Inc [2001] 2 S.C.R. 743, (2000) 204 D.L.R. (4th) 331 .... 15.01, 17.01
Lac Minerals Ltd v New Cinch Uranium Ltd (1985) 17 D.L.R. (4th) 745, H Ct (Ont) 15.01, 15.39
Lac Minerals Ltd v Vancouver Stock Exchange (1985) 17 D.L.R. (4th) 687, Sup Ct (BC) 15.01, 15.39
Lacey v Harrison [1993] P.I.Q.R. P10, Q.B.D. 19.21
Ladd v Marshall [1954] 1 W.L.R. 1489; [1954] 3 All E.R. 745; (1954) 98 S.J. 870, CA 2.53
Lagenes Ltd v It's At (UK) Ltd [1991] F.S.R. 492, Ch.D 3.16, 11.109
Lai v Customs and Excise Commissioners [2002] V. & D.R. 570; [2003] S.T.I. 221, V&DTr 20.89
Lai Pat Fong v The Chinese Chamber of Commerce, 1973 M.C. 1 .... 1.19
Lake Cumberline Pty Ltd v Effem Foods Pty Ltd (1994) 126 A.L.R. 58 .... 11.09
Lamb v Munster (1882–83) L.R. 10 Q.B.D. 110; (1882) 5 L.J. Q.B. 46, Q.B.D. 11.110, 16.61, 16.85
Lambert v Home [1914] 3 K.B. 86, CA 11.28, 11.33, 11.34
Lamey v Rice (2000) 190 D.L.R. (4th) 486, CA (New Brunswick) 11.05, 11.14, 11.44, 11.45
Lana International Ltd v Menasco Aerospace (2000) 195 D.L.R. (4th) 497, Div Ct (Ontario) 17.01
Lancaster Factoring Company Ltd v Mangone [1998] I.L. Pr. 200, Ct of Appeals (US) 2.62
Land Corp of Canada v Puleston [1884] W.N. 1 .... 11.34
Land Rover North America Inc v Windh [2005] EWHC 432, Q.B.D. 10.59
Landauer Ltd v Comins & Co, *The Times*, August 7, 1991, CA (Civ Div) 13.13, 13.35, 14.04
Landis & Gyr Ltd v Scaleo Chip ET [2007] EWHC 1880 (QB); [2007] I.L.Pr. 53 .... 3.34
Lane v Willis; sub nom. Lane v Beach (Executor of Estate of George William Willis) [1972] 1 W.L.R. 326; [1972] 1 All E.R. 430; (1971) 116 S.J. 102, CA (Civ Div) 19.22
Lang v Australian Coastal Shipping Corp [1974] 2 N.S.W.L.R 70 .... 16.50
Lang v Crowe (2000) 131 O.A.C. 26 .... 15.56
Langen v Tate (1883) L.R. 24 Ch. D. 522, CA 2.61, 17–12
Langford v Cleary [1993] 2 Tas. R. 1 .... 11.144
Langtree Group plc v Richardson. *See* Richardson v Langtree Group Plc
Lanyon Pty Ltd v Commonwealth of Australia (1973) 129 C.L.R.. 650, H Ct (Aus) 11.98
Lanzon v State Transport Authority (1985) 38 S.A.S.R.321 .... 5.41
Larke v Nugus; sub nom. Moss, In the Estate of [2000] W.T.L.R. 1033; (1979) 123 S.J. 337, CA (Civ Div) 2.07
Lask v Gloucester HA [1991] 2 Med. L.R. 379, CA (Civ Div) 11.44, 11.46
Lavallee, Rackel & Heintz v Att.-Gen. of Canada (2002) 216 D.L.R. (4th) 257, S.C.C 11.08
Law Debenture Trust Corp (Channel Islands) Ltd v Lexington Insurance Co (Application for Disclosure) [2003] EWHC 2297; (2003) 153 N.L.J. 1551, Q.B.D. (Comm.) 3.45, 15.30
Law Society of Ireland v Rawlinson & Hunter [1997] 3 I.R. 592, HC (Irl) 2.32

Law Society of Saskatchewan v Merchant (2009) 300 D.L.R. (4th) 462, CA (Sask) 11.06
Lawrence v Campbell (1859) 4 Drew. 485 .... 11.21
Lawson v Odhams Press [1949] 1 K.B. 129; [1948] 2 All E.R. 717; 64 T.L.R. 532; 92 S.J. 602, CA 16.63
Lawson v Vacuum Brake Co (1884) L.R. 27 Ch. D. 137, CA 2.61, 17.12
Layland v Fairview New Homes Plc [2002] EWHC 1350; [2003] C.P.L.R. 19; [2003] B.L.R. 20; [2002] N.P.C. 93, Ch.D 18.10
Lazenby v Zammit [1987] Tas. R. 54, Sup Ct (Full Ct) (Tasmania) 6.15
Le Compte v Belgium (A/43); Van Leuven v Belgium (A/43); De Meyere v Belgium (A/43) [1982] E.C.C. 240; (1982) 4 E.H.R.R. 1, ECHR 21.13
Leach v Chilton Transport (Bow) Ltd unreported, April 29, 1987, CA 11.60
Leahy v Dr AB (1992) 113 N.S.R. (2d) 417 .... 3.03
Leander v Sweden (A/116); sub nom. Leander v Sweden (App. No.9248/81) (1987) 9 E.H.R.R. 433, ECHR 21.08, 21.11, 21.14
Learoyd v Halifax Joint Stock Banking Co [1893] 1 Ch. 686, Ch.D 11.48
Ledwidge v Mayne (1878) I.R. 11 Eq. 463 .... 6.07
Lee v Angas (1866) L.R. 2 Eq. 59 .... 10.10, 10.23, 10.32
Lee v South West Thames RHA [1985] 1 W.L.R. 845; [1985] 2 All E.R. 385; (1985) 82 L.S.G. 2015; (1985) 135 N.L.J. 438; (1985) 128 S.J. 333, CA (Civ Div) 3.38, 11.31, 11.60, 12.02
Lee Lighting v Central Properties, unreported, September 27, 1994 .... 11.60, 11.76, 12.18
Leeke v Portsmouth Corp (1912) 106 L.T. 627 .... 16.75
LeFroy v Burnside (No.1) (1879) 4 L.R. Ir. 340 .... 16.62
Legal & General Assurance Society Ltd v Taulke-Johnson [2002] EWHC 120, Q.B.D. 6.51
Leif Hoegh & Co A/S v Petrolsea Inc; The World Era (No.2) [1993] 1 Lloyd's Rep. 363, Q.B.D. (Comm.) 11.59, 11.61, 12.08, 20.57
Leigh (Deceased) (No.3), Re; sub nom. Leigh's Estate, Re; Rowcliffe v Leigh (No.3) (1877) L.R. 6 Ch. D. 256, CA 2.33
Leitch v Abbott (1886) L.R. 31 Ch. D. 374; (1886) 34 W.R. 560, CA 2.33
Leon v Casey [1932] 2 K.B. 576; (1932) 43 Ll. L. Rep. 69, CA 2.35
Leslie v Cave [1886] W.N. 162 .... 9.13
Letpak Ltd v Harris [1997] P.N.L.R. 239, CA (Civ Div) 17.21
Letter Rogatory from Tokyo District, Re, 539 F.2d. 1216 (9th Cir., 1976) 2.63
Letters Rogatory, Re, 385 F.2d. 1017 (2d. Cir., 1967) 2.62
Lev v Lev (No.2) (1990) 64 Man.R. (2d.) 306, QB Ct (Man) 12.06
Lever v Land Securities Co Ltd (1894) 70 L.T. 323, CA 2.33
Levi Strauss & Co v Barclays Trading Corp [1993] F.S.R. 179, Ch.D ... 3.25, 11.150
Lewis v *Daily Telegraph*. *See* Rubber Improvement Ltd v Daily Telegraph Ltd
Lewis v Earl of Londesborough [1893] 2 Q.B. 191, Q.B.D. 9.35, 19.06
Lewis v Eliades (No.1) [2002] EWHC 335; [2002] C.P. Rep., Q.B.D. 2.19
Lewis v Kingsbury (1888) 4 T.L.R. 629 .... 2.61, 17.12
Lewis v Powell [1897] 1 Ch. 678, Ch.D 11.149
Lewis v Smith (1849) 1 Mac. & G. 417 .... 10.15
Lexi Holdings Plc v Luqman [2007] EWCA Civ 1501 .... 13.07
Lexi Holdings Plc (In Administration) v Luqman [2007] EWHC 1508 (Ch) 13.27
Lexi Holdings (In Administration) v Pannone & Partners [2010] EWHC 1416 (Ch) 16.51
Libby Mills v Commissioner of Police of the Metropolis [1995] P.I.Q.R. P324, CA (Civ Div) 19.23

Liberia v Roye; sub nom. Liberia v Imperial Bank (1875–76) L.R. 1 App. Cas. 139, HL 13.07, 13.20
Lichter v Rubin [2008] EWHC 450 (Ch) 2.13, 16.68
Lifecare International, Re (1989) 5 B.C.C. 755; [1990] B.C.L.C., Ch.D (Companies Ct) 4.02
Lifetime Investments Ltd v Commercial (Worldwide) Financial Services Pty Ltd [2005] F.C.A. 226, Fed. Ct. Aus. 3.03
Lillicrap v Nalder & Son [1993] 1 W.L.R. 94; [1993] 1 All E.R. 724, CA (Civ Div) 12.04
Lilly ICOS Ltd v Pfizer Ltd (Interim Application) (2000) 23(11) I.P.D. 23089, Ch.D 18.12
Lilly ICOS Ltd v Pfizer Ltd (No.2); sub nom. Lilly ICOS LLC v Pfizer Ltd (No.2); Lily ICOS Ltd v Pfizer Ltd (No.2) [2002] EWCA Civ 2; [2002] 1 W.L.R. 2253; [2002] 1 All E.R. 842; [2002] F.S.R. 54; (2002) 25(3) I.P.D. 25016; (2002) 99(10) L.S.G. 33; (2002) 146 S.J.L.B. 29, CA (Civ Div) 15.03, 15.29, 15.30
Lindsay v Gladstone (1869) L.R. 9 Eq. 132 .... 9.13, 9.30
Linfa Pty Ltd v Citibank Ltd [1995] 1 V.R. 643 .... 5.48
Lingens v Austria (No.2) (A/103); sub nom. Lingens v Austria (App. No.9815/82) (1986) 8 E.H.R.R. 407, ECHR 21.08
Linsen International Ltd v Humpuss Sea Transport PTE Ltd [2010] EWHC 303 (Comm) 11.130
Litchfield v Jones [1883] W.N. 164 .... 13.27
Little v Bennet (1900) 25 V.L.R. 645 .... 16.103
Liverpool Roman Catholic Archdiocesan Trustees Inc v Goldberg (No.3); sub nom. Liverpool Roman Catholic Archdiocesan Trust v Goldberg (No.3); Liverpool Roman Catholic Archdiocese Trustees Inc v Goldberg (No.3) [2001] 1 W.L.R. 2337; [2001] 4 All E.R. 950; [2001] B.L.R. 479; [2002] T.C.L.R. 4; (2001) 98(32) L.S.G. 37; (2001) 151 N.L.J. 1093, Ch.D 18.12
Llewellyn v Nine Network Australia Pty Ltd [2006] FCA 836; (2007) 233 A.L.R. 88, Fed. Ct of Australia 3.45
Lloyd's v Kitsons Environmental Services Ltd (1994) 64 B.L.R. 102 .. 11.125, 12.04
Lloyds Bank Ltd v Marcan [1973] 1 W.L.R. 1387; [1973] 3 All E.R. 754; 117 S.J. 761, CA (Civ Div); affirming [1973] 1 W.L.R. 339; [1973] 2 All E.R. 359; (1973) 25 P. & C.R. 65; 117 S.J. 187, Ch.D 17.07
Lobo Machado v Portugal (1997) 23 E.H.R.R. 79, ECHR 21.06
Lock International Plc v Beswick [1989] 1 W.L.R. 1268; [1989] 3 All E.R. 373; [1989] I.R.L.R. 481; (1989) 86(39) L.S.G. 36; (1989) 139 N.L.J. 644; (1989) S.J. 1297, Ch.D 2.22
Lockett v Lockett (1868–69) L.R. 4 Ch. App. 336, CA in Chancery 16.100
Logicrose Ltd v Southend United Football Club Ltd (No.1) [1988] E.G.C.S. 114; (1988) 132 S.J. 1591, Ch.D 13.05, 13.07, 13.13, 13.27, 14.04
Loizidou v Turkey (App. No.15318/89) (1997) 23 E.H.R.R. 513, ECHR 21.09
Lombard Shipping and Forwarding, Re [1992] B.C.C. 700; [1993] B.C.L.C., Ch.D 5.51, 5.53
Lombe v Pollak [2004] F.C.A. 593, Fed. Ct. Aus. 15.07
Londish v Gulf Pacify Pty Ltd (1993) 117 A.L.R. 361 .... 13.36
London & Counties Securities v Caplan, unreported, May 26, 1978 .... 2.13
London & Yorkshire Bank Ltd v Cooper (1884–85) L.R. 15 Q.B.D. 473, CA 4.38, 16.29
London and Leeds Estates Ltd v Paribas Ltd (No.2) [1995] 1 E.G.L.R. 102; [1995] 02 E.G. 134, Q.B.D. 10.11, 10.12, 10.15, 10.28, 10.29, 15.54
London and Westminster Bank v Button (1907) 51 S.J. 466 .... 10.38

London United Investments, Re [1992] Ch. 578; [1992] 2 W.L.R. 850; [1992] 2 All E.R. 842; [1992] B.C.C. 202; [1992] B.C.L.C. 285; (1992) 89(8) L.S.G. 27; (1992) 142 N.L.J. 87; (1992) 136 S.J.L.B., 1992, CA (Civ Div) 11.113
London, Corp of v Levy (1803) 8 Ves. Jun. 398 .... 3.14
Londonderry's Settlement, Re; sub nom. Peat v Walsh [1965] Ch. 918; [1965] 2 W.L.R. 229; [1964] 3 All E.R. 855; 108 S.J. 896, CA 4.22, 5.52
Long v Attorney-General [2001] 2 N.Z.L.R. 529, H Ct (NZ) 11.102, 11.103
Long v Farrer & Co [2004] EWHC 1774; [2004] B.P.I.R. 1218, Ch.D 11.74
Lonrho Ltd v Shell Petroleum Co Ltd (No.1) [1980] 1 W.L.R. 627; 124 S.J. 412, HL 5.41, 5.46, 5.47, **5,48**, 11.99
Lonrho Ltd v Shell Petroleum Co Ltd, unreported, January 25, 1980 .... 6.13
Lonrho Plc v Al-Fayed (No.2) [1992] 1 W.L.R. 1; [1991] 4 All E.R. 961, Ch.D 3.21, 11.143
Lonrho Plc v Al-Fayed (No.3), *The Times*, June 24, 1993 *Independent*, June 23, 1993, CA (Civ Div) 6.41, 6.44, 13.11, 13.13
Lonrho Plc v Al-Fayed (No.4) [1994] Q.B. 775; [1994] 2 W.L.R. 209; [1994] 1 All E.R. 870; [1994] S.T.C. 153; 66 T.C. 220, CA (Civ Div) 11.89, 11.98
Looker v Murphy (1889) 15 V.L.R. 348 .... 16.45
Loose v Williamson [1978] 1 W.L.R. 639; [1978] 3 All E.R. 89; 122 S.J. 212, Ch.D 3.14, 3.23, 16.69
L'Oréal SA v eBay International AG [2008] EWHC B13 (Ch) 3.45
Lorenzo Halcoussi, The. *See* Sunderland Steamship P and I Association v Gatoil International Inc; The Lorenzo Halcoussi
Lovell v Lovell [1970] 1 W.L.R. 1451; [1970] 3 All E.R. 721; (1970) 114 S.J. 808, CA (Civ Div) 16.41, 16.52
Lowden v Blakey (1889) L.R. 23 Q.B.D. 332, Q.B.D. 11.18
Lowdock v Edwards, The (1941) 70 Ll. Rep. 133 .... 16.54
Lubrizol Corp v Esso Petroleum Co Ltd (No.2) [1993] F.S.R. 53, Ch.D (Patents Ct) 11.163, 15.24, 15.31
Lubrizol Corp v Esso Petroleum Co Ltd (No.4) [1992] 1 W.L.R. 957; [1993] F.S.R. 64; (1992) 89(28) L.S.G. 33; (1992) 136 S.J.L.B. 165, Ch.D (Patents Ct) 11.31, 11.33, 11.146
Lucas v Barking, Havering and Redbridge Hospitals NHS Trust [2003] EWCA Civ 1102; [2004] 1 W.L.R. 220; [2003] 4 All E.R. 720; [2003] C.P. Rep. 65; [2003] Lloyd's Rep. Med. 577; (2004) 77 B.M.L.R. 13; (2003) 100(37) L.S.G. 34; (2003) 153 N.L.J. 1204, CA (Civ Div) 9.06, **12.19**, 18.16
Lucas-Box v News Group Newspapers Ltd; Lucas-Box v Associated Newspapers Group Plc [1986] 1 W.L.R. 147; [1986] 1 All E.R. 177; (1986) 83 L.S.G. 441; (1986) 130 S.J. 111, CA (Civ Div) 16.57
Ludi v Switzerland (A/238) (1993) 15 E.H.R.R., 1992, ECHR 21.07
Lukies v Ripley (No.2) (1994) 35 N.S.W.L.R. 283 .... 20.56
Lyell v Kennedy (No.1) (1882–83) L.R. 8 App. Cas. 217, HL ... 1.12, 3.05, 5.38, 8.21, 16.35, 16.43, 16.50, 16.75, 16.83
Lyell v Kennedy (No.2); sub nom. Kennedy v Lyell (No.2) (1883–84) L.R. 9 App. Cas. 81, HL; affirming (1883) L.R. 23 Ch. D. 387, CA .. 11.09, 11.38, 11.31, 11.53, 11.58, 16.79, 16.80, 16.94, 16.95, 16.107
Lyell v Kennedy (No.3) (1884) L.R. 27 Ch. D. 1, CA 5.05, 6.41, 6.44, 11.25, 11.28, 11.33, 11.53, 12.34, 16.91, 16.94, 16.107
Lyell v Kennedy (No.4) (1883) 33 W.R. 44 .... 16.41, 16.91
Lyle-Samuel v Odhams Ltd [1920] 1 K.B. 135, CA 16.63

Lynall v Inland Revenue Commissioners; sub nom. Lynall (Deceased), Re [1972] A.C. 680; [1971] 3 W.L.R. 759; [1971] 3 All E.R. 914; 47 T.C. 375; [1971] T.R. 309; 115 S.J. 872, HL 5.27, 5.28
Lyndon v Yorkshire Regional Health Authority (1991) 10 B.M.L.R. 49 .... 2.32

M v Commission of the European Communities (155/78) [1980] E.C.R. 1797, ECJ 20.37
M v L [1997] 3 N.Z.L.R. 424 .... 5.30
M v L [1999] 1 N.Z.L.R. 747, CA (NZ) 11.153
M v Plymouth HA [1993] P.I.Q.R. P223; [1993] 4 Med. L.R. 108, Q.B.D. ... 3.38
M v Ryan (1994) 119 D.L.R. (4th) 18, CA (BC) 11.06, 11.156
MCC Proceeds Inc v Bishopsgate Investments Trust plc. *See* Macmillan Inc v Bishopsgate Investment Trust Plc (No.4)
MGN Pension Trustees Ltd v Invesco Asset Management Ltd, unreported, October 1993 .... 5.09
MGN Pension Trustees Ltd v Invesco Asset Management Ltd, unreported, October 14, 1993 .... 11.81, 11.93, 11.94, 11.99
MM v Australian Crime Commission [2007] FCA 2026; (2008) 244 A.L.R. 452, Fed. Ct of Australia 10.28
MMI Research Ltd v Cellxion Ltd [2007] EWHC 2611 (Pat); [2008] F.S.R. 23 .... 5.34
MMO2 Plc v Revenue and Customs Commissioners [2006] S.T.I. 1708, V&DTr (London) 20.89
MMR and MR Vaccine Litigation, Re (No.4) [2002] EWHC 1213; [2002] All E.R. (D) 143 (Jun), Q.B.D. 18.17
M (A Child) (Care Proceedings: Best Evidence), Re [2007] EWCA Civ 589; [2007] 2 F.L.R. 1006; [2007] 2 F.C.R. 797; [2007] Fam. Law 893 ..... 18.14
M (A Child) (Children and Family Reporter: Disclosure), Re; sub nom. M (A Child) (Disclosure: Children and Family Reporter), Re [2002] EWCA Civ 1199; [2003] Fam. 26; [2002] 3 W.L.R. 1669; [2002] 4 All E.R. 401; [2002] 2 F.L.R. 893; [2002] 3 F.C.R. 208; [2003] Fam. Law 96; (2002) 99(39) L.S.G. 37, CA (Civ Div) 4.04
M (A Minor) (Disclosure of Material), Re [1990] 2 F.L.R. 36; [1990] F.C.R. 485; 88 L.G.R. 841; [1990] Fam. Law 259; (1990) 154 J.P.N. 410; (1990) 154 L.G. Rev. 496, CA (Civ Div) 11.37
M (Child: Residence), Re, *The Times*, July 24, 2002, CA (Civ Div) 4.04, 11.99, 18.22
M (Minors), Re [1995] 2 F.L.R. 57 .... 5.06, 10.15, 10.31, 11.101 Re E
M (Minors: Disclosure of Evidence), Re; sub nom. M (Minors: Disclosure of Welfare Report), Re [1994] 1 F.L.R. 760; [1995] 2 F.C.R. 1; [1994] Fam. Law 312, CA (Civ Div) 11.99
M Isaacs & Sons Ltd v Cook [1925] 2 K.B. 391, KBD 11.97, 11.137, 11.138
M&W Grazebrook Ltd v Wallens; sub nom. Wallens v M&W Grazebrook Ltd [1973] 2 All E.R. 868; [1973] I.C.R. 256; [1973] I.R.L.R. 139; [1973] I.T.R. 258, NIRC 11.41, 11.21
M(A) v Ryan (1997) 143 D.L.R. (4th) 1, Sup Ct 11.153
M(N) v Drew Estate (2003) 230 D.L.R. (4th) 697, CA (Alberta) 11.153
MacAllister v Bishop of Rochester (1880) 5 C.P.D. 194 .... 4.16
McAvan v London Transport Executive (1983) 133 N.L.J. 1101, CA (Civ Div) 11.46
McBride v Body Shop International Plc [2007] EWHC 1658 (QB) 15.03, 15.05, 15.31
McBride v Sandland (1917) S.A.L.R. 249 .... 16.45
MacBryan v Brooke [1946] 2 All E.R. 688, CA 10.17

McCabe v British American Tobacco Australia Services Ltd [2002] VSC 73, Sup Ct (Victoria), reversed [2002] V.S.C.A. 197 .... 6.32, 13.34, 14.05, 14.09
McCaskell v Mirror Newspapers Ltd [1984] 1 N.S.W.L.R. 66, Sup Ct (NSW) 11.34
McCaughey's Application for Judicial Review, Re [2004] N.I.Q.B. 2 .... 11.101
McClean's Application for Judicial Review (No.2), Re [2005] UKHL 46; [2005] N.I. 490; [2005] U.K.H.R.R. 826; (2005) 102(29) L.S.G. 32, HL (NI) 21.06
McClelland Pope & Langley v Howard [1968] 1 All E.R. 569 (Note), HL 11.113
McDonald v Ellis [2007] NSWSC 1068 .... 4.22
McDonald v Radio Telefis Eireann [2001] 1 I.E.S.C. 91, Sup Ct (Irl) 12.42
MacDonald v Thorn Plc; sub nom. Thorn Plc v MacDonald [1999] C.P.L.R. 660, CA (Civ Div) 1.32
McDougall v Black & Decker Canada Inc (2009) 302 D.L.R. (4th) 661 .... 13.34, 13.38
McDowell v Hirschfield Lipson & Rumney [1992] 2 F.L.R. 126; [1992] Fam. Law, Q.B.D. 11.129
McE v Prison Service of Northern Ireland. *See* C's Application for Judicial Review, Re
MacFarlan v Rolt (1872) L.R. 14 Eq. 580 .... 11.21
McFeely v United Kingdom (1980) 20 D.R. 44, Eur Comm. HR 21.08
McGahie v Union of Shop, Distributive and Allied Workers, 1966 S.L.T. 74, OH 3.28
McGinley v United Kingdom (App. No.21825/93); sub nom. Egan v United Kingdom (App. No.23414/94) (1999) 27 E.H.R.R. 1; 4 B.H.R.C. 421; (1998) 4 E.H.R.C. 421; (1998) 42 B.M.L.R. 123; [1998] H.R.C.D. 624, ECHR 20.62, 21.06
McGorm, Re (1989) 86 A.L.R. 275 .... 14.01
McGregor Clothing Co Ltd's Trade Mark (Disclosure) [1978] F.S.R. 353, Ch.D 11.22, 11.26, 11.42
McGuinness v Kellogg Co of Great Britain Ltd [1988] 1 W.L.R. 913; [1988] 2 All E.R. 902; (1988) 85(28) L.S.G. 45; (1988) 138 N.L.J. Rep. 150, CA (Civ Div) 19.23
McIlwain v Ramsay Food Packaging Pty Ltd [2005] F.C.A. 1233; (2006) 221 A.L.R. 785 .... 10.13
McInerney v McDonald (1992) 93 D.L.R. (4th) 415 .... 5.52
McIvor v Southern Health and Social Services Board, Northern Ireland [1978] 1 W.L.R. 757; [1978] 2 All E.R. 625; 122 S.J. 368, HL ... 3.35, 4.52, 11.159
McIvor v Southern Health and Social Servies Board [1978] N.I.1, CA (NI) ... 4.60
Mackay Sugar Co-operative Association Ltd v CSR Ltd (1996) 137 A.L.R. 183, Fed. Ct. Aus. 11.151, 11.157, 11.158
McKay v McKay [1988] N.I. 79 .... 11.31
McKenna v Cammell Laird Ship Repairers Ltd, *The Times*, May 11, 1989, CA (Civ Div) 16.49
McKerr's Application for Judicial Review, Re; sub nom. McKerr, Re [2004] UKHL 12; [2004] 1 W.L.R. 807; [2004] 2 All E.R. 409; [2004] N.I. 212; [2004] H.R.L.R. 26; [2004] U.K.H.R.R. 385; 17 B.H.R.C. 68; [2004] Lloyd's Rep. Med. 263; (2004) 101(13) L.S.G. 33; (2004) 148 S.J.L.B. 355, HL (NI) 21.01
McKinnon and Secretary, Department of Foreign Affairs and Trade [2004] A.A.T.A. 1365 .... 11.18

Mackinnon v Donaldson Lufkin & Jenrette Securities Corp [1986] Ch. 482; [1986] 2 W.L.R. 453; [1986] 1 All E.R. 653; [1987] E.C.C. 139; [1986] Fin. L.R. 225; (1986) 83 L.S.G. 1226; (1985) 130 S.J. 224, Ch.D 2.58, 3.22, 10.09, 10.44, 10.49, 10.51, 11.140
McKinnon v Donaldson Lufkin and Jenrette Securities Corp. *See* Mackinnon v Donaldson Lufkin & Jenrette Securities Corp
Maclaine Watson & Co Ltd v International Tin Council (No.2) [1989] Ch. 286; [1988] 3 W.L.R. 1190; [1988] 3 All E.R. 257; (1988) 85(41) L.S.G. 44; (1988) 132 S.J. 1495, CA (Civ Div) 2.46, 2.48, 2.51
McLean v Burns Philp Trustee Co Pty Ltd (1985) 2 N.S.W.L.R. 623 .... 1.10
McLoughlin v Dwyer (1895) Ir.R.9 C.L. 170 .... 16.61, 16.85
McMichael v United Kingdom (A/308); sub nom. McMichael v United Kingdom (16424/90) [1995] 2 F.C.R. 718; (1995) 20 E.H.R.R. 205; [1995] Fam. Law 478, ECHR 21.05, 21.06
Macmillan Inc v Bishopsgate Investment Trust Plc (No.1) [1993] 1 W.L.R. 1372; [1993] 4 All E.R. 998; (1993) 137 S.J.L.B. 174, CA (Civ Div); affirming [1993] 1 W.L.R. 837; [1993] 4 All E.R. 99; [1993] I.C.R. 385; [1993] I.R.L.R. 393, Ch.D 3.42, 5.46, 10.11, 10.12, 10.23, 10.31
Macmillan Inc v Bishopsgate Investment Trust Plc (No.4); sub nom. MCC Proceeds Inc v Bishopsgate Investment Trust Plc (No.4) [1999] C.L.C. 417, CA (Civ Div) 18.22
McNeil v Commissioner of Taxation [2003] FCA 985, (2003) 202 A.L.R. 35, Fed. Ct. Aus. 18.15
McPhilemy v Times Newspapers Ltd (Re-Amendment: Justification) [1999] 3 All E.R. 775; [1999] C.P.L.R. 533; [1999] E.M.L.R. 751, CA (Civ Div) 16.51
McPhilemy v Times Newspapers Ltd [2000] 1 W.L.R. 1732; [2000] C.P. Rep. 53; [2000] C.P.L.R. 335; [2000] E.M.L.R. 575, CA (Civ Div) 17.26
Macquarie Generation v Coal & Allied Industries Ltd [2001] F.C.A. 1349, Fed. Ct. Aus. 11.159, 11.161
McTaggart v McTaggart [1949] P. 94; [1948] 2 All E.R. 754; 64 T.L.R. 558; 46 L.G.R. 527; [1949] L.J.R. 82; 92 S.J. 617, CA 11.134, 11.153
McVeigh, O'Neill and Evans v United Kingdom (1981) 25 D.R. 15 .... 21.17
Magellan Petroleum Australia Ltd v Sagasco Amadeus Pty Ltd [1994] 2 Qd. R. 37, Sup Ct (Qld) 11.157, 11.159
Magnet, The (1874) L.R. 4 A. & E. 417 .... 19.09
Mahmood v Galloway [2006] EWHC 1286 (QB); [2006] E.M.L.R. 26 .... 21.11
Mahon v Air New Zealand [1984] A.C. 808; [1984] 3 W.L.R. 884; [1984] 3 All E.R. 201; (1984) 81 L.S.G. 3336; (1984) 128 S.J. 752, PC (NZ) 13.34
Mahon v Rahn (No.1) [1998] Q.B. 424; [1997] 3 W.L.R. 1230; [1997] 3 All E.R. 687; [1997] E.M.L.R. 558, CA (Civ Div) 2.05, 15.28
Makanjuola v Commissioner of Police of the Metropolis [1992] 3 All E.R. 617, CA (Civ Div) 11.81, 11.100
Makita (Aust) Pty Ltd v Sprowles (2001) 52 N.S.W.L.R. 705 .... 18.14
Malev Hungarian Airlines v United Technologies International Inc [1993] I.L. Pr. 422, Ct of Appeals (US) 2.62
Malhotra v Dhawan [1997] 8 Med. L.R. 319, CA (Civ Div) 13.34
Malone v United Kingdom (A/82) (1985) 7 E.H.R.R. 14, ECHR 21.10
Manatee Towing Co Ltd v Oceanbulk Maritime SA; The Bay Ridge (Discovery); Oceanbulk Maritime SA v Manatee Towing Co Ltd (Discovery); Manatee Towing Co Ltd v McQuilling Brokerage Partners Inc (Discovery) [1999] 1 Lloyd's Rep. 876; [1999] C.L.C. 1197; (1999) 143 S.J.L.B. 111, Q.B.D. (Comm.) 4.09, 4.11, 4.14, 16.27, 16.33

Manchester City Council v T; sub nom. T (A Minor) (Guardian ad Litem: Case Record), Re [1994] Fam. 181; [1994] 2 W.L.R. 594; [1994] 2 All E.R. 526; [1994] 1 F.L.R. 632; [1994] 3 F.C.R. 81; (1994) 144 N.L.J. 123, CA (Civ Div) 11.99
Manchester Corp v Manchester Palace of Varieties Ltd [1955] P. 133; [1955] 2 W.L.R. 440; [1955] 1 All E.R. 387; 119 J.P. 191; 53 L.G.R. 269; 99 S.J. 150, Ct of Chivalry 20.40
Manda (Wardship Documents) (Disclosure), Re [1993] Fam. 183; [1993] 2 W.L.R. 161; [1993] 1 All E.R. 733; [1993] 1 F.L.R. 205; [1993] Fam. Law 217; (1992) 142 N.L.J. 1233; 136 S.J.L.B. 253, CA (Civ Div) 4.04
Mandic v Phillis [2005] FCA 1279, (2006) 225 A.L.R. 760, Fed. Ct. Aus. 10.12, 10.15, 10.28
Manilal & Sons (PTE) Ltd v Bhupendra F K J Shan [1990] 2 M.L.J. 282, H Ct (Singapore) 13.12
Mann v Carnell (1999) 201 C.L.R 1, 168 A.L.R. 86, H Ct (Aus) 12.06, 12.08
Mann v Chetty & Patel [2001] C.P. Rep. 24; [2001] Lloyd's Rep. P.N. 38, CA (Civ Div) 18.04
Mantaray Pty Ltd v Brookfield Breeding Co Pty Ltd [1992] 1 Qd. R. 91 .... 9.04
Mantovanelli v France (1997) 24 E.H.R.R. 370, ECHR 21.06
Manufacturers Life Insurance Company of Canada v Harvest Hero International Ltd [2002] H.K.C.A. 83, CA (HK) 3.03
Maranda v Richer (2004) 232 D.L.R. (4th) 14, S.C.C 11.09
Marcan Shipping (London) Ltd v Kefalas [2007] EWCA Civ 463; [2007] 1 W.L.R. 1864; [2007] 3 All E.R. 365; [2007] C.P. Rep. 41; [2007] 1 C.L.C. 785; (2007) 104(22) L.S.G. 23 .... 13.10, 13.11
Marcel v Commissioner of Police of the Metropolis; Anchor Brewhouse Developments v Jaggard [1992] Ch. 225; [1992] 2 W.L.R. 50; [1992] 1 All E.R. 72; (1992) 4 Admin. L.R. 309; (1991) 141 N.L.J. 1224; (1991) 135 S.J.L.B. 125, CA (Civ Div) ... 10.13, 10.15, 10.25, 10.29, 10.31, 11.101, 11.112, 12.37, 15.01, 15.11
Marckx v Belgium (A/31) (1979–80) 2 E.H.R.R. 330, ECHR 21.08
Mare Del Nord, The [1990] 1 Lloyd's Rep. 40, Q.B.D. (Admlty) 19.09
Marine Rescue Technologies Ltd v Burchill [2007] EWHC 1976 (Ch); (2008) 31(1) I.P.D. 31006, Ch D (Patents Ct) 13.10
Marks & Spencer Plc v Freshfields Bruckhaus Deringer [2004] EWCA Civ 741; [2005] P.N.L.R. 4; (2004) 148 S.J.L.B. 788, CA (Civ Div) 15.46
Marks v Beyfus (1890) L.R. 25 Q.B.D. 494, CA 11.93, 11.103
Markt Intern Verlag GmbH v Germany (A/164); sub nom. Markt Intern Verlag GmbH v Germany (App. No.10572/83); Markt Intern and Beermann v Germany (1990) 12 E.H.R.R. 161, ECHR 21.14
Marlton v Tectronix UK Holdings Plc; sub nom. Marlton v Tektronix UK Holdings Plc [2003] EWHC 383; [2003] Info. T.L.R. 258, Ch.D 9.29
Marlwood Commercial Inc v Kozeny. *See* Omega Group Holdings Ltd v Kozeny
Marriage of Kennedy and Evans, Re (1994) 18 Fam. L.R. 472 .... 10.35
Marriott v Chamberlain (1886) L.R. 17 Q.B.D. 154, CA 11.64, 16.34, 16.36, 16.37, 16.39, 16.63
Mars UK Ltd v Waitrose Ltd [2004] EWHC 2264, Ch.D 3.31
Marsden v Amalgamated Television Services Pty Ltd [2001] N.S.W.S.C. 77 .... 10.35
Marshall v Allotts (A Firm) [2004] EWHC 1964; [2005] P.N.L.R. 11, DR (Leeds) 3.34
Marshall v Goulston Discount (Northern) [1967] Ch. 72; [1966] 3 W.L.R. 599; [1966] 3 All E.R. 994; 110 S.J. 604, CA 5.25

Marshall v Langley [1889] W.N. 222 .... 16.27
Martin & Biro Swan Ltd v H Millwood Ltd (1954) 71 R.P.C. 361 .... 5.12
Martin and Miles Martin Pen Co v Scrib (No.2) (1950) 67 R.P.C. 127, CA 5.08, 5.12
Martin v Treacher (1885–86) L.R. 16 Q.B.D. 507, CA 8.06, 8.10, 16.86
Marubeni Corporation v Alafouzos, unreported, November 6, 1986, CA (Civ Div) 12.19, 12.20, 12.25
Mascherpa v Direct [1960] 1 W.L.R. 447; [1960] 2 All E.R. 145; 104 S.J. 350, CA 8.10
Mason, Re; sub nom. Mason v Cattley (1883) L.R. 22 Ch. D. 609, Ch.D 11.72
Mason v Richard Freeman & Co [2010] EWCA Civ 287; (2010) 154(13) S.J.L.B. 29 .... 21.17
Masood v Zahoor [2009] EWCA Civ 650; [2010] 1 W.L.R. 746; [2010] 1 All E.R. 888; [2009] C.P. Rep. 44; [2010] Bus. L.R. D12 .... 13.07
Masri v Consolidated Contractors International Co SAL [2008] EWCA Civ 303; [2008] 2 Lloyd's Rep. 128; [2008] C.P. Rep. 28; [2008] 1 C.L.C. 657; [2008] I.L.Pr. 37; [2008] B.P.I.R. 531 .... 2.51
Masri v Consolidated Contractors International Co SAL [2008] EWCA Civ 876 .... 2.48, 17.14
Masri v Consolidated Contractors Company SAL [2010] EWHC 2640 (Comm) 2.39
Masson v Netherlands (A/327) (1996) 22 E.H.R.R. 491, ECHR 21.05
Matthews v Ministry of Defence [2003] UKHL 4; [2003] 1 A.C. 1163; [2003] 2 W.L.R. 435; [2003] 1 All E.R. 689; [2003] I.C.R. 247; [2004] H.R.L.R. 2; [2003] U.K.H.R.R. 453; 14 B.H.R.C. 585; [2003] P.I.Q.R. P24; [2003] A.C.D. 42; (2003) 100(13) L.S.G. 26; (2003) 153 N.L.J. 261; (2003) 147 S.J.L.B. 235, HL 21.05
Matua Finance Ltd v Equiticorp Industries Group Ltd [1993] 3 N.Z.L.R. 650, CA (NZ) 11.69
Maxwell Communications Corp Plc (No.3), Re [1995] 1 B.C.L.C. 521, Ch.D 3.41
Maxwell v Pressdram [1987] 1 W.L.R. 298; [1987] 1 All E.R. 656; (1987) 84 L.S.G. 1148; (1987) 131 S.J. 327, CA (Civ Div) 3.21
Mayne Pharma Pty Ltd v Debiopharm SA [2006] EWHC 164; [2006] F.S.R. 37; (2006) 29(3) I.P.D. 29027, Ch.D (Patents Ct) 12.19, 19.19
Mayo Associates SA v Anagram (Bermuda) Ltd 1998 J.L.R. N–4, R Ct (Jersey) 15.25, 15.28
Mealey Horgan Plc v Horgan, *The Times*, July 6, 1999, Q.B.D. 13.19, 17.21
Medcalf v Mardell (Wasted Costs Order); sub nom. Medcalf v Weatherill [2002] UKHL 27; [2003] 1 A.C. 120; [2002] 3 W.L.R. 172; [2002] 3 All E.R. 721; [2002] C.P. Rep. 70; [2002] C.P.L.R. 647; [2002] 3 Costs L.R. 428; [2002] P.N.L.R. 43; (2002) 99(31) L.S.G. 34; (2002) 152 N.L.J. 1032; (2002) 146 S.J.L.B. 175; [2002] N.P.C. 89, HL 12.05, 21.06
Medical Council v Meadow [2006] EWCA Civ 1390 .... 18.15
Medisys Plc v Arthur Andersen (A Firm) [2002] Lloyd's Rep. P.N. 323; [2002] P.N.L.R. 22, Q.B.D. 3.33
Mediterrania Raffineria v Mabanaft, unreported, December 1, 1978, CA 2.13
Meditor Capital Management Ltd v Feighan (Inspector of Taxes) [2004] S.T.C. (S.C.D.) 273; [2004] S.T.I. 1280, Sp Comm. 20.77
Medway v Doublelock Ltd [1978] 1 W.L.R. 710; [1978] 1 All E.R. 1261; 122 S.J. 248, Ch.D 15.11, 15.45
Megaleasing UK v Barrett [1993] I.R.L.M. 497 .... 3.03, 3.11
Mehra v Kilachand, 1987–88 J.L.R. 421 .... 1.17
Memarian v Ghanadian, unreported, June 23, 2000, CA (Civ Div) 19.13

Memory Corp Plc v Sidhu (No.2) [2000] Ch. 645; [2000] 2 W.L.R. 1106; [2000] 1 All E.R. 434; (2000) 97(4) L.S.G. 33; (2000) 144 S.J.L.B., Ch.D 11.109
Mendizabal v Machado (1826) 2 Russ. 540 .... 3.02
Mercantile Credit Company of Ireland Ltd v Heelan [1998] 1 I.R. 81, Sup Ct (Irl) 13.07, 13.13
Mercantile Credit Ltd v Dallhold Investments Pty Ltd (1994) 130 A.L.R. 287 .... 11.06, 12.02
Mercantile Group (Europe) AG v Aiyela [1994] Q.B. 366; [1993] 3 W.L.R. 1116; [1994] 1 All E.R. 110, CA (Civ Div) 3.14
Mercantile Mutual Custodians Pty Ltd v Village Nine Network Restaurants and Bars [1999] Q.C.A. 276, CA (Qld) 20.56
Mercer v Chief Constable of Lancashire; Holder v Chief Constable of Lancashire [1991] 1 W.L.R. 367; [1991] 2 All E.R. 504, CA (Civ Div) 17.20, 17.21, 17.25
Mercer v St. Helen's and Knowsley Hospitals [1995] C.L.Y.626 .... 11.93
Merchants & Manufacturers Insurance Co Ltd v Davies [1938] 1 K.B. 196; (1937) 58 Ll. L. Rep. 61, CA 5.24, 8.20, 16.47
Mercier v Cotton (1875–76) L.R. 1 Q.B.D. 442, CA 16.26
Merck & Co v Interpharm Inc (1992) 44 C.P.R. (3d) 440 .... 15.46
Merck & Co v Interpharm [1992] 3 F.C. 774 .... 14.15, 15.05, 15.06
Merit Finance and Investment Group Ltd, Re [1993] 1 N.Z.L.R. 152 .... 11.09
Merrell Dow Pharmaceuticals Inc's (Terfenadine) Patent [1991] R.P.C. 221, Ch.D (Patents Ct) 5.36
Merricks v Nott-Bower [1965] 1 Q.B. 57; [1964] 2 W.L.R. 702; [1964] 1 All E.R. 717; (1964) 128 J.P. 267; 108 S.J. 116, CA 11.90
Mersey Care NHS Trust v Ackroyd (No.1); sub nom. Ackroyd v Mersey Care NHS Trust (No.1) [2003] EWCA Civ 663; [2003] E.M.L.R. 36; [2003] Lloyd's Rep. Med. 379; (2003) 73 B.M.L.R. 88; (2003) 100(28) L.S.G. 30; (2003) 147 S.J.L.B. 595, CA (Civ Div) 3.21, 21.15
Mersey Care NHS Trust v Ackroyd (No.2); sub nom. Ackroyd v Mersey Care NHS Trust (No.2) [2007] EWCA Civ 101; [2008] E.M.L.R. 1; [2007] H.R.L.R. 19; [2007] Info. T.L.R. 221; (2007) 94 B.M.L.R. 84; (2007) 104(10) L.S.G. 31; (2007) 151 S.J.L.B. 298 .... 3.18, 3.21
Mertens v Haigh (1860) Johns. 735 .... 9.13, 9.16
Mertens v Haigh (1863) 1 De.G.J. & Sm. 528 .... 4.20, 14.01
Metallgesellschaft AG, Re, 121 F.3d 77 (2d. Cir., 1997) 2.62, 2.63
Metcash Trading v Bun [2010] FCA 8; (2010) 263 A.L.R. 132 .... 5.12
Meteyard v Love (2005) 224 A.L.R. 588, CA (NSW) 11.77
Metropolitan and Provincial Bank, Re, Ex p. Davis (1868) 16 W.R. 668 .... 4.36
Metropolitan Police Commissioner v Hurst. *See* R. (on the application of Hurst) v HM Coroner for Northern District London
Metropolitan Police Commissioner v Locker. *See* Commissioner of Police of the Metropolis v Locker
Metso Minerals (Australia) Ltd v Kalra (No.3) [2008] FCA 1201 .... 2.22
Mexborough v Whitwood Urban DC; sub nom. Earl of Mexborough v Whitwood Urban DC [1897] 2 Q.B. 111, CA 8.10
Mgica (1992) Ltd v Kenny & Good Pty Ltd (No.2) (1996) 135 A.L.R. 743, Fed. Ct. Aus. 12.06, 12.28
Miailhe v France (No.2) (1997) 23 E.H.R.R. 491, ECHR 21.07
Michael O'Mara Books Ltd v Express Newspapers Plc [1998] E.M.L.R. 383; [1999] F.S.R. 49; (1998) 21(7) I.P.D. 21070, Ch.D 3.05, 3.14, 3.21

Michael Wilson & Partners Ltd v Emmott; sub nom. Emmott v Michael Wilson & Partners Ltd [2008] EWCA Civ 184; [2008] Bus. L.R. 1361; [2008] 2 All E.R. (Comm) 193; [2008] 1 Lloyd's Rep. 616; [2008] C.P. Rep. 26 .... **15.47**
Microsoft Corp v Plato Technology Ltd [1999] Masons C.L.R. 370; (1999) 22(11) I.P.D. 22108, CA (Civ Div); affirming [1999] F.S.R. 834; [1999] Masons C.L.R. 87; (1999) 22(5) I.P.D. 22047, Ch.D .. 3.05, 3.11, 3.14, 3.23
Microsoft Corporation v CX Computer Pty Ltd (2002) 187 A.L.R. 326, Fed. Ct. Aus. 11.106, 11.110, 11.112
Mid East Trading Ltd, Re; sub nom. Lehman Bros Inc v Phillips; Phillips v Lehman Brothers [1998] 1 All E.R. 577; [1998] B.C.C. 726; [1998] 1 B.C.L.C. 240; (1998) 95(3) L.S.G. 24; (1998) 142 S.J.L.B. 45, CA (Civ Div) 3.22, 3.41
Middlekamp v Fraser Valley Real Estate Board (1992) 96 D.L.R. (4th) 227, CA (BC) 11.124
Milano Assicurazioni SpA v Walbrook Insurance Co Ltd [1994] 1 W.L.R. 977; [1995] L.R.L.R. 188; (1994) 91(9) L.S.G. 40; (1994) 138 S.J.L.B. 52, Q.B.D. (Comm.) 3.45, 15.21, 15.41
Milbank v Milbank [1900] 1 Ch. 376, CA 6.13, 9.07
Miley v Flood [2001] I.E.H.C. 9, H Ct (Irl) 11.13
Miller v Kirwan [1903] 2 I.R. 118 .... 16.75
Miller v Scorey; Miller v Forrest [1996] 1 W.L.R. 1122; [1996] 3 All E.R. 18, Ch.D 15.19, 15.45
Mills (John) v European Investment Bank (EIB) (110/75) [1976] E.C.R. 1613, ECJ 20.37
Minet v Morgan (1872–73) L.R. 8 Ch. App. 361, CA in Chancery 11.06
Ministry of Defences Application, Re, unreported, June 17, 1994, CA (NI) 11.96
Minnesota Mining & Manufacturing Co v Rennicks (UK) Ltd (No.1) [1991] F.S.R. 97, Ch.D 11.21, 12.33
Minnesota v Philip Morris Inc [1998] I.L.Pr. 170, CA (Civ Div) 10.56, 10.59
Minories Finance Ltd v Arthur Young, unreported, March 31, 1988 ... 6.01, 8.20
Minter v Priest [1930] A.C. 558, HL 11.07, 11.09, 11.10, 11.137, 11.138
Mireskandari v Associated Newspapers Ltd [2010] EWHC 967 (QB); (2010) 160 N.L.J. 695 .... **16.42**
Mitchell v Darley Main Colliery Co (1884) 1 Cab. & El. 215 .... 6.31
Mitsubishi Electric Australia Pty Ltd v Victorian Work Cover Authority [2002] V.S.C.A. 59 .... 11.38
Mitsubushi Electric Australia Pty Ltd v Victorian Work Cover Authority [2002] 4 V.R. 332 .... 11.14, 11.26
Mitsui & Co Ltd v Nexen Petroleum UK Ltd [2005] EWHC 625 (Ch); [2005] 3 All E.R. 511 .... **3.10**, 3.13, 3.26, 3.32, 3.33, 3.34
Moage Ltd, Re (1998) 82 F.C.R. 10, Fed. Ct. Aus. 11.67
Mobil Cerro Negro Ltd v Petroleos De Venezuela SA [2008] EWHC 532 (Comm); [2008] 1 Lloyd's Rep. 684; [2008] 1 C.L.C. 542 .... **2.19**
Modinos v Cyprus (1993) 16 E.H.R.R. 485 .... 21.08
Mogul Steamship Co v McGregor Gow & Co (1886) 2 T.L.R. 2 .... 6.41
Mole v Mole [1951] P. 21; [1950] 2 All E.R. 328; 66 T.L.R. (Pt. 2) 129; 48 L.G.R. 439; 94 S.J. 518, CA 11.134
Molloy v Kilby (1880) L.R. 15 Ch. D. 162, CA 4.15, 16.27
Molnlycke AB v Proctor & Gamble Ltd, unreported, November 20, 1991 .... 15.31
Molnlycke AB v Proctor & Gamble Ltd, April 15, 1991 .... 11.158, 11.160, 11.161, 11.162

Molnlycke AB v Procter & Gamble Ltd (No.3) [1990] R.P.C. 498, Ch.D (Patents Ct) 5.34, 5.35, 8.20
Molnlycke AB v Procter & Gamble Ltd (No.4) [1992] 1 W.L.R. 1112; [1992] 4 All E.R. 47; [1992] R.P.C. 21, CA (Civ Div) 4.46
Monsanto Co v Stauffer Chemical Co [1985] R.P.C. 515, CA (Civ Div); reversing [1985] F.S.R. 55, Ch.D (Patents Ct) 19.17
Moore v Craven (1871–72) L.R. 7 Ch. App. 94 (Note), CA in Chancery 8.25
Moore v Peachey [1891] 2 Q.B. 707, Q.B.D. 9.07
Moore v Woodman [1970] V.R. 577 .... 5.26
Moran v Erstream (Australia) Pty Ltd [2006] N.S.W.S.C. 79 .... 6.41
Moreay Nominees Pty Ltd v McCarthy (1994) 10 W.A.R. 293, Sup Ct (W Aus) 11.64, 12.06
Moresfield Ltd v Banners (A Firm); Banners v KPMG (A Firm) [2003] EWHC 1602, Ch.D 3.31, 3.33, 3.34
Morgan v Hinton Organics (Wessex) Ltd [2009] EWCA Civ 107; [2009] C.P. Rep. 26; [2010] 1 Costs L.R. 1; [2009] Env. L.R. 30; [2009] 2 P. & C.R. 4; [2009] J.P.L. 1335 .... 18.11, 18.12
Morgan v Morgan (Financial Provision) [1977] Fam. 122; [1977] 2 W.L.R. 712; [1977] 2 All E.R. 515; 121 S.J. 157, Fam Div 10.15
Morgans v Needham, unreported, October 28, 1999, CA (Civ Div) 13.06, 13.11
Mornington v Keene (1856) 4 W.R. 793 .... 13.27
Morris v Banque Arabe et Internationale d'Investissement SA (No.1) [2000] C.P. Rep. 65; [2001] I.L.Pr. 37; (1999–2000) 2 I.T.E.L.R. 492; (2000) 97(1) L.S.G. 24, Ch.D (Companies Ct) 8.26, 11.104, 11.154
Morris v Director of the Serious Fraud Office [1993] Ch. 372; [1993] 3 W.L.R. 1; [1993] 1 All E.R. 788; [1992] B.C.C. 934; [1993] B.C.L.C. 580, Ch.D 3.42
Morris v Edwards (1890) L.R. 15 App. Cas. 309, HL .. 6.13, 6.43, 11.51, 16.40, 16.75, 16.83
Morrissey v Morrissey (2000) 196 D.L.R. (4th) 94, CA (Newfoundland) ... 11.05, 11.08, 11.78, 18.16
Mortgage Corp v Halifax (SW) Ltd, *The Times*, July 15, 1998, Q.B.D. 5.29, 11.151
Mortgage Express Ltd v S Newman & Co, unreported, July 7, 1998, CA 5.30, 11.01
Morton Norwich Products Inc v Intercen Ltd (No.2); Morton Norwich Products Inc v United Chemicals (London) [1981] F.S.R. 337, Ch.D (Patents Ct) 3.24
Moseley v The Victoria Rubber Co (1886) 3 R.P.C. 351 .... 11.42
Moser v Cotton, unreported, July 31, 1990, CA (Civ Div) 11.33
Mostyn v West Mostyn Coal and Iron Co Ltd (1876) 34 L.T. 531 .. 11.14, 11.18
Moti Mahal Indian Restaurant v Customs and Excise Commissioners [1992] V.A.T.T.R. 188, VAT Tr (London) 20.88, 20.89
Motorola Credit Corp v Uzan (No.1) (Application to Stay Disclosure Order) [2002] EWCA Civ 989; [2002] 2 All E.R. (Comm.) 945; [2002] C.P. Rep. 69; (2002) 99(33) L.S.G. 21, CA (Civ Div) 2.13
Motorola Credit Corp v Uzan (No.2) (Order for Cross Examination) [2002] EWHC 2187, Q.B.D. (Comm.) 2.13, 6.44
Motorola Credit Corp v Uzan (No.6) [2003] EWCA Civ 752; [2004] 1 W.L.R. 113; [2003] C.P. Rep. 56; [2003] 2 C.L.C. 1026; (2003) 100(32) L.S.G. 34; (2003) 147 S.J.L.B. 752, CA (Civ Div) 2.13, 2.19
Mount Murray Country Club Ltd v Macleod [2003] UKPC 53; [2003] S.T.C. 1525; 75 T.C. 197; [2004] B.T.C. 76; [2003] S.T.I. 1267; (2003) 147 S.J.L.B. 1118, PC (IoM) 11.98, 11.143

Moy v Pettman Smith (A Firm) [2005] UKHL 7; [2005] 1 W.L.R. 581; [2005] 1 All E.R. 903; [2005] Lloyd's Rep. Med. 293; [2005] P.N.L.R. 24; (2005) 102(11) L.S.G. 31; (2005) 155 N.L.J. 218; (2005) 149 S.J.L.B. 180; [2005] N.P.C. 15, HL 18.05
Moynihan (Barony of), Re [2000] 1 F.L.R. 113; [2000] Fam. Law 21, HL 20.11
MS v Sweden (1999) 28 E.H.R.R. 313; 3 B.H.R.C. 248; (1999) 45 B.M.L.R. 133, ECHR 12.04, 21.10, 21.12
Mubarak v Mubarak (No.1); sub nom. Mubarak v Mubarik; Murbarak v Murbarak; Mubarak v Wani; Mubarak v Dianoor International Ltd; Mubarak v Dianoor Jewels Ltd [2001] 1 F.L.R. 698; [2001] 1 F.C.R. 193; [2001] Fam. Law 178, CA (Civ Div) 21.17
Muller v Linsley & Mortimer [1996] P.N.L.R. 74; (1995) 92(3) L.S.G. 38; (1995) 139 S.J.L.B. 43, CA (Civ Div 11.125, 11.129, 12.04
Muller v Switzerland (A/133) (1991) 13 E.H.R.R. 212, ECHR 21.14
Mulley v Manifold (1959) 103 C.L.R. 341, HC (Aus) 5.08, 5.33, 6.41
Multi Guarantee Co Ltd v Cavalier Insurance Co Ltd, *The Times*, June 24, 1986, Ch.D 10.11, 11.94, 11.98, 12.42
Multigroup Bulgaria Holdings AD v Oxford Analytica Ltd, unreported, June 30, 1999, Q.B.D. 6.49
Multiplex Constructions (UK) Ltd v Cleveland Bridge (UK) Ltd [2008] EWHC 2220 (TCC) 18.02
Mummery v Victorian Railway Commissioners (1887) 9 A.L.T. 21 .... 11.39
Murat v Inland Revenue Commissioners; sub nom. Murat v Ornoch (Inspector of Taxes); R. (on the application of Murat) v Inland Revenue Commissioners [2004] EWHC 3123; [2005] S.T.C. 184; 77 T.C. 122; [2005] B.T.C. 83; [2004] S.T.I. 2300, Q.B.D. (Admin) 20.77, 21.16
Murjani (A Bankrupt), Re [1996] 1 W.L.R. 1498; [1996] 1 All E.R. 65; [1996] B.C.C. 278; [1996] 1 B.C.L.C. 272; [1996] B.P.I.R. 325, Ch.D ... 11.77
Murphy v J Donohoe Ltd [1996] 1 I.R.123, Sup Ct (Irl) 13.10, 13.13, 13.16
Murphy v Kirwan [1993] 3 I.R. 501, Sup Ct (Irl) 11.70
Murphy v Murphy; sub nom. Murphy's Settlements, Re [1999] 1 W.L.R. 282; [1998] 3 All E.R. 1; [1998] N.P.C. 62, Ch.D 3.05, 3.06, 3.11, 3.24
Murphy v Young & Co's Brewery Plc; Murphy v Sun Alliance and London Insurance Plc [1997] 1 W.L.R. 1591; [1997] 1 All E.R. 518; [1997] 1 Lloyd's Rep. 236; [1997] C.L.C. 469; [1998] 1 Costs L.R. 94; [1997] 6 Re. L.R. 113, CA (Civ Div) 2.40
Murphy's Settlements, Re. *See* Murphy v Murphy
Murray Consultants Ltd, Re [1999] 1 I.L.R.M. 257, H Ct (Irl) 11.39
Murray v Northern Whig (1912) 46 Ir. LT 77, CA 16.62
Murray v United Kingdom (A/300–A) (1995) 19 E.H.R.R. 193, ECHR 21.09
Murray v United Kingdom (Right to Silence) (App. No.18731/91) (1996) 22 E.H.R.R. 29, ECHR 11.118, 21.07
Murray v Walter (1839) Cr. & Ph. 114 .... 4.20, 5.43
Murrell v Customs and Excise Commissioners 2 I.T.L. Rep. 936; [2001] S.T.I. 256, V&DTr 21.05
Murrell v Healy [2001] EWCA Civ 486; [2001] 4 All E.R. 345; [2002] R.T.R. 2, CA (Civ Div) 11.125
Mutch v Allen [2001] EWCA Civ 76; [2001] C.P. Rep. 77; [2001] C.P.L.R. 200; [2001] P.I.Q.R. P26, CA (Civ Div) 18.03, 18.17
Mutual Society, Re (1883) L.R. 22 Ch. D. 714, CA 4.37
Myers v Elman; sub nom. Myers v Rothfield [1940] A.C. 282, HL 6.18, 6.31, 14.01, 14.02, 14.05, 14.07, 14.09, 14.10, 14.13, 14.16, 16.104

N(K) v Alberta (1999) 174 D.L.R. (4th) 366, QB (Alberta) 5.24
Nash v Layton [1911] 2 Ch. 71, CA 16.34, 16.47
Nast v Nast and Walker [1972] Fam. 142; [1972] 2 W.L.R. 901; [1972] 1 All E.R. 1171; 116 S.J. 159, CA (Civ Div) 11.105
Nathan v Smilovitch (Application to Set Aside Permission to Appeal) [2002] EWCA Civ 759, CA (Civ Div) 6.57
National Association of Operative Plasterers v Smithies (Discovery) [1906] A.C. 434, HL 8.12, 11.106, 16.85
National Bank of Canada v Mann (1999) 37 C.P.C. (4th) 88 .... 3.03
National Bank of Egypt International Ltd v Oman Housing Bank SAOC [2002] EWHC 1760; [2003] 1 All E.R. (Comm.) 246, Q.B.D. (Comm.) 18.22
National Employers' Mutual General Insurance Association Ltd v Waind (1979) 141 C.L.R. 648, H Ct (Aus) 11.39, 11.44, 11.51, 11.57
National Grid Co Plc v Virdee [1992] I.R.L.R. 555, EAT 20.30
National Insurance Co Ltd v Whirlybird Holdings Ltd [1994] 2 N.Z.L.R. 513, CA (NZ) 11.76, 12.18
National Justice Compania Naviera SA v Prudential Assurance Co Ltd; The Ikarian Reefer (No.1) [1995] 1 Lloyd's Rep. 455, CA (Civ Div); reversing [1993] 2 Lloyd's Rep. 68; [1993] F.S.R. 563; [1993] 37 E.G. 158, Q.B.D. (Comm.) 18.02, 18.12
National Justice Compania Naviera SA v Prudential Life Assurance Co Ltd, unreported, July 30, 1999 .... 2.40
National Post v Canada, 2010 SCC 16, (2010) 318 D.L.R. (4th) 1, Supreme Court of Canada 11.103
National Tertiary Education Industry Union v Commonwealth of Australia (2001) 188 A.L.R. 614, Fed. Ct. Aus. 11.98
National Westiminster Bank plc v Rabobank Nederland [2006] EWHC 2332 (Comm) **11.02**, 11.09, 11.12, 11.14, 11.17, 11.67
Nationwide Anglia Building Society v Various Solicitors (No.1) [1999] P.N.L.R. 52; (1998) 95(6) L.S.G. 24; (1998) 148 N.L.J. 241; (1998) 142 S.J.L.B. 78, Ch.D 11.06, 11.08, 11.09, 11.11, 11.12, 12.02, 12.03, 12.08
Nationwide Building Society v Various Solicitors. *See* Nationwide Anglia Building Society v Various Solicitors (No.1)
Nationwide Mutual Insurance Co v Home Insurance Co, unreported, October 20, 1998 .... 10.29, 10.57, 10.61
Naura Phosphate Royalties Trust v Allen, Allen & Hemsley, (1997) 13 P.N. 64 .... 5.23, 11.59, 11.60
Navigators and General Insurance Co v Ringrose [1962] 1 W.L.R. 173; [1962] 1 All E.R. 97; [1961] 2 Lloyd's Rep. 415; 106 S.J. 135, CA 10.09, 11.105
Naylor v Preston AHA; Foster v Merton and Sutton HA; Thomas v North West Surrey HA; Ikumelo v Newham HA [1987] 1 W.L.R. 958; [1987] 2 All E.R. 353; (1987) 84 L.S.G. 1494; (1987) 137 N.L.J. 474; (1987) 131 S.J. 596, CA (Civ Div) 1.02, 11.08
Nea Karteria Maritime Co v Atlantic and Great Lakes Steamship Corp (No.2) [1981] Com. L.R. 138 .... 12.19, 12.28, 12.34
Neate v Duke of Marlborough (1836) 2 Y. & C. Ex. 3 .... 4.20
Nedenes, The [1925] W.N. 23 .... 16.29, 16.54
Nederlandse Reassurantie Groep Holding NV v Bacon & Woodrow (No.1) [1995] 1 All E.R. 976; [1995] 2 Lloyd's Rep. 77, Q.B.D. (Comm.) 11.13, 11.28, 12.04
Nederlandse Reassurantie Groep Holding NV v Bacon & Woodrow (No.2) [1995] 2 Lloyd's Rep. 404, Q.B.D. (Comm.) 17.20, 17.29

Neilson v Laugharne [1981] Q.B. 736; [1981] 2 W.L.R. 537; [1981] 1 All E.R. 829; 125 S.J. 202, CA (Civ Div) 11.44, 11.46, 11.100
Nene Packaging Ltd v Customs and Excise Commissioners [2001] V. & D.R. 286; [2002] S.T.I. 217, V&DTr 20.88, 21.05
Network Ten Ltd v Capital Television Holdings Ltd (1995) 36 N.S.W.L.R. 275, Sup Ct (NSW) 11.60, 11.62
New Alliance Pty Ltd, Re (1993) 118 A.L.R. 699, Fed. Ct. Aus. 2.26
New v Burns (1894) 64 L.J.Q.B. 104, CA 2.61, 17.12
New South Wales v Betfair [2009] FCAFC 160; 261 A.L.R. 311 ..... 11.09, 12.08
New South Wales Council for Civil Liberties v CRB [2006] FCA 1409; (2007) 236 A.L.R. 313, Fed. Ct of Australia 11.09, 12.04
New Victoria Hospital v Ryan [1993] I.C.R. 201; [1993] I.R.L.R. 202, EAT 11.21, 11.41
New World Alliance Pty Ltd, Re (1993) 118 A.L.R. 699, Fed. Ct. Aus. ... 11.106, 11.110
New Zealand Apple and Pear Marketing Board v Master & Sons Ltd [1986] 1 N.Z.L.R. 191 .... 11.107
New Zealand Institute of Chartered Accountants v Clarke [2009] 3 N.Z.L.R. 264 .... 11.129
New Zealand Rail Ltd v Port Marlborough New Zealand Ltd [1993] 2 N.Z.L.R. 641, CA (NZ) 5.12
Newbiggin-by-the-sea Gas Co v Armstrong (1879–80) L.R. 13 Ch. D. 310, CA 1.12
Newcastle Wallsend Coal Co Pty Ltd v Court Coal Miners Regulation (1997) 42 N.S.W.L.R. 351 .... 11.37, 12.08
Newcrest Mining (WA) Ltd v Commonwealth of Australia (1993) 113 A.L.R. 370, Fed. Ct. Aus. 12.02
News International plc v Clinger, unreported, April 6, 1998 ... 6.27, 12.17, 12.18
Nichia Corp v Argos Ltd [2007] EWCA Civ 741; [2007] Bus. L.R. 1753; [2007] F.S.R. 38; (2007) 30(8) I.P.D. 30050, CA (Civ Div) 1.31, 5.34, 5.37
Nicholl v Jones (1865) 2 H. & M. 588 .... 11.28
Nicholl v Wheeler (1886) L.R. 17 Q.B.D. 101, CA 6.43, 16.40, 16.75
Nicholls v McLevy (1971) 1 S.A.S.R. 442 .... 3.27, 19.02
Nicolardi v Daley [2002] O.J. No.595 .... 9.29
Niderost-Huber v Switzerland (1998) 25 E.H.R.R. 709, ECHR 21.06
Niemietz v Germany (A/251–B) (1993) 16 E.H.R.R. 97, ECHR 20.79, 21.09, 21.12, 21.13
Nigel Upchurch Associates v Aldridge Estates Investment Co [1993] 1 Lloyd's Rep. 535, Q.B.D. 5.23
Nikitin v Richards Butler LLP; Skarga v Richards Butler LLP [2007] EWHC 173 (QB) 3.10
Nissho Iwai Corp v Gulf Fisheries Company, unreported, July 12, 1988 ...... 2.39, 9.07
Nixon v Channel 4 [1997] EWCA Civ 1117 .... 5.52
Nokia Corp v InterDigital Technology Corp [2005] EWCA Civ 614, CA (Civ Div); affirming [2004] EWHC 2920; (2005) 28(5) I.P.D. 28039, Ch.D (Patents Ct) 5.37
Noorani v Merseyside TEC Ltd [1999] I.R.L.R. 184, CA (Civ Div) 10.11, 20.28
Nordon v Defries (1881–82) L.R. 8 Q.B.D. 508, Q.B.D. 11.38
Normanshaw v Normanshaw (1893) 69 L.T. 468 .... 11.153
Norris v Ireland (A/142); sub nom. Norris v Ireland (App. No.10581/83) (1991) 13 E.H.R.R. 186, ECHR 21.08
North Brazilian Sugar Factories, Re (1888) L.R. 37 Ch. D. 83, CA 4.36

Northumbrian Water Ltd v British Telecommunications Plc [2005] EWHC 2408; [2006] B.L.R. 38, Q.B.D. (TCC) 3.34
Norton Healthcare Ltd v Minnesota Mining & Manufacturing Co (Discovery) [1999] F.S.R. 636, Ch.D (Patents Ct) 5.35
Norway's Application (Nos 1 and 2), Re [1990] 1 A.C. 723; [1989] 2 W.L.R. 458; [1989] 1 All E.R. 745; (1989) 133 S.J. 290, HL 10.55, 10.59
Norway's Application, Re [1987] Q.B. 433; [1986] 3 W.L.R. 452; (1986) 83 L.S.G. 3248; (1986) 130 S.J. 730, CA (Civ Div) 10.59
Norwich Pharmacal Co v Customs and Excise Commissioners; sub nom. Morton-Norwich Products Inc v Customs and Excise Commissioners [1974] A.C. 133; [1973] 3 W.L.R. 164; [1973] 2 All E.R. 943; [1973] F.S.R. 365; [1974] R.P.C. 101; 117 S.J. 567, HL ... 1.12, 2.09, 2.13, 2.54, 3.03, 3.05, 3.06, 3.08, 3.11, 3.14, 3.16, 3.23, 3.24, 11.102, 15.22
Norwich Union Life Insurance Society v Waller (Tony) (1984) 270 E.G. 42; (1984) 81 L.S.G. 899; (1984) 128 S.J. 300, Ch.D 11.129
Nossen's Letter Patent, Re; sub nom. Nossen's Patent, Re [1969] 1 W.L.R. 638; [1969] 1 All E.R. 775; [1968] F.S.R. 617; 113 S.J. 445, Ch.D 19.17
Nottinghamshire CC v H (Minors) [1995] 1 F.L.R. 115; [1995] 2 F.C.R. 365; [1995] Fam. Law 63; (1995) 159 J.P.N. 318, Fam Div 4.04, 10.15, 10.23, 10.31, 11.101
Nova Scotia v Royal & Sun Alliance (2005) 251 D.L.R. (4th) 483, CA (Nova Scotia) 5.52
Novartis AG v Johnson & Johnson Medical Ltd [2008] EWHC 293 (Pat); (2008) 31(8) I.P.D. 31054, Ch D (Patents Ct) 16.72
Novo Nordisk A/S v Banco Santander (Guernsey) Ltd (1999–2000) 2 I.T.E.L.R. 557, Royal Ct (Gue) 3.03
Nowak v Sanyshyn (1979) 23 O.R. (2d.) 797, H Ct (Ont) 12.06
Nucleus Information Systems v Palmer [2003] EWHC 2013, Ch.D 9.29
Nwabueze v General Medical Council [2000] 1 W.L.R. 1760; (2000) 56 B.M.L.R. 106, PC (UK) 21.06
Nyckeln Finance Co Ltd (In Administration) v Edward Symmons & Partners (No.1) [1996] P.N.L.R. 245, CA (Civ Div) 5.24

O (Disclosure Order), Re; sub nom. O (Restraint Order: Disclosure of Assets), Re [1991] 2 Q.B. 520; [1991] 2 W.L.R. 475; [1991] 1 All E.R. 330, CA (Civ Div) 2.26
O and J (Children) (Blood Tests: Constraint), Re; sub nom. O and J (Children) (Paternity: Blood Tests), Re; J (A Child) (Blood Tests), Re [2000] Fam. 139; [2000] 2 W.L.R. 1284; [2000] 2 All E.R. 29; [2000] 1 F.L.R. 418; [2000] 1 F.C.R. 330; (2000) 55 B.M.L.R. 229; [2000] Fam. Law 324; (2000) 164 J.P.N. 839; (2000) 97(6) L.S.G. 35; (2000) 144 S.J.L.B. 85, Fam Div 19.20
O Co v M Co [1996] 2 Lloyd's Rep. 347, Q.B.D. (Comm.) 5.08, 5.12
O Ltd v Z [2005] EWHC 238, Ch.D 2.23, 11.106, 12.37, 15.11, 15.34
OCS Group Ltd v Wells [2008] EWHC 919 (QB); [2008] P.I.Q.R. P18 .... 3.34
O-M (Children) (Non-Accidental Injury: Expert Evidence), Re [2009] EWCA Civ 1405; [2010] 2 F.L.R. 58; [2010] 1 F.C.R. 305; (2010) 112 B.M.L.R. 101; [2010] Fam. Law 235; (2010) 154(1) S.J.L.B. 28 .... 18.14
O'Born v Commissioner for Government Transport (1960) 77 W.N. (N.S.W.) 81 .... 10.34
O'Brien v McKenzie (1900) 21 L.R. (N.S.W.) (Eq.) 117 .... 6.13
O'Connor v Mirror Group Newspapers (1986) Ltd, unreported, February 1, 1993, CA 15.37, 15.40

O'Reilly v State Bank of Victoria Commissioners (1983) 153 C.L.R.I, H Ct (Aus) 11.12, 11.36
Oates v Harte Reede & Co, unreported, December 17, 1998 .... 3.28
Observer v United Kingdom (A/216) (1992) 14 E.H.R.R. 153, ECHR 21.14, 21.15
Oceanbulk Shipping and Trading SA v TMT Asia Ltd [2010] EWCA Civ 79; [2010] 1 W.L.R. 1803; [2010] 3 All E.R. 282; [2010] 2 All E.R. (Comm) 176; [2010] C.P. Rep. 24; [2010] 1 C.L.C. 200; 129 Con. L.R. 35; (2010) 107(9) L.S.G. 16 .... 11.129
Oceanic Finance Corp Ltd v Norton Rose, unreported, March 26, 1997 .... 5.21, 12.04, 12.36
Ockwell International Corp v Serck Industries Ltd [1988] F.S.R. 187, CA (Civ Div); affirming [1987] R.P.C. 89, Ch.D 5.31, 11.42, 16.34, 16.38, 16.42, 16.52, 16.71
Official Receiver v Stern [2000] UKHRR 332, CA 21.05
Official Receiver v Stern. *See* Westminster Property Management Ltd (No.1), Re
Official Solicitor v K; sub nom. K (Infants), Re [1965] A.C. 201; [1963] 3 W.L.R. 408; [1963] 3 All E.R. 191; 107 S.J. 616, HL 4.04
Ofulue v Bossert [2009] UKHL 16; [2009] 1 A.C. 990; [2009] 2 W.L.R. 749; [2009] 3 All E.R. 93; [2010] 1 F.L.R. 475; [2009] 2 P. & C.R. 17; [2009] Fam. Law 1042; [2009] 11 E.G. 119 (C.S.); (2009) 106(12) L.S.G. 15; (2009) 153(11) S.J.L.B. 29; [2009] N.P.C. 40 .... 11.122, 11.125, 11.130
Ogden v London Electric Railway Co (1933) 49 T.L.R. 542 .... 11.45
Ohlsen v Terrero (1874–75) L.R. 10 Ch. App. 127, Lord Chancellor 17.06
Oldham MBC v GW [2007] EWHC 136 (Fam); [2007] 2 F.L.R. 597; [2008] 1 F.C.R. 331; (2007) 97 B.M.L.R. 146; [2007] Fam. Law 582, Fam Div (Manchester) 18.14
Ollett v Bristol Aerojet Ltd (Practice Note) [1979] 1 W.L.R. 1197; [1979] 3 All E.R. 544; 123 S.J. 705, Q.B.D. 18.02
Olympic, The and HMS Hawke. *See* Owners of the SS Olympic v Blunt
Omar (A Bankrupt), Re; sub nom. Trustee of the Estate of Omar (A Bankrupt) v Omar (Diana Bridget) [2000] B.C.C. 434; [1999] B.P.I.R. 1001, Ch.D 11.71
Omar (Mohamed) v Omar (Chiiko Aikawa) [1995] 1 W.L.R. 1428; [1995] 3 All E.R. 571; [1996] Fam. Law 20, Ch.D 3.11, 3.25
Omar v Omar, unreported, October 11, 1996, CA 10.06, 10.10, 15.22
Omega Engineering Inc v Omega SA (Extension of Time) [2003] EWHC 1482, Ch.D 1.32
Omega Group Holdings Ltd v Kozeny [2002] C.L.C. 132, Q.B.D. (Comm.) 2.63
Omega Group Holdings Ltd v Kozeny; Marlwood Commercial Inc v Kozeny [2004] EWCA Civ 798; [2005] 1 W.L.R. 104; [2004] 3 All E.R. 648; [2004] 2 C.L.C. 166; (2004) 148 S.J.L.B. 822, CA (Civ Div) ... 10.54, 15.43
Ontario Federation of Anglers & Hunters v Ontario (2001) 196 D.L.R. (4th) 367, Div Ct (Ont) 17.01
Open Door Counselling Ltd v Ireland (A/246); sub nom. Open Door Counselling Ltd v Ireland (14234/88, 14253/88); Dublin Well Woman Centre v Ireland (A/246) (1993) 15 E.H.R.R. 244, ECHR 21.14
Ophelia, The [1916] 2 A.C. 206, PC (UK) 13.34
Ophthalmological Society of New Zealand v Boulton [2003] N.Z.C.A. 26 .... 12.06, 12.09
Oppenheim & Co v Sheffield [1893] 1 Q.B. 5, CA 16.52, 16.53

Optiver Australia Pty Ltd v Tibra Trading Pty Ltd [2007] FCA 2065; (2008) 247 A.L.R. 199 .... 3.34
Optus Communications Pty Ltd v Telstra Corp Ltd [1995] F.C.A. 254 ...... 9.37
O'Reilly v Mackman 44688; Millbanks v Secretary of State for the Home Department; Derbyshire v Mackman; Dougan v Mackman; Millbanks v Home Office [1983] 2 A.C. 237; [1982] 3 W.L.R. 1096; [1982] 3 All E.R. 1124; 126 S.J. 820, HL 4.06
Orford v Rasmi Electronics Ltd [2002] EWCA Civ 1672; [2003] C.P.L.R. 213, CA (Civ Div) 19.24
Orkem SA (formerly CdF Chimie SA) v Commission of the European Communities (C–374/87); Solvay et Cie SA v Commission of the European Communities (C–27/88) [1989] E.C.R. 3283; [1989] E.C.R. 3355; [1991] 4 C.M.L.R. 502, ECJ 11.105
Ormerod Grierson & Co v St George's Ironworks Ltd [1905] 1 Ch. 505, CA 9.17
O'Rourke v Darbishire; sub nom. Whitworth, Re [1920] A.C. 581, HL 4.22, 4.23, 5.14, 5.52, 11.15, 11.23, 11.69, 11.72, 11.75
Orr v Diaper (1876–77) L.R. 4 Ch. D. 92, Ch.D 3.23
Orr v Crowe [2009] NIQB 17 .... 12.19, 12.22, 12.23
Osborne v Sparke (1907) 7 S.R.(N.S.W.) 460 .... 16.34
O'Shea v Wood [1891] P. 286, CA 4.47, 11.09
Osland v Secretary to the Department of Justice [2008] HCA 17, High Ct of Australia 12.08
Osman v United Kingdom (App. No.23452/94) [1999] 1 F.L.R. 193; (2000) 29 E.H.R.R. 245; 5 B.H.R.C. 293; (1999) 1 L.G.L.R. 431; (1999) 11 Admin. L.R. 200; [1999] Crim. L.R. 82; [1998] H.R.C.D. 966; [1999] Fam. Law 86; (1999) 163 J.P.N. 297, ECHR 13.17, 21.05
Osman, Re. *See* R. v Governor of Pentonville Prison Ex p. Osman (No.2)
Osram Lamp Works Ltd v Gabriel Lamp Co [1914] 2 Ch. 129, CA 16.34, 16.72
O'Sullivan v Commissioner of Police of the Metropolis (1995) 139 S.J.L.B. 164, Q.B.D. 11.89, 11.100
O'Sullivan v Herdmans [1987] 1 W.L.R. 1047; [1987] 3 All E.R. 129; (1987) 84 L.S.G. 2362; (1987) 131 S.J. 1003, HL 9.19, 10.23
O'Sullivan v Parkin [2008] FCAFC 134; (2008) 249 A.L.R. 507 ...... 4.07, 11.88, 11.96
Ouvaroff, Re [1997] B.P.I.R. 1712 .... 11.77
Overseas Programming Companies Ltd v Cinematographische Commerz-Anstalt; Overseas Programming Companies Ltd v Iduna Film GmbH [1985] E.C.C. 176, Q.B.D. 8.06, 10.58, 10.61, 11.109
Overseas Union Insurance Ltd v Incorporated General Insurance Ltd, unreported, July 2,1991, CA 9.09
Owen v Sambrook [1981] Crim. L.R. 329, DC 10.47
Owen v Sepro Building Services Ltd, unreported, April 16, 1991, CA 13.10
Owners of "Kamal XXVI" v Owners of "Ariela" [2010] EWHC 2531 (Comm) 2.40, 4.57, 11.68
Owners of the Bow Spring v Owners of the Manzanillo II [2004] EWCA Civ 1007; [2005] 1 W.L.R. 144; [2004] 4 All E.R. 899; [2005] 1 All E.R. (Comm.) 53; [2005] 1 Lloyd's Rep. 1; [2005] 1 C.L.C. 394, CA (Civ Div) 18.24, 18.25
Owners of the Global Mariner v Owners of the Atlantic Crusader [2005] EWHC 380; [2005] 2 All E.R. (Comm.) 389; [2005] 1 Lloyd's Rep. 699; [2005] 1 C.L.C. 413; (2005) 155 N.L.J. 594, Q.B.D. (Admlty) 18.23
Owners of the SS Olympic v Blunt; sub nom. Hawke, The [1915] A.C. 385, HL; affirming [1913] P. 214, CA 19.09

Oxford Gene Technology Ltd v Affymetrix Inc (No.2) [2001] R.P.C. 18, CA (Civ Div) 12.05

Oxfordshire CC v P (A Minor) [1995] Fam. 161; [1995] 2 W.L.R. 543; [1995] 2 All E.R. 225; [1995] 1 F.L.R. 552; [1995] 2 F.C.R. 212; 93 L.G.R. 336; (1995) 159 J.P.N. 302, Fam Div 4.04, 11.107, 15.21, 15.42

Oxley v Penwarden [2001] C.P.L.R. 1; [2001] Lloyd's Rep. Med. 347, CA (Civ Div) 18.09

Oystercatcher Commodities Ltd v J M Harwood & Co Ltd, unreported, October 29, 1986 .... 9.05

Özgür Gündem v Turkey (App. No.23144/93); sub nom. Ersoz v Turkey (App. No.23144/93) (2001) 31 E.H.R.R. 49, ECHR 21.14, 21.15

P v T Ltd; sub nom. A v B Ltd [1997] 1 W.L.R. 1309; [1997] 4 All E.R. 200; [1997] I.C.R. 887; [1997] I.R.L.R. 405, Ch.D 3.05, 3.06

P&M Quality Smallgoods Pty Ltd v Seven Network (Operations) Pty Ltd [2010] NSWSC 841 .... 10.11

PLG Research Ltd v Ardon International Ltd (1992) I.P.D. 15081 .... 11.161

P (A Minor) (Witness Summons), Re; sub nom. P (A Minor) (Care Proceedings: Witness Summons), Re [1997] 2 F.L.R. 447; [1997] 3 F.C.R. 322; [1997] Fam. Law, CA (Civ Div) 10.06, 10.13

P(D) v Wagg (2004) 239 D.L.R. (4th) 501, CA (Ont) 15.56

Pacific Investments Ltd v Christensen 1996 J.L.R. N–6, Jersey CA, 1997 J.L.R. 170, CA (Jersey) 1.17, 9.37

Packer v Deputy Commissioner of Taxation (1984) 33 A.L.R. 243, Sup Ct (Queensland) 11.09

Paddick v Associated Newspapers Ltd [2003] EWHC 2991, Q.B.D. .. 5.12, 9.20, 9.37

Pais v Pais [1971] P. 119; [1970] 3 W.L.R. 830; [1970] 3 All E.R. 491; 114 S.J. 72, PDAD 11.134, 11.153

Palermo, The (1884) L.R. 9 P.D. 6, CA 11.33

Pall Corp v Commercial Hydraulics (Bedford) Ltd (No.2) [1989] R.P.C. 703, CA (Civ Div); affirming [1990] F.S.R. 329, Ch.D (Patents Ct) .. 19.17, 19.19

Palmeira Square v Van Hoogstraten, March 28, 2001, Q.B.D. 13.37

Palmer v Fraser (1888) 7 V.L.R. 77 .... 16.62

Pammel v Germany (1998) 26 E.H.R.R. 100, ECHR 21.05

Pamplin v Express Newspapers Ltd (Costs) [1985] 1 W.L.R. 689; [1985] 2 All E.R. 185, Q.B.D. 12.30

Pan American World Airways Inc's Application, Re; sub nom. Lockerbie Air Disaster, Re [1992] Q.B. 854; [1992] 3 W.L.R. 191; [1992] 3 All E.R. 197, CA (Civ Div) 10.58

Pan Electric Industries, Re [1992] 2 S.L.R. 437, H Ct (Singapore) 4.36

Panayiotou v Sony Music Entertainment (UK) Ltd [1994] Ch. 142; [1994] 2 W.L.R. 241; [1994] 1 All E.R. 755; [1994] I.L.Pr. 241; (1993) 143 N.L.J., Ch.D 2.59, 2.60, 2.61, 10.10, 10.5, 10.57

Pankhurst v Hamilton (1886) 2 T.L.R. 862 .... 16.65

Panthalu v Ramnord Research Laboratories [1966] 2 Q.B. 173; [1965] 3 W.L.R. 682; [1965] 2 All E.R. 921; 109 S.J. 496, CA 10.63

Pantmaenog Timber Co Ltd, Re 18710; sub nom. Official Receiver v Hay; Pantmaenog Timber Co (In Liquidation), Re; Official Receiver v Meade-King (A Firm); Official Receiver v Wadge Rapps & Hunt (A Firm); Official Receiver v Grant Thornton (A Firm) [2003] UKHL 49; [2004] 1 A.C. 158; [2003] 3 W.L.R. 767; [2003] 4 All E.R. 18; [2003] B.C.C. 659; [2003] 2 B.C.L.C. 257; [2004] B.P.I.R. 139; (2003) 153 N.L.J. 1346; (2003) 147 S.J.L.B. 936, HL; reversing [2001] EWCA Civ 1227; [2002] Ch. 239; [2002] 2 W.L.R. 20; [2001] 4 All E.R. 588; [2002] B.C.C. 11; [2001] 2 B.C.L.C. 555; (2001) 98(35) L.S.G. 32; (2001) 151 N.L.J. 1212; (2001) 145 S.J.L.B. 210, CA (Civ Div) 3.43
Paragon Finance Plc (formerly National Home Loans Corp) v Freshfields [1999] 1 W.L.R. 1183; [2000] C.P. Rep. 81; [1999] Lloyd's Rep. P.N. 446; (1999) 96(20) L.S.G. 40; (1999) 143 S.J.L.B. 136; [1999] N.P.C. 33, CA (Civ Div) 11.64, 12.04
Pardy's Mozambique Syndicate Ltd v Alexander [1903] 1 Ch. 191, Ch.D 4.09, 9.07, 9.35
Parfums Yves Saint Laurent (formerly Charles of the Ritz Ltd) v Ritz Hotel Ltd [1990] F.S.R. 36, CA (HK) 16.50
Parikh v Birmingham North General Commissioners; sub nom. Parikh v General Commissioners for the Birmingham North Division [1976] S.T.C. 365; [1976] T.R. 129, CA (Civ Div) 20.74
Parker v CS Structured Credit Fund Ltd [2003] EWHC 391; [2003] 1 W.L.R. 1680; (2003) 100(15) L.S.G. 26, Ch.D 2.12, 2.32, 6.51
Parker v Wells (1880–81) L.R. 18 Ch. D. 477, CA 1.12, 16.52
Parkin v O'Sullivan [2006] FCA 1413; (2007) 235 A.L.R. 286 .... 5.30
Parnell (formerly O'Shea) v Wood [1892] P. 137, CA 10.15, 10.44, 10.47
Parnell v Walter (1890) L.R. 24 Q.B.D. 441, Q.B.D. 16.62
Parry v Bentley [1993] H.K. Digest, F89, CA (HK) 1.18, 15.22, 15.40
Parry v Boyle (1986) 83 Cr. App. R. 310; [1987] R.T.R. 282; [1986] Crim. L.R. 551, Q.B.D. 19.13
Parry v News Group Newspapers Ltd (1990) 140 N.L.J. 1719, CA (Civ Div) 11.13, 11.28, 11.45, 11.126, 12.36
Parry-Jones v Law Society [1969] 1 Ch. 1; [1968] 2 W.L.R. 397; [1968] 1 All E.R. 177; 111 S.J. 910, CA (Civ Div) 11.35, 11.37, 11.77
Partenreederei M/S Heidberg v Grosvenor Grain & Feed Co Ltd; The Heidberg (No.1) [1993] 2 Lloyd's Rep. 324; [1993] I.L.Pr. 718, Q.B.D. (Comm.) 8.26, 11.154
Pascall v Galinski [1970] 1 Q.B. 38; [1969] 3 W.L.R. 626; [1969] 3 All E.R. 1090; (1969) 20 P. & C.R. 933; 113 S.J. 607, CA (Civ Div) 11.13
Paspati v Paspati [1914] P. 110, PDAD 4.28
Paterson v Chadwick; sub nom. Paterson v Northampton and District Hospital Management Committee [1974] 1 W.L.R. 890; [1974] 2 All E.R. 772; 118 S.J. 169, Q.B.D. 3.28
Pathways Employment Services v West (2004) 212 A.L.R. 140, Sup Ct (NSW) 2.13, 11.116, 11.117
Pathways Employment Services v West [2004] N.S.W.S.C. 903; (2005) 212 A.L.R. 140 .... 2.25
Patraikos 2, The [2001] 4 S.L.R. 308, H Ct (Singapore) 11.48
Patrick v Capital Finance Corp (Australasia) Pty Ltd (2004) 211 A.L.R. 272, Fed. Ct. Aus. 11.61, 12.02, 12.08, 12.09
Patrick v Capital Finance Pty Ltd (No.3) [2003] FCA 385, (2003) 198 A.L.R. 323, Fed. Ct. Aus. 6.51, 15.37
Patrick v Capital Finance Pty Ltd (No 4) [2003] F.C.A. 436, Fed. Ct. Aus. 8.16
Patrick v Inland Revenue Commissioners [2002] EWCA Civ 1649 .... 21.16

Peach (Janet Getrude) v Commissioner of Police of the Metropolis [1986] Q.B. 1064; [1986] 2 W.L.R. 1080; [1986] 2 All E.R. 129; (1986) 83 L.S.G. 1723; (1986) 130 S.J. 448, CA (Civ Div) 11.100
Pearce v Foster (No.1) (1884–85) L.R. 15 Q.B.D. 114, CA 11.34
Pearce v Ove Arup Partnership Ltd (Copying) (2002) 25(2) I.P.D. 25011; [2002] E.C.D.R. CN2, Ch.D 18.15
Pearson Education Ltd v Prentice Hall India Pte Ltd [2006] F.S.R. 111, Q.B.D. 11.127, 11.130
Peer International Corp v Termidor Music Publishers Ltd (No.3) [2005] EWHC 1048; [2006] C.P. Rep. 2; (2005) 28(7) I.P.D. 28050, Ch.D 2.60, 17.12
Peet v Mid Kent Area Healthcare NHS Trust; sub nom. P (A Child) v Mid Kent NHS Healthcare Trust (Practice Note); MP v Mid Kent Healthcare NHS Trust [2001] EWCA Civ 1703; [2002] 1 W.L.R. 210; [2002] 3 All E.R. 688; [2002] C.P.L.R. 27; [2002] Lloyd's Rep. Med. 33; (2002) 65 B.M.L.R. 43; (2001) 98(48) L.S.G. 29; (2001) 145 S.J.L.B. 261, CA (Civ Div) 18.01, 18.09
Penfold v Pearlberg [1955] 1 W.L.R. 1068; [1955] 3 All E.R. 120; 99 S.J. 708, Ch.D 19.07
Penn Texas Corp v Anstalt (Murat); sub nom. Penn Texas Corp v English Trans-Continental [1964] 1 Q.B. 40; [1963] 2 W.L.R. 111; [1963] 1 All E.R. 258; 107 S.J. 33, CA 2.60, 10.56, 10.63
Penn v Lord Baltimore (1750) 1 Ves. Sen. 444 .... 2.17
Penn-Texas Corp v Anstalt (Murat) [1964] 2 Q.B. 647; [1964] 3 W.L.R. 131; [1964] 2 All E.R. 594; 108 S.J. 356, CA 2.60
People v Lines, 531 P.2d. 793 (1975) 12.06
Pereira v Beanlands [1996] 3 All E.R. 528; (1996) 146 N.L.J. 554, Ch.D 13.10, 13.24
Perestrello e Companhia Limitada v United Paint Co Ltd (No.1) [1969] 1 W.L.R. 570; [1969] 3 All E.R. 479; (1968) 113 S.J. 36, CA (Civ Div) 16.39
Pergamon Press, Re [1970] 3 All E.R.535 .... 11.36
Perlak Petroleum Maatschappij v Deen [1924] 1 K.B. 111, CA 16.46
Perry v Gibson (1834) 110 E.R. 1125; (1834) 1 Ad. & El. 48, KB 10.27
Perry v Phosphor Bronze Co (1895) 71 L.T. 854 .... 10.50
Perry v Smith (1842) 9 M. & W. 681 .... 11.74
Peru Republic v Wequellin (1875) L.R. 20 Eq. 140 .... 4.43
Peter Walker & Son Ltd v Hodgson [1909] 1 K.B. 239, CA 16.57, 16.65
Peters v Andrew [2009] EWHC 1511 (QB) 10.24, 20.05
Petre v Sutherland (1887) 3 T.L.R. 275, CA 8.20
Petrovic v Austria (App. No.20458/92) (2001) 33 E.H.R.R. 14; 4 B.H.R.C. 232; [1998] H.R.C.D. 366, ECHR 21.18
Pfeifer v Austria (A/227); Plankl v Austria (1992) 14 E.H.R.R. 692, ECHR 21.13
Phelps v Hillingdon LBC; sub nom. G (A Child), Re; Anderton v Clwyd CC; G (A Child) v Bromley LBC; Jarvis v Hampshire CC [2001] 2 A.C. 619; [2000] 3 W.L.R. 776; [2000] 4 All E.R. 504; [2000] 3 F.C.R. 102; (2001) 3 L.G.L.R. 5; [2000] B.L.G.R. 651; [2000] Ed. C.R. 700; [2000] E.L.R. 499; (2000) 3 C.C.L. Rep. 156; (2000) 56 B.M.L.R. 1; (2000) 150 N.L.J. 1198; (2000) 144 S.J.L.B. 241, HL 3.28
Phelps v Kemsley (1943) 168 L.T. 20 .... 16.60
Philip Donnelly vWeybridge Construction Ltd [2006] EWHC 721 (TCC) 4.12
Phillips v Barron [1876] W.N. 54 .... 16.46

Phillips v Burrows (Inspector of Taxes) (Costs); Phillips (Deceased) v Burrows (Inspector of Taxes) [2000] S.T.C. (S.C.D.) 107 (Note); [2000] S.T.I. 167, Sp Comm. 20.76
Phillips v Phillips (1879) 40 L.T. 815 .... 5.09, 5.12, 5.30, 5.38
Phillips v Symes (A Bankrupt) (Expert Witnesses: Costs) [2004] EWHC 2330; [2005] 1 W.L.R. 2043; [2005] 4 All E.R. 519; [2005] 2 All E.R. (Comm.) 538; [2005] C.P. Rep. 12; [2005] 2 Costs L.R. 224; (2005) 83 B.M.L.R. 115; (2004) 101(44) L.S.G. 29; (2004) 154 N.L.J. 1615, Ch.D 18.15
Phoenix Natural Gas Ltd v British Gas Trading Ltd [2004] EWHC 451, Q.B.D. (Comm.) 3.34
Pickering v Edmunds (1994) 63 S.A.S.R. 357 .... 12.06
Pickering, Re; sub nom. Pickering v Pickering (1884) L.R. 25 Ch. D. 247, CA 6.17, 6.44, 9.37
Pineway Ltd v London Mining Co Ltd [2010] EWHC 1143 (Comm) 3.31
Pink v JA Sharwood & Co Ltd [1913] 2 Ch. 286, Ch.D 4.28, 4.30
Pizzey v Ford Motor Co Ltd [1994] P.I.Q.R. P15, CA (Civ Div) 6.26, 12.17
Plant v Plant [1998] 1 B.C.L.C. 38; [1998] B.P.I.R. 243, Ch.D 15.29
Plattform "Arzte fur das Leben" v Austria (A/139) (1991) 13 E.H.R.R. 204, 1988, ECHR 21.14
Pleat v Perrins (1868) L.R. 3 Q.B. 658 .... 16.116
Plummers Ltd v Debenhams plc [1986] B.C.L.C. 447 .... 11.38, 11.45, 11.46
Plymouth Mutual Cooperative & Industrial Society Ltd v Traders Publishing Association Ltd [1906] 1 K.B. 403, CA 16.35, 16.63
Polanski v Conde Nast Publications Ltd [2005] UKHL 10; [2005] 1 W.L.R. 637; [2005] 1 All E.R. 945; [2005] C.P. Rep. 22; [2005] E.M.L.R. 14; [2005] H.R.L.R. 11; [2005] U.K.H.R.R. 277; (2005) 102(10) L.S.G. 29; (2005) 155 N.L.J. 245, HL; reversing [2003] EWCA Civ 1573; [2004] 1 W.L.R. 387; [2004] 1 All E.R. 1220; [2004] C.P. Rep. 13; [2004] E.M.L.R. 7; [2004] U.K.H.R.R. 278; (2003) 100(46) L.S.G. 24; (2003) 153 N.L.J. 1760; (2003) 147 S.J.L.B. 1363, CA (Civ Div) 17.02, 17.12, 17.26
Police Complaints Authority v Greater Manchester Police Authority (1991) 3 Admin. L.R. 757, Q.B.D. 11.100
Police v Campbell [2010] 1 N.Z.L.R. 483 .... 3.18
Police v Mills [1993] 2 N.Z.L.R. 592 .... 11.13
Pollock v Garle [1898] 1 Ch. 1, CA 10.37, 10.47, 10.48
Polly Peck International plc, Re [1994] B.C.C. 15 .... 3.42
Pooraka Holdings v Participation Nominees (1990) 52 S.A.S.R. 148, Sup Ct (S Aus) 11.143
Popek v National Westminster Bank Plc [2002] EWCA Civ 42; [2002] C.P.L.R. 370, CA (Civ Div) 18.10
Popwich v Saskatchewan (1998) 159 D.L.R. (4th) 756, QB Ct (Sask) 11.159
Portman Building Society v Royal Insurance Plc (t/a Fox & Sons) [1998] P.N.L.R. 672, CA (Civ Div) 5.24, 6.49, 6.50, 6.52
Porton Capital Technology Funds (A Body Corporate) v 3M UK Holdings Ltd [2010] EWHC 114 (Comm) 11.159
Portugal (Queen of) v Glyn (1840) 7 Cl. & Fin. 466 .... 4.19
Poseidon Industri AB v Cerosa Ltd (Discovery) [1975] F.S.R. 122, Ch.D ... 5.34
Post Office Counters Ltd v Mahida [2003] EWCA Civ 1583 .... 13.33
Postlethwaite, Re; sub nom. Postlethwaite v Rickman (1887) L.R. 35 Ch. D. 722, Ch.D 11.72
Potter's Sulphide Ore Treatment v Sulphide Corp (1911) 13 C.L.R. 101 ... 16.34
Potts v Mylchreest Motors Ltd (1984–86) M.L.R. 93 .... 1.17

Powell v Chief Constable of North Wales, *The Times*, February 11, 2000, CA (Civ Div) 11.93, 11.103
Powell v United Kingdom (A/172); sub nom. Powell v United Kingdom (App. No.9310/81) (1990) 12 E.H.R.R. 355, ECHR 21.05
Pozzi v Eli Lilly & Co, *The Times*, December 3, 1986 .... 12.02, 12.34
Pozzolanic Lytag Ltd v Bryan Hobson Associates [1999] B.L.R. 267; (1999) 1 T.C.L.R. 233; 63 Con. L.R. 81; [1999] Lloyd's Rep. P.N. 125; (1999) 15 Const. L.J. 135; (1999) 143 S.J.L.B. 30, Q.B.D. (TCC) 18.15
Practice Direction (Fam Div: Family Proceedings: Experts [2008] 1 W.L.R. 1027; [2009] 2 F.L.R. 1383, Fam Div 18.14
Prager and Oberschlick v Austria (A/313) (1996) 21 E.H.R.R. 1, ECHR 21.15
Pratt Holdings Pty Ltd v Commissioners of Taxation (2004) 207 A.L.R. 217, Fed. Ct. (Full Ct) Aus. 11.14, 11.26
Pratt Holdings Pty Ltd v FCT [2004] F.C.A. 122, (2004) 207 A.L.R. 217, Fed. Ct (Aus) 1.19
Prediwave Corp v New World TMT Ltd [2006] HKCA 391 .... 10.59
Premier Profiles Ltd v Tioxide Europe Ltd; EVC Compounds Ltd v Tioxide Europe Ltd [2002] B.L.R. 467; [2003] F.S.R. 20, Q.B.D. (Comm.) 11.159
Premiere Agri Technologies Asia Inc v Wong Siu Hung John [2003] UKCA 273, [2003] H.K.C.F.I. 676 .... 5.09
Prentice v Hereward Housing Association [2001] EWCA Civ 437; [2001] 2 All E.R. (Comm.) 900, CA (Civ Div) 2.53
Prentice v Phillips (1843) 2 Hare. 152 .... 9.11, 9.15
Presbyterian Church of Sudan v Taylor (2005) 256 D.L.R. (4th) 750, Sup Ct CA (Ont) 10.54
Presbyterian Church of Sudan v Taylor (2006) 275 D.L.R. (4th) 512, Ontario CA 10.54, 10.59
Prescott v Bulldog Tools [1981] 3 All E.R. 869, Q.B.D. 19.22
President of the State of Equatorial Guinea v Royal Bank of Scotland International [2006] UKPC 7 .... 3.09
Prest v Rich & Co Investment AG [2006] EWHC 927, Q.B.D. (Comm.) ... 13.13, 13.27
Prestney v Colchester Corp (1883) 24 Ch.D. 376, CA 9.11, 9.13
Preston BC v McGrath, *The Times*, May 19, 2000 *Independent*, May 19, 2000, CA (Civ Div); affirming (1999) 96(8) L.S.G. 30, Ch.D 2.05, 15.56
Price v Manning (1889) L.R. 42 Ch. D. 372, CA 10.06
Price Waterhouse v BCCI Holdings (Luxembourg) SA [1992] B.C.L.C. 583, Ch.D 11.15, 11.26, 11.46, 11.48, 11.77
PricewaterhouseCoopers v Commissioner of Taxation of the Commonwealth of Australia [2004] F.C.A. 122, Fed. Ct. (Full Ct) Aus. 11.15
Primlaks (UK) (No.2), Re [1990] B.C.L.C. 234 .... 4.35
Prioleau v United States (1866) L.R. 2 Eq. 659, Ct of Chancery 4.43
Prioleau v United States (1866) L.R. 2, Eq. 179 .... 4.42
Pritchard v Ontario (Human Rights Commission) (2004) 238 D.L.R. (4th) 1, Sup Ct (Can) 11.19, 11.77
Probatina Shipping Co Ltd v Sun Insurance Office Ltd; The Sageorge [1974] Q.B. 635; [1974] 2 W.L.R. 666; [1974] 2 All E.R. 478; [1974] 1 Lloyd's Rep. 369; 118 S.J. 331, CA (Civ Div) 2.36, 2.37
Probstmeier v Germany, unreported, July 1, 1997 .... 21.05
Process Development Ltd v Hogg [1996] F.S.R. 45; (1996) 19(2) I.P.D. 19012, CA (Civ Div) 15.11, 15.12, 15.21
Procter v Kalivis [2009] FRCA 461; (2010) 263 A.L.R. 461, Fed Ct (Aus) 6.44
Procter & Gamble Ltd v Peaudouce (UK) Ltd, unreported, November 23, 1984 .... 5.50

Procter v Smiles (1886) 55 L.J.Q.B. 467 .... 11.06, 12.02
Proctor & Gamble v Medical Research [2001] N.S.W.S.C. 183, Sup Ct (NSW) 6.41
Professional Institute of the Public Service of Canada v Canada (Director of the Canadian Museum of Nature) [1995] 3 F.C. 643 .... 12.06
Profilati Italia Srl v Painewebber Inc [2001] 1 All E.R. (Comm.) 1065; [2001] 1 Lloyd's Rep. 715; [2001] C.L.C. 672, Q.B.D. (Comm.) 13.36, 20.09
Proposed Finance Pty Ltd v Sing, *The Times*, 2, 1997, CA (Civ Div) 15.45
Protector Alarms Ltd v Maxim Alarms Ltd [1978] F.S.R. 442, Ch.D 2.22, 19.04
Prudential Assurance Co Ltd v Fountain Page Ltd [1991] 1 W.L.R. 756; [1991] 3 All E.R. 878, Q.B.D. 11.136, 12.10, 18.16
Prudential Insurance Co of America v Prudential Assurance Co [2003] EWCA Civ 1154; [2004] E.T.M.R. 29, CA (Civ Div); affirming [2002] EWHC 2809, Ch.D 11.122, 11.127, 21.14
Psalidis v Norwich Union Life Australia Ltd [2009] VSC 417 .... 5.48, 5.52, 5.54
Punjab National Bank v Jain [2004] EWCA Civ 589 .... 6.08
Purdy v Cambran [2000] C.P. Rep. 67; [1999] C.P.L.R. 843, CA (Civ Div) ... 1.32
Pyne, Re [1997] 1 Qd.R.326 (Queensland) 3.03
Pyramid Building Society v Farrow Finance Corp [1995] 1 V.R. 464 .... 10.35

QPS Consultants Ltd v Kruger Tissue (Manufacturing) Ltd, unreported, September 10, 1999, CA 13.11, 13.12
Queanbeyan City Council v ACTEW Corp [2008] FCA 1983; (2009) 253 A.L.R. 121 .... 11.98
Quilter v Heatly; sub nom. Quilter v Heatley (1883) L.R. 23 Ch. D. 42, CA 9.04, 9.05, 9.08
Quinlivan v Conroy [1999] 1 I.R. 271 .... 5.46

R. v AB; R. v Kent [1941] 1 K.B. 454; 110 L.J. K.B. 268, CCA 12.02
R. v Agar (Vincent Raymond) [1990] 2 All E.R. 442; (1990) 90 Cr. App. R. 318; (1990) 154 J.P. 89; [1990] Crim. L.R. 183; (1989) 139 N.L.J. 1116, CA (Crim Div) 11.103
R. v Albutt (1910) 6 Cr. App. R. 55, CCA 10.41
R. v Alibhai (Akbal); R. v Bakir (Nabil); R. v Collier (Adam); R. v Dias (Chaim Nathan) [2004] EWCA Crim 681, CA (Crim Div) 10.02
R. v Amray Corp (1989) 56 D.L.R. (3d.) 309, Sup Ct (Can) 11.107
R. v Andover Justices Ex p. Rhodes [1980] Crim. L.R. 644, DC 10.48
R. v Armagh (1883) 18 Ir.L.T. 2 .... 11.112
R. v Arts Council of England Ex p. Women's Playhouse Trust, *The Times*, August 20, 1997 .... 4.06
R. v Ataou [1988] Q.B. 798, CA 11.65
R. v Att.-Gen. of Northern Ireland Ex p. Devine; R. v Att.-Gen. of Northern Ireland Ex p. Breslin [1992] 1 W.L.R. 262; [1992] 1 All E.R. 609; (1992) 136 S.J.L.B. 82, HL 2.06
R. v B (Derek Anthony) [2001] Crim. L.R. 471, CA (Crim Div) 11.99
R. v Baines [1909] 1 K.B. 258, KBD 10.32
R. v Barton [1973] 1 W.L.R. 115 .... 11.65
R. v Bedfordshire Coroner Ex p. Local Sunday Newspapers Ltd (2000) 164 J.P. 283; (2000) 164 J.P.N. 370, Q.B.D. 11.101
R. v Bell Ex. p. Lees (1980) 146 C.L.R. 141, H Ct (Aus) 11.08, 11.37, 11.78

R. v Birmingham City Council Ex p.; sub nom. Birmingham City Council v O; Birmingham City Council v O'Neill [1983] 1 A.C. 578; [1983] 2 W.L.R. 189; [1983] 1 All E.R. 497; 81 L.G.R. 259; (1983) 127 S.J. 105, HL 5.52
R. v Blackledge (William Stuart) (No.2); R. v Grecian (John Paul); R. v Mason (Bryan Albert); R. v Phillips (Colin William) [1996] 1 Cr. App. R. 326; (1996) 8 Admin. L.R., CA (Crim Div) 2.05, 4.40, 5.43
R. v Board of Visitors of Hull Prison Ex p. St Germain (No.1); R. v Board of Visitors of Wandsworth Prison Ex p. Rosa [1979] Q.B. 425; [1979] 2 W.L.R. 42; [1979] 1 All E.R. 701; (1979) 68 Cr. App. R. 212; 122 S.J. 697, CA (Civ Div) 21.05
R. v Bono (1913) 29 T.L.R. 635 .... 10.46
R. v Bonython [1984] S.A.S.R. 45 .... 18.11
R. v Botmeh (Jawad); R. v Alami (Samar) [2001] EWCA Crim 2226; [2002] 1 W.L.R. 531; [2002] 1 Cr. App. R. 28; [2002] H.R.L.R. 13; [2002] Crim. L.R. 209; (2001) 98(46) L.S.G. 35; (2001) 145 S.J.L.B. 255, CA (Crim Div) 11.82
R. v Bournemouth Justices Ex p. Grey; R. v Bournemouth Justices Ex p. Rodd (1986) 150 J.P. 392; [1987] 1 F.L.R. 36; [1986] Fam. Law 337; (1986) 150 J.P.N. 588, Q.B.D. 11.99
R. v Bowden (Brian Thomas) [1999] 1 W.L.R. 823; [1999] 4 All E.R. 43; [1999] 2 Cr. App. R. 176; (1999) 163 J.P. 337; (1999) 163 J.P.N. 387; (1999) 96(10) L.S.G. 28; (1999) 143 S.J.L.B. 73, CA (Crim Div) 12.28, 12.36
R. v Boyes (1861) 1 B. & S.311 .... 11.110
R. v Brady (Paul Clement) [2004] EWCA Crim 1763; [2004] 1 W.L.R. 3240; [2004] 3 All E.R. 520; [2005] B.C.C. 357; [2005] 1 Cr. App. R. 5; [2004] B.P.I.R. 962; [2005] Crim. L.R. 224; (2004) 101(29) L.S.G. 29; (2004) 148 S.J.L.B. 1149, CA (Crim Div) 3.42
R. v Broadcasting Standards Commission Ex p. BBC [2001] Q.B. 885; [2000] 3 W.L.R. 1327; [2000] 3 All E.R. 989; [2001] B.C.C. 432; [2001] 1 B.C.L.C. 244; [2000] E.M.L.R. 587; [2000] H.R.L.R. 374; [2000] U.K.H.R.R. 624; [2000] C.O.D. 322; (2000) 97(17) L.S.G. 32; (2000) 144 S.J.L.B. 204, CA (Civ Div); reversing [1999] E.M.L.R. 858; [2000] H.R.L.R. 15; [2000] U.K.H.R.R. 158; [1999] C.O.D. 472, Q.B.D. 21.08, 21.11
R. v Bromley Magistrates Court Ex p. Smith; sub nom. R. v Bromley Justices Ex p. Wilkins; R. v Wells Street Stipendiary Magistrate Ex p. King; R. v Wells Street Magistrates Court Ex p. King [1995] 1 W.L.R. 944; [1995] 4 All E.R. 146; [1995] 2 Cr. App. R. 285; (1995) 159 J.P. 251; [1995] Crim. L.R. 248; [1995] C.O.D. 257; (1995) 159 J.P.N. 179; (1995) 92(2) L.S.G. 36; (1995) 139 S.J.L.B. 16, DC 2.05
R. v Brown (2002) 210 D.L.R. (4th) 341, SCC 11.65
R. v Brown (Winston) [1998] A.C. 367; [1997] 3 W.L.R. 447,; affirming [1994] 1 W.L.R. 1599; [1995] 1 Cr. App. R. 191; (1994) 91(31) L.S.G. 36; (1994) 138 S.J.L.B. 146, CA (Crim Div) 2.05
R. v Brushett. *See* R. v B (Derek Anthony)
R. v Central Criminal Court Ex p. Bright; sub nom. R. v Central Criminal Court Ex p. Observer; R. v Central Criminal Court Ex p. Guardian; R. (on the application of Bright) v Central Criminal Court; R. v Central Criminal Court Ex p. Alton; R. v Central Criminal Court Ex p. Rusbridger [2001] 1 W.L.R. 662; [2001] 2 All E.R. 244; [2001] E.M.L.R. 4; [2000] U.K.H.R.R. 796; [2002] Crim. L.R. 64; (2000) 97(38) L.S.G. 43, DC 11.105, 11.114, 11.118, 21.02, 21.07

R. v Central Criminal Court Ex p. Francis & Francis (A Firm) [1989] A.C. 346; [1988] 3 W.L.R. 989; [1988] 3 All E.R. 77; (1989) 88 Cr. App. R. 213; [1989] Crim. L.R. 444; [1989] C.O.D. 231; (1989) 86(1) L.S.G. 37; (1988) 138 N.L.J. Rep. 316; (1988) 132 S.J. 1592, HL 11.08, 11.68, 11.71
R. v Cheltenham Justices Ex p. Secretary of State for Trade [1977] 1 W.L.R. 95; [1977] 1 All E.R. 460; (1977) 121 S.J. 70, DC 10.11, 10.33
R. v Chief Constable of the West Midlands Ex p. Wiley; R. v Chief Constable of Nottinghamshire Ex p. Sunderland [1995] 1 A.C. 274; [1994] 3 W.L.R. 433; [1994] 3 All E.R. 420; [1995] 1 Cr. App. R. 342; [1994] C.O.D. 520; (1994) 91(40) L.S.G. 35; (1994) 144 N.L.J. 1008; (1994) 138 S.J.L.B. 156, HL 11.82, 11.86, 11.89, 11.91, 11.100, 12.42
R. v City of London Magistrates Court Ex p. Asif [1996] S.T.C. 611; [1996] Crim. L.R. 725; (1996) 140 S.J.L.B. 56, DC 20.79
R. v Clowes (Peter) (No.1) [1992] 3 All E.R. 440; [1992] B.C.L.C. 1158; (1992) 95 Cr. App. R. 440, Central Crim Ct 10.02, 10.11, 10.23, 10.31, 10.33, 11.82
R. v Colvin [1970] 3 O.R. 612, H Ct (Ont) 11.08
R. v Commissioner of Police of the Metropolis Ex p. Hart-Leverton [1990] C.O.D. 240, Q.B.D. 11.101
R. v Coventry Magistrates Court Ex p. Perks [1985] R.T.R. 74, DC 10.11
R. v Cox (Richard Cobden); R. v Railton (Richard Johnson) (1884–85) L.R. 14 Q.B.D. 153; [1881–85] All E.R. Rep. 68, Crown Cases Reserved 11.10, 11.67, 11.68, 11.71
R. v Craig [1975] 1 N.Z.L.R. 597 .... 11.65
R. v Manchester Crown Court Ex p. R (Legal Professional Privilege) [1999] 1 W.L.R. 832; [1999] 4 All E.R. 35; [1999] 2 Cr. App. R. 267; [1999] Crim. L.R. 743; (1999) 96(10) L.S.G. 31, Q.B.D. 11.05
R. v Crown Court at Manchester Ex p. Rogers. *See* R. v Manchester Crown Court Ex p. R (Legal Professional Privilege)
R. v Crown Prosecution Service Ex p. J. *See* R. v DPP Ex p. J
R. v Dadson (Peter Ernest) (1983) 77 Cr. App. R. 91; [1983] Crim. L.R. 540, CA (Crim Div) 10.40
R. v Davies (Keith) [2002] EWCA Crim 85; (2002) 166 J.P. 243; (2002) 166 J.P.N. 311; (2002) 99(10) L.S.G. 28; (2002) 146 S.J.L.B. 42, CA (Crim Div) 11.48, 12.22, 12.24, 18.16
R. v Davis (Michael George) (No.1); R. v Rowe (Raphael George) (No.1); R. v Johnson (Randolph Egbert) (No.1) [1993] 1 W.L.R. 613; [1993] 2 All E.R. 643; (1993) 97 Cr. App. R. 110; (1993) 137 S.J.L.B. 19, CA (Crim Div) 11.82
R. v Davis (Michael George) (No.2) R. v Rowe (Raphael George) (No.2); R. v Johnson (Randolph Egbert) (No.2), *The Times*, April 24, 2000, CA (Crim Div) 11.90
R. v Davis (Michael George) (No.3); R. v Rowe (Raphael George) (No.3); R. v Johnson (Randolph Egbert) (No.3) [2001] 1 Cr. App. R. 8; [2000] H.R.L.R. 527; [2000] U.K.H.R.R. 683; [2000] Crim. L.R. 1012, CA (Crim Div) 21.02
R. v Daye (Arthur John) [1908] 2 K.B. 333, KBD 5.03, 10.15, 10.34
R. v DCT, Ex p. Briggs (1987) 71 A.L.R. 86 .... 11.106
R. v Derby Magistrates Court Ex p. B [1996] A.C. 487; [1995] 3 W.L.R. 681; [1995] 4 All E.R. 526; [1996] 1 Cr. App. R. 385; (1995) 159 J.P. 785; [1996] 1 F.L.R. 513; [1996] Fam. Law 210; (1995) 159 J.P.N. 778; (1995) 145 N.L.J. 1575; [1995] 139 S.J.L.B. 219, HL .. 11.05, 11.08, 11.06, 11.65, 11.91, 12.04

R. v Director of the Serious Fraud Office Ex p. Smith; sub nom. Smith v Director of the Serious Fraud Office [1993] A.C. 1; [1992] 3 W.L.R. 66; [1992] 3 All E.R. 456; [1992] B.C.L.C. 879; (1992) 95 Cr. App. R. 191; [1992] Crim. L.R. 504; [1992] C.O.D. 270; (1992) 89(27) L.S.G. 34; (1992) 142 N.L.J. 895; (1992) 136 S.J.L.B. 182, HL 11.114
R. v Doubtfire [2001] 2 Cr. App. R. 209, CA (Crim Div) 11.94
R. v DPP Ex p. J; sub nom. R. v X Justices Ex p. J; R. v Crown Prosecution Service Ex p. J [2000] 1 W.L.R. 1215; [2000] 1 All E.R. 183), Q.B.D. ... 11.101
R. v DTT Exp. Briggs (1987) 71 A.L.R. 86 .... 16.85
R. v Dunbar and Logan (1983) 138 D.L.R. 21, CA (Ontario) 11.65
R. v Dunwoody (2005) 212 A.L.R. 103, Sup Ct (Queensland) 11.77
R. v Ealing BC Ex p. PG. *See* R. (on the application of G) v Ealing LBC (No.2)
R. v Ely Justices Ex p. Burgess (1993) 157 J.P. 484; [1992] Crim. L.R. 888; [1993] C.O.D. 21; (1993) 157 J.P.N. 189; (1992) 89(34) L.S.G. 34; (1992) 136 S.J.L.B. 244, DC 19.13
R. v Epsom Justices Ex p. Bell; sub nom. Bell, Re; R. v Epsom Magistrates Court Ex p. Bell [1989] S.T.C. 169; [1988] Crim. L.R. 684; (1988) 138 N.L.J. Rep. 165, Q.B.D. 20.79
R. v Fergus (Ivan) (1994) 98 Cr. App. R. 313; (1993) 157 J.P.N. 699, CA (Crim Div) 11.101
R. v First Lord of the Treasury Ex p. Petch, unreported January 31, 1994 ...... 11.78, 11.124
R. v First Lord of the Treasury Ex p. Petch, unreported, December 6, 1993 ... 4.06
R. v First Lord of the Treasury Ex p. Petch, unreported, January 31, 1994 .... 6.49, 12.17, 12.35
R. v G; R. v B [2004] EWCA Crim 1368; [2004] 1 W.L.R. 2932; [2004] 2 Cr. App. R. 37; (2004) 101(25) L.S.G. 27; (2004) 148 S.J.L.B. 696, CA (Crim Div) 6.26
R. v G; R. v B [2004] EWCA Crim 1368; [2004] 1 W.L.R. 2932; [2004] 2 Cr. App. R. 37; (2004) 101(25) L.S.G. 27; (2004) 148 S.J.L.B. 696, CA (Crim Div) 12.42, 15.58
R. v Gibbins (Martin) [2004] EWCA Crim 311, CA (Crim Div) 11.69
R. v Gilmore [1961] N.Z.L.R. 384 .... **10.27**
R. v Gordon (1999) 136 C.C.C. (3d) 64, Ct (Ontario) 11.103
R. v Governor of Brixton Prison Ex p. Osman (No.1); sub nom. R. v Governor of Pentonville Prison Ex p. Osman (No.4) [1991] 1 W.L.R. 281; [1992] 1 All E.R. 108; (1991) 93 Cr. App. R. 202; [1991] Crim. L.R. 533, DC 11.82, 11.87
R. v Governor of Pentonville Prison Ex p. Osman (No.1); sub nom. Osman (No.1), Re [1990] 1 W.L.R. 277; [1989] 3 All E.R. 701; (1990) 90 Cr. App. R. 281; [1988] Crim. L.R. 611; (1990) 87(7) L.S.G. 32; (1990) 134 S.J. 458, Q.B.D. 11.71
R. v Governor of Pentonville Prison Ex p. Osman (No.2); sub nom. Osman (No.2), Re [1989] C.O.D. 446; (1989) 86(7) L.S.G. 36; (1989) 133 S.J. 121, DC 4.07
R. v Gray (1992) 74 C.C.C. (3d.) 267, Sup Ct (BC) 11.08, 11.65
R. v Griffin [2001] 3 N.Z.L.R. 577, CA (NZ) 18.12
R. v Grossman (Joseph Henry) (1981) 73 Cr. App. R. 302; [1981] Crim. L.R. 396, CA (Civ Div) 10.09, 10.43, 10.44, 10.47, 10.48, 10.49, 10.51
R. v Guildhall Magistrates' Court Ex p. Primlaks Holdings Co (Panama) Inc [1990] 1 Q.B. 261; [1989] 2 W.L.R. 841; (1989) 89 Cr. App. R. 215; [1989] Crim. L.R. 448; [1989] C.O.D. 359; (1989) 133 S.J. 628, DC 11.68

R. v H; R. v C [2004] UKHL 3; [2004] 2 A.C. 134; [2004] 2 W.L.R. 335; [2004] 1 All E.R. 1269; [2004] 2 Cr. App. R. 10; [2004] H.R.L.R. 20; 16 B.H.R.C. 332; (2004) 101(8) L.S.G. 29; (2004) 148 S.J.L.B. 183, HL 11.82, 11.94
R. v Hallett [1986] Crim. L.R. 462, CA (Crim Div) 11.103
R. v Harz and Power. *See* Customs and Excise Commissioners v Harz
R. v Hay (1860 2 F. & F. 4 .... 11.153
R. v Hennessey (Timothy John); R. v Shaheen (Henry Maxamillion); R. v Alkassar (Moonzar); R. v Szarowicz (Michael Henry); R. v McDermott (John Wilfred) (1979) 68 Cr. App. R. 419, CA (Crim Div) 11.103
R. v Herefordshire Justices (1820) 3 B. & Ald. 581 .... 10.43
R. v Hertfordshire CC Ex p. Green Environmental Industries Ltd; sub nom. Green Environmental Industries Ltd, Re; Green Environmental Industries Ltd v Hertfordshire CC [2000] 2 A.C. 412; [2000] 2 W.L.R. 373; [2000] 1 All E.R. 773; [2000] Eu. L.R. 414; [2000] Env. L.R. 426; [2000] E.H.L.R. 199; [2000] H.R.L.R. 359; [2000] U.K.H.R.R. 361; (2000) 2 L.G.L.R. 754; [2000] B.L.G.R. 215; [2000] 1 P.L.R. 108; [2000] C.O.D. 223; [2000] E.G.C.S. 27; (2000) 97(9) L.S.G. 42; (2000) 150 N.L.J. 277; [2000] N.P.C. 15, HL 11.105, 11.1112, 11.118, 11.119, 21.02, 21.05, 21.07
R. v Hewitt (Peter); R. v Davis (Reginald Anthony) (1992) 95 Cr. App. R. 81; [1992] Crim. L.R. 650; (1992) 142 N.L.J. 160, CA (Crim Div) 11.103
R. v Highbury Corner Magistrates Ex p. Watkins [1992] R.A. 300, Q.B.D. 11.105
R. v HM Coroner for Hammersmith Ex p. Peach; sub nom. R. v Hammersmith Coroner Ex p. Peach; Peach v Burton; Peach (Clement Blair), Re [1980] Q.B. 211; [1980] 2 W.L.R. 496; [1980] 2 All E.R. 7; 124 S.J. 17, CA (Civ Div) 20.19
R. v HM Coroner for Lincoln Ex p. Hay; sub nom. R. v HM Coroner for Lincolnshire Ex p. Hay (1999) 163 J.P. 666; [2000] Lloyd's Rep. Med. 264; [1999] C.O.D. 192, Q.B.D. 2.27, 11.104, 12.37, 12.38, 20.19
R. v HM Coroner for South London Ex p. Thompson, *The Times*, July 9, 1982, CA (Civ Div) 2.06
R. v HM Coroner for Southwark Ex p. Hicks [1987] 1 W.L.R. 1624; [1987] 2 All E.R. 140; (1987) 151 J.P. 441; (1987) 131 S.J. 1590, Q.B.D. 20.18
R. v Home Secretary, Ex p. Daly. *See* R. (on the application of Daly) v Secretary of State for the Home Department
R. v Horseferry Road Magistrates Court Ex p. Bennett (No.2) [1994] 1 All E.R. 289; (1994) 99 Cr. App. R. 123; [1994] Crim. L.R. 370, DC 11.82
R. v Horseferry Road Magistrates Court Ex p. Bennett (No.3) [1994] C.O.D. 321, Q.B.D. 10.62
R. v Horsham DC Ex p. Wenman [1995] 1 W.L.R. 680; [1994] 4 All E.R. 681; (1992) 24 H.L.R. 669; (1995) 7 Admin. L.R. 73; [1992] C.O.D. 427; (1995) 159 L.G. Rev. 365; (1993) 143 N.L.J. 1477; [1993] N.P.C. 129, Q.B.D. 11.12
R. v Hove Justices Ex p. Donne [1967] 2 All E.R. 1253 (Note); 131 J.P. 460, DC 10.33
R. v Hundal (Avtar Singh); R. v Dhaliwal (Kesar Singh) [2004] EWCA Crim 389; [2004] 2 Cr. App. R. 19; [2004] 2 Cr. App. R. (S.) 64, CA (Crim Div) 11.107
R. Immigration Adjudicator Ex p. Secretary of State for Home Office 18399; R. v Care Ex p. Secretary of State for the Home Department [1989] C.O.D. 455, Q.B.D. 20.41

R. v Inland Revenue Commissioners Ex p. Archon Shipping Corp [1998] S.T.C. 1151; 71 T.C. 203; [1998] B.T.C. 405, Q.B.D. 20.79, 20.81

R. v Inland Revenue Commissioners Ex p. Banque Internationale a Luxembourg SA [2000] S.T.C. 708; 72 T.C. 597; [2000] B.T.C. 228; [2001] A.C.D. 21; [2000] S.T.I. 919; (2000) 97(27) L.S.G. 37, Q.B.D. 20.79, 21.12, 21.13

R. v Inland Revenue Commissioners Ex p. Davis Frankel & Mead [2000] S.T.C. 595; 73 T.C. 185; [2000] B.T.C. 203; [2000] S.T.I. 887, Q.B.D. 20.81

R. v Inland Revenue Commissioners Ex p. Goldberg [1989] Q.B. 267; [1988] 3 W.L.R. 522; [1988] 3 All E.R. 248; [1988] S.T.C. 524; (1988) 138 N.L.J. Rep. 125, Q.B.D. 11.28, 11.33, 11.34, 20.79

R. v Inland Revenue Commissioners Ex p. J Rothschild Holdings [1987] S.T.C. 163, CA (Civ Div); affirming [1986] S.T.C. 410 .... 4.06

R. v Inland Revenue Commissioners Ex p. Lorimer [2000] S.T.C. 751; 73 T.C. 276; [2000] B.T.C. 257; [2000] S.T.I. 1125, Q.B.D. ... 20.79, 20.81, 20.82

R. v Inland Revenue Commissioners Ex p. Mohammed [1999] S.T.C. 129; 73 T.C. 128; [1999] B.T.C. 20, Q.B.D. 20.79

R. v Inland Revenue Commissioners Ex p. National Federation of Self Employed and Small Businesses Ltd; sub nom. Inland Revenue Commissioners v National Federation of Self Employed and Small Businesses Ltd [1982] A.C. 617; [1981] 2 W.L.R. 722; [1981] 2 All E.R. 93; [1981] S.T.C. 260; 55 T.C. 133; 125 S.J. 325, HL 11.98

R. v Inland Revenue Commissioners Ex p. Tamosius & Partners. *See* R. v Middlesex Guildhall Crown Court Ex p. Tamosius & Partners

R. v Inland Revenue Commissioners Ex p. Taylor (No.1) [1989] 1 All E.R. 906; [1988] S.T.C. 832; 62 T.C. 562; [1988] B.T.C. 451, CA (Civ Div) 4.06, 4.07, 9.08, 20.81

R. v Inland Revenue Commissioners Ex p. Taylor (No.2) [1990] 2 All E.R. 409; [1990] S.T.C. 379; 62 T.C. 578, CA (Civ Div); affirming [1989] 3 All E.R. 353; [1989] S.T.C. 600, Q.B.D. 11.41, 15.01, 12.19, 20.74, 20.78, 20.79, 20.81

R. v Inland Revenue Commissioners Ex p. TC Coombs & Co; sub nom. TC Coombs & Co v Inland Revenue Commissioners [1991] 2 A.C. 283; [1991] 2 W.L.R. 682; [1991] 3 All E.R. 623; [1991] S.T.C. 97; (1991) 3 Admin. L.R. 501; 64 T.C. 124; [1991] C.O.D. 338, HL 20.79

R. v Inland Revenue Commissioners Ex p. Ulster Bank Ltd [1997] S.T.C. 832; 69 T.C. 211; [1997] B.T.C. 314, CA (Civ Div) 20.78

R. v Inner London Crown Court Ex p. Baines & Baines (A Firm); sub nom. Inner London Crown Court Ex p. White (Anthony Michael) [1988] Q.B. 579; [1988] 2 W.L.R. 549; [1987] 3 All E.R. 1025; (1988) 87 Cr. App. R. 111; [1988] Crim. L.R. 50; (1987) 137 N.L.J. 945; (1988) 132 S.J. 418, DC 11.12

R. v Institute of Chartered Accountants in England and Wales Ex p. Nawaz, Transcript: QBCOF 96/1583/D, CA (Civ Div); affirming [1997] P.N.L.R. 433; [1997] C.O.D. 111, Q.B.D. 11.120, 12.38

R. v Institute of Chartered Accountants in England and Wales Ex p. Nawaz, April 27, 1997, CA (Civ Div); affirming [1997] P.N.L.R. 433; [1997] C.O.D. 111, Q.B.D. 11.104, 11.106

R. v IRC Ex p. *See* R. (on the application of Morgan Grenfell & Co Ltd) v Special Commissioners of Income Tax

R. v Jack, unreported, April 7, 1998, CA 11.96

R. v Johnson (Kenneth) [1988] 1 W.L.R. 1377; [1989] 1 All E.R. 121; (1989) 88 Cr. App. R. 131; [1988] Crim. L.R. 831; (1989) 139 N.L.J. 643, CA (Crim Div) 11.103
R. v Johnson. *See* R. v Davis (Michael George) (No.3)
R. v K (TD) (1993) 97 Cr. App. R. 342; [1993] 2 F.L.R. 181; [1993] Crim. L.R. 281; [1993] Fam. Law 515; (1992) 136 S.J.L.B. 328, CA (Crim Div) 11.82, 11.94
R. v K [2006] EWCA Crim 724; [2006] 2 All E.R. 552 (Note); (2006) 103(16) L.S.G. 24, CA (Crim Div) 2.05
R. v Kansal (Yash Pal) (Change of Law); sub nom. R. v Kansal (Yash Pal) (No.2) [2001] UKHL 62; [2002] 2 A.C. 69; [2001] 3 W.L.R. 1562; [2002] 1 All E.R. 257; [2002] 1 Cr. App. R. 36; [2002] H.R.L.R. 9; [2002] U.K.H.R.R. 169; [2002] B.P.I.R. 370; [2002] Crim. L.R. 498; (2002) 99(3) L.S.G. 25; (2001) 145 S.J.L.B. 275, HL 11.113
R. v Keane (Stephen John) [1994] 1 W.L.R. 746; [1994] 2 All E.R. 478; (1994) 99 Cr. App. R. 1; [1995] Crim. L.R. 225; (1994) 144 N.L.J. 391; (1994) 138 S.J.L.B. 75, CA (Crim Div) 2.05, 11.82, 11.103
R. v Kearns (Nicholas Gary) [2002] EWCA Crim 748; [2002] 1 W.L.R. 2815; [2003] 1 Cr. App. R. 7; [2002] B.P.I.R. 1213; [2002] Crim. L.R. 653; (2002) 99(19) L.S.G. 29; (2002) 146 S.J.L.B. 101, CA (Crim Div) 11.107, 11.113, 11.118, 21.07
R. v King (David Andrew) [1983] 1 W.L.R. 411; [1983] 1 All E.R. 929; (1983) 77 Cr. App. R. 1; (1983) 147 J.P. 65; [1983] Crim. L.R. 326, CA (Crim Div) 11.48
R. v Kinghorn [1908] 2 K.B. 949, KBD 10.43
R. v Lancashire CC Ex p. Huddleston [1986] 2 All E.R. 941; (1986) 136 N.L.J. 562, CA (Civ Div) 4.06
R. v Law Society Ex p. Rosen (Arnold), *Independent*, February 19, 1990 (C.S), Q.B.D. 11.14, 11.38
R. v Lewes Justices Exp. Secretary of State for Home Department. *See* Rogers v Secretary of State for the Home Department
R. v Liverpool City Council Ex p. Horn [1997] P.N.L.R. 95, Q.B.D. ... 14.05, 14.16, 16.104
R. v Local Authority in the Midlands Ex p. LM [2000] 1 F.L.R. 612; [2000] 1 F.C.R. 736; [2000] U.K.H.R.R. 143; (2000) 2 L.G.L.R. 1043; [2000] C.O.D. 41; [2000] Fam. Law 83, Q.B.D. 4.04
R. v Long (Dennis John) [1960] 1 Q.B. 681; [1959] 3 W.L.R. 953; [1959] 3 All E.R. 559; (1960) 44 Cr. App. R. 9; 124 J.P. 4; 103 S.J. 922, CCA 10.43
R. v Loveridge (William); R. v Lee (Charles Sonny); R. v Loveridge (Christine) [2001] EWCA Crim 973; [2001] 2 Cr. App. R. 29; (2001) 98(23) L.S.G. 36; (2001) 145 S.J.L.B. 120, CA (Crim Div) 21.11
R. v Lyons (Isidore Jack) (No.3); R. v Parnes (Anthony Keith) (No.3); R. v Ronson (Gerald Maurice) (No.3); R. v Saunders (Ernest Walter) (No.3) [2002] UKHL 44; [2003] 1 A.C. 976; [2002] 3 W.L.R. 1562; [2002] 4 All E.R. 1028; [2002] B.C.C. 968; [2003] 1 Cr. App. R. 24; [2003] H.R.L.R. 6; [2003] Crim. L.R. 623; (2002) 146 S.J.L.B. 264, HL 11.113
R. v M (Wasted Costs Order) [1996] 1 F.L.R. 750; [1997] 1 F.C.R. 42; [1996] Fam. Law 350; (1997) 161 J.P.N. 40, Q.B.D. 10.30, 10.35
R. v M (Wasted Costs Order) [1996] 1 F.L.R. 750 .... 14.16
R. v Macdonald (Inspector of Taxes) Ex p. Hutchinson & Co Ltd [1998] S.T.C. 680; [1998] B.T.C. 217, Q.B.D. 20.77, 20.79
R. v MacLeod (Calum Iain) [2001] Crim. L.R. 589, CA (Crim Div) 21.05

R. v Madan (Kanhya Lal) [1961] 2 Q.B. 1; [1961] 2 W.L.R. 231; [1961] 1 All E.R. 588; (1961) 45 Cr. App. R. 80; 125 J.P. 246; 105 S.J. 160, CCA 12.02

R. v Maguire (Anne Rita); R. v Smyth (William John); R. v Maguire (Vincent John); R. v Maguire (Patrick Joseph); R. v O'Neill (Patrick Joseph); R. v Conlon (Patrick Joseph) (Deceased); R. v Maguire (Patrick Joseph Paul) [1992] Q.B. 936; [1992] 2 W.L.R. 767; [1992] 2 All E.R. 433; (1992) 94 Cr. App. R. 133, CA (Crim Div) 2.05

R. v Manchester Crown Court Ex p. Cunningham, unreported, April 19, 1991, Q.B.D. 4.06

R. v Manchester Crown Court Ex p. R (Legal Professional Privilege) [1999] 1 W.L.R. 832; [1999] 4 All E.R. 35; [1999] 2 Cr. App. R. 267; [1999] Crim. L.R. 743; (1999) 96(10) L.S.G. 31, Q.B.D. 11.09, 11.12, 11.31

R. v Manchester Crown Court Ex p. Rogers. *See* R. v Manchester Crown Court Ex p. R (Legal Professional Privilege)

R. v Marlborough Street Magistrates' Court Metropolitan Stipendiary Magistrate, exp. Simpson (1980) 70 Cr.App.R. 291 .... 10.47, 10.50

R. v Marylebone Magistrates Court Ex p. Clingham. *See* Clingham v Kensington and Chelsea RLBC

R. v McDonald (Michael Christopher) [2004] EWCA Crim 2614; (2004) 148 S.J.L.B. 1218, CA (Crim Div) 11.82

R. v Mid Glamorgan Family Health Services Ex p. Martin [1995] 1 W.L.R. 110; [1995] 1 All E.R. 356; [1995] 1 F.L.R. 282; [1995] 2 F.C.R. 578; [1995] P.I.Q.R. P103; [1994] 5 Med. L.R. 383; (1994) 91(38) L.S.G. 42; (1994) 138 S.J.L.B. 195, CA (Civ Div) 5.43, 5.52

R. v Middlesex Guildhall Crown Court Ex p. Tamosius & Partners; sub nom. R. v Inland Revenue Commissioners Ex p. Tamosius & Partners [2000] 1 W.L.R. 453; [1999] S.T.C. 1077; [1999] B.T.C. 404; [2000] Crim. L.R. 390; (1999) 96(45) L.S.G. 34; (1999) 143 S.J.L.B. 279, Q.B.D. 20.80

R. v Mills (Gary); R. v Poole (Anthony Keith) [1998] A.C. 382; [1997] 3 W.L.R. 458; [1997] 3 All E.R. 780; [1998] 1 Cr. App. R. 43; (1997) 161 J.P. 601; [1998] Crim. L.R. 64; (1997) 161 J.P.N. 858; (1997) 94(39) L.S.G. 39; (1997) 141 S.J.L.B. 211, HL 2.05

R. v Minshull Street Crown Court Ex p. Miller Gardner. *See* R. (on the application of Miller Gardner Solicitors) v Minshull Street Crown Court

R. v Mirza (Shabbir Ali); R. v Connor (Ben); R. v Rollock (Ashley Kenneth) [2004] UKHL 2; [2004] 1 A.C. 1118; [2004] 2 W.L.R. 201; [2004] 1 All E.R. 925; [2004] 2 Cr. App. R. 8; [2004] H.R.L.R. 11; 16 B.H.R.C. 279; (2004) 101(7) L.S.G. 34; (2004) 154 N.L.J. 145; (2004) 148 S.J.L.B. 117, HL 19.25

R. v Moison (2001) 141 C.C.C. (3d) 213, Q.B.D. (Alberta) 10.40, 10.42

R. v Morrisey (Ian Patrick); R. v Staines (Lorelie Marion) [1997] 2 Cr. App. R. 426; [1997] Crim. L.R. 825; (1997) 94(21) L.S.G. 32; (1997) 141 S.J.L.B. 106, CA (Crim Div) 11.119

R. v Nottingham Justices Ex p. Lynn; sub nom. R v Nottingham City Justices Ex p. Lynn (1984) 79 Cr. App. R. 238; [1984] Crim. L.R. 554, DC 10.47

R. v Nova Scotia Pharmaceutical Society (1990) 73 D.L.R. (4th) 184 .... 11.112

R. v O'Kane Ex p. Northern Bank Ltd [1996] S.T.C. 1249; 69 T.C. 187, Q.B.D. 20.79

R. v Oxford Regional Mental Health Tribunal Ex p. Secretary of State for the Home Department; sub nom. Campbell v Secretary of State for the Home Department; Secretary of State for the Home Department v Oxford Regional Mental Health Review Tribunal; R. v Yorkshire Mental Health Review Tribunal Ex p. Secretary of State for the Home Department [1988] A.C. 120; [1987] 3 W.L.R. 522, HL; affirming [1986] 1 W.L.R. 1180; [1986] 3 All E.R. 239; (1986) 83 L.S.G. 1559; (1986) 130 S.J. 505, CA (Civ Div) 20.58
R. v P. [2002] 1 A.C. 147, HL 21.10
R. v Parole Board Ex p. Bradley [1991] 1 W.L.R. 134; [1990] 3 All E.R. 828; [1990] C.O.D. 375, 1990, DC 4.06
R. v Peterborough Magistrates Court Ex p. Willis and Amos (1987) 151 J.P. 785; [1987] Crim. L.R. 692; (1987) 151 J.P.N. 542, DC 10.11
R. v PJ O'N and M O'N [2001] N.I.C.C. 5 .... 10.02
R. v R (Blood Sample: Privilege) [1994] 1 W.L.R. 758; [1994] 4 All E.R. 260; [1995] 1 Cr. App. R. 183; (1994) 138 S.J.L.B. 54, CA (Crim Div) 11.48, 12.02, 12.24
R. v R (Disclosure to Revenue); sub nom. R v R (Inland Revenue: Tax Evasion) [1998] S.T.C. 237; [1998] 1 F.L.R. 922; [1998] 1 F.C.R. 597; 70 T.C. 119; [1998] B.T.C. 53; [1998] Fam. Law 321, Fam Div 2.03
R. v Rankine (Elliston) [1986] Q.B. 861; [1986] 2 W.L.R. 1075; [1986] 2 All E.R. 566; (1986) 83 Cr. App. R. 18; [1986] Crim. L.R. 464; (1986) 130 S.J. 315, CA (Crim Div) 11.103
R. v Rathbone Ex p. Dikko; Noga Commodities (Overseas) Inc v Rijn Mass-En Zeescheepvaartkantoor NV Allied Maritime Inc [1985] Q.B. 630; [1985] 2 W.L.R. 375; (1985) 82 L.S.G. 687; (1985) 129 S.J. 85, Q.B.D. 10.63
R. v Reading Justices Ex p. Berkshire CC [1996] 1 Cr. App. R. 239; [1996] 1 F.L.R. 149; [1996] 2 F.C.R. 535; [1996] Crim. L.R. 347; [1995] C.O.D. 385; [1996] Fam. Law 84, DC 10.11, 10.33
R. v Robinson (Timothy Morgan) [2002] EWCA Crim 2489; [2003] Crim. L.R. 284; (2003) 100(2) L.S.G. 31; (2002) 146 S.J.L.B., CA (Crim Div) 21.13
R. v Rowell (Michael Charles) [1978] 1 W.L.R. 132; [1978] 1 All E.R. 665; (1977) 65 Cr. App. R. 174; [1977] Crim. L.R. 681; 121 S.J. 790, CA (Crim Div) 14.04
R. v S [2008] EWCA Crim 2177 .... 11.105, 11.108, 11.1
R. v Seaton [2010] EWCA Crim 1980 .... 12.28
R. v Saunders, unreported, January 10, 1990, CCC 11.66, 12.32
R. v Secretary of State for Defence Ex p. Sancto (1993) 5 Admin. L.R. 673; [1993] C.O.D. 144, DC 11.101
R. v Secretary of State for Education and Science Ex p. G. *See* R. v Secretary of State for Education and Science Ex p. MG
R. v Secretary of State for Education and Science Ex p. J [1993] C.O.D. 146 .... 4.06, 4.07
R. v Secretary of State for Education and Science Ex p. MG [1990] C.O.D. 65, DC 4.07
R. v Secretary of State for Foreign and Commonwealth Affairs Ex p. World Development Movement Ltd [1995] 1 W.L.R. 386; [1995] 1 All E.R. 611; [1995] C.O.D. 211; (1995) 145 N.L.J. 51, DC 4.06
R. v Secretary of State for Health Ex p. C, unreported, February 21, 2000, CA 21.05
R. v Secretary of State for Health Ex p. Association of Pharmaceutical Importers, unreported, November 15, 2000, Admin Ct 11.159

R. v Secretary of State for the Environment Ex p. Doncaster BC [1990] C.O.D. 441 .... 4.06, 4.07
R. v Secretary of State for the Environment Ex p. Islington LBC [1992] C.O.D. 67; [1991] N.P.C. 90, CA (Civ Div) 4.06, 4.07
R. v Secretary of State for the Environment Ex p. Merton LBC (No.1), *The Times*, March 22, 1990, Q.B.D. 4.06
R. v Secretary of State for the Environment Ex p. Powis [1981] 1 W.L.R. 584; [1981] 1 All E.R. 788; 79 L.G.R. 318; (1981) 42 P. & C.R. 73; (1980) 258 E.G. 57; [1981] J.P.L. 270; 125 S.J. 324, CA (Civ Div) 4.06
R. v Secretary of State for the Environment Ex p. Smith [1988] C.O.D. 3 .... 4.06
R. v Secretary of State for the Home Department Ex p. Al-Fayed (No.1) [1998] 1 W.L.R. 763; [1997] 1 All E.R. 228; [1997] I.N.L.R. 137; [1997] C.O.D. 205, CA (Civ Div) 4.06
R. v Secretary of State for the Home Department Ex p. Belgium, unreported, February 15, 2000, DC 21.10
R. v Secretary of State for the Home Department Ex p. Benson [1989] C.O.D. 329, Q.B.D. 4.06, 11.99
R. v Secretary of State for the Home Department Ex p. Doody; R. v Secretary of State for the Home Department Ex p. Pierson; R. v Secretary of State for the Home Department Ex p. Smart; R. v Secretary of State for the Home Department Ex p. Pegg [1994] 1 A.C. 531; [1993] 3 W.L.R. 154; [1993] 3 All E.R. 92; (1995) 7 Admin. L.R. 1; (1993) 143 N.L.J. 991, HL 11.99
R. v Secretary of State for the Home Department Ex p. Duggan [1994] 3 All E.R. 277; [1994] C.O.D. 258, DC 11.98, 11.99
R. v Secretary of State for the Home Department Ex p. Fininvest SpA [1997] 1 W.L.R. 743; [1997] 1 All E.R. 942; [1995] 2 B.C.L.C. 585; [1997] 1 Cr. App. R. 257; [1997] Crim. L.R. 213; [1997] C.O.D. 94, DC 10.54
R. v Secretary of State for the Home Department Ex p. Fulop (Imre); sub nom. Fulop v Secretary of State for the Home Department [1995] Imm. A.R. 323, CA (Civ Div) 20.42
R. v Secretary of State for the Home Department Ex p. Gardian [1996] Imm. A.R. 6; [1996] C.O.D. 306, CA (Civ Div) 2.53, 4.06, 20.41
R. v Secretary of State for the Home Department Ex p. Harrison, *Independent*, December 21, 1987, CA 4.06
R. v Secretary of State for the Home Department Ex p. Leech (No.2) [1994] Q.B. 198; [1993] 3 W.L.R. 1125; [1993] 4 All E.R. 539; (1993) 137 S.J.L.B. 173, CA (Civ Div) 21.13
R. v Secretary of State for the Home Department Ex p. McAvoy [1998] 1 W.L.R. 790; [1998] C.O.D. 148; (1998) 95(1) L.S.G. 23; (1998) 142 S.J.L.B. 39, CA (Civ Div) 11.99
R. v Secretary of State for the Home Department Ex p. Simms; sub nom. R. v Secretary of State for the Home Department Ex p. Main; R. v Secretary of State for the Home Department Ex p. O'Brien; R. v Governor of Whitemoor Prison Ex p. Main [2000] 2 A.C. 115; [1999] 3 W.L.R. 328, HL; reversing [1999] Q.B. 349; [1998] 3 W.L.R. 1169; [1998] 2 All E.R. 491; [1998] E.M.L.R. 431; (1998) 95(1) L.S.G. 23; (1998) 142 S.J.L.B. 38, CA (Civ Div) 21.13
R. v Secretary of State for the Home Department Ex p. Singh (Roj) [1992] Imm. A.R. 607 .... 20.42
R. v Secretary of State for the Home Department Ex p. Singh Sunder, *See* R. (on the application of Sunder (Manjit Singh)) v Secretary of State for the Home Department

R. v Secretary of State for the Home Department Ex p. Singh, *The Times*, March 28, 1988 *Independent*, April 11, 1988 (C.S.), CA (Civ Div) ... 4.06, 4.07
R. Secretary of State for the Home Department Ex p. Abdi (Khalif Mohamed); R. v Secretary of State for the Home Department Ex p. Gawe (Abdifatah Abduleh) [1996] 1 W.L.R. 298; [1996] 1 All E.R. 641, HL; affirming [1994] Imm. A.R. 402; [1995] C.O.D. 73, CA (Civ Div) 20.42
R. v Secretary of State for Trade and Industry Ex p. McCormick [1998] B.C.C. 379; [1998] C.O.D. 160; (1998) 95(10) L.S.G. 27, CA (Civ Div) 11.105, 11.119
R. v Secretary of State for Transport Ex p. Factortame Ltd (Discovery) (1997) 9 Admin. L.R. 591; [1997] C.O.D. 432; (1997) 94(22) L.S.G. 31, Q.B.D. 12.22, 12.23, 12.36
R. v Seelig (Roger Hugh); R. v Baron Spens; R v Rex (Patrick Michael) [1992] 1 W.L.R. 148; [1991] 4 All E.R. 429; [1991] B.C.C. 569; [1991] B.C.L.C. 869; (1992) 94 Cr. App. R. 17; (1991) 141 N.L.J. 638, CA (Crim Div) 11.113
R. v Shannon (John James); sub nom. R. v Alford (John James) [2001] 1 W.L.R. 51; [2001] 1 Cr. App. R. 12; [2000] Crim. L.R. 1001; (2000) 97(40) L.S.G. 41; (2000) 144 S.J.L.B. 257, CA (Crim Div) 11.103
R. v Shayler (David Michael) [2002] UKHL 11; [2003] 1 A.C. 247; [2002] 2 W.L.R. 754; [2002] 2 All E.R. 477; [2002] H.R.L.R. 33; [2002] U.K.H.R.R. 603; [2002] A.C.D. 58; (2002) 99(17) L.S.G. 34; (2002) 146 S.J.L.B. 84, HL 21.15
R. v Shirose (1999) 171 D.L.R. (4th) 193, SCC 12.04
R. v Skegness Magistrates Court Ex p. Cardy; R. v Manchester Crown Court Ex p. Williams [1985] R.T.R. 49; [1985] Crim. L.R. 237; (1985) 82 L.S.G. 929, DC 10.11, 10.23
R. v Skingley (Gordon); R. v Burrett (Brian), unreported, December 17, 1999, CA (Crim Div) 12.08, 12.32
R. v Smith (Joe) [2001] 1 W.L.R. 1031; [2001] 2 Cr. App. R. 1, CA (Crim Div) 11.94, 21.06
R. v Smith (Patrick); R. v Mercieca (Joseph) [2005] UKHL 12; [2005] 1 W.L.R. 704; [2005] 2 All E.R. 29; [2005] 2 Cr. App. R. 10; [2005] Crim. L.R. 476, HL 19.25
R. v Snaresbrook Crown Court Ex p. DPP [1988] Q.B. 532; [1987] 3 W.L.R. 1054; [1988] 1 All E.R. 315; (1988) 86 Cr. App. R. 227; [1987] Crim. L.R. 824; (1987) 131 S.J. 1487, Q.B.D. 11.45, 11.71
R. v Spens (No.1); sub nom. R. v Lord Spens; R v Rex (Patrick Michael); R v Baron Spens [1991] 1 W.L.R. 624; [1991] 4 All E.R. 421; [1991] B.C.C. 140; (1991) 93 Cr. App. R. 194, CA (Crim Div) 5.22
R. v Staines and Morrisey. *See* R. v Morrisey (Ian Patrick); R. v Staines (Lorelie Marion)
R. v Strawbridge [2003] 1 N.Z.L.R. 683, CA (NZ) 11.103
R. v Stuart (1886) 2 T.L.R. 244 .... 10.08, 10.34
R. v Stubbs (Alan David) [1982] 1 W.L.R. 509; [1982] 1 All E.R. 424; (1982) 74 Cr. App. R. 246; [1981] Crim. L.R. 701; 126 S.J. 227, CA (Crim Div) 11.143
R. v Tompkins (George Edward) (1978) 67 Cr. App. R. 181; [1978] Crim. L.R. 290, CA (Crim Div) 11.66
R. v Trutch (Stephen Anthony); R. v Trutch (Jeanne Mary) [2001] EWCA Crim 1750, CA (Crim Div) 11.61, 11.62
R. v Trutch. *See* R. v Trutch (Stephen Anthony)

R. v Turner (Paul David) [1995] 1 W.L.R. 264; [1995] 3 All E.R. 432; [1995] 2 Cr. App. R. 94, CA (Crim Div) 11.103
R. v Uljee [1982] 1 N.Z.L.R. 561, CA (NZ) 11.09, 11.66
R. v Umoh (Mfongbong) (1987) 84 Cr. App. R. 138; [1987] Crim. L.R. 258, CA (Crim Div) 11.99, 11.143, 11.153
R. v Vreones [1891] 1 Q.B. 360, Crown Cases Reserved 14.04
R. v W, *The Times*, July 12, 1996, CA 10.11, 10.32
R. v Ward (Judith Theresa) [1993] 1 W.L.R. 619; [1993] 2 All E.R. 577; (1993) 96 Cr. App. R. 1; [1993] Crim. L.R. 312; (1992) 89(27) L.S.G. 34; (1992) 142 N.L.J. 859; (1992) 136 S.J.L.B. 191, CA (Crim Div) 11.82
R. v Ward (Judith Theresa) [1993] 1 W.L.R. 619; [1993] 2 All E.R. 577; (1993) 96 Cr. App. R. 1; [1993] Crim. L.R. 312; (1992) 89(27) L.S.G. 34; (1992) 142 N.L.J. 859; (1992) 136 S.J.L.B. 191, CA (Crim Div) 2.05
R. v Wijesinha (1995) 127 D.L.R. (4th), SCC 11.69
R. v Wishart (Simon); R. v Boutcher (Todd) [2005] EWCA Crim 1337, CA (Crim Div) 12.29
R. v. Robertson Ex p. McAuley (1983) 71 Fed. L.R. 429 .... 11.83
R. (A Child), Re [2004] EWHC 2085, Fam Div 3.35, 3.39
R. (A Minor) (Blood Tests: Constraint), Re [1998] Fam. 66; [1998] 2 W.L.R. 796; [1998] 1 F.L.R. 745; [1998] 1 F.C.R. 41; [1998] Fam. Law 256, Fam Div 19.20
R. (Al-Hasan) v Home Secretary. *See* R. (on the application of Carroll) v Secretary of State for the Home Department
R. (Bennett) v Inner South London Coroner. *See* R. (on the application of A) v HM Coroner for Inner South London
R. (Bentley) v Avon Coroner. *See* R. (on the application of Bentley) v HM Coroner for Avon
R. (Bright) v Central Criminal Court. *See* R. v Central Criminal Court Ex p. Bright
R. (Cannan) v Governor of Full Sutton Prison. *See* R. (on the application of Cannan) v Full Sutton Prison Governor
R. (Carson) v Secretary of State fro Work and Pensions. *See* R. (on the application of Carson) v Secretary of State for Work and Pensions
R. (Children) (Application for Disclosure), Re [2003] EWCA Civ 19; [2003] 1 F.C.R. 193, CA (Civ Div) 4.04
R. (Daly) v Secretary of State for the Home Department. *See* R. (on the application of Daly) v Secretary of State for the Home Department
R. (DPP) v Acton Youth Court. *See* R. (on the application of DPP) v Acton Youth Court
R. (Factortame Ltd) v Transport Secretary (No.8). *See* Factortame Ltd v Secretary of State for the Environment, Transport and the Regions (Costs) (No.2)
R. (Fleurose) v Financial Services Authority. *See* R. (on the application of Fleurose) v Securities and Futures Authority Ltd
R. (Green) v Police Complaints Authority. *See* R. (on the application of Green) v Police Complaints Authority
R. (H) v IRC. *See* R. (on the application of H) v Inland Revenue Commissioners
R. (Howe) v South Durham Magistrates Court. *See* R. (on the application of Howe) v South Durham Magistrates Court

R. (Hussain) v Asylum Support Adjudicator. *See* R. (on the application of Husain) v Asylum Support Adjudicator

R. (Kent Pharmaceuticals) v Director of the Serious Fraud Office. *See* R. (on the application of Kent Pharmaceuticals Ltd) v Director of the Serious Fraud Office

R. (Lord) v Secretary of State for the Home Department. *See* R. (on the application of Lord) v Secretary of State for the Home Department

R. (Ministry of Defence) v Wiltshire and Swindon Coroner. *See* R. (on the application of the Ministry of Defence) v Wiltshire and Swindon Coroner

R. (MJ) (A Minor) (Publication of Transcript), Re; sub nom. R (MJ) (An Infant) (Proceedings: Transcripts: Publication), Re [1975] Fam. 89; [1975] 2 W.L.R. 978; [1975] 2 All E.R. 749; (1975) 5 Fam. Law 154; 119 S.J. 338, Fam Div 4.04

R. (Murat) v IRC. *See* Murat v Inland Revenue Commissioners

R. (on the application of A) v HM Coroner for Inner South London; sub nom. A v Inner South London Coroner; Bennett v A [2004] EWCA Civ 1439; [2005] U.K.H.R.R. 44; (2004) 148 S.J.L.B. 1315, CA (Civ Div) 11.101, 21.04, 21.07

R. (on the application of Abacha) v Secretary of State for the Home Department (No.2); R. (on the application of Bagudu) v Secretary of State for the Home Department [2001] EWHC Admin 787, DC 10.54

R. (on the application of Al-Sweady) v Secretary of State for Defence [2009] EWHC 2387 (Admin); [2010] H.R.L.R. 2; [2010] U.K.H.R.R. 300 ...... 4.06, 11.89, 13.37, 14.03, 14.09

R. (on the application of Bentley) v HM Coroner for Avon; sub nom. R. (on the application of Bentley) v HM Coroner for the District of Avon [2001] EWHC Admin 170; (2002) 166 J.P. 297; (2003) 74 B.M.L.R. 1; [2002] A.C.D. 1; (2002) 166 J.P.N. 390 .... 20.19

R. (on the application of Binyan Mohamed) v Secretary of State for Foreign and Commonwealth Affairs [2008] EWHC 2100 (Admin) 11.84

R. (on the application of Mohamed) v Secretary of State for Foreign and Commonwealth Affairs [2008] EWHC 2519 (Admin) 11.84

R. (on the application of Mohamed) v Secretary of State for Foreign and Commonwealth Affairs [2009] EWHC 152 (Admin); [2009] 1 W.L.R. 2653; (2009) 159 N.L.J. 234 .... 11.84

R. (on the application of Mohamed) v Secretary of State for Foreign and Commonwealth Affairs [2009] EWHC 2549 (Admin); [2009] 1 W.L.R. 2653; [2010] EWCA Civ 65; [2010] 4 All E.R. 91, CA; [2010] EWCA Civ 158; [2010] 4 All E.R. 177, CA 11.84

R. (on the application of Bozkurt) v Thames Magistrates Court; sub nom. Bozkurt v Thames Magistrates Court; R. (on the application of Bozcurt) v South Thames Magistrates Court [2001] EWHC Admin 400; [2002] R.T.R. 15, DC 11.14

R. (on the application of Brooks) v Parole Board [2004] EWCA Civ 80, (2004) 148 S.J.L.B. 233 .... 10.24

R. (on the application of Cannan) v Full Sutton Prison Governor; sub nom. Cannan v Secretary of State for the Home Department; Cannan v Governor of HMP Sutton [2003] EWCA Civ 1480, CA (Civ Div); reversing [2003] EWHC 98, Q.B.D. (Admin) 21.13

R. (on the application of Carroll) v Secretary of State for the Home Department; sub nom. R. v Secretary of State for the Home Department Ex p. Carroll; R. (on the application of Greenfield) v Secretary of State for the Home Department; R. (on the application of Al-Hasan) v Secretary of State for the Home Department [2005] UKHL 13; [2005] 1 W.L.R. 688, HL; reversing [2001] EWCA Civ 1224; [2002] 1 W.L.R. 545; [2001] H.R.L.R. 58 .... 21.05

R. (on the application of Carson) v Secretary of State for Work and Pensions; sub nom. Carson v Secretary of State for Work and Pensions; R. (on the application of Reynolds) v Secretary of State for Work and Pensions [2005] UKHL 37; [2006] 1 A.C. 173; [2005] 2 W.L.R. 1369; [2005] 4 All E.R. 545; [2005] H.R.L.R. 23; [2005] U.K.H.R.R. 1185; 18 B.H.R.C. 677 .... 21.18

R. (on the application of Corner House Research) v BAE Systems. *See* R. (on the application of Corner House Research) v Director of the Serious Fraud Office

R. (on the application of Corner House Research) v Director of the Serious Fraud Office; sub nom. R. (on the application of Corner House Research) v BAE Systems Plc [2008] EWHC 246 (Admin); [2008] C.P. Rep. 20; [2008] A.C.D. 63 .... 3.45

R. (on the application of Daly) v Secretary of State for the Home Department; sub nom. R. v Secretary of State for the Home Department Ex p. Daly [2001] UKHL 26; [2001] 2 A.C. 532; [2001] 2 W.L.R. 1622; [2001] 3 All E.R. 433; [2001] H.R.L.R. 49; [2001] U.K.H.R.R. 887; [2001] A.C.D. 79; (2001) 98(26) L.S.G. 43; (2001) 145 S.J.L.B. 156 ...... 21.12, 21.13

R. (on the application of DPP) v Acton Youth Court; sub nom. R. (on the application of Crown Prosecution Service) v Acton Youth Court; R. v Acton Youth Court Ex p. CPS [2001] EWHC Admin 402; [2001] 1 W.L.R. 1828; (2001) 165 J.P.N. 606; (2001) 98(26) L.S.G. 43; (2001) 145 S.J.L.B. 155, DC 11.82

R. (on the application of Energy Financing Team Ltd) v Bow Street Magistrates Court; sub nom. Energy Financing Team Ltd v Director of the Serious Fraud Office [2005] EWHC 1626; [2006] 1 W.L.R. 1316; [2005] 4 All E.R. 285; [2006] A.C.D. 8, Q.B.D. (Admin) 10.54

R. (on the application of Evans) v Director of the Serious Fraud Office; sub nom. Evans (Michael) v Inspector of the Serious Fraud Office [2002] EWHC 2304; [2003] 1 W.L.R. 299; (2002) 99(45) L.S.G. 34, Q.B.D. (Admin) 10.54

R. (on the application of Amro International SA) v Financial Services Authority [2010] EWCA Civ 123; [2010] Bus. L.R. 1541; [2010] 3 All E.R. 723; [2010] 2 B.C.L.C. 40; (2010) 107(10) L.S.G. 17 ...... 10.10, 10.57

R. (on the application of Fleurose) v Securities and Futures Authority Ltd; sub nom. R. v Securities & Futures Authority Ltd Ex p. Fleurose; Fleurose v Disciplinary Appeal Tribunal of the Securities & Futures Authority Ltd; R. (on the application of Fleurose) v Financial Services Authority [2001] EWCA Civ 2015; [2002] I.R.L.R. 297 .... 21.05

R. (on the application of G) v Ealing LBC (No.2); sub nom. R. (on the application of PG) v Ealing LBC [2002] EWHC 250; [2002] A.C.D. 48; (2002) 99(17) L.S.G. 37; (2002) 146 S.J.L.B. 68; (2002) 146 S.J.L.B. 209, Q.B.D. (Admin) 17.26

R. (on the application of Green) v Police Complaints Authority [2004] UKHL 6; [2004] 1 W.L.R. 725; [2004] 2 All E.R. 209; [2004] H.R.L.R. 19; [2004] U.K.H.R.R. 939; (2004) 101(12) L.S.G. 36; (2004) 148 S.J.L.B. 268 .... 11.100

R. (on the application of H) v Inland Revenue Commissioners [2002] EWHC 2164; [2002] S.T.C. 1354; 75 T.C. 377; [2002] B.T.C. 459; [2002] S.T.I. 1395; (2002) 99(46) L.S.G. 34, Q.B.D. (Admin) 11.12

R. (on the application of Hafner) v Secretary of State for the Home Department; sub nom. Hafner v Secretary of State for the Home Department [2006] EWHC 1259 (Admin); [2007] 1 W.L.R. 950; [2006] 3 All E.R. 382; [2008] Lloyd's Rep. FC 376 .... 10.54

R. (on the application of Hafner) v Westminster Magistrates' Court [2008] EWHC 524 (Admin); [2009] 1 W.L.R. 1005; [2009] Bus. L.R. 489; [2008] Lloyd's Rep. F.C. 376 .... 10.54

R. (on the application of Hallinan Blackburn-Gittings & Nott (A Firm)) v Middlesex Guildhall Crown Court [2004] EWHC 2726; [2005] 1 W.L.R. 766, Q.B.D. (Admin) 11.68, 11.69

R. (on the application of Howe) v South Durham Magistrates Court [2004] EWHC 362; (2004) 168 J.P. 424; [2005] R.T.R. 4; (2004) 168 J.P.N. 637, Q.B.D. (Admin) 11.12, 11.13

R. (on the application of Hurst) v HM Coroner for Northern District London; sub nom. Commissioner of Police of the Metropolis v Hurst; R. (on the application of Hurst) v Northern District of London Coroner [2005] EWCA Civ 890; [2005] 1 W.L.R. 3892; [2005] H.R.L.R. 31; [2005] U.K.H.R.R. 1259; [2006] A.C.D. 20; (2005) 102(31) L.S.G. 27; (2005) 155 N.L.J. 1207 .... 21.01

R. (on the application of Husain) v Asylum Support Adjudicator [2001] EWHC Admin 852; [2002] A.C.D. 10 .... 21.05

R. (on the application of Kelly) v Warley Magistrates' Court [2007] EWHC 1836 (Admin); [2008] 1 Cr. App. R. 14; [2008] 1 W.L.R. 2001; (2007) 171 J.P. 585; [2008] Crim. L.R. 643; [2007] A.C.D. 89; (2008) 172 J.P.N. 83; (2007) 157 N.L.J. 115 .... 11.08

R. (on the application of Kent Pharmaceuticals Ltd) v Director of the Serious Fraud Office [2004] EWCA Civ 1494; [2005] 1 W.L.R. 1302; [2005] 1 All E.R. 449; (2004) 101(48) L.S.G. 26 .... 2.05

R. (on the application of Lord) v Secretary of State for the Home Department [2003] EWHC 2073, Q.B.D. (Admin) 11.99, 11.152

R. (on the application of Malik) v Manchester Crown Court [2008] EWHC 1362 (Admin); [2008] 4 All E.R. 403; [2008] E.M.L.R. 19; [2008] U.K.H.R.R. 1151 .... 11.108

R. (on the application of Miller Gardner Solicitors) v Minshull Street Crown Court [2002] EWHC 3077, Q.B.D. 11.12, 11.31

R. (on the application of Mohamed) v Secretary of State for Foreign and Commonwealth Affairs [2008] EWHC 2048 (Admin); (2008) 105(34) L.S.G. 22 .... 3.07, 3.10, 3.11, 3.14

R. (on the application of Morgan Grenfell & Co Ltd) v Special Commissioners of Income Tax; sub nom. R. v Inland Revenue Commissioners Ex p. Morgan Grenfell & Co Ltd; R. v Special Commissioners of Income Tax Ex p. Morgan Grenfell & Co Ltd [2002] UKHL 21; [2003] 1 A.C. 563; [2002] 2 W.L.R. 1299; [2002] 3 All E.R. 1; [2002] S.T.C. 786; [2002] H.R.L.R. 42; 74 T.C. 511; [2002] B.T.C. 223; 4 I.T.L. Rep. 809; [2002] S.T.I. 806; (2002) 99(25) L.S.G. 35; (2002) 146 S.J.L.B. 126; [2002] N.P.C. 70 ...... 11.08, 11.17, 11.77, 20.80, 20.81, 20.84, 21.13

R. (on the application of Persey) v Secretary of State for the Environment, Food and Rural Affairs; sub nom. Persey v Secretary of State for the Environment, Food and Rural Affairs; R. (on the application of Jackson) v Secretary of State for the Environment, Food and Rural Affairs; R. (on the application of Hindmarsh) v Secretary of State for the Environment, Food and Rural Affairs [2002] EWHC 371; [2003] Q.B. 794; [2002] 3 W.L.R. 704; (2002) 99(18) L.S.G. 37; (2002) 146 S.J.L.B. 92; [2002] N.P.C. 44, Q.B.D. (Admin) 21.14

R. (on the application of Prudential Plc) v Special Commissioner of Income Tax [2010] EWCA Civ 1094; [2010] 3 W.L.R. 1042; [2010] 1 All E.R. 1113; [2010] S.T.C. 161; [2009] B.T.C. 680; [2010] A.C.D. 10; [2009] S.T.I. 2770; [2009] N.P.C. 113 .... 11.21

R. (on the application of Purja) v Ministry of Defence [2003] EWCA Civ 1345; [2004] 1 W.L.R. 289; [2004] U.K.H.R.R. 309; (2003) 100(41) L.S.G. 33 .... 21.18

R. (on the application of Quark Fishing Ltd) v Secretary of State for Foreign and Commonwealth Affairs [2002] EWCA Civ 1409 .... 4.06

R. (on the application of Rosen) v Solicitors Disciplinary Tribunal [2002] EWHC 1323, CA (Crim Div) 1.33

R. (on the application of S) v Chief Constable of South Yorkshire; R. (on the application of Marper) v Chief Constable of South Yorkshire [2004] UKHL 39; [2004] 1 W.L.R. 2196; [2004] 4 All E.R. 193; [2004] H.R.L.R. 35; [2004] U.K.H.R.R. 967; [2005] Crim. L.R. 136; (2004) 101(34) L.S.G. 29; (2004) 154 N.L.J. 1183; (2004) 148 S.J.L.B. 914 ..... 21.12, 21.18

R. (on the application of Sunder (Manjit Singh)) v Secretary of State for the Home Department; sub nom. R. v Secretary of State for the Home Department Ex p. Sunder (Manjit Singh) [2001] EWHC Admin 252, Q.B.D. (Admin) 21.05

R. (on the application of the Ministry of Defence) v Wiltshire and Swindon Coroner [2005] EWHC 889; [2006] 1 W.L.R. 134; [2005] 4 All E.R. 40, Q.B.D. (Admin) 4.07, 19.24

R. (on the application of Thompson) v Law Society [2004] EWCA Civ 167; [2004] 1 W.L.R. 2522; [2004] 2 All E.R. 113; (2004) 101(13) L.S.G. 35; (2004) 154 N.L.J. 307; (2004) 148 S.J.L.B. 265 .... 21.05

R. (on the application of Van Hoogstraten) v Governor of Belmarsh Prison [2002] EWHC 1965; [2003] 1 W.L.R. 263; [2003] 4 All E.R. 309; [2003] A.C.D. 19; (2002) 99(42) L.S.G. 38; (2002) 152 N.L.J. 1531; (2002) 146 S.J.L.B. 213), Q.B.D. (Admin) 11.21

R. (on the application of Werner) v Inland Revenue Commissioners [2002] EWCA Civ 979; [2002] S.T.C. 1213; [2002] B.T.C. 319; [2002] S.T.I. 1193, CA (Civ Div) 20.79

R. (on the application of Williams) v Secretary of State for the Home Department; sub nom. Williams v Secretary of State for the Home Department [2002] EWCA Civ 498; [2002] 1 W.L.R. 2264; [2002] 4 All E.R. 872; (2002) 99(20) L.S.G. 33; (2002) 146 S.J.L.B. 108 .... 11.99

R. (Pewsey) v Secretary of State for the Environment, Food and Rural Affairs. *See* R. (on the application of Persey) v Secretary of State for the Environment, Food and Rural Affairs

R. (PM) (An Infant), Re; sub nom. R (PM) (An Infant), Re [1968] 1 W.L.R. 385; [1968] 1 All E.R. 691 (Note); 66 L.G.R. 613; 112 S.J. 189, Ch.D 19.20

R. (Purja) v Ministry of Defence. *See* R. (on the application of Purja) v Ministry of Defence

R. (Rosen) v Solicitors Disciplinary Tribunal. *See* R. (on the application of Rosen) v Solicitors Disciplinary Tribunal
R. (S) v Chief Constable of South Yorkshire Police. *See* R. (on the application of S) v Chief Constable of South Yorkshire
R. (Thompson) v Law Society. *See* R. (on the application of Thompson) v Law Society
R. (USA) v Bow Street Magistrates' Court [2006] EWHC 2256 (Admin) 4.07
R. (Van Hoogstraten) v Governor of Belmarsh Prison. *See* R. (on the application of Van Hoogstraten) v Governor of Belmarsh Prison
RC Residuals Ltd (formerly Regent Chemicals Ltd) v Linton Fuel Oils Ltd [2002] EWCA Civ 911; [2002] 1 W.L.R. 2782; [2002] C.P. Rep. 65; [2002] C.P.L.R. 579; (2002) 99(22) L.S.G. 34; (2002) 146 S.J.L.B. 117 .... 13.24
RCA Corp v Reddingtons Rare Records; sub nom. Radio Corp of America v Reddington's Rare Records [1974] 1 W.L.R. 1445; [1975] 1 All E.R. 38; [1974] F.S.R. 509; [1975] R.P.C. 95; 118 S.J. 777, Ch.D 3.23, 16.69
RHM Foods Ltd v Bovril Ltd [1982] 1 W.L.R. 661; [1982] 1 All E.R. 673; [1983] R.P.C. 275, CA (Civ Div) 2.15, 2.32, 6.51, 8.28
Rabin v Gerson Berger Association Ltd [1986] 1 W.L.R. 526; [1986] 1 All E.R. 374; (1986) 130 S.J. 15, CA (Civ Div) 5.22
Rabin v Mendoza & Co [1954] 1 W.L.R. 271; [1954] 1 All E.R. 247; 98 S.J. 92, CA 8.08, 11.122, 11.124, 11.126
Radio Corp of America (RCA) v Rauland Corp (No.2) [1956] 1 Q.B. 618; [1956] 2 W.L.R. 612; [1956] 1 All E.R. 549; 100 S.J. 172, Q.B.D. 5.30, 10.55
Radio Ten Pty Ltd v Brisbane TV Ltd [1984] Qd.R. 113 .... 5.06
Radnorshire, The (1879–80) L.R. 5 P.D. 172, PDAD 16.53, 16.54
Rafidain Bank v Agom Universal Sugar Trading Co [1987] 1 W.L.R. 1606; [1987] 3 All E.R. 859; (1987) 84 L.S.G. 3658; (1987) 131 S.J. 1591, CA (Civ Div) 9.04, 9.08
Raiffeisen Zentralbank Österreich AG v Crosseas Shipping Ltd [2003] EWHC 1381 (Comm.) 2.40
Raja v Van Hoogstraten (Application to Strike Out Order); sub nom. Raja, In the Estate of Mohammed Sabir Raja [2006] EWHC 1315; (2006) 150 S.J.L.B. 855, Ch.D 13.07
Raja v Van Hoogstraten (Application to Strike Out) [2004] EWCA Civ 968; [2004] 4 All E.R. 793; [2005] C.P. Rep. 6, CA (Civ Div) 2.15, 13.10
Rajan v General Medical Council [2000] Lloyd's Rep. Med. 153, PC (UK) ... 2.05
Rall v Hume [2001] EWCA Civ 146; [2001] 3 All E.R. 248; [2001] C.P. Rep. 58; [2001] C.P.L.R. 239; (2001) 98(10) L.S.G. 44; (2001) 145 S.J.L.B. 54 .... 5.06, 19.24, 19.25
Ralston v Scottish Ministers. *See* Somerville v Scottish Ministers
Ramac Holdings Ltd v Brachers, unreported, August 30, 2002 .... 12.36
Ramsbotham v Senior (1869) L.R. 8 Eq. 575 .... 11.13
Ramsden v Brealey (1875) 33 L.T. 322 .... 16.61, 16.62
Ramsey v Ramsey [1956] 1 W.L.R. 542; [1956] 2 All E.R. 165; 100 S.J. 361, PDAD 16.41
Randolph M Fields v Watts, unreported, January 22, 1986, CA 11.06, 11.68, 12.02
Rank Film Distributors Ltd v ENT Ltd (1994) 4 Tas. R. 281 .... 11.60, 12.08
Rank Film Distributors Ltd v Video Information Centre [1982] A.C. 380; [1981] 2 W.L.R. 668; [1981] 2 All E.R. 76; [1981] Com. L.R. 90; [1981] E.C.C. 365; [1981] F.S.R. 363, HL 2.21, 2.24, 2.25, 11.106, 11.111, 11.116, 15.45

Rasbotham v Shropshire Union Railways & Canal Co (1883) L.R. 24 Ch. D. 110; [1881–85] All E.R. Rep. 1560, Ch.D 16.98
Rawstone v Preston Corp (1885) L.R. 30 Ch.D. 116; (1885) 33 W.R. 795; (1885) 52 L.T. 922, Ch.D 11.28
Rayment v Ministry of Defence (1999) 47 B.M.L.R. 92, Q.B.D. 17.21, 18.06
Reading BC v D (Angela); sub nom. BC v A; D, Re [2006] EWHC 1465 (Fam); [2007] 1 W.L.R. 1932; [2007] 1 All E.R. 293; [2006] 2 F.L.R. 1053; [2007] 1 F.C.R. 105; (2006) 92 B.M.L.R. 1; [2006] Fam. Law 738 .... 4.04
Real Estate Opportunities Ltd v Aberdeen Asset Managers Jersey Ltd [2007] EWCA Civ 197; [2007] Bus. L.R. 971; [2007] 2 All E.R. 791; [2008] 2 B.C.L.C. 116 .... 8.09, 11.143, 11.156
Realkredit Danmark A/S v York Montague Ltd [1999] C.P.L.R. 272, CA (Civ Div) 13.03, 13.11
Reavey v Century Newspapers [2001] N.I.Q.B. 17 .... 3.21
Redfern v O'Donnell [2009] IESC 18 .... 11.64
Redfern v Redfern [1891] P. 139, CA 4.28, 11.104
Rediffusion Simulation Ltd v Link Miles Ltd (Admissibility) [1992] F.S.R. 195, Ch.D 11.129, 11.130
Reebok International Ltd v Royal Corp [1992] 2 S.L.R 137, H Ct (Singapore) 1.19, 15.22
Reed Executive Plc v Reed Business Information Ltd (Costs: Alternative Dispute Resolution) [2004] EWCA Civ 887; [2004] 1 W.L.R. 3026; [2004] 4 All E.R. 942; [2005] C.P. Rep. 4; [2004] 4 Costs L.R. 662; [2005] F.S.R. 3; (2004) 27(7) I.P.D. 27067; (2004) 148 S.J.L.B. 881 ..... 11.132, 20.56
Reeves Brothers Inc v Lewis Reed & Co [1971] F.S.R. 17; [1971] R.P.C. 355, Ch.D 11.06
Refco Capital Markets Ltd v Credit Suisse First Boston Ltd; sub nom. Genira Trade & Finance Inc v Refco Capital Markets Ltd; Refco Capital Markets Ltd v CS First Boston and Standard Bank (London) Ltd [2001] EWCA Civ 1733; [2002] C.P. Rep. 15; [2002] C.L.C. 301 .... 10.56, 10.57
Refrigerated Express Lines (Alasia) Pty v Australian Meat and Livestock Corp (1979) 42 F.L.R. 204 .... 11.106
Reid v Howard (1993) 31 N.S.W.L.R. 298, CA (NSW) 11.120, 12.38
Reid v Howard (1995) 184 C.L.R. 1, H.Ct (Aus) 11.106, 11.111, 11.116, 12.38
Reid v Howard (1995) 69 A.L.J.R. 863, H Ct (Aus) 2.25, 2.26
Reid v Powers (1884) 28 S.J. 653 .... 19.07
Reilly v Fryer [1988] 2 F.T.L.R. 69; (1988) 138 N.L.J. Rep. 134, CA (Civ Div) 2.15
Reimer v Christmas (2003) 224 D.L.R. (4th) 635, CA (Ont) 15.05
Reiner v Marquis of Salisbury (1875–76) L.R. 2 Ch. D. 378, Ch.D 3.07
Reitler v NZI Insurance Australia (1992) 1 Tas. R. 173 .... 11.31
Renworth Ltd v Stephansen [1996] 3 All E.R. 244, CA (Civ Div) 11.115
Replication Technology Group v Gallo Africa Ltd [2009] ZAGPJHC 8 ..... 15.01, 15.05, 15.19, 15.45, 15.57
Request for Judicial Assistance from the Seoul District Criminal Court, Re, 555 F.2d. 720 (9th Cir., 1977) 2.63
Request from Ministry of Legal Affairs of Trinidad and Tobago, Re, 848 F.2d. 1151 (11th Cir., 1988) 2.62
Restom v Battenberg [2006] F.C.A. 781, Fed. Ct. Aus. 12.08
Revenue and Customs Commissioners Application (Section 20 Notice: Financial Institution), Re [2006] S.T.C. (S.C.D.) 360; [2006] S.T.I. 1497, Sp Comm. 20.78

Revenue and Customs Commissioners Application (Section 20 Notice: Tax Haven Co), Re; sub nom. Revenue and Customs Commissioners v Financial Institution [2006] S.T.C. (S.C.D.) 376; [2006] W.T.L.R. 1091; [2006] S.T.I. 1521, Sp Comm. 20.78
Revenue and Customs Commissioners Application (Section 20 Notice: Financial Institution), Re [2006] S.T.C. (S.C.D.) 71; [2006] W.T.L.R. 277; [2006] S.T.I. 241, Sp Comm. 20.78
Revenue and Customs Commissioners Application (Section 20 Notice: Investment Bank: Tax Haven Co), Re; sub nom. Tax Haven Co v Revenue and Customs Commissioners [2006] S.T.C. (S.C.D.) 310; [2006] S.T.I. 1441, Sp Comm. 20.78
Rew v Hutchins (1861) 10 C.B. (N.S.) 829 .... 8.21
Reynolds Ex p. Reynolds, Re (1881–82) L.R. 20 Ch. D. 294, CA 11.110, 11.112
Reynolds v Times Newspapers Ltd [2001] 2 A.C. 127; [1999] 3 W.L.R. 1010; [1999] 4 All E.R. 609; [2000] E.M.L.R. 1; [2000] H.R.L.R. 134; 7 B.H.R.C. 289; (1999) 96(45) L.S.G. 34; (1999) 149 N.L.J. 1697; (1999) 143 S.J.L.B. 270, 1999, HL 11.137
Rhodes Ltd, Re (1986) 2 B.C.C. 99, 284 .... 3.40, 3.43
Ricci v Chow [1987] 1 W.L.R. 1658; [1987] 3 All E.R. 534; (1987) 131 S.J. 1156, CA (Civ Div) 3.14, 16.69
Rich v Australian Securities and Investments Commission (2004) 220 C.L.R. 129, H Ct (Aus) 8.06, 8.10, 11.109
Rich v Australian Securities Exchange Commission (2003) 203 A.L.R. 671, CA (NSW) 11.109
Richard Saunders (A Firm) v Eastglen [1990] 3 All E.R. 946, Q.B.D. 17.21
Richardson v Hastings (1844) 7 Beav. 354 .... 15.02
Richardson v Langtree Group Plc [2004] EWCA Civ 1447 .... 13.11
Richbell Strategic Holdings Ltd (In Liquidation) (No.2), Re [2001] B.C.C. 409; [2000] 2 B.C.L.C. 794, Ch.D 3.40, 3.44
Richco International Ltd v International Industries Food Co SAL; The Fayrouz III [1989] 1 All E.R. 613; [1989] 2 Lloyd's Rep. 106; (1988) 138 N.L.J. Rep. 271, Q.B.D. (Comm.) 20.06
Richmark Camera Services Inc v Neilson-Hordell Ltd [1981] F.S.R. 413; 125 S.J. 462, Ch.D 8.06, 11.109
Riddick v Thames Board Mills [1977] Q.B. 881; [1977] 3 W.L.R. 63; [1977] 3 All E.R. 677, CA (Civ Div) 15.05, 15.07, 15.19, 15.45
Ridehalgh v Horsefield; Allen v Unigate Dairies Ltd; Antonelli v Wade Gery Farr (A Firm); Philex Plc v Golban; Roberts v Coverite (Asphalters) Ltd; Watson v Watson (Wasted Costs Orders) [1994] Ch. 205; [1994] 3 W.L.R. 462; [1994] 3 All E.R. 848; [1994] B.C.C. 390; [1994] 2 F.L.R. 194; [1955–95] P.N.L.R. 636; [1994] Fam. Law 560; [1994] E.G.C.S. 15; (1994) 144 N.L.J. 231; [1994] N.P.C. 7, CA (Civ Div) 12.02, 12.05
Rigg v Associated Newspapers Ltd [2003] EWHC 710; [2004] E.M.L.R. 4; [2003] All E.R. (D) 97 (Apr), Q.B.D. 2.32, 5.33, 6.51, 9.10
Rio Tinto Ltd v Commissioner of Taxation (2005) 224 A.L.R. 299, Fed. Ct. Aus. 12.06
Rio Tinto Ltd v Commissioner of Taxation [2005] F.C.A. 1335, Fed. Ct. Aus. 6.06, 9.37
Rio Tinto Ltd v Commissioner of Taxation [2006] FCA 1200; (2007) 235 A.L.R. 127, Fed. Ct of Australia 11.10, 11.19
Riyad Bank v Ahli United Bank (UK) Plc (Permission to Appeal and Amend) [2005] EWCA Civ 1419 .... 2.53
Robert Hitchins Ltd v International Computers Ltd, unreported, December 10, 1996, CA (Civ Div) 11.31, 11.32, 11.33, 11.60, 11.61, 12.08

Roberts v Jump Knitwear Ltd [1981] F.S.R. 527, Ch.D 3.16
Roberts v Oppenheim (1884) L.R. 26 Ch. D. 724, CA 9.04, 9.08, 12.12, 12.13, 12.14
Robertson Stromberg, Re (1994) 119 D.L.R.(4) 551, QB (Sask) 11.37, 11.77, 12.09, 12.19, 12.34
Robertson v Canadian Imperial Bank of Commerce [1994] 1 W.L.R. 1493; [1995] 1 All E.R. 824; [1995] E.C.C. 338; (1994) 91(41) L.S.G. 39; (1994) 138 S.J.L.B. 211, PC (StV) 10.15, 10.28
Robertson v Inland Revenue Commissioners, unreported, May 15, 2002, Sp.C 20.77
Robinson v Adskead (No.1) (1995) 12 W.A.R. 574 .... 9.04, 9.08
Robinson v Budgett [1884] W.N. 94 .... 16.40
Robinson v South Australia (Discovery) [1931] A.C. 704, PC (Aus) 11.89
Rochefoucauld v Boustead (1896) 65 L.J.Ch. 794 .... 11.74, 12.02
Rochfort v Trade Practices Commission (1982) 153 C.L.R.134, H Ct (Aus) 10.08
Rockwell Machine Tool Co Ltd v EP Barrus (Concessionaires) Ltd (Practice Note) [1968] 1 W.L.R. 693; [1968] 2 All E.R. 98 (Note); 112 S.J. 380, Ch.D 14.01, 14.03
Roe v Harvey (1769) 4 Burr. 2484 .... 10.31
Rofe v Kevorkian [1936] 2 All E.R. 1334, CA 16.43, 16.46
Rogers v Hougland (1991) Tas. R. 372 .... 5.54
Rogers v Secretary of State for the Home Department; R. v Lewes Justices Ex p. Secretary of State for the Home Department; R. v Lewes Justices Ex p. Gaming Board for Great Britain [1973] A.C. 388; [1972] 3 W.L.R. 279, HL; affirming [1972] 1 Q.B. 232; [1971] 2 W.L.R. 1466; [1971] 2 All E.R. 1126; 115 S.J. 306, Q.B.D. 10.32, 10.33, 11.82, 11.99
Rogerson v Law Society of the Northern Territory (1993) 88 N.T.R. 1 ..... 11.77
Rome v Punjab National Bank (No.1) [1989] P.C.C. 418; [1989] Fin. L.R. 380, CA (Civ Div); affirming [1989] 2 All E.R. 136; [1989] 2 Lloyd's Rep. 424, Q.B.D. (Comm.) 2.39
Ron West Motors Ltd v Broadcasting Corp of New Zealand [1989] 2 N.Z.L.R. 433 .... 9.35
Ronald A Prior & Co (Solicitors), Re. *See* Solicitor (Wasted Costs Order) (No.1 of 1994), Re
Rookes v Barnard (No.1) [1964] A.C. 1129; [1964] 2 W.L.R. 269; [1964] 1 All E.R. 367; [1964] 1 Lloyd's Rep. 28; 108 S.J. 93, HL 16.39
Ropac Ltd v Inntrepreneur Pub Co (CPC) Ltd [2001] C.P. Rep. 31; [2001] L. & T.R. 10; (2000) 97(26) L.S.G. 36, Ch.D 13.06
Rose v Lynx Express Ltd [2004] EWCA Civ 447; [2004] B.C.C. 714; [2004] 1 B.C.L.C. 455; (2004) 101(17) L.S.G. 31; (2004) 148 S.J.L.B. 477 ... 3.31
Roselle v Buchanan (1885–86) L.R. 16 Q.B.D. 656, Q.B.D. 11.64
Ross v Internet Wines Ltd [2004] N.S.W.C.A. 195, CA (NSW) 11.106
Ross v Woodford [1894] 1 Ch. 38, Ch.D 17.12
Ross v Woodford [1894] 1 Ch. 42 .... 2.61
Rothschild v Queen of Portugal (1939) 3 Y. & C. Ex. 594 .... 4.42
Roussel Uclaf v ICI (No.1) [1989] R.P.C. 59, CA (Civ Div) 11.160
Roussel Uclaf v ICI (No.2) [1990] R.P.C. 45, CA (Civ Div); affirming [1990] F.S.R. 25, Ch.D (Patents Ct) 5.37, 11.158
Roussel v Farchepro Ltd [1999] 3 I.R. 567, H Ct (Irl) 15.35, 15.39
Roux v Australian Broadcasting Commission [1992] 2 V.R. 577 .. 5.45, 5.46, 10.31
Rover International Ltd v Cannon Film Sales Ltd (Introduction of Evidence) [1987] 1 W.L.R. 1597; [1987] 3 All E.R. 986, Ch.D 10.09

Rowe v Fryers. *See* Frankson v Secretary of State for the Home Department
Rowe v United Kingdom (App. No.28901/95); Davis v United Kingdom (App. No.28901/95) (2000) 30 E.H.R.R. 1; 8 B.H.R.C. 325; [2000] Crim. L.R. 584, ECHR 2.05, 11.90, 21.06
Rowell v Pratt [1938] A.C. 101, HL 8.09, 11.143, 16.90
Rowland v Al-Fayed (Disclosure: Witness Statements), *The Times*, July 20, 1998, Ch.D 15.21, 17.21
Rowley v Liverpool City Council, *The Times*, October 26, 1989, CA (Civ Div) 5.21, 8.24, 11.152
Royal Canadian Mounted Police Public Complaints Commission v A,G. of Canada (2005) 256 D.L.R. (4th) 579, Fed CA 11.103
Roylance v General Medical Council (No.1), *The Times*, January 27, 1999, PC (UK) 11.99
Royscot Spa Leasing Ltd v Lovett, unreported, November 16, 1994, CA ... 11.69, 11.70
Rubber Improvement Ltd v Daily Telegraph Ltd; Rubber Improvement Ltd v Associated Newspapers Ltd; Lewis v Associated Newspapers Ltd; Lewis v Daily Telegraph Ltd [1964] A.C. 234; [1963] 2 W.L.R. 1063; [1963] 2 All E.R. 151; 107 S.J. 356, HL 16.57
Ruiz Torija v Spain (A/303–A) (1995) 19 E.H.R.R. 553, ECHR 21.07
Ruiz-Mateos v Spain (A/262) (1993) 16 E.H.R.R. 505, ECHR 21.05, 21.06
Rumney v Walter (1891) 61 L.J.Q.B. 149 .... 16.62
Rush & Tompkins Ltd v Greater London Council [1989] A.C. 1280; [1988] 3 W.L.R. 939; [1988] 3 All E.R. 737; 43 B.L.R. 1; 22 Con. L.R. 114; [1988] E.G.C.S. 145; (1988) 138 N.L.J. Rep. 315; (1988) 132 S.J. 1592, HL; reversing [1988] 2 W.L.R. 533; [1988] 1 All E.R. 549; 40 B.L.R. 53; (1988) 138 N.L.J. Rep. 22; (1988) 132 S.J. 265, CA (Civ Div) 11.122, 11.124, 11.125, 11.126, 11.127, 11.130, 11.131, 12.40
Russell v Jackson (1851) 9 Hare 387 .... 11.06
Russell v Stubbs Ltd [1913] 2 K.B. 200, HL 16.42, 16.60
Russell-Cooke Trust Company v Richard Prentis & Co, unreported, August 24, 2000 .... 10.52
Ryback v Langbar International [2010] EWHC 2015 (Ch) 13.10, 13.11
Rybolovleva v Rybolovlev, unreported, February 18, 2009, HC (BVI) 2.12

S, Re (Infants) [1967] 1 W.L.R. 396; [1967] 1 All E.R. 202; 65 L.G.R. 158; 110 S.J. 944, Ch.D 19.20
S v Boulton [2006] FCAFC 99; (2007) 232 A.L.R. 92, Fed. Ct of Australia ... 11.105
S v Jija 1991 (2) S.A. 52, Eastern Cape Div 11.65
S v S (Chief Constable of West Yorkshire Intervening); sub nom. Chief Constable of West Yorkshire v S [1998] 1 W.L.R. 1716; [1999] 1 All E.R. 281; [1998] 2 F.L.R. 973; [1999] 1 F.C.R. 244; [1998] Fam. Law 726; (1998) 95(35) L.S.G. 38; (1998) 142 S.J.L.B. 248, CA (Civ Div) 4.04
S v S (Judgment in Chambers: Disclosure); sub nom. S v S (Disclosure of Material) (No.2); S v S (Disclosure to Revenue); S v S (Inland Revenue: Tax Evasion) [1997] 1 W.L.R. 1621; [1997] S.T.C. 759; [1997] 2 F.L.R. 774; [1997] 3 F.C.R. 1; 69 T.C. 313; [1997] B.T.C. 333; [1997] Fam. Law 659, Fam Div 2.03, 15.45
S v Safatsa 1988(1) S.A. 868, A.D 11.65
S v Switzerland (A/220) (1992) 14 E.H.R.R. 670, ECHR 21.06, 21.13
SES Contracting Ltd v UK Coal Plc [2007] EWCA Civ 79; [2007] C.P. Rep. 46; [2007] 5 Costs L.R. 758; [2007] 33 E.G.C.S 90 .... 3.39

SITA UK Group Holdings Ltd v Serruys [2009] EWHC 869 (QB); [2009] S.T.C. 1595; [2009] B.T.C. 227; [2009] S.T.I. 1828 .... 15.42, 15.43
SKM SA v Wagner Spraytech (UK) [1982] R.P.C. 497, CA (Civ Div) .. 5.34, 5.35
SL (A Minor) (Wardship: Medical Evidence) [1987] 2 F.L.R. 412 ...... 4.04, 10.25
SL v Fiduciary Trust Ltd, September 24, 2004, CA (Gibraltar) 3.08
SMSE v KL [2009] HKCA 349 .... 2.61, 10.10
S (An Infant) v S; sub nom. S v McC (formerly S); W v W; W v Official Solicitor (acting as Guardian ad Litem for a Male Infant named PHW) [1972] A.C. 24; [1970] 3 W.L.R. 366; [1970] 3 All E.R. 107; 114 S.J. 635, HL 4.33, 19.14, 19.20, 19.21
S CC v B [2000] Fam. 76; [2000] 3 W.L.R. 53; [2000] 2 F.L.R. 161; [2000] 1 F.C.R. 536; [2000] Fam. Law 462, Fam Div 11.06, 11.37, 11.78
S&K Processors Ltd v Campbell Ave Herring Producers Ltd (1983) C.P.C. 146, Sup Ct (BC) 12.06
S&T Bautrading v Nordling, unreported, July 5, 1996, CA 2.15
Saccharin Corp v Haines, Ward & Co (1898) 15 R.P.C. 344 .... 16.72
Sagheera, The. *See* Hellenic Mutual War Risks Association (Bermuda) Ltd v Harrison; The Sagheera
Salford Corp v Lever (No.1) (1890) L.R. 24 Q.B.D. 695, Q.B.D. 16.82, 16.104
Salsbury v Woodland [1970] 1 Q.B. 324; [1969] 3 W.L.R. 29; [1969] 3 All E.R. 863; 113 S.J. 327, CA (Civ Div) 19.13
Salt v Consignia [2002] C.L.Y. 420, CC (Bow) 18.16
Saluja v Gill (t/a P Gill Estate Agents Property Services) [2002] EWHC 1435, Ch.D 2.53
Samoila v Prudential of Australia General Insurance Co (Canada) (2000) 50 O.R. (3d) 64, Sup Ct (Ont) 12.15
Sampson v John Boddy Timber Ltd (1995) 145 N.L.J. 851, CA (Civ Div) 11.124, 11.127, 12.39
Samuels v Linzi Dresses Ltd [1981] Q.B. 115; [1980] 2 W.L.R. 836; [1980] 1 All E.R. 803; 124 S.J. 187, CA (Civ Div) 13.23
Sanger v Punjab National Bank, unreported, July 19, 1994 .. 11.44, 11.60, 12.29
Sankey v Whitlam (1978) 142 C.L.R. 1, H Ct (Aus) 11.81, 11.87, 11.94, 11.98
Sarah C Getty Trust, Re; sub nom. Getty v Getty and Treves [1985] Q.B. 956; [1985] 3 W.L.R. 302; [1985] 2 All E.R. 809; (1985) 82 L.S.G. 2823; (1985) 135 N.L.J. 532; (1985) 129 S.J. 523, Q.B.D. 11.15
Sasea Finance Ltd (In Liquidation), Re [1999] B.C.C. 103; [1998] 1 B.C.L.C. 559, Ch.D 3.43
Saull v Browne (No.2) (1873–74) L.R. 9 Ch. App. 364, CA in Chancery 8.20
Saunders v Punch Ltd (t/a Liberty Publishing) [1998] 1 W.L.R. 986; [1998] 1 All E.R. 234; [1998] E.M.L.R. 18, Ch.D 3.21
Saunders v U.K. (1996) 23 E.H.R.R. 313, [1998] 1 B.C.L.C. 362, E.C.H.R 11.105, 11.113, 11.118, 11.119, 21.05, 21.07
Saunders v United Kingdom (App. No.19187/91) [1997] B.C.C. 872; [1998] 1 B.C.L.C. 362; (1997) 23 E.H.R.R. 313; 2 B.H.R.C. 358, ECHR 2.26
Saunders v Wiel (Penalties) [1892] 2 Q.B. 321; (1892) 9 R.P.C. 459, CA 8.06, 16.86
Saunderson v Von Radeck (1905) 119 L.T.J. 33, HL 16.60
Savage v Chief Constable of Hampshire; sub nom. Savage v Hoddinot [1997] 1 W.L.R. 1061; [1997] 2 All E.R. 631, CA (Civ Div) .. 11.103, 12.42
Savage v Kirk (1907) 40 Ir. L.R. 82 .... 16.49
Save Guana Cay Reef Association v Queen, The [2009] UKPC 44 .... 4.06
Savings & Investment Bank Ltd (In Liquidation) v Fincken [2003] EWCA Civ 1630; [2004] 1 W.L.R. 667; reversing [2003] EWHC 719 (Ch); [2003] 3 All E.R. 1091 .... 11.129

Saxton (Deceased), Re; sub nom. Johnson v Saxton; Saxton, Re [1962] 1 W.L.R. 968; [1962] 3 All E.R. 92; 106 S.J. 668, CA; reversing in part [1962] 1 W.L.R. 859; [1962] 2 All E.R. 618; 106 S.J. 550, Ch.D 3.27, 19.02, 19.07
Sayer v National Mutual Life Association of Australia Ltd (1994) 34 N.S.W.L.R. 132, CA (NSW) 11.99, 11.103
Scaife v Kemp & Co [1892] 2 Q.B. 319, Q.B.D. 16.39, 16.65
Schering Agrochemicals v ABM Chemicals [1987] R.P.C. 185, Ch.D (Patents Ct) 5.22, 5.25, 5.35
Schering Corp v Cipla Ltd [2004] EWHC 2587; [2005] F.S.R. 25; (2005) 28(2) I.P.D. 28009; (2004) 101(47) L.S.G. 30, Ch.D 11.127, 11.128
Schlumberger Holdings Ltd v Electromagnetic Geoservices AS [2008] EWHC 56 (Pat); (2008) 31(7) I.P.D. 31047 .... 5.48
Schmidt (Karlheinz) v Germany (A/291–B) (1994) 18 E.H.R.R. 513, ECHR 21.16
Schmidt v Rosewood Trust Ltd; sub nom. Angora Trust, Re; Everest Trust, Re; Rosewood Trust Ltd v Schmidt [2003] UKPC 26; [2003] 2 A.C. 709; [2003] 2 W.L.R. 1442; [2003] 3 All E.R. 76; [2003] Pens. L.R. 145; [2003] W.T.L.R. 565; (2002–03) 5 I.T.E.L.R. 715; (2003) 100(22) L.S.G. 31, PC (IoM) 4.22, 5.52
Schmidt v Wong [2005] EWCA Civ 1506; [2006] 1 W.L.R. 561; [2006] 1 All E.R. 677; [2006] C.P. Rep. 15; [2005] N.P.C. 143 .... 2.11
Schnabel v Austria, unreported, November 30, 1994, Eur Comm. HR 21.09
Schneider v Leigh [1955] 2 Q.B. 195; [1955] 2 W.L.R. 904; [1955] 2 All E.R. 173; 99 S.J. 276, CA 11.06, 11.48, 12.02
Schreuder v Murray (No.2) [2009] WASCA 145: (2009) 260 A.L.R. 139 .... 4.22, 6.15
Schulman v Abbott Tout Lawyers [2010] FCA 308 .... 12.06
Schwartz (Litigation Guardian of) v Schwartz Estate (2000) 189 D.L.R. (4th) 79, CA (Nova Scotia) 11.122, 15.12
Science Research Council v Nasse; sub nom. Nasse v Science Research Council; Vyas v Leyland Cars; Leyland Cars (BL Cars Ltd) v Vyas [1980] A.C. 1028; [1979] 3 W.L.R. 762; [1979] 3 All E.R. 673; [1979] I.C.R. 921; [1979] I.R.L.R. 465; 123 S.J. 768, HL 8.22, 8.23, 8.24, 8.29, 11.81, 11.102, 12.41, 20.29, 20.30
Scotch Whisky Association v Kella Distillers Ltd, *The Times*, December 27, 1996, Ch.D 18.11
Scott (otherwise Morgan) v Scott [1913] A.C. 417, HL 2.03, 21.15
Scott v Inland Revenue Commissioners [2004] EWCA Civ 400; [2004] I.C.R. 1410; [2004] I.R.L.R. 713; (2004) 148 S.J.L.B. 474 .... 5.41, 20.30
Scott v Mercantile Accident Insurance Co (1892) 8 T.L.R. 320 .... 19.07
Scott v Sampson (1881–82) L.R. 8 Q.B.D. 491, Q.B.D. 10.06
Scottish & Newcastle Plc v Raguz (No.2) [2004] EWHC 1835, Ch.D 13.11
Script Photography Co v Gregg (1890) 59 L.J.Ch.406 .... 13.23
Seabrook v British Transport Commission [1959] 1 W.L.R. 509; [1959] 2 All E.R. 15; 103 S.J. 351, Q.B.D. 11.45
Seacliff Ltd v Decca Ltd [2001] H.K.C.F.I. 275 .... 3.05, 3.11
Seacliff Ltd v Decca Ltd [2002] H.K.C.F.I. 187 .... 3.03, 3.11
Seagull Manufacturing Co Ltd (In Liquidation) (No.1), Re [1993] Ch. 345; [1993] 2 W.L.R. 872, CA (Civ Div); affirming [1992] Ch. 128; [1991] 3 W.L.R. 307; [1991] 4 All E.R. 257; [1990] B.C.C. 550; [1992] B.C.L.C. 1; 135 S.J.L.B. 18, Ch.D 10.09
Seal & Edgelow v Kingston [1908] 2 K.B. 579, CA 13.28

Seamar Holdings Ltd v Kupe Group Ltd [1995] 2 N.Z.L.R. 274, CA (NZ) 11.69, 11.71
Seattle Times Co, Re,104 S.Ct. 2199 (1984) 1.22
Sebright v Hanbury [1916] 2 Ch. 245, Ch.D 16.42, 16.53
Secilpar SL v Burgundy Consultants Ltd, unreported, August 3, 2004, Ch.D ... 3.03, 3.08
Secilpar SL v Fiduciary Trust Ltd, unreported, September 24, 2004, CA (Gibraltar) 3.03, 3.05, 3.08
Secretary for Justice v Apple Daily Ltd [2000] H.K.C.F.I. 778 .... 3.07
Secretary of State for Defence v Guardian Newspapers Ltd [1985] A.C. 339; [1984] 3 W.L.R. 986; [1984] 3 All E.R. 601; (1984) 81 L.S.G. 3426; (1984) 128 S.J. 571, HL; affirming [1984] Ch. 156; [1984] 2 W.L.R. 268; [1984] 1 All E.R. 453; (1984) 81 L.S.G. 203; (1984) 128 S.J. 172, CA (Civ Div) 3.19, 3.21
Secretary of State for the Home Department v F [2009] UKHL 28; [2009] 3 W.L.R. 74; [2009] 3 All E.R. 643; [2009] H.R.L.R. 26; [2009] U.K.H.R.R. 1177; 26 B.H.R.C. 738; (2009) 106(25) L.S.G. 14 .... 5.38A
Secretary of State for Trade and Industry v Baker (No.2); sub nom. Barings Plc (No.2), Re [1998] Ch. 356; [1998] 2 W.L.R. 667; [1998] 1 All E.R. 673; [1998] B.C.C. 888; [1998] 1 B.C.L.C. 16, Ch.D (Companies Ct) 5.14, 11.05, 11.08, 11.31, 11.39, 11.44, 11.48, 11.58
Securities and Exchange Commission v Banner Fund (Action No.85 of 1994), unreported, February 2, 1996 .... 3.03
Securities and Exchange Commission v Credit Bancorp Ltd, unreported, February 20, 2001, Q.B.D. 10.56
Securities and Exchange Commission v Stockholders of Santa Fe International, unreported, February 23, 1984, ... 10.58
Sedco International SA v Cory, 683 F.2d. 1201 (1982) 12.06
Seddon v Commercial Salt Co Ltd [1925] Ch. 187, CA 8.10
Sedgwick Group Plc v Johns-Manville Fibreboard Corp; sub nom. Asbestos Insurance Coverage Cases, Re [1985] 1 W.L.R. 331; [1985] 1 All E.R. 716; [1985] E.C.C. 531; (1985) 82 L.S.G. 1638; (1985) 129 S.J. 189, HL 10.10, 10.57
Sega Enterprises Ltd v Alca Electronics [1982] F.S.R. 516, CA (Civ Div) ... 3.23
Selvarajan v Inner London Education Authority [1980] I.R.L.R. 313, EAT ... 20.29
Senior v Holdsworth Ex p. Independent Television News [1976] Q.B. 23; [1975] 2 W.L.R. 987; [1975] 2 All E.R. 1009; 119 S.J. 393, CA (Civ Div) 5.05, 9.28, 10.12
Sentry Corp v Peat Marwick Mitchell (1990) 95 A.L.R. 11 .... 15.45
Sepa Waste Water Treatment Pty Ltd v JMT Welding Pty Ltd [1986] 6 N.S.W.L.R. 41 .... 11.22
Serious Organised Crime Agency v Scott [2010] NIQB 39 .... 5.54
Servico Pan Americano de Protection, Re, 354 F. Supp. 2d 269 (S.D.N.Y. 2004) 2.63
Sethia v Stern, *The Times*, November 4, 1987; *Independent*, October 30, 1987, CA (Civ Div) 11.89
Settebello Ltd v Banco Totta and Acores [1985] 1 W.L.R. 1050; [1985] 2 All E.R. 1025; [1985] 2 Lloyd's Rep. 448; [1986] E.C.C. 15; (1985) 82 L.S.G. 2658; (1985) 135 N.L.J. 658; (1985) 129 S.J. 683, CA (Civ Div) ... 2.61, 17.12
Seven Network Limited v News Limited [2005] F.C.A. 864, Fed. Ct. Aus. 11.17
Seven Network Ltd v News Ltd (2005) 225 A.L.R.671, Fed. Ct. Aus. 11.19
Seven Network Ltd v News Ltd (2005) 227 A.L.R. 704, Fed. Ct. Aus. 12.06
Seven Network Ltd v News Ltd (No.13) [2006] F.C.A. 354, Fed. Ct. Aus. 9.37

Seven Network Ltd v News Ltd [2005] F.C.A. 864, Fed. Ct. Aus. ... 12.08, 12.09
Seven Network Ltd v News Ltd [2006] F.C.A. 343, Fed. Ct. Aus. 11.123
Seven Network v News (No.9) [2005] F.C.A. 1394, (2006) 225 A.L.R. 256, Fed. Ct. Aus. 3.45
Seven Network v News (No.12) [2006] FCA 348; (2007) 230 A.L.R. 544, Fed. Ct of Australia 12.36
Shah v Standard Chartered Bank, unreported, February 2, 1996 .... 5.33
Shannon v Country Casuals Holdings plc, *The Times*, June 16, 1997, Q.B.D. 10.35
Shannon v Shannon [2005] N.Z.C.A. 91 .... 12.06
Sharpe & Dohme Inc v Boots Pure Drug Co (1928) 45 R.P.C. 153 .... 16.72
Sharpe v Boots Co (1927) 44 R.P.C. 69 .... 16.72
Sharpe v Smail (1975) 49 A.L.J.R. 130 .... 16.34, 16.97
Sharpe v Smail (1975) 5 A.L.R. 377 .... 16.94
Shaw v National Trust, *Independent*, February 13, 1989, CA (Civ Div) 5.24
Shaw v Skeet [1996] 7 Med. L.R. 371, Q.B.D. 12.24, 18.16, 19.22
Shaw v Smith (1887) L.R. 18 Q.B.D. 193, CA 4.09, 4.11, 4.45, 16.27
Shaw v Vauxhall Motors Ltd [1974] 1 W.L.R. 1035; [1974] 2 All E.R. 1185; 118 S.J. 347, CA (Civ Div) 3.34, 3.37
Shaw, Ex p. (1821) Jac. 270 .... 11.149
Shearson Lehman Brothers Inc v Maclaine Watson & Co Ltd [1988] 1 W.L.R. 16; [1988] 1 All E.R. 116; [1988] F.T.L.R. 225; (1988) 85(2) L.S.G. 35; (1987) 131 S.J. 1658, HL 11.139
Sheffield (Kristina) v United Kingdom (App. No.22985/93); Horsham v United Kingdom (App. No.23390/94) [1998] 2 F.L.R. 928; [1998] 3 F.C.R. 141; (1999) 27 E.H.R.R. 163; 5 B.H.R.C. 83; [1998] H.R.C.D. 758; [1998] Fam. Law 731, 1998, ECHR 21.08
Sheffield Canal Co v Sheffield & Rotherham Railway Co (1843) 1 Ph. 484 ... 9.37
Shell Pensions Trust Ltd v Pell Frischmann & Partners [1986] 2 All E.R. 911; 6 Con. L.R. 117; (1987) 3 Const. L.J. 57; (1986) 136 N.L.J. 238, Q.B.D. (OR) 18.04
Shepherd & Neame v EDF Energy Networks (SPN) Plc [2008] EWHC 123 (TCC); [2008] Bus. L.R. D43 .... 18.21
Sheward v Lord Lonsdale (1879–80) L.R. 5 C.P.D. 47, CPD 16.38
Shierson v Rastogi; sub nom. RBG Resources Plc, Re [2002] EWCA Civ 1624; [2003] 1 W.L.R. 586; [2002] B.C.C. 1005; [2003] B.P.I.R. 148; (2003) 100(2) L.S.G. 31 .... 3.43
Shipbuilders Ltd v Benson [1992] 3 N.Z.L.R. 549, CA (NZ) 13.32
Shippam (C) Ltd v Princes-Buitoni Ltd [1983] F.S.R. 427, Ch.D 6.51
Shirley v Channel Island Knitwear Company Ltd 1985–86 J.L.R. 404 ...... 1.17
Shore v Bedford (1843) 5 Man. & G. 271 .... 11.74
Shropshire, The (1922) 127 L.T. 487, CA 16.42, 16.54
Shun Kai Finance Co Ltd v Japan Leasing (Hong Kong) Ltd [2001] H.K.C.A. 481 .... 15.13
Siddeley-Deary Motor Car Co v Thompson (1916) 140 L.T. Jo. 3374 ...... 9.04
Silver v United Kingdom (A/161) (1983) 5 E.H.R.R. 347, ECHR ... 21.10, 21.12, 21.13
Simaan General Contracting Co v Pilkington Glass Ltd [1988] Q.B. 758; [1988] 2 W.L.R. 761, CA (Civ Div) [1987] 1 W.L.R. 516; [1987] 1 All E.R. 345; (1987) 3 Const. L.J. 300; (1987) 84(0) L.S.G. 819; (1986) 136 N.L.J. 824; 131 S.J. 297, Q.B.D. (OR) 11.129, 11.130
Simba-Tola v Elizabeth Fry Hostel Trustees [2001] EWCA Civ 1371, CA (Civ Div) 8.24, 11.156

Simms v Law Society (Permission to Appeal) [2005] EWCA Civ 749, CA (Civ Div) 11.37, 11.77
Singapore Airlines v Sydney Airports Corporation [2004] N.S.W.S.C. 380 .... 11.38, 11.46, 12.08
Singh v Christie. *See* Tejendrasingh v Metsons
Singh v Observer Ltd [1989] 3 All E.R. 777; (1989) 133 S.J. 485, CA (Civ Div); reversing [1989] 2 All E.R. 751, Q.B.D. 2.40
Skarga v Richards Butler LLP. *See* Nikitin v Richards Butler LLP
Skeffington v Rooney [1997] 1 I.R. 22 .... 11.100
Sketchley v Connolly (1863) 11 W.R. 573 .... 16.75
Skuse v Granada Television Ltd (Costs) [1994] 1 W.L.R. 1156, Q.B.D. ... 11.70
Slade v Tucker (1880) L.R. 14 Ch. D. 824, Ch.D 11.21
Slater Ltd v Beacontree General Commissioners (No.1) [2002] S.T.C. 246; 74 T.C. 471; [2002] B.T.C. 42; [2001] S.T.I. 1699; (2002) 99(6) L.S.G. 31, Ch.D 20.74
Sloane v Britain Steamship Co Ltd [1897] 1 Q.B. 185, CA 9.07
Smith v Berg (1877) 36 L.T. 471 .... 16.79, 16.93
Smith v Cropper (t/a HS Cropper & Co); sub nom. Cropper v Smith; Hancock v Cropper (t/a HS Cropper & Co) (1884–85) L.R. 10 App. Cas. 249, HL; reversing (1884) L.R. 26 Ch. D. 700, CA 13.05
Smith v Daniell (1874) L.R. 18 Eq. 649 .... 11.07, 11.09
Smith v Harris (1883) 48 L.T. 869 .... 5.04, 9.04, 9.09
Smith v Howard Johnson Company 615 NE 2d 1037, 1038 (1993), Sup Ct (Ohio) 13.38
Smith v Jones (1999) 132 C.C.C. (Sd.) 225, Sup Ct (Can) 11.65
Smith v Phillip Morris Companies Inc [2006] EWHC 916, Q.B.D. 10.59
Smith v Smith (1975) 5 A.L.R. 444 .... 2.61
Smith v Smith [1957] 1 W.L.R. 802; [1957] 2 All E.R. 397; 121 J.P. 391; 101 S.J. 483, DC 11.134
Smith v Southampton University Hospitals NHS Trust [2007] EWCA Civ 387; (2007) 96 B.M.L.R. 79 .... 18.22
Smith-Bird v Blower [1939] 2 All E.R. 406, Ch.D 11.10
Smith Kline & French Laboratories Ltd Cimetidine Patent (No.2); sub nom. Smith Kline & French Laboratories Ltd's Patents, Re [1990] R.P.C. 203, CA (Civ Div) 5.36
Smith Kline & French Laboratories Ltd v Global Pharmaceutics [1986] R.P.C. 394, CA (Civ Div) 3.08
Smith Myers Communications Ltd v Motorola Ltd [1991] F.S.R. 262, Ch.D ... 2.41, 19.06
SmithKline Beecham Biologicals SA v Connaught Laboratories Inc (Disclosure of Documents) [1999] 4 All E.R. 498; [1999] C.P.L.R. 505; [2000] F.S.R. 1; (2000) 51 B.M.L.R. 91; (1999) 22(10) I.P.D. 22092, CA (Civ Div) 15.30
SmithKline Beecham plc v Alphapharm Pty Ltd [2001] F.CA. 271, Fed. Ct. Aus. 11.159
SmithKline Beecham Plc v Apotex Europe Ltd [2003] EWHC 127; (2003) 26(5) I.P.D. 26031, Ch.D (Patents Ct) 11.163, 15.11
SmithKline Beecham Plc v Generics (UK) Ltd; BASF AG v SmithKline Beecham Plc [2003] EWCA Civ 1109; [2004] 1 W.L.R. 1479; [2003] 4 All E.R. 1302; [2003] C.P. Rep. 66; [2004] F.S.R. 8; (2003) 26(11) I.P.D. 26071; (2003) 100(34) L.S.G. 31 .... 8.01, 9.03, 15.03, 15.29, 15.40
Smiths Group plc v Weiss, unreported, March 22, 2002, Ch.D ... 11.124, 11.130, 11.133, 12.39, 20.56

Smolen v Solon Cooperative Housing Services Ltd [2003] EWCA Civ 1240; (2003) 147 S.J.L.B. 1087, CA (Civ Div) 18.10, 18.12
Smurfit Paribas Bank v AAB Export Finance [1990] I.R.L.M. 588, Sup Ct (Itl) 11.09
Snow v Hawthorn [1969] N.Z.L.R. 776 .... 3.27, 5.06, 19.02
Snowstar Shipping Co Ltd v Graig Shipping Plc [2003] EWHC 1367, Q.B.D. (Comm.) 3.31, 3.33, 3.34
Sociedade Nacional de Combustiveis de Angola UEE v Lundqvist [1991] 2 Q.B. 310; [1991] 2 W.L.R. 280; [1990] 3 All E.R. 283, CA (Civ Div) 2.24, 11.106, 11.110, 11.111, 11.112
Société Française Hoechst v Allied Colloids Ltd [1992] F.S.R. 66; [1991] R.P.C. 245, Ch.D (Patents Ct) 11.35, 11.39, 11.42, 11.56
Société Générale du Commerce et de L'industrie en France v Johann Maria Farina & Co [1904] 1 K.B. 794, CA 2.48
Société Immobilière St Honoré Monceau v Financial General Trust Ltd, unreported cited [1939] 2 K.B. 395, CA 11.112
Société Romanaise de la Chaussure SA v British Shoe Corp Ltd [1991] F.S.R. 1, Ch.D 3.1, 3.23
Society of Lloyd's v Jaffray (Witness Statements) [2002] EWCA Civ 235 ..... 17.26
Soden v Burns; sub nom. R. v Secretary of State for Trade and Industry Ex p. Soden [1996] 1 W.L.R. 1512; [1996] 3 All E.R. 967; [1997] B.C.C. 308; [1996] 2 B.C.L.C. 636, Ch.D 3.41, 11.102
Sofilas v Cable Sands (WA) Pty Ltd (1993) 9 W.A.R. 196, Sup Ct (WA) 15.09, 15.37, 16.117
Sogelease Australia Ltd v Griffin [2003] N.S.W.S.C. 178, overturned on other grounds [2003] N.S.W.C.A. 158 .... 2.46
Solicitor (Disclosure of Confidential Records), Re [1997] 1 F.L.R. 101; [1997] 2 F.C.R. 316; [1997] Fam. Law 162, Fam Div 10.15, 14.17
Solicitor (Wasted Costs Order) (No.1 of 1994), Re; sub nom. Ronald A Prior & Co (Solicitors), Re [1996] 1 Cr. App. R. 248; [1996] 1 F.L.R. 40; [1996] 3 F.C.R. 365; [1996] Fam. Law 83; (1996) 160 J.P.N. 514; (1995) 92(28) L.S.G. 40; (1995) 139 S.J.L.B. 157, CA (Crim Div) 10.35, 14.16
Solosky v R. (1979) 105 D.L.R. (3rd) 745, SCC 11.08
Somatra Ltd v Sinclair Roche & Temperley (No.1); Sinclair Roche & Temperley v Somatra Ltd [2000] 1 W.L.R. 2453; [2000] 2 Lloyd's Rep. 673; [2000] C.P.L.R. 601; (2000) 97(35) L.S.G. 37, CA (Civ Div); reversing in part [2000] 1 Lloyd's Rep. 311, Q.B.D. (Comm.) 12.02, 11.124, 11.130, 12.19, 12.34, 12.39, 12.40
Somervile v Australian Securities Commission (1993) 118 A.L.R. 149, Fed. Ct. Aus. 5.30, 9.38, 12.15, 12.35
Somerville v Scottish Ministers; Ralston v Scottish Ministers; Henderson v Scottish Ministers; Blanco v Scottish Ministers [2007] UKHL 44; [2007] 1 W.L.R. 2734; 2008 S.C. (H.L.) 45; 2007 S.L.T. 1113; 2007 S.C.L.R. 830; [2008] H.R.L.R. 3; [2008] U.K.H.R.R. 570; (2007) 151 S.J.L.B. 1398; 2007 G.W.D. 37–656 .... 11.94
Sonic Tape's Patent [1987] R.P.C. 251, PO 11.42
Sony Corp v Anand; Kabushika Kaisha Hattori Tokeiten v Domicrest (Fancy Goods) Ltd; Seiko Time (UK) Ltd v Domicrest (Fancy Goods) Ltd [1981] Com. L.R. 55; [1981] F.S.R. 398, Ch.D 15.22, 15.43
Sony Corp v Time Electronics [1981] 1 W.L.R. 1293; [1981] 3 All E.R. 376; [1981] F.S.R. 333, Ch.D 15.40
Sorby v Commonwealth (1983) 152 C.L.R. 281, H Ct (Aus) 11.104, 11.111

Soul v Inland Revenue Commissioners (Practice Note) [1963] 1 W.L.R. 112; [1963] 1 All E.R. 68 (Note); 40 T.C. 506; (1962) 41 A.T.C. 323; [1962] T.R. 353; 106 S.J. 957, CA 10.24
Souter v 375561 B.C. Ltd (1995) 130 D.L.R. (4th) 81, CA (BC) 12.06
South African Republic v La Compagnie Franco-Belge du Chemin de Fer du Nord (No.2) [1898] 1 Ch. 190, Ch.D 4.42
South Australia v Peat Marwick Mitchell (1995) 65 S.A.S.R. 72, Sup Ct (SA) 20.55, 20.57
South Carolina Insurance Co v Assurantie Maatshappij De Zeven Provincien NV; South Carolina Insurance Co v Al Ahlia Insurance Co; South Carolina Insurance Co v Arabian Seas Insurance Co; South Carolina Insurance Co v Cambridge Reinsurance Co Ltd [1987] A.C. 24; [1986] 3 W.L.R. 398; [1986] 3 All E.R. 487; [1986] 2 Lloyd's Rep. 317; [1987] E.C.C. 1; (1986) 83 L.S.G. 2659; (1986) 136 N.L.J. 751; (1986) 130 S.J. 634, HL 1.21, 2.58, 2.63
South Coast Shipping Co Ltd v Havant BC [2002] 3 All E.R. 779; [2002] 1 Costs L.R. 98; (2002) 152 N.L.J. 59, Ch.D 12.30
South Shropshire DC v Amos [1986] 1 W.L.R. 1271; [1987] 1 All E.R. 340; [1986] 2 E.G.L.R. 194; (1986) 280 E.G. 635; [1986] R.V.R. 235; (1986) 83 L.S.G. 3513; (1986) 136 N.L.J. 800; (1986) 130 S.J. 803, CA (Civ Div) 11.127, 11.129
South Staffordshire Tramways Co v Ebbsmith [1895] 2 Q.B. 669, CA 10.44, 10.46, 10.47, 10.48, 10.50
South Surburban Co-operative Society Ltd v Orum [1937] 2 K.B. 690, CA ... 16.63
South Tyneside MBC v Wickes Building Supplies Ltd [2004] EWHC 2428; [2004] N.P.C. 164, Q.B.D. (Comm.) 10.10
Southern Cross Airlines Holdings Ltd v Arthur Andersen & Co (1998) 84 F.C.R. 472, Fed. Ct. Aus. 12.08
Southern Equities Corporation Ltd v Arthur Andersen & Co. (1997) 70 S.A.S.R. 166, Sup Ct (Full Ct) (S Aus) 12.06
Southern Equities Corporation Ltd v West Australian Government Holdings Ltd (1993) 10 W.A.R.1, Sup Ct (Full C) (W Aus) 11.44
Southern Pacific Hotel Services Inc v Southern Pacific Hotel Corp [1984] 1 N.S.W.L.R. 710 .... 10.23
Southwark and Vauxhall Water Co v Quick (1877–78) L.R. 3 Q.B.D. 315, CA 11.05, 11.39, 16.96, 16.102
Spain (King of) v Hullett (1833) 7 Bli N.S. 359 .... 4.42
Spalding v Radio Canberra Pty Ltd [2009] ACTSC 26; 166 A.C.T.R. 14 .... 12.28
Spalla v St George Motor Finance (2004) 209 A.L.R. 703, Fed. Ct. Aus. 15.25
Spastic Estate v Imperial Tobacco Ltd (2000) 49 OR (3d) 699, CA (Ont) 13.38
Spatafora v Wiebe [1973] 1 Q.R. 93 .... 5.05
Speyside Estate and Trust Co Ltd v Wraymond Freeman (Blenders) Ltd (In Liquidation) [1950] Ch. 96; [1949] 2 All E.R. 796; 65 T.L.R. 681, Ch.D 2.32, 6.51
Sphere Drake Insurance v ME Denby; Postgate v Alexander & Alexander Services, *The Times*, December 20, 1991, Q.B.D. 10.11, 10.12
Spicers Paper (N.Z.) Ltd v Whitcoulls Group Ltd [1996] 1 N.Z.L.R. 72 ... 12.18
Spiers & Pond v John Bull (1916) 85 L.J.K.B. 992 .... 16.64
Spokes v Grosvenor Hotel Co Ltd [1897] 2 Q.B. 124, CA ... 8.12, 11.106, 16.85
Spring Salmon & Seafood Ltd v IRC, unreported, October 3, 2005, Sp C 20.77
Springall, Re [1875] W.N.225 .... 17.02
Springfield Nominees Pty Ltd v Bridgelands Securities Ltd (1992) 110 A.L.R. 685, Fed. Ct. Aus. 11.136, 15.41, 16.117
Springsteen v Masquerade Music Ltd [2001] E.M.L.R. 654, CA 13.33

Sportsbet Pty Ltd v State of **New South Wales (No.3) [2009] FCA 1283 .... 11.09, 11.98, 11.129**
SQMB v MIMIA (2004) 205 A.L.R. 392, Fed. Ct. Aus. 12.15
Sroka v Gorbal (1980) 25 S.A.S.R. 356 .... 16.97
St George v Rabo [2004] F.C.A. 1360, (2004) 211 A.L.R. 147 .... 3.34
Standen's Land v Pinkerton's of Canada Ltd (2001) 203 D.L.R. (4th) 744, Ct (Alberta) 11.103
Standrin v Yenton Minister Homes Ltd, *The Times*, July 22, 1991, CA (Civ Div) 11.127
Stanfield Properties v National Westminster Bank Plc [1983] 1 W.L.R. 568; [1983] 2 All E.R. 249, Ch.D 16.97, 16.99, 16.102, 16.103
Stanton v Callaghan [2000] Q.B. 75; [1999] 2 W.L.R. 745; [1998] 4 All E.R. 961; [1999] C.P.L.R. 31; [1999] B.L.R. 172; (1999) 1 T.C.L.R. 50; 62 Con. L.R. 1; [1999] P.N.L.R. 116; [1998] 3 E.G.L.R. 165; (1999) 15 Const. L.J. 50; [1998] E.G. 115 (C.S.); (1998) 95(28) L.S.G. 32; (1998) 95(33) L.S.G. 33; (1998) 148 N.L.J. 1355; (1998) 142 S.J.L.B. 220; [1998] N.P.C. 113· CA (Civ Div) 18.15
Star News Shops v Stafford Refrigeration Ltd [1998] 1 W.L.R. 536; [1998] 4 All E.R. 408; (1997) 94(43) L.S.G. 30; (1997) 141 S.J.L.B. 236, CA (Civ Div) 13.05, 13.06, 13.09
Starr v National Coal Board [1977] 1 W.L.R. 63; [1977] 1 All E.R. 243; 120 S.J. 720, CA (Civ Div) 19.22
State Bank of South Australia v Ferguson (1995) 64 S.A.S.R. 232, Sup Ct (S Aus) 11.08, 11.45
State Bank of South Australia v Heinrich (1989) 52 S.A.S.R. 596 .... 5.05
State Bank of South Australia v Smoothdale (No.2) Ltd (1995) 63 S.A.S.R. 224, Sup Ct (Full Ct) (S Aus) 12.08
State of New South Wales v BT Australasia Pty Ltd, unreported, July 24, 1998, Fed. Ct. (Full Ct) Aus. 12.23
State of South Australia v Barrett (1995) 64 S.A.S.R. 73, Sup Ct (Full Ct) (S Aus) 5.52, 11.28
Stateline Pty v Legal & General Assurance Society (1982) 29 S.A.S.R. 16 ..... 16.116
States Prison Board v Kirk (1991) 11 G.L.J. 62, CA (Guernsey) 1.17
Stax Claimants v Bank of Nova Scotia Channel Islands Ltd [2007] EWHC 1153 (Ch) 11.31, 11.127
Steamship Mutual Underwriting Association Trustees (Bermuda) Ltd v Baring Asset Management Ltd [2004] EWHC 202; [2004] 2 C.L.C. 628, Q.B.D. (Comm.) 3.34
Steel v Metropolitan Police Commissioner, unreported, February 18, 1993, CA 5.24
Steele v Savour (1891) 8 T.L.R. 94 .... 10.14
Steele, Re Exp. Official Trustee in Bankruptcy v Clayton Utz, Re (1994) 48 F.C.R. 236 .... 11.77
Stefan v General Medical Council (No.1) [1999] 1 W.L.R. 1293; [2000] H.R.L.R. 1; 6 B.H.R.C. 487; [1999] Lloyd's Rep. Med. 90; (1999) 49 B.M.L.R. 161; (1999) 143 S.J.L.B. 112, PC (UK) 21.07
Stein v Blake, unreported, October 24, 2000 .... 11.143
Stephens v Wanklin (1854) 19 Beav. 585 .... 17.08
Sterling v Sullivan (2004) 231 D.L.R. (4th) 344, QB (Sask) 15.11
Stern v Sevastopulo (1863) 14 C.B. (N.S.) 737 .... 16.60
Stevens v Canada (1998) 161 D.L.R. (4th) 85, Fed CA 12.35
Stevens v Gullis [2000] 1 All E.R. 527, CA 18.12, 18.15
Stjernblad (Baron), The [1918] A.C. 173, PC (UK) 20.65

Stolzenberg v CIBC Mellon Trust Co. *See* CIBC Mellon Trust Co v Stolzenberg (Sanctions: Non-compliance)
Storer v British Gas Plc [2000] 1 W.L.R. 1237; [2000] 2 All E.R. 440; [2000] I.C.R. 603; [2000] I.R.L.R. 495, CA (Civ Div) 6.58
Strachan, Re [1895] 1 Ch. 439, CA 1.02, 104, 4.31, 20.22
Straka v Humber River Regional Hospital (2000) 193 D.L.R. (4th) 680, CA (Ontario) 3.03, 3.21, 11.102
Straker Bros & Co v Reynolds (1889) L.R. 22 Q.B.D. 262, Q.B.D. 10.23
Stroh v Haringey London Borough Council, unreported, July 13, 1999, CA 17.21
Stroude v Beazer Homes Ltd [2005] EWCA Civ 265; [2005] N.P.C. 45, CA (Civ Div) 18.11
Stuart v Balkis (1884) 50 L.T. 479 .... 17.04
Sturges v Countess of Warwick (1913) 30 T.L.R. 112, CA 2.50
Subpoena (Adoption: Commissioner for Local Administration), Re; sub nom. Subpoena at the Request of the Commissioner for the Local Authority, Re; Subpoena issued by the Commissioner for Local Administration, Re [1996] 2 F.L.R. 629; [1996] 3 F.C.R. 190; (1996) 8 Admin. L.R. 577; [1996] Fam. Law 663; (1996) 140 S.J.L.B. 108, Q.B.D. 10.31, 11.99
Sullivan v West Yorkshire Passenger Transport Executive [1985] 2 All E.R. 134, CA (Civ Div) 18.11
Sumitomo Corp v Credit Lyonnais Rouse Ltd [2001] EWCA Civ 1152; [2002] 1 W.L.R. 479; [2002] 4 All E.R. 68; [2001] 2 Lloyd's Rep. 517; [2002] C.P. Rep. 3; [2001] C.P.L.R. 462; (2001) 98(34) L.S.G. 41; (2001) 145 S.J.L.B. 208 .... 9.22, 11.33
Sun Life Trust Co v Dewshi (1993) D.L.R. (4th) 232, Ont. CA 11.128
Sunday Times v United Kingdom (A/30) (1979–80) 2 E.H.R.R. 245; (1979) 76 L.S.G. 328, ECHR 21.15
Sunderland Steamship P and I Association v Gatoil International Inc; The Lorenzo Halcoussi [1988] 1 Lloyd's Rep. 180, Q.B.D. (Comm.) 10.10, 10.12, 10.31, 10.32, 10.57, 11.35, 20.05
Surface Technology Plc v Young [2002] F.S.R. 25, Ch.D 11.06
Sussmann v Germany (1998) 25 E.H.R.R. 64, ECHR 21.05
Sutherland (Duke of) v British Dominions Land Settlement Corp Ltd [1926] Ch. 746, Ch.D 16.03, 16.51
Sutton Glassworks Ltd, Re [1996] B.C.C. 174; [1997] 1 B.C.L.C. 26, Ch.D 16.26, 16.32, 16.66
Sutton Smith v Stephens, unreported, January 26, 2001 .... 18.09
Svenska Handelsbanken v Sun Alliance and London Insurance Plc (No.1) [1995] 2 Lloyd's Rep. 84, Q.B.D. (Comm.) .. 6.41, 11.01, 11.15, 11.59, 11.60, 11.62, 12.08
Sveriges Anfartygs Assurens Forening v The 1976 Eagle Assurance Co SA, unreported, March 28, 1990 .... 1.12, 6.01, 6.11, 6.13
Swain v Edlin-Sinclair Tyre Co (1903) 20 R.P.C. 435 .... 11.159
Swansea (Mayor of) v Quirk (1879–80) L.R. 5 C.P.D. 106, CPD 16.04, 16.82
Swanston v Lishman (1881) 45 L.T. 360, CA 4.20, 5.43, 8.01
Swaptronics Ltd, Re (1998) 95(36) L.S.G. 33, Ch.D (Companies Ct) 13.07
Swider & Berlin and Hamilton, Petitioners v United States, 118 S.Ct. 2081 (1998), Sup Ct (US) 11.06
Sybron Corp v Barclays Bank plc [1985] 1 Ch. 299 .... 3.25, 10.36, 15.01, 15.05, 15.11, 15.14, 15.18, 15.19, 15.22, 15.25, 15.36, 15.39

Synstar Computer Services (UK) Ltd v ICL (Sorbus) Ltd [2001] C.P. Rep. 98; [2001] U.K.C.L.R. 585; [2002] I.C.R. 112; (2001) 98(23) L.S.G. 40; (2001) 145 S.J.L.B. 119, Ch.D 15.39
Szental v Szental [2001] V.S.C. 42, Sup Ct (Victoria) 4.24, 4.26

T v T (Blood Tests: Paternity), *The Times*, July 31, 1992, CA (Civ Div) 19.20
TNT Management Pty Ltd v Trade Practice Commission (1983) 47 A.L.R. 693 .... 5.41
TSB Bank Plc v Robert Irving & Burns [2000] 2 All E.R. 826; [1999] Lloyd's Rep. P.N. 956; [2000] P.N.L.R. 384, CA (Civ Div) 11.74, 12.02, 12.03
TW Hobbs & Co Ltd v Hudson (1890) L.R. 25 Q.B.D. 232, CA .. 8.06, 11.109, 16.86
T (A Minor), Re. *See* Manchester City Council v T
T (Children) (Abuse: Standard of Proof), Re; sub nom. T (Children) (Sexual Abuse: Standard of Proof), Re [2004] EWCA Civ 558; [2004] 2 F.L.R. 838; [2004] Fam. Law 709, CA (Civ Div) 4.04, 18.14, 18.21
T (Paternity: Ordering Blood Tests), Re [2001] 2 F.L.R. 1190; [2001] 3 F.C.R. 577; [2001] Fam. Law 738, Fam Div 19.20
T (Restraint Order: Disclosure of Assets), Re [1992] 1 W.L.R. 949; (1993) 96 Cr. App. R. 194, CA (Crim Div) 2.26
Tagg v South Devon Railway Co (1849) 12 Beav. 151 .... 15.02
Tajik Aluminium Plant v Hydro Aluminium AS [2005] EWCA Civ 1218; [2006] 1 W.L.R. 767; [2005] 4 All E.R. 1232; [2006] 1 Lloyd's Rep. 155; [2006] C.P. Rep. 7; [2005] 2 C.L.C. 604 .... 10.10
Takilla Ltd v Olsen Backhurst & Dorey [2003] J.R.C. 003 .... 1.17
Tameshwar v Queen, The; Seokumar v Queen, The [1957] A.C. 476; [1957] 3 W.L.R. 157; [1957] 2 All E.R. 683; (1957) 41 Cr. App. R. 161; 121 J.P. 477; 101 S.J. 532, PC (BG) 19.13
Tanap Investments (U.K.) Ltd v Tozer, unreported, October 11, 1991, CA 12.28, 12.36
Tanfern Ltd v Cameron-MacDonald [2000] 1 W.L.R. 1311; [2000] 2 All E.R. 801; [2001] C.P. Rep. 8; [2000] 2 Costs L.R. 260; (2000) 97(24) L.S.G. 41, CA (Civ Div) 6.57
Tanner v Shergold [2004] F.C.A. 176 .... 4.06
Tarajan Overseas Ltd v Kaye [2001] EWCA Civ 1859 .... 10.19
Tarasov v Nassif, unreported, February 11, 1994, CA 11.110
Tarn Insurance Services Ltd v Kirby [2009] EWCA Civ 19; [2009] C.P. Rep. 22 .... 13.10
Tasmanian Main Life Railway Co v Clark (1879) 27 W.R. 677 .... 2.33
Tate & Lyle International v Government Trading Corp (1984) 81 L.S.G. 3341, CA (Civ Div) 12.07, 12.19, 12.20
Tate Access Floors Inc v Boswell [1991] Ch. 512; [1991] 2 W.L.R. 304; [1990] 3 All E.R. 303; (1990) 140 N.L.J. 963; (1990) 134 S.J. 1227, Ch.D 2.24, 11.106, 11.111, 11.112, 11.120, 12.38
Tate v Tate [2003] Fam. CA. 112, Fam Ct (Aus) 13.27
Tatlock v GP Worsley & Co Ltd, unreported, June 22, 1989, CA 11.78
Tau v Durie [1996] 2 N.Z.L.R. 190 .... 12.15, 12.34
Tau v Duvrie [1996] 2 N.Z.L.R. 193 .... 11.99
Taxpayer v Inspector of Taxes [1996] S.T.C. (S.C.D.) 261, Sp Comm. 20.79
Taylor v Anderton, *The Times*, October 21, 1986, Ch.D .. 3.02, 3.27, 3.36, 4.50, 11.103, 19.03
Taylor v Anderton; sub nom. Taylor v Chief Constable of Greater Manchester [1995] 1 W.L.R. 447; [1995] 2 All E.R. 420; (1995) 92(11) L.S.G. 37; (1995) 139 S.J.L.B. 66, CA (Civ Div) 11.100

Taylor v Batten (1878–79) L.R. 4 Q.B.D. 85, CA 6.11, 6.13, 6.14
Taylor v Director of the Serious Fraud Office; sub nom. Taylor v Serious Fraud Office [1999] 2 A.C. 177; [1998] 3 W.L.R. 1040; [1998] 4 All E.R. 801; [1999] E.M.L.R. 1, HL 2.05, 15.01, 15.05, 15.56, 20.69
Taylor v Oliver (1876) 45 L.J. Ch.774 .... 6.15
Taylor v Rundell (1843) 1 Ph. 222 .... 16.100
Taylor v Santos Ltd (1998) 71 S.A.S.R.434, Sup Ct (Full Ct) (S Aus) 5.48
Taylor v Taylor 1990 J.L.R. 124, CA (Jersey) ... 1.17, 11.38, 11.44, 11.45, 11.46, 11.48
Taylor-Sabori v United Kingdom (App. No.47114/99) (2003) 36 E.H.R.R. 17, ECHR 21.10, 21.12
Taylro v Clonmel Healthcare Ltd [2004] 1 I.R. 169, Sup Ct (Irl) 5.08
Tchenguiz v Imerman [2010] EWCA Civ 908; [2010] 2 F.L.R. 814; (2010) 154(30) S.J.L.B. 32 .... 4.03, 6.26
Technican Investments Ltd, Re [1985] B.C.L.C. 434, CA 5.49
Tedeschi v Singh [1948] Ch. 319; [1948] L.J.R. 1262, Ch.D 10.06
Tejendrasingh v Metsons; sub nom. Tejendrasingh v Christie; Singh (Tejendra) v Christie; Tejendrasingh v Ginn & Co; Tejendrasingh v Pickwell [1997] E.M.L.R. 597, CA (Civ Div) 15.28
Telebooth Pty Ltd v Telstra Corporation Ltd [1994] 1 V.R. 337, Sup Ct (Vic) 11.28, 11.31
Telezone Inc v Manley (2004) 235 D.L.R. (4th) 719, CA (Ontario) 10.31
Telstra Corp Ltd v B.T. Australasia Pty Ltd (1998) 156 A.L.R. 634, Fed. Ct. (Full Ct) Aus. 11.44, 12.06
Temple v South Manchester HA [2002] EWCA Civ 1406 .... 18.22
Teneria Moderna Franco Espanola v New Zealand Insurance Co; sub nom. Teneria Moderna Francoespanola SA v New Zealand Insurance Co [1924] 1 K.B. 79; (1923) 16 Ll. L. Rep. 368, CA 2.37
Teoh Pen Phe v Wan & Co [2001] 1 M.M.R. 358 .... 3.03
Testra Corporation Ltd v BT Australasia Pty Ltd (1998) 85 F.C.R. 152, Fed. Ct. (Full Ct) Aus. 12.04
Thames Housing Association Ltd v Bishop, unreported, September 2, 1991, CA 11.76, 12.18
Theaker's case (1625) Cro. Jac. 686 .... 19.20
Theodore v Australian Postal Commission [1988] V.R. 272 .... 5.54
Theodoropoulas v Theodoropoulas [1964] P. 311; [1963] 3 W.L.R. 354; [1963] 2 All E.R. 772; 107 S.J. 632, Assizes (Winchester) 11.134
Thermus v Aladdin Sales, unreported, October 25, 1999 .... 18.02, 18.08
Thomas v Palin (1882) L.R. 21 Ch. D. 360, CA 13.27
Thomason v Campbelltown Municpal Council (1939) 39 S.R.(N.S.W.) 347 .... 12.06
Thompson v Asda Stores Ltd; sub nom. Asda Stores Ltd v Thompson [2002] I.R.L.R. 245; [2002] Emp. L.R. 726, EAT 20.30
Thompson v ILEA (1977) 74 L.S. Gaz. 66 .... 11.99
Thomson v Berkhamsted Collegiate School [2009] EWHC 2374 (QB); [2010] C.P. Rep. 5; [2009] 6 Costs L.R. 859; (2009) 159 N.L.J. 1440 .... 2.46, 11.39
Thorburn v Hermon (Channel 4, Third Party), *The Times*, May 14, 1992, Q.B.D. 11.96, 12.42, 16.84
Thornett v Barclays Bank (France) Ltd [1939] 1 K.B. 675, CA 6.55
Thorpe v Chief Constable of Greater Manchester [1989] 1 W.L.R. 665; [1989] 2 All E.R. 827; 87 L.G.R. 537; (1989) 139 N.L.J. 467; (1989) 133 S.J. 750, CA (Civ Div) 5.09, 5.12, 5.24, 5.26, 5.31, 16.38

Thought Web Systems Pty Ltd v Loughnan (No.2)[2006] FCA 432; (2007) 230 A.L.R. 515, Fed. Ct of Australia 15.37
Three Rivers DC v Bank of England (Disclosure) (No.1); sub nom. Three Rivers DC v HM Treasury; Three Rivers DC v Bank of England (No.5); Three Rivers DC v Bank of England (No.4) [2002] EWCA Civ 1182; [2003] 1 W.L.R. 210; [2002] 4 All E.R. 881; [2003] C.P. Rep. 9; [2003] C.P.L.R. 181; (2002) 99(39) L.S.G. 40; affirming [2002] EWHC 1118, Q.B.D. (Comm.) 4.55, 4.56, 4.59, 5.40, 5.54, 10.05
Three Rivers DC v Bank of England (Disclosure) (No.2) [2002] EWHC 2309, Q.B.D. (Comm.) 4.56
Three Rivers DC v Bank of England (Disclosure) (No.3) [2003] EWCA Civ 474; [2003] Q.B. 1556; [2003] 3 W.L.R. 667; [2003] C.P.L.R. 349; (2003) 100(23) L.S.G. 37 ..... 11.09, 11.12, 11.15, 11.16, 11.27, 11.112, 11.16
Three Rivers DC v Bank of England (Disclosure) (No.4) [2004] UKHL 48; [2005] 1 A.C. 610; [2004] 3 W.L.R. 1274; [2005] 4 All E.R. 948; (2004) 101(46) L.S.G. 34; (2004) 154 N.L.J. 1727; (2004) 148 S.J.L.B. 1369; reversing [2004] EWCA Civ 218; [2004] Q.B. 916; [2004] 2 W.L.R. 1065; [2004] 3 All E.R. 168; (2004) 101(11) L.S.G. 36; (2004) 154 N.L.J. 382; (2004) 148 S.J.L.B. 297 .... 11.05, 11.08, 11.09, 11.10, 11.16, 11.17, 11.26, 11.31, 11.36, 11.37, 11.38, 11.48, 11.65
Three Rivers DC v Bank of England (Indemnity Costs) [2006] EWHC 816, Q.B.D. (Comm.) 6.01
Three Rivers DC v Bank of England (Restriction on Cross Examination) [2005] EWCA Civ 889; [2005] C.P. Rep. 46, CA (Civ Div) 17.29
Three Rivers District Council v Bank of England (No.6). *See* Three Rivers DC v Bank of England (Disclosure) (No.4)
Thrombosis Research Institute v Demoliou-Mason (Interrogatories) [1996] F.S.R. 785; (1996) 19(9) I.P.D. 19081, Ch.D (Patents Ct) .. 16.26, 16.51, 16.72
Thysson-Bornemisza v Thysson-Bornemisza (1999) 2 I.T.E.L.R. 467 .... 12.02
Tickell v Trifleska (1990) 24 N.S.W.L.R. 548 .... 11.10, 11.12
Tilbury Consulting Ltd v Gittins, unreported, August 15, 2003, SpC 20.75
Tirango Nominees Pty Ltd v Dairy Vale Foods Ltd (No.2) (1998) 83 F.C.R. 397, Fed. Ct. Aus. 12.24
Tito v Waddell [1975] 1 W.L.R. 1303; [1975] 3 All E.R. 997; 119 S.J. 680, Ch.D 19.12, 19.13
Tiver v Tiver [1969] S.A.S.R. 40 .... 16.34
Todd v Novotny [199] WASC 28, Sup Ct of Western Australia 11.60
Tolstoy Miloslavsky v United Kingdom (A/323) [1996] E.M.L.R. 152; (1995) 20 E.H.R.R. 442, ECHR 21.14
Tomlin v Standard Telephones & Cables Ltd [1969] 1 W.L.R. 1378; [1969] 3 All E.R. 201; [1969] 1 Lloyd's Rep. 309; 113 S.J. 641, CA (Civ Div) ... 11.130
Tomlinson, Re, Bank 2005/1, March 2, 2006, Isle of Man 2.40
Tora Tolmas v Spain (App. No.23816/94) May 17, 1995, Eur Comm. HR ... 21.05
Total E&P Soudan SA v Edmonds [2006] EWHC 1136, Q.B.D. (Comm.) 3.32
Totalise Plc v Motley Fool Ltd [2001] EWCA Civ 1897; [2002] 1 W.L.R. 1233; [2003] 2 All E.R. 872; [2002] C.P. Rep. 22; [2002] E.M.L.R. 20; [2002] F.S.R. 50; [2002] Masons C.L.R. 3; (2002) 99(9) L.S.G. 28; (2002) 146 S.J.L.B. 35 .... 3.24
Toth v Jarman [2006] EWCA Civ 1028 .... 18.13
Tournier v National Provincial and Union Bank of England [1924] 1 K.B. 461, CA 16.60
Toussaint v Mattis, unreported, May 22, 2000, CA 16.26
Trade Practices Commission v Abbco Ice Works Pty Ltd (1994) 123 A.L.R. 503, Fed. Ct. (Full Ct) Aus. 11.107

Trade Practices Commission v Ampol Petroleum (Victoria) Pty Ltd (1994) 127 A.L.R. 533, Fed. Ct. Aus. 11.28, 11.31, 11.48
Trade Practices Commission v Arnotts Ltd (1989) 88 A.L.R. 69, Fed. Ct. Aus. 12.40
Trade Practices Commission, Re v Arnotts [1989] FCA 248; (1990) 92 A.L.R. 527 .... 10.27
Trade Practices Commission v Kimberley Homes Pty Ltd (2005) 217 A.L.R. 110, Fed. Ct. Aus. 10.12, 10.28
Trade Practices Commission v Sterling (1979) 36 F.L.R. 244 .... 11.39
Trading Partners, Re. *See* Akers v Lomas
Transport Industries Insurance Co Ltd v Masel, unreported, October 19, 1998, Sup Ct (Vic) 12.06
Travelers Insurance Company Ltd v Countrywide Surveyors Ltd [2010] EWHC 2455 (TCC) 3.31, 20.04
Trinity Mirror plc v Punch Ltd, unreported, July 19, 2000 .... 3.19
Triolacan Ltd v Medway Power Drives Ltd, *The Times*, October 21, 1991, CA (Civ Div) 13.16
Triplex Safety Glass Co Ltd v Lancegaye Safety Glass (1934) Ltd [1939] 2 K.B. 395, CA 11.106, 11.107, 11.110
Tromso Sparebank v Beirne (No.2) [1989] I.L.R.M. 257 .... 1.16
Trouw UK Ltd v Mitsui & Co Plc [2007] EWHC 863 (Comm); [2007] U.K.C.L.R. 921 .... 3.34
Tsavliris Russ (Worldwide Salvage & Towage) Ltd v RL Baron Shipping Co SA; The Green Opal [2003] 1 Lloyd's Rep. 523, Q.B.D. (Admlty) 17.26
Tuck, Re; sub nom. Murch v Loosemore [1906] 1 Ch. 692, CA 2.49
Tucker (A Bankrupt) Ex p. Tucker, Re [1990] Ch. 148; [1988] 2 W.L.R. 748; [1988] 1 All E.R. 603; [1988] 1 F.T.L.R. 137; (1988) 132 S.J. 497, CA (Civ Div) **2.48**, 10.09
Tudor Accumulator Co Ltd v China Mutual Co [1931] W.N. 201, CA 19.07
Tullett Prebon Group Ltd v Davis (Jevin John) [2007] EWHC 2739 (QB) ... 5.11, 8.24, 11.151
Turkington v Times Newspapers Ltd [2000] U.K.H.L. 57 .... 11.137
Turner v Bayley (1864) 4 De G.J. & Sm. 332 .... 8.08
Turner v Davies [1981] 2 N.S.W.L.R. 324 .... 5.39, 5.46, 11.144
Turner v Jack (1871) 23 L.T. 800 .... 16.91
Turnstem Ltd v Bhanderi; Turnstem Ltd v Customs and Excise Commissioners [2004] EWHC 1318, Ch.D 2.32
Turton v Barber (1874) 17 Eq. 329 .... 11.09
Tweed v Parades Commission for Northern Ireland [2006] UKHL 53; [2007] 1 A.C. 650; [2007] 2 W.L.R. 1; [2007] 2 All E.R. 273; [2007] N.I. 66; [2007] H.R.L.R. 11; [2007] U.K.H.R.R. 456; 22 B.H.R.C. 92; (2007) 151 S.J.L.B. 24 .... 4.06, 4.07, **11.94**
Twentieth Century Fox Film Corp v Tryrare Ltd [1991] F.S.R. 58, Ch.D 2.24, 5.41, 11.105, 19.04

UCB Bank Plc v Halifax (SW) Ltd (Interrogatories) [1996] 2 E.G.L.R. 102; [1996] 36 E.G. 148, Q.B.D. 16.26
UCB Corporate Services Ltd (formerly UCB Bank Plc) v Halifax (SW) Ltd (Striking Out: Breach of Rules and Orders) [1999] C.P.L.R. 691; (2000) 97(1) L.S.G. 24; (2000) 144 S.J.L.B. 25, CA (Civ Div) 1.32
UJB Financial Corporation v Chilmark Offshore Capital Fund Ltd 1992–93 C.I.L.R. 53 (Cayman Grand Court) 3.22, 10.09, 10.57
USP Strategies Plc v London General Holdings Ltd (No.2) [2004] EWHC 373, Ch.D 11.27, 11.29, 11.32, 11.59, 11.60, 11.76, 12.07, 12.08

UYB Ltd v British Railways Board (2000) 97(43) L.S.G. 37; (2000) 97(42) L.S.G. 45; (2001) 81 P. & C.R. DG19, CA (Civ Div) 11.122
Ul-Haq v Shah [2009] EWCA Civ 542; [2010] 1 W.L.R. 616; [2010] 1 All E.R. 73; [2009] C.P. Rep. 39; [2010] 3 Costs L.R. 336; [2009] R.T.R. 27; [2010] Lloyd's Rep. I.R. 84; (2009) 159 N.L.J. 897 .... 13.07
Underwood v Cox [1912] 4 D.L.R. 66 .... 11.130
Unilateral Investments Ltd v VNZ Acquisitions Ltd [1993] 1 N.Z.L.R. 468 .... 11.15, 11.59
Unilever Plc v Chefaro Proprietaries Ltd (Discovery) [1994] F.S.R. 135, CA (Civ Div) 4.46, 5.35, 5.50
Unilever Plc v Gillette (UK) Ltd (Further Discovery) [1988] R.P.C. 416, Ch.D (Patents Ct) 5.51
Unilever Plc v Pearce [1985] F.S.R. 475, Ch.D (Patents Ct) 19.06, 19.07, 19.10, 19.11
Unilever Plc v Procter & Gamble Co [2000] 1 W.L.R. 2436; [2001] 1 All E.R. 783; [2000] F.S.R. 344; (2000) 23(1) I.P.D. 23001; (1999) 96(44) L.S.G. 40; (1999) 143 S.J.L.B. 268, CA (Civ Div); affirming [1999] 1 W.L.R. 1630; [1999] 2 All E.R. 691; [1999] F.S.R. 849; (1999) 22(5) I.P.D. 22042; (1999) 149 N.L.J. 370, Ch.D (Patents Ct) 11.125, 11.128, 11.129
Union Carbide Corp v BP Chemicals Ltd 1995 S.C. 398; 1995 S.L.T. 972; 1995 S.C.L.R. 524; [1995] F.S.R. 449, IH (1 Div) 2.32
Union Insurance Ltd v Incorporated General Assurance Ltd, unreported, July 2, 1991, CA 9.05
United Capital Corp v Bender [2005] J.R.C. 144, R. Ct (Jersey) 11.60, 12.08, 12.19, 12.20, 12.34
United Kingdom v U.S., 238 F.3d 1312 (11th Cir. 2001) 2.63
United Norwest Cooperative v Johnstone (Disclosure), *The Times*, February 24, 1994; *Independent*, March 1, 1994, CA (Civ Div) 2.25
United States v Exxon Corporation, 94 F.R.D. 246 (1981) 12.06
United States v McRae; sub nom. United States v Mcrae; United States v Macrae; United States of America v Mcrae (1867–68) L.R. 3 Ch. App. 79, CA 11.104
United States v Philip Morris Inc (No.1) [2004] EWCA Civ 330; [2004] 1 C.L.C. 811; (2004) 148 S.J.L.B. 388 .... 10.54, 10.59, 11.10, 11.38
United States v Wagner (1867) L.R. 2 Ch. App. 852 .... 4.43
United States v Woodall, 438 F. 2d. 1317 (1970) 12.06
Universal City Studios Inc v Hubbard [1984] Ch. 225; [1984] 2 W.L.R. 492; [1984] 1 All E.R. 661; [1984] R.P.C. 43; (1984) 81 L.S.G. 1291; (1984) 128 S.J. 247, CA (Civ Div) 11.116
Universal Thermosensors Ltd v Hibben [1992] 1 W.L.R. 840; [1992] 3 All E.R. 257; [1992] F.S.R. 361; (1992) 142 N.L.J. 195, Ch.D 2.22
University of Southampton v Kelly, unreported, November 14, 2005, EAT 11.10, 11.70, 12.15, 20.30
University of Western Australia v Gray (No.8) [2007] FCA 89, Fed. Ct of Australia 11.01, 11.156
Unterpertinger v Austria (A/110); sub nom. Unterpertinger v Austria (App. No.9120/80) (1991) 13 E.H.R.R. 175, ECHR 21.06
Uphill v BRB (Residuary) Ltd [2005] EWCA Civ 60; [2005] 1 W.L.R. 2070; [2005] 3 All E.R. 264; [2005] C.P. Rep. 20; (2005) 102(15) L.S.G. 35; (2005) 149 S.J.L.B. 181) 6.57
Upjohn Co v United States, 449 U.S. 383 (1981), Sup Ct (US) 11.17, 11.112
Urban Renewal Authority v Agrila Ltd [2009] HKCFI 229 .... 12.19

Urban Small Space Ltd v Burford Investment Co Ltd [1990] 2 E.G.L.R. 120; [1990] 28 E.G. 116 .... 5.28, 20.08
Uthmann v Ipswich City Council [1998] 1 Qd. R. 435, Sup Ct (Queensland) ... 4.60, 10.10, 10.12

V v C [2001] EWCA Civ 1509; [2002] C.P. Rep. 8; (2001) 98(43) L.S.G. 34; (2001) 145 S.J.L.B. 243, CA (Civ Div) 11.107
Vale v Oppert (1874–75) L.R. 10 Ch. App. 340, CA in Chancery 11.149
Van de Hurk v Netherlands (A/288) (1994) 18 E.H.R.R. 481, ECHR 21.07
Van der Mussele v Belgium (A/70) (1984) 6 E.H.R.R. 163, ECHR 21.16
Van Leuven v Belgium. *See* Le Compte v Belgium (A/43)
Van Leuven v Nielson (1993) 15 G.L.J. 79, CA (Guernsey) 1.17
Van Mechelen v Netherlands (Art.6) (1998) 25 E.H.R.R. 647; 2 B.H.R.C. 486, ECHR 21.07
Van Orshoven v Belgium (App. No.20122/92) (1998) 26 E.H.R.R. 55, ECHR 21.06
Vardas v South British Insurance Co Ltd [1984] 2 N.S.W.L.R. 652 .... 11.32
Vasiliou v Hajigeorgiou; sub nom. Hajigeorgiou v Vasiliou [2005] EWCA Civ 236; [2005] 1 W.L.R. 2195; [2005] 3 All E.R. 17; [2005] C.P. Rep. 27; (2005) 102(18) L.S.G. 22; [2005] N.P.C. 39 .... 12.10, 18.07, 19.22
Vector Transportation Services Inc v Traffic Tech Inc, 2008 Can LII 11050, Ontario Superior Ct 7.09, 9.29
Vehicle Inspectorate v Cantabrica Coach Holdings Ltd; sub nom. Cantabrica Coach Holdings Ltd v Vehicle Inspectorate [2001] UKHL 60; [2001] 1 W.L.R. 2288; [2002] 1 All E.R. 595; affirming (2000) 164 J.P. 593; [2000] R.T.R. 286; (2000) 97(18) L.S.G. 37, DC 2.22, 10.15, 21.08, 21.10, 21.12
Venables v News Group Newspapers Ltd; Thompson v News Group Newspapers Ltd [2001] Fam. 430; [2001] 2 W.L.R. 1038; [2001] 1 All E.R. 908; [2001] E.M.L.R. 10; [2001] 1 F.L.R. 791; [2002] 1 F.C.R. 333; [2001] H.R.L.R. 19; [2001] U.K.H.R.R. 628; 9 B.H.R.C. 587; [2001] Fam. Law 258; (2001) 98(12) L.S.G. 41; (2001) 151 N.L.J. 57; (2001) 145 S.J.L.B. 43, Fam Div 21.04
Ventouris v Mountain; The Italia Express (No.1) [1991] 1 W.L.R. 607; [1991] 3 All E.R. 472; [1991] 1 Lloyd's Rep. 441; (1991) 141 N.L.J. 237, CA (Civ Div); reversing [1990] 1 W.L.R. 1370; [1990] 3 All E.R. 157; [1990] 2 Lloyd's Rep. 154; (1990) 87(35) L.S.G. 40; (1990) 140 N.L.J. 666, Q.B.D. (Comm.) ... 4.32, 6.09, 6.15, 8.01, 11.05, 11.06, 11.031, 11.33, 11.34, 11.50, 11.56, 11.57, 12.02
Ventouris v Mountain; The Italia Express (No.2) [1992] 1 W.L.R. 887; [1992] 3 All E.R. 414; [1992] 2 Lloyd's Rep. 216, CA (Civ Div) 5.06
Vermeulen v Belgium, February 20, 1996, Eur Comm. HR 21.06
Vernon v Bosley (No.2) [1999] Q.B. 18; [1997] 3 W.L.R. 683; [1997] 1 All E.R. 614; [1997] R.T.R. 275; [1998] 1 F.L.R. 304; [1997] P.I.Q.R. P326; (1997) 35 B.M.L.R. 174; [1997] Fam. Law 476; (1997) 94(4) L.S.G. 26; (1997) 147 N.L.J. 89; (1997) 141 S.J.L.B. 27, CA (Civ Div) 1.16, 5.41, 13.36
Vernon v Spoudeas [2010] EWCA Civ 666 .... 13.24
Vernon v United Kingdom (App. No.38753/97), unreported September 7, 1999, Eur Comm. HR 21.06
Versailles Trade Finance Ltd, Re (in administrative receivership), *The Times*, November 1, 2001 .... 11.107
Vickers v Horsell Graphic Industries [1988] R.P.C. 421, Ch.D (Patents Ct) 5.25, 5.35, 8.20

Victor Chandler International Ltd v Customs and Excise Commissioners [2000] 1 W.L.R. 1296; [2000] 2 All E.R. 315; (2000) 97(11) L.S.G. 36; (2000) 150 N.L.J. 341; (2000) 144 S.J.L.B. 127, CA (Civ Div) 5.02
Victor Covacevich, The (1885) 10 P.D. 40 .... 19.09
Victor Hanby Associates v Oliver 1990 J.L.R. 337, CA (Jersey) 1.17, 6.41
Victory, The. *See* Antares II and Victory, The
Vimbos v Meadowcroft (1901) 46 S.J.2 .... 17.06
Visser v Netherlands, unreported, May 2, 1989, Eur Comm. HR 21.10
Vista Maritime Inc v Sesa Goa, unreported, October 24, 1997 .... 12.22, 12.23, 12.36
Visx Inc v Nidek Co Ltd (No.2) [1999] F.S.R. 91; (1998) 21(9) I.P.D. 21094, CA (Civ Div 2.323, 5.50, 11.09, 11.13, 11.21, 11.28, 11.31, 12.26, 12.32, 12.33, 16.80, 17.09
Vitol SA v Capri Marine Ltd [2008] EWHC 378 (Comm) 2.48
Von Hannover v Germany (App. No.59320/00) [2004] E.M.L.R. 21; (2005) 40 E.H.R.R. 1; 16 B.H.R.C. 545, ECHR 21.11, 21.15
Vowell v Shire of Hastings [1970] V.R. 764 .... 3.27, 19.02

WEA Records Ltd v Visions Channel 4 Ltd [1983] 1 W.L.R. 721; [1983] 2 All E.R. 589; [1984] F.S.R. 404; (1983) 127 S.J. 362, CA (Civ Div) 10.51. 10.61
WH Smith Ltd v Colman (t/a Cherished Domains) [2001] F.S.R. 9, CA (Civ Div) 11.129
W (J) (Guardian ad litem) v Yukon Territory (Comr) (1992) 85 D.L.R. (4th) 533, CA (Yukon) 11.44
W (Minors) (Social Worker: Disclosure), Re; sub nom. W (Disclosure to Police), Re [1999] 1 W.L.R. 205; [1998] 2 All E.R. 801; [1998] 2 F.L.R. 135; [1998] 2 F.C.R. 405; [1998] Fam. Law 387; (1998) 142 S.J.L.B. 132, CA (Civ Div) 4.04
W Dennis & Sons Ltd v West Norfolk Farmers' Manure & Chemical Cooperative Co Ltd [1943] Ch. 220, Ch.D 11.73
Wagstaffe v Anderson, Moss & Michell (1878) 39 L.T. 322 .... 6.07
Wah v Gold Chief Investment Ltd [2003] H.K.C.F.I. 468 .... 11.09
Wahl and Simon-Solitec Ltd v Buhler Miag (England) Ltd [1979] F.S.R. 183, Ch.D (Patents Ct) 19.11
Waind v Hill and Employers Mutual General Association Ltd [1978] 1 N.S.W.L.R. 372 .... 10.27
Waind v Hill and National Employers' Mutual General Association Ltd [1987] 1 N.S.W.L.R. 376, CA (NSW) 10.27
Wakefield v Outhwaite [1990] 2 Lloyd's Rep. 157, Q.B.D. (Comm.) .. 10.10, 10.12, 10.21, 10.32, 10.57
Waldridge v Kennison (1794) 1 Esp. 142 .... 11.129
Walker (Valerie) v Eli Lilly & Co [1986] E.C.C. 550; (1986) 136 N.L.J. 608, Q.B.D. 3.39
Walker v Daniels. *See* D (A Child) v Walker
Walker v Ost [1970] R.P.C. 151, CA 6.41
Walker v Poole (1882) L.R. 21 Ch. D. 835, Ch.D 6.19
Walker v Wilsher (1889) L.R. 23 Q.B.D. 335, CA .. 11.129, 11.130, 11.132, 12.02, 12.39
Wallace Smith Trust Co Ltd (In Liquidation) v Deloitte Haskins & Sells [1997] 1 W.L.R. 257; [1996] 4 All E.R. 403; [1997] B.C.C. 29;, CA (Civ Div); reversing [1995] C.L.C. 223, Q.B.D. 11.01, 11.02, 11.99, 11.33, 11.89, 11.151, 15.01

Walsh Automation (Europe Ltd) v Bridgeman [2002] EWHC 1344, Q.B.D. 11.69
Walton v Brignell [1875] W.N. 239 .... 16.62
Warden Burton SM, Re, Ex p. Roberts (1997) 18 W.A.R. 379, Sup Ct (Full Ct) (W Aus) 11.105, 11.107
Wardlaw v Farrar [2003] EWCA Civ 1719; [2003] 4 All E.R. 1358; [2004] P.I.Q.R. P19; [2004] Lloyd's Rep. Med. 98; (2004) 101(3) L.S.G. 33 ...... 18.14, 18.22
Wardrope v Dunn [1996] 1 Qd.R. 224, Sup Ct (Queensland) 11.64, 12.06
Warman v Wilkins-Fournier (2010) 319 D.L.R. (3d) 268, Ontario SCJ 3.11
Warner Brothers Productions Ltd v Telegraph Group Ltd, unreported, November 19, 1999 .... 6.44
Warner v Moses (1880) 16 Ch.D. 100, CA 17.02
Warner-Lambert Co v Glaxo Laboratories Ltd [1975] R.P.C. 354, CA (Civ Div) 5.37, 11.158, 11.159, 11.160, 11.163
Warren v Richard Costain Ltd, unreported, May 15, 1991 .... 10.13, 10.35
Wasted Costs Order (No.5 of 1997), Re. *See* Barristers (Wasted Costs Order: Criminal Proceedings) (No.5 of 1997), Re
Water Authority of Western Australia v AIL Holdings Pty Ltd (1992) 7 W.A.R. 135, Sup Ct (W Aus) 11.34
Waterford v Commonwealth of Australia (1986–87) 163 C.L.R. 54, H Ct (Aus) 11.19
Waterhouse v Barker [1924] 2 K.B. 759, CA 10.48, 10.50, 11.106
Watford Petroleum Ltd v Interoil Trading SA (Disclosure: Exchange of Documents) [2003] EWCA Civ 1417; [2003] All E.R. (D) 175 (Sep ... 2.33
Watkins v AJ Wright (Electrical) Ltd [1996] 3 All E.R. 31, Ch.D ... 14.15, 14.17, 15.44, 15.45
Watkins v Ross (1893) 68 L.T. 423 .... 2.47, 2.48
Watson v Cammell Laird & Co (Shipbuilders and Engineers) [1959] 1 W.L.R. 702; [1959] 2 All E.R. 757; [1959] 2 Lloyd's Rep. 175; 103 S.J. 470, CA 11.33, 11.34
Watson v Chief Constable of Cleveland [2001] EWCA Civ 1547, CA (Civ Div) 17.29
Watson v General Medical Council [2005] EWHC 1896; [2006] I.C.R. 113; [2005] Lloyd's Rep. Med. 435; (2005) 86 B.M.L.R. 152; (2005) 155 N.L.J. 1356, Q.B.D. (Admin) 18.25
Watson v Ian Snipe & Co [2002] EWCA Civ 293 .... 16.26
Watts v Raine (t/a Raine Erections), Taylor (Third Party), 115 S.J. 607, CA (Civ Div) 11.129
Waugh v British Railways Board [1980] A.C. 521; [1979] 3 W.L.R. 150; [1979] 2 All E.R. 1169; [1979] I.R.L.R. 364; 123 S.J. 506, HL 11.37, 11.38, 11.44, 11.46, 11.56
Wayne Farley Ltd v Customs and Excise Commissioners [1986] S.T.C. 487, Q.B.D. 20.90
Webb v East (1880) 5 Ex. Ch. 108 .... 6.15, 11.138, 16.85
Weber v Switzerland (A/177) (1990) 12 E.H.R.R. 508, ECHR 21.15
Webster v James Chapman & Co [1989] 3 All E.R. 939, Ch.D 11.76
Webster v Ridgeway Foundation School Governors [2009] EWHC 1140 (QB); [2009] E.L.R. 439; (2009) 153(22) S.J.L.B. 31 .... 9.05
Webster v Salloway [1931] 1 D.L.R. 831 .... 11.107
Webster v Whewall (1880) L.R. 15 Ch. D. 120, Ch.D 9.08
Wee Soon Kim Authority v UBS AG [2003] S.G.C.A. 5 .... 10.40
Welfare v Birdon Sands Pty Ltd (1997) 79 F.C.R. 220, Fed. Ct. Aus. 10.15, 15.11

Wellcome Foundation Ltd v V.R. Laboratories (Austr) Pty Ltd (1981) 148 C.L.R. 262 .... 5.08
Wellcome Foundation Ltd's Australian Applications [1981] F.S.R. 72; [1981] R.P.C. 35, HC (Aus) 5.35
Welsbach Incandescent Gas Light Co Ltd v New Sunlight Incandescent Co. (Interrogatories) [1900] 2 Ch. 1, CA ... 16.94, 16.95, 16.98, 16.102, 16.103, 16.104
Wenham Co. Ltd v Champion Gas Lamp Co Ltd (1890) 8 R.P.C. 22 .... 5.35
Wentworth v Lloyd (1864) 10 H.L.C. 589, HL 11.08
West London Pipeline & Storage Ltd v Total UK Ltd [2008] EWHC 1296 (Comm) 5.23, 16.44
West London Pipeline & Storage Ltd v Total UK Ltd [2008] EWHC 1729 (Comm) 6.41, 6.44, 11.46
West Midlands Passenger Transport Executive v Singh [1988] 1 W.L.R. 730; [1988] 2 All E.R. 873; [1988] I.C.R. 614; [1988] I.R.L.R. 186; (1988) 132 S.J. 933, CA (Civ Div) 8.20, 20.28
West Midlands Police Authority v Walsall MBC, *Independent*, February 26, 1992, Q.B.D. 11.99
West of England Bank v Canton Insurance Co (1877) 2 Ex.D. 472 .... 2.32
Western Canadian Shopping Centres Inc v Dutton [2001] 2 S.C.R. 534, Sup Ct (Canada) 4.32
Western Trust & Savings Ltd v Acland & Lensam, unreported, May 23, 2000 .... 13.10
Westinghouse Corporation and Duquesne Light Co, Re (1977) 16 O.R. (2d) 273, H Ct (Ont) 10.55
Westinghouse Electric Corp Uranium Contract Litigation MDL Docket 235 (No.2); sub nom. Rio Tinto ZinCorp v Westinghouse Electric Corp (Nos.1 and 2); RTZ Services Ltd v Westinghouse Electric Corp [1978] A.C. 547; [1978] 2 W.L.R. 81; [1978] 1 All E.R. 434; [1978] 1 C.M.L.R. 100; 122 S.J. 32, HL ... 2.23, 3.17, 8.06, 10.56, 10.55, 10.57, 11.89, 11.104, 11.105, 11.106, 11.109, 11.110, 11.111, 11.112
Westminster Airways Ltd v Kuwait Oil Co Ltd [1951] 1 K.B. 134; [1950] 2 All E.R. 596; (1950) 84 Ll. L. Rep. 297; 22 A.L.R.2d 648, CA 6.41, 11.02, 11.45, 11.60
Westminster Property Management Ltd (No.1), Re; sub nom. Official Receiver v Stern (No.1) [2000] 1 W.L.R. 2230; [2001] 1 All E.R. 633; [2001] B.C.C. 121; [2000] 2 B.C.L.C. 396; [2000] U.K.H.R.R. 332, CA (Civ Div) 11.105, 11.109, 21.05
Wheeler v Le Marchant (1881) L.R. 17 Ch. D. 675, CA 8.23, 11.08, 11.09, 11.14, 11.15, 11.18, 11.21, 11.26, 11.31, 11.39, 11.48, 11.143, 11.153
Whiffen v Hartwright (1848) 11 Beav. 111 .... 8.08
Whipman v Whipman [1951] 2 All E.R. 228; [1951] 2 T.L.R. 518; [1951] W.N. 333; 95 S.J. 383, PDAD 11.143
Whistler v Hancock (1878) 3 Q.B.D. 83 .... 13.23
Whitaker v Izod (1809) 2 Taunt. 115 .... 10.31
Whitbourne v Pettifer (1834) 4 Moo. & B. 182 .... 4.19
White v Overland [2001] F.C.A. 1835 .... 11.123
White v Watts (1862) 12 C.B.(N.S.) 267 .... 16.29
White & Co v Credit Reform Association and Credit Index Ltd [1905] 1 K.B. 653, CA 16.52, 16.62
Whitehall v Whitehall, 1957 S.L.T. 196 .... 11.134

Whitehouse v Jordan [1981] 1 W.L.R. 246; [1981] 1 All E.R. 267; 125 S.J. 167, HL 18.13
Whiteman v Whiteman, unreported, March 9, 1994 .... 2.53
White's Patent (Revocation), Re [1957] R.P.C. 405 .... 19.19
Whitmarsh v Chief Constable of Avon & Somerset, unreported, March 31, 2000, CA 11.103
Whittaker v Scarborough Post Newspaper Co [1896] 2 Q.B. 148, CA 16.62
Whittaker v Soper [2001] EWCA Civ 1462, CA (Civ Div) 13.24
Whitworth v Davis (1813) 1 Ves. & B. 545 .... 4.19
Whitworth, Re. *See* O'Rourke v Darbishire
Whyte & Co v Ahrens & Co (1884) 50 L.T. 344 .... 9.13
Whyte v Ahrens (1884) L.R. 26 Ch. D. 717; (1884) 32 W.R. 649, CA 2.33
Wieser v Austria (App. No.74336/01, October 16, 2007, ECHR 21.08
Wilden Pump v Fusfield [1985] F.S.R. 581 .... 15.20, 15.22
Wilden Pump Engineering Co v Fusfeld [1985] F.S.R. 159, CA (Civ Div) ... 11.21, 11.23, 11.42
Wildman v DPP [2001] EWHC Admin 14; (2001) 165 J.P. 453; [2001] Crim. L.R. 565; (2001) 165 J.P.N. 290, DC 21.06
Wilkinson v Kenny, unreported, February 9, 1993, CA 14.16
Wilkinson v West Coast Capital (Pre-Trial Review); sub nom. New Gadget Shop Ltd, Re; Gadget Shop Ltd, Re [2005] EWHC 1606, Ch.D 11.129
Wilks & Berks Canal Navigation v Swindon Waterworks (1872) 2 W.R. 353 .... 16.39
Williams v Barclays Bank Plc; sub nom. Williams v Williams; Tucker v Williams [1988] Q.B. 161; [1987] 3 W.L.R. 790; [1987] 3 All E.R. 257; [1988] 1 F.L.R. 455; [1987] 2 F.T.L.R. 393; [1987] Fin. L.R. 361; [1988] Fam. Law 204; (1987) 84 L.S.G. 2455; (1987) 131 S.J. 1214, CA (Civ Div) 10.23, 10.40
Williams v Bogg (1941) 57 T.L.R. 70 .... 11.130
Williams v Home Office (No.1) [1981] 1 All E.R. 1151, Q.B.D. 11.98, 15.25
Williams v Home Office (No.2) [1982] 2 All E.R. 564, CA (Civ Div) 15.25
Williams v Hull [2009] EWHC 2844 (Ch); [2009] N.P.C. 132 .... 11.127, 11.129
Williams v Ingram (1900) 16 T.L.R. 434 .... 4.47
Williams v Ingram (1990) 16 T.L.R. 451, CA 11.145
Williams v Prince of Wales (1857) 23 Beav. 336 .... 15.02
Williams v Quebrada Railway Land & Copper Co [1895] 2 Ch. 751, Ch.D 11.69
Williams v Secretary of State for the Home Department. *See* R. (on the application of Williams) v Secretary of State for the Home Department
Williams v Summerfield [1972] 2 Q.B. 512; [1972] 3 W.L.R. 131; [1972] 2 All E.R. 1334; (1972) 56 Cr. App. R. 597; [1972] Crim. L.R. 424; 116 S.J. 413, DC 10.43, 10.46, 10.48
Williams Aviation Pty Ltd v Santos Ltd (1985) 40 S.A.S.R. 272 .... 4.60
Williams & Glyn's Bank Ltd v Barnes, unreported, January 16, 1979 .... 10.10
Willis v Trequair (1906) 3 C.L.R. 912 .... 2.61
Willis & Co v Baddeley [1892] 2 Q.B. 324, CA 4.21, 4.21
Willoughby's case (1597) Cro. Eliz. 566 .... 19.20
Wilmot v Maccabe (1831) 4 Sim. 263 .... 3.14
Wilsher v Essex AHA [1988] A.C. 1074; [1988] 2 W.L.R. 557; [1988] 1 All E.R. 871; (1988) 138 N.L.J. Rep. 78; (1988) 132 S.J. 418, HL 18.22
Wilson v Church (Joinder of Defendant for Discovery) (1878) L.R. 9 Ch. D. 552, Ch.D 1.12, 3.12

Wilson v First County Trust Ltd (No.2); sub nom. Wilson v Secretary of State for Trade and Industry [2003] UKHL 40; [2004] 1 A.C. 816; [2003] 3 W.L.R. 568; [2003] 4 All E.R. 97; [2003] 2 All E.R. (Comm.) 491; [2003] H.R.L.R. 33; [2003] U.K.H.R.R. 1085; (2003) 100(35) L.S.G. 39; (2003) 147 S.J.L.B. 872 .... 21.01
Wilson v Raffalofitch (1881) 7 Q.B.D. 553, CA 13.15, 13.27
Wilson v Thornbury (1874) L.R. 17 Eq.517 .... 5.20
Wilson v White [2005] 3 N.Z.L.R. 619, CA (NZ) 15.25
Winterthur Swiss Insurance Co v AG (Manchester) Ltd (In Liquidation) [2006] EWHC 839, Q.B.D. (Comm.) 11.05, 11.06, 11.08, 12.03
Wippermann, Re; sub nom. Wissler v Wippermann; Wipperman (Deceased), Re [1955] P. 59; [1953] 2 W.L.R. 706; [1953] 1 All E.R. 764; 97 S.J. 231, PDAD 17.08
Wiszniewski v Central Manchester HA; sub nom. Wisniewski v Central Manchester HA [1998] P.I.Q.R. P324; [1998] Lloyd's Rep. Med. 223, CA (Civ Div) 17.27
Wolverhampton New Water Works v Hawksford (1859) 5 C.B.(N.S.) 703 ... 16.41
Wood v The Anglo-Italian Bank Ltd (1876) 34 L.T. 255 .... 2.33
Woodford & Ackroyd v Burgess [2000] C.P. Rep. 79; [1999] Lloyd's Rep. P.N. 231, CA (Civ Div) 18.11
Woodhouse & Co Ltd v Woodhouse (1914) 30 T.L.R. 559, CA 6.15, 11.73
Woods v Martins Bank [1959] 1 Q.B. 55; [1958] 1 W.L.R. 1018; [1958] 3 All E.R. 166; 102 S.J. 655, Assizes (Leeds) 14.02, 14.09
Woodside Energy Ltd v Commissioner of Taxation [2006] FCA 1303; (2007) 233 A.L.R. 710, Fed. Ct of Austraalia 18.11
Woodworth v Conroy; Conroy v Woodworth [1976] Q.B. 884; [1976] 2 W.L.R. 338; [1976] 1 All E.R. 107; (1975) 119 S.J. 810, CA (Civ Div) ... 11.148
Woolgar v Chief Constable of Sussex [2000] 1 W.L.R. 25; [1999] 3 All E.R. 604; (2000) 2 L.G.L.R. 340; [1999] Lloyd's Rep. Med. 335; (1999) 50 B.M.L.R. 296; (1999) 96(23) L.S.G. 33; (1999) 149 N.L.J. 857; (1999) 143 S.J.L.B. 195, CA (Civ Div) 11.80
Woolwich Building Society v Taylor [1995] 1 B.C.L.C. 132; [1994] C.L.C. 516, Ch.D 5.23
Woolworths Ltd v FELS (2002) 193 A.L.R. 1, H Ct (Aus) 11.77
Woori Bank v KDB Ireland Ltd.[2005] I.E.H.C. 451 .... 11.57
World Protector, The [1985] 1 Lloyd's Rep. 227, Q.B.D. (Admlty) 13.05
Worm v Austria (App. No.22714/93) (1998) 25 E.H.R.R. 454; 3 B.H.R.C. 180, ECHR 21.15
Worrall v Reich [1955] 1 Q.B. 296; [1955] 2 W.L.R. 338; [1955] 1 All E.R. 363; 99 S.J. 109, CA 18.16
Worrell v Woods (1999) 163 A.L.R. 195, Fed. Ct. Aus. 11.06, 11.77, 12.02
Worswick, Re; sub nom. Robson v Worswick (1888) L.R. 38 Ch. D. 370, Ch.D 11.28
Wright & Co v Mills (1890) 62 L.T. 558 .... 11.145
Wright Norman v Oversea-Chinese Banking Corp Ltd [1992] 2 S.L.R. 710 CA (Singapore) 1.19, 5.33, 16.65
Wright v Goodlake (1865) 13 L.T. 120 .... 16.39, 16.71
Wright v Wilkin (1858) 6 W.R. 643 .... 17.06

X v Austria (1972) 42 C.D. 145, Eur Comm. HR 21.06
X v Austria (1979) 18 D.R. 154 .... 21.17
X v Belgium (1982) 31 D.R. 231, Eur Comm. HR 21.10
X v Council of the European Communities (18/70) [1972] E.C.R. 1205, ECJ 20.37

X v Germany (1975) 3 D.R. 92 .... 21.17
X v Germany (1979) 17 D.R. 227, Eur Comm. HR 21.10
X v Germany (1984) 39 D.R. 90, Eur Comm. HR 21.16
X v Netherlands (A/91); sub nom. X and Y v Netherlands (App. No.8978/80); Y v Netherlands (A/91) (1986) 8 E.H.R.R. 235, ECHR ... 21.08
X v United Kingdom (1982) 5 E.H.R.R. 273 .... 21.05
X v United Kingdom (1993) 15 E.H.R.R. C.D. 113 .... 21.07
X (Children), Re [2007] EWHC 1719 (Fam); [2008] 1 F.L.R. 589; [2008] Fam. Law 23 .... 4.04
X (Children), Re; sub nom. X (Children) (Disclosure for purposes of criminal proceedings), Re [2008] EWHC 242 (Fam); [2008] 3 All E.R. 958; [2008] 3 F.C.R. 23; [2008] Fam. Law 725 .... 4.04
X (Minors) v Bedfordshire CC; M (A Minor) v Newham LBC; E (A Minor) v Dorset CC (Appeal); Christmas v Hampshire CC (Duty of Care); Keating v Bromley LBC (No.2) [1995] 2 A.C. 633; [1995] 3 W.L.R. 152; [1995] 3 All E.R. 353; [1995] 2 F.L.R. 276; [1995] 3 F.C.R. 337; 94 L.G.R. 313; (1995) 7 Admin. L.R. 705; [1995] Fam. Law 537; (1996) 160 L.G. Rev. 103; (1996) 160 L.G. Rev. 123; (1995) 145 N.L.J. 993, HL 18.15
X (Minors), Re. *See* X, Y and Z (Minors) (Wardship: Disclosure of Material), Re
X AG v Bank, A; sub nom. X,Y & Z v B [1983] 2 All E.R. 464; [1983] 2 Lloyd's Rep. 535; [1983] Com. L.R. 134; (1983) 133 N.L.J. 400, Q.B.D. (Comm.) 8.14
X Ltd v Morgan Grampian (Publishers) Ltd [1991] 1 A.C. 1; [1990] 2 W.L.R. 1000; [1990] 2 All E.R. 1; (1990) 87(17) L.S.G. 28; (1990) 140 N.L.J. 553; (1990) 134 S.J. 546, HL 2.12, 2.15, 3.19, 3.20, 11.153
X v Australian Crime Commission (2005) 212 A.L.R. 596, Fed. Ct. Aus. 11.104
X, Case of (1977) 19 D.R. 66, Eur Comm. HR 21.14
X, Y and Z (Minors) (Wardship: Disclosure of Material), Re [1992] Fam. 124; [1992] 2 W.L.R. 784; [1992] 2 All E.R. 595; [1992] 1 F.L.R. 84; [1991] F.C.R. 953; [1991] Fam. Law 318; (1991) 141 N.L.J. 708, Fam Div
XL Communications Group Plc (In Liquidation), Re; sub nom. Green v BDO Stoy Hayward LLP [2005] EWHC 2413, Ch.D 3.43
XL London Market Ltd v Zenith Syndicate Management Ltd [2004] EWHC 1182(Comm) 3.34

Yasuda Fire & Marine Insurance Co of Europe Ltd v Orion Marine Insurance Underwriting Agency Ltd [1995] Q.B. 174; [1995] 2 W.L.R. 49; [1995] 3 All E.R. 211; [1995] 1 Lloyd's Rep. 525; [1994] C.L.C. 1212; [1995] 4 Re. L.R. 217, Q.B.D. (Comm.) 4.20, 5.52
Yianni v Yianni [1966] 1 W.L.R. 120; [1966] 1 All E.R. 231 (Note); 110 S.J. 111, Ch.D 10.04, 11.109
Yokogawa v Alstom [2009] SASC 377; 262 S.L.R. 739 .... 12.06
York University v Bell Canada Enterprise (2010) D.L.R. (4th) 755, SCJ (Ont) 3.11
Yorke v Katra [2002] EWCA Civ 867 .... 18.09
Yorkshire Electricity Distribution Plc v Telewest plc [2006] EWCA Civ. 1418 .... 20.55
Yorkshire Provident Life Assurance Co v Gilbert & Rivington [1895] 2 Q.B. 148, CA 5.33, 16.65
Youell v Bland, Welch & Co Ltd [1991] 1 W.L.R. 122 .... 12.10

Yousif v Salama [1980] 1 W.L.R. 1540; [1980] 3 All E.R. 405; [1980] F.S.R. 444; 124 S.J. 480, CA (Civ Div) 2.21
Youssef v Jordan; sub nom. Youssif v Jordan [2003] EWCA Civ 1852 ...... 18.22
Yu Chee Yin v Commissioner of the Independent Commission against Corruption [2000] H.K.C.F.I. 838 .... 4.06
Yu v Chiu Wah v Gold Chief Investment Ltd [2003] H.K.C.F.I. 468 .... 14.03
Yukong Line Ltd of Korea v Rendsburg Investments Corp of Liberia; The Rialto (Mareva Proceedings: Cross Examination), *The Times*, October 22, 1996, CA (Civ Div) 2.13, 13.31, 16.114

Z v Finland (1998) 25 E.H.R.R. 371; (1999) 45 B.M.L.R. 107, ECHR 10.15, 21.10, 21.12
Z v New South Wales Crime Commission [2007] HCA 7; (2007) 231 C.L.R. 75, High Ct of Australia 11.13
Z Ltd v A-Z [1982] Q.B. 558; [1982] 2 W.L.R. 288; [1982] 1 All E.R. 556; [1982] 1 Lloyd's Rep. 240; [1982] E.C.C. 362; 126 S.J. 100, CA (Civ Div) 4.65, 19.06
Zaiwalla & Co v Union of India, unreported, November 27, 1992 ... 11.97, 11.139, 11.140, 11.141
Zakharov v White [2003] EWHC 2463 (Ch) 13.27
Zanen Dredging and Contracting Co Ltd v Costain Civil Engineering Ltd (1996) 12 Const. L.J. 129, Q.B.D. (OR) 11.129
Zierenberg v Labouchere [1893] 2 Q.B. 183, CA 16.65
Zubulake v UBS Warburg (2003) 220 F.R.D. 212 .... 13.18
ZYX Music GmbH v King [1997] 2 All E.R. 129; [1997] E.C.C. 477, CA (Civ Div); affirming [1995] 3 All E.R. 1; [1996] E.C.C. 314; [1995] E.M.L.R. 281; [1995] F.S.R. 566, Ch.D 17.30

TABLE OF STATUTES IN SUPPLEMENT

1968 Theft Act (c.60)
s.31 .... 3.17, 11.113
1975 Evidence (Proceedings in Other Jurisdictions) Act (c.34) 10.54
1978 State Immunity Act (c.33)
s.1 .... 4.44
s.3 .... 4.44
s.13 .... 4.44
s.14 .... 4.44
1981 Contempt of Court Act (c.49)
s.10 .... 10.15
Senior Courts Act (c.54)
s.51 .... 2.46
s.124 .... 3.45A
s.125 .... 3.45A
Supreme Court Act. *See* Senior Courts Act
1982 Civil Jurisdiction and Judgments Act (c.27)
s.25 .... 2.19, 3.08, 19.04
1986 Insolvency Act (c.45)
s.236 .... 3.41, 3.42
s.364 .... 21.17
1990 Access to Health Records Act (c.23) 5.52
1991 Child Support Act (c.48)
s.14 .... 11.114
1996 Arbitration Act (c.23)
s.43 .... 10.24, 20.05
s.68 .... 13.36, 20.09
(2)(g) 13.36, 20.09
1998 Human Rights Act (c.42) 21.08
2000 Financial Services and Markets Act (c.8)
s.171 .... 10.57
s.348 .... 8.09
s.391 .... 8.09
Regulation of Investigatory Powers Act (c.23)
s.27 .... 11.77
2002 Proceeds of Crime Act (c.29)
s.328 .... 11.113
s.357 .... 5.54
Enterprise Act (c.40)
s.237 .... 11.143
s.238 .... 11.143
(3) 11.143
s.241A 11.143
(3) 11.143
2003 Crime (International Co-operation) Act (c.32)
ss.13–15 .... 10.54
2005 Prevention of Terrorism Act (c.2)
s,7 .... 5.38A
2006 Fraud Act (c.35) A.54A
s.13 .... 2.25, 3.17, 11.113
(4) 2.25, 11.113
2007 Legal Services Act (c.29)
s.190 .... 11.23
2008 Counter-Terrorism Act (c.28)
s.63 .... 5.38A
Sch.7 .... 5.38A

Australia

1995 Evidence Act (Cth)
s.131 .... 11.123
2001 Health Records Act 5.52

Hong Kong

Basic Law 4.06
Companies Ordinance
s.221 .... 3.41, 3.42

Iran

Civil Procedure Code
art.51.6 .... 1.25A
art.199 .... 1.25A

New Zealand

1994 Tax Administration Act
s.81 .... 11.98

Oman

2008 Law of Evidence in Civil and Commercial Transactions (Royal Decree No.68/2008)
arts 20–22 .... 1.25A

TABLE OF STATUTORY INSTRUMENTS IN SUPPLEMENT

1965 Rules of the Supreme Court (SI 1965/1776) 15.03

Ord.24 r.10 .... 9.10

2007 Enterprise Act 2002 (Disclosure of Information for Civil Proceedings etc.) Order (SI 2007/2193) 11.143

Australia

Federal Court Rules 5.30

O.15A r.6 .... 3.34

2005 Uniform Civil Procedure Rules (NSW)

r.5.3 .... 3.34

TABLE OF CIVIL PROCEDURE RULES IN SUPPLEMENT

1998 Civil Procedure Rules (SI 1998/3132) 5.34, 12.19
r.1.1 ..... 18.23
r.3.4(2) 2.39
r.3.5(1) 11.08
r.3.9 ..... 13.10, 13.11, 18.08
r.5.4C 3.45
(4) 3.45
r.6.30(2) 2.48
Pt 7 ..... 3.23
Pt 8 ..... 3.23
Pt 18 ..... 5.23, 16.44
Pt 20 ..... 11.31, 11.127
Pt 23 ..... 3.23
r.24.2 ..... 2.39
r.25.1(1)(c) 3.34, 19.07
(g) 2.13, 16.68
Pt 31 ..... 4.06
r.31.3 ..... 9.05, 9.28
r.31.14 ..... 9.10
r.31.16 ..... 3.31, 20.04
(3)(a) 3.31
(b) 3.31
(c) 3.33
(d) 3.34
r.31.17 ..... 4.58
r.31.19 ..... 6.17
(3) 9.33
(5) 9.33, 9.39, 11.88
r.31.22(2) 15.03
Pt 35 ..... 1.31
r.35.2 ..... 18.02
(1) 18.02
r.35.5(2) 18.05
r.35.11 ..... 18.21
r.35.15 ..... 18.23
r.39.2(3) 6.58
r.48.2 ..... 2.46
r.52.9 ..... 13.17
r.54.12 ..... 4.06
Pt 71 ..... 2.48, 17.14
r.71.2 ..... 2.48, 17.14
(b) 2.48
rr.76.28–76.29 ..... 5.38A
Pt 79 ..... 5.38A

CHAPTER 1

Introduction

PARA.

A. NATURE AND PURPOSES OF DISCLOSURE 1.01

B. MEANS OF DISCLOSURE 1.05

C. HISTORY OF DISCOVERY 1.10

D. COMPARATIVE DISCOVERY 1.15*

E. DISCOVERY LITERATURE 1.26

F. REFORM AND THE CIVIL PROCEDURE RULES 1998 1.28*

G. STRUCTURE OF THIS WORK 1.33

CHAPTER 1

Introduction

D. COMPARATIVE DISCOVERY

Commonwealth

NOTE 75. In May 2010 the Australian Law Reform Commission commenced an inquiry to look into discovery of documents in litigation in federal courts. The inquiry is to focus on issues of 1.19

(1) the law, practice and management of documents in litigation before federal courts;
(2) ensuring that cost and time required for discovery of documents is proportionate to the matters in dispute, including but not limited to:
    (a) the effectiveness of different types of discovery orders;
    (b) the effectiveness and enforceability of requiring parties to identify and disclose critical documents as early as possible;
    (c) the effectiveness of different costs orders.
(3) to limit the overuse of discovery, reduce the expense of discovery and ensure key documents relevant to the real issues in dispute are identified as early as possible.
(4) the impact of technology on the discovery of documents.

In November 2010 the Australian Law Reform Commission issued its Consultation Paper (ALRC CP2), *Discovery in Federal Courts*, which is an excellent analysis of the issues in relation to discovery and potential reform. The final report is due by 31st March 2011.

Middle East

In the legal systems in the Middle East, most countries have only limited disclosure in civil cases. However, in recent years there have been some laws introducing a more extensive disclosure power in the courts in certain states. This should not be regarded as a move towards a disclosure system as in common law jurisdictions. In Iran, there was no disclosure in civil cases save that a plaintiff must declare and list all the documents and proof he wishes 1.25A

to use in support of his claim under art.51.6 of the Civil Procedure Code. Under art.199 (introduced later) the civil court has power to carry out all investigations and steps necessary to establish the truth. In theory this has given the court the power to call for documents from the parties, but in practice the judges do not use the article in this way, leaving it to the parties to simply disclose those documents on which they rely. The new Omani Law of Evidence in Civil and Commercial Transactions (Royal Decree No.68/2008) contains provisions for the parties as well as third parties to provide disclosure of specific documents in arts 20–22.

F. REFORM AND THE CIVIL PROCEDURE RULES 1998

1.31 In the context of patent actions, Jacob L.J. expressed concern about the cost of disclosure and that many in the legal profession had not grasped the concept of proportionality and the intention of the CPR to restrict disclosure: *Nichia Corp v Argos Ltd* [2007] EWCA Civ 741; [2007] F.S.R. 38, CA. His comments would appear to be well founded particularly in the context of High Court actions on the multitrack. At the District Judge and County Court level, disclosure is generally proportionate and kept within sensible bounds. For a more detailed assessment on the operation of the disclosure regime under the CPR, see Malek, H.M., 'Proportionality and Suitability of the Disclosure Regime under the CPR,' in D. Dwyer (ed.) *The Civil Procedure Rules Ten Years On* (2010, OUP), Ch.14.

In 2009 Lord Justice Jackson was appointed to conduct a fundamental review of the rules and principles governing the costs of civil litigation and to make recommendations in order to promote access to justice at proportionate cost. The result is Lord Justice Jackson's *Review of Civil Litigation: Final Report* (2010). It was noted that the traditional rules of disclosure generate massively increased costs in a world where the great majority of communications and records are preserved electronically (para.3.2.7). In chapter 37, it was recommended modifications to the disclosure rules in substantial cases. It was also recommended that legal practitioners and judges should receive specific training in relation to e-disclosure, so that they can deal with the process more efficiently and economically. The report also noted that factual and expert evidence is sometimes the cause of excessive costs in heavy cases. Even in modest cases expert evidence may generate excessive costs. In chapter 38, it was considered how the costs of factual and expert evidence might be controlled, whilst ensuring each party's case is properly disclosed before trial and presented at trial.

The practise of regularly modifying the rules and practice directions has continued. Such that it is generally advisable to check whether wordings have changed. Many of the changes are cosmetic with the practitioners having to wonder any particular change has any significance. CPR Part 35

and the accompanying Practice Direction in relation to experts was modified in 2009. There are numerous changes in wording, but mostly slight and no change in import.

Electronic disclosure has proved a challenge to legal practitioners and the courts given its potential scope, cost and technical issues. In relation to proceedings commencing from 1st October 2010, there applies *Practice Direction 31B: Disclosure of Electronic Documents* (set out in Appendix 2, B.04A to this Supplement). This adds another layer of complexity to the disclosure process and may be costly in practice to implement, despite one of its objectives being to limit costs. Practice Direction 31 is now Practice Direction 31A.

CHAPTER 2

Time of Disclosure

	PARA.
A. BEFORE PROCEEDINGS COMMENCED	2.02*
B. AT THE TIME THAT PROCEEDINGS ARE COMMENCED	2.10*
C. AFTER PROCEEDINGS HAVE BEEN COMMENCED	2.31*
D. DISCLOSURE AFTER JUDGMENT HAS BEEN GIVEN	2.46*
E. DISCLOSURE WHERE NO ENGLISH PROCEEDINGS IN EXISTENCE OR CONTEMPLATED	2.54
F. FOREIGN DISCLOSURE FOR ENGLISH PROCEEDINGS	2.57*

CHAPTER 2

Time of Disclosure

A. BEFORE PROCEEDINGS COMMENCED

Documents from previous litigation and arbitrations

NOTE 1. See also *Al Rawi v The Security Service* [2010] EWCA Civ 482. 2.03
NOTE 3. Add *AF Noonan (Architectural Practice) Ltd v Bournemouth and Boscombe Athletic Football Club Ltd* [2007] EWCA Civ 848: not contempt of court for party to reveal details of private hearing where no order made prohibiting publication.

Probate cases

2.08 As to the power of the general public to access probated wills, see para.3.45A below (in this noter-up). As to a personal representative's rights to claim delivery up of a deceased papers, see *Caudle v LD Law Ltd* [2008] EWHC 374 (QB), [2008] 1 W.L.R. 1540.

B. AT THE TIME PROCEEDINGS HAVE COMMENCED

(a) Orders ancillary to injunctions

2.12 In *Rybolovleva v Rybolovlev*, February 18, 2009, BVI High Court at [55] it was held that a disclosure order should not be wider than the freezing order. Thus where the order was limited to freezing assets within the jurisdiction that part of the disclosure order which related to assets outside the jurisdiction was set aside.

2.13 NOTE 47. Add *Lichter & Schwarz v Rubin* [2008] EWHC 450 (Ch.D.), disclosure of details of payments may be applied for under CPR r.25.1(1)(g) where there is a reasonable possibility that there will be an application for a freezing injunction.

2.15 NOTE 68. Add *JSC BTA Bank v Ablyazov (No.2)* [2009] EWCA Civ 1125, where it was held that the disclosure order in a freezing order had to be

complied with pending the determination of an application to set aside the order, however disclosure was confined to the claimant's legal representatives. In *JSC BTA Bank v Ablyazov* [2010] EWHC 2352 (Comm) an unless order was made for disclosure of assets even though there was a pending jurisdictional challenge.

2.19 The foreign proceedings to which s.25 of the Civil Jurisdiction and Judgments Act 1982 is referring are proceedings on the substance of the matter: *ETI Euro Telecom International NV v Republic of Bolivia* [2008] EWCA Civ 880, CA.

The court would only be prepared to exercise discretion to grant an application, in aid of foreign litigation or arbitration, for a freezing order affecting assets not located in England if the respondent or the dispute had a sufficiently strong link to England or, in cases not covered by the Brussels Convention, where there is some other factor of sufficient strength to justify proceeding in the absence of such a link. The presence of assets in England might in appropriate circumstances demonstrate a relevant link: *Mobil Cerro Negro Ltd v Petroleos de Venezuela SA* [2008] EWHC 532 (Comm.); [2008] 1 Lloyd's Rep. 684, Walker J. See also *Banco National SNC v Empresa de Telecommunicaciones SA* [2007] EWCA Civ 662; [2007] 1 W.L.R. 1936, CA. In *Belletti v Morici* [2009] EWHC 2316 (Comm.), [2009] 2 CLC 525, Flaux J. set aside an order against persons abroad. The absence of any connection between those persons and the jurisdiction and the impracticability of enforcing the order against them, made it inexpedient to make the order.

2.20 NOTE 81. *Admiralty and Commercial Courts Guide* (9th edn, 2009), Appendix 5 (updated citation).

(b) Search orders (*Anton Piller* orders)

2.22 NOTE 94. In Australia an applicant to a search order is normally only allowed to inspect the material seized with the leave of the court: Practice Note 24, supplementing O.25B; *Metso Minerals (Australia) Ltd v Kalra (No.3)* [2008] FCA 1201.

2.22 *Celanese Canada Inc v Murray Demolition Corp* [2006] 2 S.C.R. 189, Sup. Ct of Canada (updated citation).

2.22 In *L v L and H* [2007] EWHC 140 (QB), Tugendhat J. held that a wife who without consent used self-help to obtain a copy of the hard-drive of her husband's laptop computer, fearing that he would not disclose relevant documents in a forthcoming matrimonial dispute, could not be in a better position than if she had applied for and obtained a search order, and hence the copy should be held by the husband's solicitors pending disclosure.

The rule against self-incrimination

2.23 NOTE 100. *C Plc v P* [2007] EWCA Civ 493; [2007] 3 W.L.R. 437; [2008] Ch.7, CA; [2008] 1 W.L.R. 153, HL(E) pet.all. (updated citation for appeal).

Section 13 of the Fraud Act 2006 removes the privilege against self-incrimination on the ground that answering any question put to a person relating to property or complying with any order made in proceedings relating to property may incriminate him of any offence under the Act or a related offence. "Related offence" is defined in s.13(4) as meaning conspiracy to defraud or any other offence involving any form of fraudulent conduct or purpose. These provisions were considered in *Kensington International Ltd v Republic of Congo* [2007] EHWC 1632 (Comm.); [2007] 2 Lloyd's Rep. 382; [2008] EWCA Civ 1128, CA. The court held that corruption is a related offence. 2.25

C. AFTER PROCEEDINGS HAVE BEEN COMMENCED

NOTE 133. In an action where there was a vast amount of material to review, it was held that a party should give disclosure of an important document in advance of the rest of disclosure: *Al Rawi v Security Service* [2010] EWHC 1496 (QB). 2.33

Disclosure in interlocutory proceedings

In *Harris v The Society of Lloyd's* [2008] EWHC 1433 (Comm.) an application was refused for specific disclosure of documents for the purposes of the claimant resisting an application to strike out pursuant to CPR r.3.4(2) and/or to dismiss the claims by way of summary judgment pursuant to CPR r.24.2. Steel J. observed that there are good reasons for concluding that the approach to disclosure applications for the purpose of interlocutory proceduring is the same if not stricter than under the previous procedural rules, where it was well established that the power should be exercised sparingly and then only for such documents as can be shown to be necessary for the just disposal of the application (at [10], citing this paragraph in *Disclosure*). In *Masri v Consolidated Contractors Company SAL* [2010] EWHC 2640 (Comm), an application for general specific disclosure of documents for the purposes of an abuse of process argument (in the context of contempt proceedings) was refused. 2.39

Disclosure of funding third party

This passage in *Disclosure*, 2nd edn, was quoted in *Re Tomlinson*, Bank 2005/1, March 2, 2006, Isle of Man, Doyle J. A respondent to an application against a funder to pay costs under s.51 of the Senior Courts Act 1981, may be ordered to provide disclosure: *Owners of "Kamal XXVI" v Owners of "Ariela"* [2010] EWHC 2531 (Comm). 2.40

D. DISCLOSURE AFTER JUDGMENT HAS BEEN GIVEN

2.46 The court may order disclosure in relation to applications for costs, *eg* where the successful defendant proposes to make an application for costs against a third party funder under Senior Courts Act 1981 s.51 and CPR r.48.2: *Thomson v Berkhamstead Collegaite School* [2009] EWHC 2374 (QB).

Oral examination

2.48 In *Masri v Consolidated Contractors International Co. SAL* [2009] UKHL 43, [2009] 3 W.L.R. 385, [2009] 2 Lloyd's Rep. 473, the House of Lords held that CPR r.71.2 does not enable an order for examination to be made against an officer of a company who is outside the jurisdiction, and CPR Pt 6 provides no basis for service out of the jurisdiction of any such order, had it been possible to make one. The House of Lords in overturning the Court of Appeal [2008] EWCA Civ 876, [2009] 1 Lloyd's Rep 42, followed *Vitol SA v Capri Marine Ltd* [2008] EWHC 378 (Comm.), [2009] Bus. L.R. 271. However, in *Kuwait Airways v Iraq Airways Corporation* [2010] EWCA Civ 740, the Court of Appeal made on appeal an ex parte order against a foreign officer of the judgment debtor in support of a worldwide freeze order. The order was a restraining order against the officer who was temporarily within the jurisdiction providing for his arrest, surrender of passport, and prohibiting him from leaving the jurisdiction until he had provided disclosure of assets of the judgment debtor. This unprecedented order was untested by any opposition and had been refused by the Commercial Court judge.

Where the judgment debtor is a company or other corporation, "an officer of that body" within CPR r.71.2(b) is not wide enough to include a director of a corporate director of the judgment debtor: *Masri v Consolidated Contractors International Co. SAL* [2008] EWCA Civ 876, [2009] 1 Lloyd's Rep. 42 at [20]. It is also not wide enough to include someone who was no longer an existing officer of the company at the time when the order for the examination was made: *Vitol SA v Capri Marine* [2008] EWHC 378 (Comm.) at [23].

Inherent jurisdiction

2.51 NOTE 200. Add *Masri v Consolidated Contractors International Co. SAL* [2008] EWHC 3010 (Comm.) and [2008] EWCA Civ 303; [2008] 1 Lloyd's Rep. 128, CA (post-judgment freeze order in relation to assets abroad); see also *Kuwait Airways v Iraq Airways Corporation* [2010] EWCA Civ 740 (noted under para.2.48 above).

F. FOREIGN DISCLOSURE FOR ENGLISH PROCEEDINGS

For a case where the English court restrained a party to English proceedings from deposing witnesses for the purposes of pending US proceedings, on the basis that this would disrupt the English proceedings and would be unfair and oppressive to a defendant, see *Benfield Holdings Ltd v Richardson* [2007] EWHC 171 (QB). 2.58

NOTE 249. Add *Honda v KJM Superbikes Ltd* [2007] EWCA Civ 313; [2007] C.P. Rep. 28, CA overturning refusal to issue letter of request on ground of delay [2007] EWHC 581 (Ch). 2.60

NOTE 241. *Charman v Charman* [2005] EWCA Civ 1606, [2006] 1 W.L.R. 1053, CA was referred to in the context of a subpoena for documents in *SMSE v KL* [2009] HKCA 349 at [36] and followed in the context of an incoming request in support of ancillary relief divorce proceedings in *Jennings v Jennings* [2009] SC (Bda) 62 Civ. 2.61

NOTE 269. See also *Benfield Holdings Ltd v Richardson* [2007] EWHC 171 (QB). 2.63

CHAPTER 3

Norwich Pharmacal and other Pre-Action Disclosure

	PARA.
A. NORWICH PHARMACAL ORDERS	3.02*
B. PRE-ACTION DISCLOSURE: CPR RULE 31.16	3.26*
C. CORPORATE INSOLVENCY	3.40*
D. APPLICATION TO INSPECT COURT FILE	3.45*

CHAPTER 3

Norwich Pharmacal and other Pre-Action Disclosure

A. NORWICH PHARMACAL ORDER

Requirements

NOTE 32. Add *R. (on the application of Mohamed) v Secretary of State for Foreign & Commonwealth Affairs* [2008] EWHC 2048 (Admin), [2009] 1 W.L.R. 2579 at [95–96]. It is not a condition that the person seeking the documents needs them for a civil action. In that case the documents were needed to defend or challenge terrorist charges before a US military commission. In *Aamer v Secretary of State for Foreign and Commonwealth Affairs* [2009] EWHC 3316 (Admin) at [51], the documents were required for a person detained by the US military in Afghanistan to make submissions to the Task Force against his detention. 3.07

NOTE 38. Add *Al-Rushaid Petroleum v TSJ Engineering*, April 20, 2010, BVI High Court (proceedings in BVI in aid of UK proceedings to locate secret commissions). 3.08

NOTE 39. Section 25 of the Civil Jurisdiction and Judgments Act 1982 only applies where the foreign proceedings are proceedings on the substance of the matter: *ETI Euro Telecom International NV v Republic of Bolivia* [2008] EWCA Civ 880, CA. 3.08

Norwich Pharmacal relief is intended to be an exceptional though flexible remedy. The court should not require a respondent to provide information unless it is necessary. However, in *R. (on the application of Mohamed) v Secretary of State for Foreign and Commonwealth Affairs* [2008] EWHC 2048 (Admin), [2009] 1 W.L.R. 2579 the Court took the view at [94] that Lightman J. in *Mitsui v Nexen Petroleum* [2005] EWHC 625 (Ch) and Langley J. in *Nikitin v Richards Butler* [2007] EWHC 173 (QB) had taken a too restrictive view. The court rejected a more stringent requirement than necessity by elevating the test to the information being a missing piece of the jigsaw or to it being a remedy of last resort. This approach to the requirement of necessity was followed in *Aamer v Secretary of State for Foreign* 3.10

and Commonwealth Affairs [2009] EWHC 3316 (Admin) at [49–50]. In *GEA Group AG v Ventra Group Co* (2010) 312 D.L.R. (4th) 160, the Ontario CA considered that necessity is not a free standing requirement for this flexible remedy.

3.11 The extent of the information that may be required to be disclosed depends on the circumstances, bearing in mind that *Norwich Pharmacal* is a flexible remedy. Although the action cannot be one used for wide-ranging discovery or the gathering of evidence and is strictly confined to necessary information, and the court must always consider what is proportionate and the expense involved, the scope of what can be ordered must depend on the factual circumstances of each case. The range of information was not to be construed narrowly in a case where a person's liberty and life was at stake: *R. (on the application of Mohammed) v Secretary of State for Foreign and Commonwealth Affairs* [2008] EWHC 2048 (Admin), [2009] 1 W.L.R. 2579 at [33–34]. In that case the Court concluded that the *Norwich Pharmacal* jurisdiction could be exercised for the purposes of ordering disclosure to a detainee at Guantanamo Bay facing possible criminal proceedings, of information capable of supporting his claim that confessions on which the prosecution intended to rely had been obtained by torture. For a similar application of the principle, see *Aamer v Secretary of State for Foreign and Commonwealth Affairs* [2009] EWHC 3316 (Admin). For cases where the court ordered disclosure of information intended to identify so far as possible the sender of an email (including computer routing and addressing information), see *Campaign against Arms Trade v BAE Systems Plc* [2007] EWHC 330 (QB), and *Applause Store Productions Ltd v Raphael* [2008] EWHC 1781 (QB). In a number of cases internet providers have been ordered to disclose information which would enable to identify the party posting messages or sending emails: *G and G v Wikimedia Foundation Inc* [2009] EWHC 3148 (QB) (order for IP address of registered user of website who had posted confidential information); *York University v Bell Canada Enterprise* (2010) D.L.R. (4th) 755, Ontario SCJ (order for information necessary to obtain identity of author of allegedly defamatory emails and a website posting); cp *Warman v Wilkins-Fournier* (2010) 319 D.L.R. (3d) 268, Ontario SCJ (order for information, including email and IP addresses refused as no prima facie case of defamation shown).

3.14 It is sufficient that the respondent became involved in the wrongdoing (even if innocently) by facilitating that wrongdoing. It is not necessary to show that the respondent's actions were causative of the occurrence of the wrongdoing: *R. (on the application of Mohammed) v Secretary of State for Foreign and Commonwealth Affairs* [2008] EWHC 2048 (Admin), [2009] 1 W.L.R. 2579 at [69–70]. It is not necessary to show that the respondent had knowledge of the wrongdoing (at [71]). For a case where the receipt of an email deliberately sent to the recipient was enough to involve the recipient as more than a mere witness, so that the court ordered disclosure of information intended to identify so far as possible the sender of that email,

see *Campaign against Arms Trade v BAE Systems Plc* [2007] EWHC 330 (QB).

Bankers Trust

NOTE 69. Add *B (A) v D (C)* (2008) 291 D.L.R. (4th) 359, Alberta CA (*Norwich Pharmacal* order against banks refused, where information would be available in ordinary disclosure process in the action); *Al-Rushaid Petroleum v TSJ Engineering*, April 20, 2010, BVI High Court (*Norwich Pharmacal*. Order made against BVI company in respect of receipt of commission payments, where such information not likely to be readily forthcoming in related UK proceedings). 3.15

Defences

In *Kensington International Ltd v Republic of Congo* [2007] EWCA Civ 1128, the Court of Appeal held that s.13 of the Fraud Act 2006 deprived some of the third parties of the right to claim the privilege against self-incrimination in relation to the disclosure of information to which the *Norwich Pharmacal* order referred. The court declined to construe the section restrictively, or to hold that it only applied to future conduct by the defendant, and held that it was directed to the same kind of proceedings as s.31 of the Theft Act 1968. However, for this purpose the *Norwich Pharmacal* proceedings were not separate from the substantive claim. 3.17

NOTE 78. See also *Mersey Care NHS Trust v Ackroyd* [2007] EWCA Civ 101; c.f. *Police v Campbell* [2010] 1 N.Z.L.R. 483. Note that in *Financial Times Ltd v United Kingdom,* Application 821/03, 15 December 2009, the ECtHR held that the UK had violated Art 10 of the ECHR by virtue of the *Interbrew* decision requiring the delivery up of documents under the *Norwich Pharmacal* principle which might identify a journalist's source. 3.18

NOTES 86, 88. See also *Mersey Care NHS Trust v Ackroyd* [2007] EWCA Civ 101. 3.21

NOTE 87. Note that in *Financial Times Ltd v United Kingdom,* Application 821/03, 15 December 2009, the ECtHR held that the UK had violated Art 10 of the ECHR by virtue of the *Interbrew* decision requiring the delivery up of documents under the *Norwich Pharmacal* principle which might identify a journalist's source.

Procedure

The Chancery Guide (6th edn, 2009), para.4.2 provides that although *Norwich Pharmacal* applications may be made under CPR Parts 7 or 8, nevertheless if the application is or is thought likely to be uncontested the court may entertain an application under Part 23 supported by evidence. 3.23

In deciding whether to make an order requiring disclosure of customers' names in interlocutory proceedings in a patent infringement action, the court approached the question of making the order in a similar way to considering the granting of an interim injunction. In making a disclosure 3.23

order the court considered the questions of irreparable damage and balance of convenience: *Eli Lilly & Co. Ltd v Neopharma Ltd* [2008] EWHC 415 (Ch) following *Sega v Alca Electronics* [1982] F.S.R. 516.

3.24 NOTE 108. Even where the costs of compliance with the order may be substantial, the court may still make an order on the basis that it is for the applicant to pay the reasonable costs of compliance: *BNP Paribas v TH Global Ltd* [2009] EWHC 37 (Ch) at [47]. In that case the court made an order for disclosure of documents, but declined to make orders for affidavits as well. Provision was made in the order to enable third parties to intervene to prevent disclosure of information which they claim to be confidential or protected by legal professional privilege (at [53]).

3.25 For the form of an express undertaking as to use, see *Al-Rushaid Petroleum v TSJ Engineering*, April 20 2010, BVI High Court.

B. PRE-ACTION DISCLOSURE: CPR RULE 31.16

Requirements for pre-action disclosure

3.31 The proceedings which are contemplated must be proceedings between the parties in the High Court and not arbitral proceedings. Thus where the respondent has a right to have the dispute referred to arbitration which he is entitled to exercise, the court will refuse pre-action disclosure under CPR r.31.16: *EDO Corporation v Ultra Electronics Ltd* [2009] EWHC 682 (Ch), [2009] Bus. LR 1306; *Travelers Insurance Company Ltd v Countrywide Surveyors Ltd* [2010] EWHC 2455 (TCC).

3.31 NOTE 139. Add *Gwelhayl Ltd v Midas Construction Ltd* [2008] EWHC 2316 (TCC).

3.31 NOTE 140. Add *Anglo Irish Bank Corporation Plc v West LB AG* [2009] EHWC 207 (Comm.), not appropriate to express views on the merits in a complex case. In *Kneale v Barclays Bank (t/a Barclaycard)* [2010] EWHC 1900 (Comm.), Flaux J.considered the extent to which an applicant for pre-action disclosure under CPR r.31.16 has to demonstrate an arguable case in order to satisfy the jurisdiction criteria of sub-rules (3)(a) and (b). He declined to follow “real prospect of success” as the jurisdictional criterion which had been adopted in *Rose v Lynx Express* [2004] 1 BCLC 455 and itself followed in *Pineway Limited v London Mining Company Limited* [2010] EWHC 1143 (Comm.). Instead he followed the test of the applicant having to show some sort of prima facie case which is more than a merely speculative punt. This approach accords with principle as often the whole purpose of the application is to ascertain whether to bring a claim or not and accords with *Black v Sumitomo* [2002] 1 W.L.R. 1562 and *BSW Limited v Balltec Limited* [2006] EWHC 822 (Ch). The strength of any case can be taken into account when considering whether or not to exercise the discretion to order disclosure.

As to the requirement of CPR r.31.16(c), the applicant must show that if he brought proceedings, the documents or classes of documents included in the application would fall within the respondent's duty by way of standard disclosure. All the documents within a category or class must be subject to standard disclosure and the applicant must show that it is more probable than not that the documents are within the scope of standard disclosure in regard to issues that are likely to arise: *Hutchinson 3G UK Ltd v O2 (UK) Ltd* [2008] EWHC 50 (Comm.) at [38 and 44]; *Hays Specialist Recruitment (Holdings) Ltd v Ions* [2008] EWHC 745 (Ch) at [33]. A need for a highly focused application which clearly does not encompass categories of documents that will simply prove to be relevant (if at all) as part of the background (let alone of course documents that might merely lead to a train of enquiry) was emphasised in *Hutchinson 3G UK Ltd v O2 (UK) Ltd* [2008] EWHC 50 (Comm.) at [39]. 3.33

As to the requirement of CPR r.31.16(d), in *Hays Specialist Recruitment (Holdings) Ltd v Ions* [2008] EWHC 745 (Ch) at [44] it was held that disclosure sought in that case would satisfy the jurisdictional requirement in that it would enable there to be fully pleaded particulars of claim from the start and should make resolution easier to achieve as it would enable the parties to have a real appreciation of the extent of any claim. In *Hutchinson 3G UK Ltd v O2 (UK) Ltd* [2008] EWHC 50 (Comm.) at [55], it was observed that, in almost every dispute, a case could be made out that pre-action disclosure would be useful in achieving a settlement or otherwise saving costs. In order to obtain pre-action disclosure, the circumstances must be outside "the usual run" to allow the hurdle to be surmounted: *Trouw UK Ltd v Mitsui & Co. (UK) Plc* [2007] EWHC 863 (Comm.) at [43]. In any event, the absence of any convincing grounds for distinguishing the case from the normal run would be telling grounds for not exercising the court's discretion. 3.34

NOTE 153. Add *Dartberg Pty Ltd v Wealthcare Financial Planning Pty Ltd* [2007] FCA 1216 and *Optiver Australia Pty Ltd v Tibra Trading Pty Ltd* [2007] FCA 2065, (2008) 247 A.L.R. 199; [2008] FCAFC 133, (2008) 249 A.L.R. 495, preliminary disclosure under O.15A r.6 of the Federal Court Rules in Australia; *Hatfield v TCN Channel Nine Pty Ltd* [2010] NSWCA 69, preliminary discovery pursuant to Uniform Civil Procedure Rules 2005 (NSW) r.5.3 (refused where sought was discovery of episodes of programme in order to determine whether claimant had a defamation claim). 3.34

NOTE 156. In *OCS Group Ltd v Wells* [2008] 919 (QB), [2009] 1 W.L.R. 1895 the Court refused an application for pre-action disclosure of a claimant's medical records, on the ground that such disclosure was not desirable prior to the commencement of proceedings. There is no obligation on a claimant to disclose documents under the personal injury pre-action protocol. There is such an obligation on defendants. 3.34

NOTE 157. Add *Gwelhayl Ltd v Midas Construction Ltd* [2008] EWHC 2316 (TCC), where pre-action disclosure refused where no arguable cause 3.34

of action identified. However the court did order delivery up to certain records under CPR r.25.1(1)(c)(i) on the basis they were the applicant's property held by the respondent as agent. See also *Kneale v Barclays Bank (t/a Barclaycard)* [2010] EWHC 1900 (Comm.) pre-action disclosure was refused because of the speculative nature of the application and any possible claim. Further, to obtain the document sought was not necessary to establish whether or not the applicant had a claim.

3.34 NOTE 161. A separate factor, particularly important in the context of pre-action disclosure, is that disclosure might involve the provision by the respondents of commercially sensitive information to a competitor: *Hays Specialist Recruitment (Holdings) Ltd v Ions* [2008] EWHC 745 (Ch) at [48]. The availability of other means of obtaining the relevant documents may be a factor militating against disclosure, but this will not be a valid objection if this will be inadequate or far more expensive: *Hays* at [49–50].

3.34 NOTE 163. In *Landis & Gyr Ltd v Scaleo Chip ET* [2007] EWHC 1880 (QB) pre-action disclosure was ordered where it was accepted that it would be possible to plead a case before disclosure, but any such pleading would be short on particulars and virtually meaningless prior to disclosure.

3.34 NOTE 169. Add *Anglo Irish Bank Corporation Plc v West LB AG* [2009] EWHC 207 (Comm.), pre-action disclosure refused as such order is unusual and would be a burdensome exercise to impose it unilaterally on a party against whom no proceedings have been taken.

Procedure

3.39 NOTE 189. Add *SES Contracting Ltd v UK Coal Plc* [2007] EWCA Civ 791; [2007] C.P. Rep. 46, order that respondent be ordered to pay costs found to be wrong, order each party bear own costs substituted. An order requiring the respondent to pay the costs would only be expected where it was clearly unreasonable for the respondent to oppose the application for pre-action disclosure or where the manner of his opposition was so unreasonable as to make it appropriate to require him to bear both parties' costs. See also *Kneale v Barclays Bank (t/a Barclaycard)* [2010] EWHC 1900 (Comm.) at [59–66], which explains that even where opposition has been unreasonable the court may order each party bear their own costs rather than making the respondent pay both sides costs.

C. CORPORATE INSOLVENCY

3.41 The purpose and rationale of s.221 of the Companies Ordinance, Cap. (Hong Kong equivalent to s.236 of Insolvency Act 1996) was dealt with fully by Lord Millett in *Joint & Several Liquidators of Kong Wah Holdings Ltd v Grande Holdings Ltd* (2006) 9 HKCFAR 766 at 780–782.

In *Akai Holdings Ltd (in liquidation) v Ernst & Young* [2009] HKCFA 14, the Hong Kong Court of Final Appeal set aside a disclosure order against a company in liquidation which was suing its former auditors. The order had required it to disclose transcripts and notes of a series of private examinations and interviews conducted pursuant to or under threat of s.221 of the Companies Ordinance, Cap.32 (Hong Kong equivalent of s.236 Insolvency Act 1996). The HKCA held that litigation privilege can apply to cover such transcripts and notes. In that case the private examinations and interviews were privileged as they were conducted for the dominant purpose of obtaining legal advice for contemplated litigation. **3.42**

D. APPLICATIONS TO INSPECT COURT FILE

Under CPR r.5.4C there is a right in non-parties not only to have sight of a claim form, but also an acknowledgment of service and detailed grounds in judicial review proceedings. This is because "defence" includes the judicial review equivalent to a defence: *R. (on the application of Corner House Research) v Director of Serious Fraud Office* [2008] EWHC 246 (Admin). **3.45**

In *L'Oréal SA v eBay International AG* [2008] EWHC B13 (Ch), the court ordered that certain defendants could (in the first instance by their lawyers only) see confidential Tomlin orders relating to other parties, in order to see what effect (if any) the terms contained in them had on their own positions. **3.45**

NOTE 228. In *G and G v Wikimedia Foundation Inc* [2009] EWHC 3148 (QB) an order was made under CPR r.5.4 C (4) that a non-party may not (without further order) inspect the statement of case unless it was edited to remove the name of the claimants. **3.45**

NOTE 229. CPR, Pt.31, Practice Direction 31B, para.12 answers to the Electronic Documents Questionnaire will only be available for inspection by non-parties if permission is given under CPR, r.5.4C(2). **3.45**

NOTE 231. Add *Llewellyn v Nine Network Australia Pty Ltd* [2006] FCA 836; (2007) 233 A.L.R. 88, Fed. Ct of Australia: inspection of court file permitted to allow journalist to inspect statement of claim after claim had settled despite contentions by parties it should remain confidential. **3.45**

Sections 124 and 125 of the Supreme Court Act 1981 (renamed the Senior Courts Act 1981) deal with access to wills (and other documents) that are under the control of the High Court. Wills are to be open to inspection "subject to the control of the High Court". Rule 58 of the NCPR makes provision for the court to determine that a will shall not be open to inspection if such inspection "would be undesirable or otherwise inappropriate". For an application to inspect the will of HM Queen Elizabeth **3.45A**

the Queen Mother, which had been subject to an order of the President to be sealed and not open to inspection without the consent of the President for the time being, see *Brown v Executors of the Estate of the Queen Elizabeth, The Queen Mother* [2008] EWCA Civ 56.

CHAPTER 4

Persons Who Must Give Disclosure

	PARA.
A. GENERAL POSITION OF SUBSTANTIVE PARTIES TO PROCEEDINGS	4.01*
B. SPECIAL CASES	4.18*
C. PARTIES JOINED TO AN EXISTING ACTION FOR THE PURPOSES OF DISCLOSURE	4.45
D. NON-PARTIES	4.47*

CHAPTER 4

Persons Who Must Give Disclosure

A. GENERAL POSITION OF SUBSTANTIVE PARTIES TO PROCEEDINGS

Claimants and defendants, petitioners and respondents

Matrimonial causes

Procedure in ancillary relief cases is regulated by the Family Proceedings Rules. As explained in *Tchenguiz v Imerman* [2010] EWCA Civ 908 at [33]: 4.03

"In relation to these Rules we make two general observations. First, that the Rules do not provide for any disclosure of information or disclosure (discovery) of documents until a spouse has lodged his Form E. Second, and even more significantly, that the process of disclosure (discovery) of documents both then and thereafter is closely regulated by the Rules and, in accordance with the Rules, by the court. Although there is a general and continuing duty to make full disclosure of all relevant information, there is, despite the duty imposed on the court by section 25 of the 1973 Act, no duty of general disclosure (discovery) of documents of the kind required in ordinary civil proceedings by the Civil Procedure Rules. And whereas in ordinary civil proceedings the parties can normally choose what documentary evidence to tender, it is the court which controls what documents are to be disclosed and tendered by way of evidence in ancillary relief proceedings."

A practice grew up whereby the Family Court generally refused to condemn when a spouse obtains and copies the other spouses documents, even though they were confidential, provided no force was used. These became known as the *Hildebrand* rules (a reference to *Hildebrand v Hildebrand* [1992] 1 F.L.R. 244). In *Tchenguez v Imerman* [2010] EWCA Civ 908, this practice was disapproved and the court may take steps to restrain such a breach of confidence and make an order for delivery up of any originals and copies of such documents.

Wardship and other children cases

4.04 See also *A Borough Council v A (Chief Constable of Thames Valley Police intervening)* [2007] 1 W.L.R. 1932, where guidance was given for police and social workers on the disclosure and permissible use of confidential information and documents relating to family proceedings.

4.04 NOTE 35. Add *Re X (Children)* [2007] EWHC 1719 (Fam) (disclosure of documents in family proceedings to CPS for Crown Court criminal proceedings) and *Re X (Children)* [2008] EWHC 242 (Fam); [2008] 3 All E.R. 958, Munby J. (disclosure of documents to CPS and police in connection with criminal proceedings; to Criminal Injuries and Compensation Authority; and to local authority's adult services).

Judicial review

4.06 In January 2010 the Treasury Solicitor's Department issued its *Guidance on Discharging the Duty of Candour and Disclosure in Judicial Review Proceedings*. This is practical guidance addressed to government departments and litigation case handlers. The guidance notes that CPR Part 31 will not normally apply on an application for judicial review. Disclosure is not required unless the court otherwise orders: CPR r.54.12. However, all public authorities who are respondents to applications for judicial review are subject to the duty of candour. The effect of this duty is to require the public authority, when presenting its evidence in response to the application for judicial review to set out fully and fairly all matters that are relevant to the decision that is under challenge, or are otherwise relevant to any issue arising in the proceedings (para.1.2): *R. v Lancashire County Council ex p. Huddleston* [1986] 2 All E.R. 941, CA; *Secretary of State for Commonwealth Affairs v Quark Fishing* [2002] EWCA Civ 1409; *R (on the application of Al Sweady) v Secretary of State for Defence* [2009] EWHC 2387 (Admin).

The guidance also emphasises the types of case where disclosure is likely to be required. In particular:

(1) Where a court is required to consider whether the actions of a public body were proportionate, and where there are documents which are directly material to that issue of proportionality, it will more often be necessary to disclose documents by exhibiting them to relevant witness statements (para.1.2). This is consistent with *Tweed v Parades Commission for Northern Ireland* [2007] 1 A.C. 950, HL.

(2) Where there is to be cross-examination or in a case where the Court is required to make findings of fact, the case handler has a duty to ensure that proper disclosure is given as emphasised in *R (on the*

application of Al Sweady) v Secretary of State for Defence [2009] EWHC 2387 (Admin) (para.1.4). Examples of where complex issues of disputed fact are central to the claim requiring a disclosure exercise may be where the claim alleges breaches of the substantive obligations arising under ECHR Articles 2 or 3 (para.1.5).

The guidance contains useful advice as to how searches for documents are to be conducted, material is to be reviewed and the form of disclosure (para.3).

The guidance reflects a greater willingness of the Administrative Court to make orders for disclosure than in the past, albeit the position remains that a disclosure order is not the norm in judicial review proceedings.

In *R (on the application of Al Sweady) v Secretary of State for Defence* [2009] EWHC 2387 (Admin) the court ordered cross-examination of persons who had made witness statements, in such a case disclosure was needed to enable an effective cross-examination to take place (at [22]). The Court noted that in practice orders for disclosure in judicial review cases have usually been unnecessary because, not only the defendant normally complies with its duty of candour/disclosure (set out in *R. v Secretary of State for the Home Department ex p. Fayed* [1988] 1 W.L.R. 763 at 775 per Lord Woolf MR and *R (Quark Fishing Limited) v Secretary of State for Foreign & Commonwealth Affairs* [2002] EWCA Civ 1409 at [50] per Laws LJ), but also because judicial review applications typically raise issues of law with the facts either not being in dispute or only being relevant to explain the context in which the issue of law arises. The position is different in many human rights cases brought under the ECHR because these tend to be very fact-specific and a judgment on proportionality may be called for (at [23]). The parties have a clear obligation in any judicial review case to consider at all times whether there is a crucial issue in the case in the form of a hard-edged issue, because this will be relevant in determining whether the court should make orders for cross-examination and disclosure. If the parties cannot reach agreement, an application should be made for an order (at [64]). In that case the court was critical of the Secretary of State's approach to disclosure and made an order for indemnity costs.

In *Save Guana Cay Reef Association Ltd v R* [2009] UKPC 44 orders for cross-examination and disclosure were refused as being unnecessary and no more than a fishing expedition. In the Privy Council, Lord Walker stated (at [47]):

"It is no longer the rule that disclosure should be ordered only where the affidavit evidence put in on behalf of the decision-maker can be shown to be inaccurate or misleading: *Tweed v Parades Commission for Northern Ireland* [2007] 1 A.C. 650. Nevertheless, orders for disclosure and cross-examination are still exceptional in judicial review proceedings, for good reason. Such proceedings are essentially a review of official decision-making, and need to be determined without any avoidable delay. On a realistic

analysis the only arguable ground for judicial review in this case was the alleged inadequacy of the public consultation, a topic on which there was quite a lot of documentary evidence. The judge's refusal of orders for discovery and cross-examination were well within the scope of his discretion."

4.06 NOTE 51. In *Chan Mei Yiu v Secretary for Justice* [2007] HKCFI 664 the Court refused to order disclosure of a foreign criminal letter of request on a challenge to search warrants issued pursuant to such request. The court followed *Tweed v Parades Commission for Northern Ireland* [2007] 1 A.C. 650; [2007] 2 W.L.R. 1, HL whereby a more flexible and less prescriptive approach is adopted than hitherto in the context of judicial review proceedings. The court balanced a refusal of disclosure, a decision that would potentially restrict rights under Hong Kong's Basic Law, against the risk of any real damage being caused to the proper administration of justice, including the investigation of serious offences, by disclosure.

4.07 NOTE 61. Add *O'Sullivan v Parkin* [2008] FCAFC 134, (2008) 249 A.L.R. 507.

B. SPECIAL CASES

(c) Trustees and beneficiaries

4.22 NOTE 118. *Schmidt v Rosewood Trust Ltd* [2003] UKPC 26, [2003] 2 A.C. 709 was followed in *Avanes v Marshall* [2007] NSWSC191, (2007) 69 N.S.W.L.R. 595 in holding that a beneficiary has no entitlement as of right to disclosure of anything which can plausibly be described as a trust document. However, a contrary view was taken in *McDonald v Ellis* [2007] NSWSC1068. The issue dealt with in *Schmidt* related to the right of a beneficiary of a trust to inspect trust documents. It said nothing about whether a trustee could refuse to disclose to a beneficiary, in proceedings between them, documents containing legal advice about the due administration of the trust on the ground of legal professional privilege. Such a claim to privilege was rejected on the grounds that the trustee and beneficiaries had joint privilege which may not be maintained against each other in *Schreuder v Murray (No.2)* [2009] WASCA 145 (2009) 260 A.L.R. 139. It is necessary to distinguish between

(1) legal proceedings by a beneficiary against the trustee where the cause of action is based on the trustee's alleged breach of duty in failing to provide the beneficiary with access to "trust documents" or information. This was the situation in *Schmidt*, where the Privy Council held that a beneficiary's right to inspect "trust documents" or receive information in the procession of a trustee was merely a

procedural right for the court to make an order in its discretion as part of its supervisory jurisdiction in relation to trusts.

(2) legal proceedings by a beneficiary against the trustee on other causes of action and, in the course of the proceedings, the beneficiary makes an application against the trustee for disclosure of and inspection of "trust documents" which are relevant to the pleaded causes of action in respect of which legal professional privilege exists as against strangers to the trust. It is this second situation and the applicable principles that were considered in detail in *Schreuder v Murray (No.2)* [2009] WASA 145, (2009) 260 A.L.R. 139.

The whole question of disclosure of letters of wishes by trustees to beneficiaries was considered in detail in *Breakspear v Ackland* [2008] EWHC 220 (Ch); [2008] 3 W.L.R. 698; [2008] W.T.L.R. 777 (discussed in A.J. Oakley, *Parker and Mellows: The Modern Law of Trusts*, 9th edn (London: Sweet & Maxwell, 2008), para.14–46). This is a matter calling for the exercise of discretion rather than the adjudication upon a proprietary right. At least in the context of family discretionary trusts, the *Londonderry* principle applies. Trustees need not disclose a letter of wishes to beneficiaries merely because they request it unless, in their view, disclosure is in the interests of the sound administration of the trust, and the discharge of their powers and discretions. 4.23

(l) Foreign states or sovereigns

On *Koo Golden East Mongolia v Bank of Nova Scotia* [2008] Q.B. 717, CA, *Norwich Pharmacal* disclosure was sought against a central bank and sections 1, 3, 13 and 14 of the State Immunity Act 1978 was considered. The court of Appeal set aside the order as against the central bank/agent bank of the central bank on the grounds of state immunity. 4.44

D. NON-PARTIES

(a) Supreme Court Act 1981, s.34 and CPR, r.31.17

Requirements for non-party disclosure

The distinction between a single document or a class of documents was considered in *Fanmail.com Ltd v Cooper* [2010] EWHC 2647 (Ch). This is relevant to the approach to be adopted for the purpose of ascertaining relevance. If disclosure of a single document is sought, then the court must consider whether all or any part of that single document is relevant. If what is sought is disclosure of a collection or class of documents then the court must consider whether each individual document, or part of that document, is relevant (at [48]). 4.56

4.57 In *Fanmail.com Ltd v Cooper* [2010] EWHC 2647 (Ch) the disclaimant sought non-party disclosure against SCB which it was considering seeking a non-party costs order. Dislcosure was refused as the materials sought were not likely to support the case against the dependent or save costs. The disclosure was in reality sought to support a costs claim against the non-party SCB. Once a person has been made a respondent to an application under s.51 Senior Courts Act 1981 for a non-party to the litigation to be ordered to pay the costs of a claim or defence, then disclosure can be sought against that person in the normal way: see *Owners of "Kamal XXVI" v Owners of "Ariela"* [2010] EWHC 2531 (Comm).

4.58 As to the residual discretion as to whether or not to make an order for non-party disclosure, it is at this stage that broader considerations come into play, such as where the public interest lies and whether or not disclosure would infringe third party rights in relation, for example, to privacy or confidentiality. Where documents relate to the confidential affairs of a non-party, he may be heard on an application for an order under CPR, r.31.17 or on his own application to set aside an order already made or to restrain the use of such documents once disclosed: *Flood v Times Newspapers Ltd* [2009] EWHC 411 (QB).

CHAPTER 5

What Must be Disclosed

	PARA.
A. WHAT IS A DOCUMENT	5.02
B. SCOPE OF THE OBLIGATION	5.08*
C. PARTICULAR INSTANCES	5.19*
D. SPECIAL CASES	5.33*
E. "POSSESSION, CUSTODY OR POWER"/ "CONTROL"	5.39*

CHAPTER 5

What Must be Disclosed

B. SCOPE OF THE OBLIGATION

Matters in question

Add *EAA Securities Ltd v Chan Lin Mui* [2008] HKDC 205 at [16] (citing opening sentence in this paragraph of main work). 5.09

Standard disclosure

NOTE 35. *Chancery Guide* (6th edn, 2009), para.4.3 (updated citation). 5.10
NOTE 36. *Chancery Guide* (6th edn, 2009), paras.4.5–4.7 (updated citation). 5.10
NOTE 37. *Admiralty and Commercial Courts Guide* (9th edn, 2009), para.E4.2 (updated citation). In *Berezovsky v Abramovich* [2010] (Comm), Gloster J refused to order enhanced disclosure pursuant to CPR, r. 31.5(1). Whilst the sums at stage were enormous and allegations of serious dishonesty were being made, it was considered premature to make such an order prior to seeing what was disclosed on standard disclosure. The court left open the possibility of such an order in relation to specific issues or categories at a later stage in the proceedings. 5.10

Although the parties can agree to limit disclosure that would otherwise have to be given, it is not open to one party unilaterally to seek to summarise the effect of a number of otherwise disclosable documents in a schedule created specifically for the purpose and to disclose only that, and not the underlying documents: *Tullett Prebon Ltd v Davis* [2007] EWHC 2739 (QB), [28]–[32]. Nor will it normally be appropriate for the court to decline to order disclosure of documents after deciding that they are disclosable merely on the basis of a concession at the hearing designed to draw the sting of the application for specific disclosure: *Tullett Prebon Ltd v Davis* [2007] EWHC 2739 (QB), [26]. 5.11

Statements of case

EAA Securities Ltd v Chan Lin Mui [2008] HKDC 205 at [26], pleadings not necessarily decisive in determining whether documents are in existence 5.12

that ought to be disclosed because they relate to a matter in question, but are a crucial reference point (citing this paragraph of main work). In *Metcash Trading v Bunn* [2010] FCA 8, (2010) 263 A.L.R. 132 at [8], Lander J stated that "the extent of a party's obligations to give discovery is above all regulated by the pleadings." In *Ashley v Chief Constable of Sussex Police* [2008] EWHC 3152 (QB) at [3], Eady J judged the matter according to the outstanding issues on the parties' statements of case.

C. PARTICULAR INSTANCES

(d) Insurance and legal aid

5.23 NOTE 69. Add *West London Pipeline and Storage Ltd v Total UK Ltd* [2008] EWHC 1296 (Comm.); cf. *Harcourt v FEF Griffin* [2007] EWHC 1500 (QB), both applications for information as to insurance cover under CPR Pt 18.

(e) Other transactions and incidents

5.24 NOTE 78. Add *EAA Securities Ltd v Chan Lin Mui* [2008] HKDC 205 at [33].

(g) Fishing

5.30 In Australia the reluctance of the court to allow a fishing expedition is not as great as it once was. This is because the Federal Court Rules do not provide for discovery as of right (unlike before in most jurisdictions) and now preliminary and non-party discovery is permitted: *Parkin v O'Sullivan* [2006] FCA 1413; (2007) 235 A.L.R. 286 at [36], citing *Caltex Refining Co. Pty Ltd v Amalgamated Metal Workers Union* (1990) 51 IR 113 at 116.

D. SPECIAL CASES

Patents

5.34 In *Nichia Corp v Argos Ltd* the majority of the Court of Appeal held that there was no special rule in patent infringement cases that disclosure should not be ordered where the defence was obviousness. Standard disclosure under the CPR was a real change from the old *Peruvian Guano* test, and

concerns of over-disclosure could be met by a rigorous application of the rationale of standard disclosure. See also *M.M.I. Research Ltd v Cellxion Ltd* [2007] EWHC 3464 (Pat). In *Hospira Inc v Amgen Inc* [2010] EWHC 176 (Pat), in a patent action where allegations of obviousness were made, the court declined the defendant's application for standard disclosure be dispensed with altogether without prejudice to any application for specific disclosure.

The need for proportionality in the context of patent disputes was stressed in *Nichia Corp v Argos Ltd* [2007] EWCA Civ 741; [2007] F.S.R. 38, CA. Standard disclosure no longer requires automatic wholesale disclosure of all the inventor's work. Jacob L.J. (dissenting) was of the view that proportionality requires that disclosure should not be ordered from the patentee (or objector) when the objection is straightforward obviousness. The majority held that a limited reasonable search for documents should be undertaken. Nevertheless the members of the Court of Appeal were agreed in the desire to cut down the costs of disclosure in patent actions. 5.37

Terrorism

CPR Part 79 contains provisions applicable in relation to, inter alia, applications under Section 63 of the Counter-Terrorism Act 2008 to set aside a direction placing restrictions on dealings made pursuant to Schedule 7 of the Act. CPR Part 79 provides for a closed material, with the involvement of special advocates. The Treasury is obliged to disclose sufficient information to enable the person restricted to enable it to give effective instructions about the essential allegations against it: *Bank Mellat v HM Treasury* [2010] EWCA Civ 483 [2010] 3 W.L.R. 1090 applying *Secretary of State for the Home Department v AF (No.3)* [2009] UK HL 28, [2009] 3 W.L.R. 74. Disclosure obligations may also arise in respect of control orders against suspected terrorists and their modification, where a closed material and special advocates procedure may be adopted: *BX v Secretary of State for the Home Department* [2010] EWCA Civ 481; s.7 Prevention of Terrorism Act 2005, CPR rr.76.28–29. 5.38A

E. "POSSESSION, CUSTODY OR POWER"/"CONTROL"

NOTE 138. Add *Psalidis v Norwich Union Life Australia Ltd* [2009] VSC 417. 5.39

"Power" and "right to inspect/take copies"

In *Schlumberger Holdings Ltd v Electromagnetic Geoservices* [2008] EWHC 56 (Pat), the claimant disclosed records in its list of documents of 5.48

other companies and individuals within the same group. On an application for specific disclosure of further records held by those third parties, the claimant argued that those records were not within its control, relying on *Lonrho v Shell* [1980] 1 W.L.R. 627, HL. The claimant was ordered to undertake a further search on the basis that the records were within its control, based upon the original consent of those third parties to permit the claimant to search for documents.

5.48 NOTE 180. Some aspects of the reasoning in *Linfa Pty Ltd v Citibank Ltd* [1995] 1 V.R. 643 have been doubted: see *Taylor v Santos* (1998) 71 S.A.S.R. 434; *Psalidis v Norwich Union Life Australia Ltd* [2009] VSC 417 at [31–34]. Documents which a party would be likely to obtain if it made a request (but which it had no presently enforceable legal right to obtain) are not within its power: *Psalidis* at [33]; *Bova v Avati* [2009] NSWSC 921.

5.52 NOTE 189. Add *Breakspear v Ackland* [2008] EWHC 220 (Ch); [2008] W.T.L.R. 777 on beneficiaries claim for inspection and production of letters of wishes from trustees, see para.4.23 noted above.

5.52 NOTE 193. Add *Psalidis v Norwich Union Life Australia Ltd* [2009] VSC 417 medical records not in power of patient as the "right" of access under the Health Records Act 2001 was subject to restrictions and limitations. See also *Nixon v Channel 4* [1997] EWCA Civ 1117 which under the old rules held that the right of a patient to have access to medical records under the Access to Health Records Act 1990 did not render them discoverable by the patient as he had no right to demand possession or custody of the original documents. However, the test under the CPR includes where a party has a right to inspect or take copies. Unlike in UK or Australia, individuals in Canada have a common law right to have access to their medical records: *McInerney v McDonald* (1992) 93 D.L.R. (4th) 415. In *Breen v Williams* (1996) 186 C.L.R. 71 the High Court of Australia refused to follow the Canadian case of *McInerney*.

5.54 NOTE 207. Add *Psalidis v Norwich Union Life Australia Ltd* [2009] VSC 417.

5.54 The power of SOCA to apply for disclosure of documents in the hands of a third party under s.357 of the Proceeds of Crime Act 2002 is to be used for the purposes of the Act. It would be an impermissible use of that power to obtain documents simply for the purposes of disclosing them in civil proceedings, hence such documents do not fall within the power of SOCA for the purposes of a party to an action seeking disclosure from SOCA: *Serious Organised Crime Agency v Scott* [2010] NIQB 39.

CHAPTER 6

Means of Disclosure

	PARA.
A. LISTS OF DOCUMENTS	6.01*
B. CHALLENGING ADEQUACY OF DISCLOSURE	6.35
C. VERIFICATION ON AFFIDAVIT	6.37*
D. ORDER THAT PARTY COMPLY	6.39
E. CONCLUSIVENESS OF LIST OR AFFIDAVIT	6.41*
F. APPLICATION FOR SPECIFIC DISCLOSURE	6.45*
G. APPEALS	6.57
H. PUBLICITY	6.58*

CHAPTER 6

Means of Disclosure

A. LISTS OF DOCUMENTS

Form and contents of list

NOTE 1. *Admiralty and Commercial Courts Guide* (9th edn, 2009), para.E3.7 (updated citation). 6.01
NOTE 4. *Admiralty and Commercial Courts Guide* (9th ed, 2009), no longer features para.E2.1(v).

Disclosure statement

NOTE 10. *Admiralty and Commercial Courts Guide* (9th edn, 2009), paras.E3.4–6 (updated citation). 6.05
NOTE 10. *Admiralty and Commercial Courts Guide* (9th edn, 2009), paras.E3.4–6 (updated citation). 6.06
NOTE 15. *Admiralty and Commercial Courts Guide* (9th edn, 2009), para.E3.7 (updated citation). 6.06
NOTE 17. *Admiralty and Commercial Courts Guide* (9th edn, 2009), para.E3.8. It is now specifically stated at para.3.8(d) that a person holding an office or position in the disclosing party but who is not in a position responsibly and authoritively to make the statements contained in the disclosure statement will not be regarded as an appropriate person to make the disclosure statement of the party. 6.06

List

In relation to disclosure of Electronic Documents, CPR, Pt.31, Practice Direction 31A has been modified in relation to disclosure pursuant to CPR, Pt.31 Practice Direction 31B, para.30 (as noted under para.7.13 in this Supplement). 6.08

Enumeration and description

6.12 NOTE 37. *Admiralty and Commercial Courts Guide* (9th edn, 2009), para.E3.1 (updated citation).

6.12 NOTE 38. *Admiralty and Commercial Courts Guide* (9th edn, 2009), para.E3.3 (updated citation).

Claims to withhold disclosure and inspection

6.14 NOTE 41. In the context of a claim to disclose documents in a form redacted for privilege or irrelevance, see *Atos Consulting Ltd v Avis plc* [2007] EWHC 323 (TCC).

6.15 NOTE 52. Add *Schreuder v Murray (No.2)* [2009] WASCA 145, (2009) 260 A.L.R. 139 at [60–63].

6.15 NOTE 53. The English and Australian cases on the extent to which a list needs to specify privileged documents was considered in detail in *Joint & Several Liquidators of Kong Wah Holdings v HSBC* [2007] HKCFI 1056. In that case a party was ordered to provide a list of documents for which legal professional privilege was claimed. The Australian cases that were followed demonstrate that there can be a middle ground in requiring an adequate description of privileged documents to enable the other side to assess the propriety of the claim that stops short of disclosure, directly or indirectly, of the contents of the documents.

Sealed up documents

6.17 CPR, Pt.31, Practice Direction 31B, para.35 provides that if a party is providing in electronic form copies of disclosed documents and wishes to redact or otherwise make alterations to a document then the party redacting or altering the document must inform the other party in accordance with CPR, r.31.19 that redacted or altered versions are being supplied and ensure that the original unredacted or unaltered version is perceived, so that it remains to be inspected if required. This does not apply where the only alteration made to the document is an alteration to the Metadata as a result of the ordinary process of copying and/or accessing the document.

6.18 In the context of a claim to disclose documents in a form redacted for privilege or irrelevance, see *Atos Consulting Ltd v Avis plc* [2007] EWHC 323 (TCC).

Service/exchange of lists

6.22 As regards challenges to authenticity or dates of documents, see *Admiralty and Commercial Courts Guide* (9th edn, 2009), para.E5.1.

Correction of errors

It may be noted that in the Family Division a practice had grown up of tolerating the deployment in ancillary relief proceedings of reelvant information from confidential documents belonging to one spouse having been surreptitiously removed and copied by the other without the owner's consent. These are known as the *Hildebrand* rules, after *Hildebrand v Hildebrand* [1992] 1 FLR 244. But in *Tchenguiz v Imerman* [2010] EWCA Civ 908, the court held that the so-called rules were not good law. He law on this point was the same as in the other Divisions of the High Court. 6.26

Supplementary lists

NOTE 92. *Admiralty and Commercial Courts Guide* (9th edn, 2009), para.E1.2 (updated citation). 6.31

Duty of search

The first sentence of this paragraph was cited in *Digicel (St Lucia) Ltd v Cable & Wireless Plc* [2008] EWHC 2522 (Ch), [48], [51]. 6.33

NOTE 97. CPR, Pt.31, Practice Direction has been amended to omit para.2A.4, which has been replaced by Practice Direction 31B, para.21 (as noted under para.7.07 in this Supplement). 6.33

C. VERIFICATION ON AFFIDAVIT

NOTE 110. *Admiralty and Commercial Courts Guide* (9th edn, 2009), para.E3.7 (updated citation). 6.38

E. CONCLUSIVENESS OF LIST OR AFFIDAVIT

The authorities on challenges to claims to privilege were considered in detail in *West London Pipeline and Storage Ltd v Total UK Ltd* [2008] EWHC 1729 (Comm.). Beatson J. at [86] distilled the following propositions from authorities on challenges to claims to privilege: 6.41

"(1) The burden of proof is on the party claiming privilege to establish it: see *Matthews & Malek on Disclosure* (2007) 11–46, and paragraph [50] above. A claim for privilege is an unusual claim in the sense that the party claiming privilege and that party's legal advisers are, subject to the power of the court to inspect the documents,

the judges in their or their own client's cause. Because of this, the court must be particularly careful to consider how the claim for privilege is made out and affidavits should be as specific as possible without making disclosure of the very matters that the claim for privilege is designed to protect: *Bank Austria Akt v Price Waterhouse*; *Sumitomo Corp v Credit Lyonnais Rouse Ltd* (*per* Andrew Smith J).

(2) An assertion of privilege and a statement of the purpose of the communication over which privilege is claimed in an affidavit are not determinative and are evidence of a fact which may require to be independently proved: *Re Highgrade Traders Ltd*; *National Westminster Bank plc v Rabobank Nederland*.

(3) It is, however, difficult to go behind an affidavit of documents at an interlocutory stage of proceedings. The affidavit is conclusive unless it is reasonably certain from:

(a) the statements of the party making it that he has erroneously represented or has misconceived the character of the documents in respect of which privilege is claimed: *Frankenstein v Gavin's House to House Cycle Cleaning and Insurance Co*, per Lord Esher MR and Chitty LJ; *Lask v Gloucester Health Authority*.

(b) the evidence of the person who or entity which directed the creation of the communications or documents over which privilege is claimed that the affidavit is incorrect: *Neilson v Laugharane* (the Chief Constable's letter), *Lask v Gloucester HA* (the NHS Circular), and see *Frankenstein v Gavin's House to House Cycle Cleaning and Insurance Co*, per A L Smith LJ.

(c) the other evidence before the court that the affidavit is incorrect or incomplete on the material points: *Jones v Montivedeo Gas Co; Birmingham and Midland Motor Omnibus Co. v London and North West Railway Co; National Westminster Bank plc v Rabobank Nederland.*

(4) Where the court is not satisfied on the basis of the affidavit and the other evidence before it that the right to withhold inspection is established, there are four options open to it:

(a) It may conclude that the evidence does not establish a legal right to withhold inspection and order inspection: *Neilson v Laugharane; Lask v Gloucester Health Authority.*

(b) It may order a further affidavit to deal with matters which the earlier affidavit does not cover or on which it is unsatisfactory: *Birmingham and Midland Motor Omnibus Co. Ltd v London and North West Railway Co*; *National Westminster Bank plc v Rabobank Nederland.*

(c) It may inspect the documents: see CPR 31.19(6) and the discussion in *National Westminster Bank plc v Rabbo Bank Nederland* and *Atos Consulting Ltd v Avis plc (No. 2)*. Inspection should be a solution of last resort, in part because of the danger of looking at documents out of context at the interlocutory stage. It should not be undertaken unless there is credible evidence that those claiming privilege have either misunderstood their duty, or are not to be trusted with the decision making, or there is no reasonably practical alternative.

(d) At an interlocutory stage a court may, in certain circumstances, order cross-examination of a person who has sworn an affidavit, for example, an affidavit sworn as a result of the order of the court that a defendant to a freezing injunction should disclose his assets: (*House of Spring Gardens Ltd v Wait; Yukong Lines v Rensburg; Motorola Credit Corp v Uzan (No. 2)*). However, the weight of authority is that cross-examination may not be ordered in the case of an affidavit of documents: *Frankenstein's* case; *Birmingham and Midland Motor Omnibus Co. Ltd v London and North Western Railway Co* and *Fayed v Lonrho*. In cases where the issue is whether the documents exist (as it was in *Frankenstein's* case and *Fayed v Lonrho*) the existence of the documents is likely to be an issue at the trial and there is a particular risk of a court at an interlocutory stage impinging on that issue."

Even if there is no jurisdictional bar to ordering cross-examination of a deponent on his affidavit as to disclosure, the exercise of that power should be reserved to extreme cases where there is no alternative relief. It will only be in the rarest of cases that it would be appropriate to permit cross-examination at an interlocutory stage as to a claim to privilege: *West London Pipeline and Storage Ltd v Total UK Ltd* [2008] EWHC 1729 (Comm.) at [88–91]. See also *Procter v Kalivis* [2009] FCA 461, (2010) 263 A.L.R. 461, Fed. Ct. of Aus. (cross examination refused, but order to file further and better affidavits of discovery). 6.44

F. APPLICATION FOR SPECIFIC DISCLOSURE

NOTE 134. *Admiralty and Commercial Courts Guide* (9th edn, 2009), para.E2.1 (updated citation). 6.47

Mode of application

In *Canadian Imperial Bank of Commerce v Beck* [2009] EWCA Civ 619, [2009] I.R.L.R. 740, CA it was held that the test for specific disclosure in the 6.53

Employment Tribunal is whether it is necessary for disposing fairly of the proceedings (at [22]). On appeal the test for a review of the decision below is whether the exercise of discretion exceeds the generous ambit within which reasonable disagreement is possible (at [23]).

In *Fiddes v Channel 4 TV Corporation* [2010] EWCA Civ 516, the CA refused to disturb a cost management decision to reuse to order specific disclosure of back-up texts containing emails and attachments on the basis that the judge had considered the relevant factors and the appellate court should not interfere.

6.53 NOTE 149. *Admiralty and Commercial Courts Guide* (9th edn, 2009), paras.E4.2 and E2.5(d) (updated citation); *Chancery Guide* (6th edn, 2009), paras.4.5–4.7 (updated citation).

H. PUBLICITY

6.58 Where a winding-up petition was heard in private under r.39.2(3) (but the judge did not prohibit the publication of information about the hearing), and subsequently the company made statements to the media about what happened in court, the company was not in contempt of court: *AF Noonan (Architectural Practice) Ltd v Bournemouth and Boscombe Athletic Football Club Ltd* [2007] EWCA Civ 848.

CHAPTER 7

Electronic Disclosure

CHAPTER 7

Electronic Disclosure

The cost and practical difficulties with electronic disclosure are considered in Lord Justice Jackson's Review of Civil Litigation: Final Report (2010), Chapter 37. It was concluded that lawyers and judges require further training on electronic disclosure and that the then forthcoming Practice Direction on Electronic Disclosure was to be commended. The new Practice Direction 31B came into effect in October 2010 and is set out in this Supplement at Appendix 2, B.04A. It applies in respect of proceedings which started on or after 1st October 2010 and, unless the court otherwise orders, it only applies to proceedings that are (or are likely to be) allocated to the multi-track (paras.3 and 4). Paragraph 2A.1 of Practice Direction 31A continues to apply to proceedings started before that date (para.4). 7.01

Practice Direction 31B, para.6 sets out the following general principles in relation to disclosure of Electronic Documents:

(1) Electronic Documents should be managed efficiently in order to minimise the cost incurred;
(2) technology should be used in order to ensure that document management activities are undertaken efficiently and effectively;
(3) disclosure should be given in a manner which gives effect to the overriding objective;
(4) Electronic Documents should generally be made available in a form which allows the party receiving the documents the same ability to access, search, review and display the documents as the party giving disclosure; and
(5) disclosure of Electronic Documents which are of no relevance to the proceedings may place an excessive burden in time and cost on the party to whom disclosure is given.

Practice Direction 31B is a response to the problems in practice with disclosure of Electronic Documents, one of which is the sheer complexity and cost involved. If Practice Direction 31B is to be followed without qualification and considering what is truly needed in any given case, electronic disclosure will be a costly exercise. Whilst the steps in the Practice Direction are suitable for high value cases with a significant amount of

Electronic Documents in many cases it may prove to be unnecessary. Hence it only applies to cases on the multi-track and the court may wish to consider the extent to which it should apply (if at all) in any given case.

7.01 NOTE 1. Delete reference to *Admiralty and Commercial Courts Guide* (6th edn, 2006), para.3.11.

7.01 NOTE 4. See also *Digicel (St Lucia) Ltd v Cable & Wireless Plc* [2008] EWHC 2522 (Ch), [37]–[43].

A. WHAT ARE ELECTRONIC DOCUMENTS?

7.02 Practice Direction 31B, para.5 defines Electronic Documents as meaning:

"... any document held in electronic form. It includes, for example, email and other electronic communications such as text messages and voicemail, word-processed documents and databases, and documents stored on portable devices such as memory sticks and mobile phones. In addition to documents that are readily accessible from computer systems and other electronic devices and media, it includes documents that are stored on servers and back-up systems and documents that have been deleted. It also includes Metadata and other embedded data which is not typically visible on screen or a print out."

7.02 NOTE 5. *Admiralty and Commercial Courts Guide* (9th edn, 2009), para.E2.5(a) (updated citation).

7.03 In *Hellard v Money* Unreported, April 28, 2008, Ch.D., a non-party was ordered to provide disclosure of the meta-data in relation to a note of a meeting which had already been disclosed, but had been created long after the meeting had been held.

B. DUTY OF SEARCH

7.06 NOTE 20. Delete references to *Admiralty and Commercial Courts Guide* (7th edn, 2006), para.E3.11.

7.07 The duty of search in relation to Electronic Documents is dealt with in Practice Direction 31B, paras.20–27. The parties should consider a staged approach and the use of keyword searches supplemented as appropriate. Metadata may require separate consideration (paras.28, 29 and 33).

7.07 NOTE 22. Practice Direction 31, has been renamed Practice Direction 31A. Paragraphs 2A.2 to 2A.5 have now been deleted and with effect from 1st October 2010 replaced by the following:

"2A.2 Practice Direction 31B contains additional provisions in relation to the disclosure of electronic documents in cases that are or are likely to be allocated to the multi-track."

Practice Direction 31B, para.21 lists the factors that may be relevant in deciding the reasonableness of a search for Electronic Documents include (but are not limited to) the following—

(1) the number of documents involved;
(2) the nature and complexity of the proceedings;
(3) the case and expense of retrieval of any particular document. This includes:

  (a) the accessibility of Electronic Documents including email communications on computer systems, servers, back-up systems and other electronic devices or media that may contain such documents taking into account alterations or developments in hardware or software systems used by the disclosing party and/or available to enable access to such documents;
  (b) the location of relevant Electronic Documents, data, computer systems, servers, back-up systems and other electronic devices or media that may contain such documents;
  (c) the likelihood of locating relevant data;
  (d) the costs of recovering any Electronic Documents;
  (e) the cost of disclosing and providing inspection of any relevant Electronic Documents; and
  (f) the likelihood that Electronic Documents will be materially altered in the course of recovery, disclosure or inspection;

(4) the availability of documents or classes of documents from other sources, and
(5) the significance of any document which is likely to be located during the search.

See also *Admiralty and Commercial Courts Guide* (9th edn, 2009), para.E2.5(d).

In *Earles v Barclays Bank* [2010] EWHC 2500 (Mercantile) at [41], the judge criticised a bank for not engaging an IT expert to retrieve ESI from back up sources and commented: 7.08

"One expects a major high street Bank in this day and age of electronic records and communication with an in-house litigation department to have an efficient and effective information management system in place to provide identification, preservation, collection, processing, review analysis and production of its ESI in the disclosure process in litigation and regulation."

NOTE 24. CPR Pt 31, Practice Direction, para.2A.5 has been deleted—see now Practice Direction 31B, paras.22–24; *Admiralty and Commercial Courts Guide* (9th edn, 2009), para.E2.5(e). 7.08

7.09 NOTE 25. In *Vector Transportation Services Inc v Traffic Tech Inc*, 2008 Can LII 11050, the Ontario Superior Court ordered a party to produce a laptop so it could be examined by an expert to see if he could find relevant deleted emails. See further under para.9.29 below.

7.11 In *Digicel (St Lucia) Ltd v Cable & Wireless Plc* [2008] EWHC 2522 (Ch), where allegations of conspiracy to injure the claimants were made, Morgan J. ordered the defendants to restore back up tapes which might contain documents from the email accounts of former employees, and also ordered further key-word searches to be made in addition to those already performed. In *Fides v Channel 4 TV Corporation* [2010] EWCA Civ 516, the Court of Appeal refused to interfere with the judge's refusal to order a search of a party's IT systems' backup tapes to look for relevant emails which had been deleted but may have been retrievable from back up tapes.

7.12 In *Goodale v Ministry of Justice* [2010] EWHC B40 (QB), Master Whitaker reviewed the approach to electronic disclosure and in that case adopted an incremental or staged approach. He ordered an initial search of electronic data of 4 main witnesses by means of a keyword search. He stressed the need for parties to co-operate when it comes to electronic disclosure. The advent of the electronic age has meant that in practice there are difficulties with the potential scope and extent of disclosure.

Practice Direction 31B now provides a framework for co-operation between the parties in relation to Disclosure of Electronic Disclosure. The parties and their legal representatives in cases in which the Practice Direction applies must discuss the use of technology in the management of Electronic Documents and the conduct of proceedings (para.8) and disclosure of Electronic Documents (para.9). Where appropriate the discussions should include the categories of Electronic Documents and storage systems, the scope of the reasonable search, tools and techniques to reduce the burden and cost of disclosure, and preservation of Electronic Documents. The Schedule to Practice Direction 31B contains the Electronic Disclosure Questionnaire which may be used to assist the parties to exchange information.

Practice Direction 31B makes provision for the resolution of any disputes between the parties as to Electronic Disclosure. In advance of the first case management conference the parties should submit a summary of the matters on which the parties agree in relation to the disclosure of Electronic Documents and a summary of matters on which they disagree (para.14). In cases of disagreement, the court can then give written directions in relation to disclosure o order a separate hearing, and may direct exchange of completed Electronic Questionnaires (para.15). The person signing the Electronic Questionnaire should attend the first case management conference, and any subsequent hearing at which disclosure is likely to be considered (para.16). The Practice Direction is in terms which appears to require such attendance, even where there is no dispute as to Electronic Disclosure.

If at any time it becomes apparent that the parties are unable to reach agreement in relation to disclosure of Electronic Documents, the parties should seek directions from the court at the earliest practical date (para.17). The court may give directions as to disclosure if it considers the parties agreement in relation to the disclosure of Electronic Documents is inappropriate or inefficient (para.18). If a party gives disclosure of Electronic Documents without discussions with the other party in advance, the court may require the party to conduct further searches and repeat steps (para.19).

C. FORM OF DISCLOSURE

Practice Direction 31B, para.30 provides that Practice Direction 31A, para.3 in respect of listing of documents is to be read subject to the following: 7.13

(1) Form N265 may be amended to accommodate the sub-paragraphs which follow;
(2) a list of documents may by agreement between the parties be an electronic file in .csv (comma-separated values) or other agreed format;
(3) documents may be listed otherwise than in date order where a different order would be more convenient;
(4) save where otherwise agreed or ordered, documents should be listed individually if a party already possesses data relating to the document (for example, type of document and date of creation) which make this possible (so that as far as possible each document may be given a unique reference number);
(5) a party should be consistent in the way documents are listed;
(6) consistent column headings should be repeated on each page of the list on which documents are listed, where the software used for preparing the list enables this to be carried out automatically; and
(7) the disclosure list number used in any supplemental list of documents should be unique and should run sequentially from the last number used in the previous list.

Specific provision is made as to the format of Disclosure Data in electronic form (para.31).

Practice Direction 31B, paras.32 to 35 deals with the provision of electronic copies of disclosed documents (noted under paras.9.27–9.28 in this Supplement). 7.15

NOTE 32. *Admiralty and Commercial Courts Guide* (9th edn., 2009), para. E2.5(c) (updated citation). 7.15

CHAPTER 8

Objections to Disclosure

PARA.

A. INTRODUCTION 8.01

B. OBJECTIONS AS OF RIGHT 8.06*

C. PRIVILEGE FROM PRODUCTION 8.11

D. INJUNCTIONS 8.13

E. DOCUMENTS FROM PREVIOUS CASES 8.16

F. OTHER OBJECTIONS 8.18*

CHAPTER 8

Objections to Disclosure

B. OBJECTIONS AS OF RIGHT

Sections 348 and 391 of the Financial Services and Markets Act 2000 were considered in detail in the context of disclosure by the Court of Appeal in *Real Estate Opportunities Ltd v Aberdeen Asset Management Jersey Ltd* [2007] EWCA Civ 197; [2007] 2 All E.R. 791. Section 348 does not forbid the disclosure and inspection of documents in the hands of a party if the party already had the information provided by the FSA. A person cannot be said to "obtain" information for the purpose of s.348 if he already knew that information or, in the case of a body corporate, knowledge of that information was attributed to it under the general rules as to attribution. Section 391 only prohibits the publishing of information. Making documents available for inspection does not of itself result in the publication of the information contained in those documents. 8.09

F. OTHER OBJECTIONS

(d) Confidentiality of third parties

In *Chan Mei Yiu v Secretary for Justice* [2007] HKCFI 664 the court inspected a foreign criminal letter of request before deciding that disclosure was not necessary in the context of a judicial review challenge to warrants issued pursuant to the request. The court adopted the view that the court should inspect the letter of request if a case is made out that the documents may be necessary. 8.24

NOTE 101. In *Cadogan Petroleum v Tolley* [2009] EWHC 3291 (Ch) and [2010] EWHC 1107 (Ch), the remaining defendants' sought production of a settlement agreement between the claimants and certain former defendants. In view of its confidentiality, the judge ordered production of those parts which were relevant, the judge having inspected the whole and an independent counsel instructed to make submissions on the issue. 8.24

NOTE 107. Confidentiality is a relevant matter in the exercise of the court's discretion whether or not to order production. If a document is both 8.24

relevant and confidential, disclosure should be ordered if its disclosure is in accordance with the over-riding objective, and in particular, if disclosure is proportionate and necessary to ensure that the case is dealt with fairly: *Tullett Prebon Group Ltd v Davis* [2007] EWHC 2739 (QB) at [13].

(e) Exposure of the party's trade secrets or other confidential information

8.25 This paragraph was cited with approval in *Koger Inc v O'Donnell* [2009] IEHC 385, which reviewed both English and Irish authorities on restricted inspection. The Court concluded that limiting disclosure to experts or experts and legal advisors, but to deny it to even a limited number of persons in the plaintiffs' organisation is exceptional. In that case the judge ordered disclosure to the plaintiffs' legal advisors and to a nominated officer of the plaintiffs under strict conditions.

8.25 NOTE 109. See Ch.11, paras.11.157–11.163, below (correct cross-reference).

CHAPTER 9

Inspection of Documents

	PARA.
A. INTRODUCTION	9.01
B. NOTICE TO INSPECT	9.02
C. DOCUMENTS MENTIONED IN STATEMENTS OF CASE ETC.	9.04*
D. PLACE OF INSPECTION	9.11
E. TIME OF INSPECTION	9.15
F. COPIES	9.17
G. TRANSLATIONS	9.22*
H. ELECTRONICALLY HELD DOCUMENTS AND EQUIPMENT	9.23*
I. WHO MAY INSPECT?	9.30
J. THE EFFECT OF INSPECTION	9.32
K. APPLICATIONS TO THE COURT	9.33
L. RSC, ORDER 24, RULE 12: PRODUCTION TO THE COURT	9.35

CHAPTER 9

Inspection of Documents

C. DOCUMENTS MENTIONED IN STATEMENTS OF CASE ETC.

In *Expandable Ltd v Rubin* [2008] EWCA Civ 59 [2008] 1 W.L.R. 1099, at [24], Rix L.J. stated that if a party thinks it worthwhile to mention a document in his pleadings, witness statements or affidavits, he did not see why, subject to the question of privilege, the court should put difficulties in the way of inspection. Where a document has been mentioned, inspection can be resisted not only on grounds of privilege, but also on the more general grounds in CPR r.31.3. Thus where in a statement there was a reference to a database, inspection was successfully resisted on grounds that it would be disproportionate to do so and would be an unjustified interference with Article 8 ECHR rights: *Webster v Ridgeway Foundation School Governors* [2009] EWHC 1140 (QB) at [31–36]. 9.05

NOTE 34. This sentence was cited in *Expandable Ltd v Rubin* [2008 EWCA Civ 59; [2008] 1 W.L.R. 1099 at [35]. 9.05

In *Expandable Ltd v Rubin* [2008] EWCA Civ 59; [2008] 1 W.L.R. 1099 the Court of Appeal was content to assume that there is no effective or substantive difference in the meaning of CPR r.31.14 which speaks of "mentioned" and RSC Ord.24 r.10 which spoke of "reference" in the pleadings or affidavit to the document concerned (at [23]). The court adopted the test of direct allusion as an elucidation of CPR r.31.14 language which speaks of "mentioned". It was considered that the change in the rule's language does underline two matters. The first is to confirm the test of "direct allusion" or "specifically mention". Secondly, the expression "mentioned" is as general as could be. The document in question does not have to be relied on, or refereed to in any particular way or for any particular purpose, in order to be mentioned (at [24]). The expression "he wrote to me" was found to be a direct illusion to a document (at [25]). 9.10

G. TRANSLATIONS

In *Han v Cho* (2008) 297 D.L.R. (4th) 572 (British Columbia Supreme Court), it was held that the disclosing party is under no obligation to 9.22

provide translations. The court also suggested that unofficial translations done in-house as a result of the legal teams efforts were privileged, however *Sumitomo v Credit Lyonnais Rouse* [2002] 1 W.L.R. 479, CA was not cited.

H. ELECTRONICALLY HELD DOCUMENTS AND EQUIPMENT

9.27 Practice Direction 31B which applies to proceedings on the multi-track starting on or after 1st October 2010 make provision for the format and inspection of Electronic Documents. Before the first case management conference the parties should discuss the format in which Electronic Documents are to be provided on inspection and the methods to be used (para.9(6)). The parties are expected to co-operate at an early stage about format. In the case of difficulty or disagreement, the matter should be referred to the court for directions at the earliest practical date, if possible at the first case management conference (para.32).

Save where otherwise agreed or ordered, electronic copies of disclosed documents should be provided in their Native Format (i.e. original form in which it was created by a computer software programme), in a manner which preserves Metadata relating to the date of the creation of each document (para.33). A party should provide any available searchable OCR versions of Electronic Documents with the original, but may choose not to do so in respect of redacted documents (para.34). Where electronic disclosure is being given of redacted documents, then the redacting party should inform the other party that redacted versions are being supplied and the original unredacted or unaltered version must be retained (para.35).

9.28 Practice Direction 31B, para.6(h) expressly provides that Electronic Documents should generally be made available for inspection in a form which allows the party receiving the documents the same ability to access, search, review and display the documents as the party giving disclosure. If Electronic Documents are best accessed using technology which his not readily available to the party entitled to disclosure, and that party reasonably requires additional inspection facilities, the party making disclosure shall co-operate in making available to the other party such reasonable additional inspection facilities as may be appropriate in order to afford inspection in accordance with CPR r.31.3 (para.36).

9.29 In *Vector Transportation Services Inc v Traffic Tech Inc*, 2008 Can LII 11050, the Ontario Superior court ordered a party to produce a laptop so it could be examined by an expert to see if he could find relevant deleted emails. The court took into account a variety of factors, including the importance of the emails and the plaintiff's willingness to pay for the costs of inspection. The court cited at [14] the following passage in *Nicolardi v Daley* [2002] O.J. No.595:

"Since the definition of document in the Rules includes data stored electronically, then if production for inspection of a document stored on computer is ordered, then such production can only be made if the court orders a hard copy of all documents to be printed, or orders a duplicate of the electronic data be reproduced and delivered on diskette, or allows an inspection of the storage device in which the electronic information resides. Where a party on proper evidence convinces the court that documents that have not been produced are likely stored on a computer's hard drive or other electronic storage medium, but the party in possession of the computer asserts it has printed and produced all that it has, then the only solution that would allow inspection of a document, would be inspection of the storage medium itself, in this case the firm's hard drive, with proper safeguards".

In *Innovative Health Group Inc. Calgary Health Region* (2008) 294 D.L.R. (4th) 83, the Alberta Court of Appeal held that it is only in an exceptional cases where a court would order production *in specie* of a computer hard drive. An example would be where it is apparent that one of the parties is deliberately trying to thwart the discovery process by not disclosing relevant and material information.

K. APPLICATIONS TO THE COURT

An application may also be made by a party under CPR r 31.19(5) to ask the court to decide on a claim under CPR r 31.19(3) to withhold inspection of a document or a part of a document: see *Atos Consulting Ltd v Avis plc* [2007] EWHC 323 (TCC), and para.9.39 below. 9.33

N. SEALING UP

In *Egglishaw v ACC (No.2)* [2009] FCA 12, (2009) 253 A.L.R. 354, Fed. Ct. of Aus. A distinction was made between where there is an order for general discovery, as opposed to limited discovery. It was held that in the former case a party is entitled to seal up irrelevant parts of a document without the consent of the other party or the permission of the court. Where the order is for limited discovery a party in Australia requires consent or permission to do so. 9.37

Whether the claim to redaction of material is based on irrelevance or privilege, the matter may be decided by the court on an application under CPR r 31.19(5). In *Atos Consulting Ltd v Avis plc* [2007] EWHC 323 (TCC), [37], Ramsey J said: 9.39

1. "In my judgment the appropriate course to be adopted in an application under rule 31.19 (5) where the right being relied on is privilege

or irrelevance, is for the Court to proceed by way of stages as follows:

(1) The Court has to consider the evidence produced on the application.
(2) If the Court is satisfied that the right to withhold inspection of a document is established by the evidence and there are no sufficient grounds for challenging the correctness of that asserted right, the Court will uphold the right.
(3) If the Court is not satisfied that the right to withhold inspection is established because, for instance, the evidence does not establish a legal right to withhold inspection then the Court will order inspection of the documents.
(4) If sufficient grounds are shown for challenging the correctness of the asserted right then the Court may order further evidence to be produced on oath or, if there is no other appropriate method of properly deciding whether the right to withhold inspection should be upheld, it may decide to inspect the documents.
(5) If it decides to inspect then having inspected the documents it may invite representations."

CHAPTER 10

Production by Non-Parties

	PARA.
A. GENERAL	10.01
B. WITNESS SUMMONS	10.02*
C. BANKER'S BOOKS EVIDENCE ACT 1879	10.37*
D. EVIDENCE (PROCEEDINGS IN OTHER JURISDICTIONS) ACT 1975	10.54*

CHAPTER 10

Production by Non-Parties

B. WITNESS SUMMONS

Requirements

(b) Actual possession or custody

In the Australian case of *Dorajay Pty Ltd v Aristocrat Leisure Ltd* [2006] FCA 335, (2007) 230 A.L.R. 549 it was held that an addressee of a subpoena must produce that which he has in his possession, power or control but he is not obliged to take steps to bring documents that do not fall within these concepts into his power or control. On the facts it was held that documents held by foreign affiliated practices of the accounting firm PWC were not within its control. 10.08

(d) Identification

NOTE 27. *Tajik Aluminium Plant v Hydro Aluminium* [2005] EWCA Civ 1218, [2006] 1 W.L.R. 767, CA was distinguished in the very different context of the FSA's statutory powers to investigate and assist a foreign regulator: *Financial Services Authority v Amro* [2010] EWCA Civ 123, [2010] 3 All E.R. 723. In *SMSE v KL* [2009] HK CA 349 at [36] reference was made to *Charman v Charman* [2005] Civ 1606, [2006] 1 W.L.R. 1053 as authority to the effect that the family courts are more relaxed in their approach to the test of particularly for documents. This approach is doubtful. 10.10

NOTE 33. Add *Assistant Deputy Coroner for Inner West London v Channel 4 Television Corporation* [2007] EWHC 2513 (QB): witness summons for documents held by television company for coroner's inquest. 10.10

(e) Relevance and admissibility

In Attorney General for New South Wales v Chidgey [2008] NSWCCA65 the test for disclosure pursuant to a subpoena was considered in a criminal 10.11

context. This was considered in *P & M Quality Smallgoods Pty Ltd v Seven Network (Operations) Pty Ltd* [2010] NSWSC841 at [17] where it was noted that:

"On the one hand, there is clearly to be recognised, the obvious danger of permitting a party by the use of the subpoena procedure, to investigate issues of credit having no conceivable relevance to the issues pleaded, in the sense that to permit subpoenas of that type to be called would open up matters falling outside the legitimate field of enquiry raised by the issues in contest. On the other hand, it seems to me quite clear that inspection should be granted, so far as is necessary, in the proper conduct of litigation, where the court forms the view that the material falls within the legitimate field of enquiry raised by the issues in contest and is reasonably likely to add in the end in some way or other to the relevant evidence in the case."

See also *Campaign Master v Forty Two* [2010] FCA 398, (2010) 269 ALR 7, fed. Ct. of Aus, which considers relevance and the test for abuse of process, where documents are sought for a pre-dominant or improper or collateral purpose.

10.11 NOTE 33. Add *ACCC v Pratt* (2009) 250 A.L.R. 661, Fed. Ct. of Aus. (subpoena for documents for purposes of an application to stay criminal proceedings as an abuse of process).

(g) Necessity

10.15 Where documents as to a journalist's sources are sought, then s.10 of the Contempt of Court 1981 may come into play. The need for the coroner to have the fullest picture outweighed the need to protect such sources in *Assistant Deputy Coroner for Inner West London v Channel 4 Television Corporation* [2007] EWHC 2513 (QB). The court stressed that disclosure in the first instance would be limited to providing the documents to the coroner, who would only reveal such information as he obtained if it were necessary and proportionate to do so.

Inferior courts and tribunals

10.24 For an example of a witness summons in the context of a coroner's inquest see *Assistant Deputy Coroner for Inner West London v Channel 4 Television Corporation* [2007] EWHC 2513 (QB). Unlike in ordinary civil litigation, with coroner's inquests there are no pleadings with which to define both relevance and to an extent necessity. Further the disclosure is to the coroner, who in turn can then make a final decision as to whether the material he receives should be disseminated further having regard to both necessity and proportionality.

10.24 NOTE 90. Where the arbitral tribunal has given permission pursuant to section 43 of the Arbitration Act 1996 for a party to seek a witness summons from the Court of documents, the affirmative decision of the

arbitrators on the issue of necessity and relevance is entitled to respect: *Peters v Andrew* [2009] EWHC 1511 (QB) at [4].

Production

Where the witness summons is one merely to provide documents and not oral testimony, the party issuing the summons need not call the witness for him to be sworn and thus be subject to cross-examination: *Davis v Dale* (1830) 173 E.R. 142; *Perry v Gibson* (1834) 110 E.R. 1125; *R. v Gilmore* [1961] N.Z.L.R. 384; *Re Trade Practices Commission v Arnotts* [1989] FCA 248. 10.27

NOTE 100. *Waind v Hill and Employers Mutual General Association Ltd* [1978] 1 N.S.W.L.R. 372 (corrected citation). 10.27

Responding to and challenging witness summons

NOTE 102. Add *Campaign Master v Forty Two* [2010] FCA 76, (2010) 269 ALR 76 at [31], where it was noted that whilst there is authority to the effect that if documents contain information which a person seeking to challenge a subpoena claims to be confidential to him, then such claim should be supported by appropriate evidence. The case also considers the objection to a subpoena that it was obtained predominantly for an improper or collateral purpose.

NOTE 104. In a different context of a compulsory notice for production of documents that may be privileged, see *MM v Australian Crime Commission* [2007] FCA 2026; (2008) 244 A.L.R. 452, Fed. Ct of Australia. It was stated that the recipient of a notice would be obliged to make claims for privilege in respect of documents where privilege might reasonably be expected to exist to ensure that such a claim for privilege would not be lost. 10.28

NOTE 135. Add *Farm Assist Ltd v Secretary of State for the Environment, Food and Rural Affairs (No 2)* [2009] EWHC 1102 (TCC), [53]. 10.32

Costs

NOTE 152. Add *Akiba on Behalf of the Torres Strait Regional Sea Claim Group v State of Queensland* [2010] FCA 321, Fed. Ct. of Australia, where recipient of subpoena awarded reasonable costs of taking steps to comply, including costs of legal advice and appearing in court. 10.35

C. BANKER'S BOOKS EVIDENCE ACT 1879

Sections 1–6

For a discussion on the meaning of bankers books and whether it includes account-opening documentation and correspondence, see *Bernarus v Haughton* [2005] IEHC 240, High Court of Ireland. 10.40

D. EVIDENCE (PROCEEDINGS IN OTHER JURISDICTIONS) ACT 1975

Introduction

10.54 In *Presbyterian Church of Sudan v Taylor* (2006) 275 D.L.R. (4th) 512 at [20], the Ontario CA set out the relevant principles as enunciated by Osborne J. in *Re Friction Division Products Inc v E.I. DuPont de Nemours & Co. (No.2)* (1986) 32 D.L.R. (4th) 105, namely before an order giving effect to a letter of request may be made, the evidence (including the letter rogatory) must establish that:

(1) the evidence sought is relevant;
(2) the evidence sought is necessary for trial and will be adduced at trial, if admissible;
(3) the evidence is not otherwise obtainable;
(4) the order sought is not contrary to public policy;
(5) the documents sought are identified with reasonable particularity;
(6) the order sought is not unduly burdensome, having in mind the relevant witnesses would be required to do, and produce, were the action to be pursued here.

Whilst not exhaustive, the above list is still a useful statement of relevant principles.

10.54 NOTE 209. On disclosure of a foreign criminal letter of request on a judicial challenge to warrants issued pursuant to such request, see *Chan Mei Yiu v Secretary for Justice* [2007] HKCFI 664 (disclosure refused), following *R. (on the application of Evans) v Director of the Serious Fraud Office* [2003] 1 W.L.R. 299, CA. On the Crime (International Co-operation) Act 2003, ss.13–15, see *R. (on the application of Hafner) v Secretary of State for the Home Department* [2006] EWHC 1259 (Admin); [2007] 1 W.L.R. 950 (letter of request not disclosed); *R. (on the application of Hafner) v City of Westminster Magistrates' Court* [2008] EWHC 524 (Admin); [2008] Lloyd's Rep. FC 376; [2009] 1 W.L.R. 1005. See generally *Phipson on Evidence* (17th edn, 2010), paras.8.51–8.52.

Limitations imposed by the Act

10.57 So long as the classes of documents are specified, it is not necessary for the FSA to specify particular documents when seeking documents in aid of a foreign request under Section 171 of the Financial Services and Markets Act 2002: *Financial Services Authority v Amro* [2010] EWCA Civ 123. In the context of ancillary relief applications in divorce proceedings, there is a line of authority that the requirement to specify documents is relaxed. It is

sufficient, given the quasi-inquisitorial role of the judge in ancillary relief litigation for the request to refer to conjectural documents: *Jennings v Jennings* [2009] SC (Bda) 62 at [18–19] applying *Charman v Charman* [2006] 1 W.L.R. 1053, CA.

Save in the clearest of cases, the court will usually accept the statements contained in the letter of request that the evidence sought is relevant admissible evidence for trial in the requesting state: *Prediwave Corporation v New World TMT Ltd* [2006] HKCA 391 at [39], (letter of request from USA to Hong Kong seeking bank records): cf. *Presbyterian Church of Sudan v Taylor* (2006) 275 D.L.R. (4th) 512, Ontario CA, where it was found that the relevance criterion had not been met with a broadly framed request. Confidentiality between a bank and its customer is a matter to be considered in a balancing exercise against the public interest of the court in giving assistance to a foreign court in its administration of justice on the latter's request for evidence in aid of its proceedings: *Prediwave* at [53–54]. **10.59**

NOTE 245. Add *Honda v KJM Superbikes Ltd* [2007] EWCA Civ 313; [2007] C.P. Rep. 28: outgoing letter of request not fishing where seeking relevant oral testimony. **10.59**

CHAPTER 11

Objections to Inspection

	PARA.
A. THE GENERAL RULE	11.01*
B. OBJECTIONS TO INSPECTION GENERALLY	11.03
C. LEGAL PROFESSIONAL PRIVILEGE	11.05*
D. LEGAL ADVICE PRIVILEGE	11.09*
E. LITIGATION PRIVILEGE	11.30*
F. EXCEPTIONS TO LEGAL PROFESSIONAL PRIVILEGE	11.63*
G. PUBLIC INTEREST IMMUNITY	11.81*
H. PRIVILEGE AGAINST INCRIMINATION	11.104*
I. "WITHOUT PREJUDICE" PRIVILEGE	11.121*
J. WITNESS STATEMENTS	11.136
K. DOCUMENTS PRIVILEGED BY THE LAW OF DEFAMATION	11.137
L. DIPLOMATIC PRIVILEGE	11.139

CHAPTER 11

Objections to Inspection

A. THE GENERAL RULE

Unlike in England, there may be no automatic right to inspect in some other common law jurisdictions: see, eg. *The University of Western Australia v Gray (No.8)* [2007] FCA 89. 11.01

For recent cases on whether a judge should inspect documents where there is a disputed claim to a privilege, see *National Westminster Bank Plc v Rabobank Nederland* [2006] EWHC 2332 (Comm.); *Financial Services Compensation Scheme Ltd v Abbey National* [2007] EWHC 2868 (Ch). 11.02

C. LEGAL PROFESSIONAL PRIVILEGE

See also *Brookfield Multiplex Limited v International Litigation Funding Partners Pte Ltd (No 2)* [2009] FCA 449. 11.05

Professional legal associations such as the Law Society cannot take over the position of the lawyer and therefore cannot penetrate the privilege unless statute so permits: *Law Society of Saskatchewan v Merchant* (2009) 300 DLR (4th) 462, Sask CA. 11.06

In Canada it has been held that legal professional privilege cannot apply to the functions of Crown counsel in considering whether and what criminal charges to bring against a person; any confidentiality would be adequately protected by public interest immunity: *AG of British Columbia v Davies* (2009) 308 DLR (4th) 577, CA of BC. In *Brookfield Multiplex Limited v International Litigation Funding Partners Pte Ltd (No 2)* [2009] FCA 449, where the issue was the status of communications between a law firm and prospective members of a class to bring or join in class litigation, the court said: 11.07

"20. What kind of communication between a lawyer and a 'client' with whom there is no retainer can be protected? If the communication is *to* the lawyer it will be privileged if it is confidential and provided to the lawyer in his professional capacity. A communication may be so characterised in a

variety of circumstances, most usually if the person believes he is consulting a lawyer in that capacity and his manifest intention is to seek legal advice or legal services. [. . .]

21. In the case of a communication *from* the lawyer, in my view the following (non-exhaustive) rule is appropriate. If a lawyer provides a person with unsolicited legal advice, the advice cannot be privileged. It cannot be privileged because the communication is not made during the course of a professional relationship; nor can it be characterised as confidential. If, on the other hand, the advice is given in pursuance of a request, whether express or implied, made of the lawyer in his professional capacity, or if the circumstances are such that the 'client' would reasonably expect to be given such advice, then it will be privileged."

The information given to the prospective members about developments in the case was therefore privileged.

11.08 NOTE 49. Add *Canada (Privacy Commissioner) v Blood Tribe Department of Health* (2008) 294 DLR (4th) 385, SCC; *Akai Holdings Ltd v Ernst & Young* [2009] HKCFA 14.

11.08 NOTE 50. See also *R. (on the application of Kelly) v Warley Magistrates' Court* [2007] EWHC 1836 (Admin); [2008] 1 Cr.App.R. 14; [2008] 1 W.L.R. 2001, where it was held that a requirement under r.3.5(1) of the Criminal Procedure Rules for a defendant to identify the witnesses he intended to call infringed the defendant's right to legal professional privilege. The fundamental right to legal professional privilege could only be intruded upon by subordinate legislation if the statute providing those subordinate instruments made it plain that such an authority was intended to be conveyed.

D. LEGAL ADVICE PRIVILEGE

The basic rule

11.09 "If a client writes to his lawyer in terms asking for advice on a particular question, the communication is privileged, whether or not any advice is then given. Likewise, any internal record of the advice requested is privileged"

(para 11): *Financial Services Compensation Scheme Ltd v Abbey National Treasury Services Plc* [2007] EWHC 2868 (Ch), David Richards J.

11.09 NOTE 66. See also *BBGP Managing General Partner Ltd v Babcock & Brown Global Partners* [2010] EWHC 2176 (Ch).

11.09 NOTE 68. See also *Dadourian Group International Inc v Simms* [2008] EWHC 1784 (Ch), Patten J. (communication in issue need not contain the legal advice as such), *C v C* [2007] W.T.L.R. 753 (relevant parts of conveyancing file privileged as wife failed to show that transaction intended to

defeat claim for ancillary relief), and *New South Wales Council for Civil Liberties v CRB* [2006] FCA 1409; (2007) 236 A.L.R. 313, Fed. Ct of Australia (advice to review board is covered by LPP).

NOTE 69. *AWB Ltd v Cole (No.5)* [2006] FCA 1234; 234 A.L.R. 651 (updated citation). 11.09

NOTE 73. Add *New South Wales v Betfair* [2009] FCAFC 160, 261 ALR 311, [38]–[40]; *Sportsbet Pty Limited v State of New South Wales (No 3)* [2009] FCA 1283. 11.09

See also *Rio Tinto Ltd v Commissioner of Taxation* [2006] FCA 1200; (2007) 235 A.L.R. 127, Fed. Ct of Australia (draft company resolutions prepared by general counsel: held privileged). 11.10

NOTE 80. *AWB Ltd v Cole (No.5)* [2006] FCA 1234; 234 A.L.R. 651 (updated citation). 11.10

NOTE 84. See also *Brookfield Multiplex Limited v International Litigation Funding Partners Pte Ltd (No 2)* [2009] FCA 449, [25]. But a funding agreement may be privileged: *Brookfield Multiplex Limited v International Litigation Funding Partners Pte Ltd (No 2)* [2009] FCA 449, [27]. 11.10

In *C v C* [2007] W.T.L.R. 753, Munby J. held that the parts of a conveyancing file recording a conveyancing lawyer's dealings with his client were protected by legal advice privilege. 11.12

NOTE 99. See also the discussion in *Z v New South Wales Crime Commission* [2007] HCA 7; (2007) 231 C.L.R. 75, High Court of Australia, and also *The Author of a Blog v Times Newspapers Ltd* [2009] EWHC 1358 (QB) (not a privilege case, but one of confidentiality/privacy). 11.13

Third parties

NOTE 107. See also *BBGP Managing General Partner Ltd v Babcock & Brown Global Partners* [2010] EWHC 2176 (Ch) (limited partnership obtained legal advice through corporate managing partner, itself acting through a director).

NOTE 110. Where non-lawyers prepare a draft document containing legal advice and circulate it to others (including lawyers) for comment, neither the original draft nor any version revised to take account of any lawyer's advice is privileged, except to the extent it sets out the legal advice received from the lawyer: *Atos Consulting Ltd v Avis plc* [2007] EWHC 323 (TCC), [58], Sch 1, para 3. 11.14

What kind of lawyer?

In *Dadourian Group International Inc v Simms* [2008] EWHC 1784 (Ch), Patten J. held that a client who in good faith instructs someone whom he mistakenly believes to be a qualified lawyer does not forfeit the protection 11.18

of the legal privilege which he would otherwise obtain in relation to the disclosures he has made or the advice he has received, but also that the burden lies on that client to show that he held that belief at the material time.

11.19 See also *Rio Tinto Ltd v Commissioner of Taxation* [2006] FCA 1200; (2007) 235 A.L.R. 127, Fed. Ct of Australia (draft company resolutions prepared by general counsel: held privileged).

11.19 NOTE 141. See also *Akzo Nobel Chemicals Ltd v Commission of the European Communities* (T-125/03, T-253/03) September 17, 2007, EC Court of First Instance, affirmed by the ECJ, 14 September 2010.

11.21 In *R (Prudential plc) v Special Commissioner of Income Tax* [2010] EWCA Civ 1094, the CA held that the clients of accountants could not claim any privilege equivalent to legal privilege over and above the statutory privilege referred to, in relation to auditors and tax advisers.

11.23 Section 63 of the Courts and Legal Services Act 1990 will be replaced by section 190 of the Legal Services Act 2007 when the latter is brought into force. Section 190 is wider in scope, and applies to any 'authorised person' (not being an English barrister or solicitor) who provides advocacy, litigation, conveyancing or probate services, but also to any licensed body acting through a UK lawyer, an authorised person, a registered foreign lawyer or a European lawyer.

Client acting in person

11.25 In *Dadourian Group International Inc v Simms* [2008] EWHC 1784 (Ch), Patten J. regarded it as "an open question" whether a litigant in person could claim litigation privilege.

Confidentiality

11.28, 11.31 In *Stax Claimants v Bank of Nova Scotia* [2007] EWHC 1153 (Ch), Warren J. held that it was difficult to see why a note by a solicitor of a conversation with his opponent should not be privileged if it went beyond merely recording the conversation and contained "the note-taker's own thoughts and comments on what he is recording with a view to advising his client".

E. LITIGATION PRIVILEGE

The basic rule

11.31 In *Stax Claimants v Bank of Nova Scotia* [2007] EWHC 1153 (Ch), Warren J. held that, where discussions took place between claimants and Pt 20

defendants about the litigation, documents relating to and recording the meeting could be protected by litigation privilege, at least in the hands of the claimants (against whom alone the application for disclosure was made).

The Federal Court of Australia has held that the claim to privilege has to be determined at the time that the document concerned came into existence: *Barnes v F.C.T.* [2007] FCAFC 88, 242 A.L.R. 601. **11.31, 11.32**

Copies

NOTE 215. *AWB Ltd v Cole (No.5)* [2006] FCA 1234; 234 A.L.R. 651 [updated citation]. **11.32**

On litigation privilege in Canada, see *Blank v Canada (Minister of Justice)* 2006 SCC 31, SCC; reviewed by Ives and Pitel (2007) 11 E&P 49–56. **11.33**

NOTE 222. *Cf Han v Cho* (2008) 297 DLR (4th) 572, BC Sup. Ct. (*Sumitomo* not cited). **11.33**

See also *Hudson Bay Mining and Smelting Co. v Cummings* (2007) 272 D.L.R. (4th) 419, Manitoba CA (no litigation privilege in transcripts of Crown Counsel with potential witnesses at non-adversarial coroner's inquest), and also *Ingot v MacQuarie* [2006] NSWSC 530; (2007) 233 A.L.R. 369 (litigation privilege does not apply to documents prepared for purposes of Administrative Appeals Tribunal as proceedings are not adversarial). **11.37**

When is litigation contemplated?

In Australia, the test for the reasonable anticipation of litigation is that there must be a real prospect of litigation, as distinct from a mere possibility; but it does not need to be more likely than not: *ACCC v Visy (No.2)* [2007] FCA 444; 239 A.L.R., Fed. Ct Australia. **11.38, 11.44**

Directly or indirectly

NOTE 257. Add *Thomson v Berkhampstead Colegaite School* [2009] EWHC 2374 (QB), [38]. **11.39**

The question of purpose

In *Hansfield Developments v Irish Asphalt* [2009] IEHC 90, the Irish High Court held that communications between a builder and a consumer warranty company were not made for the dominant purpose of litigation and hence not privileged. **11.44**

11.45 NOTE 300. Add *Akai Holdings Ltd v Ernst & Young* [2009] HKCFA 14.

11.46 The first sentence of this paragraph was approved by Beatson J in *West London Pipeline & Storage Ltd v Total UK Ltd* [2008] EWHC 1729 (Comm.), [50], [86].

11.46 NOTES 311, 312. Add *West London Pipeline & Storage Ltd v Total UK Ltd* [2008] EWHC 1729 (Comm.), [86].; *Atos Consulting Ltd v Avis plc* [2007] EWHC 323 (TCC). As to procedure, see paras 9.33, 9.39.

Communications between persons with a "common interest"

11.59 NOTE 366. See also *Dadourian Group International Inc v Simms* [2008] EWHC 1784 (Ch), Patten J.

11.60 See also *Griffiths McBurney & Partners v Ernst & Young YBM Inc* (2000) ABCA 284, Alberta CA. See also *Todd v Novotny* [1999] WASC 28, Sup. Ct of Western Australia (if the parties are potential adversaries or if they are acting from purely selfish motives, then comment interest privilege will not arise). The bulk of this paragraph was cited by the Irish High Court in *Hansfield Developments v Irish Asphalt* [2009] IEHC 90, [10], where it was held that a builder and a consumer warranty company did not have a common interest.

F. EXCEPTIONS TO LEGAL PROFESSIONAL PRIVILEGE

(a) Material fact in itself

11.64 In *Farm Assist Ltd v Secretary of State for the Environment, Food and Rural Affairs* [2008] EWHC 3079 (TCC), Ramsey J held that there was no such genral principle as suggested in the first sentence. He also disagreed with the final sentence ("Where in litigation . . . "), on the basis that *Paragon Finance* overruled *Hayes v Dowding* completely and not merely in part. See also *Redfern Ltd v O'Donnell* [2009] IESC 18, and paras 12.04–12.06 below.

(b) Documents to prove innocence in a criminal trial

11.65 See also *Goodis v Ontario*, 2006 SCC 31, Sup. Ct of Canada (court can interfere with legal advice privilege only where absolutely necessary).

(c) Fraud or illegality

11.67 In *Kimber v Brookman Solicitors* [2004] 2 F.L.R. 221, Coleridge J. held that a husband who had disappeared, in serious breach of his duty to make full disclosure to the court of his means, and who was "cocking a snook" at the court, lost his legal privilege and his solicitor was ordered to produce even privileged material to the court. The judge commented that:

"It is not just a question as between two clients. It is a question between the court and the parties. The court has an inquisitorial function, not merely an arbitration function as between the two parties. That puts the court, it seems to me, in a different position to that more conventionally found in civil litigation generally".

It is however submitted that this is special pleading and unjustified. In some respects the family courts do have an inquisitorial function (eg. where considering what are the best interests of a child). But to say that because, in addition to the parties, *the court* is involved in what is otherwise purely adversarial litigation, it becomes inquisitorial, is mere sophistry. The court is involved in every piece of adversarial litigation in all the courts, and that does not make it inquisitorial and help to justify removing legal privilege. On the other hand, in *C v C* [2007] W.T.L.R. 753, Munby J. held that, although the fraud exception to privilege extended to a transaction intended to defeat a spouse's claim for ancillary relief on divorce, the wife in the present case had failed to show a prima facie case to justify the forfeiture of the privilege. Although the court had the power to look at the documents before deciding whether they were privileged, that power should be exercised very sparingly:

"Those who cannot meet that demanding test [ie. for ousting privilege] should not be allowed to go on a fishing expedition—and it makes no difference for this purpose that it is the judge rather than the litigant who is casting the net and inspecting the catch".

The decision in *Kimber v Brookman Solicitors* was cited to Munby J., but he said that that case was very different, as the husband in his case was

"not accused of litigation misconduct of the type let alone on the scale of that which Coleridge J. was considering".

R. v Central Criminal Court ex p. Francis [1989] 1 AC 346 was applied in *Owners of "Kamal XXVI" v Owners of "Ariela"* [2010] EWHC 2531 (Comm). The fraud exception applies even where both a solicitor and the client giving instructions to the client are innocent, but are being used as instruments by third parties to facilitate a fraud. **11.68**

See, to the same effect, *National Westminster Bank plc v Rabobank* [2006] EWHC 2332, [55], [58], and *BBGP Managing General Partner Ltd v Babcock & Brown Global Partners* [2010] EWHC 2176 (Ch), [71]–[72].

NOTE 459. But see *BBGP Managing General Partner Ltd v Babcock & Brown Global Partners* [2010] EWHC 2176 (Ch), holding that the court should not look at the documents concerned unless there is present "some exceptional factor of real weight" ([72]). **11.71**

NOTES 454 and 457. See also *Dadourian Group International Inc v Simms* [2008] EWHC 1784 (Ch), Patten J. **11.71**

11.74 NOTE 462. See also *BBGP Managing General Partner Ltd v Babcock & Brown Global Partners* [2010] EWHC 2176 (Ch).

11.76 In *Dadourian Group International v Simms* [2007] EWHC 2634 (Ch) there were collateral proceedings. In the Queen's Bench Division A sued a former employee, B, and obtained an order that B deliver up confidential information to A and not make any use of it. But before the order was made B had provided copies of some of the material to the solicitors for C, who in the Chancery Division (the present claim) was suing D (the managing director of A) and others, for use in that litigation. Other defendants in the chancery litigation claimed an injunction restraining C from using that information against them in those proceedings. No application had been made against them in the QBD action and C had not applied for any variation of the order in those proceedings. Warren J held that the QBD order did not require C (not a partiy to those proceedings) to hand over material obtained before they learned of it, but might have the effect that actual deployment of the material in the chancery proceedings after it knew of the order could be a contempt of court. It would be necessary to look at the documents in question in order to decide. If it were a contempt, the court could refuse to allow the material to be deployed in this claim.

11.76 NOTE 469. See also *ASIC v Lindberg* [2009] VSCA 234, 261 ALR 207.

11.77 In *McE v Prison Service of Northern Ireland* [2009] UKHL 15, the House of Lords by a majority held that s.27 of the Regulation of Investigatory Powers Act 2000 permitted the covert surveillance of prisoners during consultations with legal advisers.

G. PUBLIC INTEREST IMMUNITY

11.82A In the absence of statutory authority (or possible agreement between the parties), it is not open to the civil courts to order a 'closed material' procedure in relation to the trial of an ordinary civil claim, *eg* on the basis that conducting a traditional PII exercise will take too long and cost too much. The court relied on the principles that justice be done in public, that each party should see and hear the evidence and arguments given and made to the court, that a party should know his opponent's case in advance, and that he should know of the relevant documents in the hands of his opponent: *Al Rawi v Security Service* [2010] EWCA Civ 482 [2010] 3 W.L.R. 1069. *Cf Cadogan Petroleum plc v Tolley* [2010] EWHC 1107 (Ch), a case of specific disclosure of a confidential settlement agreement, decided two weeks after *Al Rawi* (which however appears not to have been cited).

"Class" claims and "Contents" claims

11.84 The December 1996 Paper was discussed by the Divisional Court in *R. (on the application of Mohamed) v Secretary of State for Foreign and Commonwealth Affairs* [2008] EWHC 2100 (Admin); further [2008] EWHC

2519 (Admin); [2009] EWHC 152 (Admin); [2009] EWHC 2549 (Admin), [2009] 1 WLR 2563; [2010] EWCA Civ 65, [2010] 4 All E.R. 91, CA; [2010] EWCA Civ 158, [2010] 4 All E.R. 177, CA. In *DCT v Law Institute of Victoria* [2010] VSCA 127, (2010) 267 ALR 127, it was held at [49] that there is a heavy burden of proof on any authority making a claim based only on the class of documents.

The three stage approach in considering to claim

See also *Chan Mei Yiu v Secretary for Justice* [2007] HKCFI 664 (judge did not decide point but found argument based on whether "disclosure would cause real damage" attractive). 11.85

Procedure

See also *Atos Consulting Ltd v Avis plc* [2007] EWHC 323 (TCC) (application under CPR r.31.19(5) in relation to redaction, though not a PII case); *Al Rawi v Security Service* [2010] EWHC 1496 (QB) (questions of timing of disclosure given the large scale of the PII exercise to be gone through). 11.88

In *Parkin v O'Sullivan* [2008] FCAFC 134, 249 ALR 507, the Full Courtof the Federal Court of Australia held that part of the evidence in support of a claim to PII should not in the circumstances be shown even to the lawyers for the other side. 11.88

The importance of the accuracy of the certificate of the minister was stressed by the Administrative Court in *R (Al Sweady) v Secretary of State for Defence* [2009] EWHC 1687 (Admin), where it was discovered that a partly false certificate had been placed before the court: 11.89

"14. [. . .] As Laws LJ made clear at paragraph 50 of the judgement in *R (Quark Fishing) v Secretary of State for Foreign and Commonwealth Affairs* [2002] EWCA Civ 1409, there is a very high duty on central government to assist the court with full and accurate explanations of all the facts relevant to the issue that the court must decide. To state the obvious, the systems for dealing with PII claims in the Courts of England and Wales depend, if a Ministerial Certificate and Schedule are advanced in support of a claim, upon the scrupulous accuracy of the whole of the content of those documents. The more so if the content of the Schedule is sensitive (as is invariably the case), and cannot therefore be disclosed to the party seeking disclosure of the underlying material, who thus cannot contest its content. Especially so, if (as here) that Schedule deals with issues of national security, in relation to which (in accordance with well-established principles) the Court must accord the Minister's assertions considerable weight in the balancing exercise.

15. The Courts necessarily proceed upon the basis that Ministerial Certificates and Schedules are the product of a scrupulous process of preparation and checking, designed to ensure the complete accuracy of their whole content. Indeed, one member of the Court has experience over many years, as a practitioner, of participation in that process mostly in relation to other Ministries. Clearly, something went badly wrong in this case. [. . .]

46. We have set out at length the lamentable history of what occurred in this case in order to ensure that nothing similar happens in future. The complete integrity of PII Certificates and the Schedules attached to them, signed by Ministers of the Crown, is absolutely essential in all cases in which they are put forward. The Courts must be able to have complete confidence in the credibility and reliability of such Certificates and Schedules. Nothing less is acceptable.

47. We have already noted that as a result of events in this case a senior civil servant has now been given specific responsibility in the MOD for policy for PII, and that he is urgently considering the need for a written redaction policy. We find it astonishing that no such person was already in post, and this suggests a serious lack of oversight, or at the very least inadequate procedures, at a senior level in the MOD. The failures in the present case demonstrate an apparent inability in the MOD to understand the importance and significance of PII applications in the judicial process. The lack of internal co-ordination and communication within the MOD could have led to very much more serious consequences than in the event resulted in this case.

48. Not the least of our concerns is that even when it became apparent within the MOD that there were failures, nothing was done to put matters right until far too late in the day. Well before the end of May it was apparent to MOD officials that the original PII Certificate and Schedule could not be maintained and that the Court had been misled, and yet it was not until 1 July 2009 that the Court was told anything about the existence of a problem. When the Court has been misled, or even may have been misled, it should be notified immediately that there is a possible problem and that the matter is under investigation.

49. As we have said in paragraph 25, until such time as the MOD has demonstrated that its procedures have remedied the risk of the kind of errors occurring that occurred in this case it will, in our view, be incumbent on the Courts to approach the content of any Ministerial Certificate and Schedule from it with very considerable caution."

11.94 In *Somerville v Scottish Ministers (Scotland)* [2007] UKHL, 44, the House of Lords in a judicial review case held, following *Tweed v Parades Commission for Northern Ireland* [2007] 1 A.C. 650, that there should be have been a public interest immunity inspection of material by the court before ordering production: see at paras 63, 83–86, 151–156, 205–207. Moreover, two of their Lordships commented that it had been unwise to

permit counsel for the applicant to see the material on terms of confidentiality, even from his own clients: see at 152–153, 203–204.

See also *Parkin v O'Sullivan* [2009] FCA 1096, 260 ALR 503, Fed Ct Aus. 11.96

Workings of central government

In *Betfair Pty Limited v Racing New South Wales (No 7)* [2009] FCA 1140 at [44], 260 ALR 538, the Federal Court of Australia held that documents from a working party at which the state consulted industry bodies about changes to legislation were not covered by PII. The case went to appeal but not on this point: [2009] FCAFC 160, 261 ALR 311, [8]. See also *Sportsbet Pty Limited v State of New South Wales (No 3)* [2009] FCA 1283. 11.98

NOTE 581. Add *Queanbeyan City Council v ACTEW Corp* [2008] FCA 1983, (2009) 253 A.L.R. 121, Fed. Ct. of Aus. (disclosure of cabinet papers refused; not relevant). 11.98

NOTE 582. Add *BNZ Investments Ltd v Commissioner of Inland Revenue* [2008] 2 N.Z.L.R. 709, Sup. Ct of New Zealand (disclosure of documents relating to affairs of other banks not subject to public interest immunity principles, as covered by s.81 of Tax Administration Act 1994). 11.98

Other branches of public service

In *DCT v Law Institute of Victoria* [2010] VSCA 73 (2010) 127 ALR 127, it was held that public interest immunity may exist in records by a regulatory body regulating the legal profession but in fact the class of documents was not of such high signficance or importance that they would be protected from disclosure irrespective of their contents. 11.99

Confidentiality

Some US courts accept the existence of a "self-evaluative" privilege, as a kind of private PII (if such a thing can be imagined). It allows a corporation to commission reports on risks to itself and its business without the fear of having to disclose these in any subsequent litigation. See, eg. Ronald G. Blum and Andrew J. Torro, The Self-Evaluative Privilege in the Second Circuit: Dead or Alive?, *New York State Bar Association Journal*, June 2003, 75, No.5; Christine A. Edwards and John E. Court, Good Corporation Behaviour Redu —The Federal Self-Evaluative Privilege, *The Metropolitan Corporate Counsel*, June 2007, p.13. 11.102

Informants

For a review of the Australian cases in relation to public interest immunity and informants, see *ASIC v P Dawson Nominees Pty Ltd* [2008] FCAFC 11.103

123; (2008) 247 A.L.R. 646, Fed. Ct of Australia (public interest immunity for documents which would have revealed informers' identities). For a review of the Canadian cases in relation to informants and disclosure, see *National Post v Canada*, 2010 SCC 16, (2010) 318 D.L.R. (4th) 1, Supreme Court of Supreme.

H. PRIVILEGE AGAINST INCRIMINATION

11.105 See also *Breslin v McKenna* [2007] NICA 14 at [42], where the Northern Ireland Court of Appeal held that:

> "[. . .] the purpose of the measure in question provides the key to the question whether it constitutes a penalty. In this context, the expressed intention of the plaintiffs in pursing the civil claim cannot be taken as the authoritative statement of the purpose of the proceedings. This is supplied by the nature of the proceedings themselves. An action for damages is in its essential nature a requirement to pay compensation for a civil wrong. This is not a penalty as that term requires to be construed for the purposes of article 7 [of the ECHR]. The purpose of the proceedings is to obtain due recompense for the wrong that the plaintiff has suffered. We are satisfied that the order to produce documents does not involve the imposition of a penalty on the appellants."

11.105 In *S v Boulton* [2006] FCAFC 99; (2007) 232 A.L.R. 92, Fed. Ct of Australia. It was held that the common law recognises a privilege against spousal incrimination, but this does not extend to de facto spouses.

11.105 In the sentence beginning "In purported pursuance of the principle . . . " delete "purported" and the words from "but this" to the end. To footnote 670 add *C plc v P* [2007] EWCA Civ 493; *R v S & A* [2008] EWCA Crim 2177, [18].

11.105 NOTE 672. *C Plc v P* [2007] EWCA Civ 493; [2007] 3 W.L.R. 437; [2008] Ch.1, CA; [2008] 1 W.L.R. 153, HL(E) pet.all. (updated citation for appeal).

11.106 NOTE 682. *C Plc v P* [2007] EWCA Civ 493; [2007] 3 W.L.R. 437; [2008] Ch.1, CA; [2008] 1 W.L.R. 153, HL(E) pet.all. (updated citation for appeal).

11.108 The first instance decision in *C plc v P* [2006] 4 All ER 311 was affirmed by the Court of Appeal, but on different grounds. The critical distinction according to Longmore LJ (with whom Sir Martin Nourse agreed) was between evidence provided by the statement of the party required to speak and evidence existing independently of the order that he speak. Only the former infringed the privilege. See also *R v S & A* [2008] EWCA Crim 2177, where the court held that an order to disclose an encryption key which would enable police to read computer files seized under terrorism legislation

does not infringe the privilege as the key did not incriminate anyone. The information which might incriminate was already in the hands of the police.

NOTE 695. *C Plc v P* [2007] EWCA Civ 493; [2007] 3 W.L.R. 437; [2008] Ch.1, CA; [2008] 1 W.L.R. 153, HL(E) pet.all. (updated citation for appeal). See also *Re A* [2008] EWHC 1362 (Admin). **11.108**

NOTE 696. See also *R. v S* [2008] EWCA Crim 2177, [2009] 1 All E.R. 716, CA.

Exceptions to the privilege

11.113 Section 13 of the Fraud Act 2006 removes the privilege against self-incrimination on the ground that answering any question put to a person relating to property or complying with any order made in proceedings relating to property may incriminate him of any offence under the Act or a related offence. "Related offence" is defined in s.13(4) as meaning conspiracy to defraud or any other offence involving any form of fraudulent conduct or purpose. These provisions were considered in *Kensington International Ltd v Republic of Congo* [2007] EHWC 1632 (Comm.); [2007] 2 Lloyd's Rep. 382; [2008] EWCA Civ 1128, CA. The court held that corruption is a related offence. The court also declined to construe the section restrictively, or to hold that it only applied to future conduct by the defendant, and held that it was directed to the same kind of proceedings as s.31 of the Theft Act 1968. However, for this purpose the *Norwich Pharmacal* proceedings were not separate from the substantive claim. In *JSC BTA Bank v Ablyazov* [2009] EWCA Civ 1124, the Court of Appeal held that the offence under s.328 of the Proceeds of Crime Act 2002 was likewise arelated offence for the purposes of s.13 of the Fraud ASct 2006.

11.113, 11.118 In *Breslin v McKenna* [2007] NICA 14, the Northern Ireland Court of Appeal held that:

"We therefore reject the claim that the privilege against self incrimination advanced by the appellants can only be overridden by a statutory provision. On the contrary, we consider that where, as in this case, there are compelling reasons that the documents should be produced in the interests of justice, the rights of the appellants must defer to those wider interests. Moreover, we are of the view that the documents sought in this case come within the first category adumbrated in paragraph 53 (4) of *Kearns* [ie. documents having an existence independently of the will of the suspect or accused] and on that account also are exigible".

11.114 In *Child Maintenance Enforcement Commission v Forrest* [2010] EWHC 1264 (Admin)e Divisional Court held that a father who failed to provide information under s.14 of the Child Support Act 1991 in order to protect

his wife from the risk of prosecution did not have a reasonable excuse for the failure.

11.118 The first instance decision in *C plc v P* [2006] 4 All ER 311 was affirmed by the Court of Appeal, but on different grounds. The critical distinction according to Longmore LJ (with whom Sir Martin Nourse agreed) was between evidence provided by the statement of the party required to speak and evidence existing independently of the order that he speak. Only the former infringed the privilege. See also *R v S & A* [2008] EWCA Crim 2177, where the court held that an order to disclose an encryption key which would enable police to read computer files seized under terrorism legislation does not infringe the privilege as the key did not incriminate anyone. The information which might incriminate was already in the hands of the police.

11.118 NOTE 771. *C Plc v P* [2007] EWCA Civ 493; [2007] 3 W.L.R. 437; [2008] Ch.1, CA; [2008] 1 W.L.R. 153, HL(E) pet.all. (updated citation for appeal).

I. "WITHOUT PREJUDICE" PRIVILEGE

11.122 NOTE 783. Add *Ofulue v Bossert* [2009] 1 AC 990.

11.123 NOTE 790. Section 131 of the Evidence Act 1995 (Cth); *Korean Airlines v ACCC (No.3)* [2008] FCA 701; (2008) 247 A.L.R., 781, Fed. Ct of Australia; *ACCC v Allphones (No 3)* [2009] FCA 1075, 259 ALR 541, Fed Ct Aus.

Impact on disclosure

11.125 In *Cumbria Waste Management Ltd v Baines & Wilson* [2008] EWHC 786 (QB); [2008] B.L.R. 330, the issue was whether the defendant was entitled to disclosure of documents arising out of or in connection with two mediations between the claimants and the Department for Environment, Food and Rural Affairs, and which were not subject to legal professional privilege. The judge held that she was:

"not persuaded that disclosure of documents within the mediations falls within the exception to the without prejudice rule enunciated in *Muller.* The circumstances in *Muller* are different from those which obtain here. In that case, it was the plaintiffs who sought to deny disclosure of without prejudice material. Here, the question is whether a third party's without prejudice material should be disclosed. The Court of Appeal in *Muller* gave no consideration to the position of a third party. In this case the privilege belongs not only to the claimants but also to DEFRA. There are public policy reasons why DEFRA should be entitled to assert that privilege:

DEFRA are entitled to protect from disclosure material which may embarrass them in other disputes. Further, in this case there was express (not just implied) agreement between the claimants and DEFRA that the without prejudice rule apply".

NOTE 801. And see *Ofulue v Bossert* [2009] 1 AC 990, where the majority of the House of Lords disapproved Lord Hoffmann's view in *Rashid*. 11.125

Extent of the evidential rule

In *Framlington Group Ltd v Barnetson* [2007] EWCA Civ 502; [2007] 1 W.L.R. 2443, the Court of Appeal held that "without prejudice" privilege applied to discussions between the parties about contractual entitlement even before litigation had been commenced or indeed threatened. Auld L.J. said: 11.127

"the claim to privilege cannot, in my view, turn on purely temporal considerations. The critical feature of proximity for this purpose, it seems to me, is one of the subject matter of the dispute rather than how long before the threat, or start, of litigation it was aired in negotiations between the parties. Would they have respectively lowered their guards at that time and in the circumstances if they had not thought or hoped or contemplated that, by doing so, they could avoid the need to go to court over the very same dispute? On that approach, which I would commend, the crucial consideration would be whether in the course of negotiations the parties contemplated or might reasonably have contemplated litigation if they could not agree. Confining the operation of the rule, as the Judge did, to negotiations of a dispute in the course of, or after threat of, litigation on it, or by reference to some time limit set close before litigation, does not, with respect, fully serve the public policy interest underlying it of discouraging recourse to litigation and encouraging genuine attempts to settle whenever made".

In *Stax Claimants v Bank of Nova Scotia* [2007] EWHC 1153 (Ch), Warren J. held that "without prejudice" privilege could not be extended to cover discussions between a claimant and a Pt 20 defendant about the proceedings generally. The public policy on which the privilege is based is directed at avoiding litigation by settling disputes, and not at enabling litigants to conduct their cases more privately. Protection for communications that are not aimed at settling disputes must be found (if at all) in other types of privilege. On the other hand, in *Williams v Hull* [2009] EWHC 2844 (Ch), Arnold J held that a letter between the parties headed 'without prejudice' and asserting the rights of the sender in the course of negotiations between them was protected by without prejudice privilege. It was not 11.127

necessary that it contain any concession or offer of compromise, only that it evinced a genuine desire to settle the dispute.

11.128 In *Cadogan Petroleum plc v Tolley* [2009] EWHC 3291 (Ch) Peter Smith J held that a confidentiality clause which purported to prevent disclosure of documents which was necessary for the fair disposal of a trial would be contrary to public policy, and void. In the same case subsequently, [2010] EWHC 1107 (Ch), he ordered production for inspection of parts of a settlement agreement between the claimant and certain defendants which were relevant to the continuing dispute between the claimant and other defendants.

11.129 In *Brunel University v Webster* [2007] EWCA 482; [2007] I.R.L.R. 592, the Court of Appeal declined to rule on how far the "unabiguous impropriety" principle applied in cases of unlawful discrimination and victimisation. But the court added:

> "We can understand a possible submission that it may sometimes be difficult to prove victimisation if the general rule (that remarks made in the course of 'without prejudice' discussions cannot be referred to) applies in its full width. In the present case, however, it is not at all surprising that the University in defending itself against the allegations should have felt the need to adopt the claimants' approach that the 'without prejudice' discussions needed to be referred to. That must be a very common position for parties to victimisation claims to find themselves in and analysis in this court of the dicta in *Mezzotero* should only take place in a case where one of the parties has made it clear at an appropriate early stage that it seeks to exclude any reference to 'without prejudice' discussions".

11.129 In *Williams v Hull* [2009] EWHC 2844 (Ch), Arnold J refused to treat the writing of a letter (held to be without prejudice) as an 'unambiguous impropriety' merely because it may have been inconsistent with the party's pleaded case. But at worst there was a serious risk of exposure to perjury proceedings. The judge relied on the decision of the Court of Appeal in *Savings & Investment Bank v Fincken.*

11.129 In *New Zealand Institute of Chartered Accountants v Clarke* [2009] 3 NZLR 264, it was held that certain features of a without prejudice letter, namely the date, the signature and the use of letters to denote the status of chartered accountant, lay outside the privileged contents of the letter and hence were not protected by privilege. Similarly, in *Betfair Pty Limited v Racing New South Wales (No 7)* [2009] FCA 1140, 260 ALR 538, [74], the Federal Court of Australia held that documents arising out of settlement negotiations were not covered by WP privilege, "as Betfair seeks to make use of them for the purpose not of proving the truth of any admissions made about the operation of the Racing Distribution Agreement but of proving the commercial relationship between Racing NSW and Tabcorp". The case went to appeal but not on this point: [2009] FCAFC 160, 261 ALR 311, [8].

See also *Sportsbet Pty Limited v State of New South Wales (No 3)* [2009] FCA 1283.

NOTE 826. The decision of Patten J in *Savings & Investment Bank v Fincken* was reversed by the Court of Appal [2003] EWCA Civ 1630, [2004] 1 WLR 667. 11.129

In *Cf Oceanbulk Shipping v TMT Asia* [2010] UKSC 44, the Supreme Court held that, as an exception to the without prejudice rule, facts communicated between the parties in the course of without prejudice negotiations which resulted in an agreement were admissable where such facts would otherwise be admissale as part of the factual matrix surrounding circumstances in order to construe the agreement. 11.129

In *Linsen International Ltd v Humpuss Sea Transport* [2010] EWHC 303 (Comm.), the question was whether the applicants for a without notice freezing order should have disclosed without prejudice documents to the judge. Christopher Clarke J said: 11.130

"51 The basic rule is that the fact and content of without prejudice communications are not to be disclosed . . .

52 . . . The rule is not without exception. The obligation of a party seeking *ex parte* relief to ensure that the Court is not misled means that he cannot regard the basic rule as determinative on the question of disclosure . . . .

53 . . . At the same time, as it seems to me, considerable care needs to be taken in holding that a claimant is bound (and, therefore, entitled) to disclose without prejudice material. A decision whether or not to disclose may well have to be taken within a short timescale. More importantly there is a real danger of defendants being disadvantaged by the *ex parte* disclosure (which the defendant is powerless to prevent) of such material by claimants on the basis that they are only fulfilling a duty when the material consists of or amounts to admissions—the very risk that the first principle seeks to avoid.

55 I do not, however, accept that the test as to whether reference should be made to without prejudice communications is that the need to do so was compellingly obvious. In *Pearson* Crane, J rejected a test of "*manifest impropriety*" and I would reject a test that comes close to that. It is sufficient to say that some disclosure of without prejudice communication will be necessary if it is clear that without it the court may be misled."

In *Ofulue v Bossert* [2009] 1 AC 990 the majority of the House of Lords held that, as a result of the without prejudice rule, a without prejudice offer by a squatter to buy the land concerned from the owner, made in the context of earlier proceedings to recover possession, could not be relied on by the owner as an acknowledgement within the Limitation Act 1980 sufficient to stop time running so as to bar a second action to recover possession. 11.130

11.130 NOTE 836. Add *Brown v Patel* [2007] EWHC 625 (Ch) (without prejudice communications could be considered to resolve the question whether settlement occurred in context of mediation; clause in mediation agreement that settlement during mediation not legally binding until reduced to writing and signed did not affect this conclusion).

Third parties

11.133 In *Brown v Patel* [2007] EWHC 625 (Ch), where the question arose whether a settlement had been come to in the course of a mediation, the judge held that it was not necessary in that case to decide whether there was a special mediation privilege preventing admission of evidence about what happened during it. But he added that in the future it might require to be considered either by the legislature or the courts. See also *Cumbria Waste Management Ltd v Baines Wilson (A Firm)* [2008] EWHC 786 (QB); [2008] B.L.R. 330, where the judge said:

> "In my judgment, whether on the basis of the without prejudice rule or as an exception to the general rule that confidentiality is not a bar to disclosure, the court should support the mediation process by refusing, in normal circumstances, to order disclosure of documents and communications within a mediation.
>
> I note that the disclosure sought by the defendant is of such wide scope that it would include documents held by the mediator. In my judgement, the court should be very slow to order such disclosure. Mediators should be able to conduct mediations confident that, in normal circumstances, their papers could not be seen by the parties or others".

11.133 NOTE 851. The reference to discussion of mediation should read "Ch 20, paras 20.55–20.57".

L. DIPLOMATIC PRIVILEGE

11.141 The court cannot make an order requiring the central bank of a foreign state to disclose information or documents in relation to a commercial transaction where the central bank entered into the transaction as an exercise of sovereign authority, by virtue of the State Immunity Act 1978, ss 1, 3, and likewise cannot make an order against the agent of such central bank: *KOO Golden East v Bank of Nova Scotia* [2008] QB 717, CA.

M. OTHER STATUTORY OBJECTIONS TO INSPECTION

11.143 The Enterprise Act 2002, s.237, restricts disclosure of 'specified information', ie information coming to a public authority in connection with the

exercise of certain public regulatory functions (s.238). But this is subject to exceptions. One is where the information has already been lawfully disclosed to the public (sub-s (3)). Another is where another provision in that part of the Act permits. This brings in s.241A, which provides that a public authority may disclose 'prescribed information' (*ie* prescribed by statutory instrument: sub-s(3)) for certain purposes relating to 'prescribed civil proceedings'. The Enterprise Act 2002 (Disclosure of Information for Civil Proceedings etc) Order 2007, SI 2007/2193, prescribes all 'specified information' under s.237, with some exceptions, and prescribes proceedings relating to the rights or obligations of consumers, the infringement of uintellectual property rights, and passing off or misuse of trade secrets. But in any event another exception to s.237 provides that the restrictions on disclosure in this part of the Act do not affect "any power or duty to disclose information which exists apart from this Act". This should mean that disclosure under the CPR, *Norwich Pharmacal etc* is not affected.

NOTES 895, 897, 898. *Real Estate Opportunities Ltd v Aberdeen Asset Management Jersey Ltd* [2007] EWCA Civ 197; [2007] 2 All E.R. 791, CA (updated reference), doubting *Arbuthnott v Fagan* [1996] 1 L.R.L.R. 143, CA. **11.143**

N. DISCRETIONARY OBJECTIONS TO INSPECTION

It may be impossible for the judge to decide whether or not confidentiality outweighs production without inspecting the documents concerned: *Tullett Prebon Goup Ltd v Davis* [2007] REHC 2739 (QB); *Cadogan Petroleum plc v Tolley* [2009] EWHC 3291 (Ch), [2010] EWHC 1007 (Ch). **11.151**

NOTE 934. For "paras 8.8–8.25" read "paras 8.18–8.25" **11.151**

NOTE 938. See also *Tullett Prebon Goup Ltd v Davis* [2007] REHC 2739 (QB); *Ashley v Chief Constable of Sussex Police* [2008] EWHC 3151 (QB); *Cadogan Petroleum plc v Tolley* [2009] EWHC 3291 (Ch), [2010] EWHC 1007 (Ch). **11.151**

O. DISPROPORTIONALITY

In *The University of Western Australia v Gray (No.8)* [2007] FCA 89, the Federal Court of Australia ordered inspection of voluminous discovery despite objections that it would put the defendant to disproportionate expense, when the solicitors had earlier certified that the documents were available for inspection. **11.156**

NOTE 966. *Real Estate Opportunities Ltd v Aberdeen Asset Management Jersey Ltd* [2007] EWCA Civ 197; [2007] 2 All E.R. 791, CA (updated reference). **11.156**

P. CONDITIONAL OR RESTRICTED INSPECTION

11.157, 11.159 See also *Interdigital Technology Corp v Nokia Corporation* [2008] EWHC 969 (Pat) (access to sensitive commercial documents limited to legal advisors, with undertaking), *Koger Inc v O'Donnell* [2009] IEHC 385 (disclosure to legal advisers and named officer of plaintiff, with conditions), *Porton Capital Technology Funds v 3M UK Holdings Ltd* [2010] EWHC 114 (Comm.) (creation of 'confidentiality club'), and *Croft House Care Ltd v Durham County Council* [2010] EWHC 909 (TCC) (access to confidential documents only at solicitors' office or in solicitors' presence; no copies).

CHAPTER 12

Loss of Privilege

	PARA.
A. INTRODUCTION	12.01
B. WHO CAN WAIVE?	12.02*
C. WHAT IS A WAIVER?	12.03*
D. REFERENCE IN PLEADINGS	12.11
E. INCLUSION IN LIST OF DOCUMENTS	12.16*
F. REFERENCE IN AFFIDAVIT OR WITNESS STATEMENT	12.19*
G. REFERENCE IN EXPERT'S REPORT OR WITNESS STATEMENT	12.21
H. REFERENCE IN CORRESPONDENCE AND DISCLOSED DOCUMENTS	12.25
I. INCLUSION IN TRIAL BUNDLE	12.27
J. WAIVER AT TRIAL	12.28
K. WAIVER ON TAXATION OF COSTS	12.30*
L. EXTENT OF WAIVER	12.31*

CHAPTER 12

Loss of Privilege

B. WHO CAN WAIVE?

See also *Griffiths McBurney v Parnters v Ernst & Young YBM Inc* (2000) ABCA 284, Alberta CA (receiver may ask court for directions as to waiving privilege). 12.02
NOTE 17. Add *BBGP Managing General Partner Ltd v Babcock & Brown Global Partners* [2010] EWHC 2176 (Ch).

C. WHAT IS A WAIVER?

See also *New South Wales Council for Civil Liberties v CRB* [2006] FCA 1409; (2007) 236 A.L.R. 313, Fed. Ct of Australia (no implied waiver). 12.04
NOTE 34. Add *Farm Assist Ltd v Secretary of State for the Environment, Food and Rural Affairs* [2008] EWHC 3079 (TCC). 12.04
NOTE 50. Add *Schulman v Abbott Tout Lawyers* [2010] FCA 308. 12.06
NOTE 52. Add *Yokogawa v Alstom* [2009] SASC 377, 262 ALR 739. 12.06
NOTE 53. *AWB Ltd v Cole (No.5)* [2006] FCA 1234; 234 A.L.R. 651 (updated citation). 12.06
NOTE 57. *AWB Ltd v Cole (No.5)* [2006] FCA 1234; 234 A.L.R. 651 (updated citation). 12.07
NOTE 61. Add *Double K Oil v Neste Oy* [2009] EWHC 3380 (Comm.), [2010] 1 Lloyd's Rep 141. 12.07

In *Osland v Secretary to the Department of Justice* [2008] HCA 37, (2008) 234 C.L.R. 275, the High Court of Australia held that where the substance of legal advice in relation to denying a petition for mercy was put into a press release, legal privilege had not thereby been waived. However waiver was found in another case where a redacted document was disclosed which included passages based on legal advice; in that case there was found to be an inconsistency with maintaining confidence in the privileged advice in such circumstances: *Zentai v O'Connor* (No.2) [2010] FCA 252, (2010) 268 ALR 7. In *Farm Assist Ltd v Secretary of State for the Environment, Food and Rural Affairs (No 2)* [2009] EWHC 1102 (TCC), [31], Ramsey J held that privilege was not waived if a document was shown to the mediator 12.08

in confidence. In *New South Wales v Betfair* [2009] FCAFC 160, 261 ALR 311, [46]-[59] the Full Court of the Federal Court of Australia held that there had been no waiver of privileged documents relating to the drafting of legislation by reason of sharing them with industry bodies at a working party under a confidentiality obligation.

12.09 NOTE 83. *AWB Ltd v Cole (No.5)* [2006] FCA 1234; 234 A.L.R. 651 (updated citation).

12.10 NOTE 87. See also *Australian Competition and Consumer Commission v Cadbury Schweppes Pty Ltd* [2009] FCAFC 32.

E. INCLUSION IN LIST OF DOCUMENTS

12.18 The third sentence in this paragraph was approved by the Irish High Court in *Byrne v Shannon Foynes Port* [2007] IEHC 315 at [4.2].

12.18 NOTE 126. See also *Canada Post Corp v Euclide Cormier Plumbing and Heating Inc* (2008) 296 DLT (4th) 738, New Brunswick CA (court declined to remove counsel to whom privileged documents had been inadvertently disclosed).

F. REFERENCE IN AFFIDAVIT OR WITNESS STATEMENT

12.19 In *Expandable Ltd v Rubin* [2008] EWCA Civ 59; [2008] 1 W.L.R. 1099, the Court of Appeal held that the CPR had not effected a change in the rule under the RSC that a mere mention of a privileged document in a witness statement did not amount to a waiver of the privilege. See also *Brennan v Sunderland City Council* [2009] ICR 479, EAT, and *Digicel (St Lucia) Ltd v Cable & Wireless plc* [2009] EWHC 1437 (Ch).

12.19 The two sentences beginning "A mere reference . . . " were cited with approval by the High Court of Northern Ireland in *Orr v Crowe* [2009] NIQB 17, [15], and in *Re Donaldson Judicial Review* [2010] NIQB 47, [15]. See also *AXA China Region Insurance Co. Ltd v Pacific Century Insurance Co. Ltd & Ors (No.2)* [2005] 3 HKC 359, 372 and *Urban renewal Authority v Agrila Ltd* [2009] HKCFI 229, [46].

12.19 NOTE 134. The quotation and the remainder of the paragraph were cited with approval by Waller LJ in *Lucas v Barking, Havering & Redbridge Hospitals NHS Trust* [2004] 1 WLR 220, 227. See also *Dadourian Group International Inc v Simms* [2008] EWHC 1784 (Ch), Patten J.

G. REFERENCE IN EXPERT'S REPORT OR WITNESS STATEMENT

12.22 The first two sentences were cited with approval by the High Court of Northern Ireland in *Orr v Crowe* [2009] NIQB 17, [16], and in *Re Donaldson Judicial Review* [2010] NIQB 47, [16].

NOTE 160. *Clough* was not followed by the High Court of Northern Ireland in *Orr v Crowe* [2009] NIQB 17. 12.23

J. WAIVER AT TRIAL

See also *Spalding v Radio Canberra Pty Ltd* [2009] ACTSC 26, 166 ACTR 14 (privilege in proof of evidence held waived by answering questions in cross-examination to effect that plaintiff-witness had read proof in preparation for giving evidence; full examination of Australian authorities), and *R v Seaton* [2010] EWCA Crim 1980 (D's explanation in evidence that his first witness statement had been prepared by his solicitor, and had contained an error, amounted to a waiver of privileges). 12.28

K. WAIVER ON TAXATION OF COSTS

See also *Gower Chemicals Group Litigation v Gower Chemicals Ltd* [2008] EWHC 735 (QB), where receiving parties in a costs assessment were put to their election as to disclosing experts' reports not previously disclosed in the litigation, but in respect of which they sought substantial costs recovery. 12.30

L. EXTENT OF WAIVER

NOTE 211. Add *Dore v Leicestershire County Council* [2010] EWHC 34 (Ch). 12.34

See also *Seven Network v News (No.12)* [2006] FCA 348; (2007) 230 A.L.R. 544, Fed. Ct of Australia (privilege waived in legal advice where gist or conclusion of advice set out in document voluntarily disclosed). 12.36

NOTE 216. Add *Atos Consulting Ltd v Avis plc* [2007] EWHC 323 (TCC); and see para 9.39. 12.36

NOTE 218. Add *Dore v Leicestershire County Council* [2010] EWHC 34 (Ch). 12.36

NOTE 225. *AWB Ltd v Cole (No.5)* [2006] FCA 1234; 234 A.L.R. 651 (updated citation). See also *Dore v Leicestershire County Council* [2010] EWHC 34 (Ch). 12.36

M. PRIVILEGE AGAINST SELF-INCRIMINATION

NOTE 234. *C Plc v P* [2007] EWCA Civ 493; [2007] 3 W.L.R. 437; [2008] Ch.1, CA; [2008] 1 W.L.R. 153, HL(E) pet.all. (updated citation for appeal). 12.37

N. "WITHOUT PREJUDICE" PRIVILEGE

12.39 In *Brunel University v Webster* [2007] EWCA 482, the Court of Appeal held in an employment case that without prejudice privilege for certain communications between the parties (employer and employee) had been waived in two different ways: first, where both parties had relied on those communications at a hearing of an internal adjudication panel composed of persons who were not aware of those communications previously; and secondly, because both parties had referred to those communications in their pleadings in the employment tribunal proceedings.

12.39 NOTE 243. Add *Galliford Try Construction Ltd v Mott MacDonald Ltd* [2008] EWHC 603 (TCC); [2008] T.C.L.R. 6, Coulson J.

CHAPTER 13

Failure to Comply with Disclosure Obligation

	PARA.
A. APPLICATION	13.02
B. PURPOSE	13.05
C. STRIKING OUT	13.07*
D. CONDITIONS	13.19
E. REVOCATION AND VARIATION OF ORDERS	13.22
F. CONTEMPT	13.27*
G. OTHER CONSEQUENCES	13.30*

CHAPTER 13

Failure to Comply with Disclosure Obligation

C. STRIKING OUT

In *Lexi Holdings Plc v Luqman* [2007] EWCA Civ 1501, the Court of Appeal held that the judge had been wrong not to make an "unless" order debarring the defendant accused of misappropriating company funds from defending the proceedings unless he complied with earlier worldwide freezing orders requiring disclosure of his assets. The defendant's evidence was incredible, and there was no need (as the judge had thought) to order cross-examination to prove it so. Moreover, the standard to which the judge had to be satisfied that the evidence was incredible was the civil standard of the balance of probabilities, rather than any higher standard. 13.07

NOTE 19. Add *Blerim Ethemi v Robert Shiels* [2008] EWHC 291 (QB): action struck out where claimant had failed to comply with orders for disclosure and where a costs award would not adequately meet further delay nor reflect earlier defaults. 13.07

NOTE 23. *Arrow Nominees Inc v Blackledge* [2000] 2 B.C.L.C. 167 has been explained in *Dadourian Group International Inc v* Simms [2009] EWCA Civ 169 at [221–236]; Al *Haq v Shah* [2009] EWCA Civ 542, [2009] 1 W.L.R. 616, CA; *Masood v Zahoor (Practice Note)* [2009] EWCA Civ 650, [2010] 1 W.L.R. 745, CA; amd *Alhamrani v Alhamrani*, 2009 JLR 301, Jersey CA. It must be very rare for a judge to strike out a case at the end of a trial for misconduct rather than dismiss it in a judgment on the merits in the usual way. 13.07

NOTE 29. Add *Barbados Redifusion v Asha Mirchandani (No.2)* [2006] CCJ1 (AJ); (2006) 69 W.I.R.52 on consequences of failing to comply with unless order, where *Stolzenberg v CIBC Mellon Trust Co* [2004] EWCA Civ 827 was applied and the authorities considered extensively. See also *Marine Rescue Technologies Ltd v Burchill* [2007] EWHC 1976 (Ch); *Marcan Shipping (London) Ltd v Kefalas* [2007] EWCA Civ 463; [2007] 1 W.L.R. 1864; *Blerim Ethemi v Robert Shiels* [2008] EWHC 291 (QB); *Tarn Insurance Services Ltd v* Kirby [2009] EWCA Civ 19, CA *Ryback v Langbar International* [2010] EWHC 2015 (Ch): actions struck out for failing to 13.10

comply with unless order, relief from sanction applications under CPR r.3.9 refused. In *Tarn Insurance Services Ltd v* Kirby [2009] EWCA Civ 19 at [82] it was noted that in a case of deliberate and persistent non-compliance with orders to provide information and deliver documents made in order to safeguard proprietary claims, a proper administration of justice requires that, save in very exceptional circumstances, sanctions imposed should take effect. In *Ryback v Langbar International* [2010] EWHC 2015 (Ch), the claimant was the subject of an unless order to make available for inspection by a computer expert various computer hard drives, but before delivering up the material items were deleted. This was held to be a deliberate breach of the order and relief from sanctions was refused.

13.11 NOTE 36. Add *Marcan Shipping (London) Ltd v Kefalas* [2007] EWCA Civ 463; [2007] 1 W.L.R. 1864, CA where there has been clear non-compliance with an unless order, the statement of case is struck out without more; it is then for the defaulting party to seek to persuade the court to grant relief from the sanction taking into account the factors listed in CPR r.3.9 at [34]. A conditional order striking out a statement of case or dismissing the claim or counterclaim is one of the most powerful weapons in the court's case-management armoury and should not be deployed unless its consequences can be justified (at [36]). *Marcan Shipping* was applied in *Ryback v Langbar International* [2010] EWHC 2015 (Ch) at [48].

13.17 In *Dadourian Group International Inc v Simms* [2009] EWCA Civ 169 at [211–236] an application was made to strike out an appeal on the ground that failures in disclosure rendered the appeal an abuse of process. The Court of Appeal refused the application on the facts, whilst holding that in an appropriate case there was jurisdiction to do so under CPR r.52.9. The court was not satisfied that the respondent was prejudiced which might be compensated in some other way. The Court of Appeal examined the application and extent of the principles enunciated in *Arrow Nominees Inc v Blackledge* [2000] 2 B.C.L.C. 167, CA.

Destruction of documents pre-litigation

13.18 In *Earles v Barclays Bank* [2010] EWHC 2500 (Mercantile) at [28], the view was expressed that in respect of documents not preserved pre-litigation, one would have to have evidence of deliberate spoliation in anticipation of litigation before one could draw evidential adverse inferences in such circumstances.

E. REVOCATION AND VARIATION OF ORDERS

13.24 NOTE 73. Where the lower court failed to rule on whether a failure to comply with an unless order for disclosure was intentional, the Court of Appeal remitted the case back to the lower court to determine that issue as

it was a key factor in determining whether relief from the sanction of striking out should be granted: *Vernon v Spoudear* [2010] EWCA Civ 666, CA.

F. CONTEMPT

NOTE 82. For the principles to be applied in deciding whether or not to grant permission to commence committal proceedings for the punishment of an alleged contempt of court by the making of a false statement in a document verified with a statement of truth and in a false disclosure statements. See *Barnes v Seabrook* [2010] EWHC 1849 (Admin). 13.27

NOTE 85. Add *Lexi Holdings Plc v Shaid Luqman* [2007] EWHC 1508 (Ch): custody for contempt where failure to provide disclosure pursuant to asset tracing order, part of a freezing injunction (18 months' imprisonment). 13.27

G. OTHER CONSEQUENCES

Restriction on use of documents at trial

In *Jones v Money Expert Ltd* [2008] UKEAT 0231 08 2208, the respondent relied at the substantive employment tribunal hearing (at which the claimant was not present, he having by then emigrated) on documents that had not been disclosed to the claimant, in breach of a case management order. This was a material irregularity that cried out for review, with the claimant being able to make a fresh witness statement dealing with the points raised in the new documents. 13.32

Adverse inferences at trial

In *McDougall v Black & Decker Canada Inc* (2009) 302 D.L.R. (4th) 661, Alberta CA it was held that the presumption that documents are adverse to the party destroying them would only apply where the destruction was deliberate. The presumption was no more than a rebuttable presumption. In *Earles v Barclays Bank* [2009] EWHC 2500 (Mercantile), the Court criticised a bank for its failure to preserve and disclose electronic records, however the judge declined to draw an adverse inference as there was no evidence that it had been done deliberately or constitutes spoliation in order to gain tactical advantage at the trial. 13.34

Retrial

NOTE 133. Add *L Brown & Sons Ltd v Crosby Mones (North West) Ltd* [2008] EWHC 817 (TCC) applying *Profilati v Paine Webber* [2001] 1 13.36

Lloyd's Rep. 715 in refusing to interfere with an arbitration award under s.68 of the Arbitration Act 1996. In that case Akenhead J. summarised the relevant principles at [36] as follows:

(i) The deliberate withholding of documents that had been ordered to be disclosed in the arbitration may in certain circumstances be considered to be reprehensible conduct and thus contrary to public policy under s.68(2)(g);
(ii) It must, at least, be less reprehensible (if reprehensible at all) for a party to withhold disclosure where disclosure has not as such been ordered by the arbitrator. Under some agreed or standard procedures for disclosure (for instance the IBA Rules) disclosure is voluntary unless specific documents are either agreed or ordered to be disclosed;
(iii) On balance, I consider that the withholding or non-disclosure of documents that have not been ordered to be disclosed by the arbitrator, or have not been agreed to be disclosed, cannot be described as reprehensible or fraudulent unless such non-disclosure is clearly part of some other fraud or reprehensible conduct on the part of the non-disclosing party;
(iv) Lying, being not uncommon in arbitration or in civil proceedings in general, can be a basis upon which an award is obtained by fraud or in a way that is contrary to public policy, but where the credibility of the witness in question was a primary feature of the arbitration or the arbitration hearing it is less likely that it will be considered to be a serious irregularity;
(v) If there are grounds under s.68(2)(g) based on lying or deception on the part of the respondent to the application, it is necessary to demonstrate that the award was dependent upon or was reached as a result of the lying or deception;
(vi) If the grounds under s.68(2)(g) are established, it is still necessary to show that substantial injustice would be caused to the applicant as a result thereof. That may prove not to be very difficult to establish if the grounds under s.68(2)(g) are established.

Costs

13.37 In *Dadourian Group International Inc v Simmons* [2009] EWCA Civ 169 at [149–166] the trial judge awarded indemnity costs against the defendants on the basis that inter alia, there had been serious failings in disclosure. The Court of Appeal refused to interfere with that exercise of discretion. In *R (on the application of Al Sweady) v Secretary of State for Defence* [2009] EWHC 2387 (Admin) indemnity costs of the proceedings were awarded against the defendant as the whole of the cost of the proceedings had been

wasted by the inadequate disclosure process conducted on behalf of the Secretary of State [at [13]).

NOTE 119. *Hedrich v Standard Bank London Ltd* [2008] EWCA Civ 905, CA no wasted costs order against solicitors when disclosure chaotic and inadequate, where no negligence by solicitor. **13.37**

Other remedies

In *Holland v Marshall* (2009) 301 D.L.R. (4th) 371, the New Brunswick Court of Appeal left open the question of whether a tort of spoilation should be recognised. It noted that a strong argument against recognition of an independent tort for spoliation is its inherently speculative nature with respect to injury, causation and damages (at [71]). See also *McDougall v Black & Decker Canada Inc* (2009) 302 D.L.R. (4th) 661, Alberta CA. **13.38**

CHAPTER 14

Solicitor's Obligations

CHAPTER 14

Solicitor's Obligations

B. SOLICITOR'S DUTIES

General

The duties of solicitors with regard to disclosure were considered in *Hedrich v Standard Bank London Ltd* [2008] EWCA Civ 905 which cited paragraphs 14.02, 14.03, 14.07, 14.09 and 14.10 of this work as setting out the relevant principles. 14.02

Explanation to the client

A solicitor has a duty to take steps to ensure that his client knows what documents have to be disclosed: *R (on the application of Al Sweady) v Secretary of State for Defence* [2009] EWHC 2387 (Admin) at [42]. 14.03

Preservation of documents

Practice Direction 31B, para.7 now expressly provides that as soon as litigation is contemplated, the parties' legal representatives must notify their clients of the need to preserve disclosable documents. The documents to be preserved include Electronic Documents which would otherwise be deleted in accordance with a document retention policy or otherwise deleted in the ordinary course of business. 14.04

NOTE 16. See now Solicitors *Code of Conduct*, r.11.01 and Guidance to r.11. The *Code of Conduct* replaced the *Guide to the Professional Conduct of Solicitors* with effect from July 2007. 14.05

Checking the documents

In *R (on the application of Al Sweady) v Secretary of State for Defence* [2009] EWHC 2387 (Admin) the failure to carry out important searches for 14.09

no good reason was categorised as a serious breach of the duty to give proper disclosure (at [42]).

14.10 NOTE 29. See now Solicitors *Code of Conduct*, r.11, and Guidance to r.11.

Restriction on collateral use of documents or information

14.15 NOTE 37. Add *British Sky Broadcasting Group Plc v Virgin Media* [2008] EWCA Civ 612, [2008] 1 W.L.R. 2854, *The Times*, June 11, 2008, CA. Where a solicitor has obtained information from disclosure subject to a restriction on collateral use in separate proceedings, the court will usually decline to preclude the solicitor from acting in other proceedings involving the same parties or one of them. The Court of Appeal at [23] endorsed the observations of Giles A.S.P. in the Federal Court of Canada in *Merck & Co. v Interpharm* [1992] 3 F.C. 774:

"In my view the implied undertaking would be most impractical if it resulted in an ability to remove from a case any solicitor who was bound by the undertaking. The implied undertaking is not of sufficient public interest when balanced against the right of a party to choose his own solicitors and the public interest in the efficient administration of justice to require the court to disqualify any solicitors who might wrongly deploy information subject to the undertaking. If the solicitor fails to observe the undertaking the remedy is to cite him for contempt, not to remove him".

CHAPTER 15

Collateral Use of Documents

	PARA.
A. THE UNDERTAKING	15.01
B. CPR RULE 31.22	15.03*
C. RATIONALE	15.05*
D. TO WHOM OWED	15.07
E. ON WHOM BINDING	15.09*
F. DOCUMENTS OR INFORMATION	15.11*
G. COLLATERAL OR ULTERIOR PURPOSE	15.18
H. EXPRESS UNDERTAKING	15.24
I. DURATION OF OBLIGATION	15.25*
J. RELEASE FROM OR MODIFICATION OF OBLIGATION	15.33*
K. ENFORCEMENT OF OBLIGATION	15.44
L. ARBITRATION	15.47*

M. TAXATION OF COSTS 15.55

N. CRIMINAL PROCEEDINGS 15.56*

CHAPTER 15

Collateral Use of Documents

A. THE UNDERTAKING

NOTE 2. The first part of this paragraph was cited with approval by Malan J in *Replication Technology Group v Gallo Africa Ltd* [2009] ZAGPJHC 8, [9] 15.01

B. CPR RULE 31.22

It is no longer necessary, as it was under the RSC, to show that there are special reasons for seeking a court order under CPR 31.22(2) to restrict or prohibit the use of a document that has been disclosed: see *McBride v The Body Shop International Plc* [2007] EWHC 1658 (QB) at [46]. The court prohibited the claimant from using a document disclosed as part of employment tribunal proceedings as the foundation for a libel claim against her employer. 15.03

In Australia, the implied undertaking is now regarded as a substantive legal obligation: *Hearne v Street* [2008] HCA 36, (2008) 235 C.L.R. 125, (2008) 248 A.L.R. 609; *Daniels v TAB Ltd* [2009] FMCA 148. 15.03

C. RATIONALE

This paragraph was referred to with apparent approval by Eady J. in *McBride v The Body Shop International Plc* [2007] EWHC 1658 (QB) at [41], and in large part by Malan J in *Replication Technology Group v Gallo Africa Ltd* [2009] ZAGPJHC 8, [9]. 15.05

NOTE 23. Add *Kitchenham v AXA Insurance* (2009) 306 DLR (4th) 68, Ont CA. 15.05

See also *British Sky Broadcasting Group Plc v Virgin Media* [2008] EWCA Civ 612, [2008] 1 W.L.R. 2854, *The Times*, June 11, 2008, CA: where a solicitor has obtained information from disclosure subject to a restriction on collateral use in separate proceedings, the court will usually 15.05, 15.06

decline to preclude the solicitor from acting in other proceedings involving the same parties or one of them. The Court of Appeal at [23] endorsed the observations of Giles A.S.P. in the Federal Court of Canada in *Merck & Co. v Interpharm* [1992] 3 F.C. 774:

> "In my view the implied undertaking would be most impractical if it resulted in an ability to remove from a case any solicitor who was bound by the undertaking. The implied undertaking is not of sufficient public interest when balanced against the right of a party to choose his own solicitors and the public interest in the efficient administration of justice to require the court to disqualify any solicitors who might wrongly deploy information subject to the undertaking. If the solicitor fails to observe the undertaking the remedy is to cite him for contempt, not to remove him".

E. ON WHOM BINDING

15.09 In Australia, the implied undertaking is binding directly on the servant or agent of a party, rather than the servant or agent being potentially liable for breach as an accessory: *Hearne v Street* [2008] HCA 36.

F. DOCUMENTS OR INFORMATION

15.11 NOTE 39. *C Plc v P* [2007] EWCA Civ 493; [2007] 3 W.L.R. 437; [2008] Ch.7, CA; [2008] 1 W.L.R. 153, HL(E) pet.all. (updated citation for appeal).

15.12 See also *Brookfield Multiplex Limited v International Litigation Funding Partners Pte Ltd (No 2)* [2009] FCA 449.

15.18 In Canada it has been held hat the obligation is not to use the documents or information, not to refrain from disclosing them in the later proceedings: *Kitchenham v AXA Insurance* (2009) 306 DLR (4th) 68, [32], Ont CA.

15.19 This paragraph was cited with approval by Malan J in *Replication Technology Group v Gallo Africa Ltd* [2009] ZAGPJHC 8, [9]

I. DURATION OF OBLIGATION

15.25 NOTE 90. The British Columbia Court of Appeal has now decided that the implied undertaking ends when the document is read out in court: *IBEW Local 213 v Hochstein* (2010) 11 DLR (4th) 389.

15.31 NOTE 112. See also *McBride v The Body Shop International Plc* [2007] EWHC 1658 (QB) at [46], where the court prohibited the claimant from using a document disclosed as part of employment tribunal proceedings as the foundation for a libel claim against her employer.

J. RELEASE FROM OR MODIFICATION OF OBLIGATION

See also *Breslin v McKenna* [2007] NICA 14 at [36]. 15.34

NOTE 127. *C Plc v P* [2007] EWCA Civ 493; [2007] 3 W.L.R. 437; [2008] Ch.7, CA; [2008] 1 W.L.R. 153, HL(E) pet.all. (updated citation for appeal). 15.34

In *Thought Web Systems Pty Ltd v Loughnan (No.2)* [2006] FCA 432; (2007) 230 A.L.R. 515, Fed. Ct of Australia, the judge refused to allow documents disclosed in other proceedings to be used in a winding up petition, emphasising that there were no special circumstances in the present case. 15.37

See also *Juman v Doucette* 2008 SCC 8 (criminal authorities refused access to documents disclosed in civil discovery without a court order; the public interest in the prosecution of crime will not necessarily trump a citizen's privacy interest in statutorily compelled information). In *SITA UK Group Holdings Ltd v Serruys* [2009] STC 1595, Jack J considered that it was not necessary to give permission under r 31.22 at this stage. 15.42

NOTE 159. Add *SITA UK Group Holdings Ltd v Serruys* [2009] STC 1595. 15.43

NOTE 160. *C Plc v P* [2007] EWCA Civ 493; [2007] 3 W.L.R. 437; [2008] Ch.7, CA; [2008] 1 W.L.R. 153, HL(E) pet.all. (updated citation for appeal). 15.43

K. ENFORCEMENT OF OBLIGATION

Add *Dadourian Group International* v *Simms* [2007] EWHC 2634 (Ch); *Brookfield Multiplex Limited v International Litigation Funding Partners Pte Ltd (No 2)* [2009] FCA 449; *Replication Technology Group v Gallo Africa Ltd* [2009] ZAGPJHC 8. 15.45

L. ARBITRATION

In *Emmott v Michael Wilson & Partners Ltd* [2008] EWCA Civ 184, Lawrence Collins L.J. summarised the position in this way: 15.47

"[. . .] case law over the last 20 years has established that there is an obligation, implied by law and arising out of the nature of arbitration, on both parties not to disclose or use for any other purpose any documents prepared for and used in the arbitration, or disclosed or produced in the course of the arbitration, or transcripts or notes of the evidence in the arbitration or the award, and not to disclose in any other way what evidence

has been given by any witness in the arbitration. The obligation is not limited to commercially confidential information in the traditional sense.

As I have said above, this is in reality a substantive rule of arbitration law reached through the device of an implied term. That approach has led to difficulties of formulation and reliance (perhaps, over-reliance) on the banking principles in *Tournier.*

In my judgment the content of the obligation may depend on the context in which it arises and on the nature of the information or documents at issue. The limits of that obligation are still in the process of development on a case-by-case basis. On the authorities as they now stand, the principal cases in which disclosure will be permissible are these: the first is where there is consent, express or implied; second, where there is an order, or leave of the court (but that does not mean that the court has a general discretion to lift the obligation of confidentiality); third, where it is reasonably necessary for the protection of the legitimate interests of an arbitrating party; fourth, where the interests of justice require disclosure, and also (perhaps) where the public interest requires disclosure".

See also *Replication Technology Group v Gallo Africa Ltd* [2009] ZAGPJHC 8.

N. CRIMINAL PROCEEDINGS

15.56 In *Breslin v McKenna* [2008] IEHC 122 the Irish High Court left open the question whether there was an implied undertaking in respect of documents disclosed for the purposes of criminal proceedings.

CHAPTER 16

Information Requests

	PARA.
A. BACKGROUND	16.01*
B. OBJECTIVES OF REQUEST	16.06
C. THE PRELIMINARY REQUEST	16.08
D. APPLICATIONS FOR ORDER UNDER PART 18	16.20*
E. BETWEEN WHOM AVAILABLE	16.27
F. RELEVANCE	16.33
G. PARTICULAR INSTANCES	16.38*
H. NECESSITY AND PROPORTIONALITY	16.51*
I. OPPRESSIVE, PROLIX, SCANDALOUS, VAGUE AND IRRELEVANT REQUESTS	16.52
J. SPECIAL CASES	16.54*
K. OBJECTIONS TO REQUESTS	16.76
L. PRIVILEGE AND STATUTORY PROHIBITION	16.78
M. RESPONSE	16.91

CHAPTER 16

Information Requests

A. BACKGROUND

The current version of CPR Pt 18 Practice Direction is included in Appendix 2 below, para.B.02. This has only been slightly modified at para.1.7.

D. APPLICATIONS FOR ORDERS UNDER PART 18

The Application

NOTE 47. (9th edn, 2009), para.D15.1 (updated citation) 16.23

G. PARTICULAR INSTANCES

Fishing

In *Mireskandari v Associated Newspapers* [2010] EWHC 967 (QB), the court refused an application requiring the defendant to a libel action to provide details of any occasions on which a particular judge had acted for it whilst at the bar. The request did not go to any pleaded issue. The Court found that the claimant was seeking an opportunity to "fish" for further information in the hope that something more substantive may turn up, so as to enable him to argue at some stage that a particular judge should recuse herself if the litigation comes before her again. 16.42

Insurance

Where insurance does not relate to any matter in dispute in the proceedings, there is no jurisdiction under CPR Pt 18 to order a party to provide details of his insurance cover simply to permit the claimant to decide whether or not it is worth pursuing the proceedings against a defendant of limited 16.44

financial means: *West London Pipeline and Storage v Total UK Ltd* [2008] EWHC 1296 (Comm.), Steel J. who was correct in not following *Harcourt v FEF Griffin* [2007] EWHC 1500 (QB), Irwin J.

H. NECESSITY AND PROPORTIONALITY

16.51 NOTE 137. *McPhilemy v Times Newspapers* [1999] 3 All E.R. 755 at 792–3 was followed in *Lexi Holdings (in administration) v Pannone and Partners* [2010] EWHC 1416 (Ch) at [9], noting that the CPR takes a more restrictive approach to what used to be regarded as an entitlement to particulars under the RSC. The judge allowed some of the requests, but rejected those which failed to pass the necessity and proportionality tests.

J. SPECIAL CASES

Admiralty

16.54 NOTE 154. (9th edn, 2009), para.D15 (updated citation).

Commercial Court

16.55 NOTE 159. (9th edn, 2009), para.D15 (updated citation).

Injunctions and *Anton Piller* orders

16.68 NOTE 215. Add *Lichter & Schwartz v Rubin* [2008] EWHC 450 (Ch) application under CPR r.25.1(1)(g) for details of various payments where reasonable possibility that an application for a freezing order would be made.

Patent and copyright actions

16.72 In *Novartis AG v Johnson & Johnson Medical Ltd* [2008] EWHC 293 (Pat), the claimant in a patent infringement action was ordered to disclose further information, which would assist the defendant to design an effective experiment.

CHAPTER 17

Other Disclosure of Facts

CHAPTER 17

Other Disclosure of Facts

B. LETTERS OF REQUEST

(1) Witness out of jurisdiction (non-EU)

NOTE 67. *Admiralty and Commercial Courts Guide* (9th edn, 2009) para. H4.2 (updated citation). 17.13

NOTE 68. *Admiralty and Commercial Courts Guide* (9th edn, 2009), paras. H4 and H4 (updated citation). 17.13

(2) Witness in another EU Member State

17.14 The Evidence Regulation applies where the requesting court wants another Member State court to take evidence, or itself to take evidence directly in another Member State. It does not apply to the situation where an order is made against a judgment debtor to provide evidence to the English court as to the nature and location of his assets. There is no evasion of the Evidence Regulation in such circumstances. In addition CPR Pt 71 requests for the examination of a director of a judgment debtor do not fall within the Evidence Regulations: *Masri v Consolidated Contractors International Company SAL* [2008] EWCA Civ 876, [2009] 1 Lloyd's Rep. 42 at [38–54]. However, as the House of Lords held on appeal, CPR r.71.2 does not enable an order for examination to be made against an officer who is outside the jurisdiction: [2009] UKHL 43, [2009] 3 W.L.R. 385, [2009] 2 Lloyd's Rep. 473. This may not prevent an order being made against an officer who is temporarily within the jurisdiction, but care should be exercised before exercising such a jurisdiction against a foreigner: c.f. *Kuwait Airways v Iraq Airways Corporation* [2010] EWCA Civ 740 (ex parte order made by Court of Appeal against a foreign officer of a judgment debtor temporarily within the jurisdiction).

C. WITNESS STATEMENTS

Form and contents of witness statements

17.22 NOTE 127. *Admiralty and Commercial Courts Guide* (9th edn, 2009), para. H1.1(i) (updated citation).

Amendment and supplementary statements

17.24 NOTE 134. *Admiralty and Commercial Courts Guide* (9th edn. 2009), para. H1.7(b) permission is required for the service of a supplemental statement.

Procedure at trial

17.25 NOTE 137. *Admiralty and Commercial Courts* Guide (9th edn, 2009), para. H1.6(b) (updated citation).

17.26 NOTE 141. *Admiralty and Commercial Court Guide* (9th edn, 2009), para. H1.8(b) (updated citation).

17.30 A witness (whether expert or factual) has in general immunity from civil suit in respect of what is contained in a witness statement or expert report, however this does not extend to exhibits: *Accident Exchange Ltd v Autofocus Ltd* [2009] EWHC 3304 (QB) applying *Darker v Chief Constable of West Midlands Police* [2001] 1 A.C. 435, HL. See also *Wynne Jones v Kaney* [2010] EWHC 61 (QB), noted under para.18.15 in this supplement.

CHAPTER 18

Experts' Reports

	PARA.
A. GENERAL	18.01*
B. DIRECTION OF THE COURT	18.04*
C. SINGLE JOINT EXPERTS	18.09*
D. RULING ON ADMISSIBILITY	18.11*
E. DUTIES OF EXPERT	18.12*
F. PRIVILEGE	18.16*
G. QUESTIONS FOR EXPERT	18.17*
H. REQUESTS FOR INFORMATION	18.18*
I. MEETING OF EXPERTS	18.19*
J. EXPERT'S REQUEST FOR DIRECTIONS	18.20*
K. PROCEDURE AT TRIAL	18.21*
L. ASSESSORS	18.23*

CHAPTER 18

Experts' Reports

A. GENERAL

For a more comprehensive discussion of expert evidence in civil cases under the CPR see Hodgkinson and James, *Expert Evidence: Law and Practice* (3rd edn, 2010, *Phipson on Evidence* (17th edn, 2010), Ch.33. For an assessment of the success of the courts in dealing with experts see Jacob, R., 'Experts and Woolf: Have Things Got Better' and Dwyer, D., 'The Role of the Expert under CPR Pt.35' in D. Dwyer (ed)., *The Civil Procedure Rules Ten Years On* (2010, OUP), Chapters 15 and 16. See also Lord Justice Jackson's *Review of Civil Litigation: Final Report* (2010), chapter 38 on the cost of expert evidence. 18.01

CPR Part 35 and the Practice Direction were revised in 2009. The amended version is set out at Appendix 2, B.11 to this Supplement. Most of the changes to CPR Part 35 are minor and not substantive, but it is not always wholly clear whether such changes are meant to change the meaning and import of the relevant paragraphs. The numbering of the paragraphs has changed in the Practice Direction and paragraphs 7 (single joint expert) and 9 (discussions between experts) are new. The *Protocol for the Instruction of Experts to give Evidence in Civil Claims* was revised in October 2009. The revised version is set out at Appendix 2, B.12 to this Supplement.

NOTE 2. *Chancery Guide* (6th Edn, 2009), paras. 4.8–4.21; *Admiralty and Commercial Courts Guide* (9th Edn, 2009), para.H2 and Appendix 11 (updated citations). 18.01

NOTE 8. CPR, r.35.2(1) now provides that a reference to an "expert" is to a person who has been instructed to give or prepare expert evidence for the purpose of "proceedings" (the former rule referred to "*Court* proceedings). 18.02

Sometimes an issue will arise as to whether a particular witness is a factual witness or an expert as in the latter case permission of the court will be needed to adduce such evidence. The lack of a clear definition of "expert" may encourage some to try to reclassify the evidence as one of fact. For recent cases on whether a particular witness evidence was one of expert opinion or fact, see *Gall v Chief Constable of the West Midlands* [2006] 18.02

EWHC 2638 (QB) and *Kirkman v Euro Exide Corporation* [2007] EWCA Civ 66; [2007] C.P. Rep. 19 discussed in D. Dwyer, "The effect of the fact/opinion distinction on CPR, r.35.2" (2008) 12 E&P 141. In both cases it was held that medical witnesses were witnesses of fact and not experts within CPR r.35.2.

In many construction disputes of the kind considered in the Technology and Construction Court, as well as medical negligence actions, witnesses of fact will also be experts in the matters covered in their statements. Thus a statement may include both factual and opinion evidence. Whether this is permissible depends on the circumstances. For a useful discussion of this issue, see *Multiplex Constructions (UK) Ltd v Cleveland Bridge (UK) Ltd* [2008] EWHC 2220 (TCC), Jackson J. at [657–676].

18.03 NOTE 11. *Chancery Guide* (6th edn, 2009), para.4.8 (updated citation).

B. DIRECTION OF THE COURT

18.05 NOTE 27. *Admiralty and Commercial Courts Guide* (9th edn, 2009), para. H2.1 (updated citation).

18.05 NOTE 32. CPR, r. 35.5(2) provides that if a claim is on the small claims track or the fast track, the court will not direct an expert to attend a hearing unless it is necessary to do so in the interests of justice. (The earlier version of this rule made no reference to claims on the small claims track).

18.05 NOTE 33. *Admiralty and Commercial Courts Guide* (9th edn, 2009), para. H2.11; *Chancery Guide* (6th edn, 2009) para.4.15 (updated citations).

18.08 NOTE 43. *ES v Chesterfield and North Derbyshire Royal Hospital NHS Trust* [2003] EWCA Civ 1284, [2004] Lloyd's Rep. Med. 50 was distinguished in *Beaumont v Ministry of Defence* [2009] EWHC 1258 (QB). In the latter case each party had one obstetric expert witness and the defendant was to call a consultant as a factual witness (albeit with an expert element). The court refused to depart from the normal rule and thus refused the claimant permission to call a second obstetric expert.

18.08 NOTE 46. Add *Gallaher International NV v Tlais Enterprises Ltd* [2007] EWHC 527 (Comm.): failure to comply with unless order for service of expert report, relief under CPR r.3.9 from sanction of debarring calling such expert evidence on terms party pays costs on indemnity basis.

C. SINGLE JOINT EXPERTS

18.09 CPR, r.35.2(2) defines "single joint expert" as being an expert instructed to prepare a report for the court on behalf of two or more of the parties (including the claimant) to the proceedings.

18.09 NOTE 48. *Chancery Guide* (6th edn, 2009) para.4.13 (updated citation).

NOTE 49. *Chancery Guide* (6th edn, 2009), para.4.12 (updated citation). 18.09

NOTE 53. CPR, Pt. 35, Practice Direction—Experts and Assessors, para.7 provides that when considering whether to give permission for the parties to rely on expert evidence and whether that evidence should be from a single joint expert the court will take into account the circumstances. Particular factors (a) to (i) are listed. This replaces what was para.6 of the former version of the Practice Direction. 18.09

NOTE 55. *Admiralty and Commercial Courts Guide* (9th edn, 2009), para. H2.3; *Chancery Guide* (6th edn, 2009), para.4.14 (updated citations). 18.09

NOTE 57. Add *Childs v Vernon & Butcher* [2007] EWCA Civ 305 (inappropriate for single joint expert to have discussions with one party in the absence of the other in boundary dispute); *Edwards v Bruce & Hyslop (Brucast) Ltd* [2009] EWHC 2790 (QB) (joint expert inappropriately communicating with one party's solicitor; other party given permission to rely upon another expert). 18.09

D. RULING ON ADMISSIBILITY

NOTE 63. Add *Woodside Energy Ltd v Commissioner of Taxation* [2006] FCA 1303; (2007) 233 A.L.R. 710, Fed. Ct of Australia (expert economists and expert account evidence admissible in relation to treatment of hedging losses). 18.11

NOTE 64. Add *Morgan v Hinton Organics (Wessex) Ltd* [2009] EWCA Civ 107 (undesirable to leave it to the course of trial to rule as inadmissible expert evidence on ground of an actual or apparent interest). 18.11

E. DUTIES OF EXPERT

NOTE 68. CPR, Pt 35, Practice Direction, paras. 2.1–2.5 (updated citation). 18.12

NOTE 71. Add *Gallaher International Ltd v Tlais Enterprises Ltd* [2007] EWHC 464 (Comm.), expert report from employee of claimant's related company permitted as safeguards taken and such expertise scarce. 18.12

NOTE 74. Add *Morgan v Hinton Organics (Wessex) Ltd* [2009] EWCA Civ 107, it is highly undesirable to leave it to the course of the trial to rule that an expert's evidence is inadmissible on the ground of an actual or apparent interest. This should be determined in the course of case management (on the facts CA held no interest or lack of independence). 18.12

NOTE 79. CPR, Pt 35, Practice Direction, para.,3.1 (updated citation). 18.13

NOTE 80. CPR, Pt 35, Practice Direction, para.3.2; *Admiralty and Commercial Guide* (9th edn, 2009), para.H2.6, App. 11 (updated citations). 18.13

NOTE 82. *Admiralty and Commercial Courts Guide* (9th edn, 2009), para. H2.6(a) (updated citation). 18.14

18.14 NOTE 84. CPR, Pt 35, Practice Direction, para.2.4 (updated citation). Delete reference to *Chancery Guide* (5th edn. 2005), para.4.9).

18.14 NOTE 87. *Admiralty and Commercial Courts Guide* (9th edn, 2009), para. H2.20 (updated citation).

18.14 NOTE 88. *Admiralty and Commercial Courts Guide* (9th edn, 2009), para. H2.21 (updated citation).

18.14 NOTE 89. CPR, Pt 35, Practice Direction, para.3.3 (updated citation).

18.14 NOTE 90. Delete reference to *Chancery Guide* (5th edn, 2006), para.4.9. CPR, Pt 35, Practice Direction, para.2.5 (updated citation).

18.14 In *Oldham Metropolitan Borough Council v GW* [2007] EWHC 136 (Fam); [2007] 2 F.L.R. 597 difficulties arose from relying on a single expert in care proceedings. After analysing the lessons to be learned, Ryder J. recommended that (at [91]):

"(i) Local authorities should always write a letter of instruction when asking a potential witness for a report or an opinion, whether that request is within proceedings or pre-proceedings e.g. when commissioning specialist assessment materials, reports from a treating expert or other evidential materials and the letter of instruction should conform to the principles set out by the Family Justice Council at www.family-justice-council.org.uk and the Chief Medical Officer at Annex B para [21] of 'Bearing Good Witness' (2006) 30 October and Charles J. in *A County Council v K, D and L* (supra) at para [89];

(ii) When requesting and collating existing materials, all parties should be vigilant to record requests of third parties for disclosure and their responses, so that the spectre of partial disclosure which tends only to prove a case rather than give full and frank information can be dispelled. Furthermore, great care must be exercised when placing reliance on materials that have not been produced either as 'original medical (or other professional) records' or in response to an instruction from a party as these materials may contain an assumption as to the standard of proof, the admissibility or otherwise of hearsay evidence and other important procedural and substantive questions that relate to the differing purposes of other enquiries (e.g. criminal or disciplinary proceedings);

(iii) Once instructed, experts in their advice to the court should conform to the best practice of their clinical training and, in particular, should describe their own professional risk assessment process and/or the process of differential diagnosis that has been undertaken, highlighting factual assumptions, deductions there from and unusual features of the case. They should set out contradictory or inconsistent features. They should identify the range of opinion on the question to be answered, giving reasons for the opinion they hold. They should highlight whether a proposition is an hypothesis

(in particular a controversial hypothesis) or an opinion deduced in accordance with peer reviewed and tested technique, research and experience accepted as a consensus in the scientific community. They should highlight and analyse within the range of opinion an 'unknown cause', whether that be on the facts of the case (e.g. there is too little information to form a scientific opinion) or whether by reason of limited experience, lack of research, peer review or support in the field of skill and expertise that they profess. The use of a balance sheet approach to the factors that support or undermine an opinion can be of great assistance;

(iv) An expert should be asked at the earliest stage and in any event should volunteer an opinion whether another expert is required to bring a skill or expertise not possessed by those already involved or in the rare case a second opinion to a key issue that has been identified by the court and, if possible, what the question is that should be asked of that expert. In any event, far greater heed should be paid to advice from experts as to the questions that they are able to answer and that might be relevant to the court's determination;

(v) The 'Code of Guidance for Expert Witnesses in Family Proceedings' at Appendix C to the Protocol (supra) should be amended to incorporate the recommendations made above".

In children proceedings the *Practice Direction: Experts in Family Proceedings relating to Children* [2009] 2 FL.R. 1383 applies. See also *Re M (Care proceedings: Best Evidence)* [2007] EWCA Civ 589, [2007] 2 F.L.R. 2006; *O-M (Children) v Local Authority* [2009] EWCA Civ 1405, CA (permission to instruct a consultant paediatrician and geneticist refused).

NOTE 96. CPR, Pt 35, Practice Direction, para.3.3; *Admiralty and Commercial Courts Guide* (9th edn, 2009), para H2.9(b) (updated citations). **18.15**

For a discussion on the remedies and consequences of negligent expert evidence, see D. Dwyer, "Legal remedies for the negligent expert" (2008) 12 E&P 93. In *Wynne Jones v Kaney* [2010] EWHC 61 (QB), it was held that the principle of witness immunity from being sued in *Stanton v Callaghan* [2000] QB 75, CA was binding so an action by a claimant against an expert who had allegedly negligently signed a joint expert statement was struck out. The judge considered that this was an issue which needed to be reviewed by the Supreme Court. **18.15**

F. PRIVILEGE

NOTE 105. CPR, Pt 35, Practice Direction, para.5 (updated citation). **18.16**

G. QUESTIONS FOR EXPERT

18.17 NOTE 110. CPR, Pt 35, Practice Direction, para.6; *Chancery Guide* (6th edn, 2009), para.4.19; *Admiralty and Commercial Courts Guide* (9th edn, 2009), para.H2.19 (updated citations).

H. REQUESTS FOR INFORMATION

18.18 NOTE 114. CPR, Pt, Practice Direction, para.4 (updated citation).

I. MEETINGS OF EXPERTS

18.19 NOTE 117. Add CPR, Pt 35, Purchase Direction, para.9 which now contains detailed provisions as to discussions between experts. *Admiralty and Commercial Courts Guide* (9th edn, 2009), para.H2.12–H2.18; *Chancery Guide* (6th edn, 2009), para.4.16–4.18 (updated citations).

J. EXPERT'S REQUEST FOR DIRECTIONS

18.20 NOTE 121. *Admiralty and Commercial Courts Guide* (9th edn, 2009), H2.10; *Chancery Guide* (6th edn, 2009), para.4.20 (updated citations).

18.20 NOTE 122. *Chancery Guide* (6th, 2009), para.4.20 (updated citation).

K. PROCEDURE AT TRIAL

18.21 NOTE 126. *Admiralty and Commercial Courts Guide* (9th edn, 2009), para.H2.22 (updated citation). This also provides that experts' supplementary reports must be exchanged not later than the progress monitoring date and the introduction of additional expert evidence after that date will only be permitted upon application to the trial judge and if there are very strong grounds for admitting it.

18.21 NOTE 128. Add *Shepherd Neame v EDF Energy Networks (SPN) Ltd* [2008] EWHC 123 (TCC): CPR r.35.11 applies to permit every party to rely upon a report disclosed by another party to the proceedings, it does not matter that the party who had commissioned and disclosed it had withdrawn from the proceedings.

18.22 NOTE 131. However, if a trial judge incorrectly excludes relevant expert evidence, then on appeal a new trial may be ordered if the excluded evidence may have had an impact on the result: for an example, see *Cadbury*

Schweppes Pty Ltd v Darrell Lea Chocolate Shops Pty Ltd [2007] FCAFC 70, Fed. Ct of Australia.

NOTE 136. Add *Smith v Southampton University Hospital NHS Trust* [2007] EWCA Civ 387 (trial judge failed to explain why rejected evidence of one expert; not enough merely to say other expert was highly reputable and representative of a responsible body of medical opinion). 18.22

L. ASSESSORS

In *Balcombe Group Plc v London Development Agency* [2008] EWHC 1392 (TCC), Coulson J. refused an application pursuant to CPR r.35.15 for the appointment of an assessor to assist at the trial of quantum. He concluded that it would be both disproportionate and unnecessary to require the parties to pay for the costs of an assessor. He summarised the relevant principles as follows (at [6]): 18.23

"(a) The court must have regard to the overriding principle (CPR 1.1), and in particular to all questions of proportionality, when considering appointing an assessor. Since the parties will have to pay the costs of an assessor, a court should think twice about imposing an extra layer of cost on the parties, and evaluate the potential benefit of an assessor against that cost, and the amount at stake in the proceedings.

(b) The appointment of an assessor may be appropriate if the subject matter of the proceedings is technically complex or involves a particular activity which will be unfamiliar to the court. In nautical collision cases, an assessor will often be appointed; see, by way of example, **The Owners of the Ship 'Bow Spring' v The Owners of the Ship Manzanillo II** [2004] EWCA Civ 1007; and **The Owners and Bareboat Charterers of the Vessel 'Global Marina' v The Owners and Bareboat Charterers of the Vessel 'Atlantic Crusader'** [2005] EWHC 380 (Admlty). Assessors can sometimes be appropriate in detailed or complex costs disputes although, depending on the circumstances, their own costs will often be met by the court service, rather than by the parties.

(c) Where assessors are appointed, it will be important to ensure that both the questions put to the assessor, and the assessor's answers to those questions are shared with the parties and made the subject of counsel's submissions. This can lead to the risk of increased cost and delay which will be "inherent in the ping-pong of post-hearing exchanges"; see paragraph 16 of the judgment of Gross J. in **Global Marina.**

(d) In TCC cases in recent years, the appointment of an assessor has been very much the exception rather than the rule. In *McAlpine Humberoak v MacDermott* (1990)51 BLR 34, although His Honour Judge Davies QC sat with two assessors, they played no separate part in the proceedings, produced no reports, and their influence was not obviously discernible in the judge's judgment".

18.23 NOTE 137. CPR, Pt 35, Practice Direction, para.10; *Admiralty and Commercial Courts Guide* (9th edn, 2009), para.N.14; *Chancery Guide* (6th edn, 2009), para.4.21 (updated citations).

18.26 NOTE 145. *Admiralty and Commercial Courts Guide* (9th edn, 2009), para.N14.1 (updated citation).

CHAPTER 19

Disclosure of Real Evidence

	PARA.
A. INSPECTION OF PROPERTY	19.02*
B. SAMPLES AND EXPERIMENTS	19.14
C. MEDICAL EXAMINATIONS	19.20
D. PLANS, PHOTOGRAPHS AND MODELS	19.23

CHAPTER 19

Disclosure of Real Evidence

A. INSPECTION OF PROPERTY

Before substantive proceedings commenced

NOTE 24. Section 25 of the Civil Jurisdiction and Judgments Act 1982 only applies where the foreign proceedings are proceedings on the substance of the matter: *ETI Euro Telecom International NV v Republic of Bolivia* [2008] EWCA Civ 880, CA. 19.04

After substantive proceedings commenced

In *Gwelhayl Ltd v Midas Construction Ltd* [2008] EWHC 2316 (TCC), Coulson J. ordered the defendant to deliver up documents in its possession to the claimant (its former principal), pursuant to CPR r.25.1(1)(c)(i), upon security being provided for its (disputed) claim for its outstanding fees. 19.07

CHAPTER 20

Disclosure in other Courts and Tribunals

PARA.

A. INTRODUCTION 20.01

B. AGRICULTURAL LAND TRIBUNALS 20.02

C. ARBITRATIONS 20.04*

D. BARMOTE COURTS 20.10

E. COMMITTEE OF PRIVILEGES OF THE HOUSE OF LORDS 20.11

F. COMMONS COMMISSIONERS 20.12

G. COMPETITION COMMISSION APPEAL TRIBUNAL 20.13

H. COPYRIGHT TRIBUNAL 20.15

I. CORONERS' COURTS 20.17

J. COURT OF ADMIRALTY OF THE CINQUE PORTS 20.21

K. COURT OF PROTECTION 20.22

L. ECCLESIASTICAL COURTS 20.23

M. EMPLOYMENT TRIBUNALS (FORMERLY INDUSTRIAL TRIBUNALS) 20.27*

N. EUROPEAN COURT OF JUSTICE AND THE EUROPEAN COURT OF FIRST INSTANCE 20.32*

O. FINANCIAL SERVICES AND MARKETS TRIBUNAL 20.38*

P. HIGH COURT OF CHIVALRY 20.40

Q. IMMIGRATION APPEALS 20.41

R. INFORMATION TRIBUNAL 20.44

S. INTERNATIONAL TRIBUNALS 20.47

T. LAND REGISTRY 20.48

U. LANDS TRIBUNAL 20.49

V. LLOYD'S DISCIPLINARY COMMITTEE AND APPEAL TRIBUNAL 20.54

W. MEDIATION 20.55*

X. MENTAL HEALTH REVIEW TRIBUNALS 20.58

Y. PENSIONS APPEAL TRIBUNALS 20.61

Z. PRIZE COURTS 20.65

AA. PUBLIC INQUIRIES 20.66

BB. RENT ASSESSMENT COMMITTEES 20.70

CC. SOCIAL SECURITY ADJUDICATIONS AND APPEALS 20.72

DD. SPECIAL AND GENERAL COMMISSIONERS 20.73

CHAPTER 20

Disclosure in other Courts and Tribunals

C. ARBITRATIONS

The Court has no power to order pre-action disclosure under CPR r.31.16 against a respondent which is entitled to have any proceedings stayed in favour of arbitration: *ECO Corporation v Ultra Electronics Ltd* [2009] EWHC 682 (Ch), [2009] Bus. LR 1306; *Travelers Insurance Company Ltd v Countrywide Surveyors Ltd* [2010] EWHC 2455 (TCC). CPR r. 31.16 contemplates that any substantive proceedings be brought in the High Court. 20.04

NOTE 24. Where the arbitral tribunal has given permission pursuant to section 43 of the Arbitration Act 1996 for a party to seek a witness summons for the Court for documents (in that case telephone records), the affirmative decision of the arbitrators on the issue of necessity and relevance is entitled to respect: *Peters v Andrew* [2009] EWGC 1511 (QB) at [4]. The court declined to set aside the witness summons and rejected the argument that the applicant was fishing. 20.05

See also *L Brown & Sons Ltd v Crosby Mones (North West) Ltd* [2008] EWHC 817 (TCC) applying *Profilati v Paine Webber* [2001] 1 Lloyd's Rep. 715 in refusing to interfere with an arbitration award under s.68 of the Arbitration Act 1996. In that case Akenhead J. summarised the relevant principles at [36] as follows: 20.09

(i) The deliberate withholding of documents which had been ordered to be disclosed in the arbitration may in certain circumstances be considered to be reprehensible conduct and thus contrary to public policy under s.68(2)(g);

(ii) It must, at least, be less reprehensible (if reprehensible at all) for a party to withhold disclosure where disclosure has not as such been ordered by the arbitrator. Under some agreed or standard procedures for disclosure (for instance the IBA Rules) disclosure is voluntary unless specific documents are either agreed or ordered to be disclosed;

(iii) On balance, I consider that the withholding or non-disclosure of documents which have not been ordered to be disclosed by the arbitrator or have not been agreed to be disclosed, cannot be described as reprehensible or fraudulent unless such non-disclosure is clearly part of some other fraud or reprehensible conduct on the part of the non-disclosing party;

(iv) Lying, being not uncommon in arbitration or in civil proceedings in general, can be a basis upon which an award is obtained by fraud or in a way which is contrary to public policy but where the credibility of the witness in question was a primary feature of the arbitration or the arbitration hearing it is less likely that it will be considered to be a serious irregularity;

(v) If there are grounds under s.68(2)(g) based on lying or deception on the part of the respondent to the application, it is necessary to demonstrate that the award was dependent upon or was reached as a result of the lying or deception;

(vi) If the grounds under s.68(2)(g) are established, it is still necessary to show that substantial injustice would be caused to the applicant as a result thereof. That may prove not to be very difficult to establish if the grounds under s.68(2)(g) are established.

M. EMPLOYMENT TRIBUNALS (FORMERLY INDUSTRIAL TRIBUNALS)

20.31 In *Jones v Money Expert Ltd* [2008] UKEAT 0231 08 2208, the respondent relied at the substantive employment tribunal hearing (at which the claimant was not present, he having by then emigrated) on documents that had not been disclosed to the claimant, in breach of a case management order. This was a material irregularity that cried out for review, with the claimant being able to make a fresh witness statement dealing with the points raised in the new documents.

N. EUROPEAN COURT OF JUSTICE AND THE EUROPEAN COURT OF FIRST INSTANCE

20.37 In *Akzo Nobel Chemicals Ltd v Commission of the European Communities* (T-125/03, T-253/03) September 17, 2007, the EC Court of First Instance held that the Commission, in carrying out a search of the applicants' premises for evidence of anti-competitive practices, had infringed the procedures to be followed in such searches, in that it had (i) forced the applicants to allow the Commission to take a cursory look at documents claimed to be protected by legal privilege, and also (ii) read certain documents similarly

claimed to be privileged without having first afforded an opportunity to the applicants to contest the Commission's view that the documents were not privileged. Internal company documents may be privileged even before they have been sent to a lawyer or in some cases even if they were not intended to be sent to a lawyer. But the court rejected the argument that the privilege should be widened to cover cases where the lawyer concerned is "in-house". Only where the lawyer is independent can the privilege apply. The decision was affirmed by the European Court of Justice on 14 September 2010.

NOTE 227. Add *IFAW v European Commission* (C-64/05P) [2008] 3 W.L.R. 756, ECJ. 20.37

O. FINANCIAL SERVICES AND MARKETS TRIBUNAL

20.38 The Financial Services and Markets Tribunal has been abolished and its function subsumed by the Upper Tribunal.

W. MEDIATION

20.56 In *Brown v Patel* [2007] EWHC 625 (Ch) the court held that without prejudice communications could be considered to resolve the question whether a settlement had been reached during a mediation, and that a clause in the mediation agreement that any settlement during the mediation was not legally binding until it was reduced to writing and signed did not affect this conclusion. The judge also held that it was not necessary in that case to decide whether there was a special mediation privilege preventing admission of evidence about what happened during it. But he added that in the future it might need to be considered either by the legislature or the courts. See also *Cattley v Pollard* [2007] 2 All ER 1086. On the other hand, in *Cumbria Waste Management Ltd v Baines Wilson (A Firm)* [2008] EWHC 786 (QB), the judge said:

> "In my judgment, whether on the basis of the without prejudice rule or as an exception to the general rule that confidentiality is not a bar to disclosure, the court should support the mediation process by refusing, in normal circumstances, to order disclosure of documents and communications within a mediation.
>
> I note that the disclosure sought by the defendant is of such wide scope that it would include documents held by the mediator. In my judgement, the court should be very slow to order such disclosure. Mediators should be able to conduct mediations confident that, in normal circumstances, their papers could not be seen by the parties or others".

In *Farm Assist Ltd v Secretary of State for Environment, Food & Rural Affairs (No.2)* [2009] EWHC 1102 (TCC), [2009] B.L.R. 399, the court

upheld a witness summons directed at a mediator to give oral evidence in an action to set aside a settlement reached at the mediation. However, the facts of that case were unusual and both parties had waived the without prejudice privilege.

The European Union Directive on Mediation (2008/52/EC of 21 May 2008), Art 7, requires that member states ensure (by 21 May 2011: Art 12(1)) that mediators are not compellable to give evidence in civil proceedings or arbitrations regarding information arising out of or in connection with a mediation, except where overriding considerations of public policy otherwise require, or where disclosure of the content of a settlement agreement is necessary in order to implement or enforce it. See an article by Briggs J in (2009) 159 NLJ 506, 550.

CHAPTER 21

The Impact of the Human Rights Act 1998

PARA.

A. INTRODUCTION 21.01

B. THE RIGHT TO A FAIR HEARING 21.05

C. THE RIGHT TO RESPECT FOR PRIVATE LIFE 21.08*

D. THE RIGHT TO FREEDOM OF EXPRESSION 21.14*

E. OTHER MISCELLANEOUS RIGHTS 21.16

CHAPTER 21

The Impact of the Human Rights Act 1998

B. THE RIGHT TO A FAIR HEARING

NOTE 71. Add *Brown v Stott* [2003] 1 AC 681; *R v S & A* [2008] EWCA Crim 2177, [23]. 21.07

C. THE RIGHT TO RESPECT FOR PRIVATE LIFE

In *Wieser v Austria*, App. No.74336/01, October 16, 2007, ECtHR, the offices of a lawyer and a company that belonged to him were searched by the local Economic Police on the warrant of the local court, which had been requested to assist by an Italian court, in the context of pending Italian criminal proceedings. Certain documents or files were seized by the officers, and sealed in accordance with local law, but after only having been shown to the lawyer and the representative of the local bar association. Certain computer files were downloaded to disks, but no complete copy was made of the hard drive. Subsequently the investigating judge opened the sealed documents, and returned some to the lawyer. The ECtHR considered that the search and seizure of electronic data constituted an interference with the applicants' rights to respect for their "correspondence" within the meaning of art.8 of the ECHR. The court held that the procedural safeguards under local law were fully complied with as regards the seizure of physical documents. But they were not observed in relation to the electronic data. The court concluded: 21.08

"In conclusion, the Court finds that the police officers' failure to comply with some of the procedural safeguards designed to prevent any abuse or arbitrariness and to protect the lawyer's duty of professional secrecy rendered the search and seizure of the first applicant's electronic data disproportionate to the legitimate aim pursued.

Furthermore, the Court observes that a lawyer's duty of professional secrecy also serves to protect the client. Having regard to its above findings

that the first applicant represented companies whose shares were held by the second applicant and that the data seized contained some information subject to professional secrecy, the Court sees no reason to come to a different conclusion as regards the second applicant".

21.11 In *The Author of a Blog v Times Newspapers Ltd* [2009] EWHC 1358 (QB), Eady J held that the anonymous author of an internet 'blog' had no reasonable expectation of privacy in relation to his identity, just like a journalist who writes under a pseudonym (see *Mahmood v Galloway* [2006] EMLR 26), "because essentially blogging is a public rather than a private activity".

D. THE RIGHT TO FREEDOM OF EXPRESSION

21.15 See also *Commissioner of Police v Bermuda Broadcasting Ltd* [2008] UKPC 5 (injunction against newspaper publishing extracts from documents stolen from police refused at interlocutory stage; balancing competing interests of police in confidentiality and of the press and public in freedom of expression), and *Al Rawi v Security Service* [2010] EWCA Civ 482 (court hearing civil claim has no jurisdiction to adopt 'closed material' procedure using special advocates, instead of adopting normal procedures involving claims to PII for a large number of documents).

21.15 NOTE 164. Add *The Author of a Blog v Times Newspapers Ltd* [2009] EWHC 1358 (QB)

21.15 In *Financial Times Ltd v United Kingdom*, Application 821/03, 15 December 2009, the ECtHR held that the Uk had violated the ECHR Art 10 by virtue of the decision of the Court of Appeal in *Interbrew Ltd v Financial Times Ltd* [2002] EWCA Civ 274, ordering media organisations to deliver up documents under the *Norwich Pharmacal* principle which might identify their sources. The ECtHR held that although the order was authorised by law, with a legitimate aim, it was not "necessary in a democratic society", because "the court emphasises that a chilling effect will arise wherever journalists are seen to assist in the identification of anonymous sources" (at [70]).

21.17 In *Hickling v Baker* [2007] EWCA Civ 287 the Court of Appeal held that the procedure adopted in obtaining an order for the arrest of a bankrupt under s.364 of the Insolvency Act 1986 and following the execution of that order did not comply with Art 5 of the ECHR (right to liberty and security of person).

APPENDIX 1

Statutes

Fraud Act 2006

1 Fraud

(1) A person is guilty of fraud if he is in breach of any of the sections listed in subsection (2) (which provide for different ways of committing the offence). A.54A

(2) The sections are—

(a) section 2 (fraud by false representation),
(b) section 3 (fraud by failing to disclose information), and
(c) section 4 (fraud by abuse of position).

(3) A person who is guilty of fraud is liable—

(a) on summary conviction, to imprisonment for a term not exceeding 12 months or to a fine not exceeding the statutory maximum (or to both);
(b) on conviction on indictment, to imprisonment for a term not exceeding 10 years or to a fine (or to both).

(4) Subsection (3)(a) applies in relation to Northern Ireland as if the reference to 12 months were a reference to 6 months.

2 Fraud by false representation

(1) A person is in breach of this section if he— A.54B

(a) dishonestly makes a false representation, and
(b) intends, by making the representation—
  (i) to make a gain for himself or another, or
  (ii) to cause loss to another or to expose another to a risk of loss.

(2) A representation is false if—

(a) it is untrue or misleading, and
(b) the person making it knows that it is, or might be, untrue or misleading.

(3) "Representation" means any representation as to fact or law, including a representation as to the state of mind of—

(a) the person making the representation, or
(b) any other person.

(4) A representation may be express or implied.

(5) For the purposes of this section a representation may be regarded as made if it (or anything implying it) is submitted in any form to any system or device designed to receive, convey or respond to communications (with or without human intervention).

3 Fraud by failing to disclose information

A.54C A person is in breach of this section if he—

(a) dishonestly fails to disclose to another person information which he is under a legal duty to disclose, and
(b) intends, by failing to disclose the information—
   (i) to make a gain for himself or another, or
   (ii) to cause loss to another or to expose another to a risk of loss.

4 Fraud by abuse of position

A.54D (1) A person is in breach of this section if he—

(a) occupies a position in which he is expected to safeguard, or not to act against, the financial interests of another person,
(b) dishonestly abuses that position, and
(c) intends, by means of the abuse of that position—
   (i) to make a gain for himself or another, or
   (ii) to cause loss to another or to expose another to a risk of loss.

(2) A person may be regarded as having abused his position even though his conduct consisted of an omission rather than an act.

5 "Gain" and "loss"

A.54E (1) The references to gain and loss in sections 2 to 4 are to be read in accordance with this section.

(2) "Gain" and "loss"—

(a) extend only to gain or loss in money or other property;
(b) include any such gain or loss whether temporary or permanent;

and "property" means any property whether real or personal (including things in action and other intangible property).

(3) "Gain" includes a gain by keeping what one has, as well as a gain by getting what one does not have.

(4) "Loss" includes a loss by not getting what one might get, as well as a loss by parting with what one has.

6 Possession etc. of articles for use in frauds

A.54F (1) A person is guilty of an offence if he has in his possession or under his control any article for use in the course of or in connection with any fraud.

(2) A person guilty of an offence under this section is liable—

(a) on summary conviction, to imprisonment for a term not exceeding 12 months or to a fine not exceeding the statutory maximum (or to both);
(b) on conviction on indictment, to imprisonment for a term not exceeding 5 years or to a fine (or to both).

(3) Subsection (2)(a) applies in relation to Northern Ireland as if the reference to 12 months were a reference to 6 months.

7 Making or supplying articles for use in frauds

(1) A person is guilty of an offence if he makes, adapts, supplies or offers to supply any article— A.54G

(a) knowing that it is designed or adapted for use in the course of or in connection with fraud, or
(b) intending it to be used to commit, or assist in the commission of, fraud.

(2) A person guilty of an offence under this section is liable—

(a) on summary conviction, to imprisonment for a term not exceeding 12 months or to a fine not exceeding the statutory maximum (or to both);
(b) on conviction on indictment, to imprisonment for a term not exceeding 10 years or to a fine (or to both).

(3) Subsection (2)(a) applies in relation to Northern Ireland as if the reference to 12 months were a reference to 6 months.

8 "Article"

(1) For the purposes of— A.54H

(a) sections 6 and 7, and
(b) the provisions listed in subsection (2), so far as they relate to articles for use in the course of or in connection with fraud,

"article" includes any program or data held in electronic form.

(2) The provisions are—

(a) section 1(7)(b) of the Police and Criminal Evidence Act 1984 (c. 60),
(b) section 2(8)(b) of the Armed Forces Act 2001 (c. 19), and
(c) Article 3(7)(b) of the Police and Criminal Evidence (Northern Ireland) Order 1989 (S.I. 1989/1341 (N.I. 12));

(meaning of "prohibited articles" for the purposes of stop and search powers).

9 Participating in fraudulent business carried on by sole trader etc.

(1) A person is guilty of an offence if he is knowingly a party to the carrying on of a business to which this section applies. A.54I

(2) This section applies to a business which is carried on—

(a) by a person who is outside the reach of section 458 of the Companies Act 1985 (c. 6) or Article 451 of the Companies (Northern Ireland) Order 1986 (S.I. 1986/1032) (N.I. 6)) (offence of fraudulent trading), and
(b) with intent to defraud creditors of any person or for any other fraudulent purpose.

(3) The following are within the reach of section 458 of the 1985 Act—

(a) a company (within the meaning of that Act);
(b) a person to whom that section applies (with or without adaptations or modifications) as if the person were a company;
(c) a person exempted from the application of that section.

(4) The following are within the reach of Article 451 of the 1986 Order—

(a) a company (within the meaning of that Order);
(b) a person to whom that Article applies (with or without adaptations or modifications) as if the person were a company;
(c) a person exempted from the application of that Article.

(5) "Fraudulent purpose" has the same meaning as in section 458 of the 1985 Act or Article 451 of the 1986 Order.

(6) A person guilty of an offence under this section is liable—

(a) on summary conviction, to imprisonment for a term not exceeding 12 months or to a fine not exceeding the statutory maximum (or to both);
(b) on conviction on indictment, to imprisonment for a term not exceeding 10 years or to a fine (or to both).

(7) Subsection (6)(a) applies in relation to Northern Ireland as if the reference to 12 months were a reference to 6 months.

10 Participating in fraudulent business carried on by company etc.: penalty

A.54J (1) In Schedule 24 to the Companies Act 1985 (punishment of offences), in column 4 of the entry relating to section 458 of that Act, for "7 years" substitute "10 years".

(2) In Schedule 23 to the Companies (Northern Ireland) Order 1986 (punishment of offences), in column 4 of the entry relating to Article 451 of that Order, for "7 years" substitute "10 years".

Obtaining services dishonestly

11 Obtaining services dishonestly

A.54K (1) A person is guilty of an offence under this section if he obtains services for himself or another—

(a) by a dishonest act, and
(b) in breach of subsection (2).

(2) A person obtains services in breach of this subsection if—

(a) they are made available on the basis that payment has been, is being or will be made for or in respect of them,
(b) he obtains them without any payment having been made for or in respect of them or without payment having been made in full, and
(c) when he obtains them, he knows—
    (i) that they are being made available on the basis described in paragraph (a), or
    (ii) that they might be,

but intends that payment will not be made, or will not be made in full.

(3) A person guilty of an offence under this section is liable—

(a) on summary conviction, to imprisonment for a term not exceeding 12 months or to a fine not exceeding the statutory maximum (or to both);
(b) on conviction on indictment, to imprisonment for a term not exceeding 5 years or to a fine (or to both).

(4) Subsection (3)(a) applies in relation to Northern Ireland as if the reference to 12 months were a reference to 6 months.

Supplementary

[. . .]

13 Evidence

(1) A person is not to be excused from— A.54L

(a) answering any question put to him in proceedings relating to property, or
(b) complying with any order made in proceedings relating to property,

on the ground that doing so may incriminate him or his spouse or civil partner of an offence under this Act or a related offence.

(2) But, in proceedings for an offence under this Act or a related offence, a statement or admission made by the person in—

(a) answering such a question, or
(b) complying with such an order,

is not admissible in evidence against him or (unless they married or became civil partners after the making of the statement or admission) his spouse or civil partner.

(3) "Proceedings relating to property" means any proceedings for—

(a) the recovery or administration of any property,
(b) the execution of a trust, or
(c) an account of any property or dealings with property,

and "property" means money or other property whether real or personal (including things in action and other intangible property).

[. . .]

APPENDIX 2

Rules of Court

Practice Direction — further information

This Practice Direction supplements CPR Part 18
Attention is also drawn to Part 22 (Statement of Truth).

Preliminary Request for Further Information or Clarification

1.1 Before making an application to the court for an order under Part 18, the party seeking clarification or information (the first party) should first serve on the party from whom it is sought (the second party) a written request for that clarification or information (a Request) stating a date by which the response to the Request should be served. The date must allow the second party a reasonable time to respond. B.02

1.2 A Request should be concise and strictly confined to matters which are reasonably necessary and proportionate to enable the first party to prepare his own case or to understand the case he has to meet.

1.3 Requests must be made as far as possible in a single comprehensive document and not piecemeal.

1.4 A Request may be made by letter if the text of the Request is brief and the reply is likely to be brief; otherwise the Request should be made in a separate document.

1.5 If a Request is made in a letter, the letter should, in order to distinguish it from any other that might routinely be written in the course of a case,

(1) state that it contains a Request made under Part 18, and
(2) deal with no matters other than the Request.

1.6 (1) A Request (whether made by letter or in a separate document) must—

(a) be headed with the name of the court and the title and number of the claim,
(b) in its heading state that it is a Request made under Part 18, identify the first party and the second party and state the date on which it is made,
(c) set out in a separate numbered paragraph each request for information or clarification,
(d) where a Request relates to a document, identify that document and (if relevant) the paragraph or words to which it relates,

(e) state the date by which the first party expects a response to the Request.

(2) (a) A Request which is not in the form of a letter may, if convenient, be prepared in such a way that the response may be given on the same document.

(b) To do this the numbered paragraphs of the Request should appear on the left hand half of each sheet so that the paragraphs of the response may then appear on the right.

(c) Where a Request is prepared in this form an extra copy should be served for the use of the second party.

1.7 Subject to the provisions of rule 6.23(5) and (6) and paragraphs 4.1 to 4.3 of Practice Direction A supplementing Part 6, a request should be served by e-mail if reasonably practicable.

Responding to a Request

2.1 A response to a Request must be in writing, dated and signed by the second party or his legal representative.

2.2 (1) Where the Request is made in a letter the second party may give his response in a letter or in a formal reply.

(2) Such a letter should identify itself as a response to the Request and deal with no other matters than the response.

2.3 (1) Unless the Request is in the format described in paragraph 1.6(2) and the second party uses the document supplied for the purpose, a response must:

(a) be headed with the name of the court and the title and number of the claim,

(b) in its heading identify itself as a response to that Request,

(c) repeat the text of each separate paragraph of the Request and set out under each paragraph the response to it,

(d) refer to and have attached to it a copy of any document not already in the possession of the first party which forms part of the response.

(2) A second or supplementary response to a Request must identify itself as such in its heading.

2.4 The second party must when he serves his response on the first party serve on every other party and file with the court a copy of the Request and of his response.

Statements of Truth

3 Attention is drawn to Part 22 and to the definition of a statement of case in Part 2 of the rules; a response should be verified by a statement of truth.

General Matters

4.1 (1) If the second party objects to complying with the Request or part of it or is unable to do so at all or within the time stated in the Request he must inform the first party promptly and in any event within that time.

(2) He may do so in a letter or in a separate document (a formal response), but in either case he must give reasons and, where relevant, give a date by which he expects to be able to comply.

4.2 (1) There is no need for a second party to apply to the court if he objects to a Request or is unable to comply with it at all or within the stated time. He need only comply with paragraph 4.1(1) above.

(2) Where a second party considers that a Request can only be complied with at disproportionate expense and objects to comply for that reason he should say so in his reply and explain briefly why he has taken that view.

Applications for Orders under Part 18

5.1 Attention is drawn to Part 23 (Applications) and to the Practice Direction which supplements that Part.

5.2 An application notice for an order under Part 18 should set out or have attached to it the text of the order sought and in particular should specify the matter or matters in respect of which the clarification or information is sought.

5.3 (1) If a Request under paragraph 1 for the information or clarification has not been made, the application notice should, in addition, explain why not.

(2) If a Request for clarification or information has been made, the application notice or the evidence in support should describe the response, if any.

5.4 Both the first party and the second party should consider whether evidence in support of or in opposition to the application is required.

5.5 (1) Where the second party has made no response to a Request served on him, the first party need not serve the application notice on the second party, and the court may deal with the application without a hearing.

(2) Sub-paragraph (1) above only applies if at least 14 days have passed since the Request was served and the time stated in it for a response has expired.

5.6 Unless paragraph 5.5 applies the application notice must be served on the second party and on all other parties to the claim.

5.7 An order made under Part 18 must be served on all parties to the claim.

5.8 Costs:

(1) Attention is drawn to the Costs Practice Direction and in particular the court's power to make a summary assessment of costs.

(2) Attention is also drawn to rule 44.13(1) which provides that the general rule is that if an order does not mention costs no party is entitled to costs relating to that order.

Part 31

Disclosure and Inspection of Documents

Amended September 28, 2000, in force October 2, 2000

Contents

31.1 Scope of this Part B.03
31.2 Meaning of disclosure
31.3 Right of inspection of a disclosed document
31.4 Meaning of document
31.5 Disclosure limited to standard disclosure
31.6 Standard disclosure—what documents are to be disclosed

31.7 Duty of search
31.8 Duty of disclosure limited to documents which are or have been in a party's control
31.8 Duty of disclosure limited to documents which are or have been in a party's control
31.9 Disclosure of copies
31.10 Procedure for standard disclosure
31.11 Duty of disclosure continues during proceedings
31.12 Specific disclosure or inspection
31.13 Disclosure in stages
31.14 Documents referred to in statements of case etc.
31.15 Inspection and copying of documents
31.16 Disclosure before proceedings start
31.17 Orders for disclosure against a person not a party
31.18 Rules not to limit other powers of the court to order disclosure
31.19 Claim to withhold inspection or disclosure of a document
31.20 Restriction on use of a privileged document inspection of which has been inadvertently allowed
31.21 Consequence of failure to disclose documents or permit inspection
31.22 Subsequent use of disclosed documents
31.23 False Disclosure Statements
[Inserted September 28, 2000, in force October 2, 2000]

Scope of this part

31.1—(1) This Part sets out rules about the disclosure and inspection of documents.

(2) This Part applies to all claims except a claim on the small claims track.

Meaning of disclosure

31.2 A party discloses a document by stating that the document exists or has existed.

Right of inspection of a disclosed document

31.3—(1) A party to whom a document has been disclosed has a right to inspect that document except where—

(a) the document is no longer in the control of the party who disclosed it;
(b) the party disclosing the document has a right or a duty to withhold inspection of it; or
(c) paragraph (2) applies.

(Rule 31.8 sets out when a document is in the control of a party)
(Rule 31.19 sets out the procedure for claiming a right or duty to withhold inspection)

(2) Where a party considers that it would be disproportionate to the issues in the case to permit inspection of documents within a category or class of document disclosed under rule 31.6(b)—

(a) he is not required to permit inspection of documents within that category or class; but
(b) he must state in his disclosure statement that inspection of those documents will not be permitted on the grounds that to do so would be disproportionate.

(Rule 31.6 provides for standard disclosure)

(Rule 31.10 makes provision for a disclosure statement)
(Rule 31.12 provides for a party to apply for an order for specific inspection of documents)

Meaning of document

31.4 In this Part—

"document" means anything in which information of any description is recorded; and

"copy", in relation to a document, means anything onto which information recorded in the document has been copied, by whatever means and whether directly or indirectly.

Disclosure limited to standard disclosure

31.5—(1) An order to give disclosure is an order to give standard disclosure unless the court directs otherwise.

(2) The court may dispense with or limit standard disclosure.

(3) The parties may agree in writing to dispense with or to limit standard disclosure.

(The court may make an order requiring standard disclosure under rule 28.3 which deals with directions in relation to cases on the fast track and under rule 29.2 which deals with case management in relation to cases on the multi-track)

Standard disclosure—what documents are to be disclosed

31.6 Standard disclosure requires a party to disclose only—

(a) the documents on which he relies; and
(b) the documents which—

  (i) adversely affect his own case;
  (ii) adversely affect another party's case; or
  (iii) support another party's case; and

(c) the documents which he is required to disclose by a relevant practice direction.

Duty of search

31.7—(1) When giving standard disclosure, a party is required to make a reasonable search for documents falling within rule 31.6(b) or (c).

(2) The factors relevant in deciding the reasonableness of a search include the following—

(a) the number of documents involved;
(b) the nature and complexity of the proceedings;
(c) the ease and expense of retrieval of any particular document; and
(d) the significance of any document which is likely to be located during the search.

(3) Where a party has not searched for a category or class of document on the grounds that to do so would be unreasonable, he must state this in his disclosure statement and identify the category or class of document.

(Rule 31.10 makes provision for a disclosure statement)

Duty of disclosure limited to documents which are or have been in a party's control

31.8—(1) A party's duty to disclose documents is limited to documents which are or have been in his control.

(2) For this purpose a party has or has had a document in his control if—

(a) it is or was in his physical possession;
(b) he has or has had a right to possession of it; or
(c) he has or has had a right to inspect or take copies of it.

Disclosure of copies

31.9—(1) A party need not disclose more than one copy of a document.
(2) A copy of a document that contains a modification, obliteration or other marking or feature—

(a) on which a party intends to rely; or
(b) which adversely affects his own case or another party's case or supports another party's case;

shall be treated as a separate document.
(Rule 31.4 sets out the meaning of a copy of a document)

Procedure for standard disclosure

31.10—(1) The procedure for standard disclosure is as follows.
(2) Each party must make and serve on every other party, a list of documents in the relevant practice form.
(3) The list must identify the documents in a convenient order and manner and as concisely as possible.
(4) The list must indicate—

(a) those documents in respect of which the party claims a right or duty to withhold inspection; and
(b) (i) those documents which are no longer in the party's control; and
(ii) what has happended to those documents.

(Rule 31.19(3) and (4) require a statement in the list of documents relating to any documents inspection of which a person claims he has a right or duty to withhold)
(5) The list must include a disclosure statement.
(6) A disclosure statement is a statement made by the party disclosing the documents—

(a) setting out the extent of the search that has been made to locate documents which he is required to disclose;
(b) certifying that he understands the duty to disclose documents; and
(c) certifying that to the best of his knowledge he has carried out that duty.

(7) Where the party making the disclosure statement is a company, firm, association or other organisation, the statement must also—

(a) identify the person making the statement; and
(b) explain why he is considered an appropriate person to make the statement.

(8) The parties may agree in writing—

(a) to disclose documents without making a list; and
(b) to disclose documents without the disclosing party making a disclosure statement.

(9) A disclosure statement may be made by a person who is not a party where this is permitted by a relevant practice direction.

Duty of disclosure continues during proceedings

31.11—(1) Any duty of disclosure continues until the proceedings are concluded.

(2) If documents to which that duty extends come to a party's notice at any time during the proceedings, he must immediately notify every other party.

Specific disclosure or inspection

31.12—(1) The court may make an order for specific disclosure or specific inspection.

(2) An order for specific disclosure is an order that a party must do one or more of the following things—

(a) disclose documents or classes of documents specified in the order;
(b) carry out a search to the extent stated in the order;
(c) disclose any documents located as a result of that search.

(3) An order for specific inspection is an order that a party permit inspection of a document referred to in rule 31.3(2).

(Rule 31.3(2) allows a party to state in his disclosure statement that he will not permit inspection of a document on the grounds that it would be disproportionate to do so)

Disclosure in stages

31.13 The parties may agree in writing, or the court may direct, that disclosure or inspection or both shall take place in stages.

Documents referred to in statements of case etc.

31.14—(1) A party may inspect a document mentioned in—

(a) a statement of case;
(b) a witness statement;
(c) a witness summary;
(d) an affidavit; or
(e) [. . .]*

(2) Subject to rule 35.10(4), a party may apply for an order for inspection of any document mentioned in an expert's report which has not already been disclosed in the proceedings.

(Rule 35.10(4) makes provision in relation to instructions referred to in an expert's report)

Inspection and copying of documents

31.15 Where a party has a right to inspect a document—

(a) that party must give the party who disclosed the document written notice of his wish to inspect it;
(b) the party who disclosed the document must permit inspection not more than 7 days after the date on which he received the notice; and
(c) that party may request a copy of the document and, if he also undertakes to pay reasonable copying costs, the party who disclosed the document must supply him with a copy not more than 7 days after the date on which he received the request.

(Rules 31.3 and 31.14 deal with the right of a party to inspect a document)

* Revoked by Civ Proc (Amdt No 5) Rules 2001 SI 2001/4015.

Disclosure before proceedings start

31.16—(1) This rule applies where an application is made to the court under any Act for disclosure before proceedings have started.[1]

(2) The application must be supported by evidence.

(3) The court may make an order under this rule only where—

(a) the respondent is likely to be a party to subsequent proceedings;
(b) the applicant is also likely to be a party to those proceedings;
(c) if proceedings had started, the respondent's duty by way of standard disclosure, set out in rule 31.6, would extend to the documents or classes of documents of which the applicant seeks disclosure; and
(d) disclosure before proceedings have started is desirable in order to—

(i) dispose fairly of the anticipated proceedings;
(ii) assist the dispute to be resolved without proceedings; or
(iii) save costs.

(4) An order under this rule must—

(a) specify the documents or the classes of documents which the responent must disclose; and
(b) require him, when making disclosure, to specify any of those documents—

(i) which are no longer in his control; or
(ii) in respect of which he claims a right or duty to withhold inspection.

(5) Such an order may—

(a) require the respondent to indicate what has happened to any document which are no longer in his control; and
(b) specify the time and place for disclosure and inspection.

Orders for disclosure against a person not a party

31.17—(1) This rule applies where an application is made to the court under any Act for disclosure by a person who is not a party to the proceedings.[2]

(2) The application must be supported by evidence.

(3) The court may make an order under this rule only where—

(a) the documents of which disclosure is sought are likely to support the case of the applicant or adversely affect the case of one of the other parties to the proceedings; and
(b) disclosure is necessary in order to dispose fairly of the claim or to save costs.

(4) An order under this rule must—

(a) specify the documents or the classes of documents which the respondent must disclose; and
(b) require the respondent, when making disclosure, to specify any of those documents—

(i) which are no longer in his control; or

[1] An application for disclosure before proceedings have started is permitted under section 33 of the Supreme Court Act 1981 (c.54) or section 52 of the County Courts Act 1984 (c. 28).

[2] An application for disclosure against a person who is not a party to proceedings is permitted under section 34 of the Supreme Court Act 1981 or section 53 of the County Courts Act 1984.

(ii) in respect of which he claims a right or duty to withhold inspection.

(5) Such an order may—

(a) require the respondent to indicate what has happened to any documents which are no longer in his control; and
(b) specify the time and place for disclosure and inspection.

Rules not to limit other powers of the court to order disclosure

31.18 Rules 31.16 and 31.17 do not limit any other power which the court may have to order—

(a) disclosure before proceedings have started; and
(b) disclosure against a person who is not a party to proceedings.

Claim to withhold inspection or disclosure of a document

31.19—(1) A person may apply, without notice, for an order permitting him to withhold disclosure of a document on the ground that disclosure would damage the public interest.

(2) Unless the court orders otherwise, an order of the court under paragraph (1)—

(a) must not be served on any other person; and
(b) must not be open to inspection by any person.

(3) A person who wishes to claim that he has a right or a duty to withhold inspection of a document, or part of a document must state in writing—

(a) that he has such a right or duty; and
(b) the grounds on which he claims that right or duty.

(4) The statement referred to in paragraph (3) must be made—

(a) in the list in which the document is disclosed; or
(b) if there is no list, to the person wishing to inspect the document.

(5) A party may apply to the court to decide whether a claim made under paragraph (3) should be upheld.

(6) For the purpose of deciding an application under paragraph (1) (application to withhold disclosure) or paragraph (3) (claim to withhold inspection) the court may—

(a) require the person seeking to withhold disclosure or inspection of a document to produce that document to the court; and
(b) invite any person, whether or not a party, to make representations.

(7) An application under paragraph (1) or paragraph (5) must be supported by evidence.

(8) This Part does not affect any rule of law which permits or requires a document to be withheld from disclosure or inspection on the ground that its disclosure or inspection would damage the public interest.

Restriction on use of a privileged document inspection of which has been inadvertently allowed

31.20 Where a party inadvertently allows a privileged document to be inspected, the party who has inspected the document may use it or its contents only with the permission of the court.

Consequence of failure to disclose documents or permit inspection

31.21 A party may not rely on any document which he fails to disclose or in respect of which he fails to permit inspection unless the court gives permission.

Subsequent use of disclosed documents and completed Electronic Documents *Questionnaires*

31.22—(1) A party to whom a document has been disclosed may use the document only for the purpose of the proceedings in which it is disclosed, except where—

(a) the document has been read to or by the court, or referred to, at a hearing which has been held in public;
(b) the court gives permission; or
(c) the party who disclosed the document and the person to whom the document belongs agree.

(2) The court may make an order restricting or prohibiting the use of a document which has been disclosed, even where the document has been read to or by the court, or referred to, at a hearing which has been held in public.

(3) An application for such an order may be made—

(a) by a party; or
(b) by any person to whom the document belongs.

(4) For the purpose of this rule, an Electronic Documents Questionnaire which has been completed and served by another party pursuant to Practice Direction 31B is to be treated as if it is a document which has been disclosed.

[False disclosure statements

31.23—(1) Proceedings for contempt of court may be brought against a person if he makes, or causes to be made, a false disclosure statement, without an honest belief in its truth.

(2) Proceedings under this rule may be brought only—

(a) by the Attorney General; or
(b) with the permission of the court.][3]

PRACTICE DIRECTION 31B: DISCLOSURE OF ELECTRONIC DOCUMENTS

This Practice Direction supplements CPR Part 31

Purpose, scope and interpretation

1. Rule 31.4 contains a broad definition of "document". This extends to Electronic Documents.
2. The purpose of this Practice Direction is to encourage and assist the parties to reach agreement in relation to the disclosure of Electronic Documents in a proportionate and cost-effective manner.
3. Unless the court orders otherwise, this Practice Direction only applies to proceedings that are (or are likely to be) allocated to the multi-track.
4. Unless the court orders otherwise, this Practice Direction only applies to proceedings started on or after 1st October 2010. Paragraph 2A.2 to 2A.5 of Practice Direction 31A in force immediately before that date continues to apply to proceedings started before that date.

[3] Added by the Civil Procedure (Amendment) Rules 2000, r.16.

5. In this Practice Direction—

(1) "Data Sampling" means the process of checking data by identifying and checking representative individual documents;
(2) "Disclosure Data" means data relating to disclosed documents, including for example the type of document, the date of the document, the names of the author or sender and the recipient, and the party disclosing the document;
(3) "Electronic Document" means any document held in electronic form. It includes, for example, e-mail and other electronic communications such as text messages and voicemail, word-processed documents and databases, and documents stored on portable devices such as memory sticks and mobile phones. In addition to documents that are readily accessible from computer systems and other electronic devices and media, it includes documents that are stored on servers and back-up systems and documents that have been deleted. It also includes Metadata and other embedded data which is not typically visible on screen or a print out;
(4) "Electronic Image" means an electronic representation of a paper document;
(5) "Electronic Documents Questionnaire" means the questionnaire in the Schedule to this Practice Direction;
(6) "Keyword Search" means a software-aided search for words across the text of an Electronic Document;
(7) "Metadata" is data about data. In the case of an Electronic Document, Metadata is typically embedded information about the document which is not readily accessible once the Native Electronic Document has been converted into an Electronic Image or paper document. It may include (for example) the date and time of creation or modification of a word-processing file, or the author and the date and time of sending an e-mail. Metadata may be created automatically by a computer system or manually by a user;
(8) "Native Electronic Document" or "Native Format" means an Electronic Document stored in the original form in which it was created by a computer software program; and
(9) "Optical Character Recognition (OCR)" means the computer-facilitated recognition of printed or written text characters in an Electronic Image in which the text-based contents cannot be searched electronically.

General principles

6. When considering disclosure of Electronic Documents, the parties and their legal representatives should bear in mind the following general principles—

(1) Electronic Documents should be managed efficiently in order to minimise the cost incurred;
(2) technology should be used in order to ensure that document management activities are undertaken efficiently and effectively;
(3) disclosure should be given in a manner which gives effect to the overriding objective;
(4) Electronic Documents should generally be made available for inspection in a form which allows the party receiving the documents the same ability to access, search, review and display the documents as the party giving disclosure; and
(5) disclosure of Electronic Documents which are of no relevance to the proceedings may place an excessive burden in time and cost on the party to whom disclosure is given.

Preservation of documents

7. As soon as litigation is contemplated, the parties' legal representatives must notify their clients of the need to preserve disclosable documents. The documents to be preserved include Electronic Documents which would otherwise be deleted in accordance with a document retention policy or otherwise deleted in the ordinary course of business.

Discussions between the parties before the first Case Management Conference in relation to the use of technology and disclosure

8. The parties and their legal representatives must, before the first case management conference, discuss the use of technology in the management of Electronic Documents and the conduct of proceedings, in particular for the purpose of—

   (1) creating lists of documents to be disclosed;
   (2) giving disclosure by providing documents and information regarding documents in electronic format; and
   (3) presenting documents and other material to the court at the trial.

9. The parties and their legal representatives must also, before the first case management conference, discuss the disclosure of Electronic Documents. In some cases (for example heavy and complex cases) it may be appropriate to begin discussions before proceedings are commenced. The discussions should include (where appropriate) the following matters—

   (1) the categories of Electronic Documents within the parties' control, the computer systems, electronic devices and media on which any relevant documents may be held, storage systems and document retention policies;
   (2) the scope of the reasonable search for Electronic Documents required by rule 31.7;
   (3) the tools and techniques (if any) which should be considered to reduce the burden and cost of disclosure of Electronic Documents, including—

      (a) limiting disclosure of documents or certain categories of documents to particular date ranges, to particular custodians of documents, or to particular types of documents;
      (b) the use of agreed Keyword Searches;
      (c) the use of agreed software tools;
      (d) the methods to be used to identify duplicate documents;
      (e) the use of Data Sampling;
      (f) the methods to be used to identify privileged documents and other non-disclosable documents, to redact documents (where redaction is appropriate), and for dealing with privileged or other documents which have been inadvertently disclosed; and
      (g) the use of a staged approach to the disclosure of Electronic Documents;

   (4) the preservation of Electronic Documents, with a view to preventing loss of such documents before the trial;
   (5) the exchange of data relating to Electronic Documents in an agreed electronic format using agreed fields;
   (6) the formats in which Electronic Documents are to be provided on inspection and the methods to be used;
   (7) the basis of charging for or sharing the cost of the provision of Electronic Documents, and whether any arrangements for charging or sharing of

costs are final or are subject to re-allocation in accordance with any order for costs subsequently made; and

(8) whether it would be appropriate to use the services of a neutral electronic repository for storage of Electronic Documents.

The Electronic Documents Questionnaire

10. In some cases the parties may find it helpful to exchange the Electronic Documents Questionnaire in order to provide information to each other in relation to the scope, extent and most suitable format for disclosure of Electronic Documents in the proceedings.
11. The answers to the Electronic Documents Questionnaire must be verified by a statement of truth.
12. Answers to the Electronic Documents Questionnaire will only be available for inspection by non-parties if permission is given under rule 5.4C(2).
13. Rule 31.22 makes provision regulating the use of answers to the Electronic Documents Questionnaire.

Preparation for the first Case Management Conference

14. The documents submitted to the court in advance of the first case management conference should include a summary of the matters on which the parties agree in relation to the disclosure of Electronic Documents and a summary of the matters on which they disagree.
15. If the parties indicate that they have been unable to reach agreement in relation to the disclosure of Electronic Documents and that no agreement is likely, the court will give written directions in relation to disclosure or order a separate hearing in relation to disclosure. When doing so, the court will consider making an order that the parties must complete and exchange all or any part of the Electronic Documents Questionnaire within 14 days or such other period as the court may direct.
16. The person signing the Electronic Documents Questionnaire should attend the first case management conference, and any subsequent hearing at which disclosure is likely to be considered.

Where the parties are unable to reach an appropriate agreement in relation to the disclosure of Electronic Documents

17. If at any time it becomes apparent that the parties are unable to reach agreement in relation to the disclosure of Electronic Documents, the parties should seek directions from the court at the earliest practical date.
18. If the court considers that the parties' agreement in relation to the disclosure of Electronic Documents is inappropriate or insufficient, the court will give directions in relation to disclosure. When doing so, the court will consider making an order that the parties must complete and exchange all or any part of the Electronic Documents Questionnaire within 14 days or such other period as the court may direct.
19. If a party gives disclosure of Electronic Documents without first discussing with other parties how to plan and manage such disclosure, the court may require that party to carry out further searches for documents or to repeat other steps which that party has already carried out.

The reasonable search

20. The extent of the reasonable search required by rule 31.7 for the purposes of standard disclosure is affected by the existence of Electronic Documents. The extent of the search which must be made will depend on the circumstances of

the case including, in particular, the factors referred to in rule 31.7(2). The parties should bear in mind that the overriding objective includes dealing with the case in ways which are proportionate.

21. The factors that may be relevant in deciding the reasonableness of a search for Electronic Documents include (but are not limited to) the following—

    (1) the number of documents involved;
    (2) the nature and complexity of the proceedings;
    (3) the ease and expense of retrieval of any particular document. This includes:

        (a) the accessibility of Electronic Documents including e-mail communications on computer systems, servers, back-up systems and other electronic devices or media that may contain such documents taking into account alterations or developments in hardware or software systems used by the disclosing party and/or available to enable access to such documents;
        (b) the location of relevant Electronic Documents, data, computer systems, servers, back-up systems and other electronic devices or media that may contain such documents;
        (c) the likelihood of locating relevant data;
        (d) the cost of recovering any Electronic Documents;
        (e) the cost of disclosing and providing inspection of any relevant Electronic Documents; and
        (f) the likelihood that Electronic Documents will be materially altered in the course of recovery, disclosure or inspection;

    (4) the availability of documents or contents of documents from other sources; and
    (5) the significance of any document which is likely to be located during the search.

22. Depending on the circumstances, it may be reasonable to search all of the parties' electronic storage systems, or to search only some part of those systems. For example, it may be reasonable to decide not to search for documents coming into existence before a particular date, or to limit the search to documents in a particular place or places, or to documents falling into particular categories.
23. In some cases a staged approach may be appropriate, with disclosure initially being given of limited categories of documents. Those categories may subsequently be extended or limited depending on the results initially obtained.
24. The primary source of disclosure of Electronic Documents is normally reasonably accessible data. A party requesting under rule 31.12 specific disclosure of Electronic Documents which are not reasonably accessible must demonstrate that the relevance and materiality justify the cost and burden of retrieving and producing it.

Keyword and other automated searches

25. It may be reasonable to search for Electronic Documents by means of Keyword Searches or other automated methods of searching if a full review of each and every document would be unreasonable.
26. However, it will often be insufficient to use simple Keyword Searches or other automated methods of searching alone. The injudicious use of Keyword Searches and other automated search techniques—

(1) may result in failure to find important documents which ought to be disclosed, and/or
(2) may find excessive quantities of irrelevant documents, which if disclosed would place an excessive burden in time and cost on the party to whom disclosure is given.

27. The parties should consider supplementing Keyword Searches and other automated searches with additional techniques such as individually reviewing certain documents or categories of documents (for example important documents generated by key personnel) and taking such other steps as may be required in order to justify the selection to the court.

Disclosure of Metadata

28. Where copies of disclosed documents are provided in Native Format in accordance with paragraph 33 below, some Metadata will be disclosed with each document. A party requesting disclosure of additional Metadata or forensic image copies of disclosed documents (for example in relation to a dispute concerning authenticity) must demonstrate that the relevance and materiality of the requested Metadata justify the cost and burden of producing that Metadata.
29. Parties using document management or litigation support systems should be alert to the possibility that Metadata or other useful information relating to documents may not be stored with the documents.

Lists of Documents

30. If a party is giving disclosure of Electronic Documents, paragraph 3 of Practice Direction 31A is to be read subject to the following—

(1) Form N265 may be amended to accommodate the sub-paragraphs which follow;
(2) a list of documents may by agreement between the parties be an electronic file in .csv (comma-separated values) or other agreed format;
(3) documents may be listed otherwise than in date order where a different order would be more convenient;
(4) save where otherwise agreed or ordered, documents should be listed individually if a party already possesses data relating to the document (for example, type of document and date of creation) which make this possible (so that as far as possible each document may be given a unique reference number);
(5) a party should be consistent in the way in which documents are listed;
(6) consistent column headings should be repeated on each page of the list on which documents are listed, where the software used for preparing the list enables this to be carried out automatically; and
(7) the disclosure list number used in any supplemental list of documents should be unique and should run sequentially from the last number used in the previous list.

Provision of Disclosure Data in electronic form

31. Where a party provides another party with Disclosure Data in electronic form, the following provisions will apply unless the parties agree or the court directs otherwise—

(1) Disclosure Data should be set out in a single, continuous table or spreadsheet, each separate column containing exclusively one of the following types of Disclosure Data—

(a) disclosure list number (sequential)
(b) date
(c) document type
(d) author/sender
(e) recipient
(f) disclosure list number of any parent or covering document;

(2) other than for disclosure list numbers, blank entries are permissible and preferred if there is no relevant Disclosure Data (that is, the field should be left blank rather than state "Undated");
(3) dates should be set out in the alphanumeric form "01 Jan 2010"; and
(4) Disclosure Data should be set out in a consistent manner.

Provision of electronic copies of disclosed documents

32. The parties should co-operate at an early stage about the format in which Electronic Documents are to be provided on inspection. In the case of difficulty or disagreement, the matter should be referred to the court for directions at the earliest practical date, if possible at the first case management conference.
33. Save where otherwise agreed or ordered, electronic copies of disclosed documents should be provided in their Native Format, in a manner which preserves Metadata relating to the date of creation of each document.
34. A party should provide any available searchable OCR versions of Electronic Documents with the original. A party may however choose not to provide OCR versions of documents which have been redacted. If OCR versions are provided, they are provided on an "as is" basis, with no assurance to the other party that the OCR versions are complete or accurate.
35. (1) Subject to sub-paragraph (2) below, if a party is providing in electronic form copies of disclosed documents and wishes to redact or otherwise make alterations to a document or documents, then—

(a) the party redacting or altering the document must inform the other party in accordance with rule 31.19 that redacted or altered versions are being supplied; and
(b) the party redacting or altering the document must ensure that the original unredacted and unaltered version is preserved, so that it remains available to be inspected if required.

(2) Sub-paragraph (1) above does not apply where the only alteration made to the document is an alteration to the Metadata as a result of the ordinary process of copying and/or accessing the document. Sub-paragraph (1) does apply to the alteration or suppression of Metadata in other situations.

Specialised technology

36. If Electronic Documents are best accessed using technology which is not readily available to the party entitled to disclosure, and that party reasonably requires additional inspection facilities, the party making disclosure shall co-operate in making available to the other party such reasonable additional inspection facilities as may be appropriate in order to afford inspection in accordance with rule 31.3.

SCHEDULE

ELECTRONIC DOCUMENTS QUESTIONNAIRE

Part 1—Your disclosure

Extent of a reasonable search

Date range and custodians

1. What date range do you consider that your searches for Electronic Documents should cover ("the date range")?
2. Identify the custodians or creators of your Electronic Documents whose repositories of documents you consider should be searched.[1]

Communications

3. Which forms of electronic communication were in use during the date range (so far as is relevant to these proceedings)?

A Communication	B In use during the date range? (yes/no)	C Are you searching for relevant documents in this category? (yes/no)	D Where and on what type of software/equipment/media is this communication stored?[2]	E (a) Are backups or archives of this communication available, and (b) if so, are you searching the backups or archives?
i) E-mail[3]				
ii) Other (provide details for each type[4]) . . .				

Electronic Documents

4. Apart from attachments to e-mails, which forms of Electronic Documents were created or stored by you during the date range?

[1] Include names of all those who may have or have had custody of disclosable documents, including secretaries, personal assistants, former employees and/or former participants. It may be helpful to identify different dates for particular custodians.

[2] State the geographical location (if known). Consider (at least) servers, desktop PCs, laptops, notebooks, handheld devices, PDA devices, off-site storage, removable storage media (for example, CD-ROMs, DVDs, USB drives, memory sticks) and databases.

[3] Consider all types of e-mail system (for example, Outlook, Lotus Notes, web-based accounts), whether stored on personal computers, portable devices or in web-based accounts (for example, Yahoo, Hotmail, Gmail).

[4] For example, instant messaging, voicemail, VOIP (Voice Over Internet Protocol), recorded telephone lines, text messaging, audio files, video files.

A Document Type	B In use during the date range? (yes/no)	C Are you searching for relevant documents in this category? (yes/no)	D Where and on what type of software/ equipment/ media are these documents?[5]	E (a) Are back-ups or archives of these documents available, and (b) if so, are you searching the back-ups or archives?
i) Word (or equivalent – state which)				
ii) Excel (or equivalent – state which)				
iii) Electronic Images[6]				
iv) Other[7] (state which)				

Databases of Electronic Documents

5. In the following table identify database systems, including document management systems, used by you during the date range and which may contain disclosable Electronic Documents.

A Name	B Brief description	C Nature of data held	D Are you disclosing documents held in this database? (yes/no)	E Proposals for provision of relevant documents to or access by other parties to this litigation
1.				
2. (etc)				

Method of search

Key words

6. Do you consider that Keyword Searches should be used as part of the process of determining which Electronic Documents you should disclose?

[5] State the geographical location (if known). Consider (at least) servers, desktops and laptops.
[6] For example, .pdf. .tif, .jpg.
[7] For example, Powerpoint or equivalent, specialist documents (such as CAD Drawings).

If yes, provide details of—

(1) the keywords used or to be used (by reference, if applicable, to individual custodians, creators, repositories, file types and/or date ranges)[8]; and
(2) the extent to which the Keyword Searches have been or will be supplemented by a review of individual documents.

Other types of automated searches

7. Do you consider that automated searches or automated techniques other than Keyword Searches (for example, concept searches or clustering) should be used as part of the process of determining which Electronic Documents you should disclose?
If yes, provide details of—

(1) the process(es) used or to be used (by reference, if applicable, to individual custodians, creators, repositories, file types and/or date ranges);
(2) the extent to which the processes have been or will be supplemented by a review of individual documents; and
(3) how the methodology of automated searches will be made available for consideration by other parties.

8. If the answer to Question 6 or 7 is yes, state whether attachments to (a) e-mails (b) compressed files (c) embedded files and (d) imaged text will respond to your Keyword Searches or other automated search.
9. Are you using or intending to use computer software for other purposes in relation to disclosure? If so, provide details of the software, processes and methods to be used.

Potential problems with the extent of search and accessibility of Electronic Documents

10. Do any of the sources and/or documents identified in this Electronic Documents Questionnaire raise questions about the reasonableness of the search which ought to be taken into account?[9] If so, give details.
11. Are any documents which may be disclosable encrypted, password-protected or for other reasons difficult to access, or do you have any reason to believe that they may be?[10] If so, state which of the categories identified at Questions 3, 4 and 5 above are affected, and your proposals for making them accessible.
12. Are you aware of any other points in relation to disclosure of your Electronic Documents which require discussion between the parties? If so, give details.

Preservation of Electronic Documents

13. Do you have a document retention policy?
14. Have you given an instruction to preserve Electronic Documents, and if so, when?

[8] Where Keyword Searches are used in order to identify irrelevant documents which are to be excluded from disclosure (for example a confidential name of a client or customer), a general description of the type of search may be given.

[9] See Practice Direction 31B, which refers to the following matters which may be relevant: (a) the number of documents involved; (b) the nature and complexity of the proceedings; (c) the ease and expense of retrieval of any particular document; (d) the availability of documents or contents of documents from other sources; and (e) the significance of any document which is likely to be located during the search.

[10] For example, back-ups, archives, off-site or outsourced document storage, documents created by former employees, documents stored in other jurisdictions, documents in foreign languages.

Inspection

15. Subject to re-consideration after receiving the responses of other parties to this Electronic Documents Questionnaire, (a) in what format and (b) on what media do you intend to provide to other parties copies of disclosed documents which are or will be available in electronic form?
16. Subject to re-consideration after receiving the responses of other parties to this Electronic Documents Questionnaire, do you intend to provide other parties with Disclosure Data electronically, and if so, (a) in what format and (b) on what media?
17. Insofar as you have available or will have available searchable OCR versions of Electronic Documents, do you intend to provide the searchable OCR version to other parties?[11] If not, why not?

Part 2—The disclosure of other parties

The extent and content of their search

18. Do you at this stage have any proposals about the date ranges which should be searched by other parties to the proceedings? If so, provide details.
19. Do you at this stage have any proposals about the custodians or creators whose repositories of documents should be searched for disclosable documents by other parties to the proceedings? If so, provide details.[12]
20. Do you consider that the other party(ies) should disclose all available Metadata[13] attaching to any documents? If yes, provide details of the documents or categories of documents.

Proposals for the method to be adopted for their searches

21. Do you at this stage have any proposals about the Keyword Searches, or other automated searches, which should be applied by other parties to their document sets? If so, provide details.

Inspection

22. Subject to re-consideration after receiving the responses of other parties to this Electronic Documents Questionnaire, (a) in what format and (b) on what media do you wish to receive copies of disclosed documents which are or will be available in electronic form?

[11] There is no requirement that you should obtain OCR versions of documents, and this question is directed only to OCR versions which you have available or expect to have available to you. If you do provide OCR versions to another party, they will be provided by you on an "as is" basis, with no assurance to the other party that the OCR versions are complete or accurate. You may wish to exclude provision of OCR versions of documents which have been redacted.

[12] Include names of all those who may have or have had custody of disclosable documents, including secretaries, personal assistants, former employees and/or former participants. It may be helpful to identify different dates for particular custodians.

[13] "Metadata" is information about the document or file which is recorded in the computer, such as the date and time of creation or modification of a word-processing file, or the author and the date and time of sending of an e-mail. The question is directed to the more extensive Metadata which may be relevant where for example authenticity is disputed.

23. Subject to re-consideration after receiving the responses of other parties to this Electronic Documents Questionnaire, do you wish to receive Disclosure Data electronically, and if so, (a) in what format and (b) on what media?

STATEMENT OF TRUTH

[I believe][The [claimant][defendant] believes] that the facts stated in the answers to this Electronic Documents Questionnaire are true.

I am duly authorised by the [claimant][defendant] to sign this statement.

Full name ....

Name of legal representative's firm ....

Signed...

Position or office held (if signing on behalf of firm or company) ....

Date...

delete as appropriate

WARNING: Unless the court makes some other order, the answers given in this document may only be used for the purposes of the proceedings in which the document is produced unless it has been read to or by the court or referred to at a hearing which has been held in public or the Court gives permission or the party who has completed this questionnaire agrees.

Guidance Notes:

1. Technical expressions are defined in Practice Direction 31B.
2. The questions in the Electronic Documents Questionnaire are not intended to give rise to any implication about how disclosure should or should not be carried out. They are intended only to provide information to other parties and to the court.
3. Further facts and matters may come to parties' attention over the course of the proceedings which affect the answers to the Electronic Documents Questionnaire. Where detailed information is not yet available at the time the Electronic Documents Questionnaire is first answered, parties should give such information as they can, and supplement or amend their answers when further information is available. Answers should be updated by notifying other parties and the court without undue delay, and in any event before each case management conference at which disclosure is likely to be considered.
4. Some of the questions in the Electronic Documents Questionnaire require only a brief answer which may need to be elaborated after Electronic Documents Questionnaires have been exchanged. The purpose of such questions is to assist the parties in identifying the points which may require elaboration in order for meaningful discussions to take place between them.
5. Questions which refer to sources of Electronic Documents that are not considered to be relevant may be answered with a statement to that effect.
6. Questions about "your" documents and about software, hardware or systems used by "you" are directed, in the case of solicitors, to the solicitor's lay client's documents or to documents prepared on the lay client's behalf.

Part 35 Experts and Assessors

Contents of this Part

Interpretation and definitions	Rule 35.2
Experts—overriding duty to the court	Rule 35.3
Court's power to restrict expert evidence	Rule 35.4
General requirement for expert evidence to be given in a written report	Rule 35.5
Written questions to experts	Rule 35.6
Court's power to direct that evidence is to be given by a single joint expert	Rule 35.7
Instructions to a single joint expert	Rule 35.8
Power of court to direct a party to provide information	Rule 35.9
Contents of report	Rule 35.10
Use by one party of expert's report disclosed by another	Rule 35.11
Discussions between experts	Rule 35.12
Consequence of failure to disclose expert's report	Rule 35.13
Expert's right to ask court for directions	Rule 35.14
Assessors	Rule 35.15

Duty to restrict expert evidence

35.1

Expert evidence shall be restricted to that which is reasonably required to resolve the proceedings.

Interpretation and definitions

35.2

(1) A reference to an 'expert' in this Part is a reference to a person who has been instructed to give or prepare expert evidence for the purpose of proceedings.

(2) 'Single joint expert' means an expert instructed to prepare a report for the court on behalf of two or more of the parties (including the claimant) to the proceedings.

Experts—overriding duty to the court

35.3

(1) It is the duty of experts to help the court on matters within their expertise.

(2) This duty overrides any obligation to the person from whom experts have received instructions or by whom they are paid.

Court's power to restrict expert evidence

35.4

(1) No party may call an expert or put in evidence an expert's report without the court's permission.

(2) When parties apply for permission they must identify—

(a) the field in which expert evidence is required; and

(b) where practicable, the name of the proposed expert.

(3) If permission is granted it shall be in relation only to the expert named or the field identified under paragraph (2).

(3A) Where a claim has been allocated to the small claims track or the fast track, if permission is given for expert evidence, it will normally be given for evidence from only one expert on a particular issue.

(Paragraph 7 of Practice Direction 35 sets out some of the circumstances the court will consider when deciding whether expert evidence should be given by a single joint expert.)

(4) The court may limit the amount of a party's expert's fees and expenses that may be recovered from any other party.

General requirement for expert evidence to be given in a written report

35.5

(1) Expert evidence is to be given in a written report unless the court directs otherwise.

(2) If a claim is on the small claims track or the fast track, the court will not direct an expert to attend a hearing unless it is necessary to do so in the interests of justice.

Written questions to experts

35.6

(1) A party may put written questions about an expert's report (which must be proportionate) to—

(a) an expert instructed by another party; or
(b) a single joint expert appointed under rule 35.7.

(2) Written questions under paragraph (1)—

(a) may be put once only;
(b) must be put within 28 days of service of the expert's report; and
(c) must be for the purpose only of clarification of the report, unless in any case—

(i) the court gives permission; or
(ii) the other party agrees.

(3) An expert's answers to questions put in accordance with paragraph (1) shall be treated as part of the expert's report.

(4) Where—

(a) a party has put a written question to an expert instructed by another party; and
(b) the expert does not answer that question,

the court may make one or both of the following orders in relation to the party who instructed the expert—

(i) that the party may not rely on the evidence of that expert; or
(ii) that the party may not recover the fees and expenses of that expert from any other party.

Court's power to direct that evidence is to be given by a single joint expert

35.7

(1) Where two or more parties wish to submit expert evidence on a particular issue, the court may direct that the evidence on that issue is to be given by a single joint expert.

(2) Where the parties who wish to submit the evidence ('the relevant parties') cannot agree who should be the single joint expert, the court may—

(a) select the expert from a list prepared or identified by the relevant parties; or

(b) direct that the expert be selected in such other manner as the court may direct.

Instructions to a single joint expert

35.8

(1) Where the court gives a direction under rule 35.7 for a single joint expert to be used, any relevant party may give instructions to the expert.
(2) When a party gives instructions to the expert that party must, at the same time, send a copy to the other relevant parties.
(3) The court may give directions about—

(a) the payment of the expert's fees and expenses; and
(b) any inspection, examination or experiments which the expert wishes to carry out.

(4) The court may, before an expert is instructed—

(a) limit the amount that can be paid by way of fees and expenses to the expert; and
(b) direct that some or all of the relevant parties pay that amount into court.

(5) Unless the court otherwise directs, the relevant parties are jointly and severally liable[(GL)] for the payment of the expert's fees and expenses.

Power of court to direct a party to provide information

35.9

Where a party has access to information which is not reasonably available to another party, the court may direct the party who has access to the information to—

(a) prepare and file a document recording the information; and
(b) serve a copy of that document on the other party.

Contents of report

35.10

(1) An expert's report must comply with the requirements set out in Practice Direction 35.
(2) At the end of an expert's report there must be a statement that the expert understands and has complied with their duty to the court.
(3) The expert's report must state the substance of all material instructions, whether written or oral, on the basis of which the report was written.
(4) The instructions referred to in paragraph (3) shall not be privileged[(GL)] against disclosure but the court will not, in relation to those instructions—

(a) order disclosure of any specific document; or
(b) permit any questioning in court, other than by the party who instructed the expert,

unless it is satisfied that there are reasonable grounds to consider the statement of instructions given under paragraph (3) to be inaccurate or incomplete.

Use by one party of expert's report disclosed by another

35.11

Where a party has disclosed an expert's report, any party may use that expert's report as evidence at the trial.

Discussions between experts

35.12

(1) The court may, at any stage, direct a discussion between experts for the purpose of requiring the experts to—

(a) identify and discuss the expert issues in the proceedings; and
(b) where possible, reach an agreed opinion on those issues.

(2) The court may specify the issues which the experts must discuss.
(3) The court may direct that following a discussion between the experts they must prepare a statement for the court setting out those issues on which—

(a) they agree; and
(b) they disagree, with a summary of their reasons for disagreeing.

(4) The content of the discussion between the experts shall not be referred to at the trial unless the parties agree.
(5) Where experts reach agreement on an issue during their discussions, the agreement shall not bind the parties unless the parties expressly agree to be bound by the agreement.

Consequence of failure to disclose expert's report

35.13

A party who fails to disclose an expert's report may not use the report at the trial or call the expert to give evidence orally unless the court gives permission.

Expert's right to ask court for directions

35.14

(1) Experts may file written requests for directions for the purpose of assisting them in carrying out their functions.
(2) Experts must, unless the court orders otherwise, provide copies of the proposed requests for directions under paragraph (1)—

(a) to the party instructing them, at least 7 days before they file the requests; and
(b) to all other parties, at least 4 days before they file them.

(3) The court, when it gives directions, may also direct that a party be served with a copy of the directions.

Assessors

35.15

(1) This rule applies where the court appoints one or more persons under section 70 of the Senior Courts Act 1981[1] or section 63 of the County Courts Act 1984[2] as an assessor.
(2) An assessor will assist the court in dealing with a matter in which the assessor has skill and experience.
(3) An assessor will take such part in the proceedings as the court may direct and in particular the court may direct an assessor to—

[1] 1981 c. 54.
[2] 1984 c. 28.

(a) prepare a report for the court on any matter at issue in the proceedings; and
(b) attend the whole or any part of the trial to advise the court on any such matter.

(4) If an assessor prepares a report for the court before the trial has begun—

(a) the court will send a copy to each of the parties; and
(b) the parties may use it at trial.

(5) The remuneration to be paid to an assessor is to be determined by the court and will form part of the costs of the proceedings.
(6) The court may order any party to deposit in the court office a specified sum in respect of an assessor's fees and, where it does so, the assessor will not be asked to act until the sum has been deposited.
(7) Paragraphs (5) and (6) do not apply where the remuneration of the assessor is to be paid out of money provided by Parliament.

Practice Direction 35—Experts and Assessors

This Practice Direction supplements CPR Part 35

Contents of this Practice Direction

Title	Number
Introduction	Para. 1
Expert Evidence—General Requirements	Para. 2.1
Form and Content of an Expert's Report	Para. 3.1
Information	Para. 4
Instructions	Para. 5
Questions to Experts	Para. 6.1
Single joint expert	Para. 7
Orders	Para. 8
Discussions between experts	Para. 9.1
Assessors	Para. 10.1
Annex	

Introduction

1

Part 35 is intended to limit the use of oral expert evidence to that which is reasonably required. In addition, where possible, matters requiring expert evidence should be dealt with by only one expert. Experts and those instructing them are expected to have regard to the guidance contained in the Protocol for the Instruction of Experts to give Evidence in Civil Claims annexed to this practice direction. (Further guidance on experts is contained in Annex C to the Practice Direction (Pre-Action Conduct)).

Expert Evidence—General Requirements

2.1

Expert evidence should be the independent product of the expert uninfluenced by the pressures of litigation.

2.2

Experts should assist the court by providing objective, unbiased opinions on matters within their expertise, and should not assume the role of an advocate.

2.3

Experts should consider all material facts, including those which might detract from their opinions.

2.4

Experts should make it clear—

(a) when a question or issue falls outside their expertise; and
(b) when they are not able to reach a definite opinion, for example because they have insufficient information.

2.5

If, after producing a report, an expert's view changes on any material matter, such change of view should be communicated to all the parties without delay, and when appropriate to the court.

Form and Content of an Expert's Report

3.1

An expert's report should be addressed to the court and not to the party from whom the expert has received instructions.

3.2

An expert's report must:

(1) give details of the expert's qualifications;
(2) give details of any literature or other material which has been relied on in making the report;
(3) contain a statement setting out the substance of all facts and instructions which are material to the opinions expressed in the report or upon which those opinions are based;
(4) make clear which of the facts stated in the report are within the expert's own knowledge;
(5) say who carried out any examination, measurement, test or experiment which the expert has used for the report, give the qualifications of that person, and say whether or not the test or experiment has been carried out under the expert's supervision;
(6) where there is a range of opinion on the matters dealt with in the report—

    (a) summarise the range of opinions; and
    (b) give reasons for the expert's own opinion;

(7) contain a summary of the conclusions reached;
(8) if the expert is not able to give an opinion without qualification, state the qualification; and
(9) contain a statement that the expert—

    (a) understands their duty to the court, and has complied with that duty; and
    (b) is aware of the requirements of Part 35, this practice direction and the Protocol for Instruction of Experts to give Evidence in Civil Claims.

3.3

An expert's report must be verified by a statement of truth in the following form—

I confirm that I have made clear which facts and matters referred to in this report are within my own knowledge and which are not. Those that are within my own knowledge I confirm to be true. The opinions I have expressed represent my true and complete professional opinions on the matters to which they refer.

(Part 22 deals with statements of truth. Rule 32.14 sets out the consequences of verifying a document containing a false statement without an honest belief in its truth.)

Information

4

Under rule 35.9 the court may direct a party with access to information, which is not reasonably available to another party to serve on that other party a document, which records the information. The document served must include sufficient details of all the facts, tests, experiments and assumptions which underlie any part of the information to enable the party on whom it is served to make, or to obtain, a proper interpretation of the information and an assessment of its significance.

Instructions

5

Cross-examination of experts on the contents of their instructions will not be allowed unless the court permits it (or unless the party who gave the instructions consents). Before it gives permission the court must be satisfied that there are reasonable grounds to consider that the statement in the report of the substance of the instructions is inaccurate or incomplete. If the court is so satisfied, it will allow the cross-examination where it appears to be in the interests of justice.

Questions to Experts

6.1

Where a party sends a written question or questions under rule 35.6 direct to an expert, a copy of the questions must, at the same time, be sent to the other party or parties.

6.2

The party or parties instructing the expert must pay any fees charged by that expert for answering questions put under rule 35.6. This does not affect any decision of the court as to the party who is ultimately to bear the expert's fees.

Single joint expert

7

When considering whether to give permission for the parties to rely on expert evidence and whether that evidence should be from a single joint expert the court will take into account all the circumstances in particular, whether:

(a) it is proportionate to have separate experts for each party on a particular issue with reference to—

(i) the amount in dispute;
(ii) the importance to the parties; and

(iii) the complexity of the issue;

(b) the instruction of a single joint expert is likely to assist the parties and the court to resolve the issue more speedily and in a more cost-effective way than separately instructed experts;
(c) expert evidence is to be given on the issue of liability, causation or quantum;
(d) the expert evidence falls within a substantially established area of knowledge which is unlikely to be in dispute or there is likely to be a range of expert opinion;
(e) a party has already instructed an expert on the issue in question and whether or not that was done in compliance with any practice direction or relevant pre-action protocol;
(f) questions put in accordance with rule 35.6 are likely to remove the need for the other party to instruct an expert if one party has already instructed an expert;
(g) questions put to a single joint expert may not conclusively deal with all issues that may require testing prior to trial;
(h) a conference may be required with the legal representatives, experts and other witnesses which may make instruction of a single joint expert impractical; and
(i) a claim to privilege(GL) makes the instruction of any expert as a single joint expert inappropriate.

Orders

8

Where an order requires an act to be done by an expert, or otherwise affects an expert, the party instructing that expert must serve a copy of the order on the expert. The claimant must serve the order on a single joint expert.

Discussions between experts

9.1

Unless directed by the court discussions between experts are not mandatory. Parties must consider, with their experts, at an early stage, whether there is likely to be any useful purpose in holding an experts' discussion and if so when.

9.2

The purpose of discussions between experts is not for experts to settle cases but to agree and narrow issues and in particular to identify:

(i) the extent of the agreement between them;
(ii) the points of and short reasons for any disagreement;
(iii) action, if any, which may be taken to resolve any outstanding points of disagreement; and
(iv) any further material issues not raised and the extent to which these issues are agreed.

9.3

Where the experts are to meet, the parties must discuss and if possible agree whether an agenda is necessary, and if so attempt to agree one that helps the experts to focus on the issues which need to be discussed. The agenda must not be in the form of leading questions or hostile in tone.

9.4

Unless ordered by the court, or agreed by all parties, and the experts, neither the parties nor their legal representatives may attend experts discussions.

9.5

If the legal representatives do attend—

(i) they should not normally intervene in the discussion, except to answer questions put to them by the experts or to advise on the law; and
(ii) the experts may if they so wish hold part of their discussions in the absence of the legal representatives.

9.6

A statement must be prepared by the experts dealing with paragraphs 9.2(i)—(iv) above. Individual copies of the statements must be signed by the experts at the conclusion of the discussion, or as soon thereafter as practicable, and in any event within 7 days. Copies of the statements must be provided to the parties no later than 14 days after signing.

9.7

Experts must give their own opinions to assist the court and do not require the authority of the parties to sign a joint statement.

9.8

If an expert significantly alters an opinion, the joint statement must include a note or addendum by that expert explaining the change of opinion.

Assessors

10.1

An assessor may be appointed to assist the court under rule 35.15. Not less than 21 days before making any such appointment, the court will notify each party in writing of the name of the proposed assessor, of the matter in respect of which the assistance of the assessor will be sought and of the qualifications of the assessor to give that assistance.

10.2

Where any person has been proposed for appointment as an assessor, any party may object to that person either personally or in respect of that person's qualification.

10.3

Any such objection must be made in writing and filed with the court within 7 days of receipt of the notification referred to in paragraph 10.1 and will be taken into account by the court in deciding whether or not to make the appointment.

10.4

Copies of any report prepared by the assessor will be sent to each of the parties but the assessor will not give oral evidence or be open to cross-examination or questioning.

ANNEX TO PART 35 PRACTICE DIRECTION

PROTOCOL FOR THE INSTRUCTION OF EXPERTS TO GIVE EVIDENCE IN CIVIL CLAIMS

(**June 2005**, amended October 2009)

PROTOCOL FOR THE INSTRUCTION OF EXPERTS TO GIVE EVIDENCE IN CIVIL CLAIMS

1. Introduction

Expert witnesses perform a vital role in civil litigation. It is essential that both those who instruct experts and experts themselves are given clear guidance as to what they are expected to do in civil proceedings. The purpose of this Protocol is to provide such guidance. It has been drafted by the Civil Justice Council and reflects the rules and practice directions current [in June 2005], replacing the Code of Guidance on Expert Evidence. The authors of the Protocol wish to acknowledge the valuable assistance they obtained by drawing on earlier documents produced by the Academy of Experts and the Expert Witness Institute, as well as suggestions made by the Clinical Dispute Forum. The Protocol has been approved by the Master of the Rolls.

2. Aims of Protocol

2.1 This Protocol offers guidance to experts and to those instructing them in the interpretation of and compliance with Part 35 of the Civil Procedure Rules (CPR 35) and its associated Practice Direction (PD 35) and to further the objectives of the Civil Procedure Rules in general. It is intended to assist in the interpretation of those provisions in the interests of good practice but it does not replace them. It sets out standards for the use of experts and the conduct of experts and those who instruct them. The existence of this Protocol does not remove the need for experts and those who instruct them to be familiar with CPR35 and PD35.

2.2 Experts and those who instruct them should also bear in mind para 1.4 of the Practice Direction on Protocols which contains the following objectives, namely to:

(a) encourage the exchange of early and full information about the expert issues involved in a prospective legal claim;
(b) enable the parties to avoid or reduce the scope of litigation by agreeing the whole or part of an expert issue before commencement of proceedings; and
(c) support the efficient management of proceedings where litigation cannot be avoided.

3. Application

3.1 This Protocol applies to any steps taken for the purpose of civil proceedings by experts or those who instruct them on or after 5th September 2005.

3.2 It applies to all experts who are, or who may be, governed by CPR Part 35 and to those who instruct them. Experts are governed by Part 35 if they are or have been instructed to give or prepare evidence for the purpose of civil proceedings in a court in England and Wales (CPR 35.2).

3.3 Experts, and those instructing them, should be aware that some cases may be "specialist proceedings" (CPR 49) where there are modifications to the Civil Procedure Rules. Proceedings may also be governed by other Protocols. Further, some

courts have published their own Guides which supplement the Civil Procedure Rules for proceedings in those courts. They contain provisions affecting expert evidence. Expert witnesses and those instructing them should be familiar with them when they are relevant.

3.4 Courts may take into account any failure to comply with this Protocol when making orders in relation to costs, interest, time limits, the stay of proceedings and whether to order a party to pay a sum of money into court.

Limitation

3.5 If, as a result of complying with any part of this Protocol, claims would or might be time barred under any provision in the Limitation Act 1980, or any other legislation that imposes a time limit for the bringing an action, claimants may commence proceedings without complying with this Protocol. In such circumstances, claimants who commence proceedings without complying with all, or any part, of this Protocol must apply, giving notice to all other parties, to the court for directions as to the timetable and form of procedure to be adopted, at the same time as they request the court to issue proceedings. The court may consider whether to order a stay of the whole or part of the proceedings pending compliance with this Protocol and may make orders in relation to costs.

4. Duties of experts

4.1 Experts always owe a duty to exercise reasonable skill and care to those instructing them, and to comply with any relevant professional code of ethics. However when they are instructed to give or prepare evidence for the purpose of civil proceedings in England and Wales they have an overriding duty to help the court on matters within their expertise (CPR 35.3). This duty overrides any obligation to the person instructing or paying them. Experts must not serve the exclusive interest of those who retain them.

4.2 Experts should be aware of the overriding objective that courts deal with cases justly. This includes dealing with cases proportionately, expeditiously and fairly (CPR 1.1). Experts are under an obligation to assist the court so as to enable them to deal with cases in accordance with the overriding objective. However the overriding objective does not impose on experts any duty to act as mediators between the parties or require them to trespass on the role of the court in deciding facts.

4.3 Experts should provide opinions which are independent, regardless of the pressures of litigation. In this context, a useful test of 'independence' is that the expert would express the same opinion if given the same instructions by an opposing party. Experts should not take it upon themselves to promote the point of view of the party instructing them or engage in the role of advocates.

4.4 Experts should confine their opinions to matters which are material to the disputes between the parties and provide opinions only in relation to matters which lie within their expertise. Experts should indicate without delay where particular questions or issues fall outside their expertise.

4.5 Experts should take into account all material facts before them at the time that they give their opinion. Their reports should set out those facts and any literature or any other material on which they have relied in forming their opinions. They should indicate if an opinion is provisional, or qualified, or where they consider that further information is required or if, for any other reason, they are not satisfied that an opinion can be expressed finally and without qualification.

4.6 Experts should inform those instructing them without delay of any change in their opinions on any material matter and the reason for it.

4.7 Experts should be aware that any failure by them to comply with the Civil Procedure Rules or court orders or any excessive delay for which they are responsible may result in the parties who instructed them being penalised in costs and even,

in extreme cases, being debarred from placing the experts' evidence before the court. In[1] *Phillips v Symes* Peter Smith J held that courts may also make orders for costs (under section 51 of the Supreme Court Act 1981) directly against expert witnesses who by their evidence cause significant expense to be incurred, and do so in flagrant and reckless disregard of their duties to the Court.

5. Conduct of Experts instructed only to advise

5.1 Part 35 only applies where experts are instructed to give opinions which are relied on for the purposes of court proceedings. Advice which the parties do not intend to adduce in litigation is likely to be confidential; the Protocol does not apply in these circumstances[2] [3].

5.2 The same applies where, after the commencement of proceedings, experts are instructed only to advise (e.g. to comment upon a single joint expert's report) and not to give or prepare evidence for use in the proceedings.

5.3 However this Protocol does apply if experts who were formerly instructed only to advise are later instructed to give or prepare evidence for the purpose of civil proceedings.

6. The Need for Experts

6.1 Those intending to instruct experts to give or prepare evidence for the purpose of civil proceedings should consider whether expert evidence is appropriate, taking account of the principles set out in CPR Parts 1 and 35, and in particular whether:

(a) it is relevant to a matter which is in dispute between the parties.
(b) it is reasonably required to resolve the proceedings (CPR 35.1);
(c) the expert has expertise relevant to the issue on which an opinion is sought;
(d) the expert has the experience, expertise and training appropriate to the value, complexity and importance of the case; and whether
(e) these objects can be achieved by the appointment of a single joint expert (see section 17 below).

6.2 Although the court's permission is not generally required to instruct an expert, the court's permission is required before experts can be called to give evidence or their evidence can be put in (CPR 35.4).

7. The appointment of experts

7.1 Before experts are formally instructed or the court's permission to appoint named experts is sought, the following should be established:

(a) that they have the appropriate expertise and experience;
(b) that they are familiar with the general duties of an expert;
(c) that they can produce a report, deal with questions and have discussions with other experts within a reasonable time and at a cost proportionate to the matters in issue;
(d) a description of the work required;
(e) whether they are available to attend the trial, if attendance is required; and
(f) there is no potential conflict of interest.

[1] *Phillips v Symes* [2004] EWHC 2330 (Ch)
[2] *Carlson v Townsend* [2001] 1 WLR 2415
[3] *Jackson v Marley Davenport* [2004] 1 WLR 2926

7.2 Terms of appointment should be agreed at the outset and should normally include:

(a) the capacity in which the expert is to be appointed (e.g. party appointed expert, single joint expert or expert advisor);
(b) the services required of the expert (e.g. provision of expert's report, answering questions in writing, attendance at meetings and attendance at court);
(c) time for delivery of the report;
(d) the basis of the expert's charges (either daily or hourly rates and an estimate of the time likely to be required, or a total fee for the services);
(e) travelling expenses and disbursements;
(f) cancellation charges;
(g) any fees for attending court;
(h) time for making the payment; and
(i) whether fees are to be paid by a third party.
(j) if a party is publicly funded, whether or not the expert's charges will be subject to assessment by a costs officer.

7.3 As to the appointment of single joint experts, see section 17 below.

7.4 When necessary, arrangements should be made for dealing with questions to experts and discussions between experts, including any directions given by the court, and provision should be made for the cost of this work.

7.5 Experts should be informed regularly about deadlines for all matters concerning them. Those instructing experts should promptly send them copies of all court orders and directions which may affect the preparation of their reports or any other matters concerning their obligations.

Conditional and Contingency Fees

7.6 Payments contingent upon the nature of the expert evidence given in legal proceedings, or upon the outcome of a case, must not be offered or accepted. To do so would contravene experts' overriding duty to the court and compromise their duty of independence.

7.7 Agreement to delay payment of experts' fees until after the conclusion of cases is permissible as long as the amount of the fee does not depend on the outcome of the case.

8. Instructions

8.1 Those instructing experts should ensure that they give clear instructions, including the following:

(a) basic information, such as names, addresses, telephone numbers, dates of birth and dates of incidents;
(b) the nature and extent of the expertise which is called for;
(c) the purpose of requesting the advice or report, a description of the matter(s) to be investigated, the principal known issues and the identity of all parties;
(d) the statement(s) of case (if any), those documents which form part of standard disclosure and witness statements which are relevant to the advice or report;
(e) where proceedings have not been started, whether proceedings are being contemplated and, if so, whether the expert is asked only for advice;
(f) an outline programme, consistent with good case management and the expert's availability, for the completion and delivery of each stage of the expert's work; and

(g) where proceedings have been started, the dates of any hearings (including any Case Management Conferences and/or Pre-Trial Reviews), the name of the court, the claim number and the track to which the claim has been allocated.

8.2 Experts who do not receive clear instructions should request clarification and may indicate that they are not prepared to act unless and until such clear instructions are received.

8.3 As to the instruction of single joint experts, see section 17 below.

9. Experts' Acceptance of Instructions

9.1 Experts should confirm without delay whether or not they accept instructions. They should also inform those instructing them (whether on initial instruction or at any later stage) without delay if:

(a) instructions are not acceptable because, for example, they require work that falls outside their expertise, impose unrealistic deadlines, or are insufficiently clear;
(b) they consider that instructions are or have become insufficient to complete the work;
(c) they become aware that they may not be able to fulfil any of the terms of appointment;
(d) the instructions and/or work have, for any reason, placed them in conflict with their duties as an expert; or
(e) they are not satisfied that they can comply with any orders that have been made.

9.2 Experts must neither express an opinion outside the scope of their field of expertise, nor accept any instructions to do so.

10. Withdrawal

10.1 Where experts' instructions remain incompatible with their duties, whether through incompleteness, a conflict between their duty to the court and their instructions, or for any other substantial and significant reason, they may consider withdrawing from the case. However, experts should not withdraw without first discussing the position fully with those who instruct them and considering carefully whether it would be more appropriate to make a written request for directions from the court. If experts do withdraw, they must give formal written notice to those instructing them.

11. Experts' Right to ask Court for Directions

11.1 Experts may request directions from the court to assist them in carrying out their functions as experts. Experts should normally discuss such matters with those who instruct them before making any such request. Unless the court otherwise orders, any proposed request for directions should be copied to the party instructing the expert at least seven days before filing any request to the court, and to all other parties at least four days before filing it. (CPR 35.14).

11.2 Requests to the court for directions should be made by letter, containing.

(a) the title of the claim;
(b) the claim number of the case;
(c) the name of the expert;
(d) full details of why directions are sought; and
(e) copies of any relevant documentation.

12. Power of the Court to Direct a Party to Provide Information

12.1 If experts consider that those instructing them have not provided information which they require, they may, after discussion with those instructing them and giving notice, write to the court to seek directions (CPR 35.14).

12.2 Experts and those who instruct them should also be aware of CPR 35.9. This provides that where one party has access to information which is not readily available to the other party, the court may direct the party who has access to the information to prepare, file and copy to the other party a document recording the information. If experts require such information which has not been disclosed, they should discuss the position with those instructing them without delay, so that a request for the information can be made, and, if not forthcoming, an application can be made to the court. Unless a document appears to be essential, experts should assess the cost and time involved in the production of a document and whether its provision would be proportionate in the context of the case.

13. Contents of Experts' Reports

13.1 The content and extent of experts' reports should be governed by the scope of their instructions and general obligations, the contents of CPR 35 and PD35 and their overriding duty to the court.

13.2 In preparing reports, experts should maintain professional objectivity and impartiality at all times.

13.3 PD 35, para 2 provides that experts' reports should be addressed to the court and gives detailed directions about the form and content of such reports. All experts and those who instruct them should ensure that they are familiar with these requirements.

13.4 Model forms of Experts' Reports are available from bodies such as the Academy of Experts or the Expert Witness Institute.

13.5 Experts' reports must contain statements that they—

(i) understand their duty to the court and have complied and will continue to comply with it; and
(ii) are aware of the requirements of Part 35 and Practice Direction 35, this protocol and the practice direction on pre-action conduct.

Experts' reports must also be verified by a statement of truth. The form of the statement of truth is as follows—

" I confirm that I have made clear which facts and matters referred to in this report are within my own knowledge and which are not. Those that are within my own knowledge I confirm to be true. The opinions I have expressed represent my true and complete professional opinions on the matters to which they refer."

This wording is mandatory and must not be modified.

Qualifications

13.6 The details of experts' qualifications to be given in reports should be commensurate with the nature and complexity of the case. It may be sufficient merely to state academic and professional qualifications. However, where highly specialised expertise is called for, experts should include the detail of particular training and/or experience that qualifies them to provide that highly specialised evidence.

Tests

13.7 Where tests of a scientific or technical nature have been carried out, experts should state:

(a) the methodology used; and
(b) by whom the tests were undertaken and under whose supervision, summarising

their respective qualifications and experience.

Reliance on the work of others

13.8 Where experts rely in their reports on literature or other material and cite the opinions of others without having verified them, they must give details of those opinions relied on. It is likely to assist the court if the qualifications of the originator(s) are also stated.

Facts

13.9 When addressing questions of fact and opinion, experts should keep the two separate and discrete.

13.10 Experts must state those facts (whether assumed or otherwise) upon which their opinions are based. They must distinguish clearly between those facts which experts know to be true and those facts which they assume.

13.11 Where there are material facts in dispute experts should express separate opinions on each hypothesis put forward. They should not express a view in favour of one or other disputed version of the facts unless, as a result of particular expertise and experience, they consider one set of facts as being improbable or less probable, in which case they may express that view, and should give reasons for holding it.

Range of opinion

13.12 If the mandatory summary of the range of opinion is based on published sources, experts should explain those sources and, where appropriate, state the qualifications of the originator(s) of the opinions from which they differ, particularly if such opinions represent a well-established school of thought.

13.13 Where there is no available source for the range of opinion, experts may need to express opinions on what they believe to be the range which other experts would arrive at if asked. In those circumstances, experts should make it clear that the range that they summarise is based on their own judgement and explain the basis of that judgement.

Conclusions

13.14 A summary of conclusions is mandatory. The summary should be at the end of the report after all the reasoning. There may be cases, however, where the benefit to the court is heightened by placing a short summary at the beginning of the report whilst giving the full conclusions at the end. For example, it can assist with the comprehension of the analysis and with the absorption of the detailed facts if the court is told at the outset of the direction in which the report's logic will flow in cases involving highly complex matters which fall outside the general knowledge of the court.

Basis of report: material instructions

13.15 The mandatory statement of the substance of all material instructions should not be incomplete or otherwise tend to mislead. The imperative is transparency. The term "instructions" includes all material which solicitors place in front of

experts in order to gain advice. The omission from the statement of 'off-the-record' oral instructions is not permitted. Courts may allow cross-examination about the instructions if there are reasonable grounds to consider that the statement may be inaccurate or incomplete.

14. After receipt of experts' reports

14.1 Following the receipt of experts' reports, those instructing them should advise the experts as soon as reasonably practicable whether, and if so when, the report will be disclosed to other parties; and, if so disclosed, the date of actual disclosure.

14.2 If experts' reports are to be relied upon, and if experts are to give oral evidence, those instructing them should give the experts the opportunity to consider and comment upon other reports within their area of expertise and which deal with relevant issues at the earliest opportunity.

14.3 Those instructing experts should keep experts informed of the progress of cases, including amendments to statements of case relevant to experts' opinion.

14.4 If those instructing experts become aware of material changes in circumstances or that relevant information within their control was not previously provided to experts, they should without delay instruct experts to review, and if necessary, update the contents of their reports.

15. Amendment of reports

15.1 It may become necessary for experts to amend their reports:

(a) as a result of an exchange of questions and answers;
(b) following agreements reached at meetings between experts; or
(c) where further evidence or documentation is disclosed.

15.2 Experts should not be asked to, and should not, amend, expand or alter any parts of reports in a manner which distorts their true opinion, but may be invited to amend or expand reports to ensure accuracy, internal consistency, completeness and relevance to the issues and clarity. Although experts should generally follow the recommendations of solicitors with regard to the form of reports, they should form their own independent views as to the opinions and contents expressed in their reports and exclude any suggestions which do not accord with their views.

15.3 Where experts change their opinion following a meeting of experts, a simple signed and dated addendum or memorandum to that effect is generally sufficient. In some cases, however, the benefit to the court of having an amended report may justify the cost of making the amendment.

15.4 Where experts significantly alter their opinion, as a result of new evidence or because evidence on which they relied has become unreliable, or for any other reason, they should amend their reports to reflect that fact. Amended reports should include reasons for amendments. In such circumstances those instructing experts should inform other parties as soon as possible of any change of opinion.

15.5 When experts intend to amend their reports, they should inform those instructing them without delay and give reasons. They should provide the amended version (or an addendum or memorandum) clearly marked as such as quickly as possible.

16. Written Questions to Experts

16.1 The procedure for putting written questions to experts (CPR 35.6) is intended to facilitate the clarification of opinions and issues after experts' reports have been served. Experts have a duty to provide answers to questions properly put. Where they fail to do so, the court may impose sanctions against the party instructing the expert, and, if, there is continued non-compliance, debar a party from relying on the report. Experts should copy their answers to those instructing them.

16.2 Experts' answers to questions automatically become part of their reports. They are covered by the statement of truth and form part of the expert evidence.

16.3 Where experts believe that questions put are not properly directed to the clarification of the report, or are disproportionate, or have been asked out of time, they should discuss the questions with those instructing them and, if appropriate, those asking the questions. Attempts should be made to resolve such problems without the need for an application to the court for directions.

Written requests for directions in relation to questions

16.4 If those instructing experts do not apply to the court in respect of questions, but experts still believe that questions are improper or out of time, experts may file written requests with the court for directions to assist in carrying out their functions as experts (CPR 35.14). See Section 11 above.

17. Single Joint Experts

17.1 CPR 35 and PD35 deal extensively with the instruction and use of joint experts by the parties and the powers of the court to order their use (see CPR 35.7 and 35.8, PD35, para 5).

17.2 The Civil Procedure Rules encourage the use of joint experts. Wherever possible a joint report should be obtained. Consideration should therefore be given by all parties to the appointment of single joint experts in all cases where a court might direct such an appointment. Single joint experts are the norm in cases allocated to the small claims track and the fast track.

17.3 Where, in the early stages of a dispute, examinations, investigations, tests, site inspections, experiments, preparation of photographs, plans or other similar preliminary expert tasks are necessary, consideration should be given to the instruction of a single joint expert, especially where such matters are not, at that stage, expected to be contentious as between the parties. The objective of such an appointment should be to agree or to narrow issues.

17.4 Experts who have previously advised a party (whether in the same case or otherwise) should only be proposed as single joint experts if other parties are given all relevant information about the previous involvement.

17.5 The appointment of a single joint expert does not prevent parties from instructing their own experts to advise (but the costs of such expert advisers may not be recoverable in the case).

Joint instructions

17.6 The parties should try to agree joint instructions to single joint experts, but, in default of agreement, each party may give instructions. In particular, all parties should try to agree what documents should be included with instructions and what assumptions single joint experts should make.

17.7 Where the parties fail to agree joint instructions, they should try to agree where the areas of disagreement lie and their instructions should make this clear. If separate instructions are given, they should be copied at the same time to the other instructing parties.

17.8 Where experts are instructed by two or more parties, the terms of appointment should, unless the court has directed otherwise, or the parties have agreed otherwise, include:

(a) a statement that all the instructing parties are jointly and severally liable to pay the experts' fees and, accordingly, that experts' invoices should be sent simultaneously to all instructing parties or their solicitors (as appropriate); and

(b) a statement as to whether any order has been made limiting the amount of experts' fees and expenses (CPR 35.8(4)(a)).

17.9 Where instructions have not been received by the expert from one or more of the instructing parties the expert should give notice (normally at least 7 days) of a deadline to all instructing parties for the receipt by the expert of such instructions. Unless the instructions are received within the deadline the expert may begin work. In the event that instructions are received after the deadline but before the signing off of the report the expert should consider whether it is practicable to comply with those instructions without adversely affecting the timetable set for delivery of the report and in such a manner as to comply with the proportionality principle. An expert who decides to issue a report without taking into account instructions received after the deadline should inform the parties who may apply to the court for directions. In either event the report must show clearly that the expert did not receive instructions within the deadline, or, as the case may be, at all.

Conduct of the single joint expert

17.10 Single joint experts should keep all instructing parties informed of any material steps that they may be taking by, for example, copying all correspondence to those instructing them.

17.11 Single joint experts are Part 35 experts and so have an overriding duty to the court. They are the parties' appointed experts and therefore owe an equal duty to all parties. They should maintain independence, impartiality and transparency at all times.

17.12 Single joint experts should not attend any meeting or conference which is not a joint one, unless all the parties have agreed in writing or the court has directed that such a meeting may be held[4] and who is to pay the experts' fees for the meeting.

17.13 Single joint experts may request directions from the court—see Section 11 above.

17.14 Single joint experts should serve their reports simultaneously on all instructing parties. They should provide a single report even though they may have received instructions which contain areas of conflicting fact or allegation. If conflicting instructions lead to different opinions (for example, because the instructions require experts to make different assumptions of fact), reports may need to contain more than one set of opinions on any issue. It is for the court to determine the facts.

Cross-examination

17.15 Single joint experts do not normally give oral evidence at trial but if they do, all parties may cross-examine them. In general written questions (CPR 35.6) should be put to single joint experts before requests are made for them to attend court for the purpose of cross-examination[5].

18. Discussions between Experts

18.1 The court has powers to direct discussions between experts for the purposes set out in the Rules (CPR 35.12). Parties may also agree that discussions take place between their experts.

[4] *Peet v Mid Kent Area Healthcare NHS Trust* [2002] 1 WLR 210
[5] *Daniels v Walker* [2000] 1 WLR 1382

18.2 Where single joint experts have been instructed but parties have, with the permission of the court, instructed their own additional Part 35 experts, there may, if the court so orders or the parties agree, be discussions between the single joint experts and the additional Part 35 experts. Such discussions should be confined to those matters within the remit of the additional Part 35 experts or as ordered by the court.

18.3 The purpose of discussions between experts should be, wherever possible, to:

(a) identify and discuss the expert issues in the proceedings;
(b) reach agreed opinions on those issues, and, if that is not possible, to narrow the issues in the case;
(c) identify those issues on which they agree and disagree and summarise their reasons for disagreement on any issue; and
(d) identify what action, if any, may be taken to resolve any of the outstanding issues between the parties.

Arrangements for discussions between experts

18.4 Arrangements for discussions between experts should be proportionate to the value of cases. In small claims and fast-track cases there should not normally be meetings between experts. Where discussion is justified in such cases, telephone discussion or an exchange of letters should, in the interests of proportionality, usually suffice. In multi-track cases, discussion may be face to face, but the practicalities or the proportionality principle may require discussions to be by telephone or video conference.

18.5 The parties, their lawyers and experts should co-operate to produce the agenda for any discussion between experts, although primary responsibility for preparation of the agenda should normally lie with the parties' solicitors.

18.6 The agenda should indicate what matters have been agreed and summarise concisely those which are in issue. It is often helpful for it to include questions to be answered by the experts. If agreement cannot be reached promptly or a party is unrepresented, the court may give directions for the drawing up of the agenda. The agenda should be circulated to experts and those instructing them to allow sufficient time for the experts to prepare for the discussion.

18.7 Those instructing experts must not instruct experts to avoid reaching agreement (or to defer doing so) on any matter within the experts' competence. Experts are not permitted to accept such instructions.

18.8 The parties' lawyers may only be present at discussions between experts if all the parties agree or the court so orders. If lawyers do attend, they should not normally intervene except to answer questions put to them by the experts or to advise about the law[6].

18.9 The content of discussions between experts should not be referred to at trial unless the parties agree (CPR 35.12(4)). It is good practice for any such agreement to be in writing.

18.10 At the conclusion of any discussion between experts, a statement should be prepared setting out:

(a) a list of issues that have been agreed, including, in each instance, the basis of agreement;
(b) a list of issues that have not been agreed, including, in each instance, the basis of disagreement;

[6] *Hubbard v Lambeth, Southwark and Lewisham HA* [2001] EWCA 1455

(c) a list of any further issues that have arisen that were not included in the original agenda for discussion;
(d) a record of further action, if any, to be taken or recommended, including as appropriate the holding of further discussions between experts.

18.11 The statement should be agreed and signed by all the parties to the discussion as soon as may be practicable.

18.12 Agreements between experts during discussions do not bind the parties unless the parties expressly agree to be bound by the agreement (CPR 35.12(5)). However, in view of the overriding objective, parties should give careful consideration before refusing to be bound by such an agreement and be able to explain their refusal should it become relevant to the issue of costs.

19. Attendance of Experts at Court

19.1 Experts instructed in cases have an obligation to attend court if called upon to do so and accordingly should ensure that those instructing them are always aware of their dates to be avoided and take all reasonable steps to be available.

19.2 Those instructing experts should:

(a) ascertain the availability of experts before trial dates are fixed;
(b) keep experts updated with timetables (including the dates and times experts are to attend) and the location of the court;
(c) give consideration, where appropriate, to experts giving evidence via a video-link.
(d) inform experts immediately if trial dates are vacated.

19.3 Experts should normally attend court without the need for the service of witness summonses, but on occasion they may be served to require attendance (CPR 34). The use of witness summonses does not affect the contractual or other obligations of the parties to pay experts' fees.